Family Law and Practice

The Paralegal's Guide

Second Edition

Grace A. Luppino, Esq.

Justine FitzGerald Miller, Esq.

PEARSON
Prentice
Hall

Upper Saddle River, New Jersey 07458

Library of Congress Cataloging-in-Publication Data

Luppino, Grace A.
    Family law and practice: the paralegal's guide / by Grace A. Luppino and Justine
FitzGerald Miller. — 2nd ed.
        p. cm.
    Includes bibliographical references and index.
    ISBN 0-13-238199-0
    1. Domestic relations—United States.   I. Miller, Justine FitzGerald.   II. Title.   III.
Title: Family law and practice.
    KF505.Z9L87 2008
    346.7301'5—dc22   2007001436

Editor-in-Chief: Vernon R. Anthony
Senior Acquisitions Editor: Gary Bauer
Associate Editor: Linda Cupp
Development Editor: Deborah Hoffman
Marketing Manager: Leigh Ann Sims
Marketing Coordinator: Alicia Dysert
Managing Editor—Production: Mary Carnis
Manufacturing Buyer: Ilene Sanford
Production Liaison: Denise Brown
Full-Service Production and Composition: Emily
  Bush/Carlisle Publishing Services
Media Production Project Manager: Lisa Rinaldi

Director, Image Resource Center: Melinda Patelli
Manager, Rights and Permissions: Zina Arabia
Manager, Visual Research: Beth Brenzel
Manager, Cover Visual Research & Permissions: Karen
  Sanatar
Image Permission Coordinator: Joanne Dippel
Senior Design Coordinator: Christopher Weigand
Cover Design: Rob Aleman
Cover Image: Getty Images/Coco Masuda
Printer/Binder: Edwards Brothers, Inc.
Cover Printer: Phoenix Color

Photo Credits:

Page 2: Michael Newman PhotoEdit Inc.; page 4: AP Wide World Photos; page 18: Jim Pickerell/The Stock Connection; page 37: John Neubauer/PhotoEdit Inc.; page 40: Michael Newman/PhotoEdit Inc.; page 48: Esbin/Anderson/Ommi-Photo Communications, Inc.; page 60: Scott T. Baxter/Getty Images, Inc.—Photodisc; page 69: Corbis Digital Stock; page 75: Brian Smith, Photographer; page 142: Getty Images Inc.—Hulton Archive Photos; page 152: Scott Cunningham/Merrill Education; page 157: Bob Daemmrich Photography, Inc.; page 174: Getty Images—Stockbyte; page 190: Irene Springer/Pearson Education/PH College; page 209: A Ramey/PhotoEdit Inc.; page 224: Laima Druskis/Pearson Education/PH College; page 225: Krista Greco/Merrill Education; page 233: Ken Karp/Pearson Education/PH College; page 251: Krista Greco/Merrill Education; page 274: Rhoda Sidney/Pearson Education/PH College; page 286: Patrick White/Merrill Education; page 341: Todd Yarrington/Merrill Education.

Pearson Education Ltd.
Pearson Education Singapore Pte. Ltd.
Pearson Education Canada, Ltd.
Pearson Education—Japan

Pearson Education Australia PTY. Limited
Pearson Education North Asia Ltd.
Pearson Educación de Mexico, S.A. de C.V.
Pearson Education Malaysia Pte. Ltd.

10 9 8 7 6 5 4 3
ISBN 13: 978-0-13-238199-4
ISBN 10:   0-13-238199-0

DEDICATION

This book is dedicated to my niece Grace and my nephews Rocco and Jhonnatan.

Grace A. Luppino

Dedicated to my children, Justine and George.

Justine FitzGerald Miller

BRIEF CONTENTS

CONTENTS

PREFACE

The first edition of *The Paralegal's Guide to Family Law and Practice* was written with the intent to fill the need for an understandable and interesting family law textbook for students in paralegal studies programs. It was a challenge to combine the theoretical and practical aspects of the subject. Our goal was to prepare students to enter the workplace both knowledgeable in aspects of family law and equipped with a grasp of the procedural law requirements of family law practice, including the types of documents filed with courts and the tools used to facilitate the information gathering needed to determine financial issues and custody and visitation dispositions.

We have approached this second edition with the same intent and goal, as well as the additional aim that our textbook be relevant and responsive to the needs of a broader student population in a variety of legal studies degree and certificate programs. To realize our goals to the fullest, we have attempted to refine our presentation, generally using the same framework and emphasis, but augmenting the practical sections. To this end, in many of the chapters, we have included a survey of legal procedures and extrajudicial methods employed by various states to promote the individual citizen's interests and the state's interest in the orderly disposition of disputes arising in a marital and family setting.

Again, the major focus is on the process of marital dissolution and the issues of property distribution, custody, visitation, alimony, and child support. However, attention is also given to enforcement of the orders entered to resolve those issues and other postjudgment matters such as a modification of one or more of the court's "final" orders.

As in the previous edition, the book is logically ordered to provide the student with the various theories underlying family law and the procedures that translate these theories into practice. There have been some changes in both the presentation and the sequencing of topics. Specifically, Chapter 1 and Chapter 2 have been combined into a new Chapter 1 that includes those parts of both chapters that are critical to family law practice in the twenty-first century and eliminates sections less relevant. Although somewhat condensed, there is still a section providing a historical perspective on the evolution of family law and the changing views regarding marriage, the roles and responsibilities of each spouse, the status of children in the family, and, last but not least, what constitutes a family.

"Ethics in Family Law," formerly Chapter 3, is now Chapter 2. This chapter continues to provide the theoretical basis for rules of professional responsibility and examples of their practical application. Again, the paralegal's ethical responsibilities are emphasized. Also discussed is the ever-expanding impetus to license paralegals and the recent efforts of some lawmakers to promote legislation that would extend liability for ethical breaches to the paralegal when warranted. The section on the *pro se* litigant addresses the resources available to parties who are representing themselves, including the availability of useful and affordable "unbundled legal services."

"The Client Interview," formerly Chapter 9, is now Chapter 3. This change in sequencing has been made to draw students into the practical aspects of the course much earlier so that as the different aspects of the dissolution process and post-judgment proceedings are introduced, students can better visualize their role at each stage.

Chapter 4, "Premarital Agreements, Cohabitation, and Same-Sex Marriage," covers these additional and related topics. New information is provided on the now generally accepted criteria for determining the validity of a premarital agreement, and on how to prepare and execute an agreement that will be legally enforceable. The section on same-sex marriage has been updated to include an account of the legalization of same-sex marriage in Massachusetts and the opposition to this landmark legislation.

Chapters 5 through 8 provide the substantive law that is applied to resolve issues arising in a dissolution proceeding as well as the policy concerns underlying the law. Separate chapters are devoted to alimony, property and debt distribution, child custody, and child support. Changes from our first edition include, in Chapter 6, "Property and Debt Distribution," an expanded explanation of the difference between individual property and marital property and more intensive coverage of the "how's" and "why's" of property distribution and debt allocation in community property states. Chapter 7, "Child Custody, Visitation and Rights of Third Parties," provides an update on grandparents' rights and the parental alienation syndrome, and includes new topics such as the increasing instances of allegations of sexual abuse raised by one parent against another in custody battles. Chapter 8, "Child Support," introduces information regarding the latest computerized methods of locating and keeping track of delinquent payer parents as well as more effective methods of collection of arrearages.

Chapters 9 through 14 focus on the practice of family law and the paralegal's role in the process. These chapters include samples of complaints, motions, orders, agreements, and discovery-related documents. Major changes to Chapter 11, "The Discovery Process in Family Law," include an expanded and more detailed section on the paralegal's role in the discovery process. Chapter 12, "Separation Agreements," features an updated sample separation agreement that introduces new clauses that have recently become standard provisions in separation agreements.

Chapter 13 contains significant changes. Previously titled "The Divorce Trial," the new title, "Alternative Dispute Resolution and the Divorce Trial," heralds the expansion of the chapter to include a comprehensive section on mediation and other alternative methods of dispute resolution used to diminish the instances of protracted and unpleasant litigation arising from custody and property disputes. Chapter 14, "Postjudgment Divorce Matters," identifies the various methods used to facilitate enforcement of court orders, especially support enforcement methods and remedies. This chapter also includes a discussion of instances where courts may modify "nonmodifiable" sections of a settlement agreement.

Chapter 15, formerly Chapter 16, has been renamed "Child Protection and Adoption." It continues to cover state intervention in family matters. The section on adoption now contains a subsection on the lengthy and intricate process of stepparent adoption, and a subsection on the "second parent" adoption process through which some states confer co-parent status on the same-sex partner of an adoptive parent. The topic of open adoption is discussed extensively, and a sample open adoption agreement is provided.

To make this edition relevant and interesting to more students throughout the country, we have included cases, statutes, and legal forms from a variety of states.

Nevertheless, we stress the need for students to familiarize themselves with the forms of these materials specific to their respective jurisdictions. To this end, many of the end-of-chapter exercises require students to investigate the resources and materials in their states that contain the substantive law and procedural tools necessary to facilitate the resolution of clients' family law issues.

Finally, we hope that our revisions, updates, and additions to this, our second edition, offer our students greater knowledge, understanding, and skill development in the area of family law and practice.

Grace A. Luppino
Justine FitzGerald Miller

ACKNOWLEDGMENTS

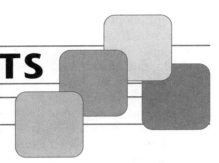

We wish to thank the following people for their support and encouragement in making this book a reality:

Dana Meltzer, Linda Cupp, and Gray Bauer at Prentice Hall; our colleagues and students at Branford Hall Career Institute and Briarwood College, Adelia (Dee) Silva, Barbara Fay, Melissa Naughton, Toni Esposito, Dawn A. Chuley, Heather Bell, Connie Luppino, Margaretann Antonelli, Katharine Hunt, and Swami Sarasvatyananda; our friends and families; and the following paralegal students for their legal research: Amy L'Heurevx, Debra Williams, Marie Gerrie, Eileen Viglione, Marchell Sinanis, Diane Allen, Sherrian Benson, Kelly Butler, Christy Cash, Domenica Colavolpe, Laurie Coppola, Raymond Daley, Lori DiGiovanni, Connie Esposito, Mia Garmizo, Andrew Gister, Cheryl Granoff, Joann Gleason, Gail LaGreca, Deanna Lozowski, Susan McClintock, Linda McCue, Cynthia McQueen, Mary Notarangelo, Joann O'Leary, Melanie Rieder, Margaret Sabilla, Christine Van Vliet, and Elizabeth Young.

We wish also to thank the following reviewers: Robert Diotalevi, Florida Gulf Coast University; Rosalia G. Barone, Norwalk Community College, CT; Lisa Schaffer, Corinthian Colleges, Inc., CA; Wesley S. Marion, Ivy Tech Community College of Indiana; and Beverly C. Campbell, Interboro Institute, Law Division, NY.

Our special thanks to paralegal Pamela Robicheau for her countless hours of legal research, editing, and preparation of the manuscript. This book could not have been completed without her hard work, expertise, and devotion to this project. We are also grateful to paralegal Christine Averill for her many hours of research for the second edition, and to paralegal Joanne O'Leary for additional research and for editing and reformating chapters.

Special thanks to the American Bar Association, the National Association of Legal Associates, Inc., and W. Kelsea Wilbur Eckert for their permission to reprint documents in this book, and to Carol Swenson, Esq., and Eileen Jenetopulos, Esq., for their technical assistance on cutting-edge legal issues.

Grace A. Luppino
Justine FitzGerald Miller

CHAPTER 1

Introduction to Family Law and Practice

KEY TERMS

affinity	marriage certificate
annulment	marriage license
bigamy	marriage
Child support enforcement amendments	migratory divorces
	no-fault divorce
civil unions	polygamy
common law marriage	putative spouse
consanguinity	separate maintenance
covenant marriage	sham or green card marriage
Defense of Marriage Act (DOMA)	simplified divorce procedure
dissolution of marriage	summary dissolution of marriage
domestic partnerships	void ab initio
emancipation	void marriage
legal separation	voidable marriage

Family law is one of the most interesting, exciting, and dynamic areas of legal practice. If you like boxing, wrestling, or any of the other pugilistic arts, you will certainly enjoy being part of a legal team that tackles the knotty problems

and ever-changing cultural, social, and economic issues that affect the American family.

Family law as a specialty evolved slowly, but now, in many jurisdictions, family law cases occupy more space on the civil court docket than any other type of matter. This increase has occurred because of changes in our society during the past forty years that have affected attitudes toward marriage, family, divorce, and parenting.

During the first half of the twentieth century in the United States, divorce was far less common than it is today. At the turn of the twentieth century, less than one in twenty marriages ended in divorce; since the mid-1970s, for every two marriages that took place in a given year, one divorce has occurred. Today, more than one-half of children under the age of eighteen are growing up in one-parent homes. As a result of this trend, many law firms devote their practice exclusively to family law; for other firms, the practice of family law comprises a large segment of the work produced. Both types of law firms increasingly employ paralegals in their family law department. These paraprofessionals, with the guidance of their supervisory attorneys, complete the myriad of tasks needed to provide thorough and effective representation to clients on family matters.

A paralegal who is both competent in and enthusiastic about family law practice can provide valuable assistance to attorneys who spend all or most of their time practicing family law. Employment opportunities for paralegals in this field of law will abound as long as individuals continue to seek attorneys to help them resolve their marital and family conflicts, and as long as there are paralegals whose training has provided them with a solid background in both family law theory and practice. The goal of this book is to provide the paralegal student, in a comprehensive and understandable manner, with just that type of theoretical and practical education.

FAMILY LAW THEORY

Family law theory provides the analytical framework for the body of substantive law used in courts to decide marital and family-related matters. These laws determine, regulate, and enforce the obligations of marriage and parenthood. They are made by the legislature branch as state legislators fashion and exact statute's and upheld by the judicial branch as judges make decisions in the courtroom. These common law and statutory decisions are not made arbitrarily, nor are they made in a vacuum without considering what is taking place in the society in which the laws will be enforced. When a law is being made, it is fashioned in a way that promotes the dominant views of the time on the proper, fair, or most enlightened way to handle the issues at hand. Legislation and judicial opinions reflect the values and attitudes of society. These values and attitudes produce the ideas that provide the theory or underlying rationale for resolving a legal issue in a particular manner. As values and attitudes change and as society acquires new information and knowledge related to various aspects of family law issues, new theories emerge and replace the earlier rationales for resolving disputes.

In the area of family law, courts and legislatures use many different approaches to address marital disputes and the issues arising from such disputes. These issues include:

- support and maintenance of family members,
- care and custody of minor children, and
- division of property upon the breakup of the marital unit.

Over time, family law theory has grown and evolved as society has changed. The history of American family law presented in this chapter demonstrates how differently family law issues have been treated during different time periods.

FAMILY LAW PRACTICE

COURT PROCEDURES

In every jurisdiction, the judicial system provides specific procedures for bringing disputed substantive family law issues before the court. These include procedures for:

- initiating family-related actions in a court,
- acquiring and presenting evidentiary information,
- providing temporary solutions to issues of support, custody, and visitation while a matter is pending,
- enforcing or modifying a court's orders,
- conducting alternative dispute resolution,
- processing uncontested matters by streamlining process, and
- litigating contested matters.

Every state or jurisdiction has its own particular set of procedural rules to follow in the practice of family law. These rules are part of the jurisdiction's larger body of civil procedural law that governs how private parties may enforce their substantive legal rights through the court system. In the practice of family law, knowledge of the family court's procedural rules is essential.

OFFICE PROCEDURES

It is equally essential to know the procedures that a law firm uses within its office to handle family law matters. Every law office has its own particular methods and practices for the following aspects of managing family law cases:

- obtaining and recording information from clients,
- setting up files,

- preparing legal documents for filing in court,
- docketing court dates,
- recording the amount of time spent working on each file, and
- billing clients for work done.

APPLYING FAMILY LAW THEORY TO FAMILY LAW PRACTICE

It is also very important to understand how family law theory is actually applied in the real world of family law practice. In many instances in a marital dispute, the issues such as property division, alimony, child support, and even child custody are worked out by the parties in a manner that is not consistent with the prevailing theoretical view or even the substantive statutory or common law guidelines. This happens when the parties work out an agreement to settle their differences through settlement, mediation, or collaborative law. These forms of alternative dispute resolution will be discussed in a later chapter.

THE FAMILY PRACTITIONER'S ROLE IN THE DISSOLUTION PROCESS

The practice of family law involves as much negotiating as it does litigating. For instance, a common saying is that there are no winners in a divorce, and the children are the biggest losers. The family practice law firm that strives to favorably resolve its client's legal problems in a manner that creates the least amount of additional damage and pain to all individuals affected—and does so successfully—provides the greatest degree of service to the client. Whether the service involves the initial divorce proceeding or a subsequent need to enforce or modify the alimony, child support, or custody order, the family practice lawyer who can meet the client's objectives with the least amount of court intervention will serve a client well.

All litigation is adversarial and can only escalate hostility between the adverse parties. In a family law practice, the clients' need for legal assistance arises from

FIGURE 1–2
With the assistance of a trained mediator, the parties attempt to resolve the issues surrounding the dissolution of their marriage.

discord in the most personal and intimate areas of their lives. Much attention and concern should be given to the manner in which the controversy is handled and the consequences for all concerned of mishandling or insensitively handling the issues underlying the dispute. All staff members of the law office should be aware of the need to handle delicate matters with great care. With the very high divorce rate that exists today, both the many members of the court system and the attorneys who practice a considerable amount of family law have become adept at treating all parties with respect and with understanding of the turmoil that accompanies the breakup of a marriage.

Divorces are much easier to obtain in the new millenium than they were in the 1890s. Most of the stigma attached to divorce has disappeared, and today's communities offer many resources to help divorcing spouses and their children deal with the difficult changes taking place. Community support for families going through this type of crisis is readily available today because of our society's acceptance of divorce. This was not always the case. For many centuries and for a number of decades in the twentieth century, there was enormous pressure from social, cultural, and certain religious institutions to preserve the marital union and nuclear family at almost any cost. We now turn to an historical glimpse of the nature of marriage and divorce over time and the values and attitudes that contributed to past and present views of both marriage and divorce.

THE ROOTS AND TRADITIONS OF AMERICAN FAMILY LAW

Much of American legal tradition has its roots in the common law decisions of England. However, centuries before the creation of the English common law, ancient legal systems developed rules to govern the rights and responsibilities of spouses and other family members. These ancient rules left their mark on later legal systems. In ancient Greece, a married woman was chattel, the legal property of her husband with no rights of her own. For centuries afterward, marriage was a formal arrangement in society in which women were subservient to men. Although in various cultures, at different points in history, women did possess some legal rights, they generally occupied a legal status that was inferior to that of men. In the United States, it was not until the passage of the Married Women's Property Acts that American women were allowed to own property in their own name. For this and many other equally compelling reasons, women were often reluctant to initiate legal proceedings to end their marriages.

Marriage, for many centuries, was a very strong social institution that contributed to the stability of society. Christianity transformed marriage from a mere social institution into a sacrament, a holy union lasting for eternity—"What God has brought together, let no man put asunder." Marriage was a legally and morally sanctioned relationship between a man and a woman, functioning as one social and economic unit. Spouses were responsible for the care of each other and jointly responsible for the care and maintenance of children, the issue of their union. However, divorce was not unheard of even in the earliest of times. In ancient times, a form of divorce took place when a woman left her husband or when a husband cast out his wife. In both instances, the husband remained in the family home and retained possession and control of the children of the marriage since they were regarded as chattel, pieces of personal property owned by the husband. In the Christian Western European civilizations of the Middle Ages, church and state were intertwined and the state enforced the doctrines of the Christian church, including the proscription against divorce.

Until the mid-1500s, there was one Christian church for all of Western Europe. This was the Roman Catholic Church with its seat of power vested in the pope in Rome. In the 1530s when King Henry VIII wished to divorce his queen, Catherine of Aragon, and marry Anne Boleyn, the Roman Catholic Church refused to give Henry VIII a dispensation to divorce and remarry. Henry VIII, as the head of the church in England, broke from Rome and established the Church of England. During the second half of the sixteenth century, several different religious groups arose in England, Scotland, Germany, and France, eventually resulting in the establishment of many new Christian sects, separate from the Church of Rome, which became branches of the Protestant movement. Originally, in the European countries where Protestantism prevailed, the church and state continued their close connection and the national religion became the prevailing Protestant denomination in the country. For instance, in Scotland, the established religion was Presbyterianism. In the American colonies settled by the Puritans, such as the Massachusetts Bay Colony, Puritanism became the state religion. In other of the thirteen original American colonies such as Virginia and the Carolinas, which were settled by Englishmen who remained loyal to the established Church of England, the Anglican religion became the official religion of the colony. However, despite the continuing connection of church and state, many of the now largely Protestant European nations and the Protestant colonies in America allowed at least what came to be called civil divorce. On the other hand, in the European countries where Roman Catholicism remained either the state religion or the religion embraced by the majority of inhabitants, civil divorce was much slower in coming. In Italy and the Republic of Ireland, civil divorce was not legally authorized until the second half of the twentieth century!

MARRIAGE, DIVORCE, AND FAMILY LAW FROM COLONIAL AMERICA TO THE TWENTIETH CENTURY

In colonial America, although marriage was regarded as a sacred union, the Puritans who had settled the New England colonies recognized and allowed divorce. They also sanctioned a form of legal separation known as "divorce of bed and board" under which the couple's sacred union remained intact but they no longer cohabited. When a couple divorced or separated, colonial governments imposed on the husband the continuing obligation of economic support of his wife and their children.

When the thirteen original colonies broke away from England and formed a new nation, the state governments assumed the power to legally authorize and legally dissolve marriages. The new American nation provided specifically for the separation of church and state in its Constitution. There was to be no national religion, nor were any of the new states allowed to establish any one religion as the official religion of that state. Henceforth, marriage and divorce as civil matters became separated from marriage and divorce as religious issues. In the eyes of the state, marriage was now viewed as a civil contract between two parties.

Under the marriage contract, each party had obligations to the other party. When one of the parties failed to perform an obligation of the marriage, he or she had breached the marital contract. The nonbreaching party could sue for a termination of the marriage contract and for damages from the other party as compensation for the harm caused by the breach. If the nonbreaching or "innocent" party proved that the marital contract had been breached, the court could terminate the marriage and, under the civil law, both parties were free to remarry. The state, through its court system, could order the offending or breaching party to compensate the other party and enter orders for the continuing support of the minor children of the marriage.

When each state government established either legislative or common law grounds for establishing breach of the marriage contract, these were commonly referred to as the grounds for divorce. When the female spouse alleged and proved grounds for divorce, the court almost always ordered the male spouse to continue to provide financial support to his former wife and his children. In many instances, even when a husband brought and won a divorce action against his wife, if the wife had been financially dependent on her husband for subsistence, the court ordered the husband to continue to provide for her financial support. However, enforcing these obligations was not always possible. Many ex-husbands disappeared from the court's jurisdiction and many divorced women and their children suffered economic deprivation and frequently social isolation as well. As long as women lacked the ability to support themselves, divorce was not a practical alternative. Societal pressures from many avenues, including the church, the extended family, and the local community, were also exerted to keep the family intact.

Political and economic forces also promoted the advantages of staying married. During the eighteenth century and for a good part of the nineteenth century, the intact family was the basic economic unit of the new American nation. When the United States was mainly an agrarian society, its financial health and political strength depended on the production and sale of agricultural products from thousands of small family farms. All family members were essential to the operation of these farms. Family members, even young children, contributed to the economic advancement of their family and the nation by performing one or more of the many chores needed to keep the farm running.

THE INDUSTRIAL REVOLUTION AND THE FAMILY

The Industrial Revolution of the nineteenth century gave rise to the factory system in the United States and shifted the centers of economic activity from the country towns to the cities. In the early and middle years of the nineteenth century, many individuals left the family farms in the New England and Middle Atlantic states to work in the cities. Throughout the second half of the 1800s the large influx of immigrants from Europe added to the population of urban centers. Frequently, mothers, fathers, and even young children worked in city factories. Eventually laws were passed to protect children from working at early ages.

Some women then began to stay at home to care for their children. When this occurred, the husband became the person primarily responsible for the family's financial support. He also usually became the family member with predominant economic power. Men had the ability to obtain credit in their own names, whereas women could only obtain credit under their husband's, father's, or brother's signature. Even married women who continued to work in mills and factories and later in offices and stores had inferior economic power because these women were frequently paid far less than their male counterparts. Single women fared no better in the workplace. In fact, except for low-paying jobs in factories or low-paying positions as domestic servants, there were few employment opportunities for women in nineteenth-century America.

FIGURE 1–3
As time went by, respectable married women were not expected to work, but rather stay home, do housework, and take care of the children.

As time went by, "respectable" married women were not expected to work. Even well-educated, married women who, when single, had held positions as schoolteachers or nursing professionals had few or no opportunities to work for pay. Many school systems prohibited married women from working as teachers; other school systems would not hire women with young children. Hospitals frequently instituted similar exclusionary policies for staff nurses.

As a result of these constraints, married women did not often consider divorce as a solution to a failing or unhappy marriage. Many women feared that they would have no means of supporting themselves or their children. Further, divorce carried a social stigma. Divorced women were not well accepted in many communities. The children of divorced mothers were often excluded from neighborhood play and not welcome in the homes of their friends who came from intact families.

Despite the many negative consequences of divorce for both women and men, and especially for children, the divorce rates rose at a slow but steady pace throughout the nineteenth century and into the early decades of the twentieth century. In the 1880s, one out of sixteen American marriages ended in divorce.

FAMILY LAW FROM THE DAWN OF THE TWENTIETH CENTURY TO THE PRESENT DAY

By 1900, there was one divorce for every twelve marriages. Undoubtedly, industrialization and urbanization played some part in this increase, if for no other reason than that these social and economic developments decreased the value of the intact family as an economic unit while providing women a meager increase in opportunities for paid employment outside the home.

However, divorce did occur during the first half of the twentieth century. Courts, when granting a divorce, usually ordered a husband to make weekly alimony payments and support payments for the maintenance of his former spouse and his children. Mothers were always awarded custody of children unless they were deemed in some way unfit or unless they abandoned the children and did not seek custody. Society continued to frown on divorce. To get a legal divorce, one party had to bring a civil suit and prove one of a limited number of grounds before the court would grant a decree of divorce. Typically, most states granted a divorce if one party proved the other committed adultery, abandoned them, or was a habitual drunkard. Eventually many states added grounds known as intolerable cruelty and mental cruelty. Even if parties agreed to divorce, one party had to sue the other party alleging one of these grounds. If the other party did not challenge the allegations, the judge would grant a divorce.

By the 1960s attitudes toward divorce were changing. Many young people no longer feared the severe sanctions imposed by their religious faith. Also some religious groups took a more compassionate view of couples in a bad marriage. Traditional religious institutions lost much influence over individuals and society in the 1960s when people began to question all aspects of American culture, including women's roles and women's rights, constraints on employment opportunities for women, and constraints on sexual freedom and reproductive choices.

Prior to the 1960s, fault played a central role in both the granting of divorce and in the determination of the amounts set for alimony awards and the distribution of marital property. Beginning in the mid-1960s and growing strong in the 1970s, public support emerged for what came to be known as **no-fault divorce.** Beginning in the 1970s, a number of state legislatures modified existing divorce laws to include the ground that the marital union or marital relationship had broken down irretrievably. This ground did not place fault for the breakdown on either party. The spouse seeking the divorce and bringing the legal action had merely to testify under oath that the marriage had broken down irretrievably and that there was no possibility of reconciliation. This change plus the many societal changes mentioned earlier resulted in many more divorces than previously.

In addition, the 1970s witnessed the beginnings of a trend toward awarding custody to fathers even when mothers were not deemed unfit. Many custody battles ensued as mothers' work schedules paralleled fathers' in terms of time spent away from home.

Divorce actions also increased dramatically in segments of the married population where individuals previously never considered severing their marital ties. Older women, frequently with the support of and at the urging of their adult children, sought divorces after decades of troubled marriages. These women demanded a fair share not only of what they and their husbands had acquired during the marriage, but also a fair share of their husbands' pensions and Social Security benefits.

Another development arising from new social conditions dealt with health care provisions. With the advent of comprehensive health insurance and the skyrocketing costs of health care, courts routinely ordered the noncustodial spouse, often the father, to maintain his minor children and sometimes his former spouse on his health plan. Women with superior health plans through their employers also sometimes were required to cover former spouses and children even if they were not the children's custodial parent. Further, with women making large salaries, men began to seek alimony from former wives and courts began awarding it to them!

The increase in the number of divorces gave rise to an increase in second and third marriages. With this higher rate of divorce and remarriage, prenuptial agreements also increased in both number and complexity.

The trend toward easy and frequent divorce continued through the 1980s and 1990s. The mid-1990s saw the beginnings of social and political action to once again make divorces harder to obtain. Laws surrounding the severing of the marital relationship may well come full circle during the twenty-first century.

Family Law Attorneys Reject Return to Fault-Based Divorce, Finds ABA Survey

WASHINGTON, DC, Oct. 18—Eighty-four percent of family lawyers oppose rescinding no-fault divorce laws according to a survey released today by the American Bar Association Section of Family Law.

"No-fault" divorce, available in some form in all 50 states, allows spouses to divorce without the assignment of blame. Prior to the adoption of no-fault laws in the 1970s, spouses were required to establish such fault-based grounds as adultery or mental or physical cruelty to obtain a divorce.

Legislatures in states such as Idaho, Michigan, and Iowa are among those currently examining their divorce laws and considering new legislation that is termed more "pro-family." Proposals typically include the establishment or extension of waiting periods before the divorce can be finalized; special education for parents so they understand the impact of divorce on their children; and returning to fault-based divorces. "Bad idea" say most of the more than 1,400 attorneys who responded to the ABA survey, when asked if there should be a return to fault-based divorce.

The overwhelming majority of respondents, nearly 84 percent, say they do not support a return to fault-based divorces. Further, more than two-thirds (69 percent) of the respondents do not agree that there is a direct correlation between the increase in the divorce rate in this country and the advent of the no-fault divorce 20 years ago.

"Divorce is one of the most complex issues of our time," says Los Angeles attorney Ira Lurvey, chair of the 11,000-member ABA Family Law Section. "No single magic bullet is the answer. Fault was taken out of divorce 25 years ago to promote harmony and reduce fighting. Putting it back in will do little more than return those evils, plus an increased divorce rate. We don't get progress by going back to the past."

However, nearly one-third (30 percent) of respondents support two systems of divorce based on whether the divorcing spouses were parents, while 66 percent do not support such a differentiation.

Respondents indicate support for the idea that no-fault divorce helps families weather the storm of divorce better than they did under fault-based systems.

Two-thirds of respondents (67 percent) agree that no-fault divorces are typically quicker than fault-based divorces; More than two-thirds indicate that no-fault divorces are less expensive than fault divorces (69 percent); and 65 percent agree that no-fault divorces typically are less acrimonious than fault divorces.

Proponents of a return to fault-based divorce say it will cure a host of ills related to the dissolution of marriage. Most respondents in the ABA survey, however, disagree. When asked whether or not these problems would be solved by divorce by fault the percentage of lawyers saying "no" were:

financial disparity between the divorcing spouses—women consistently fare worse (86 percent);

the abandonment of the family by those who are unwilling or cannot abide the mandatory waiting periods currently in place in 24 states (88 percent); and

unfairness to victims of domestic violence who occasionally are treated with bias by the courts and/or in the mediation process (85 percent).

"What may help is a retraining program for all of us. We live in a world of false expectations and mixed messages. Marriage is not necessarily bells and whistles forever. It is hard work, caring and being selfless. Those are commodities often in short supply these days," said Lurvey. Respondents are more split on whether no-fault divorces are emotionally easier on the children involved. While nearly 58 percent agree that no-fault divorces are emotionally easier on children from the marriage, more than one-third (37 percent) do not agree.

When asked to consider the impact of no-fault divorce on the fathers' rights movement in custody, just over one-fourth (26 percent) of survey participants agree that no-fault divorce is more equitable in custody, while 59 percent do not agree.

More than half of respondents (54 percent) agree that judges still do consider fault in divorce today.

"Judges do consider fault, and in some states are required to do so, but almost exclusively in the division of property, not in granting the divorce," said Lurvey.

The survey of approximately 6,000 of the nation's top matrimonial lawyers was conducted via fax. 1,462 attorneys participated in the survey, yielding an approximate response rate of 24 percent.

Source: ABA Press Release, "Family Law Attorneys Reject Return to Fault-Based Divorce. Finds ABA Survey," American Bar Association, 750 N. Lake Shore Dr., Chicago, IL, 60611; 312-988-5000, info@abanet.org.Copyright American Bar Association. All rights reserved. Reprinted by permission

Tremendous changes have taken place in American family law over the last half-century. Divorced persons and their children are no longer stigmatized in the eyes of society. The consciousness of the country has changed to where many believe that it is better for all parties involved to get divorced rather than to stay in a bad marriage. The most significant change over the last half-century, however, has been the high divorce rate, which is currently twice as high as it was in the 1960s. It reached its peak in the 1980s and has slowly been declining. The reason for this decline, however, is that marriage itself is declining. More couples in the United States are opting out of marriage and choosing to cohabitate instead. We do not know the failure rate of these relationships because they are severed by mutual agreement and not judicial intervention. Most marriages entered into today still have a 40 to 50 percent chance of surviving.

If you ask the question "Why is there such a high divorce rate?" in legal circles, the answer is the shift from fault to no-fault divorce. In order to obtain a divorce, a litigant traditionally had to prove one of the statutory fault grounds, or no divorce was granted. Traditional fault grounds included physical or mental cruelty, adultery, desertion, confinement to a prison or mental institution for a specified period of time, commission of a felony, and intemperance. Because fault grounds were difficult to prove, parties often colluded for the sole purpose of obtaining a divorce. Where the state fault grounds included mental and physical cruelty, mental cruelty was the easiest fault ground to fabricate. The parties understood that in order to get divorced, they had to play by the state's rules, and that a certain amount of lying was necessary if the goal was to dissolve a marriage. In 1969, the California legislature enacted the first no-fault divorce, which required parties only to prove that they had irreconcilable differences and there was no hope of reconciliation. The concept of no-fault divorce spread throughout the entire United States. Currently, all fifty states have some form of no-fault divorce provisions. Statutes vary from jurisdiction to jurisdiction, so it is important for attorneys and paralegals practicing family law to be familiar with their state requirements. New York State, for example, has one of the strictest no-fault statutes in the country. New York law requires a one-year period of separation as well as the filing of a written, notarized separation agreement. If the parties cannot resolve matters amicably, they must file for a divorce under the fault system and allege one of the statutory fault grounds.

Changes have also occurred in the American family with the advent of the women's movement. Prior to this era, fathers financially supported their daughters until the responsibility was passed on to husbands. In a traditional marriage, the husband was the head of the household and worked to support the family. The wife's function was to tend to the needs of the husband, home, and children. She was subordinate to her husband and dependent upon him for fulfillment of all her needs. The women's movement not only raised women's consciousness regarding the elevation of their status in society to that of men, it also helped open doors for economic opportunity. Many women have pursued the goal of becoming financially independent by working outside of the home, with some making more money than their husbands and commanding more status in the workplace. With more opportunities open to women, they are less likely to stay in unhappy marriages because they know they can take care of themselves and their children.

With the exception of resolving child custody and visitation issues, modern divorce law requires a shift in focus from proving fault to determining property and debt division; divorces are increasingly becoming financial accountings. For a couple with substantial assets, not only must they have attorneys representing them, they also must rely on the assistance of accountants, pension valuation experts, appraisers, and so on. Those without substantial assets have to learn how to live on what they have or work harder and longer to make ends meet. Most jurisdictions rely on the system of equitable distribution to divide property. Under the common law system of the past, judges looked at who actually held title to the property and determined its division in a divorce case based on who owned it. This system was extremely unfair to the traditional homemaker spouse, whose noneconomic contributions were not recognized. Many courts today look at the marital property of the parties, its value, and who has contributed to its acquisition, preservation, appreciation, or depreciation. The concept of equitable distribution assumes that marriage is an economic partnership, valuing not only the contributions of the employer spouse, but also the efforts of the homemaker spouse.

Changes have also occurred in spousal support awards. Traditionally, wives who were married for over ten years were awarded permanent or lifetime alimony. This was because of the financial position of women. They did not work outside the home and did not acquire Social Security or pension benefits. Without permanent alimony, a woman would become a charge on the taxpayers. The concept of alimony shifted as attitudes toward men, women, and social mores changed. Permanent alimony currently is a dying horse, and is not awarded to a spouse unless it was a long-term marriage of over twenty years, the spouse suffers from ill health, or the spouse has been out of the workforce for so long that climbing any kind of corporate ladder is not possible. Permanent alimony was replaced by rehabilitative alimony, which afforded the wife alimony in the short term for the purpose of becoming self-sufficient. Additionally, husbands may now ask for alimony from their wives, where as in the past, this was legally and socially unacceptable.

The reality of divorce, however, is that women usually fare much worse economically after a divorce. Women are most likely to be awarded custody of the children and must pick up the slack when the child support enforcement system fails to provide a solution. The amount of child support awarded was traditionally left up to the discretion of the trial court judge. It wasn't until the early 1990s that federal intervention prompted states to enact standard formulas to determine the amount of child support subject to strict deviation criteria. In 1984, Congress passed the **Child Support Enforcement Amendments** to enable mothers to collect child support and ease the social welfare burden on taxpayers. Some of these measures include federal and state income tax refund interception, wage withholding, revocation of professional licenses, and interstate enforcement. Despite these efforts, most women still find the system frustrating.

Changes in residency requirements in the last half-century have also impacted divorce in the United States. Historically, in many jurisdictions, a prospective divorce litigant had to wait either one or two years before a divorce could be filed. The purpose behind these requirements was that the state had to have a vested interest in the marriage before the courts would intervene in the divorce. States wanted to prevent **migratory divorces**—people flocking to a particular jurisdiction because of the short divorce residency requirements. The trend today is shorter residency requirements, making divorces easier to obtain.

Another recent trend is the increased number of *pro se* litigants dominating the divorce dockets due to the high cost of divorce. Many jurisdictions are creating *pro se* resource centers in courthouses, posting forms and instructions online, and enlisting lawyers from the private bar to take on cases *pro bono* or reduced rates to alleviate the burden. Paralegals, under lawyer supervision, may also assist in helping prepare documents. Courts are also simplifying and streamlining the process for uncontested divorces, and requiring parties involved in contested cases to participate in alternative dispute resolution as opposed to knock-down-drag-out divorce trials. In cases where the parties have little or no assets, no children, were married for a relatively short period of time, and both want the divorce, simplified procedures are being adopted by many jurisdictions. Legislatures in California, Colorado, Indiana, Minnesota, Nevada, and Oregon have enacted **summary dissolution of marriage.** All that is required in these jurisdictions, if you meet the requirements, is the filing of official documents with the appropriate court without the assistance of attorneys. Another form of low-cost divorce enacted by a number of states is a **simplified divorce procedure,** which is sometimes referred to as summary process or divorce by mutual consent. Unlike the summary dissolution of marriage, the parties in these states must appear before the court to dissolve their marriage. The process, however, is simplified and the courts make user-friendly forms and guidebooks available. The following states have adopted some type of simplified divorce procedure: Alaska, Arizona, Connecticut, Florida, Hawaii, Illinois, Mississippi, Montana, Ohio, Tennessee, Washington, and Wisconsin.

MARRIAGE: FROM CREATION TO DISSOLUTION

MARRIAGE DEFINED

"But for man no suitable helper was found. So the Lord God caused the man to fall into a deep sleep; and while he was sleeping, he took one of the man's ribs and closed up the place with flesh. Then the Lord God made a woman from the rib he had taken out of man, and he brought her to the man. The man said,

'This is now bone of my bones, and flesh of my flesh;
She shall be called 'woman' for she was taken out of man.'

For this reason, a man will leave his father and mother and be united to his wife and they will become one flesh". Genesis 2: 21–24 (New International Version.)

While *Black's Law Dictionary* defines marriage as a "legal union of a couple as husband and wife," its definition is also deeply rooted in our Judeo-Christian culture. Attempts to change the definition of marriage in the last decade have buttressed against its Judeo-Christian definition, with both the state and federal governments turning to the legislative drawing board in its defense. In the United States, a marriage is defined as the joining together of one man and one woman in a civil contract called **marriage.** On September 21, 1996, President Bill Clinton signed the **Defense of Marriage Act (DOMA)** into law in response to attempts on the part of gay-rights activists to require states to recognize same-sex marriages. DOMA provides that:

- The states have the right to deny recognition of a same-sex marriage or any marriage-like relationship recognized in another state.
- For federal purposes, marriage is defined as "a legal union of one man and one woman as husband and wife," and the term *spouse* as used in the statutes refers "only to a person of the opposite sex who is a husband or a wife." This means that same-sex couples are denied any benefits or rights afforded to heterosexual couples under federal law.

With the exception of Massachusetts, which recognizes same-sex marriage, the majority of states have enacted laws denying recognition of or banning same-gender unions. A small number of jurisdictions have established laws recognizing separate categories of legal recognition for same-sex couples called **civil unions** and **domestic partnerships.** Civil unions and domestic partnerships are a way for same-sex couples to formalize their relationship and take advantage of some state rights afforded to heterosexual couples. The most significant difference is that only heterosexual married couples may benefit from the more than 1,100 federal rights and privileges accruing from marriage such as Social Security and immigration benefits. (An in-depth discussion of the history of same-sex marriage is found in Chapter 4.)

In addition to its role as a social and religious institution, marriage affords the couple important rights in the eyes of the law. The legal benefits of marriage include:

- Elective share protection
- Estate and gift tax exemptions benefits

- Family court jurisdiction for dissolving marital relationship and obtaining orders in the area of alimony, property and debt division, child custody, visitation, and child support
- Family leave
- The ability to file joint income tax returns for state and federal tax purposes
- Guardianship rights
- Hospital visitation rights
- Immigration benefits
- Insurance benefits
- Intestate succession protection
- Joint adoptions
- Military benefits
- Appointment as conservator for a disabled spouse
- Decision making power for an incapacitated spouse
- Retirement benefits
- Spousal or marital communications privilege in court proceedings
- Loss of consortium claims in personal injury suits
- Right to file wrongful death lawsuits
- Possession of deceased spouse's remains at death
- Social Security, Medicare, and disability benefits
- Spousal or widow's allowance
- Stepparent adoptions
- Veterans' benefits
- Workers' compensation benefits

CREATING A VALID MARRIAGE

In order to create a valid marriage, a couple must comply with the laws of their jurisdiction. Barring some variations, most jurisdictions impose the following requirements:

Age Requirement: Anyone who has reached the age of majority in their state, usually age eighteen, may marry without the consent of their parents. If one or both of the individuals seeking to marry are under the age of eighteen, state law may require parental consent or **emancipation** by a court. Youths may be emancipated by operation of law, that is, on their birthday by reaching the age of majority or by court order at a younger age, usually age 16 or 17. Emancipation by court order is where a judge declares a minor an adult in the eyes of the law.

Blood Test Requirement: Most states, except for Indiana and Montana, have repealed mandatory blood tests for couples planning to marry. The original purpose for premarital blood testing was to screen for syphilis, rubella, and genetic disorders such as sickle-cell anemia or Tay-Sachs disease. In October of 2003, the State of Connecticut repealed premarital blood tests on the advice of the Centers for Disease Control and Prevention. Testifying in support of the repeal, Norma Gayle,

Connecticut's Department of Public Health commissioner, said the that premarital blood tests are expensive, inconvenient, and have little impact on prevention.

Marriage License Requirement: To get married, many state laws require both parties to personally appear before the county clerk in the county in which the wedding will take place, fill out and sign an application, and pay a nominal fee. The prospective bride and groom swear under oath to issues regarding age, prior marriages, and the legal relationship between the spouses, if any. The clerk then issues a **marriage license.** A marriage license is a document issued by the county clerk that authorizes a couple to get married. It is important to differentiate between a marriage license and a **marriage certificate.** While a marriage license is a legal document issued by the clerk that will eventually be filed with the state once the marriage is performed, the marriage certificate is a document prepared by the official performing the marriage. Most jurisdictions require the bride and groom, the person officiating the marriage, and one or two witnesses to sign the marriage certificate after the completion of the ceremony. In some jurisdictions, the marriage certificate is filed with the clerk upon completion of the marriage, and in others it is incorporated into the marriage license. All states now require the parties to disclose their respective Social Security numbers so that in the event of divorce, they may be located for child support enforcement purposes.

Solemnization Requirement: The marriage must be solemnized by a person authorized under state law. Clergy and justices of the peace generally carry out this function in most jurisdictions.

Connecticut General Statutes Sec. 46b-22

(a) All judges and retired judges, either elected or appointed and including federal judges and judges of other states who may legally join persons in marriage in their jurisdictions, family support magistrates, state referees and justices of the peace may join persons in marriage in any town in the state and all ordained or licensed clergymen, belonging to this state or any other state, so long as they continue in the work of the ministry may join persons in marriage. All marriages solemnized according to the forms and usages of any religious denomination in this state, including marriages witnessed by a duly constituted Spiritual Assembly of the Baha'is, are valid. All marriages attempted to be celebrated by any other person are void.

Recording Requirement: The person officiating the wedding ceremony has the responsibility of recording the marriage license and the marriage certificate with the county clerk within a specific statutory period. The couple may then obtain an official copy of the marriage license from the appropriate state agency.

MARRIAGES PERFORMED ABROAD

Most jurisdictions recognize marriages created in other states or foreign countries as long as the marriage was validly created in the state or country of origin and does not violate the public policy of the state. Same-sex marriages created in foreign countries where such unions are valid will probably not be recognized given the effect of the DOMA.

No Steps, No Marriage

In *Singh v. Singh*, the Supreme Court of New York set Mrs. Singh free from an arranged marriage. Her refusal to take the traditional seven steps called the "saptapadi" invalidated her marriage under India's Hindu Marriage Act of 1955 and New York law as well.

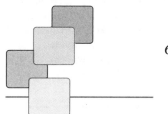

VIJAI P. SINGH V. VIMLA SINGH

67 Misc.2d 878, 325 N.Y.S.2d 590 (1971)

Supreme Court, Special Term, Tompkins County

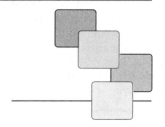

FREDERICK B. BRYANT, J.

This is an action brought by the plaintiff to have his purported marriage to the defendant declared null and void pursuant to section 5 of the Hindu Marriage Act (Act. No. 25 of the Laws of India, 1955).

The complaint alleges that the purported marriage took place in Allahabad, India, on January 19, 1964 when both parties were residents of India. The plaintiff asserts that he is now and has been for more than two years prior to the commencement of this action a resident of the State of New York. The complaint and the evidence submitted show that the marriage was arranged by the respective parents of the plaintiff and the defendant without the consent of either of the parties and that certain ceremonies and rites customary and essential in marriages performed according to the Hindu Marriage Act were not observed. The plaintiff asserts that because of this the purported marriage was a nullity. These ceremonies include the invocation before the sacred fire and the "saptapadi"—that is, the taking of seven steps by the bride and bridegroom before the sacred fire. The plaintiff alleges that the defendant refused to participate in these two rites and that the purported marriage was never consummated. The parties have never lived together as husband and wife.

Service of the summons in the action by personal service upon the defendant in India is shown by affidavit in accordance with section 232 Dom. Rel. of the Domestic Relations Law. The plaintiff appeared and testified before the court together with a co-operating witness and the proof required by section 144 Dom. Rel. of the Domestic Relations Law has been completed. The defendant has not appeared in the action nor answered the complaint. The court finds that it has jurisdiction of the subject matter of the action by reason of the plaintiff's uncontested allegation of residence in the State required by subdivision 5 of section 230 Dom. Rel. of the Domestic Relations Law.

Section 7 of the Hindu Marriage Act of 1955 reads as follows:

> "*Ceremonies for a Hindu marriage:* (1) A Hindu marriage may be solemnized in accordance with the customary rites and ceremonies of either party thereto."
>
> "(2) Where such rites and ceremonies include the Saptapadi (that is, the taking of seven steps by the bridegroom and the bride jointly before the sacred fire), the marriage becomes complete and binding when the seventh step is taken."

The meaning and effect of the quoted section is the principal question before this court. Plainly, where the customary ceremonies of either party to the marriage include the saptapadi the marriage is complete when the saptapadi is performed. But when the saptapadi is not performed the question arises as to whether the marriage is thereby invalid. Numerous Indian authorities on this point have been studied, including "The Hindu Marriage Act of 1955" by D.H. Chandhari; "Hindu Law of Marriage" by S.V. Gupte; "Indian Law of Marriage and Divorce" by Kumaid Desai; "The Hindu Marriage Act" by P.V. Deolalkar; "The Hindu Marriage Act" by Kashi Prasad; "The Hindu Marriage Act" by P.S.B. Bendra; "The Hindu Code" by Shiva Gopal; "The Hindu Law and Usage" by Nirmal Kumar Roy; and "The Hindu Marriage Act, 1955" by S.K. Shanglo. While these writers are not completely unanimous in their view as to the absolute necessity for performance of the saptapadi in order that a valid marriage be contracted, it seems to be the consensus that if the saptapadi is included among the customary rites and ceremonies of the parties to a marriage a marriage without the saptapadi is invalid and no marriage at all. Apparently, the customary beliefs and practices of the parties are determinative on this issue.

In the present case the plaintiff established that his purported marriage to the defendant was to be a Hindu marriage, solemnized by a Hindu priest. In such circumstances the saptapadi was an essential part of the rite. The refusal of the defendant to take the seven steps, although urged by the priest and her father several times to do so, amounted in effect to a refusal of her consent to the marriage. The plaintiff later learned that the reason for this refusal was that the defendant was in love with someone else and did not want to marry the plaintiff. She told the plaintiff she was not his wife and did not consider him to be her husband

and another witness testified to the defendant's failure to perform the saptapadi and to her present refusal to acknowledge herself the plaintiff's wife.

Under all of these circumstances it is this court's opinion that the defendant's failure to perform the saptapadi—an essential element in the marriage rites—makes the marriage invalid under New York law and likewise invalid under the Hindu Marriage Act of 1955. This is not a situation of a voidable marriage. The marriage in the present case was void *ab initio* in accordance with the Hindu Marriage Act and this annulment action merely declares that to be the fact.

The plaintiff is therefore entitled to a decree declaring his purported marriage to the defendant on January 19, 1964 to be null and void.

MARRIAGE PROHIBITIONS

RESTRICTING MARRIAGE BETWEEN FAMILY MEMBERS

A marriage between family members related by **consanguinity** (blood) or **affinity** (marriage) is **void ab initio,** or from its inception. All jurisdictions prohibit marriage between close relatives related by blood or consanguinity and do not allow marriage to a parent, grandparent, child, grandchild, aunt, uncle, niece, or nephew. States regulate intrafamilial relationships through marriage statutes and criminal statutes prohibiting incest. From a public policy standpoint, states justify such laws based on claims that children conceived in an incestuous relationship are born with genetic defects. The image of the uncivilized hillbilly who marries his sister and produces cross-eyed children is widely frowned upon in our society and a source of ridicule on daytime talk shows. More important, laws prohibiting incest prevent the exploitation of children and establish a social order within the family unit. Intrafamilial relationships are also prohibited because they disrupt family harmony and violate social norms. From a religious perspective, incest is considered a sin under biblical law and is strictly prohibited in Judeo-Christian traditions.

Marriage laws also restrict unions between family members related by affinity or marriage. Laws regarding marriage between cousins, in-laws, and step-relatives however, vary from state to state. In 1957, rock legend Jerry Lee Lewis created a scandal when he married his first cousin, and such marriages are still considered taboo today. Marriage between first cousins is banned in twenty-four states. Nineteen states have no restrictions, and the others place either a sterility requirement or mandate genetic counseling to ensure that the couple is well aware of the risks of reproducing children who may be born with genetic abnormalities. New scientific evidence, however, may support repealing laws that prohibit marriage between cousins. A report in the *Journal of Genetic Counseling*, published in April of 2002, entitled "Genetic Counseling and Screening of Consanguineous Couples and Their Offspring: Recommendations of the National Society of Genetic Counselors," concluded that children born of first cousins have a 2 to 3 percent greater risk of birth defects and a slightly over 4 percent greater risk of early death than the general population, and such risks may be detected early through genetic testing.

California Family Code, Section 2200–2201

2200. Marriages between parents and children, ancestors and descendants of every degree, and between brothers and sisters of the half as well as the whole blood, and between uncles and nieces or aunts and nephews, are incestuous, and void from the beginning, whether the relationship is legitimate or illegitimate.

Florida Statute Sec. 741.21

Incestuous marriages prohibited. A man may not marry any woman to whom he is related by lineal consanguinity, nor his sister, nor his aunt, nor his niece. A woman may not marry any man to whom she is related by lineal consanguinity, nor her brother, nor her uncle, nor her nephew.

Texas Family Code Sec. 6.201

Consanguinity. A marriage is void if one party to the marriage is related to the other as:

1. an ancestor or descendant, by blood or adoption;
2. a brother or sister, of the whole or half blood or by adoption;
3. a parent's brother or sister, of the whole or half blood or by adoption; or
4. a son or daughter of a brother or sister, of the whole or half blood or by adoption.

BIGAMOUS OR POLYGAMOUS MARRIAGES

Bigamy is defined as being married to two people at the same time. **Polygamy** is defined as having multiple spouses. All jurisdictions prohibit bigamous and polygamous marriages. Contrary to popular belief, Utah also prohibits polygamous and bigamous marriages, which were once sanctioned by the Mormon Church many years ago. These practices are punishable under criminal law throughout the country.

We live in a culture where being married two to three times in a lifetime is not unheard of. Once a client is legally divorced, he or she is free to remarry immediately, as long as state requirements are satisfied. Divorced persons who wish to remarry should make sure that they are legally divorced from their previous spouse. If this is overlooked or the person lies to the city official, is granted a marriage license, and goes through a ceremony, the second marriage may be declared invalid. The second spouse is referred to as a **putative spouse.** The first spouse is in a stronger legal position. If a previous marriage was not legally dissolved, this may be "cured" by legally dissolving the first marriage. Once the divorce to the first spouse is final, the second marriage has been "cured" and is now valid.

COVENANT MARRIAGE

Covenant marriage is a response to the rising divorce rate in the United States as a result of changes from fault to no-fault divorce. In addition, the U.S. Census of 2000 reveals that many couples are avoiding marriage and opting to cohabitate instead. Our society has also accepted divorce as another adult passage. Many go into marriage with the feeling that if it doesn't work out, divorce is always an option. Social stigma is no longer attached to divorce. Some feel that opposite-sex marriages are too easy to get into and too easy to terminate. Covenant marriage is an alternative type of marriage that can be summarized as requiring premarital counseling, a return to fault-based grounds in order to dissolve the marriage, counseling before going through divorce, adherance to a covenant contract, and longer mandatory waiting periods. This type of marriage is supported by religious groups who view marriage as a covenant between God and the spouses.

The end result is to reduce the divorce rate and make marriages harder to dissolve. People will be discouraged from going into marriage too quickly and divorcing too quickly. It is intended to reinforce the commitment to marriage. Three states have covenant marriage as an option. Louisiana was the first to enact covenant marriage in 1997, followed by Arizona in 1998 and Arkansas in 2001. Covenant marriage has not "caught on" and has not become popular even in the jurisdictions that enacted it.

LOUISIANA COVENANT MARRIAGE ACT

Under Louisiana's covenant marriage law, the couple must sign a statement of intent, recite a declaration, and provide proof of participation in a premarital course. In the event the parties wish to dissolve their marriage, they could obtain a divorce by proving the fault grounds of adultery, imprisonment for a felony, abandoning the marital home for at a period of at least one year, or physically or sexually abusing a family member. If such fault grounds are not available, the parties may be divorced if they have lived separate and apart for a specified period of time. There is a provision in the law that allows couples who are already married to convert to a covenant marriage.

> **Declaration, Louisiana Civil Code Annotated; Title V, Article 103 and Louisiana Revised Statutes, Section 9–308**
>
> We do solemnly declare that marriage is a covenant between a man and a woman who agree to live together as husband and wife for so long as they both may live. We have chosen each other carefully and disclosed to one another everything which could adversely affect the decision to enter into this marriage. We have received premarital counseling on the nature, purposes, and responsibilities of marriage. We have read the Covenant Marriage Act, and we understand that a Covenant Marriage is for life. If we experience martial difficulties, we commit ourselves to take all reasonable efforts to preserve our marriage, including marital counseling.
>
> With full knowledge of what this commitment means, we do hereby declare that our marriage will be bound by Louisiana law on Covenant Marriages and we promise to love, honor, and care for one another as husband and wife for the rest of our lives.

COMMON LAW MARRIAGE

By the end of the nineteenth century, the institution known as common law marriage was recognized in most states in the United States as a legal form of marriage that carried with it all of the rights and obligations of a ceremonial and statutorily memorialized union. Common law marriages were numerous in frontier states and in rural areas where the parties were often geographically distant from the county or municipal offices that issued marriage licenses. However, common law marriages also existed in urban areas. Today, many states have statutorily abolished common law marriage. Legal proceedings that affect common law marriages are becoming increasingly rare because so few states permit or recognize the formation of a common law marriage within their boundaries. However, states that do recognize common law marriages do adjudicate their dissolution. In addition, some states do not recognize the formation of a common law marriage within the state, but will recognize as legally valid a common law marriage formed in a state where common law marriage is legal. In these states, the courts will adjudicate the dissolution of these marriages as long as other jurisdictional requirements have been met.

What is a Common Law Marriage?

A **common law marriage** is a marriage created without a license or ceremony. According to popular myth, simply living with a member of the opposite gender for a period of time creates this form of marriage. Requirements vary from state to state, but creating a common law marriage requires more than living together with someone.

In general, the requirements for a valid common law marriage are:

- The parties must live together for a significant period of time.
- This means that they refer to each other as "my wife" or "my husband" and by the same last name hold assets, bills, and leases in joint name; file a joint tax return, and so on.
- The parties intend to be married.

States That Recognize Common Law Marriage

Alabama, Colorado, Iowa, Kansas, Montana, Rhode Island, South Carolina, Texas, and Utah all recognize common law marriage. New Hampshire recognizes common law marriages for inheritance purposes only. Georgia, Idaho, and Ohio recognize common law marriages created before certain dates in an effort to phase them out over time.

Love Hurts

It sure does, especially when you're trying to claim a common law marriage exists between you and one of the stars of 'The Big Chill' and 'Syriana.'

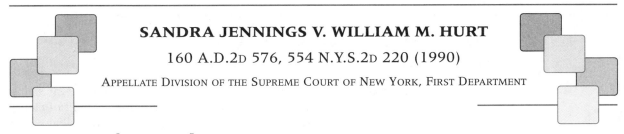

SANDRA JENNINGS V. WILLIAM M. HURT

160 A.D.2D 576, 554 N.Y.S.2D 220 (1990)

APPELLATE DIVISION OF THE SUPREME COURT OF NEW YORK, FIRST DEPARTMENT

SILBERMANN, J

In her amended complaint, plaintiff alleged that she and defendant had entered into a common-law marriage by virtue of having held themselves out as husband and wife in South Carolina from October 31, 1982 to January 10, 1983. After meeting in 1981, the parties began living together in New York City. On October 31, 1982, plaintiff joined defendant in South Carolina where he was filming a movie. When plaintiff became pregnant in 1982, defendant, who was married to another woman, commenced divorce proceedings with the divorce becoming final on December 3, 1982. During that same year, defendant's counsel drafted a financial agreement for the parties. The relationship between the parties in South Carolina became somewhat volatile but plaintiff alleged that during one of their arguments, defendant told her that "as far as he was concerned, we were married in the eyes of God" and that they had "a spiritual marriage." He also purportedly told her that "[w]e were more married than married people." Plaintiff's claim that she is defendant's common-law wife is based on these events. Defendant's testimony directly contradicted that of plaintiff.

The record fails to support plaintiff's claim that she is defendant's common-law wife. Notably, plaintiff never mentioned the conversation regarding the "spiritual marriage" at her deposition. The record also reveals that a statement in which plaintiff allegedly signed her name as "Sandra Cronsberg Hurt" was an altered copy in which the name "Hurt" had been inserted.

In 1983, defendant filed an affidavit with the Putative Fathers' Registry in New York which acknowledged his paternity of plaintiff's child. Filing this document, designed to ensure the child's legitimacy, would have been unnecessary had the parties in fact been married. Moreover, in 1984, one year after the parties left South Carolina, drafts of a relationship agreement continued to state "whether or not the parties hereafter marry each other." Other documents introduced into evidence listed defendant as single and plaintiff as his "friend" rather than his spouse. Of the many witnesses who testified and of the numerous affidavits offered into evidence, almost all demonstrated that the parties never held themselves out as being married nor were they perceived as husband and wife.

To establish a common-law marriage in South Carolina, the proponent must establish "an intention on the part of both parties to enter into a marriage contract" *(Ex Parte Blizzard*, 185 S.C. 131, 133, 193. S.E. 633, 635). The mutual agreement necessary to create such a marriage "must be conveyed with such a demonstration of intent and with such clarity on the part of the parties that marriage does not creep up on either of them and catch them unawares. One cannot be married unwittingly or accidentally" *(Collier v. City of Milford*, 206 Conn. 242, 251, 537 A.2d 474, 479). The evidence in the instant case clearly demonstrates that there was neither a mutual intent nor an agreement to enter into a marriage contract. Consequently, there was no common-law marriage.

We further find that the Supreme Court properly denied plaintiff's motion for leave to amend her complaint to allege three new causes of action since these causes of action were insufficient as a matter of law *(see, East Asiatic Co. v Corash*, 34 A.D.2d 432). The first proposed cause of action, to impose a constructive trust on an apartment owned by defendant, cannot stand since plaintiff failed to establish that she had a property interest in the apartment. Nor did she establish all of the necessary elements for a constructive trust *(see, Onorato v Lupoli*, 135 A.d.2d 693).

The second proposed cause of action, relating to defendant's alleged breach of a promise to support plaintiff in the future, is too vague to sufficiently state a cause of action *(see, Dombrowski v. Somers*, 41 N.Y.2d 858). Moreover, while plaintiff claims that this cause of action sounds in fraud, it arose directly from the breach of contract and is therefore a contract claim instead of a cause of action in fraud *(Marks v. Nassau County Assn. for Help of Retarded Children*, 135 A.D.2d 512). The third proposed cause of action, that defendant falsely promised to support plaintiff if she would have his child and give up her career, is void as against public policy *(see, McCall v. Frampton*, 81 A.D.2d 607). The law does not recognize a cause of action for sacrificing career opportunities in order to act as a "wife" *(see, Baron v. Jeffer*, 98 A.D.2d 810). Concur—Sullivan, J.P., Carro, Milonas, Rosenberger and Smith, JJ.

WHY CHOOSE COMMON LAW MARRIAGE?

People may opt for a common law marriage for these reasons:

- **Convenience.** In the nineteenth century, while the frontier was being settled, parties pledged themselves to each other without benefit of clergy or state officials because they were miles away from either religious or governmental institutions.

- **Personal preference.** Some couples opposed and wished to avoid intrusion by either church or state. For instance, in the early decades of the twentieth century, many free-spirited individuals known as *Bohemians* lived in the Greenwich Village section of New York and scorned the legal and religious trappings of conventional society as bourgeois and artificial. Their common law marriages were often political or societal statements. Some Bohemians went even further with their protests and embraced living together instead of any legally binding arrangement.

- **Poverty.** Some couples simply had no money for a church wedding or for an official ceremony and the attendant costs of a marriage license and blood tests.

DISSOLVING THE MARITAL UNION

DISSOLUTION OF MARRIAGE

Excluding the death of a spouse, there are three ways to terminate a marriage: (1) dissolution of marriage, (2) legal separation, and (3) annulment. **Dissolution of marriage** is the phrase many jurisdictions use to formally define the word "divorce." It is the complete legal severance of the marital relationship. After the conclusion of a divorce proceeding, the parties are legally free to remarry if they so choose. Be it a ceremonial or common law marriage, it is the state that must legally dissolve the marital union. State intervention is required to protect the rights of the parties, provide a forum where grievances can be aired instead of encouraging couples to resort to self-help, and formally end a legal status that carries many rights and obligations. Major issues such as child support, custody, visitation, alimony, and property and debt division must be resolved either by mutual agreement of the parties, with assistance from attorneys or mediators, or by judicial order.

LEGAL SEPARATION

Clients inquiring about a divorce will very often ask about a **legal separation,** or **separate maintenance,** as it is known in some jurisdictions. Instead of asking for a dissolution of marriage, the client's petition or complaint requests a legal separation: a status that allows the parties to live separate and apart, but unable to remarry. Once clients hear that they cannot remarry, many abandon the idea. While not as common today, legal separations are available in most jurisdictions and may be chosen for some of the following reasons:

Religious: If the client's religion objects to divorce, a legal separation may be an option.

Medical Insurance Coverage: If a client has serious health problems, is the nonemployee spouse, and is currently covered under a spouse's health insurance, it is important to examine whether a divorce or legal separation is in the client's best interest. Most insurance coverage ceases upon divorce; however, some policies may allow continued coverage in cases of legal separation. Ask for a copy of the client's group policy to determine when coverage ceases.

Financial: Parties may want to delay obtaining a formal divorce in order to qualify for certain Social Security and pension rights. If a couple has been married for ten years, for example, they qualify for a divorced spouse benefit under federal Social Security law. Therefore, reaching the ten-year mark is important, especially in cases where they may be very close. If this is the situation, the couple may obtain a legal separation and later convert it to a divorce, while preserving their rights.

Trial Separation: The parties may wish to enter into a trial separation and live separate and apart during this interim period. They may view the legal separation as a cooling-off period with the prospect of possibly reconciling in the near future. A legal separation may be a solution, especially if they want a formal agreement on issues of custody, support, and property division. There are procedural mechanisms available to convert legal separations to dissolutions in cases where the parties wish to change their status later on.

An action for a legal separation is similar to a divorce or dissolution action in that specific grounds must be alleged and proven. The grounds that can be alleged are usually the same grounds that can be alleged in a divorce proceeding. Historically, an action for legal separation was brought by a spouse who desired to avoid the legal, social, or religious ramifications of a divorce but nevertheless wished to live apart from the other spouse. Legal separations are not as common today, but the action has survived and is still available to the spouse who wishes to pursue that course of action rather than divorce.

Courts granting legal separations may, when appropriate, order one spouse to provide for the financial support of the other spouse by making periodic payments to the spouse. Most courts will order the noncustodial spouse to pay child support to the custodial spouse for the minor children. Courts may also order an equitable distribution of marital property or may incorporate into the separation decree the parties' separation agreement in which the parties themselves have negotiated a division of the marital estate.

After a legal separation, both parties retain certain marital rights and obligations that are extinguished after a divorce is final. For instance, a spouse may still have to provide medical insurance coverage for the other spouse and will still be able to have that spouse covered under any family policy. Similarly, if an individual's pension plan, on that individual's death, calls for the payment of either a lump sum or partial or full periodic pension payments to the person's spouse, the spouse who has obtained a legal separation rather than a divorce will be eligible for such a benefit. In addition, if one party to a legal separation dies intestate, his or her spouse will be entitled to a statutory spousal share of the estate. If the deceased spouse had a will, then the other spouse may elect to receive either what was bequeathed to him or her in the will or to receive the statutory spousal share, and will usually select whichever amount is greater.

A legal separation also places limitations on spouses. The most restrictive limitation is that because the parties are still legally married, neither party is free to remarry.

SEPARATE MAINTENANCE

An action for separate maintenance is similar to a legal separation. The marriage is still valid and neither party is legally free to remarry. In addition, an action for separate maintenance affirms the continuation of the marriage and enforces the legal obligations of each spouse in the marriage. An action for separate maintenance does not expressly or necessarily authorize a husband or wife to live apart; however, a wife's refusal to cohabit with her husband is sanctioned and authorized. Actions for separate maintenance are less common today than in the nineteenth century and during the first half of the twentieth century. Sometimes they were initiated by a wife whose husband was about to go abroad or to another part of this country to work or to perform military service. On other occasions, the action for separation was a precursor to a divorce action brought during a period of marital discord or during a trial separation.

ANNULMENTS

An **annulment** is a court order terminating a marriage by declaring it void from its inception. There are two types of annulments. A civil annulment is obtained through a court order, and laws vary from state to state. A religious annulment is obtained through a religious body and is separate and distinct from a civil annulment, which is obtained through a civil court proceeding. For example, Roman Catholics who divorce must obtain a religious annulment or an "ecclesiastical declaration of nullity" in accordance with Church law before they can remarry or receive Holy Communion. A religious annulment does not affect issues such as legal dissolution of the marriage, alimony, child custody, property division, and child support. These matters must be dealt with in a civil court, either through a divorce or civil annulment, *before* an ecclesiastical declaration of nullity may be obtained in the Roman Catholic Church. If there is no civil divorce or annulment, the Church tribunal will most likely encourage the parties to reconcile their differences.

In order to obtain a civil annulment, the moving party must prove that a defect existed at the time of the marriage that rendered it invalid. Some clients think that annulments are easier to obtain than divorces, especially if they were in a short-term marriage. This could not be farther from the truth, as the grounds for obtaining an annulment may be very difficult to prove. In addition, annulments cannot be obtained simply because one or both of the parties feel as though they made a horrible mistake.

GROUNDS FOR ANNULMENT—VOID VERSUS VOIDABLE MARRIAGE

A **void marriage** is invalid at the time of its creation. A **voidable marriage** is invalid at its inception but remains in effect unless the court terminates it. When a court is satisfied that the petitioning party has proven that a legal impediment existed at the time the marriage ceremony took place, the court may declare a marriage null and void. In some jurisdictions, the court may be limited to declaring the marriage "voidable" rather than void. The invalid marriage may become valid once the impediment to marriage has been removed. For instance, where a petitioning party has brought an annulment action based on legal incapacity due to minority age, if both parties are now of legal age, the court may issue a decision giving the petitioning party the legal right to void the marriage if they wish. However, if that party has reconsidered their decision to annul the marriage, the marriage may continue because the court will not void the marriage on its own initiative. Conversely, a court will always declare a marriage void on proof that one or both parties entered into a prior valid marriage and is (are) still legally married to the party of the prior marriage. Existence of the following grounds on the part of one or both parties allows a court to declare a marriage null and void or voidable, under some circumstances. Remember, grounds for annulment vary from state to state, so check local statutes.

- A valid prior existing marriage that was never legally terminated. If the previous marriage is legally terminated and the couple is still cohabitating, the void marriage may become valid.
- Close relation by blood or consanguinity.

- One or both of the parties lacked the mental capacity or were mentally disabled to the extent of not being able to understand or appreciate the nature of the marriage.
- One or both of the parties entered the marriage with no intention of living in a marital relationship or residing together as husband and wife. For example, at one time in the United States, a noncitizen could acquire U.S. citizenship by marrying a U.S. citizen, in what is known as a **sham or green card marriage.** In many cases, the citizen agreed to the marriage for monetary compensation, and sometimes did not meet the person until the day of the ceremony and never saw the person again.
- Under the legal age of consent in their jurisdiction. In many states, parents may consent to the marriage of a sixteen-or seventeen-year-old child. Teenagers who are legally emancipated by a court of law may also marry without parental consent. If one or both of the parties were underage at the time of the marriage, reach the age of majority, and then continue to cohabitate, the once-void marriage may be valid.
- One or both parties were forced to enter into the marriage through fraud, duress, or coercion. An example of a marriage entered into under duress is the "shotgun wedding." There was a time in the history of our country when getting pregnant out of wedlock was not acceptable. Many men were forced into a what became known as a "shotgun wedding" in order to protect the honor of the woman and her family. Fraud is also a basis for annulment. Failure to disclose infertility, a criminal history of felonious conduct, an incurable illness, or a history of severe mental illness to a prospective spouse may be grounds for an annulment if such vital information disclosed prior to the marriage would have resulted in a refusal to enter into the marriage.
- One or both parties were under the influence of drugs or alcohol.
- One or both parties are physically unable to consummate the marriage.

Annulments are alive and well in the United States today, as the accompanying recent and much-publicized cases illustrate.

On May 9, 2005, after having known each other for a brief four months, Renee Zellweger, star of '*Jerry McGuire*' and '*The Bridget Jones Diary*', married country singer Kenny Chesney on a trip to the Virgin Islands. As with many celebrity marriages, blink and you'll miss it. On September 15, 2005, Zellweger filed papers with the Los Angeles Superior Court asking for an annulment and citing "fraud" as grounds. In later statements, Zellweger clarified the term *fraud* as only a legal term, having no reflection on Chesney's character. A later statement by both parties released to the public said that they both had different objectives at the start of the marriage, but these conflicting objectives were not specified.

Another celebrity marriage with an extremely short shelf life concerns pop star Britney Spears. On January 5, 2004, a Clark County family court judge granted Spears an annulment, declaring her five-hour marriage to childhood friend Jason Allen Alexander null and void. Spears and Alexander entered into marriage at the Little White Chapel in Las Vegas, Nevada, only to regret it five hours later. In her annulment petition, Spears alleged the following grounds:

> . . . Plaintiff Spears lacked understanding of her actions to the extent that she was incapable of agreeing to the marriage because before entering into the marriage the Plaintiff and Defendant did not know each others' likes and dislikes, each others' desires to have or not have children, and each others' desires as to state of

1 COMA

2 JOHN D. HANOVER, ESQ., Nevada Bar No. 6672
   RICHARD A. CALEEL, ESQ., Nevada Bar No. 6585
3 LAW OFFICES OF JOHN D. HANOVER
   3753 Howard Hughes Parkway, Suite 200
4 Las Vegas, Nevada 89109
   Telephone: (702) 836-8499
5

6 Attorneys for Plaintiff

7

8

9   EIGHTH JUDICIAL DISTRICT COURT

10   CLARK COUNTY, NEVADA

11   )
12 Darva Conger.   )
)
13   Plaintiff,   )
)
14   vs.   )   CASE NO. D251297
)   DEPT NO. C
15 Richard Scott Rockwell,   )
)
16   Defendant.   )
)
17 ——————————————————————————)

18

19   COMPLAINT FOR ANNULMENT

20

21   I.

22   Plaintiff entered into marriage ceremony in the City of Las Vegas, County of

23 Clark, State of Nevada, on or about the 8th day of February 2000, having first secured a

24 marriage license from the County Clerk of Clark County Nevada.

25

26   II.

27 There are no minor children the issue of said purported marriage.

28

III.

There is no community property of the parties hereto.

IV.

The marriage has not been consummated and the parties to the marriage have not cohabitated at any time.

V.

The grounds for the annulment are fraud, pursuant to N.R.S. 125.340, and all equitable grounds pursuant to N.R.S. §125.350, including, but not limited to, mutual mistake in that the contract of marriage does not express the true intentions of the parties with regard to the marriage.

VI.

Plaintiff was a contestant on a televised show entitled "Who Wants to Marry A Millionaire" which was broadcast on February 15, 2000 (hereinafter the "Show"). The producers of the Show and the Fox Network (hereinafter "Fox"), the network that aired the Show, brought fifty female contestants to Las Vegas, Nevada, from all over the United States to compete on the Show for "the opportunity to marry a millionaire" and in exchange for certain gifts and prizes. The Defendant was the "millionaire" for whom the contestants competed. Each of the fifty contestants applied for a marriage license in Nevada so that if chose, the Show could conclude with a marriage ceremony, to be broadcast live, purporting to unite the perfect strangers as man and wife. The wedding ceremony, and the contest, were intended to draw millions of viewers and thereby generate significant revenues for the producers of the Show and Fox. Neither the contestants nor the Show's producers seriously contemplated creating a proper marriage. In fact, the Show's producers and Fox had each of the contestants and the defendant sign an annulment agreement prior to the Show as a guaranty of the contestants' right to an annulment.

VII.

As part of the Show and for entertainment purposes, Plaintiff and Defendant agreed to be married on television with the understanding that the marriage was not of legal force and effect and could be annulled following the show's televised broadcast. Plaintiff, at the time she entered into the marriage, did not intend to become the actual wife of the Defendant in law or in fact. Plaintiff is informed and believes that Defendant did not intend to become the husband of Plaintiff in law or fact.

VIII.

At the time she entered into the purported marriage, Plaintiff relied in good faith on the erroneous assertions of the Defendant and/or the Show's producers regarding Defendant and his background. Defendant and/or the Show's producers misrepresented material facts regarding Defendant's personality and his background to Plaintiff. Plaintiff was unaware that Defendant had a history of problems with his prior girlfriends and was the subject of at least one restraining order for threatening and dangerous behavior. Had Plaintiff known the true and complete material facts at the time she entered into the purported marriage, she would not have taken the action that she did. Plaintiff could not reasonably discover the true facts regarding Defendant prior so the marriage since even Defendant's identity was concealed from her until its revelation on live television just moments before the purported marriage.

IX.

The marriage is the result of a mutual mistake of fact and was entered into solely for an entertainment purpose. The parties did not intend that the marriage should be of

1   operative legal force or effect. Moreover, Plaintiff's purported consent is invalidated by

2   the misrepresentations upon which she reasonably relied.

3

4   WHEREFORE, Plaintiff prays that said purported marriage of plaintiff and

5   defendant may be, by an Order of the above-entitled Court, declared to be null and void

6   *ab initio* for the reasons hereinabove set forth, and for such other and further relief as to

7   the Court may deem just and proper.

8

9   DATED: March 3, 2000   LAW OFFICES OF JOHN D. HANOVER

10

11   By: *John D. Hanover*

12   John D. Hanover, Esq., Bar No. 6672

13   Richard A. Caleel, Esq., Bar No. 6585

14   3753 Howard Hughes Parkway

15   Suite 200

16   Las Vegas, NV 89109

17   Telephone (702)836-8489

18   Attorney for Plaintiff

19

20

21

22

23

24

25

26

27

28

residency. Upon learning of each others' desires, they are so incompatible that there was a want of understanding of each others' actions in entering into this marriage.

In another example of short-lived celebrity marriages, the winning contestant on the *Who Wants to Marry a Millionaire* television show soon discovered that sometimes it's not easier to *stay* married to a rich man than a poor man.

Although *annulment* is not a totally unfamiliar term to the average layperson, most people do not know how an annulment differs from a marital dissolution or divorce action. The legal theory underlying an annulment action is quite different from the action for divorce or dissolution of marriage. A person institutes a divorce or dissolution of marriage action to end a valid existing marriage. A person initiates an annulment proceeding to obtain a judicial decision that a valid marriage does not exist nor ever existed between that person and another party.

Just as a common law marriage may be legally formed without a formal ceremony, a formal ceremony does not always establish legal marriage. In an annulment action the court is called on to legally declare that despite ceremonial and state procedures, no legal marriage was formed or exists. A court may grant an annulment even if the parties obtained a marriage license and went through a marriage ceremony, provided that the petitioning party alleges and proves that at the time of the marriage ceremony, an impediment existed to the forming of a legally valid marriage. The petitioning party must introduce evidence of facts or circumstance that the state legislature or state common law has determined constitute an impediment to the forming of a valid marital union.

Typical grounds for annulment can include incapacity because of minority age status, mental incompetence, one or both parties' involvement in the existence of a still legally valid marriage, the inability of one party to consummate the marital union through sexual intercourse, and fraud that is material to the decision to marry (such as lying about one's reproductive ability, withholding knowledge of one's own infertility, or withholding material information about one's criminal history or the state of one's health).

A person seeking an annulment must be one of the parties to the marriage, unless a party is legally a minor or mentally incompetent. In such instance, the party's parent, legal guardian, or conservator can bring the action. The person bringing the annulment action must institute an annulment proceeding in a family court.

END-OF-CHAPTER EXERCISES

Crossword Puzzle

Across

2. a marriage that is invalid at its inception but remains in effect unless the court terminates it

4. acquiring adult status by reaching the age of majority or by court order at a younger age

6. an alternative type of marriage that can be summarized as requiring premarital counseling, a return to fault-based grounds in order to dissolve the marriage, counseling before going through divorce, adherance to a covenant contract, and longer mandatory waiting periods

8. a document issued by the county clerk that authorizes a couple to get married

9. related by blood

10. a court order terminating a marriage by declaring it void from its inception

11. the joining together of one man and one woman in a civil contract

12. related by marriage

Down

1. people flocking to a particular jurisdiction to get divorced because of the short divorce residency requirements

3. a marriage created without a license or ceremony

5. a status that allows the parties to live separate and apart, but unable to remarry

7. a U.S. citizen agrees to a marriage for monetary compensation

Review Questions

1. What changes have taken place in American family law over the last half-century?

2. What are the legal advantages of being married?

3. What is meant by the term "grounds" for divorce, and what were some of the traditional grounds in the United States?

4. Do you believe that no-fault divorce is to blame for the high divorce rate in the United States?

5. Why do you think covenant marriages have not become popular in this country despite the high divorce rate?

Case for Briefing

RANIERI v. RANIERI, 146 A.D.2d 34, 539 N.Y.S.2d 382 (2d Dept 1989)

Exploring the Workplace: Activities

1. What are the requirements for a valid marriage in your state? See **http://usmarriagelaws.com.**

2. Your clients are first cousins and residents of the State of Arizona. She is thirty-one and he is thirty-five. They wish to get married and want to know the requirements for marriage in the state. Using the website **http://usmarriagelaws. com,** what are the Arizona requirements? Are there any other jurisdictions that allow first cousins to marry?

3. What are the requirements for a valid common law marriage in Pennsylvania, Texas, and Alabama? See **http://www. unmarried.org/common.html.**

4. Your client lives in Iowa and has lived with her boyfriend for over ten years. She wants out of the relationship and he says to her "it won't be that easy because you are my common law wife!" What are the requirements for a valid common law marriage in Iowa, and what questions do you want to ask the client to determine whether this relationship is or is not a common law marriage?

5. It was a dull day in the law firm of Appletts & Antonelli, where you work as a family law paralegal, until Precious Pendergast walked in. Mrs. Pendergast is an action film star who recently married the famous televangelist Reverend Billy Bullion. The wedding took place several months ago on the same day Mrs. Pendergast converted and was baptized by the reverend himself in a highly televised ceremony. After the baptism, they were overcome with emotion and ran off to Las Vegas for a quickie marriage. They returned to the State of California, where they currently reside in his large mansion in Beverly Hills.

   Sobbing uncontrollably, Mrs. Pendergast, who is pushing thirty-five, said that despite his countless sermons on family and encouraging his flock to "be fruitful and multiply," Reverend Bullion hates kids and doesn't want to be a father. He refers to children as "rugrats" and believes they should be seen, in someone else's house, and not heard. Upon learning of his true feelings toward children, she immediately made an appointment to see Attorney Appletts, who came highly recommended by Mrs. Pendergast's Pilates teacher, Baby Atia. Mrs. Pendergast would like to have this marriage annulled and hopes to resume her film career until either her biological clock stops ticking or the right man comes along.

   Attorney Appletts has asked you to review the statute on annulments in California and prepare a client opinion letter regarding the feasibility of an annulment in the case of *Pendergast v. Bullion.*

6. Roman Catholics who divorce must obtain a religious annulment or an "ecclesiastical declaration of nullity" in accordance with Church law before they can remarry or receive Holy Communion. What about those who follow the Jewish or Islamic faith? Check out the following websites for

information: **http://www.jewfaq.org/divorce.htm#Attitude, http://al-islam1.org/laws/divorce.html,** and **http://home.swipnet.se/islam/articles/divorce.htm.**

California Family Code § 2210

A marriage is voidable and may be adjudged a nullity if any of the following conditions existed at the time of the marriage:

a) The party who commences the proceeding or on whose behalf the proceeding is commenced was without the capability of consenting to the marriage as provided in Section *301* or *302*, unless, after attaining the age of consent, the party for any time freely cohabited with the other as husband and wife.

b) The husband or wife of either party was living and the marriage with that husband or wife was then in force and that husband or wife (1) was absent and not known to the party commencing the proceeding to be living for a period of five successive years immediately preceding the subsequent marriage for which the judgment of nullity is sought or (2) was generally reputed or believed by the party commencing the proceeding to be dead at the time the subsequent marriage was contracted.

c) Either party was of unsound mind, unless the party of unsound mind, after coming to reason, freely cohabited with the other as husband and wife.

d) The consent of either party was obtained by fraud, unless the party whose consent was obtained by fraud afterwards, with full knowledge of the facts constituting the fraud, freely cohabited with the other as husband or wife.

e) The consent of either party was obtained by force, unless the party whose consent was obtained by force afterwards freely cohabited with the other as husband or wife.

f) Either party was, at the time of marriage, physically incapable of entering into the marriage state, and that incapacity continues, and appears to be incurable.

CHAPTER 2

Ethics in Family Law

KEY TERMS

Administrative Procedure Act	integrated bar association
attorney/client privilege	legal advice
authorized practice of law	limited scope retainer agreement
billable hours	living expenses
code	Model Rules of Professional Conduct
	multiple representation
competency	National Association of Legal Assistants, Inc.
complaint	National Federation of Paralegal Associations
confidentiality	padding
conflict of interest	premium
contingent fees	*pro hac vice*
costs	*pro per*
costs of litigation	*pro se*
deep pocket	reciprocity
disciplinary board	release
	representation
discrete tasks	*respondeat superior*

earned retainer   retainer

ethical wall   rules of ethics

freelance paralegal   sanction

fee   solicitation

fee agreement   time sheet

flat fee   time slip

former client–current   unauthorized practice of law

opponent   unbundled legal services

grievance   unearned retainer

grievance committees   vicarious liability

hourly basis   work product

During the course of a typical workday, the family law paralegal will come in contact with a variety of people: clients, supervising attorneys, office staff, opposing counsel and their staff, sheriffs, lay and expert witnesses, and court personnel. In addition, they will also encounter a variety of situations in which they will have to make decisions regarding their professional conduct. Whatever paralegals do or say during the course of their employment will impact the client, their supervisor, and themselves. The statutes regulating the unauthorized practice of law and the rules of ethics are two aspects of the law that paralegals must become familiar with in order to conduct themselves properly on a daily basis. This chapter addresses the principles regulating paralegal conduct and provides paralegals with guidelines that will help them maneuver confidently through their busy schedules.

AUTHORIZED PRACTICE OF LAW

Every state has enacted statutes that establish the requirements necessary to obtain a license to "practice law" in that jurisdiction. The general criteria for obtaining a license to practice law require that an individual be a graduate of an accredited law school, possess a good moral character, and successfully pass the state bar exam. Once all statutory requirements have been met, the individual is admitted to the bar of that state and is **authorized to practice law** in that state only. If he or she wishes to practice law in another jurisdiction, he or she must meet that particular state's requirements for admission to the bar. This may include taking another bar exam. Some states do not require an attorney licensed to practice in another jurisdiction to take the state bar exam. One state may extend to attorneys in a different state the right to practice law in its jurisdiction in exchange for the other state's granting the same privilege to attorneys in their state. This is called **reciprocity.**

FIGURE 2–1
Statutory requirements for obtaining a license to practice law are imposed to protect the public from unqualified legal representation.

A state may allow out-of-state attorneys to practice law in its jurisdiction as long as the attorney has been practicing law in another state for a specified time and is a member in good standing of that state's bar. Other requirements must also be met, but they vary from state to state. A state may also grant an attorney special permission to handle one particular case. This is known as appearing *pro hac vice.*

UNAUTHORIZED PRACTICE OF LAW

Statutory requirements for obtaining a license to practice law are imposed to protect the public from unqualified legal representation. Although there has been considerable discussion about licensing paralegals, as of 2006, California is the only jurisdiction that makes it illegal to identify oneself as a paralegal, unless he or she has met certain educational standards. Even if paralegals were to be licensed by the state, they could not engage in the practice of law. Only those individuals who have met the state's statutory criteria may engage in the activities that constitute the practice of law.

In addition to statutes regulating the practice of law, most jurisdictions have enacted laws prohibiting the **unauthorized practice of law,** or "UPL statutes," as they are commonly referred to in the paralegal profession. These statutes define the unauthorized practice of law. Violation of the UPL statutes is a criminal offense. This means that a nonattorney can be prosecuted in criminal court for engaging in any activity that a UPL statute prohibits.

UPL VIOLATIONS

Violations of the UPL statute may have additional consequences for the paralegal including civil liability and may give rise to disciplinary proceedings against the supervising attorney, which is addressed later in this chapter. The paralegal may also suffer loss of employment and experience difficulty finding a new job if word gets around in the legal community that the paralegal has engaged in the unauthorized practice of law. The activities discussed in the following subsections define the practice of law.

STATUTES

Illustrated below are the UPL statutes of Connecticut, Florida, California, and Texas. Each statute imposes a criminal penalty for its violation.

CONNECTICUT GENERAL STATUTES

Sec. 51–88. *Practice of law by persons not attorneys.*
(a) A person who has not been admitted as an attorney under the provisions of section 51-80 shall not: (1) Practice law or appear as an attorney-at-law for another, in any court of record in this state, (2) make it a business to practice law, or appear as an attorney-at-law for another in any such court, (3) make it a business to solicit employment for an attorney-at-law, (4) hold himself out to the public as being entitled to practice law, (5) assume to be an attorney-at-law, (6) assume, use or advertise the title of lawyer, attorney and counselor-at-law, attorney-at-law, counselor-at-law, attorney, counselor, attorney and counselor, or an equivalent term, in such manner as to convey the impression that he is a legal practitioner of law, or (7) advertise that he, either alone or with others, owns, conducts or maintains a law office, or office or place of business of any kind for the practice of law.

(b) Any person who violates any provision of this section shall be fined not more than two hundred and fifty dollars or imprisoned not more than two months or both. . . .

FLORIDA STATUTES ANNOTATED (WEST)

454.23. Penalties Any person not licensed or otherwise authorized by the Supreme Court of Florida who shall practice law or assume or hold himself or herself out to the public as qualified to practice in this state, or who willfully pretends to be, or willfully takes or uses any name, title, addition, or description implying that he or she is qualified, or recognized by law as qualified, to act as a lawyer in this state, and any person entitled to practice who shall violate any provisions of this chapter, shall be guilty of a misdemeanor of the first degree, punishable as provided in s. 775.082 or s. 775.083.

CALIFORNIA CODE

BUSINESS AND PROFESSIONS CODE SECTION 6125–6126

6125. No person shall practice law in California unless the person is an active member of the State Bar.

6126. (a) Any person advertising or holding himself or herself out as practicing or entitled to practice law or otherwise practicing law who is not an active member of the State Bar, is guilty of a misdemeanor.

VERNON'S TEXAS CODES ANNOTATED

Sec. 38–123. *Unauthorized Practice of Law*

(a) A person commits an offense if, with intent to obtain an economic benefit for himself or herself, the person:
  (1) contracts with any person to represent that person with regard to personal causes of action for property damages or personal injury;
  (2) advises any person as to the person's rights and the advisability of making claims for personal injuries or property damages;

(3) advises any person as to whether or not to accept an offered sum of money in settlement of claims for personal injuries or property damages;

(4) enters into any contract with another person to represent that person in personal injury or property damage matters on a contingent fee basis with an attempted assignment of a portion of the person's cause of action; or

(5) enters into any contract with a third person which purports to grant the exclusive right to select and retain legal counsel to represent the individual in any legal proceeding.

(b) This section does not apply to a person currently licensed to practice law in this state, another state, or a foreign country and in good standing with the State Bar of Texas and the state bar or licensing authority of any and all states and foreign countries where licensed.

(c) Except as provided by Subsection (d) of this section, an offense under Subsection (a) of this section is a Class A misdemeanor.

(d) An offense under Subsection (a) of this section is a felony of the third degree if it is shown on the trial of the offense that the defendant has previously been convicted under Subsection (a) of this section.

REPRESENTING SOMEONE IN COURT OR AT ADMINISTRATIVE PROCEEDINGS

Only attorneys are allowed to represent clients in court proceedings or administrative proceedings unless a specific state or federal statute or regulation allows a nonattorney to appear. There are limited circumstances in which a nonattorney may represent another person. The **Administrative Procedure Act,** 5 U.S.C.A. § 555 (1967), is a federal statute that allows a person appearing before a federal administrative agency to be represented by an attorney or, if the agency permits, "by other qualified individual." This means that you must consult the federal statutes and regulations to determine (1) if the particular agency allows nonattorneys to practice before it and, if so, (2) what requirements the nonattorney must meet in order to be deemed a "qualified representative" (e.g., testing, applications). Examples of agencies that allow nonattorneys to practice before them on an administrative level are the Internal Revenue Service, Social Security Administration, and Immigration and Naturalization Service.

Many states have similar statutes that allow nonattorneys to represent individuals before state agencies. In addition, nonattorneys are always allowed to represent themselves before any court or administrative body. These individuals who represent themselves are known as *pro se* or *pro per* litigants.

LEGAL ADVICE

This involves advising a client of his or her specific legal rights and responsibilities, and either predicting an outcome or recommending that the client pursue a particular course of action. Paralegals must be very careful so that they do not render **legal advice,** either to clients or to the public in general. A paralegal may experience pressure from family, friends, or clients to render a legal opinion. The best way to avoid this is to tell the individual that the rendering of legal advice by a nonattorney is a violation of the law and that the paralegal may be subject to criminal prosecution.

FIGURE 2–2
Paralegals may prepare legal documents under the supervision of attorneys.

Paralegals are allowed to relay legal advice from the attorney to the client but must be careful not to add any additional advice to the clients that was not mentioned by the attorney. Paralegals must also be careful not to put legal advice in letters to a client that are signed by the paralegal and not the attorney.

PREPARATION OF LEGAL DOCUMENTS AND PLEADINGS

Paralegals may prepare legal documents and pleadings under the supervision of attorneys. It is the responsibility of the attorney to review the documents and make sure they have been drafted correctly. The attorney is also responsible for signing legal documents and pleadings. Paralegals may sign a letter, but must indicate their paralegal status at the end of the letter. Preparation of legal documents without attorney supervision constitutes the unauthorized practice of law.

Lawyer's Supervision Required

In the following case, a paralegal advertised to prepare uncontested divorce papers for clients. The U.S. District Court was not swayed by the paralegal's constitutional arguments.

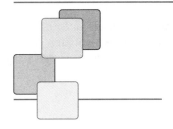

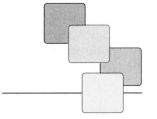

NADINE O. MONROE V. DANIEL B. HORWITCH ET AL.

820 F. SUPP. 682 (D. CONN. 1993)

UNITED STATES DISTRICT COURT, CONNECTICUT

RULING ON PENDING MOTIONS

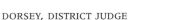

DORSEY, DISTRICT JUDGE

Plaintiff sues under 42 U.S.C. § 1983 alleging deprivation of her rights under the United States Constitution. Defendants move to dismiss.

I. BACKGROUND

Facts alleged in the complaint are assumed for purposes of a motion to dismiss. Plaintiff alleges that

Conn. Gen. Stat. §51-88,[1] forbidding the unauthorized practice of law, violates the First Amendment, freedom of speech, and the Fourteenth Amendment, equal protection and due process. Plaintiff further alleges that Conn. Gen. Stat. §51-90a(2) and §51-90c(b)[2] unconstitutionally grant defendants, the Statewide Grievance Committee (SGC) and the Statewide Bar Counsel (SBC), respectively, criminal jurisdiction.

In October 1991, plaintiff, a paralegal, advertised an offer to prepare papers for parties representing themselves in uncontested divorce actions. In November 1991, defendant Horwitch, acting for SGC was investigating her, under Conn. Gen. Stat. §51-88, for the unauthorized practice of law. Plaintiff did not testify at a March 1993 hearing, refusing to recognize the SGC's authority to conduct or to subpoena her to said hearing.

The SGC found, based on her advertisement, that plaintiff's actions constituted the unauthorized practice of law. Because plaintiff had ceased running the advertisement and had not served any clientele, the SGC recommended dismissing the complaint without prejudice. It recommended pursuit of the complaint under Practice Book 31(c) if she resumes offering the services.[3] In June 1992, defendant informed plaintiff of the SGC's decision. Plaintiff alleges that since that time, Horwitch has threatened her with prosecution for criminal contempt if she resumes the practice in question. . . .

1. FIRST AMENDMENT FREEDOM OF EXPRESSION

The prohibition against unauthorized practice of law does not violate plaintiff's First Amendment right to freedom of speech . . . (citation omitted). "The practice

of law is above that of a mere privilege. It cannot be treated as a matter of grace or favor. But it may be granted only upon fulfillment of certain rigid qualifications established by this court. The defendant had not fulfilled these qualifications and he is not therefore entitled to exercise the privilege bestowed upon those who have . . ." (citation omitted).

FOURTEENTH AMENDMENT

Due Process

Statutes forbidding the "unauthorized practice of law" are "sufficiently definite" to withstand constitutional scrutiny . . . (citation omitted). An activity on the "outerboundaries" of the "practice of law" might be impermissibly vague. *Hackin*, 102 Ariz. at 221, 427 P.2d at 913. [P]reparation "of legal documents fall squarely within the boundaries.

. . . Plaintiff's vulnerability to Conn. Gen. Stat. § 51-88 arises from her offer to prepare court documents in uncontested divorce actions. Preparation of legal documents is "commonly understood to be the practice of law." *Grievance Committee v. Dacey*, 222 A.2d at 349. What constitutes "preparation of legal documents" is construed broadly. Preparation of instruments, even with *pre-printed forms* involves more than a "mere scrivener's duties" and, therefore, constitutes the practice of law. *State v. Buyers Service Co.*, 292 S.C. 426, 357 S.E.2d 15, 17 (1987). *See also Pulse v. North Am. Land Title Co.*, 218 Mont. 275, 707 P.2d 1105, 1109 (1985) ("drafting or filling in of blanks in printed forms of instruments dealing with land" constitutes the practice of law); *Kennedy v. Bar Ass'n*, 316 Md. 646, 561 A.2d 200, 208 (1989) (preparation of legal documents in patent case constitutes the practice of law). Legal documents purport to allocate legal obligation.

The preparation of documents in simple divorce actions unequivocally constitutes the practice of law. *See United States v. Hardy*, 681 F. Supp, 1326, 1328–29 (N.D. Ill. 1988) ("Common sense dictates that the drafting of even a simple complaint or an uncomplicated petition for dissolution of marriage requires at least some degree of legal knowledge or skill"); *McGiffert v. State ex rel. Stowe*, 366 So. 2d 680, 683 (Ala.1979) ("It would seem to be clear that only a licensed lawyer may obtain an uncontested divorce for another person without violating the statute"); *Florida Bar v. Brumbaugh*, 355 So. 2d. 1186, 1194 (Fla.1978) (assistance in preparation of dissolution of marriage forms constitutes the practice of law); *State Bar v. Cramer*, 399 Mich. 116, 249 N.W.2d 1, 9 (1976) (preparation of a client's no-fault divorce documents constitutes the practice of law).

---

[1]Conn. Gen. Stat. § 51-88 proscribes the practice of law by persons not attorneys. Subsection (b) provides: "Any person who violates any provision of this section shall be fined not more than two hundred and fifty dollars or imprisoned not more than two months or both."

[2]Conn. Gen. Stat. §§ 51-90a and 51-90c(b) each delineate the powers and duties of the State-wide Bar Committee and Counsel, respectively, to include "investigate and prosecute complaints involving the violation by any person of any provision of section 51-88."

[3]Conn. Prac. Book 31(c) provides in part: "A petition to restrain any person from engaging in the unauthorized practice of law not occurring in the actual presence of the court may be made by written complaint to the superior court in the judicial district where the violation occurs. . . . Such complaint may be prosecuted by the state's attorney, by the statewide bar counsel, or by any member of the bar by direction of the court. . . . Such complaints shall be proceeded with as civil action."

Such documents may assert, fail to assert or acknowledge legal rights.

Equal Protection

. . . The states have a "compelling interest" in the practice of professions. *Goldfarb v. Virginia State Bar,* 421 U.S. 773,793, 95 S. Ct. 2004, 2015–16, 44 L. Ed. 2d. 572 (1975). "As part of their power to protect the public health, safety and other valid interests they have broad power to establish standards for licensing practitioners and regulating the practice of professions." *Id.* The limitation of the practice of law to bar members "protects the public against rendition of legal services by unqualified persons." Conn. Prac. Book Rule 5.5 (comment). Such a limitation constitutes "protection" in that "the public can better be assured of the requisite responsibility and competence if the practice of law is confined to those who are subject to the requirements and regulations imposed upon members of the legal profession." ABA

Model Code of Professional Responsibility, EC3-1 (1987).

A lawyer may delegate functions to a paralegal "so long as the lawyer supervises the delegated work and retains responsibility for their work." Conn. Prac. Book Rule 5.5 (comment). Oversight and accountability guarantee, so far as practicable, that the "requirements and regulations" imposed on lawyers will also ensure the quality of work of supervised paralegals (footnotes omitted). Prohibiting unsupervised paralegals from work with legal consequences is rationally related to public protection. *See Lawline v. American Bar Ass'n,* 956 F.2d 1378, 1385–86 (7th Cir. 1992). . . .

VI. CONCLUSION

Defendant's motion to dismiss (document #10) is granted.

Negotiating with Opposing Attorney in Pending Litigation

It is the attorney's job to negotiate with the opposing party's attorney in pending litigation. Paralegals may relay messages between their supervising attorney and opposing counsel, but must be careful not to use their independent judgment in making or accepting offers.

Accepting and Rejecting Cases

Only the attorney can determine whether or not to accept or reject cases. The paralegal must leave this task up to the attorney and cannot use independent judgment in deciding whether or not to accept a case. Paralegals may screen prospective clients upon instruction by attorneys in limited and specific instances. For instance, if a person calls the law office requesting representation in a personal injury matter, and the law office limits its practice to family law, the paralegal may communicate this information to the caller without referring the call to the attorney.

Setting and Collecting Fees

It is the attorney's responsibility to establish fees for legal services or collect fees from delinquent clients.

Maintaining an Office to Render Legal Services

Only attorneys may operate an office for the practice of law. Many paralegals run paralegal services companies, which generally provide paralegal services to attorneys or law firms on an as-needed basis. When a paralegal is retained, the attorney or firm that hired the paralegal will supervise him. In some jurisdictions, paralegal businesses may prepare legal documents for nonattorney individuals but must be careful not to render legal advice in the course of providing this service.

DUTY TO DISCLOSE PARALEGAL STATUS

It is the attorney's responsibility to identify the nonattorney status of his or her paralegals when introducing them to clients, opposing counsel, judges, and any other third parties. Conversely, a paralegal has the duty to identify his or her nonattorney status whenever meeting a third party for the first time. The reason for this requirement is so third parties do not assume that the paralegal is an attorney who is authorized to give legal advice. Paralegals in family law offices have a lot of client contact and it is common for clients to find the paralegal much more accessible than the attorney. A family law practitioner is often in court trying cases or arguing motions, so the paralegal is often in the position of liaison between the two. It is very important for paralegals to make it clear to clients that they are unauthorized to give legal advice.

RULES OF ETHICS

Every profession has **rules of ethics.** Rules of ethics are standards of conduct that a profession demands from its members. Adherence to these standards of conduct is not limited only to attorneys. Attorneys often employ other attorneys, law students, paralegals, secretaries, clerks, and investigators to assist them in rendering legal services to clients. Supervising attorneys are obligated to see to it that all those employed by them are cognizant of the rules of ethics. Attorneys also hire **freelance paralegals** who are not employees of the attorney, but independent contractors who work for a number of attorneys on an as-needed basis. Attorneys supervise freelance paralegals in the course of performing each particular assignment. Freelance paralegals are also responsible for knowledge of the rules of ethics.

Attorneys and paralegals must work within the confines of the professional rules of ethics. Rules of ethics govern the manner in which the members of a profession conduct themselves. The legal profession holds itself to a high standard of conduct in order to facilitate a sense of trust and confidence among the general public and to preserve the integrity and respectability of the profession. The legal profession has a set of written rules called a **code** that establishes the guidelines for attorneys in their interactions with clients, courts, staff, and their obligations to the general public.

The American Bar Association (ABA) has established the **Model Rules of Professional Conduct** as a prototype for attorney ethics. Because the ABA is a national, voluntary bar association that does not have jurisdiction to oversee the legal profession, it has written the Model Rules of Professional Conduct (MRPC) as a model for states that wish to adopt them. A majority of the states have adopted the MRPC as their ethical code. Some states have not adopted the MRPC but follow the Model Rules of Professional Responsibility, which is the ABA's older model code.

The legal profession and licensed attorneys are under the control of the state's highest court, commonly referred to in most jurisdictions as the supreme court. Some states have **integrated bar associations** in which membership is mandatory. Other states require attorneys to register and pay fees to state bar associations or to the court or designated agency. State bar associations regulate the legal profession through disciplinary bodies known as **grievance committees** or **disciplinary boards.** These disciplinary bodies may **sanction** or punish attorneys for engaging in conduct that violates the state's code of professional conduct.

If a **complaint** or **grievance** is filed with the disciplinary body, attorneys have the right to a hearing and to an appeals process in order to defend their privilege to practice law in that jurisdiction. Attorney grievance proceedings may result in a variety of dispositions. If the allegations against an attorney are unsubstantiated, the grievance committee may dismiss the complaint. This is equivalent to "dropping the charges." If the allegations against an attorney are substantiated, the attorney may be reprimanded, put on probation, suspended, or even disbarred, depending on the seriousness of the offense.

Paralegals are not members of the bar and cannot join, vote, or hold office. In some jurisdictions paralegals may become associate members. The state agency or authority responsible for disciplining attorneys for unethical conduct does not have the same authority to impose sanctions on paralegals for engaging in unethical behavior. Therefore, it is important for paralegals to have a thorough knowledge of their jurisdiction's rules of professional conduct, which regulate attorneys, and of any ethical guidelines their state has established for paralegals. While national, state, and local paralegal associations such as the **National Association of Legal Assistants, Inc.** (NALA) and the **National Federation of Paralegal Associations** (NFPA) have established their own ethical codes, membership in these organizations is voluntary. These organizations do not have any disciplinary authority over paralegals. The most that one of these paralegal associations can do is revoke a paralegal's membership in the association.

While the state bar association cannot discipline paralegals for violating the rules of ethics, their supervisors will be held responsible for any unethical conduct by paralegals. Attorneys who employ paralegals are obligated to supervise their employees' conduct and **work product.** Work product consists of the notes, materials, memoranda, and written records generated by the attorney, as well as the written records of the attorney's mental impressions and legal theories concerning the case. Attorneys are also ultimately responsible for the quality and accuracy of their paralegal's work product.

As mentioned, if paralegals violate an ethical rule, it is the attorneys who have to answer to the state disciplinary body, not the paralegals. Although grievance committees can punish only attorneys for unethical conduct, violation of certain ethical rules may expose not only the attorney but also the paralegal to civil lawsuits and/or criminal prosecution.

EXAMPLE

Johnny Swift, Esq., and his paralegal, Nona Williams, get bored one afternoon. They conspire to raid the Mary Smith Client Trust Account and go gambling in Atlantic City. They withdraw $50,000 from the account and take off for the casino. They lose the entire $50,000 at the roulette wheel. Mary finds out that her money was stolen by Swift and Williams.

What are Mary's remedies?

1. **Grievance.** Smith may file a grievance against Swift with the state disciplinary body. A lawyer is obligated under the ethical rules to safekeep his

client's property and to maintain a fiduciary relationship of trust and confidence with the client. Although the grievance committee can reprimand, suspend, or disbar Swift, it has no authority to discipline the paralegal, Nona Williams. The consequences of a grievance will affect the attorney's privilege to practice law.

2. **Criminal.** Because Williams and Swift conspired to take the client's money, they committed a crime and may be subject to criminal prosecution. If a paralegal knowingly assists an attorney in committing a crime during the course of representation, both the paralegal and the attorney can be prosecuted. If a paralegal commits a crime on her own during the course of employment, both she and the attorney may be prosecuted. The consequence of a criminal prosecution is fine, imprisonment, or both, or at the very least a criminal record.

3. **Civil.** Smith may also bring civil action against Swift and Williams alleging both the torts of civil conversion of Smith's money and malpractice. An aggrieved client may sue the attorney for injuries caused by the attorney or paralegal. An attorney and his staff owe a duty to effectively and ethically represent a client. In addition, an attorney is in a fiduciary relationship with the client. In this case, Swift owed Smith a fiduciary duty to safekeep her money. When the attorney breaches that duty and in the course of that breach the client suffers some type of loss, the client can sue the attorney for damages. The duty to Smith was breached when the money was removed from the client's trust account for personal use without the client's consent. Because the client's money was lost and the client was damaged, Smith can sue both Swift and Williams. The consequence of a civil suit is the payment of money damages to the client, if she prevails in the case.

What if Williams acted on her own in this case? Would attorney Swift be civilly responsible for her actions? The answer is yes. An employer is **vicariously liable** or responsible for the negligence and other torts committed by his employees when the acts are committed during the scope of their employment. This is known as the doctrine of *respondeat superior.* Even if Williams acted alone in this scenario, Smith may bring a civil action naming both the attorney and paralegal as defendants.

Although the client may sue both the attorney and the paralegal, the attorney is eventually the best defendant in the case because of his deep pocket. **Deep pocket** is the term applied to characterize the defendant in a lawsuit who has the financial resources to absorb a civil suit for monetary damages. Attorneys ordinarily carry malpractice insurance, which will cover them in civil lawsuits brought by their clients for their negligent acts or mistakes. However, malpractice insurance will not cover an attorney in a civil action based on a criminal act or for an intentional tort. Some states, such as Connecticut and New Jersey, require contributions from attorneys to fund accounts to reimburse clients in this type of situation.

Malpractice insurance usually covers the negligent acts of attorneys and sometimes the negligent actions of the attorney's staff; however, this is not always the case. Paralegals should inquire as to whether or not they are covered under a firm's malpractice insurance. Attorneys pay a **premium,** which is a monetary sum paid on an annual or installment basis for malpractice insurance coverage. The policy is renewable on a yearly basis. Attorneys must notify their malpractice carrier immediately on becoming aware that they have committed an act, error, or omission that could result in a civil lawsuit.

This chapter does not intend to exhaust all of the ethical rules that apply to attorneys. It only provides a general overview of the basic ethical principles paralegals must become familiar with in the course of a family law practice. As stated earlier, paralegals must become thoroughly familiar with the rules of ethics that apply to attorneys in their jurisdiction and any ethical guidelines the state bar associations of their states have developed for them. Ethical codes established by paralegal associations also provide excellent guidelines. Paralegals should review the ethical rules on a regular basis in order to refresh their knowledge and update themselves on any changes in the rules or opinions interpreting them. If a paralegal has even the slightest concern about an ethical issue, the paralegal should always consult with the supervising attorney before taking action. Communication is a good way to minimize problems that could expose the firm to a grievance or malpractice suit. While supervising styles differ in the legal profession, conscientious attorneys will appreciate the paralegal's attention and cautiousness.

There are many ethical challenges in the area of family practice. This area of the law is emotionally draining because it thrusts two people who once shared a life together into an adversarial system that is normally not conducive to amicable resolutions. Almost 50 percent of today's marriages end in divorce, and the proceedings involved may represent the first time a client is exposed to the legal system. Their expectations of what the legal system can do may be based on bad legal advice obtained from talk shows, magazine articles, or friends. When the results of a dissolution case do not live up to these expectations, an attorney may become the target of a disgruntled client. Paralegals should keep this in mind when performing their daily activities, and their conduct should conform to a strict adherence to the rules of ethics and UPL statutes.

In addition to knowing and observing ethical boundaries, the following office procedure tips will assist paralegals in protecting their supervising attorneys from malpractice claims and grievance proceedings:

1. Promptly return client phone calls, log client contact in the client file, and reduce client conversations to writing to avoid any misunderstandings that can later be used against the attorney or paralegal. The attorney should review the file entries and client correspondence and maintain the attorney/client relationship.
2. Perform assignments in a timely fashion to avoid delays.
3. Identify professional status at all times and explain to those unfamiliar with the paralegal profession the limitations the law has placed on nonattorneys.
4. Keep track of all important court dates and make sure they are promptly and appropriately marked in the office master calendar and the attorney's personal calendar.
5. Disclose any conflicts of interest relating to the paralegal to the attorney.
6. Promptly relay client information to the attorney so action can be taken on a client's case.

OVERVIEW OF BASIC ETHICAL PRINCIPLES

CONFIDENTIALITY

The ethical rule of **confidentiality** protects communications between attorneys and their clients. Paralegals working for attorneys, either as employees or freelance independent contractors, are equally obligated to be guardians of client information revealed during the course of representation. Attorneys cannot disclose information related to the representation of a client. There are two exceptions to this rule. The attorney may reveal such information after obtaining the client's consent. This means that the client has given his or her attorney the permission to disclose information to another party. This permission should always be obtained in writing, in the form of a document called a **release,** which the paralegal may be asked to draft. Paralegals should also be very careful when disclosing information under the consent exception. The file should be consulted at all times to verify the existence of a release, to whom the information may be disclosed, and to what extent. Under most circumstances, the attorney may disclose most information to the paralegal who is working on the client's file. The paralegal, as an employee of the attorney or law firm, will have the same obligation to maintain client confidentiality.

Under the second exception, attorneys may reveal client confidences when they have a reasonable belief that clients will engage in conduct that is likely to result in substantial bodily harm or death. The purpose of this rule is to prevent such crimes from occurring rather than reporting them to the authorities after the fact.

EXAMPLE

During an office visit with his attorney, a very distraught client pulls out a .357 magnum pistol and reveals his plans to kill his wife.

In this scenario, if the attorney reasonably believes that her client will engage in conduct that may result in death or a serious physical injury, she may have an ethical obligation to inform the authorities of her client's plans for the purpose of stopping the crime before it takes place. If, however, the client first committed the murder and then broke down and confessed his crime to the lawyer, the attorney is under no ethical obligation to notify anyone! The communications between the attorney and client are confidential, privileged, and protected by law.

Paralegals must take special precautions to protect client confidentiality. If clients arrive early for an office appointment and start talking about their case in the reception area, paralegals should politely instruct clients to wait until they have privacy with the attorney before they discuss their case. Other clients or delivery or repair persons may be within earshot of the client's personal business, and once clients have disclosed information in the presence of a third party, that disclosure is not protected by the rules of confidentiality.

Paralegals should also be protective of client files, correspondence, or other materials and should not leave them in open view where other clients or visitors may see them. Therefore, reception areas, interview rooms, and any other area where clients or visitors may roam should be free of client information.

Paralegals should also avoid taking calls from clients while in the presence of other clients. If it is an emergency, the paralegal should use a separate room that

FIGURE 2–3
Paralegals should refrain from engaging in unethical conduct such as gossiping about clients' cases.

lends itself to privacy. If no separate room is available, the call should be very short and paralegals should not reveal the caller's name or any other information. Care should also be taken when visitors such as repair, delivery, or cleaning personnel are in the office. Again, client documents should be kept out of sight and oral communications should be brief and discreet.

The paralegal who works in a family practice office will often be privy to the most intimate details of a client's marital relationship. Sometimes these details may be shocking, scandalous, or simply humorous or ridiculously funny. The paralegal may be tempted to share with friends or family some of the spicier portions of clients' files. Paralegals should avoid doing so, at all costs! Technically, an attorney, paralegal, or any other employee of a law firm will not violate client confidentiality if they disclose information that is already a matter of public record in the court system or in any other office of public records such as the town land records office or town tax assessor. However, even when questioned about this already public information, the wisest and most prudent course of action for the paralegal to pursue is to refrain from any disclosures of a client's business.

The client's right to confidentiality also extends to the courtroom. Attorneys or paralegals may find themselves summoned to testify in a case involving the client. Whether or not the attorney or paralegal may provide testimony is based on evidentiary rule called the **attorney/client privilege.** In a judicial proceeding, it is up to the client to decide whether or not she will allow the attorney or any of his staff to disclose confidential client information on the witness stand. The client is the holder of the privilege and unless the client consents, the attorney or paralegal must not answer any questions, but simply assert the attorney/client privilege.

Conflict of Interest

"You can't serve two masters" best describes this rule of ethics. Attorneys owe their clients a duty of loyalty and must exercise their independent judgment in the course of representation. Any activity that may divide an attorney's loyalty and compromise her independent judgment is a **conflict of interest.** The following subsections present an overview of the various activities that might result in a conflict of interest situation.

MULTIPLE REPRESENTATION

Sometimes divorcing couples decide to save money by hiring one lawyer to represent both spouses. This is known as **multiple representation** and presents unique ethical problems for attorneys.

Legal Services Out of Control

Not only do we have a serious conflict of interest in the accompanying multiple representation case, but also documents forged by the firm's paralegal!

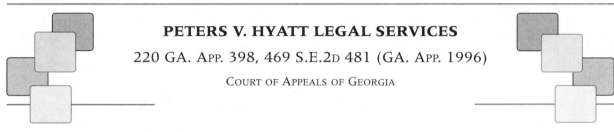

PETERS V. HYATT LEGAL SERVICES

220 GA. APP. 398, 469 S.E.2D 481 (GA. APP. 1996)

COURT OF APPEALS OF GEORGIA

POPE, PRESIDING JUDGE

This is the second appearance of this legal malpractice, breach of contract, breach of fiduciary duty, breach of statutory duty case before this court. See *Peters v. Hyatt Legal Svcs.*, 211 Ga. App. 587, 440 S.E.2d 222 (1990). After a bifurcated trial, the jury awarded plaintiff Richard Peters $10,000 in nominal damages, $35,545.10 in attorney's fees and expenses to litigation, and $175,000 in punitive damages against Hyatt Legal Services (Hyatt). The trial court granted Hyatt's motion for judgment notwithstanding the verdict on punitive damages, and Peters appeals.

Richard E. Peters brought suit against Hyatt, Hyatt attorney Linda Gross and the Hyatt legal assistant and notary public Kasonya M. Storey for damages resulting from Hyatt's representation of Peters in an uncontested divorce action. Although defendant Gross died after Peters filed the complaint, she was aware that legal action had been threatened.

Peters and his former wife were married on July 2, 1986, and had one child. Both were enlisted personnel in the United States Army with Mr. Peters stationed in West Germany. In January 1988, Peters discovered his wife in bed with another man. Peters and his wife took steps to separate legally that same month. Counsel for Mrs. Peters in West Germany prepared a proposed settlement agreement which Mrs. Peters executed on June 24, 1988. However, Peters did not agree to the proposed terms and did not sign the agreement.

On October 14, 1988, Peters returned to the United States on military leave to obtain a divorce. He consulted Hyatt attorney Linda Gross, paying $222.50, half the total fee for an uncontested divorce. Peters signed a fee agreement with Hyatt and signed his name on the signature line titled "client."[1] Peters returned to West Germany and expected the paperwork would be sent to him within 30 days, and that he would then receive a bill for the balance of the fee. He testified he told Gross if she provided him with 30 days' notice he expected that he could obtain the military leave necessary to be present in court. When Mrs. Peters asked him about the status of the pending divorce, Peters provided her with the name and address of Gross. Although Peters told his wife he would send the remaining money to Hyatt, Mrs. Peters indicated to him she would satisfy the balance while she was in the United States later in the month. Peters testified he did not authorize his wife to consult with Gross, but only to pay the balance so the divorce could proceed.

In December 1988, Mrs. Peters paid the outstanding balance and Gross began representing her. Although Peters thought that Hyatt continued to represent him, Gross had no contact with him after his initial visit. Instead, Gross filed the complaint for divorce with Mrs. Peters as plaintiff on December 29, 1988, the day after Mrs. Peters went to Hyatt and paid the remainder

---

[1]The Hyatt Legal Services Fee Statement provided. "When half the total attorney fee and costs is paid, we will complete preparation of the paperwork. When your account is paid in full, we will file the case. This is not binding until you make a payment. Your signature allows us to represent you after payment is made."

of the fee. It is undisputed that the acknowledgment of service of the complaint dated December 29, 1988, contains a forged signature of Richard E. Peters, notarized by Kasonya M. Storey, a Hyatt employee. Nor is it disputed that the consent to final hearing dated December 29, 1988, witnessed by Linda M. Gross, the Hyatt attorney, contains a forged signature of Richard E. Peters.

The forged acknowledgment and forged consent were filed with the petition for divorce on December 29, 1988. A final judgment and decree was thereafter entered on January 31, 1989. After Peters discovered the divorce was final, he contacted Hyatt to find out what had transpired and Hyatt informed him that the file had been lost. Peters then obtained the paperwork directly from the court, discovered the forged signatures, and realized something was wrong.

Peters first contends that the trial court erred in granting j.n.o.v. on the issue of punitive damages. We agree. . . .

OCGA § 51-12-5.1(b) provides that "[p]unitive damages may be awarded in only such tort actions in which it is proven by clear and convincing evidence that the defendant's actions showed willful misconduct, malice, fraud, wantonness, oppression, or *that entire want of care which would raise the presumption of conscious indifference to consequences.*" (Emphasis supplied)

Peters presented the following evidence of Hyatt's entire want of care from which the jury could have determined the evidence raised the presumption of conscious indifference to consequences. It is undisputed that the forged documents were at all times in Hyatt's sole custody and control. It is undisputed that Hyatt represented adverse parties in a divorce proceeding without obtaining the informed consent of both. Peters presented evidence of a conflict of interest and breach of fiduciary duty. Mrs. Peters testified that the Army Legal Center refused to represent both her and her husband. Hyatt's own expert testified he would not allow an attorney in his office to represent both parties to a divorce. Peters' expert testified Gross' conduct was "unethical," "improper," "illegal," and constituted a breach of her agreement with Peters. Peters' expert also claimed Gross had a duty to inform Peters of his case. Yet Peters testified that after he paid half the fee, Hyatt never sent him any paperwork or contacted him in any way. Peters also testified that when he returned stateside and contacted Hyatt, he was told his file had been lost. Hyatt's employee, Storey, admitted she sometimes notarized documents without people signing in her presence, a violation of the statutory duty impose by OCGA § 45-17-8(e). No evidence was presented that Hyatt's socalled audit procedure properly detected the conflict problem. For the foregoing reasons, we reject Hyatt's contention that there was insufficient factual evidence to support an award of punitive damages.

Hyatt argues that neither dual representation nor witnessing the forging of Peters' signature supports the imposition of punitive damages because punitive damages are not allowed for violation of an ethical rule. *Allen v. Lefkoff, Duncan, Grimes & Dermer, P.C.,* 265 Ga. 374, 453 S.E.2d 719 (1995). However, Hyatt has distorted the holding of *Allen.* The Supreme Court held that *standing alone,* an alleged violation of the Code of Professional Responsibility or the Standards of Conduct cannot serve as a legal basis for a legal malpractice action. Moreover, evidence of even a potential conflict of interest is sufficient to raise a jury issue on punitive damages in a legal malpractice case. *Read v. Benedict,* 200 Ga. App, 4, 6(2), 406 S.E.2d 488 (1991).

Although attorneys may represent two opposing parties, provided that both parties consent, this could be disastrous in cases involving family relations. Parties may wish to retain a single lawyer's services on the promise that they have come to an agreement as to the distribution of their assets, the disposition of custody, and so on. The parties may represent that they merely need someone to act as a scribe for their agreement and to get them through the court system. The problem is that the amicable divorce of today can turn into the World War III of tomorrow. In addition, a client may find that after having consulted an attorney and learning of his or her legal rights, the agreement originally made with the other spouse may not be in his or her best interest. This puts the lawyer in an awkward position as both an advocate and as a counselor.

The parties may also have revealed confidential information to one attorney that can be used against them later. If attorneys have heard confidential information regarding the case, it would be unethical for them to represent one spouse versus the other. Before hearing any confidential information, attorneys may take on the representation of one spouse and direct the other spouse to obtain independent representation.

FORMER CLIENT–CURRENT OPPONENT

Attorneys and paralegals who switch jobs and go from one firm to another present special ethical problems. During their course of employment, attorneys and paralegals are privy to clients' confidential information. Upon switching jobs, an attorney or paralegal may discover that a former client is now the adversary of one of the clients in the new firm, termed **former client–current opponent.**

EXAMPLE

John Doe is a paralegal who works at Law Firm A. Law Firm A represents Mrs. Smith in the divorce matter of Smith v. Smith. *John Doe leaves Law Firm A and is now employed at Law Firm B, who represents Mr. Smith in the divorce case. John must immediately inform his new supervisor of the existence of a conflict. Because he previously worked on this case at Law Firm A, he cannot work on the same case in Law Firm B.*

If John were allowed to work on the case, the danger exists that he could use the confidential information obtained in Mrs. Smith's case against her interests, in favor of Mr. Smith. Law Firm B must now build an **ethical wall** around John. This means that John cannot discuss the case with anyone in the office, nor can he have access to the file.

Another activity that may raise a conflict of interest is the commonly used tactic by one spouse seeking a divorce to obtain a free consultation from a variety of well-known divorce attorneys in the community. Confidential information is then revealed during the course of these initial consultations so as to preclude their spouses from retaining those attorneys' services. The unscrupulous spouse will then raise a conflict of interest claim alleging that he is the former client of the attorney and request that the attorney be disqualified from representing his spouse. The paralegal should carefully log the names of all clients, even if they just come to the office for an initial consultation, to avoid any conflict of interest challenges.

SEXUAL RELATIONS WITH CLIENTS

Attorneys and paralegals should not engage in sexual relations with clients during the course of the client's representation! Clients going through a divorce may be very vulnerable and emotionally devastated. Unfortunately, unscrupulous attorneys take advantage of clients in this position and may engage in romantic relations or actual sexual harassment. Such a dynamic may influence attorneys to act contrary to a client's best interest. Sometimes paralegals work very closely with divorce clients over an extended period of time. The intimacy of working together may lead to a mutual personal attraction. If this attraction is acted on during the course of the representation of the client, the paralegal has put herself in an ethically precarious position. Only after representation has been completed should a paralegal consider having any sort of personal relationship with a client.

SEX AND THE LEGAL ASSISTANT

The following *Logan* case illustrates the serious breach of client confidentiality and conflict of interest problems involved when a legal assistant has an affair with a client's husband.

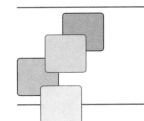
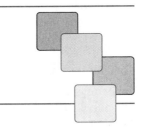

GERALDINE L. LOGAN V. HYATT LEGAL PLANS, INC.

874 S.W.2D 548(MO. APP. W.D. 1994)

MISSOURI COURT OF APPEALS, WESTERN DISTRICT

PER CURIAM:

Geraldine Logan appeals from the trial court's order dismissing with prejudice her first amended petition for damages against Hyatt Legal Plans, Inc., a Delaware corporation. Her petition asserted that Hyatt Legal Plans, Inc., is liable for the tortious conduct of Dori Dolinar, a secretary and legal assistant who worked in the "Hyatt Legal Services" office during the time that an attorney in that office represented Logan in an action for dissolution of marriage. The trial court, concluding there could be no basis of vicarious liability against Hyatt Legal Plans, Inc., dismissed the action with prejudice. We now reverse and remand.

Prior to and during the time of her dissolution proceeding in October 1991, Logan was employed by American Telephone & Telegraph (AT&T). One of the benefits offered to eligible non-management AT&T employees was a group legal services plan which provided pre-paid personal legal services. . . .

. . . Logan claims that she was referred to Jay Crotchett of "Hyatt Legal Services" in Kansas City after calling the 800 number listed in the plan. Crotchett was employed in the law office operating under the name "Hyatt Legal Services." Logan apparently assumed that Crotchett was employed by Hyatt.

On May 16, 1991, Logan retained Crotchett as her attorney to represent her in a dissolution proceeding. Although she and her husband, John Gragg, were separated, they both attended the initial meeting at the Hyatt Legal Services office. At that meeting, Logan and Gragg met Dori Dolinar, a secretary and legal assistant, employed by the law firm. Shortly thereafter, Dolinar allegedly began a sexual relationship with Gragg that continued throughout the dissolution proceedings. There is no allegation in the petition that either Jay Crotchett or Allen Lebovitz were aware of Dolinar's involvement with Gragg during Crotchett's representation of Logan. Logan alleges that during the time she was being represented by Crotchett, Dolinar secretly disclosed to Gragg various confidential communications between Logan and her attorney as to her negotiating posture, and that Dolinar counseled and encouraged Gragg to refuse to pay certain portions of the marital debt, to renege on previous commitments,

to threaten bankruptcy, and to refuse any offers of reconciliation with his wife.'[1]

Following the dissolution of her marriage, Logan learned of Dolinar's involvement with Gragg and brought suit against Hyatt alleging that the corporation was vicariously liable for the tortious conduct of Dolinar. Hyatt filed a motion to dismiss, contending that Hyatt could have no liability because "Hyatt Legal Services" was a separate entity from Hyatt and that neither Dolinar nor Crotchett were agents or employees of Hyatt. The motion to dismiss was sustained by the court and Logan was granted thirty days to file an amended petition. . . .

. . . An employer may be held liable for the negligent acts or omissions of his employee under the doctrine of respondeat superior if those acts are committed within the scope of employment. *Studebaker v. Nettie's Flower Garden, Inc.*, 842 S.W.2d 227, 229 (Mo. App. 1992). In this case, all of the alleged misconduct of which Logan complains is attributed to Dolinar. The affidavit of Andrew Kohn, General Counsel of Hyatt, asserts that at the time of the alleged misconduct, Dolinar was employed by Allen Lebovitz, a sole proprietor of a law firm using the trade name "Hyatt Legal Services." The affidavit states that Dolinar was not paid and had never been an employee or agent of Hyatt and offers the conclusion that Hyatt had no actual control or right to control the activities of Ms. Dolinar. . . .

. . . On this appeal, Plaintiff argues that, based on the content of the summary plan booklet, defendant is estopped from denying liability for Dolinar's conduct. Plaintiff essentially argues that the content of the summary plan booklet created an impression, upon which plaintiff reasonably relied, that the legal services would be provided by an employee of Hyatt Legal Plans. . . . At this early stage of the case, we will give plaintiff's

---

[1]Logan alleges Dolinar was guilty of various acts of a tortious nature. Some of the alleged tortious conduct is no longer cognizable in Missouri. *See Thomas v. Siddiqui*, 869 S.W.2d 740 (Mo. banc 1994) (where the Missouri Supreme Court abolished the tort of criminal conversation). Stripped to its basics, the claim would seem to be essentially a claim of legal malpractice based on Dolinar's conduct, which was disloyal to Logan.

pleadings (and proposed pleadings) the broadest possible intendment for purposes of our review, in view of the finality of a disposition by summary judgment.

A provision in the plan booklet states that "Hyatt Legal Plans or the law firms providing services under the plan are responsible for all services provided by their attorneys." This provision could be interpreted as a statement that Hyatt *is at least contingently responsible* for legal services provided under the plan. Also, the plan booklet states that service of process "concerning legal services provided under the plan should be directed to" Hyatt. Another provision of the booklet, which concerns liability with regard to legal services and attorney conduct, states: "[y]ou should understand that AT&T, the unions, the Plan and their directors, officers, and employees have no liability for the conduct of any plan attorney or the services provided." This sentence does *not* say that *Hyatt Legal Plans, Inc.* has no liability in connection with such services, and the term "the Plan" is not synonymous with Hyatt Legal Plans, Inc., in the definitions set forth in the booklet (footnote omitted). Since the summary plan booklet is not entirely supportive of the idea that Hyatt has no relationship to Dolinar upon which liability could be imputed, there remained some reasonable question as to the nature of the relationship between Hyatt Legal Plans, Inc. and "Hyatt Legal Services."

Plaintiff's intention to plead a theory of vicarious liability was cut short by the action of the court in dismissing the case without prior notice to plaintiff that the court was considering, in effect, a summary judgment ruling. . . . It is difficult to imagine how plaintiff intends to show that Dolinar's actions were within the scope of her employment or agency when there is no apparent reason to believe that Dolinar's actions were undertaken in the interest of her employer, or were encouraged or tolerated by her employer. Crotchett, who was engaged in representing Logan, ordinarily would have no reason to countenance Dolinar's involvement with Gragg, which was disloyal to Logan and could have interfered with Crotchett's ability to secure a favorable result for Logan. However, we cannot say that it is impossible to imagine a set of facts in which Crotchett or Lebovitz could hypothetically have involved themselves in the matter to such a degree that vicarious liability is appropriate. . . . Plaintiff should be given an opportunity to explore the possibility of any malfeasance by Crotchett or Lebovitz, and to explore the relationship between Hyatt and "Hyatt Legal Services." Consequently, we reverse and remand the case. We conclude that there remain some genuine issues of material fact.

Loaning Money to a Client

Attorneys may advance the **costs of litigation** to a client. These costs include filing fees, sheriff's fees, deposition costs, expert witness fees, and excessive photocopying and mailing costs. **Living expenses,** however, may not be advanced to a client. This includes any monies for a client's personal use.

Gifts from a Client

Clients may often show their appreciation by making a gift to attorneys or paralegals. There is nothing wrong with accepting a gift from a client as long as the transferring of that gift does not include the preparation of legal documents such as a deed, will, trust, or letter. An attorney may prepare a document that includes in it a bequest or transfer of property to that attorney if the attorney is related to the donor. If the attorney is not related to the donor, it is best for the attorney to send the donor to another lawyer to avoid later allegations of undue influence.

Communicating with Opposing Party

Attorneys and paralegals may not communicate directly with the opposing party if that party is represented by legal counsel. It is unethical to communicate directly with a represented adversary without the opposing attorney's permission, which is rarely obtained. This ethical rule protects represented individuals from being approached by the opposing party and gathering information to be used against them.

Sometimes defendants who have been served with "divorce papers" may call the plaintiff's attorney and demand to speak to someone. If an opposing party contacts the office by telephone, paralegals should instruct that party to have his or her attorney contact the office. The conversation should go no further.

If an opposing party contacts the office in writing, the paralegal should inform the supervising attorney immediately.

THE *PRO SE* LITIGANT

As you learned in the previous section, legal professionals cannot communicate with opposing parties if they are represented by counsel; instead they must communicate directly with the opposing party's legal representative. Sometimes, an individual may elect to self-representation, acting as a *pro se* or *pro per* litigant in order to save money, or he may just wish to handle his own representation. It is important to navigate carefully when dealing with persons who are not represented by counsel. First, it is prudent to ask the *pro se* party to forward a letter confirming the self-representation. In addition, if there is a pending proceeding, the opposing party must file an appearance with the court indicating self-representation. The office should request a copy of the appearance from the *pro se* party and verification of its filing through the clerk's office. While this procedure may seem like a cumbersome formality, it enables attorneys to formally confirm the opposing party's status as a *pro se* litigant.

It is also prudent to communicate with a *pro se* party in writing when at all possible so that the office has a record of the communication. While many *pro se* litigants represent themselves with dignity and a high degree of professionalism, some *pro se* litigants abuse the legal system and resort to unethical conduct. Having communications in writing avoids the "he said, she said" situations that can occur when the office relies on telephone communications as opposed to written documentation. When telephone communications do occur, paralegals must carefully log all phone calls to keep the file current.

Attorney and paralegals must also take care not to offer legal advice to *pro se* parties or take unfair advantage of them because of their lack of knowledge of the legal system. Paralegals should also avoid engaging the *pro se* party in any unnecessary communications.

PRO SE RESOURCES AND UNBUNDLED LEGAL SERVICES

Read any family court docket and you will find that half of the appearances filed belong to *pro se* parties. Many have no choice. Many appear as *pro se* litigants because they are unable to afford the high cost of divorce, while a small number of *pro se* litigants don't trust attorneys, judges, and the entire system. The increase in *pro se* litigants presents special problems for the judicial system:

- Lack of legal knowledge (substantive family law, court procedure, and rules of evidence)
- Inability to preserve a record for appeal
- Constant need to ask for legal advice or help from clerks, judges, or opposing counsel
- Inability to navigate in an increasingly complex field
- Execution of mistakes that will cost them later on

- Abusive behavior and an "axe" to grind against the spouse and/or the legal system
- Slow down for the court system

Many jurisdictions have responded to the growing number of *pro se* litigants by offering a variety of self-help resources. In some jurisdictions, paralegals, under attorney supervision, may volunteer at legal aid clinics to assist *pro se* litigants in preparing the legal documents necessary to process a divorce case. Many jurisdictions offer simplified and standardized family law forms and how-to guides online, as well as self-help centers in courthouses and self-help seminars offered by local bar associations, to help alleviate the *pro se* burden. (A great website for *pro se* litigants is **www.selfhelpsupport.org,** which provides links to state-by-state legal aid services, state court websites, court forms, self-help centers, and online legal information.)

Another form of assistance for *pro se* parties is called **unbundled legal services**. Traditionally, a client who hires a divorce attorney is entitled to a full bundle of services. This means that the attorney, along with the assistance of his or her paralegal, will interview the client, gather the relevant facts of the case, prepare and file relevant documents, conduct discovery, research relevant legal issues, go to court, and do whatever is necessary to process the client's case from start to finish. Attorneys enjoy this method because it allows them to control all aspects of the case. Unbundled legal services, or **discrete tasks representation,** allows the client to purchase legal services on a task-by-task basis, sort of a pick-and-choose menu approach to legal representation. The client and attorney agree by contract as to what services the lawyer will provide in exchange for a fee. A list of unbundled legal services may consist of:

- Advising the client regarding the feasibility of self-representation depending on the complexity of the case
- Advising the client on maneuvering through the court system
- Educating the client on the divorce process
- Ghostwriting or preparation of legal documents as well as monitoring deadlines for filing
- Advising the client on legal issues impacting the case
- Coaching the client through the process by providing information on an as-needed basis
- Reviewing and responding to documents
- Conducting legal research on relevant issues
- Developing strategy for the case
- Introducing or objecting to evidence
- Dissecting and resolving legal problems
- Preparation for trial
- Advising the client on how to negotiate a settlement
- Advising the client on alternative dispute resolution options

For clients, unbundled legal services allow clients to represent themselves while providing legal expertise in certain areas without a large financial commitment. For legal professionals, unbundled legal services serve as a new source of revenue, as well as raise some ethical worries. Many state ethical codes allow an attorney to limit the scope of representation, if the client consents after consultation. This means that the attorney must explain to the client the services she will provide, not provide, and how this arrangement may affect the client's case. While the ethical rules may provide some leeway, attorneys are concerned that performing small tasks could eventually lead to responsibility for the whole matter. Clients can also be very demanding and expect the attorney and his or her staff to take on more services than originally contracted for. A client may, for example, purchase the preparation of the initial documents from the attorney and then call constantly for information on how to proceed in the case. Attorneys are also worried that clients who rely on unbundled legal services may do more harm because of lack of knowledge in how to maneuver strategically or misuse of the services they purchased. States such as Colorado, Oregon, New York, Alaska, and California have addressed the matter of unbundled legal services and provide some guidance to the bar in how to proceed ethically. Due to the large number of *pro se* litigants dominating court dockets, we foresee unbundled legal services as the wave of the future in divorce litigation.

Under the supervision of a licensed attorney, paralegals will play an integral part in offering unbundled legal services. It is important to check your state bar association's rules on the topic and determine if your state allows attorneys to offer such services and integrate such rules into practice. Most state rules of professional conduct indicate that an attorney owes a duty of candor toward the tribunal. Basically, this means that an attorney must be truthful to the court. In Iowa, for example, "ghostwriting," or an attorney preparing documents for a *pro se* client without signing the pleadings, is a "deception on the court" (Iowa Opinion 94-35, May 23, 1995). In New York, pleadings prepared by attorneys for *pro se* litigants require the words "prepared by counsel" to be on the document (New York Bar Association Opinion 1987-2). In Maine and Alaska, no disclosure is necessary (Maine Ethics Commission No. 89, 8/31/88, Alaska Bar Association No. 93-1, 3/19/93).

The paralegal may also assist the attorney by preparing a contract for legal services or engagement letter for the client to sign. In cases where the attorney is providing unbundled legal services, this agreement is called a **limited scope retainer agreement.** This is a contract for legal services between the attorney and client where the attorney limits the scope of representation with the client's consent. This is vital, especially in clarifying the role of the attorney and his or her office. The contract may contain:

- An explanation of the client's options—full bundled services, unbundled services, alternative dispute resolution (ADR) options, risks of *pro se* representation—and that the attorney explained these options to the client.
- Explicit details concerning what the lawyer will do for the client and the limits of the attorney's representation. Here we must be clear to indicate that the attorney will not be filing a court appearance on behalf of the client and that we are assisting a *pro se* litigant by providing unbundled legal services. Remember, once an attorney files an appearance, he or she may "own" the case. This means that an attorney will be responsible for the whole case and the judge will require his or her appearance at every court hearing.
- Fee for services. Usually unbundled legal services are paid for by the client at the time of service and the attorney charges a flat or fixed fee per session to control costs.
- A clause that says the client has fully disclosed the facts of the case to the attorney.

- An option for client to go from an unbundled service agreement to full bundled representation and how much this will cost.
- A notice that client will be responsible for all expenses.
- It may also be a good idea to prepare a state-specific list of the steps in the divorce process as well as a timeline for filing various forms.

Finally, remember that attorneys who engage in offering unbundled legal services are just as open to malpractice allegations as any other attorney. Make sure to keep very good notes regarding all interactions with the client—they may one day prove to be crucial in a grievance procedure against your supervising attorney.

COMPETENCE

Attorneys have a duty to render competent legal representation to their clients. **Competency** is the duty to exercise a reasonable degree of care and skill commonly used by other attorneys engaged in a similar area of practice. Paralegals must also deliver competent services in assisting attorneys in client representation.

Competency is attained by engaging in activities that educate attorneys as to the most efficient and effective manner of representing a particular client. The following activities help educate attorneys:

1. **Attendance at continuing legal education seminars.** Such seminars are provided by local bar associations, local paralegal associations, and by private entities.

2. **Associating with more experienced attorneys.** Experienced attorneys who possess adequate knowledge and skill in their particular area of practice frequently, either informally or through organized legal mentor programs, share their knowledge and expertise with attorneys who are new to their area of practice.

3. **Consulting statutes, case law, legal periodicals, journals, and other legal publications.** The practice of law is flexible in that attorneys can practice in a variety of areas as long as they become competent in those areas. Paralegals also enjoy this flexibility and work in different areas of practice as long as they too become competent and are supervised by attorneys. The ethical duty of competency is ongoing and imposes on attorneys and paralegals the obligation of continually educating themselves and upgrading their skills.

It is important for paralegals involved in family practice to review their jurisdiction's domestic relations statutes and relevant case law and to attain familiarity with the forms used in their state. State bar associations and local paralegal associations may periodically offer seminars in family practice, of which the paralegal should take full advantage. In addition, state bar publications and legal periodicals focusing on the jurisdictional law and procedures should be read on a regular basis to keep current on changing legal developments.

REASONS FOR HIGH COST OF DIVORCE

Why are divorce costs so high? One reason, and you will learn this quickly if you venture into the field of family law, is that the initial retainer is often all that a family lawyer will see in the course of representing a client. Many clients will not pay monies owed to the attorney, even in long, drawn-out cases where the attorney and staff have worked numerous hours on the client's file. Lawyers hesitate to sue clients for breach of contract over legal fees for fear that the client will file a grievance with the state bar association, or worse, sue the attorney for legal malpractice, which will result in an increase to his or her insurance premiums. If lawyers do get paid, it is after the divorce settlement, which requires the attorneys to carry the client's unpaid balance until the end of the case without interest. A piece of advice one of the authors of this book received from a legal mentor upon venturing into the family law arena was "Get all you can up front, because that's all you may ever see in this case!"

Society blames "shark" or "gladiator" attorneys for making divorces unbearable. While some divorce lawyers fit this profile, many reject this form of family practice. As a paralegal, you may find that the reverse is true. Many clients contemplating divorce seek out attorneys who are aggressive at the recommendation of their friends, coworkers, and family. A lawyer who encourages settlements and does not advocate "scorched earth" tactics is perceived as weak. One of the authors of this book recalls a case where a prospective female client with children was contemplating divorce. She came to the office for an interview and was advised by the attorney to resolve the matter amicably and avoid a long case that would not only damage her financially, but cause stress to the children. The next day, the prospective client called the attorney and said, "I've decided to hire someone tougher. I think you're nice, but way too soft." Surely enough, one year later, she and her husband were still on the short calendar docket, fighting over temporary orders.

Many divorce clients are very demanding and place a great burden on the lawyer and his or her staff. Clients who promise "this will be easy" or "my husband would never take my kids away from me," lull the novice attorney into a virtual Pandora's box of endless court hearings, failures to comply with discovery requests, contempt hearings, phone calls, negotiation attempts, failure to follow the lawyer's advice, and exposure to malpractice if things don't go their way.

Many divorce clients make a lot of phone calls to the office over trivial matters such as complaints about the father arriving five minutes late to pick up the kids, or the mother spending all the child support money on manicures and not on the children. And guess who has to deal with these calls when the lawyer doesn't want to hear it anymore? The paralegal! Clients also rely on the paralegal for moral as well as legal support. Clients may find the paralegal more accessible and cheaper to talk to than the lawyer since paralegals are billed out at lower rates.

FEES

Attorneys should charge "reasonable" **fees.** The factors considered when determining what is "reasonable" are the skill and experience of the attorney, the simplicity or complexity of the client's matter, the cost of similar service in the community, the result obtained, the reputation of the attorney, and whether the matter is contested or uncontested.

Divorce attorneys may be compensated for their legal services by employing any one of the following fee arrangements.

FLAT FEE

Under a **flat fee** arrangement, a fixed dollar amount is agreed on and charged for the entire case. Flat fees are sometimes charged in uncontested divorce cases where the parties have no children, no property, and no disputed issues between them.

HOURLY RATES

Attorneys may also charge clients on an **hourly basis.** This means that they will bill the client for each hour of time spent working on a client's file, including, but not limited to, research, drafting documents, phone calls, travel, office visits, trial preparation, and interviewing witnesses. Attorneys often bill in tenth or quarter hours.

Attorneys will also charge for expenses or **costs,** such as filing fees, sheriff's fees, and court reporter fees for transcripts and depositions.

RETAINER ARRANGEMENT

Another type of fee arrangement is the requiring of a **retainer** prior to the attorney committing himself or herself to representation of a client. A retainer is a payment made in advance to an attorney. The attorney will deposit the retainer in a client trust account and withdraw amounts from the retainer in proportion to the amount of work expended on the client's file. For example, a client gives his attorney a retainer of $2,000 to represent him in a divorce matter. The attorney bills at the rate of $200 an hour. Once the attorney has completed ten hours of work on the case, he is entitled to withdraw the **earned retainer.** If the attorney spent only five hours on the client's case, the attorney would be entitled to an earned retainer of $1,000 and would be obligated to return the **unearned retainer** to the client.

CONTINGENT FEE ARRANGEMENT

Attorneys may also be paid under a **contingent fee** arrangement, which entitles attorneys to a percentage of the financial outcome of the case, be it a judgment or settlement. Contingent fee arrangements are frequently used in personal injury cases and in other areas of civil litigation where the plaintiff lacks the financial resources to provide a retainer or pay the customary hourly rates. Many contingent fee arrangements provide that the attorney will receive one-third of the judgment or settlement amount the client recovers. Contingent fees are unethical in divorce cases because they discourage attorneys from accepting a settlement if they do not feel that the offer is adequate enough to cover their fee. They may push the parties to trial in order to seek a better disposition. Under these circumstances, they are acting in their best interests, not the client's.

FEE AGREEMENTS: PUTTING IT IN WRITING

Attorneys should always enter into written **fee agreements** with their clients so as to avoid any confusion regarding the attorney's billing practices. In fact, many jurisdictions require fee agreements between attorneys and clients to be in writing.

The fee agreement should specify the services to be performed by the attorney, the charge to the client, and the costs of litigation to be paid by the client. If the attorney uses paralegals in her law practice, the attorney should specify the paralegal's hourly rate for the performance of paralegal duties and the hourly rate for routine clinical tasks such as excessive photocopying, typing, and filing. Charging a client the attorney's rate for performing paralegal or clerical tasks is unethical.

Paralegal Fees

The following *McMacklin* case outlines the criteria for setting paralegal fees and the importance of differentiating between attorney, paralegal, and secretarial work in client billing practices.

FIGURE 2–4
It is important for family law paralegals to review their state's domestic relations law and attain familiarity with the forms used in their jurisdiction.

JAMES H. MCMACKLIN V. MARIANNE C. MCMACKLIN

651 A.2D 778 (1993)

FAMILY COURT OF DELAWARE, NEW CASTLE COUNTY

OPINION

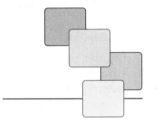

CROMPTON, JUDGE.

The following is my decision regarding attorney's fees in the above-entitled matter. I have reviewed Affidavits for Fees submitted by counsel for both James H. McMacklin (hereinafter "Husband") and Marianne C. McMacklin (hereinafter "Wife"). Wife's total attorney's fees, paralegal fees and costs amount to $12,785.50. Husband's total attorney fees, paralegal fees and costs are $9,768.35.

. . . In the past, Family Court Judges have treated paralegal fees in a variety of ways. Some Judges have permitted them. Others have steadfastly denied them. In my view, paralegal costs should be uniformly allowed, so long as certain information is specifically addressed by the supervising attorney in the fee affidavit presented to the Court.

13 *Del.C* § 1515 is the controlling statute regarding an award of fees following a division of marital assets and debts. That statute reads as follows:

The Court from time to time after considering the financial resources of both parties may order a party to pay all or part of the cost to the other party of maintaining or defending any proceeding under this title and for attorney's fees, including sums for legal services rendered and costs incurred prior to the commencement of the proceeding or after the entry of judgment. The Court may order that the amount be paid directly to the attorney, who may enforce the order in his name.

The phrase "all or part of the costs of the other party of maintaining or defending" has previously been found broad enough to include fees incurred by a legal assistant or paralegal (citation omitted). . . .

. . . The United States Supreme Court has found that the term "attorney's fee" refers not only to the work performed by members of the Bar but also to reasonable fees for the work product of an attorney, which includes the work of paralegals, law clerks and recent law graduates at market rates for their services. *Missouri v. Jenkins*, 491 U.S. 274, 109 S. Ct. 2463, 105 L. Ed. 2d 229 (1989). . . .

. . . Paralegal fees are not a part of the overall overhead of a law firm. Paralegal services are billed separately by attorneys, and these legal assistants have the potential for greatly decreasing litigation expenses and, for that matter, greatly increasing the efficiency of many attorneys. By permitting paralegal fees, the danger of charging these fees off as the attorney's work is hopefully extinguished. By the same token, the danger of charging off a secretary's services as those of a paralegal is very real and present, thereby mandating that certain information be provided by the supervising attorney before paralegal fees can be awarded by this Court in the future. Those criteria are as follows:

1. The time spent by the person in question on the task;
2. The hourly rate as charged to clients (will vary based on expertise and years of experience);
3. The education, training or work experience of the person which enabled him or her to acquire sufficient knowledge of legal concepts. The Court recognizes that not all those who work in a paralegal capacity have a paralegal degree or license, but many of these people do possess expertise, which should be recognized in family law matters;
4. The type of work involved in detail. The work must *not* be purely clerical or secretarial in nature. Such work would fall under costs and may not be charged as paralegal fees at the market rate. The task must contain substantive legal work under the direction or supervision of an attorney such that if that assistant were not present, the work would be performed by the attorney and not a secretary. However, the assistant may not do work that only an attorney is allowed to do under the rules of practice and ethics. Substantive legal work which may be performed by legal assistants and billed at the market rate includes, but is not limited to, such activities as:
   (a) Factual investigation, including locating and interviewing witnesses;
   (b) Assistance with depositions, interrogations and document preparation;
   (c) Compilation of statistical and financial data;
   (d) Checking legal citations;
   (e) Correspondence with clients/opposing counsel/ courts; and
   (f) Preparing/reviewing/answering petitions and other pleadings.

. . . Applying the above standards to the two Affidavits received in the matters *sub judice,* it is evident that both of them contain the required information. Both affidavits clearly comply with all four criteria previously discussed. For example, they describe the time spent by the paralegal, the hourly rate, and the education training or work experience of the paralegal. The type of affidavit submitted by Husband's counsel is exactly what this Court expects when reviewing fees. The affidavit of Wife's counsel leaves a bit to be desired in that it merely attaches invoices sent to the client. These invoices are very difficult to read and should be consolidated into one document with a separate affidavit attached by the paralegal. Husband's affidavit complies in every respect, but Wife's affidavit is certainly within the guidelines. Both attorneys have described in detail the type of work performed by the paralegal. This work includes such activities as reviewing depositions, preparing subpoenas, reviewing discovery, assisting in preparing Rule 52(d) Submissions, conferences with clients and correspondence. Clearly the type of work involved is that which would normally have been prepared or accomplished by the attorney and not a secretary.

Having made the decision that paralegal fees are and will be henceforth permissible by this Court, and having also decided that the Affidavits presented by counsel in this specific case rise to the required standards, I nevertheless must make a determination of counsel fees in accordance with 13 *Del. C.* § 1515, supra. . . .

. . . Husband has stated in his answer to Wife's Motion for Counsel Fees that he has no cash available to pay her fees. It is my opinion that his substantial income of approximately $82,000.00 per year versus Wife's income of approximately $35,000.00 per year mandates that he pay 60% of her fees or $7,671.30. This amount is to be added to the lump sum which Husband owes to Wife and is to be paid at the same time.

IT IS SO ORDERED.

In a law office, time is money; therefore there is a lot of emphasis on **billable hours.** This is the amount of time expended on a particular case, which can later be billed to that client. There is a lot of pressure in many firms to achieve a certain number of billable hours on a yearly basis. Attorneys and even paralegals are under similar pressure to produce billable hours. This pressure may lead some attorneys and paralegals to engage in unethical billing practices.

Paralegals record the time spent working on client files on forms called **time sheets** or **time slips.** Time sheets and time slips are used as a record of work performed on behalf of a client that will be billed to them on a periodic basis (see Exhibit 2–2). These documents should include the client's name, file number, spaces to log the date, activity performed on the client's file, and time actually spent. Every time the paralegal performs a task on the client's file, it is important to log the appropriate information on the client's time sheet. The time sheet should be completed at the same time the work is done. Several risks arise if time sheets are not completed in a timely manner. The paralegal may forget to include tasks performed, which would cheat the law firm out of earned revenue. Conversely, the paralegal may increase the time spent on a particular task, which would cheat the client and risk engaging in the unethical practice of **padding.** Padding means unjustifiably increasing the number of hours actually spent on a client's case. Padding is not only fraudulent, but also illegal since you are, in effect, stealing from the client.

ESTABLISHING LEGAL FEES

Just as it is the attorney's role to accept or reject cases, the attorney is also the only one who may set legal fees. Paralegals cannot set legal fees. This is for the attorney to determine after he has consulted with the client. Attorneys are also prohibited from splitting fees with nonattorneys. For example, attorneys and paralegals may not enter into an agreement whereby the paralegal is paid a percentage on each client file. Attorneys may compensate paralegals through a weekly salary or on an hourly basis. In addition, the attorney may also offer the paralegal fringe benefits such as bonuses, retirement plans, and health insurance coverage.

SOLICITATION

Paralegals cannot be paid for cases that they refer to the office. While paralegals may hand out the attorney's business cards and be a source of referral, paralegals cannot be compensated for the cases referred. The ethical rule prohibiting this practice is called **solicitation.** The public commonly uses the phrase "ambulance chasing" to describe this conduct. Attorneys cannot actively seek out persons they know are in need of legal services, either by mail or in person, unless there already exists an attorney/client relationship or a family relationship. However, attorneys may solicit clients if they wish to volunteer their legal services for free. In addition, attorneys may advertise their services to the general public through the media, by having listings and advertisements in the telephone directory and on the Internet, and by having advertising spots on television and the radio.

WORKPLACE VIOLENCE

Divorces deal with heavy emotional issues—love, anger, money, jealousy, possessiveness, shattered dreams and expectations. Divorce-related anger can be dangerous because it is often fueled by rage, vindictiveness, and a desire to punish or get even. This anger is sometimes expressed in the courts and toward the attorneys. Divorce practice is the most dangerous field of practice and is becoming high-risk work for lawyers, as the following examples note.

- In 1997, the American Bar Association conducted an informal survey of its Family Law Section and found that 12 percent of the 253 members who responded had been victims of violence perpetrated by either their client or the opposing party, 17 percent had been threatened by their clients, and 60 percent had been threatened by the opposing party.

■ In 1997, attorney Bud Zilaff of Sacramento, California, was shot and killed by a client's ex-husband. That same year, divorce attorney Ron Weiss was murdered in his office.

■ In May of 1984, Kenneth Spargo shot and killed his wife while she sat in Connecticut's Norwich Superior Court awaiting a hearing in their pending divorce case. Spargo was able to bypass the court's metal detector by entering through an unlocked back door in the courthouse.

■ On June 15, 2005, Connecticut attorney Julie M. Porzio was thrust into the national spotlight on what would have started off as a very routine day for a divorce practitioner. On that morning, Attorney Porzio did what many family lawyers do. . . she drove her client to court. At approximately 9:30 AM, Attorney Porzio arrived at the municipal parking garage next to Middlesex Superior Court in Middletown, Connecticut, along with her client, Donna Bochicchio, for the twelfth day of trial over a heated child custody and financial dispute in a divorce that had originally been filed in April of 2003. Michael Bochicchio, a retired Connecticut state trooper, the plaintiff and *pro se* litigant, approached the women and fatally shot his wife, seriously wounded Attorney Porzio, and finally killed himself.

■ On June 20, 2005, Perry L. Manley, dressed in camouflage and carrying a backpack, arrived at a Seattle, Washington, federal courthouse, threatening to set off a grenade to settle his grudge with the government over a bitter divorce case and court orders to pay child support. Taking his threat seriously and unaware that the grenade was inactive, police officers finally shot and killed Manley after unsuccessful attempts to convince him to put down the weapon. A month prior to the incident that led to his death, Manley protested on the federal courthouse steps by trying to burn the American flag.

Many divorce litigants feel as though their cases and lives are spinning out of control in the adversarial system designed to dissolve their marriage. Attorneys and paralegals practicing in this field should take any threats very seriously and take steps to diffuse an already combustible situation. Here are some suggestions:

■ Practice civility. See law practice as a profession, not a grudge match between attorneys and litigants. Help clients get through the process fairly and sanely for the sake of themselves and the children.

■ Take precautions at the office if you feel threatened. The entire staff should meet to develop a safety plan when dealing with highly volatile cases. If the attorney or staff has been threatened, call the police. Lock doors at all times and only admit clients with an appointment.

■ Seek out court ordered protection in the form of restraining orders

■ Ask if the client or spouse has a history of violence. Is there access to weapons? Drug or alcohol abuse? Stalking? Threats to hurt self or others?

■ Inquire about clients' and opposing party's ability to resolve conflicts. Do they resort to verbal or physical assaults or threats?

- You may have to arrange for court security personnel to escort clients to their cars. Don't do it yourself. It could be dangerous.

- It is also dangerous to give clients rides to court. Meet at the courthouse instead. If they are uncomfortable waiting for the attorney in the courthouse, have them wait near security personnel or near the metal detectors at the entrance. Avoid parking garages and isolated areas around courthouse.

- Seat clients as far as possible from abusive persons while waiting for the case to be called. Alert court security personnel to potential problems.

- Encourage angry clients to keep tempers under control and to seek counseling for anger issues.

- Encourage participation in mediation or collaborative divorce to resolve problems with the help of mental health professionals. The goal should be to seek a resolution, and not endless litigation that will damage the parties and their children long after the case is over.

Finally, we must accept that there are many divorces where no amount of mediation, collaborative efforts, or counseling will help. Cases involving domestic violence are not appropriate for mediation because the abused spouse may be intimidated and unable to speak due to fear. Some cases involve mentally ill individuals or those with a deep distrust of the courts and the law, and attempts to reach a resolution in such cases are literally impossible. As long as there are divorces, these types of cases will exist and will always pose a potential threat.

EXHIBIT 2–1 Sample time sheet.

CLIENT _____			PHONE _____	
ADDRESS _____				
DOCKET # _____	IN RE: _____	TYPE OF CASE _____		
NOTES _____				
_____				
_____				

DATE	IN	OUT	HRS	DESCRIPTION OF SERVICES
	:	:		
	:	:		
	:	:		
	:	:		
	:	:		
	:	:		
	:	:		
	:	:		
	:	:		
	:	:		
	:	:		
	:	:		
	:	:		
	:	:		
	:	:		
	:	:		
	:	:		
	:	:		
	:	:		
	:	:		
	:	:		
	:	:		
	:	:		
	:	:		
	:	:		

TOTAL HRS _____

END-OF-CHAPTER EXERCISES

Crossword Puzzle

1. clients purchase legal services on a task-by-task basis

2. actively seeking out persons in need of legal services for the purpose of providing them with legal representation

3. notes, materials, memoranda, and written records generated by an attorney, as well the attorney's mental impressions and legal theories concerning a case

4. a term characterizing the defendant in a lawsuit who has the financial assets to pay the monetary damages in a civil suit

5. the process of prohibiting a paralegal from discussing a case or having access to the file because of a conflict of interest

6. advising a client of his specific rights and responsibilities

7. a record of work performed on behalf of a client that is billed to the client on a periodic basis

8. acronym for National Association of Legal Assistants

9. acronym for National Federation of Paralegal Associations

10. a fixed dollar amount charged for the entire case

11. the ethical rule that protects communications between attorney and client

12. unjustifiably increasing the number of hours actually spent on a client's case

Review Questions

1. Why are divorces so expensive?

2. What are some of the ethical issues involved in performing unbundled legal services for clients? List five tasks that may be "unbundled."

3. In a divorce case, what is the problem with one attorney representing both parties?

4. Why do many divorce lawyers cringe when they hear the opposing party is appearing *pro se*?

5. Why is family law the most dangerous practice specialty for attorneys?

Case for Briefing

CARLSON v. CARLSON, 639 So.2d 1094 (Fla.App. 4 Dist. 1994)

Exploring the Workplace: Activities

1. You work as a paralegal for the Law Office of Jonathan Coleman. Attorney Coleman just interviewed Lorraine Newsome, a client who wants to represent herself *pro se* in a divorce matter. She would like to hire Attorney Coleman for the limited purpose of giving her legal advice at different stages of the case. She is a businesswoman and has enough savvy to see the case through. Attorney Coleman has asked you to prepare a limited scope retainer agreement in which he agrees to give Mrs. Newsome legal advice on an as-needed basis for a fixed fee of $250.00 per hour. You have never drafted one of these documents, so you may want to check out these websites as a starting point:

http://www.unbundledlaw.org/retainer_agreements/legal_services.htm and http://www.unbundledlaw.org/retainer_agreements/agreement_limited.htm

2. You just got a job as family law paralegal with the Law Office of Rocco & Rocco in your state. You are aware that it is your responsibility to be competent and stay current in this area of practice. Develop a game plan outlining the organizations, continuing legal education resources, publications, and groups that will help you achieve this goal.

3. You work as a paralegal for Marie Chase, an attorney who was just admitted to the Texas bar. She wants to include you on her letterhead and business cards. Read the following ethics opinion and write Attorney Chase a memo regarding your findings on this issue. Go to **http://www.txethics.org** and read Opinion 403 (Tex. Comm. on Professional Ethics, Op. 403, V. 45 Tex. B.J. 78 [1982]).

4. You work as a paralegal in the State of Florida for the Law Office of Anita Velez. A prospective client, Gertie Howard, comes to the office and asks if she could hire Attorney Velez to prepare the necessary documents she needs to represent herself *pro se* in a divorce. Attorney Velez wants you to check the state's ethical rules to determine if the office could prepare these documents for Mrs. Howard and prepare pleadings without signing as attorney for the party. Go to **http://www.floridabar.org** and read Ethics Opinion 79-7 Reconsideration. Prepare a short memo informing Attorney Velez of your findings.

CHAPTER

3

The Client Interview

KEY TERMS

financial worksheet
initial client intake form
initial client interview
jurisdictional requirement

legal advice
retainer agreement
retainer letter

THE PARALEGAL'S ROLE IN THE INITIAL SCREENING PROCESS

The divorce process begins with a potential client contacting the law office for the purpose of obtaining legal representation in the dissolution of his marriage. Clients also seek attorney representation in obtaining some type of postjudgment remedy such as contempt actions and modification proceedings. The client's first contact with the law office will ordinarily be through the telephone. Family law paralegals may often find themselves answering the phone and fielding phone calls from prospective clients.

Use of an **initial client intake form** will help the paralegal obtain important information during the prospective client's first call to the family law office (see Exhibit 3–1). The initial client intake form will aid the paralegal in obtaining data from the client and relaying information to the client. In addition to the prospective client's name, address, phone number, and reasons for seeking an attorney, the paralegal may:

1. Schedule an appointment for the client with the attorney, and log the appointment in the attorney's master calendar system and in the attorney's individual daily diary.
2. Inform the client of the cost of an initial consultation (which is determined by the attorney). If the initial consultation is free, inform the client of the time limits of this initial meeting.

FIGURE 3–1
Many clients' first
contact with a law
office will be made
via telephone.

3. Give the client travel instructions to the office and tell the client where to park.

4. If the prospective client was served with legal papers or has received any correspondence regarding possible litigation, tell the client to bring this material to the initial interview.

PREPARING FOR THE CLIENT INTERVIEW

The next step in the divorce process is the **initial client interview.** The initial interview is the first meeting between the client and the attorney.

The purposes of the initial interview are as follows:

1. To give the client the opportunity to meet the attorney.

2. To give the client some preliminary legal advice regarding his problem.

3. To give the attorney and the attorney's support staff (the attorney's secretary, paralegal, and law clerks) an opportunity to become acquainted with the client.

4. To enable the attorney to establish a relationship of trust and confidence with the client.

5. To give the attorney the opportunity to discuss fees and fee payment arrangements with the client, and to determine and communicate to the client the scope of the attorney's representation.

6. To give the attorney the chance to assess the client's needs and determine whether he or she is willing and able to represent this particular client.

7. To enable the attorney to obtain enough information to commence the client's legal action.

UNDERSTANDING THE EMOTIONAL ASPECTS OF DIVORCE

Before proceeding further with a discussion of the interview process, it is important for the paralegal to comprehend the emotional aspects of divorce. Marriages are entered into with high expectations. They can range from mutual promises to be faithful to each other and stay together forever, to somber resolves to maintain a sober and responsible lifestyle, to undying pledges to always be there for each other to provide emotional support, financial support, intimacy, companionship, love, caring, and mutual respect. When a client is at the threshold of seeking legal representation in a divorce matter, it is important to understand that some of the expectations of marriage have been shattered in one way or another.

An impending divorce signals the rupture of a dream. This event can literally turn a client's life upside down, and start the client on an emotional roller coaster. Throughout the process, clients experience everything from anger, jealousy, rage, and hopelessness to depression, frustration, and distrust. Furthermore, the adversarial nature of our legal system and litigious family law practitioners can exacerbate an already volatile situation.

Paralegals will have contact with clients at various stages in the divorce process, either by phone or in person. The paralegal should provide emotional support for a stressed-out client in a professional and limited manner. While a paralegal should acknowledge clients' feelings and give them an opportunity to express themselves, it may be appropriate, in some cases, to refer a client to a therapist or support group. It is not the function of the law office to provide therapeutic services to clients. The law office must remain within the confines of its role to provide legal services efficiently and competently and refer clients to therapists when they are in need of professional mental health services.

DEVELOPING A RELATIONSHIP OF TRUST AND CONFIDENCE

One of the most important goals of the client interview is developing a relationship of trust and confidence with the client. At the beginning of the interview, the client should be assured that all communications with the office are strictly confidential. While the ethical standard of confidentiality applies to any situation where an attorney/client relationship has been established, it is particularly important to verbally explain this duty to a client, especially a family law client. Divorce or family-related matters may present very sensitive issues that a client may be too embarrassed to discuss with an attorney or paralegal. Assure the client that the information will not be disclosed to third parties unless the client has consented or the disclosure is required by one of the exceptions to the confidentiality rule. A thorough knowledge of your state's confidentiality rule is extremely important.

A proficiently managed law office and a competent staff responding to clients' needs also helps inspire trust and confidence. Returning phone calls and following through on promises made to clients is essential. If you have told a client that documents will be forwarded for her review, do so. Take good notes when speaking with a client, either in person or on the telephone. Transfer any tasks to be completed on behalf of the client to your "Things to Do" list. This will ensure that this information will not get lost and that these tasks will be completed. Attorneys are very busy and may also need to be reminded to complete certain tasks or return a client's phone call.

DEVELOPING GOOD LISTENING SKILLS

A good interviewer develops listening skills over time and experience with a variety of clients. There are, however, some techniques that are worth discussing and applying when interviewing a client. One such technique is active listening. When interviewing a client, it is important to pay close attention to what he is saying and to convey to him that you are actually listening. If the interviewer is not engaged in the interview the mind may wander and vital information that could be useful to the client's case will be missed. The following are some guidelines to help you develop active listening skills:

1. **Refrain from passing judgment on your clients.** You will encounter clients with a wide range of life experiences and backgrounds that may conflict with your own values. It is not your function to judge the client, but rather to assist the attorney in the client's representation. You may empathize with the client, if appropriate, but refrain from expressing an opinion on her choices or lifestyle.

2. **Be aware of your body language.** We communicate nonverbally through the use of our bodies. As interviewers, it is important that we maintain eye contact with the client. If you keep looking at the clock, for instance, it may show that you are either bored or in a rush. Maintaining eye contact shows that you are interested in what the client has to say. Another way to show a client that you are engaged in the conversation is to be conscious of your body position. Avoid placing barriers (i.e., a desk) between you and the client. Sit across from the client at a reasonable distance and lean forward to show interest. Clients also communicate with body language. There are numerous books on the market that can help you learn how to interpret visual cues and how to respond to them.

3. **Provide feedback.** Repeat some key facts back to the client or summarize a series of events. Politely do this during a break in the conversation. This conveys that you are actually hearing what the client is saying and gives him the opportunity to correct any misunderstandings.

4. **Empathize with your clients.** Be sensitive to your client's emotional needs and acknowledge his feelings. Do not, however, share your personal experiences. Not only is this unprofessional, but getting too personal will disrupt your professional relationships. If you find that interviewing divorce clients raises certain issues in your own life, seek professional help or a support group.

PREINTERVIEW PREPARATIONS

Determine the scope of the interview with your supervisor. Is the client seeking a divorce or is it a postjudgment matter? Next, make sure that the interviewing room or area is private, neat, and free from confidential information pertaining to other clients. Facial tissues are also important to have on hand in case the client becomes emotional. You will also need a copy of the preprinted form used by your office, a legal pad for notes, and any releases or other documents necessary.

THE CLIENT INTERVIEW

THE CLIENT'S ARRIVAL

When the client arrives, make sure that you are not interrupted. Greet the client with a smile and a handshake. Introduce yourself and identify your paralegal status. Take the client's coat and engage in small talk in order to put the client at ease. Chatting about the weather or asking if the client had difficulty locating the office are some ways of initiating a conversation. Many offices keep hot and cold beverages for their clients' enjoyment. Offer the client something to drink if this is the procedure in your office.

THE ACTUAL INTERVIEW

Once the client is comfortably seated, explain your role. Tell the client that for her own protection, the ethical rules of the state prohibit you from giving legal advice.

The client's communication level will dictate how you approach the interview. Some clients are more verbal than others. For clients who talk too much, it is important to focus them on the purpose of the interview. Others are very nervous and need to be prompted with a lot of questions. Give the client an overview of the interview process and tell her that it is important that you hear her story and collect the necessary data. Tell the client that you will be taking notes so that you can preserve the information for the file.

GATHERING INFORMATION

Start with open-ended questions that will illicit more than a one-word response. For instance:

- "You contacted us about a divorce matter. Could you tell me what is going on in your marriage?"
- "What can we help you with today?"

These questions will encourage the client to start talking.

Tape recording client interviews is not recommended. When the recorder is on, your mind will relax, knowing that you are getting all the information on tape. The problem is that you may not be alert to sections of the interview where you need to ask questions. Focus on the client and listen. Only when you listen can you ask relevant questions. Jot down notes about questions or areas on which you may want the client to elaborate.

NARROWING ISSUES

Once you have a general idea of the client's situation, it is time to focus on specific issues. For example:

- "Can you elaborate on your child's educational problems?"
- "You mentioned that your wife was unfaithful during your marriage. Can you be more specific?"

Once you have a general picture of the marriage and the causes of the breakdown it is now time to focus on the preprinted form. Say to the client, "I think I have enough for now. I'd like to go through our questionnaire so that we can take down some important information the attorney will need in order to adequately represent you."

CONCLUDING THE INTERVIEW

Tell the client what will happen next: "I'll pass this information on to Attorney Jones" or "We'll draft the initial document and send you a copy." Take care of any documents that need to be signed at this time, such as releases or retainer agreements. (Retainer agreements are discussed later in this chapter.)

Explain to the clients what is expected from them. Do they need to gather additional information? Do they need to perform certain tasks? Ask the clients if they have any questions and tell them to feel free to call the office.

Whenever conducting a client interview, the interviewer must remember to obtain the essential information: where, when, who, what, why, and how. If a client has trouble remembering specific facts such as date, time, and place, it may be helpful to have the client go through his personal calendar, which may jar his memory. In addition to the initial interview, paralegals will often conduct subsequent follow-up interviews with the client during the course of the attorney's representation of the client. The basic skills of listening, actively asking questions, and gathering information from the client are equally as important in follow-up interviews.

REFERRING CLIENT TO SUPPORT SERVICES

Referring a client to a therapist or support group must be done in a sensitive, diplomatic manner, to avoid insulting or talking down to a client. Fortunately, the stigma of consulting a counseling professional or support group has waned in recent years, but it still may be difficult for some clients to accept. A good way to broach the subject is to ask clients if they think it would help them to talk to someone about their feelings. It is also helpful to convey to the client that during periods of extreme stress, many individuals seek the professional help of an objective person who can provide them with some healing advice.

Encouraging a client to seek counseling can also help the client cope throughout the divorce process, which will have its ups and downs. The client who is getting professional help and has a sounding board will be stronger and better emotionally able to handle the divorce process. This client will rely less on the divorce process to solve his or her emotional problems. This client will also rely less on the legal staff to address his or her emotional needs, thus allowing the law office to concentrate on the client's legal matter.

A family law paralegal should become familiar with the local services available to clients. Local newspapers, hotline telephone information lines, and hospitals can provide appropriate referrals. A client should also be encouraged to explore her medical insurance coverage to determine whether or not such services are provided under her plan. If insurance will not cover therapy or the client is without insurance and cannot afford to pay a private therapist, the law office can make the client aware of agencies that offer sliding-scale counseling services and of community support groups that are free or that charge a nominal fee to help defray the cost of the meeting space.

The paralegal should create a list of resources, updating it regularly, that provides a quick reference for client referrals. The list should include a variety of services for an array of client needs such as domestic violence services, twelve-step groups, substance abuse counselors, support groups, displaced homemaker services, mental health clinics, pastoral counselors, and private mental health counselors. Clients themselves may also have resources available to them that they have not considered. They may have had a friend who went through a divorce and can recommend either a therapist or support group. Other clients may be in the position to take advantage of employee assistance programs at their place of employment. If a client has religious affiliations, these institutions may also provide services or referrals to the client.

The paralegal should keep the following client information in a Rolodex or other type of filing system:

- name of agency,
- address,
- phone number,
- name of contact person, and
- what services are provided, dates, times, and cost.

Some organizations or professionals may also provide the office with business cards or brochures describing their services, which can be distributed to clients.

REFERRALS FOR CHILDREN

In addition to assisting and encouraging the client to seek professional help, an inquiry should also be made regarding the status of the children. Divorce is devastating for most children and their needs should be addressed, because this stressful event may have long-term effects on them. In addition to information hotlines, schools may also provide resources for children whose parents are going through a divorce.

CONDUCTING THE INITIAL INTERVIEW

No set rule dictates who should conduct the initial client interview. It will depend on the preference of the supervising attorney or, in an emergency situation, who is available. In some offices, the attorney will conduct the initial interview; in others, the paralegal will be the first person with whom the client has contact. The most ideal situation is to have both the attorney and the paralegal available for the client.

The presence of the attorney during the initial client interview is extremely important. Attorneys can perform a function that a paralegal cannot: give **legal advice.** Clients seeking a divorce from a spouse will have many questions regarding how the law will impact on *their* particular case and how it will effect *their* family. **Legal advice can only be provided by an attorney.** Giving legal advice means that you are applying the law to a particular client's particular circumstances and either predicting an outcome or advising the client to take a particular course of action. A paralegal may relay legal advice from the lawyer to the client, may provide nonlegal advice, and may give information by describing the law. Once the paralegal has applied the specific facts of the client's case, the paralegal has crossed the line into the unauthorized practice of law. Any paralegal conducting *any* client interview must be very careful to refrain from giving legal advice to the client.

In offices where the attorney conducts the initial interview, the attorney will obtain enough information to commence the representation of the client. This information will then be passed on to the paralegal, who will begin the drafting of the initial pleadings. Sometimes the attorney will introduce the paralegal to the client so they may become acquainted and the role of the paralegal in the representation of the client explained.

In some law offices, both the attorney and paralegal are present at the initial interview. This enables the client to observe the attorney and paralegal as a team working toward the client's representation. The attorney can explain the paralegal's role and allow the client and paralegal to form a professional relationship that will benefit the client. Because family attorneys are often in court representing clients, the client may find the paralegal more accessible. The paralegal will have a considerable amount of contact with the client during the divorce process for purposes of gathering information, drafting documents, answering client phone calls, and relaying messages from the attorney. A client's ability to communicate with the attorney, even through the paralegal, will increase the client's satisfaction and decrease his level of anxiety. A client who has to wait until the attorney gets around to answering his phone calls or attending to his case will be a frustrated and dissatisfied customer.

In some law offices, the paralegal will conduct the initial interview. In this situation, the paralegal must be ever so careful not to render legal advice in the course of the interview. Even though a paralegal may know the answer to the client's question and be 100 percent correct, she must resist the temptation. In some instances, either unexpected or planned, the paralegal may be conducting the initial interview alone. For instance, a client will have a scheduled appointment with the attorney and the attorney is delayed in court. If this happens, the paralegal should contact the client to reschedule the appointment. If the client is already en route to the office, the paralegal will have to take over the initial interview. The paralegal should politely explain that the attorney has been delayed and

FIGURE 3–2
A paralegal may conduct initial interview, but must refrain from ever giving legal advice. That can only be done by the attorney.

that she will instead obtain all the necessary information, but that the client will be contacted later that day by the attorney, who will answer all legal questions.

MAINTAINING A HIGH DEGREE OF PROFESSIONALISM

At all times during *any* client contact, the paralegal should maintain a professional demeanor. It is important that boundaries be set with the client so as to keep the relationship on a professional level at all times. Paralegals should never discuss personal information with the client, either about themselves, the attorney, or the law firm. Paralegals should also refrain from making moral judgments about clients and telling them what to do with their lives. The paralegal must always remember that the goal of the law office is to process the client's matter and achieve the client's ultimate legal goals. Client's other needs should be provided for by mental health professionals or the client's support network.

PREPARING FOR THE CLIENT INTERVIEW

The paralegal should make adequate preparations for the client interview. The actual time and date of the interview will have been set in advance at the time the client made the initial contact with the office. The paralegal should check the office calendar in order to refresh his recollection as to the name of the client and the date and time of the appointment. Steps should be taken to make the interview area neat and tidy and ensure that other client's files and correspondence are kept out of view for confidentiality purposes. The paralegal should also make sure that a box of tissues is readily available for the client's convenience in the event the client becomes emotional.

Upon the client's arrival, he or she should be greeted as "Mr._____" or "Mrs._____." The paralegal should introduce herself and indicate her professional status; for example, "I am Mary Jones, a paralegal with this office." The client may be nervous at the first meeting, so the paralegal may want to engage the client in light conversation regarding the weather or compliment a client's outfit and offer the client a beverage to ease the client's anxiety.

FUNDAMENTALS OF CLIENT INTERVIEWING IN THE FAMILY LAW OFFICE

At the outset of the interview, the paralegal should explain his role in the family law office. Some clients will not be familiar with the paralegal profession and will need to be educated on what services the paralegal provides under the supervision of an attorney. The paralegal should also make it clear to the client that he cannot give legal advice. The issue of confidentiality should also be addressed. The client should be ensured that all communications made to any law office personnel are confidential, barring certain exceptions, particular to the jurisdiction's rules of ethics.

It is also important to encourage the client to disclose all information, whether positive or negative, to the attorney and paralegal. Clients will often withhold embarrassing or damaging information for fear of being judged by the interviewer. It is imperative that the client disclose any information that can impact the divorce proceedings. If the attorney is made aware of this information in advance, she will be better equipped to deal with it instead of being surprised on the day of trial, or having the opposing side ambush her in the course of negotiation. Learning about negative information at an advanced stage in the proceedings may be too late, and the attorney may be unable to counteract its effects.

Once the client is comfortably seated, the paralegal may encourage him or her to give a brief synopsis of the problem. At this time, the paralegal should not take notes, because it is important to actively listen and develop a trust relationship with the client. The paralegal should get a general idea of what caused the breakdown of the marriage, the extent of the marital estate, and the number and ages of the children. Tape recorders should be avoided because the interviewer tends to relax and be less active if he is aware that a machine is preserving the data. This will make him less interactive with the client and he may fail to ask probing questions.

Once some general information has been exchanged, the paralegal should tell the client that he will have to obtain some essential information in order for the office to adequately represent the client. Then the paralegal can use a preprinted form as a guideline for obtaining the necessary information. Moving to the use of a form too quickly may insult a client and give him or her the impression that the office is sterile and uncaring.

OBTAINING ESSENTIAL INFORMATION FROM THE CLIENT

One of the primary purposes of the initial interview is to obtain enough information to commence representation of the client in her family matter. Most family law offices use preprinted initial intake sheets to garner these facts from the client (see Exhibit 3–2). The advantage of a preprinted form is that the paralegal will not miss obtaining any relevant information because the form serves as a guideline. A legal pad should also be kept on hand to jot down other notes in the course of the interview.

Some paralegals may find themselves working for new attorneys or attorneys with very busy schedules that have not had the opportunity to draft preprinted forms. In such a case, the following is an overview of what information the initial interview should elicit about both spouses:

1. **Name.** The names of both the client spouse and the other spouse should be obtained and spelled correctly. The wife's maiden name should also be elicited.

2. **Current address.** Physical address is important for the purpose of personal or abode service. Post office boxes or mailbox services are not sufficient for service, but the client may request that correspondence be forwarded to a P.O. box for security purposes. For example, the client may fear that his correspondence will be intercepted by his spouse or other third party. The office should have a system of alerting any office personnel who happen to pick up the file on any given day that care should be taken in terms of forwarding correspondence to the client, perhaps using a special colored sticker to serve as a "red flag."

3. **Telephone numbers.** Obtain home and work numbers. Sometimes clients cannot receive phone calls at work so you should avoid making

calls to their workplace, except in emergency situations. On the other hand, some clients may not be comfortable receiving calls at home if they are still residing with their spouse, especially in cases where domestic violence is a problem. Clients may also request that you leave phone messages with family members or friends, while others will use beepers in this electronic age to keep attorney communications confidential.

4. **Jurisdiction.** How long has the client resided in the state? Each state has a **jurisdictional requirement** indicating how long a party must reside in the state before the state courts have the power to dissolve the marriage.

5. **Social Security numbers.** Social Security numbers are useful for many reasons. Some jurisdictions may require Social Security numbers on initial pleadings. They are also important for tax purposes or when engaging the services of an investigator to conduct asset searches or track down a "deadbeat" parent. Social Security numbers are also useful in debt collection proceedings against delinquent clients.

6. **Military service.** Did either spouse serve in the military? This question is important, because military pensions may qualify as marital property. Also, if a spouse is currently in the military, care must be taken so service of process will be adequate.

7. **Employer.** Where is the client employed? What is the address? What is the client's occupation? How long has the client been employed in his current position? Similarly, where is the client's spouse employed and what is her occupation? This information will be helpful for purposes of service, subpoenaing employment records, and obtaining pension information.

8. **Date and place of marriage.** This will establish where and when the marriage took place.

9. **Education, race, and age.** This data may be necessary for statistical information to be made available to the state's bureau of vital statistics. Education will also indicate how far a client has gone through school, which may be relevant in terms of his ability to earn income.

10. **City or state welfare assistance.** Has the state or city welfare system ever provided financial support for the spouse and the children? Many jurisdictions require this information and require that the governmental entity be notified of the proceedings and appear for purposes of collecting monies owed to them.

11. **Date of separation.** When did the parties separate and what were the reasons for the separation?

12. **Cause of breakdown of the marriage.** All jurisdictions have adopted some form of no-fault divorce where the grounds for divorce are commonly referred to as irretrievable breakdown or irreconcilable differences. It is still important, however, to illicit the cause of the breakdown of the marriage from the client.

13. **Reconciliation.** Is there any hope of reconciliation? Divorce is a devastating life event, not only for the spouses, but more importantly for the children. It is the ethical responsibility of the attorney or paralegal to make sure that a divorce is what the client wants. Most clients who have made their way to an attorney's office are confident in their decision to dissolve the marriage. A client who is reluctant or may be having second thoughts should be encouraged to seek professional counseling services.

14. **Children.** How many children were born during the marriage? What are their names and dates of birth? Were any children born to the spouses prior to their marriage? Were there any children born to the spouses during the marriage who are not issue of the marriage? Is the wife pregnant? These questions are important to ask for purpose of allocating child support responsibilities and determining the custody and visitation rights of the parents. Paternity may also be at issue if challenged.

15. **Previous marriage(s).** Was either of the parties previously married? How, why, and when did the previous marriage(s) end? Is the spouse currently paying alimony or child support to a former spouse pursuant to a court order? What, if any, orders are in effect?

16. **Prenuptial agreement.** Did the parties sign a prenuptial agreement? If the answer is yes, be sure to obtain a copy from the client. The existence of a prenuptial agreement will raise several issues. Is the agreement valid? What rights did the parties give up? What did they obligate themselves to do?

17. **Was a divorce action previously initiated in the course of this marriage?** If the client tells you that a divorce was previously initiated, the paralegal should review any paperwork the client may have. The paralegal should then follow it up with a review of the court file in the appropriate courthouse where the actions were filed. The client may be surprised to find out that he may already be divorced or that the initial pleadings may have been filed. If the file is still active, a client seeking a divorce may save on filing and sheriff's fees. If this is the case, the filing of responses will be sufficient.

18. **Disability/illness.** The interviewer should ask whether either spouse or children suffer from any disabilities or illnesses. Issues regarding medical care and expenses, insurance coverage, and support may require special attention.

19. **Date of the interview.** When did the interview take place?

20. **Name of the interviewer.** Who conducted the interview?

21. **Source of referral.** Who referred the client to the attorney? This will help track the attorneys advertising dollars and zero in on where business is being generated. Thank-you cards or letters should be sent to individuals and organizations who refer business to the office.

22. **Legal fees.** If the attorney is conducting the interview, she will quote the client a fee for her services. If the paralegal is conducting the interview, he cannot quote a fee. Remember that a paralegal cannot set fees; this is the attorney's responsibility. In this instance, inform the client that he can discuss the fee structure with the attorney.

23. **Type of relief.** The interviewer should ask the client what type of legal relief he is seeking as a result of the family action. First and foremost, the attorney must determine the legal cause of action to be filed. Does the client want a dissolution of marriage, legal separation, or annulment? An attorney's legal advice is essential in making this selection. Additional relief includes child custody, child support, property and debt distribution, alimony, and attorney's fees.

24. **Name change.** A wife may seek to resume the use of her maiden name as part of the final divorce decree. It was a long-standing custom for women to assume their husband's surname upon marriage. Some states went as far as requiring women to assume their husband's last names through court

decisions. Gender discrimination laws, however, prohibit this judicial mandate. The Equal Protection Clause of the U.S. Constitution prohibits states from requiring women to assume the husband's surname since their is no rational basis for women, but not men, to change their last names upon marriage. Today, women are free to follow custom or to retain their own maiden names. Some couples create a new last name using the wife's maiden name and the husband's surname. A married woman's legal name is determined by what she actually calls herself *after* the marriage ceremony. She is basically free to use whatever she pleases as long as her choice is not intended to defraud her creditors or use her name for unlawful purposes. In preparing the initial divorce pleadings, the wife may include restoration of her maiden name in her prayer for relief. The court will automatically grant the wife's wishes despite objections from the husband. Some women choose to retain their husband's surname as a matter of preference. Many women with young children choose to retain their married name until the children have finished school and may later return to court to restore their maiden name. Change of name after the divorce is final is considered a postjudgment matter. The wife must file a petition in the proper state court. A hearing date is scheduled by the court and a notice is published in the legal section of the newspaper. Courts generally allow former spouses to change their names as long as the change is not being made to advance fraudulent or illegal purposes. The wife must then obtain a certified copy of the court's final decree and notify her creditors and the Social Security Administration of the change. The children of the marriage will also assume their biological father's last name. Problems arise when the wife remarries. Sometimes the children develop a close relationship with their new stepfather and wish to take his name. Mother may also push for a change of the children's last names for various reasons. Because the change of names, even for minor children, requires a court hearing, the biological father must be notified of the proceedings. If the parties disagree regarding the children's name change, the court will have to decide. The court will determine whether the name change is in the children's best interest. The court will focus on the wishes of the parents, stepparent, and children, and on the name that has been historically used by the child. While the best-interest standard is often applied, many courts still believe that it is in the children's best interest to use their biological father's surname.

Whenever conducting any client interview the interviewer must remember to obtain the essential information: where, when, who, what, why, and how. If a client has trouble remembering specific facts such as date, time, and place, it may be helpful to have the client go through his personal calendar, which may jar his memory. In addition to the initial interview, paralegals will often conduct subsequent follow-up interviews with the client during the course of the attorney's representation of the client. The basic skills of listening, actively asking questions, and gathering information from the client are equally as important in follow-up interviews.

Once the initial interview form has been completed, the attorney or paralegal may give the client a **financial worksheet** to take home and fill out (see Exhibit 3–3). This worksheet should focus on the client's income, expenses, assets, and liabilities, be they joint or separate. The financial worksheet will enable the attorney to begin assessing the extent of the marital estate. The client should also be instructed to write a history of the marriage, which will be helpful in illuminating issues that may be of relevance in the divorce action. The client should be instructed to complete these documents before the next meeting.

If the paralegal has conducted the interview without the attorney present, an appointment should be scheduled for a meeting with the attorney, which will enable the client to obtain legal advice and go over the material obtained by the paralegal at the initial interview. The attorney can also address the legal course of action to be taken and review the fee structure.

If the attorney has conducted the interview with or without the presence of the paralegal, he will now turn over the initial interview form to the paralegal for the purpose of having the paralegal draft the initial pleadings.

REPRESENTING THE DEFENDANT SPOUSE

In a family law practice, the office will either be representing the plaintiff or the defendant spouse. With a plaintiff spouse, the divorce proceedings are basically starting at square one, which requires the drafting and service of the writ, summons, and complaint. When representing the defendant spouse, the paralegal must make sure in initial phone consultation to instruct the client to bring in any papers that were served on her and all correspondence received in conjunction with the divorce matter. At the initial interview he must make sure to photocopy all paperwork the client brings. Determine whether service was properly made either through abode or in-hand service. He may also want to go over the complaint or petition with the client to determine whether the information contained is accurate. This will enable the paralegal to obtain the data necessary to prepare the responsive pleadings.

PREPARING RELEASES

Another task the paralegal may be asked to perform is to prepare a release of information or have the client sign a preprinted release. As explained in Chapter 2, the confidential relationship of the attorney and client, just as the doctor and patient relationship, prohibits the professional from disclosing information without the client's consent. In family matters, an attorney may need a client's consent to communicate with any one of the following:

- client's physician or therapist,
- children's pediatrician, teachers, or therapists,
- client's accountant,
- client's employer, and
- hospital or treatment centers.

The paralegal should be sure to check the federal and state statutes that concern the release of confidential information, especially when dealing with drug treatment or HIV- and AIDS-related information (see Exhibits 3–4 and 3–5).

THE RETAINER LETTER

Before the client interview ends, the supervising attorney will review the law office's fee schedule for providing legal services to clients. The law firm's projected costs for handling a dissolution matter or any other related family law matter should be disclosed, with realistic figures presented. The client should fully understand the financial obligation he or she is undertaking by retaining the law firm and must be willing to assume this obligation. The client must also feel comfortable in other respects with having that particular law firm provide representation. Similarly, the law firm and the individual attorney who will be in charge of the case must also feel comfortable taking on the client. Sometimes an attorney may have reservations about dealing with a particular client. The attorney may feel that the prospective client may not honor the financial arrangement to be made, or the attorney may sense that the client is not being honest in disclosing information about marital assets, in revealing events leading up to the dissolution, or in revealing events that could cause controversy about the client's fitness as a custodial parent. If, on the other hand, neither the attorney nor the prospective client have such reservations, then the relationship will be formalized. The law office will prepare a retainer letter for the prospective client to sign. Once this document is executed, the law firm will actively begin work on the client file.

A **retainer letter** or **retainer agreement** is a contract between the law firm and the client whereby the law firm agrees to provide specified legal services in exchange for monetary compensation (see Exhibit 3–6). As discussed in an earlier chapter, there are different types of fee arrangements, such as flat fees, contingency fees, and hourly fees assessed for time spent working on the file.

Most of the time, in a complex family matter, firms charge by the hour. When this is the case, the retainer letter will state the firm's hourly rate schedule. There may be one hourly rate specified for work done on the file by a partner, a different and lower hourly rate for work done by associates in the firm, and there will be hourly rates listed for work done by paralegals and law clerks.

The retainer letter will also specify the terms of payment. If interest or late fees are to be charged for tardy payments, that fact will be stated and agreed to. Sometimes a retainer letter will state that if a client defaults on payment of a balance owed, the firm may take legal actions and the client will be responsible for attorney's fees and collection costs. The retainer letter, as a contract, is signed by both parties. Each party has rights and obligations. Like other legal contracts, if either party breaches the agreement by failing to execute their obligations, the injured party may seek relief in the court system.

Retainer letters should not be entered into lightly by either the client or the law firm. The client must consider whether he or she can afford the anticipated cost of representation. The attorney must gauge whether the prospective client actually has the financial means to pay for services. In addition, the attorney must decide whether his or her firm has the legal expertise and technical resources to properly handle a case of the complexity and time the matter requires.

If the prospective client and the law firm agree to go forward with representation of the client, the parties will sign the agreement. When the retainer letter is finalized, the attorney in charge of the file will assign a staff person to prepare the documents that will initiate the court action being contemplated.

EXHIBIT 3–1 Sample initial telephone interview.

Client Intake Form
Initial Telephone Interview/Family Matters

Date_____   Referred by: ____Friend/coworker/relative

                                                                    ____Legal referral source

Interviewed by:_____   ____Yellow Pages

                                                                    ____Bar association

                                                                    ____Other:_____

1. Client's Name:_____

   Address:_____

   City/State/Zip:_____

   Phone: Work_____   Home_____

2. Reason for Calling: Dissolution_____   Postjudgment_____

3. Client's Occupation:_____

   Employer:_____

   Yearly income:_____

4. Length of Marriage:_____   Date Married:_____

5. Number of Children and Ages:_____

6. Brief Description of Assets:_____

7. Are there issues of:____ adultery ____alcoholism/drug abuse

   _____domestic violence _____gambling

8. Initial appointment scheduled for: Date:_____ Time:_____

                          With Attorney:_____

Inform the client of the following:

    Directions to the office and parking instructions

    Bring the following documents: _____ Marriage certificate

                                            _____ Copy of deed

                                            _____ Current pay stub

                                            _____ Income tax returns

                                            _____ Police incident reports

                                            _____ List of assets and debts

                                            _____ Certified copy of judgment (if postjudgment)

                                            _____ Separation agreement (if postjudgment)

EXHIBIT 3–2 Sample preprinted initial client interview form.

Client Intake Form
Initial Interview/Family Matters

Date_____

Check one:_____ Dissolution of Marriage   Representing: _____Plaintiff

_____ Legal Separation   _____Defendant

_____ Annulment   _____Third party

_____ Postjudgment   Intervenor

I.   *General Information:*

A.   Client's Name:_____   Maiden Name:_____

Address: _____

City/State/Zip:_____

Phone: (Home) _____ (Work) _____ Best time to call:_____

DOB _____ Place of birth:_____

SSN _____ Race:_____

Education:_____ Military Service:_____

B.   Spouse's Name:_____   Maiden Name:_____

Address: _____

City/State/Zip:_____

Phone: (Home)_____ (Work) _____

Best time to call:_____

DOB _____ Place of birth:_____

SSN _____ Race:_____

Education:_____ Military Service:_____

Represented by:_____

_____

_____

II.   *History of the Marriage:*

A.   Place of marriage:_____

Date of marriage:_____ Date of separation:_____

Reason for breakdown: _____

EXHIBIT 3–2 Continued

B. Children born of the marriage:

Name   D.O.B.   Birthplace

_____

_____

_____

Is wife currently pregnant? _____Yes _____No

C. Public Assistance:

Have you or your spouse ever received public assistance?_____

Are you or your spouse currently receiving public assistance? _____

D. Employment:

Client's Employer:_____

　　　Address:_____

　　　City/State/Zip:_____

Occupation: _____

Years Employed:_____ Salary:_____

Benefits: _____

Spouse's Employer:_____

　　　Address:_____

　　　City/State/Zip:_____

Occupation: _____

Years Employed:_____ Salary:_____

Benefits: _____

E. What would you describe as the cause of the breakdown of your marriage?

Have you or your spouse sought marital counseling?

Is there any hope of reconciliation?

Did you sign a prenuptial agreement?

F. Have you or your spouse had any prior marriages?

EXHIBIT 3–2 Continued

G. Disability/Illness (either spouse/children):_____

H. How long have you resided in this state?

III. *Client Claims:*

Pendente lite	*Final orders*
_____ Alimony	_____ Dissolution of marriage
_____ Child custody	_____ Legal separation
_____ Child support	_____ Annulment
_____ Visitation	_____ Alimony
_____ Attorney's fees	_____ Property division
_____ Exclusive possession	_____ Child custody ___ Sole
of the marital residence	___ Joint
_____ Restraining order	_____ Visitation
_____ Other	_____ Attorney's fees
_____	_____ Name change to:_____
	_____ Contempt citation
	_____ Modification
	_____ Other:
	_____

IV. *Postjudgment Matters*

Contempt Citations

Date of the original order: _____

Court where order entered: _____

Original order: _____

Date of last payment: _____

Modification:

Date of the original order: _____

Court where order entered: _____

Original order: _____

Modification sought: _____

Specify the substantial change in circumstances since the date of the original order:

EXHIBIT 3–2 Continued

V. *Service of Process*

Where to serve spouse:_____

Best time to serve:_____ a.m./p.m.

Brief description of spouse:_____

_____

Description of spouse's car: _____

VI. *Documents to Prepare*

_____ Summons/complaint   _____ Financial affidavit

_____ Pendente lite motions   _____ Lis pendens

_____ Subpoena   _____ Contempt citation

_____ Reopen and modify judgment

_____ Other: _____

VII. *Legal Fees*

Fee quoted: $_____   Costs: $_____

Initial retainer amount required before services are commenced: $ _____

Terms of payment: _____

Fee agreement signed? _____ Yes_____ No

VIII. *Referral Source*

_____ Friend/coworker/relative   _____ Legal referral service

_____ Yellow Pages   _____ Bar association

_____ Other _____

EXHIBIT 3–3 Sample financial worksheet to determine assets and liabilities.

Financial Worksheet

Client's name: _____ Date: _____

I. *INCOME*

(Indicate weekly income and deductions. If paid monthly, divide monthly figure by 4.3 to determine weekly amount.)

A. Gross weekly income

Salary, wages, commissions $_____

Bonuses   _____

Tips   _____

Pensions/retirement   _____

Public assistance   _____

Social Security   _____

Unemployment insurance   _____

Disability   _____

Dividends/interest   _____

Rental income   _____

Alimony/child support   _____

Other: _____   _____

TOTAL GROSS WEEKLY INCOME $_____

B. Deductions

Federal withholding tax $_____

State withholding tax   _____

F.I.C.A.   _____

Medicare   _____

Health insurance   _____

Union dues   _____

Credit union   _____

Pension   _____

Other: _____   _____

TOTAL WEEKLY DEDUCTIONS $_____

TOTAL NET WEEKLY INCOME $_____

(A minus B)

EXHIBIT 3–3 Continued

II. *EXPENSES*

(Indicate weekly expenses. If expenses incurred on a monthly basis, divide monthly figure by 4.3 to determine weekly amount.)

A. Rent/Mortgage/Household

    1. Rent/mortgage $_____

    2. Homeowner's/renter's insurance   _____

    3. Property taxes   _____

    4. Household repairs   _____

    5. Trash collection   _____

    6. Other:_____   _____

        TOTAL RENT/MORTGAGE/HOUSEHOLD $_____

B. Utilities

    1. Electricity $_____

    2. Heat   _____

    3. Gas   _____

    4. Telephone   _____

    5. Water   _____

    6. Cable TV   _____

    7. Other:_____ $_____

        TOTAL UTILITIES $_____

C. Groceries $_____

D. Clothing $_____

E. Dry Cleaning/Laundry $_____

F. Transportation

    1. Car payments $_____

    2. Parking   _____

    3. Tolls   _____

    4. Gas/oil   _____

    5. Repairs   _____

    6. Car taxes   _____

    7. License/registration/emissions   _____

EXHIBIT 3–3 Continued

8. Bus	_____
9. Train	_____
10. Car insurance	_____
11. Other:_____	_____
TOTAL TRANSPORTATION	$_____
G. Medical (out-of-pocket expenses)	
1. Medical insurance	$_____
2. Dental insurance	_____
3. Doctor visits	_____
4. Dentist visits	_____
5. Prescriptions/medicine	_____
6. Optometrist	_____
7. Orthodontist	_____
8. Counseling/therapy	_____
9. Other:_____	_____
TOTAL MEDICAL	$_____
H. Life Insurance Premium	$_____
I. Children's Expenses	
1. School lunches	$_____
2. School books/school supplies	_____
3. Tutors	_____
4. School tuition	_____
5. Camps	_____
6. Class trips	_____
7. Lessons (piano, karate, etc.)	_____
8. Allowance	_____
9. Religious instruction	_____
10. Day care/babysitter	_____
TOTAL CHILDREN'S EXPENSES	$_____

EXHIBIT 3–3 Continued

J.   Payment on Outstanding Debts

    1.   Credit cards:_____ $_____

                  _____   _____

                  _____   _____

                  _____   _____

    2.   Student loans   _____

    3.   Installment contracts   _____

    4.   Personal loans   _____

    TOTAL PAYMENTS ON OUTSTANDING $_____
    DEBTS

K.   Miscellaneous Expenses

    1.   Haircuts $_____

    2.   Newspapers/magazines   _____

    3.   Eyeglasses   _____

    4.   Charitable contributions   _____

    5.   Subscriptions   _____

    6.   Gifts   _____

    7.   Bank fees   _____

    8.   Postage   _____

    9.   Vacations   _____

    10.   Entertainment   _____

    11.   Pet care   _____

    12.   Cigarettes   _____

    13.   Toiletries   _____

    14.   Other:_____   _____

    TOTAL MISCELLANEOUS EXPENSES $_____

TOTAL EXPENSES $_____

EXHIBIT 3–3 Continued

III. *ASSETS*

(Provide the following information for each home, vacation home, condominium, farm, or parcel of real estate.)

A. Real Estate:

1. Address:_____

City/State/Zip: _____

2. Date acquired:_____

3. Mortgage institution:_____

4. How is property owned? (specify exact names on deed)

_____

_____

_____

5. Estimated value $_____

6. Outstanding mortgage   _____

7. Equity   _____

TOTAL REAL ESTATE $_____

(Include only your one-half undivided interest if property jointly owned.)

B. Bank/Checking Accounts

Name of Bank	Account Number	How Held (Joint or Individual)	Balance
_____	_____	_____	$_____
_____	_____	_____	_____
_____	_____	_____	_____
_____	_____	_____	_____
TOTAL BANK/CHECKING ACCOUNTS			$_____

C. Stocks and Bonds

Number of Shares	Company or Fund	Value
_____	_____	$_____
_____	_____	$_____
_____	_____	$_____
TOTAL STOCKS and BONDS		$_____

EXHIBIT 3–3 Continued

D. Deferred Compensation (401k, SEP, Keogh, IRA, etc.)

(provide the following information for each plan)

1. Name of company:_____

2. Name of plan:_____

3. Account number:_____

4. Estimated value:_____

5. Name and address of plan administrator:_____

_____

_____

TOTAL DEFERRED COMPENSATION $ _____

E. Motor Vehicles (provide the following information for each motor vehicle, including boats, airplanes, and motorcycles).

1. Year:_____

2. Model:_____

3. Estimated value $_____

4. Loan balance   _____

5. Equity   _____

TOTAL MOTOR VEHICLES $_____

F. Business Interests

1. Name of business:_____

2. Type of business:_____

3. Type of business interest: _____ Sole proprietorship

     _____ Partnership

     _____ Limited liability corporation

     _____ Professional corporation

     _____ Joint venture

     _____ Corporation

4. Estimated value of your interest $_____

TOTAL BUSINESS INTERESTS $_____

EXHIBIT 3–3 Continued

G. Insurance

Insured	Company	Beneficiary	Face Value	Cash Surrender Value
_____	_____	_____	$ _____	$ _____
_____	_____	_____	$ _____	$ _____
_____	_____	_____	$ _____	$ _____

TOTAL CASH SURRENDER VALUE (minus loans) $ _____

H. Personal Property

    1. Household furniture $ _____

    2. Antiques   _____

    3. Jewelry   _____

    4. Artwork   _____

    5. Collectibles   _____

    6. Stereo/electronic equipment   _____

    7. Clothing   _____

    8. Furs   _____

    9. Family heirlooms   _____

   10. Silver   _____

   11. Crystal   _____

   12. Other_____   _____

                _____   _____

                _____   _____

     TOTAL PERSONAL PROPERTY $_____

TOTAL ASSETS $_____

EXHIBIT 3–3 Continued

IV.   LIABILITIES

        Outstanding Debts

Date Debt Incurred	Creditor	Incurred by Payment	Monthly	Current Balance
_____	_____	_____	$_____	$_____
_____	_____	_____	$_____	$_____
_____	_____	_____	$_____	$_____
_____	_____	_____	$_____	$_____
TOTAL LIABILITIES				$_____

EXAMPLE 3–4 Sample information release form.

Authorization for Release of Information

I, EVELYN BRONSON, of NEW HAVEN, CONNECTICUT, hereby give permission to DOREEN HUNT, CPA, of NEW

HAVEN, CONNECTICUT, to allow my attorney, GRACE A. LUPPINO, to review, inspect, and otherwise photocopy any

documents or files, or obtain any information pertaining to me currently in my accountant's possession.

_____

Evelyn Bronson

_____

Date

_____

Witness

EXAMPLE 3–5 Sample medical information release form.

Medical Authorization for Release of Information

I, EVELYN BRONSON of NEW HAVEN, CONNECTICUT, hereby give permission to CLAYTON REEVES, M.D., of NEW HAVEN, CONNECTICUT, to permit my attorney, GRACE A. LUPPINO, to review, inspect, and otherwise photocopy my medical records, including laboratory records and reports, all tests of any type, and all of my records pertaining to medical care, history, condition, treatment, diagnosis, prognosis, etiology, and expenses.

_____

Evelyn Bronson

_____

Date

_____

Witness

EXAMPLE 3–6 Sample retainer agreement (author unknown).

Retainer Agreement

A. EVELYN BRONSON ("Client") hereby employs GRACE A. LUPPINO, an attorney licensed to practice law in the State of Connecticut ("Attorney"), to represent her in a dissolution of marriage action: RODNEY BRONSON v. EVELYN BRONSON, Docket No. FA 96-123456.

B. In consideration of the services rendered, the Client shall pay the Attorney in the following manner:

　1. The Attorney shall commence work on the Client's dissolution matter upon receipt of an initial retainer of $3,000.00 (Three Thousand dollars) from the Client.

　2. The total number of hours expended by the Attorney will be billed at a rate of $200.00 (Two Hundred dollars) per hour.

　3. Upon expending the initial retainer, the Attorney shall bill the Client for any additional hours expended at a rate of $200.00 (Two Hundred dollars) per hour.

　4. Upon completion or termination of the Attorney's representation of Client, the Attorney shall return any unearned retainer to the Client.

C. The Client shall pay for all costs and expenses incurred by the Attorney in the course of representing the Client. Costs and expenses include, but are not limited to, court entry fees, sheriff's fees, process server fees, transcripts, subpoenas, and expert witnesses.

D. The Client authorizes the Attorney to engage the services of accountants, appraisers, evaluators, investigators, court reporters, sheriffs, experts, and process servers deemed necessary by the Attorney in rendering legal services to the Client. (The Client shall be directly responsible for the fees and bills of these service providers.) The Attorney shall obtain the Client's approval prior to engaging the services of such persons or incurring such costs and expenses.

E. The Attorney shall bill the Client for all legal fees, costs, and expenses on a monthly basis. Such bill shall be paid by the Client within 30 days from the date of the invoice.

F. If this Agreement is terminated by the Client prior to completion of the Attorney's services, the Client shall pay any Attorney's fees, costs, and expenses accrued to that date.

G. The Attorney shall not be required to deliver any reports, investigations, appraisals, evaluations, or other documents prepared by third parties that have not been paid for by the Client.

H. In the event that the Attorney must enforce this Agreement through any legal collection proceedings, the Attorney shall be entitled to recover reasonable attorney's fees and court costs in conjunction with such proceeding.

The undersigned parties have read the above Agreement and agree to abide by its terms and conditions.

Signed this _____ day of _____, 2001.

_____
Evelyn Bronson, Client

_____
Grace A. Luppino, Esq. Attorney

END OF CHAPTER EXERCISES

Crossword Puzzle

Across

2. a contract between the law firm and client where the law firm agrees to provide specified legal services in exchange for monetary compensation

4. a letter outlining the law firm's agreement to provide legal services to the client in exchange for monetary compensation

5. a form used by attorneys to collect information regarding a client's income, assets, expenses, and liabilities

6. advising a client of his or her specific legal rights and responsibilities

Down

1. the amount of time a party must reside in a state before the state courts have the power to dissolve a marriage

3. the first meeting between a client and the attorney and/or paralegal

Review Questions

1. Why is it important for the family law paralegal to comprehend the emotional aspects of divorce?

2. Explain the importance of locating the appropriate support services for clients.

3. What steps should the paralegal take in preparing for the initial client interview?

4. What is the purpose of a retainer agreement? What terms should a retainer agreement include? Why is it important to have the client prepare a detailed financial worksheet?

5. Explain the differences between conducting an initial interview with a plaintiff spouse and a defendant spouse.

Case for Briefing

Doe v. Condon, 341 S.C. 22, 532 S.E. 2d 879 (2000)

Exploring the Workplace: Activities

If you plan on working as a family law paralegal, you will see many clients who are dealing with the issue of domestic violence. The following exercises help give you a basic understanding of the issue, acquaint you with the resources available in your community, and educate you regarding the court-ordered legal protections available in your state.

1. Go to **http://www.ncadv.org/** and read the Violence Against Women Act, signed into law by President George Bush on January 6, 2006. Briefly, describe the purpose of the legislation and how it impacts survivors of domestic violence. List five points you find interesting.

2. Read "Law Enforcement Response to Domestic Violence—Understanding Domestic Violence" at **http://www.mc. maricopa.edu/dept/d52/ajs/vaw/under standingdv.htm**.

After reading the article, answer the following questions:

a) List three myths of domestic violence and the facts that destroy each myth.

b) Describe the cycle of violence.

c) Answer the question "why doesn't she just leave?"

d) List three common characteristics of the domestic violence victim.

e) Your client has been in and out of an abusive relationship for over five years. You are getting impatient with her. Apply what you have learned from **Section E** of this article, entitled "**Dealing with Victims,**" and note how you would adjust your response based on what you have read in this section.

f) List five common characteristics of an abuser

g) Discuss one excuse used by a batterer.

h) What are the effects of domestic violence on the children?

3. Go to **http://www.ndvh.org/** and find out what services are available for victims of domestic violence in the state and city where you intend to work as a paralegal. Use "Search" at the bottom of first page to find services in your community.

4. Go to **http://www.batteredmen.com/ gjdvneut.htm**. What are some of the problems battered men face when trying to get help from the system? What services are available in your community for male victims of domestic violence?

5. Go to **http://www.aardvarc.org/dv/ orders.shtml—"An Abuse, Rape, Domestic Violence and Resources for Children."** This site gives you state-by-state links to court-ordered protection for victims. What is available in your jurisdiction? This is a great site with many resources that will be of use to you in practice.

CHAPTER 4

Premarital Agreements, Cohabitation, and Same-Sex Marriage

KEY TERMS

antenuptial agreement

beneficiary

civil unions

cohabitation agreement

constructive trust

Defense of Marriage Act

domestic partnership

express contract

expressed trust

Federal Marriage Amendment

full faith and credit clause

fundamental right

implied partnership

implied trust

implied-in-fact contract

marriage statute

miscegenation laws

palimony

Posner

post-nuptial agreement

premartial agreement

prenuptial agreement

public policy

quasi-contract

reciprocal beneficiaries law

religious freedom and civil
marriage protection act

resulting trust

same-sex marriage

second glance doctrine

trustee

unconscionable

Uniform Premarital
Agreement Act (UPAA)

PREMARITAL AGREEMENTS

INTRODUCTION

Prior to marriage, the parties involved may choose to enter into a contract that determines their respective rights upon dissolution of the marriage or the death of one of the parties. These arrangements are called **antenuptial agreements, premarital agreements,** or **prenuptial agreements.** A premarital agreement is a contract entered into between two parties who intend to marry. Occasionally, this document addresses how the responsibilities and property rights will be handled during the marriage—who will pay the bills, who will support children from a prior marriage, who will pay the mortgage, how the children's upbringing will be handled, and who will care for the children's day-to-day needs. Frequently, the premarital agreement focuses on the disposition of the parties' estates in the event of divorce or death.

Once exclusively a staple in the legal arsenal of the rich and famous, more and more couples are now considering premarital agreements. These contracts were historically entered into by older men who married younger women. These men wished to protect their assets from potential "gold diggers" who were arguably marrying them for their money. Today, premarital agreements are popular among people who are entering into second or third marriages. In these cases, one or both parties may come with baggage. The husband, for instance, may be obligated to pay alimony and child support to the former wife. The wife may have children from a previous relationship. Premarital agreements are also used by parties who have more assets or income than their spouse-to-be, and by those who wish to protect the inheritance rights of their adult children. Premarital agreements are also considered a means of financial and emotional self-defense in a society with a high divorce rate. In addition, young professionals who have postponed marriage until their thirties or forties resort to prenuptial agreements to protect assets they have accumulated.

Some parties enter into such agreements *after* the marriage has been performed. These contracts are called **post-nuptial agreements** and the elements are similar to those of premarital agreements.

A premarital agreement is not a very romantic topic to discuss with a prospective partner, even if it can save the parties a great deal of grief in the long run. Money is also a very delicate topic to discuss under any circumstances and even more difficult to interject into a personal relationship. Talk of money can dredge up old childhood wounds and expose embarrassing habits that have formed in adulthood.

Prior to 1970, premarital agreements were frowned on by the courts. Judges often found these contracts void against public policy because they contemplated the end of the marital relationship. The state government had an interest in preserving the institution of marriage. The prevailing view was that premarital agreements facilitated divorce because they encouraged the spouse in the position to benefit most from the contract to put less effort into preserving the marital relationship. Courts were also protective of women's interests, fearing that men, who traditionally had more assets and business savvy, would leave women destitute in the event of divorce. For many centuries, a woman's traditional position was that of homemaker and child rearer. Many women lacked the education and finances to negotiate on an equal level with men. Premarital agreements were introduced into our legal system by men who had greater assets and greater business sophistication in legal matters. The courts feared that if premarital agreements were enforced, women would be unable to support themselves and would have to rely on public assistance.

The 1960s and 1970s brought many social changes to the institution of marriage, such as the advent of the women's liberation movement and no-fault divorce. No-fault divorce removed the traditional fault grounds that were once required to be proven by the moving spouse in order to obtain a divorce (i.e., abandonment, adultery, intemperance). The changing role of women propelled them to pursue higher education, greater opportunities in the workplace, and, as a result, economic independence. The women's liberation movement also demanded equal treatment under the law. Courts eventually did away with the legal presumptions that aimed to protect women in the legal system. Judicial attitudes progressed to the point where premarital agreements were enforced because it made sense in this era. Premarital agreements allowed prospective spouses to enter into a marriage with more predictability since they could now get their legal and financial house in order.

In 1970, the Florida Supreme Court, in *Posner v. Posner*, 233 So.2d 381 (Fla. 1970), paved the way for family courts around the country to hold that premartial agreements made in contemplation of marriage were not invalid *per se*. While the premarital agreement in this case was invalidated because of nondisclosure of assets, it was not struck down on public policy grounds. The following *Posner* excerpt illustrates the historical progression of premarital agreements in our legal system.

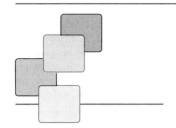

VICTOR POSNER, PETITIONER V. SARI POSNER, RESPONDENT

233 So.2d 381 (1970)

Supreme Court of Florida

March 25, 1970

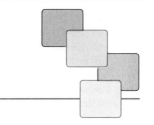

Roberts, Justice.

. . . Both parties had appealed to the appellate court for reversal of the decree of the Chancellor entered in a divorce suit—the wife having appealed from those portions of the decree awarding a divorce to the husband and the sum of $600 per month as alimony to the wife pursuant to the terms of an antenuptial agreement between the two parties. . . .

. . . The three appellate judges . . . each took a different position respecting the antenuptial agreement concerning alimony. Their respective views were (1) that the parties may validly agree upon alimony in an antenuptial agreement but that the trial court is not bound by their agreement; (2) that such an agreement is void as against public policy; and (3) that an antenuptial agreement respecting alimony is entitled to the same consideration and should be just as binding as an antenuptial agreement settling the property rights of the wife in her husband's estate upon his death. They have certified to this court, as one of great

public interest, the question of the validity and binding effect of an antenuptial agreement respecting alimony in the event of the divorce or separation of the parties. . . .

. . . At the outset we must recognize that there is a vast difference between a contract made in the market place and one relating to the institution of marriage.

It has long been the rule in a majority of the courts of this country and in this State that contracts intended to facilitate or promote the procurement of a divorce will be declared illegal as contrary to public policy. . . .

. . . At common law. The so-called "matrimonial causes," including divorce, were cognizable only in the Ecclesiastical Courts. Because of the Church's view of the sanctity of the nuptial tie, a marriage valid in its inception would not be dissolved by an absolute divorce *a vinculo matrimonii*, even for adultery—although such divorces could be granted by an Act of Parliament. Therefore, the divorce was only from bed and board, with an appropriate allowance for sustenance of the wife out of the husband's estate. See Ponder v. Graham, 1851, 4 Fla. 23; *Chitty's Blackstone*, Vol. I, Ch. XV, 432, 431. We have, of course, changed by statute the common-law rule respecting the indissolubility of a marriage valid in its inception; but the concept of marriage as a social institution that is the foundation of the family and of society remains unchanged. . . . Since marriage is of vital interest to society and the state, it has frequently been said that in every divorce suit the state is a third party whose interests take precedence over the private interests of the spouses. . . .

. . . The state's interest in the preservation of the marriage is the basis for the rule that a divorce cannot be awarded by consent of the parties . . . this court said that it "would be aiming a deadly blow at public morals to decree a dissolution of the marriage contract merely because the parties requested it;". . .

. . . And it is the same policy that is the basis for the rule that an antenuptial agreement by which a prospective wife waives or limits her right to alimony or to the property of her husband in the event of a divorce or separation, regardless of who is at fault, has been in some states held to be invalid . . . Crouch v. Crouch, 1964, 53 Tenn.App. 594. . . . The reason that such an agreement is said to "facilitate or promote the procurement of a divorce" was stated in Crouch v. Crouch, *supra*, as follows: "Such contract could induce a mercenary husband to inflict on his wife any wrong he might desire with the knowledge his pecuniary liability would be limited. In other words, a husband could through ill treatment of his wife force her to bring an action for divorce and thereby buy a divorce for a small fee less than he would otherwise have to pay."

Antenuptial or so-called "marriage settlement" contracts by which the parties agree upon and fix the property rights which either spouse will have in the estate of the other upon his or her death have, however, long been recognized as being conducive to marital tranquility and thus in harmony with public policy. See Del Vecchio v. Del Vecchio, Fla.1962, 143 So. 2d 17, in which we prescribed the rules by which the validity of such antenuptial or postnuptial property settlement agreements should be tested. Such an agreement has been upheld after the death of the spouse even though it contained also a provision settling their property rights in the event of divorce or separation—the court concluding that it could not be said this provision "facilitated or tended to induce a separation or divorce." . . .

. . . In this view of an antenuptial agreement that settles the right of the parties in the event of divorce as well as upon death, it is not inconceivable that a dissatisfied wife—secure in the knowledge that the provisions for alimony contained in the antenuptial agreement could not be enforced against her, but that she would be bound by the provisions limiting or waiving her property rights in the estate of her husband—might provoke her husband into divorcing her in order to collect a large alimony check every month, or a lump-sum award (since, in this State, a wife is entitled to alimony, if needed, even though the divorce is awarded to the husband) rather than take her chances on being remembered generously in her husband's will. In this situation, a valid antenuptial agreement limiting property rights upon death would have the same meretricious effect, insofar as the public policy in question is concerned, as would an antenuptial divorce provision in the circumstances hypothesized in Crouch v. Crouch, *supra*, 385 S.W.2d 288.

There can be no doubt that the institution of marriage is the foundation of the familial and social structure of our Nation and, as such, continues to be of vital interest to the State; but we cannot blind ourselves to the fact that the concept of the "sanctity" of a marriage—as being practically indissoluble, once entered into—held by our ancestors only a few generations ago, has been greatly eroded in the last several decades. This court can take judicial notice of the fact that the ratio of marriages to divorces has reached a disturbing rate in many states; and that a new concept of divorce—in which there is no "guilty" party—is being advocated by many groups and has been adopted by the State of California in a recent revision of its divorce laws providing for the dissolution of a marriage upon pleading and proof of "irreconcilable differences" between the parties, without assessing the fault for the failure of the marriage against either party.

With divorce such a commonplace fact of life, it is fair to assume that many prospective marriage partners whose property and familial situation is such as to generate a valid antenuptial agreement settling their property rights upon the death of either, might want to consider and discuss also—and agree upon, if possible—the disposition of their property and the alimony rights of the wife in the event their marriage, despite their best efforts, should fail. . . .

We know of no community or society in which the public policy that condemned a husband and wife to a lifetime of misery as an alternative to the opprobrium of divorce still exists. And a tendency to recognize this change in public policy and to give effect to the antenuptial agreements of the parties relating to a divorce is clearly discernable. . . .

. . . We have given careful consideration to the question of whether the change in public policy toward divorce requires a change in the rule respecting antenuptial agreements settling alimony and property rights of the parties upon divorce and have concluded that such agreements should no longer be held to be void *ab initio* as "contrary to public policy." If such an agreement is valid when tested by the stringent rules prescribed in Del Vecchio v. Del Vecchio, *supra*, 143 So. 2d 17, for ante-and post-nuptial agreements settling the property rights of the spouses in the estate of the other upon death, and if, in addition, it is made to appear that the divorce was prosecuted in good faith, on proper grounds, so that, under the rules applicable to postnuptial alimony and property settlement agreements referred to above, it could not be said to facilitate or promote the procurement of a divorce, then it should be held valid as to conditions existing at the time the agreement was made. . . .

LEGAL REQUIREMENTS OF A VALID PREMARITAL AGREEMENT

The content of a premarital agreement, as well as any other contract, will depend on the intent of the parties. Some are very detailed documents covering specific aspects of married life, such as who will pay the bills and who will do the household chores. Exhibit 4–1 at the end of the chapter shows a sample premarital agreement. Premarital agreements, however, cannot bind parties during the marriage. For example, assume the parties agree in a premarital agreement that the husband will wash the dishes and take out the trash. This provision will not be enforced by the court. The court will not enforce those portions of a premarital agreement that govern the spouse's respective duties during an intact marriage. These provisions are useful only to provide the couple with guidelines as to how they wish to conduct their day-to-day affairs.

ACQUIRING THE NECESSARY DOCUMENTATION

The following information should be obtained from the client for review, whether the office is representing the spouse seeking the premarital agreement or the spouse reviewing the agreement. For each party, obtain

1. A list of assets and their current fair market value;
2. Income, both earned and unearned;
3. Debts and liabilities;
4. Previous divorce obligations owed to a former spouse, such as the following:
   - Alimony—What is the amount and duration of payments?
   - Child support—What is the amount and what are the ages of the children?
   - College expenses—Is the party obligated to pay higher education costs?
   - Insurance premiums—Must the party pay health, life, or disability insurance premiums?
   - Qualified Domestic Relations Orders (QDRO)—Are there any future rights to an employee pension that the client will receive or be required to pay out?
   - Tax obligations—Do either of the parties owe money to a local, state, or federal tax entity?
   - Lawsuits—Does either party anticipate receiving money damages or a settlement amount from a pending lawsuit?
   - Legal judgments—Have any legal judgments been entered against the parties requiring payment of damages?
   - Credit history—Have there been previous or pending bankruptcies?

WHO SHOULD HAVE A PREMARITAL AGREEMENT?

The following parties should consider having a premarital agreement prepared:

- parties who have children from a previous marriage whose financial interests they wish to protect,
- parties who have significant assets or are very well compensated,
- parties who anticipate a family inheritance, and
- parties who wish to protect their separate property (property acquired prior to marriage).

If a party wants to ensure that assets pass to the children of a previous marriage, a premarital agreement is essential. A spouse enjoys statutory protections, such as :

- an elective statutory share of the deceased spouse's estate (this share is usually elected if the deceased spouse left the surviving spouse nothing or very little in the will);
- intestacy succession rights;
- homestead rights in the principal; and
- widow's allowance.

These rights are automatically conferred on the spouse by virtue of the legal marital status. A spouse may, however, waive these rights in the prenuptial agreement. Without a properly executed premarital agreement in effect, a surviving spouse is legally entitled to claim a portion of the deceased spouse's estate. An attorney may advise a client to sign a Qualified Terminal Interest Trust (QTIP). A QTIP is a trust naming the children as beneficiaries of the client's estate while allowing the surviving spouse access to the assets acquired during his or the deceased spouse's lifetime. In addition, the attorney should also advise the client to write a new will, and change beneficiary designations on insurance policies, trusts, annuities, and other retirement plans to safeguard the current spouse.

Parties who are well compensated or have significant assets may also seek the protection of a premarital agreement. The client may be well advised by the attorney to keep the money he or she has already amassed in a separate account and not to commingle these funds with marital property.

PREMARITAL AGREEMENTS—POST *POSNER*

As the landmark case upholding premarital agreements that included provisions contemplating divorce, ***Posner*** was cited as precedent in other states in determining the validity of such contracts. In 1976, the **Uniform Premarital Agreement Act (UPAA),** a model act, was drafted by the National Conference of Commissioners on Uniform State Laws. It provides states with model legislation that addresses the issues necessary to create a valid premarital agreement. States have the option of whether to adopt the model act as is, adopt a revised version, or ignore it. Remember that a premarital agreement is a contract and all contracts require some type of consideration. The consideration in a premarital agreement, as recognized in all jurisdictions, is the marriage. A *promise* to marry, on the other hand, is not valid consideration.

The UPAA states that to be enforceable, a premarital agreement must be:

- in writing,
- signed by both parties,
- parties must have the contractual capacity to enter into a contract and must do so voluntarily,
- each spouse must provide a fair and reasonable disclosure of their financial assets and obligations prior to execution, and
- the agreement must not be unconscionable at the time of execution.

The UPAA states that a premarital agreement may address issues such as waiver or modification of alimony and the disposition of property upon divorce, death, or separation. Generally, parties are free to contract regarding these issues as long as the agreement does not violate public policy or involve the commission of a crime. When it comes to matters dealing with the custody of children and their support, the court always retains jurisdiction to override the agreement based on the best interest of the children. For example, while the parties may agree that children will be raised within a certain religion, an agreement that gives the mother sole custody in the event of divorce is unenforceable. It is up to the courts to decide the custody issue based on what is in the best interest of the children.

DRAFTING AND EXECUTING VALID PREMARITAL AGREEMENTS

1. **Checking State Law.** When drafting a premarital agreement, paralegals must check state law to determine whether their state has adopted some version of the UPAA, permits premarital agreements through statutory or case law, or has no definitive case law or statute on the issue. The following states have passed a state version of the UPAA:
   Arizona, Arkansas, California, Connecticut, Delaware, District of Columbia, Hawaii, Idaho, Illinois, Indiana, Iowa, Kansas, Maine, Montana, Nebraska, Nevada, New Jersey, New Mexico, North Carolina, North Dakota, Oregon, Rhode Island, South Dakota, Texas, Utah, Virginia, and Wisconsin.

   The text of Arizona's Uniform Premarital Agreement Act and **California's Premarital Agreement Act** is located in Appendix A.

2. **Determining Intent of the Parties.** When drafting a premarital agreement, it is important to be very clear on the intention of the party or parties. It may be necessary to prepare and review several drafts of the agreement before the final document is ready for execution. If your client is proposing the agreement to his or her prospective spouse, it is important for the attorney to review a draft with the client to determine if the client's objectives have been met and to explain legal terms so they are fully understood. If your client is on the receiving end of the agreement, it may be possible that portions of the proposed agreement may have to be negotiated and that several drafts will have to be written until the intent of the parties is clearly indicated.

3. **Document Must Be in Writing.** Promises made in contemplation of marriage must be made in writing and signed by the parties.

4. **Adequate Financial Disclosure.** Prospective spouses entering into a premarital agreement have a duty to fully disclose their property and financial obligations. Clients may want to hide, falsify, or misrepresent their financial information; however, if the jurisdiction requires disclosure, the agreement may be rendered unenforceable if this requirement is not satisfied. Many jurisdictions require the parties to attach an accurate financial statement to the agreement. The extent of disclosure is different from one jurisdiction to another, so it is important to review state law.

5. **Advice of Independent Counsel.** The proponent of a premarital agreement must give his or her prospective spouse the opportunity to have an independent attorney of his or her choice review the agreement. The reviewing attorney will advise the client of the rights he or she is relinquishing by signing the premarital agreement and may also be involved in renegotiating certain provisions. It is not advisable for the attorney drafting the premarital agreement to refer the opposing party to an attorney or draft a premarital agreement on behalf of both parties, as this would present a conflict of interest. Additionally, a prospective spouse should be given ample time to find an attorney and to consider the ramifications of the agreement. The bride, for example, should not be accosted in the vestibule of the church on the day of the wedding and forced to sign a document she has not been able to review with her own attorney. If a party waives the right to seek independent counsel, this waiver should be obtained in writing to avoid any future problems.

6. **Fairness.** A basic principle of contract law is that **unconscionable** contracts will not be enforced. Premarital agreements are no exception to the general rule. An agreement is unconscionable when it is so unfair to one party that the court will refuse to enforce it. Courts regularly review contracts on the basis of "fairness." In business environments, the parties enter into contracts as arm's length transactions. Prospective spouses, however, are in a confidential relationship and may be pressured into signing for fear that the marriage will not go forward. Therefore, prospective spouses are more susceptible to undue influence, thus alerting the courts to the possibility of unconscionability.

   Courts will generally enforce a premarital agreement unless one party can prove that it promotes divorce (e.g., a large, enticing property settlement upon divorce) or the contract was entered into with the intent to divorce.

   A court will determine fairness at the time the agreement was executed and at the time of enforcement. Provisions that seemed fair at the time of drafting may be invalid at the time of execution. For example, it would be unconscionable to enforce an agreement where a spouse who has become recently disabled waived alimony at the time of the signing of the agreement. In this case, the spouse's health and the unwillingness on the part of many courts to allow the spouse to become a charge on the taxpayers may render the agreement unenforceable due to unconscionability. Unconscionability is determined by the courts based on the particular facts and circumstances of the case.

   A proponent spouse may wish to include a provision in the prenuptial agreement that will give the prospective spouse some type of support or property in the event of a divorce. The courts may frown upon agreements that leave the less economically disadvantaged spouse without any reasonable means of support.

7. **Voluntariness.** Another principle of contract law applicable to premarital agreements is a "meeting of the minds." This means that each party must understand and agree to the terms of a contract. If a person is forced or pressured to sign, or signs for fear that the marriage will be called off, the contract may later be declared unenforceable by the court.

8. **Choice of Governing Law.** A premarital agreement should include a clause indicating which state law controls in the event of a dispute. Language such as "this premarital agreement shall be construed under the laws of the State of " should be incorporated into the document. Under traditional contract law, an agreement that is silent regarding governing law will be construed under the laws of the jurisdiction where the agreement was originally signed. The UPAA, however, allows the parties to choose the governing law as long as there is some type of connection to the chosen state—either one of the parties lives, plans to live, or plans to marry in that particular state.

9. **Unenforceable Provisions.** Parties are generally free to waive or modify the financial rights and obligations affecting the adults in the relationship. Provisions dealing with child custody or child support, however, are always within the control of the court and cannot be contracted away by the parties. The court decides these issues based on what is in the best interest of the child. Let's say, for example, the agreement read that in the event of divorce, the wife shall have custody of the minor children. The couple marries and divorces ten years later. Mom is now addicted to drugs, but still seeks to enforce the provision in the premarital agreement giving her custody of the minor children. This provision is unenforceable and the question regarding child custody will be determined by the court.

Provisions that are illegal or against **public policy** will also be deemed unenforceable. For example, a provision stating that the wife will agree to a ménage à trois at least once a month will be deemed void against public policy as it promotes adultery. Here is the California judicial definition of "public policy," cited from the case of *Noble v. City of Palo Alto*, 89 Cal. App. 47, 50-51 (1928):

By "public policy" is intended that principle of law which holds that no citizen can lawfully do that which has a tendency to be injurious to the public or against the public good, which may be termed the policy of the law. Likewise, it has been defined as the principles under which freedom of contract or private dealing are restricted by law for the good of the community"—the foregoing definitions being supported by respectable authority (32 Cyc. 1251). Public policy means the public good. Anything which tends to undermine that sense of security for individual rights, whether of personal liberty or private property, which any citizen ought to feel is against public policy. It is the evil tendency and not the actual result which is the test of illegality. (*Maryland Trust Co. v. National Bank*, 102 Md. 608 [62 Atl. 79])

BAD BARGAIN

In *Waton v. Waton*, the Florida District Court of Appeal held that the premarital agreement was enforceable because Mrs. Waton received full disclosure of her prospective husband's assets and had enough time to seek the advice of independent counsel before signing the agreement. Despite the bad bargain made by Mrs. Waton, this case illustrates how paying close attention to the requirements necessary to execute a premarital agreement protects the proponent spouse, no matter how unfair the results.

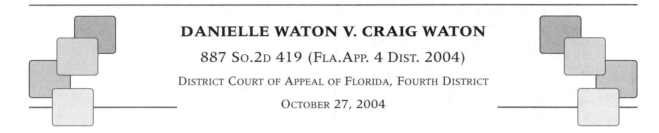

DANIELLE WATON V. CRAIG WATON

887 So.2d 419 (Fla.App. 4 Dist. 2004)

District Court of Appeal of Florida, Fourth District

October 27, 2004

STONE, J.

We affirm the trial court's order upholding the validity of an antenuptial agreement.

We recognize that the result in this dissolution after eighteen years of marriage is harsh. Wife has not worked full time in thirteen years, while Husband is now making a very large salary and has a net worth of over three million dollars. As a result, Husband is left with considerable wealth and income, while Wife waived all rights to alimony and equitable distribution by signing an antenuptial agreement. It is undisputed that the agreement is patently unreasonable. However, if an unreasonable agreement is freely entered into, it is enforceable. *Casto v. Casto*, 508 So.2d 330, 334 (Fla. 1987).

The primary issue considered in this appeal is whether Husband made a full and fair disclosure of his net worth and income to Wife at the time of the antenuptial agreement, allowing Wife to make a free and voluntary relinquishment of her property rights to Husband's assets. As there is substantial, competent evidence supporting the trial court's decision, we find no abuse of discretion.

The parties decided to get married after living together for six months. The marriage date was set to be six weeks after their decision. Husband had been previously married and divorced. Due to the prior divorce experience, Husband insisted upon an antenuptial agreement. Wife, a native of Morocco, was 34-years-old when she decided to marry Husband. In the face of conflicting testimony, the trial court expressed reluctance to believe Wife's evidence as to the extent to which she understood English. Husband testified that English was the only language spoken by the couple throughout the relationship. Although Wife spoke four languages,

English was the only language Husband understood. Wife also obtained a "GED" degree and passed a cosmetology exam and a licensing exam for insurance sales agents in English. At no time prior to, or during, the signing of the agreement did Wife indicate that she did not understand the legal consequences and terms of the agreement. The agreement provided that Husband was entitled to all the property he currently owned and "any hereinafter acquired, including any salary or income or dividends from such assets or interests." Similarly, Wife was to retain all the property she owned and any later acquired property. The agreement also stated that in the event the marriage dissolved, neither party would be entitled to any sort of monetary support from the other.

Exhibit A to the antenuptial agreement is a list of assets owned by Husband. This list included all of Husband's assets with their corresponding values. Several of the assets, however, although described, did not include an expressed valuation, but stated: "value unknown as of the date hereof," "exact value unknown," or "value unknown and undetermined." Two such valuation descriptions applied to Husband's interest in two businesses that have never had any significant value and are essentially moot. However, a major asset with such non-stated value was the interest Husband owned in America's No. Life and Health Insurance, Inc., the company where he worked. The agreement recognized that Husband owned a 25% interest, soon to be 33 1/3% interest, in that business. At trial, a certified public accountant, called by Husband, testified that at the time of the marriage, the value of Husband's interest in the business was $386,000.

The antenuptial agreement was prepared two weeks before the wedding date. Both parties were represented by counsel when the antenuptial agreement was executed, although Wife selected her attorney from a list of names suggested by Husband's attorney. Wife's attorney testified that he did not specifically remember her, but is certain of his representation because he signed the certificate of attorney. He confirmed the accuracy of his certificate, essentially stating that the attorney went over the antenuptial agreement with Wife and that he advised her of the legal significance of the agreement and its impact on her property rights.

In its ruling, the trial court emphasized it did not find Wife's testimony credible and concluded: First, that the subject antenuptial agreement was not the product of fraud, overreaching, misrepresentation, undue influence, duress or coercion by Husband. Second, that Wife had a reasonable and proximate knowledge of Husband's net worth and income based upon the information provided to the Wife by Husband at the time the antenuptial agreement was signed...

...We initially conclude that the trial court did not abuse its discretion in rejecting Wife's claim that the agreement was induced by duress and coercion. Wife claims her case is similar to *Hjortaas v. McCabe*, 656 So.2d 168 (Fla. 2d DCA 1995). In *Hjortaas*, the wife was asked to sign a prenuptial agreement two days before the wedding, leaving her "only one day to seek counsel from her own attorney, to make an independent evaluation of the contract, or to cancel her wedding." *Id.* Further, she did not previously know the agreement's terms and no information was in the agreement regarding her husband's finances. *Id.* "The timing of the signing of the document indicates that . . . [the wife's] signature was the product of duress." *Id.*

This case is clearly distinguishable. Here, Wife received the agreement two weeks before the wedding; Husband had told Wife about the proposed terms long before the agreement was prepared; he made a list of his assets and showed them to Wife before contacting a lawyer to draft the antenuptial agreement. We note that the court, in *Hjortaas*, indicated that if the wife in that case had known of the proposed terms three weeks earlier, when the couple met with the husband's attorney, that fact would have made it less likely that she signed under duress. *Id.*

Further, here, Husband told Wife that before they could get married, there would have to be an antenuptial agreement in which she would agree that she would not receive anything from him. There is also testimony that even if the parties did not get married because Wife did not agree to sign the antenuptial agreement, Husband would not have terminated the relationship and the couple would have continued to live together. Furthermore, unlike *Hjortaas*, the actual agreement in this case does contain Husband's financial information.

Wife also argues that the agreement was a product of overreaching. *See Tenneboe v. Tenneboe*, 558 So.2d 470 (Fla. 4th DCA 1990); *McGregor v. McGregor*, 447 So.2d 994 (Fla. 4th DCA 1984). However, we find each of the authorities relied on to be distinguishable.

Unlike *Tenneboe*, this case does not involve a situation where Wife agreed to pay her income to Husband. At the most, this agreement withdraws Husband's support from Wife, anticipating that she would support herself. Here, also, Wife was represented by counsel and she has not made any allegations that Husband, or his attorney, made misrepresentations to her. Here, unlike the circumstances in *McGregor*, the property in question was never Wife's property, and the agreement provides that each spouse will keep their property separate.

This court has previously recognized that even though an agreement is one-sided and unfair, that alone does not make it the result of overreaching. *Schreiber.*

Wife asserts that even if she does not prevail as a result of her claims of duress, coercion, and overreaching, she is entitled to prevail under the second ground recognized in *Casto* and *Del Vecchio v. Del Vecchio*, 143 So.2d 17 (Fla. 1962).

For guidance, we look to *Del Vecchio* and *Casto*. These authorities require that, under these circumstances, the challenging spouse have "a general and approximate knowledge of . . .[the other spouse's] property and resources," *Del Vecchio*, 143 So.2d at 21, and "a general knowledge of the income of the parties." *Casto*, 508 So.2d at 333. Here, there is no dispute that Wife had knowledge of Husband's income at the time of execution. Therefore, our focus is on whether there is record support for a conclusion that Wife had a general and approximate knowledge of Husband's property and resources.

Under this second ground, to establish that an agreement is unenforceable, the challenging spouse must satisfy a two-prong test. First, that the agreement makes an unfair or unreasonable provision for that spouse, given the circumstances of the parties. *Casto*, 508 So.2d at 330 (citing *Del Vecchio*, 143 So. 2d at 20). Second, after establishing the agreement is unreasonable, a rebuttable presumption arises conceding that there was either concealment by the defending spouse or a presumed lack of knowledge by the challenging spouse of the defending spouse's finances at the time the agreement was reached. *Id.* The presumption shifts the burden to the defending spouse, who may rebut these presumptions by showing that there was either:

(a) a full, frank disclosure to the challenging spouse by the defending spouse before the signing of the agreement relative to the value of all marital property and the income of the parties, or (b) a general and approximate knowledge by the challenging spouse of the character and extent of the marital property sufficient to obtain a value by reasonable means, as well as a general knowledge of the income of the parties. *Id.* at 333.

In this case, the antenuptial agreement was indisputably unfair and unreasonable, and the agreement is certainly "disproportionate to the means" of Husband. *Id.* (quoting *Del Vecchio*, 143 So.2d at 19-20); *see also Fleming v. Fleming*, 474 So.2d 1247, 1248, (Fla. 4th DCA 1985) (stating that if "an instrument provided for the wife to get nothing at all, it would be simple to find it unfair on its face."). Therefore, the first prong of the test is satisfied and the presumption arises that Husband attempted to conceal his finances or that Wife had no knowledge of Husband's finances. The burden, then, falls on Husband to prove that he disclosed his assets or that Wife had knowledge of them.

As to the disclosure, "there must be a full, frank disclosure as to the value of all the marital property." *Casto*, 508 So.2d at 330. This includes a "good faith disclosure by the prospective husband of the material facts relating to the character and value of his property." Stated otherwise, Husband is required to disclose such information regarding his assets as to provide Wife with: a general and approximate knowledge by her of the prospective husband's property. The term "approximate" is, for this purpose, held synonymous with "near," "close to" or "approaching". . . . And while the disclosure should be full, fair, and open, it need not be minutely detailed nor exact. The test is the adequacy of the knowledge of the woman—she must have had some understanding of her rights and a general and approximate knowledge of his property and resources. The basic issue is concealment, not the absence of disclosure, and the wife may not repudiate if she is not prejudiced by lack of information. *Del Vecchio*, 143 So.2d at 20.

The disclosure is necessary to show that the spouse *"possessed such general and approximate knowledge of his property as to enable [the spouse] to reach an intelligent decision to enter into the agreement."* *Del Vecchio*, 143 So.2d at 21 (emphasis added). *See also Casto*, 508 So.2d at 333 (two alternative means of rebutting the presumption of concealment or lack of knowledge, one is full frank disclosure by the defending spouse and the other is general and approximate knowledge of the "character and extent of the marital property sufficient to obtain a value by reasonable means, as well as a general knowledge of the income of the parties.").

Here, Husband listed the actual value of his various accounts and holdings except for his three business interests. As to the only one of significant value, the question is whether the following language may be construed by the trial court as a full, frank disclosure:

> 25% interest soon to be 33 1/3% interest in America's No. Life and Health Agency, Inc., which has an address of 4624 Hollywood Boulevard, Hollywood, Florida
>
> * * *
>
> Exact value unknown but see note below:
>
> * * *
>
> * * Stock ownership interest:

Note on America's No. Life and Health Agency, Inc.— Corporation itself makes approximately $750,000.00, a year gross on renewal commissions on current policies, deductions are made from the gross commissions to pay the respective agents their proportionate or required commissions. Corporation makes approximately $1,000,000.00 a year gross on new policies, but from these sums payments are made to cover, salaries, office overhead, and general operating expenses of the office.

Here, as Wife knew that Husband owned part of the business and knew his income, the remaining question is whether her general knowledge was sufficient for one to obtain a value "by reasonable means." *Id.* Significantly, there is no indication in the record that Husband had any more information as to valuation than that disclosed to Wife, and there is no suggestion that any equity or assets of the business were in any way secretly set aside for the future benefit of Husband. Here, also, Wife did not make trade offs in the agreement, or otherwise rely upon misleading disclosure information to her detriment. Wife also never sought clarification or additional information. The court could conclude from the record that, whatever an appraised value might be, Wife accepted that she would receive nothing.

Further, the record reflects that an expert would have been needed to accurately value the business. We do not read into *Del Vecchio* or *Casto* a requirement imposing a duty on Husband to hire an expert to determine a valuation of his interest in the agency before the parties could marry. To so hold would mandate that all parties entering into such agreements first obtain a professional appraisal of business or professional interests, even without proof that such appraisal could be accomplished within the time remaining prior to the marriage, and at reasonable cost, and with the data and information available.

We cannot conclude, on this record, that the court could not reasonably conclude that Wife was provided with sufficient general and approximate knowledge of Husband's net worth and income, or that the order is an abuse of discretion.

Therefore, the order is affirmed.

ASSESSING THE CLIENT'S POSITION REGARDING THE ENFORCEABILITY OF THE PREMARITAL AGREEMENT

The law office will either be representing the party who originally proposed that a premarital agreement be prepared and executed and now seeks its enforcement or the party who agreed to its execution but who now seeks legal representation to oppose the enforcement. In either case, the first aspect to review is what circumstances existed during the formation of the contract. The court will generally uphold a premarital agreement unless the parties possessed unequal bargaining power. If both parties had similar financial and educational backgrounds at the time of the execution, the court will most likely uphold the agreement.

The second aspect to consider is what circumstances exist at the time one of the parties seeks enforcement of the agreement. The courts apply the **"second glance doctrine"** in order to protect spouses from changes in circumstances that occurred since the date of the formation of the premarital agreement. The courts will not enforce the contract due to unconscionability if enforcing the contract "today" would be unfair in light of the current circumstances. The contract must be fair and reasonable to the relinquishing spouse. The court may overrule the premarital agreement if enforcement would cause a spouse to become a charge of the state or greatly reduce his standard of living.

EXAMPLE

Jonathan and Shannon enter into a prenuptial agreement. Shannon waives away her right to alimony. Later, Shannon gets sick with Parkinson's disease and cannot work or support herself. Is the prenuptial agreement enforceable? No.

Provisions may not take effect for years. Fairness and reasonableness are subjective tests to be determined by the courts after reviewing the totality of circumstances, such as the parties' health, financial status, intellectual and business savvy, existence of dependent children, and current standard of living.

COHABITATION—A MARRIAGE ALTERNATIVE

INTRODUCTION

The U.S. Census for the year 2000 reveals that the number of households consisting of unmarried couples, both same-sex and heterosexual, has increased by 72 percent over the last ten years, from 3,187,772 in 1992 to 5,475,768 in 2000. Theses statistics indicate that more and more people view cohabitation either as a trial marriage or as an alternative to getting married. The emergence of the cohabitating couple as a marriage alternative presents new challenges for family law practitioners and paralegals.

Couples who plan to live together should have a **cohabitation agreement** in writing that specifically delineates their respective rights and responsibilities. While matters regarding the custody and support of children may be resolved in the family courts by unmarried parents, issues involving property, debts, and other obligations must be dealt with in civil court. Our population has become familiar with the term **palimony**, a lawsuit for support filed against a cohabitating partner. In palimony cases, one partner may have agreed to cohabitate with someone who was financially well off. They may have quit their job or career on the promise that their partner would take care of them. If the relationship terminates, this promise could result in a court granting support or property division by virtue of a contractual arrangement. A cohabitation agreement would outline the parties' rights and obligations and possibly avoid unnecessary litigation.

A cohabitation agreement should be in writing, signed by both parties, and should include the terms of the parties' cohabitation arrangement and how they will deal with their finances. Both parties should hire their own independent attorney who may assist in negotiating an agreement and drafting and reviewing the finished product. Very often, the paralegal will be asked to draft a cohabitation agreement.

Begin the drafting of the agreement by clarifying the client's expectations and terms of the agreement with the partner. It is best that the parties specifically determine their financial obligations. Remember that agreements where sexual acts or relations are used as consideration are unenforceable.

MARVIN V. MARVIN

In response to the very sharp increase in cohabitation arrangements that occurred in the late 1960s and early 1970s, the law had to change to make some accommodations for resolving disputes between cohabiting partners. The first case to recognize the rights of cohabitants was *Marvin v. Marvin*, 18 Cal. 3d 660, 557 P.2d 106, 134 Cal. Rptr. 815 (1976). In *Marvin*, the plaintiff and the defendant had lived together for a period of seven years. During this period, the plaintiff agreed to give up her career and provide domestic services for the defendant. In exchange, the defendant agreed to financially support the plaintiff and share any assets that were accumulated. This agreement was *not* memorialized in writing.

When the relationship ended, the plaintiff sued the defendant on a contractual basis for support and a division of the assets. The trial court dismissed her case and she appealed. On appeal, the California Supreme Court held that the contract between the parties was valid and remanded the case to the trial court to be judged on its merits. The parties had accumulated approximately one million dollars in assets. However, these assets were titled in the name of the defendant.

The defendant attacked the validity of the contract by raising the long-standing public policy argument. According to the defendant, a contract that included sexual relations was void. The California Supreme Court held that as long as sexual relations were not the sole consideration, the court should disregard that provision and enforce the lawful provisions of the agreement.

The next step was to determine the remedies available to the parties. While *Marvin* is a landmark case in the area of cohabitation, these remedies vary from state to state. First, the court had to decide what type of contract was in effect:

1. **Express contract.** This would require an express agreement between the parties regarding the specific terms. The high court recognized that in a romantic relationship, parties do not generally negotiate the terms of their roles and expectations, let alone reduce them to a written document.

2. **Implied-in-fact contract.** In an implied-in-fact contract, the intention of the parties is inferred by their conduct. For example, a person goes to a restaurant and orders ham and eggs. The waiter brings him his food and he consumes the meal. There is an implied contract that the consumer intends to pay for the meal. In supporting an implied contract action in a cohabitation case, examining the conduct of the parties is essential. How did the parties conduct themselves during their relationship? What contributions,

both monetary and nonmonetary, did the parties bring to the relationship? Were assets commingled in joint accounts?

3. **Quasi-contract.** Quasi-contracts are contractual obligations that are imposed upon the parties by the court. No actual contract has been entered into by the parties. The court takes this position when it appears that one party has been so unjustly enriched that the court creates a contract to avoid unfairness to the other party.

4. **Implied partnership.** When a cohabiting couple works on a business enterprise that is owned by one of the parties, the court creates an implied partnership. The court assesses the financial status of the business and distributes the assets and liabilities just as such a distribution would occur upon the dissolution of a business partnership.

5. **Implied trust.** A trust is a legal relationship where one party, the **trustee,** holds legal title to property for the benefit of the **beneficiary.** Most trusts are **expressed trusts,** in which the terms have been negotiated by the parties. Implied trusts are created by the court to avoid an injustice. One type of trust is a **resulting trust.** In a resulting trust, one party provides the funds for property, while title is in the other party's name.

   EXAMPLE

   Mary has enough money for a down payment on a house, but has poor credit. John has excellent credit and can qualify for a mortgage in his sole name. With Mary's down payment, John agrees to split the mortgage payments and purchases the house, which is titled in his name only. John and Mary move into the house and live there for ten years together. During this time, Mary contributes to the mortgage payments and household expenses. The relationship deteriorates and Mary and John break up. Mary moves out of the house because John has become verbally abusive. Mary may sue for her interest in the house on a resulting trust theory.

6. **Constructive trust.** A constructive trust is imposed by the court to avoid unjust enrichment when there is no intent between the parties to create a trust.

While the *Marvin* court established a variety of legal remedies for litigating cohabitants, it did not approve of treating cohabiting couples as married couples:

> . . . [W]e take this occasion to point out that the structure of society itself largely depends upon the institution of marriage and nothing we have said in this opinion should be taken to derogate from that institution. [*Marvin v. Marvin,* 557 P.2d 106, 122 (1976)]

SAME-SEX MARRIAGE

INTRODUCTION

Same-sex couples find themselves in the same legal position as cohabiting heterosexual couples. The one difference between the two is that, if they so choose, heterosexual couples have the option of legalizing their union, while same-sex couples do not.

The sexual revolution brought about many social changes, one of which has been the opening of the "closet door." The current headlines indicate that members of the gay community are demanding not only social acceptance and equal rights, but also the right to enter into marital relationships. This idea, however, is not yet widely accepted by society, and triggers many emotional reactions from those who wish to preserve the traditional type of marriage—a union between a man and a woman.

Every social movement has a defining moment in its history. The gay liberation movement was born during the Stonewall riots in New York City in 1969. Since then, the gay-rights movement has sought to remove the stigma that has so long been attached to this lifestyle. This stigma affects familial, legal, economic, and social aspects for a gay person. Legal and religious institutions in particular have condemned the gay lifestyle. While many state laws have been repealed, there are still laws on the books that criminalize sodomy or other gay conduct. Homosexuality is also considered a sin in many religious traditions.

To date, only the state of Massachusetts has legalized **same-sex marriage**— a legal marriage between members of the same sex who are entitled to the same rights and privileges as heterosexual married couples.

Marriage Statutes

Every state has a **marriage statute**. This is a law passed by a state legislature that indicates who may marry. This is the same statute that tells us, for instance, that a man cannot marry his niece because they are too close in consanguinity and this union could violate public policy. Marriage statutes vary from state to state. Some statutes explicitly forbid a marriage between members of the same sex by specifying that marriage must be between a man and a woman. In these jurisdictions, same-sex marriages are prohibited.

In other jurisdictions, the marriage statute is silent as to who may marry. When the statute is silent as to definitions, these jurisdictions also prohibit same-sex marriage because they apply the "plain meaning" and dictionary definition of the word "marriage."

The Legal Battle for Recognition of Same-Sex Marriage

The advocates of same-sex marriage contend that the prohibition against same-sex marriage violates the Establishment Clause of the First Amendment of the Constitution because the state is establishing a religion (i.e., the prohibition reflects Judeo-Christian biblical views against homosexual conduct). Courts have rejected this argument, ruling that a legitimate governmental interest is served by prohibiting marriages between members of the same sex. It is the view of many courts that states should sanction only marriages that are capable of procreating— reproducing children. The courts have also believed that preserving the traditional family unit will discourage children and youth from viewing homosexuality as an acceptable lifestyle.

The Fourteenth Amendment Argument

Marriage is considered a **fundamental right** in our system of jurisprudence. Advocates of same-sex marriage have argued that denying homosexuals the right to marry on the basis of their sex violates the Fourteenth Amendment. A classification resulting in the denial of a fundamental right may only be upheld where it is necessary to accomplish a compelling state interest and achievement of that goal cannot be done by less restrictive means.

In 1967, the U.S. Supreme Court struck down a Virginia statute that prohibited interracial marriages. This statute and similar legislation were know as **miscegenation laws** and were enforced in many states. The Virginia statute at the time read as follows:

> All marriages between a white person and a colored person shall be absolutely void without any decree of divorce or other legal process. (Virginia Code Ann. 750-57)

In *Loving v. Virginia*, 388 U.S. 1 (1967), the Supreme Court held that marriage is a fundamental right that cannot be restricted by states unless there is a compelling state interest. Courts have rejected this application of this holding to decide the legality of same-sex marriage and routinely uphold laws passed by state legislatures that prohibit same-sex marriage. Many courts employ the rationale that upholding such statutes discourages the illegal activity of sodomy and encourages procreation.

THE STATE EQUAL RIGHTS AMENDMENT ARGUMENT

Another theory of attack used by same-sex marriage advocates has been states' Equal Rights Amendments.

> Equality of rights under the law shall not be denied or abridged on account of sex. (Ex. **Colo.Const.Art. II Section 29.**)

A state's Equal Rights Amendment would bar sex-based classifications, even though the classification may be based on a compelling state interest. There is no federal equal rights amendment (ERA). Efforts to pass an ERA to the U.S. Constitution failed on several occasions, with protestors alleging that it would lead to women serving in military combat, unisex toilets, and . . . same-sex marriage.

One state that has received a lot of attention in the same-sex marriage controversy has been Hawaii particularly, because of the case of *Baehr v. Miike* (formerly *Baehr v. Lewin*), 74 Haw. 530, 852 P.2d 44 (1993). Hawaii was the first state in the country in which a court of law was asked to determine if same-sex couples have the right to a legally recognized marriage. In December 1990, several same-sex couples applied for marriage licenses and were denied. The couples filed a lawsuit against the Hawaii State Department of Health contending that the marriage statute was unconstitutional because it prohibited same-sex couples from obtaining marriage licenses on the basis of sex and sexual orientation. In October 1991, the plaintiffs' complaint was dismissed by the trial court on the grounds of failure to state a claim on which relief could be granted. The plaintiffs appealed this decision to the Supreme Court of Hawaii. On May 1, 1993, Hawaii's highest court stunned the nation when it reversed the trial court's ruling and remanded the case for a new trial. The court held that restrictions on same-sex marriages may violate the state's Equal Protection Clause because they prohibit same-sex couples from obtaining a marriage license on the basis of gender. Couples were entitled to protection under the state's Equal Rights Amendment and could not be denied a marriage license based on compelling state interests. This would require the legal test of strict scrutiny.

On remand, it was up to the Hawaii State attorney general to prove a compelling state interest—that the state of Hawaii was justified in its restrictions. The state's position was that marriage is for the promotion and rearing of children by heterosexuals only. It is in the children's best interest to be raised by their biological parents and states have interests in promoting the development of children.

The plaintiffs presented expert testimony that confirmed that children of gay parents are no different developmentally than children raised by heterosexual couples. In addition, the plaintiffs argued that the State's argument is flawed because the state places children in foster care and because many children are raised in single-parent homes.

While the *Baehr* case progressed through the Hawaiian court system, the Hawaii legislature in 1994 reacted to the decision by amending its marriage statute to expressly state that marriage is between a man and a woman.

STATUTES

HAWAII REVISED STATUTES §572-1

§572-1 Requisites of valid marriage contract.
In order to make valid the marriage contract, which shall be only between a man and a woman, it shall be necessary that:

1. The respective parties do not stand in relation to each other of ancestor and descendant of any degree whatsoever, brother and sister of the half as well as the whole blood, uncle and niece, aunt and nephew, whether the relationship is the result of the issue of parents married or not married to each other;

2. Each of the parties at the time of contracting the marriage is at least sixteen years of age; provided that with the written approval of the family court of the circuit within which the minor resides, it shall be lawful for a person under the age of sixteen years, but in no event under the age of fifteen years, to marry, subject to 572-2;

3. The man does not at the time have any lawful wife living and that the woman does not at the time have any lawful husband living;

4. Consent of neither party to the marriage has been obtained by force, duress, or fraud;

5. Neither of the parties is a person afflicted with any loathsome disease concealed from, and unknown to, the other party;

6. The man and woman to be married in the State shall have duly obtained a license for that purpose from the agent appointed to grant marriage licenses; and

7. The marriage ceremony be performed in the State by a person or society with a valid license to solemnize marriages and the man and the woman to be married and the person performing the marriage ceremony by all physically present at the same place and time for the marriage ceremony.

In December 1996, the trial court ruled in favor of the plaintiffs and issued an injunction ordering the state to issue marriage licenses to the same-sex couples. The next day, the state filed a motion to stay the injunctions until the State had the opportunity to appeal the case. The motion was granted and no licenses were issued to the plaintiffs.

In April 1997, the Hawaii legislature closed this issue by passing a constitutional amendment stating that the legislature could limit marriage to a man and a woman.

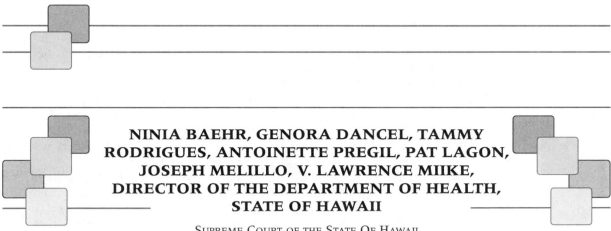

NINIA BAEHR, GENORA DANCEL, TAMMY RODRIGUES, ANTOINETTE PREGIL, PAT LAGON, JOSEPH MELILLO, V. LAWRENCE MIIKE, DIRECTOR OF THE DEPARTMENT OF HEALTH, STATE OF HAWAII

SUPREME COURT OF THE STATE OF HAWAII

CIV. NO 91-1394-05

FILED ON DECEMBER 11, 1995

SUMMARY OF DISPOSITION ORDER

Pursuant to Hawaii Rules of Evidence (HRE) Rules 201 and 202 (1993), this court takes judicial notice of the following: On April 29, 1997, both houses of the Hawaii legislature passed, upon final reading, House Bill No. 117 proposing an amendment to the Hawaii Constitution (the marriage amendment). *See* 1997b House Journal at 922; 1997 Senate Journal at 766. The bill proposed the addition of the following language to article I of the Constitution: "**Section 23.** The legislature shall have the power to reserve marriage to opposite-sex couples." *See* 1997 Haw. Sess. L. H.B. 117 §2, at 1247. The marriage amendment was ratified by the electorate in November, 1998.

In light of the foregoing, and upon carefully reviewing the record and the briefs and supplemental briefs submitted by the parties and amicus curiae and having given due consideration to the arguments made and the issues raised by the parties, we resolve the defendant-appellant Lawrence Miike's appeal as follows:

On December 11, 1996, the first circuit court entered judgment in favor of plaintiffs-appellees Ninia Baehr, Genora Dancel, Tammy Rodrigues, Antoinette Pregil, Pat Lagon, and Joseph Melillo (collectively, "the plaintiffs") and against Miike, ruling (1) that the sex-based classification in Hawaii Revised Statutes (HRS) §572-1 (1985) was "unconstitutional" by virtue of being "in violation of the equal protection clause of article I, section 5 of the Hawaii Constitution," (2) that Miike, his agents, and any person acting in concert with or by or through Miike were enjoined from denying an application for a marriage license because applicants were of the same sex, and (3) that costs should be awarded against Miike and in favor of the plaintiffs. The circuit court subsequently stayed enforcement of the injunction against Miike.

The passage of the marriage amendment placed HRS §572-1 on new footing. The marriage amendment validated HRS §572-1 by taking the statute out of the ambit of the equal protection clause of the Hawaii Constitution, at least insofar as the statute, both on its face and as applied, purported to limit access to the marital status to opposite-sex couples. Accordingly, whether or not in the past it was violative of the equal protection clause in the foregoing respect, HRS §572-1 no longer is. In light of the marriage amendment, HRS §572-1 must be given full force and effect.

The plaintiffs seek a limited scope of relief in the present lawsuit, i.e., access to applications for marriage licenses and the consequent legally recognized marital status. Inasmuch as HRS §572-1 is now a valid statute, the relief sought by the plaintiffs is unavailable. The marriage amendment has rendered the plaintiffs' complaint moot.

Therefore,

IT IS HEREBY ORDERED that the judgment of the circuit court be reversed and that the case be remanded for entry of judgment in favor of Miike and against the plaintiffs.

IT IS FURTHER ORDERED that the circuit court shall not enter costs or attorney's fees against the plaintiffs.

DATED: Honolulu, Hawaii, December 9, 1999.

Baehr sent shockwaves throughout the country. In response, many jurisdictions amended their marriage statutes, defining marriage as a union between a man and a woman. States feared that if Hawaii legalized gay marriage, same-sex partners would go to Hawaii, get married, then return to their state of domicile and demand that their marriage be recognized under the **full faith and credit clause** of the U.S. Constitution. The full faith and credit clause states that states must honor the public acts, records, and judicial proceedings of every other state. U.S. Const. Art. IV, §1. If a heterosexual couple marries in Hawaii, then moves to Ohio, the state of Ohio must legally recognize the marriage.

In May 1996, the U.S. Congress enacted the **Defense of Marriage Act** (DOMA). The act protects the traditional definition of marriage as a union between a man and a woman in the United States Code and bars same-sex couples from enjoying federal benefits, regardless of how their states redefine marriage, either through statute or judicial act. Marriage is referenced in many federal laws such as tax, bankruptcy, immigration, Social Security, and military justice. DOMA also ensures that states would not be forced to recognize same-sex marriages performed in states that have sanctioned such unions.

Defense of Marriage Act, 28 U.S.C. Section 1738C (1996)
Sec. 2. Powers Reserved to the States.

(a) IN GENERAL—Chapter 115 of title 28 United States Code, is amended by adding after section 1738B the following:

"Sec. 1738C. Certain acts, records, and proceedings and the effect thereof
No State, territory, or possession of the United States, or Indian tribe, shall be required to give effect to any public act, record, or judicial proceeding of any other State, territory, possession, or tribe respecting a relationship between person of the same sex that is treated as a marriage under the laws of such other State, territory, possession, or tribe, or a right or claim arising from such relationship."

Sec. 3. Definition of Marriage

IN GENERAL—Chapter 1 of Title 1, United States Code, is amended by adding at the end the following:

"Sec. 7. Definition of 'marriage' and 'spouse'
In determining the meaning of any Act of Congress, or of any ruling, regulation, or interpretation of the various administrative bureaus and agencies of the United States, the word 'marriage' means only a legal union between one man and one woman as husband and wife, and the word 'spouse' refers only to a person of the opposite sex who is a husband or a wife."

Another battle for the recognition of same-sex marriage is being waged in the state of Vermont. On December 20, 1999, the Vermont Supreme Court reached a landmark decision is the case of *Baker v. State*. Vermont's highest court held that three same-sex couples who applied for marriage licenses and were denied had the right to the same benefits of marriage as their heterosexual counterparts—that is, an absolute right to legal marriage benefits under Vermont law. The court extended the Common Benefits Clause of the Vermont Constitution to include the right of same-sex couples to marry. The court also retained jurisdiction in the case. Therefore, if the Vermont legislature is unable to provide a remedy to samesex couples according to the court's ruling, the court will do so on its own. As of April 2000, the Vermont legislature passed Bill H-847, creating civil unions for same-sex couples. This statute will grant same-sex couples numerous state benefits of marriage, including tax benefits, inheritance rights, and the right to make medical decisions.

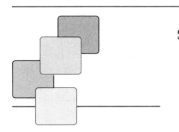

STAN BAKER, ET AL. V. STATE OF VERMONT, ET AL.

Vermont Supreme Court

DOCKET NO. 98-032

November Term, 1998

December 20, 1999

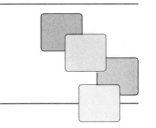

AMESTOY, C. J.

May the State of Vermont exclude same-sex couples from the benefits and protections that its laws provide to opposite-sex married couples? That is the fundamental question we address in this appeal, a question that the Court knows arouses deeply-felt religious, moral, and political beliefs. Our constitutional responsibility to consider the legal merits of the issues properly before us provides no exception for the controversial case. The issue before the Court, moreover, does not turn rather on the statutory and constitutional basis for the exclusion of same-sex couples from the more secular benefits and protections offered married couples.

We conclude that under the Common Benefits Clause of the Vermont Constitution, which, in pertinent part, reads that government is, or ought to be, instituted for the common benefit, protection, and security of the people, nation, or community, and not for the particular emolument or advantage of any single person, family, or set of persons, who are a part only of that community, Vt. Const., ch. I, art. 7. plaintiffs may not be deprived of the statutory benefits and protections afforded persons of the opposite sex who choose to marry. We hold that the State is constitutionally required to extend to same-sex couples the common benefits and protections that flow from marriage under Vermont law. Whether this ultimately takes the form of inclusion within the marriage laws themselves or a parallel "domestic partnership" system or some equivalent statutory alternative, rests with the Legislature. Whatever system is chosen, however, must conform with the constitutional imperative to afford all Vermonters the common benefit, protection, and security of the law.

Plaintiffs are three same-sex couples who have lived together in committed relationships for periods ranging from four to twenty-five years. Two of the couples have raised children together. Each couple applied for a marriage license from their respective town clerk, and each was refused a license as ineligible under the applicable state marriage laws. Plaintiffs thereupon filed this lawsuit against defendants—the State of Vermont, the Towns of Milton and Shelburne, and the City of South Burlington—seeking a declaratory judgment that the refusal to issue them a license violated the marriage statutes and the Vermont Constitution.

The State, joined by Shelburne and South Burlington, moved to dismiss the action on the ground that plaintiffs had failed to state a claim for which relief could be granted. The Town of Milton answered the complaint and subsequently moved for judgment on the pleadings. Plaintiffs opposed the motions and cross-moved for judgment on the pleadings. The trial court granted the State's and Town of Milton's motions, denied plaintiffs' motion, and dismissed the complaint. The court ruled that the marriage statutes could not be construed to permit the issuance of a license to same-sex couples.

The court further ruled that the marriage statutes were constitutional because they rationally furthered the State's interest in promoting "the link between procreation and child rearing." This appeal followed.

I. THE STATUTORY CLAIM

Plaintiffs initially contend the trial court erred in concluding that the marriage statutes render them ineligible for a marriage license. It is axiomatic that the principal objective of statutory construction is to discern the legislative intent. . . . While we may explore a variety of sources to discern that intent, it is also a truism of statutory interpretation that where a statute is unambiguous we rely on the plain and ordinary meaning of the words chosen. . . . ". . . [W]e rely on the plain meaning of the words because we presume they reflect the Legislature's intent. . . ."

. . . Vermont's marriage statues are set forth in Chapter 1 of Title 15, entitled "Marriage," which defines the requirements and eligibility for entering into a marriage, and Chapter 105 of Title 18, entitled "Marriage Records and Licenses," which prescribes the forms and procedures for obtaining a license and solemnizing a marriage. Although it is not necessarily the only possible definition there is no doubt the plain and ordinary meaning of "marriage" is the union of one man and one woman as husband and wife. . . .

. . . Further evidence of the legislative assumption that marriage consists of a union of opposite genders may be found in the consanguinity statutes, which expressly prohibit a man from marrying certain female relatives. . . . In addition, the annulment statutes explicitly refer to "husband and wife" . . . as do other statutes relating to married couples. . . .

. . . These statutes, read as a whole, reflect the common understanding that marriage under Vermont law consists of a union between a man and a woman. . . .

II. THE CONSTITUTIONAL CLAIM

Assuming that the marriage statutes preclude their eligibility for a marriage license, plaintiffs contend that the exclusion violates their right to the common benefit and protection of the law guaranteed by Chapter I, Article 7 of the Vermont Constitution. They note that in denying them access to a civil marriage license, the law effectively excludes them from a broad array of legal benefits and protections incident to the marital relation, including access to a spouse's medical, life, and disability insurance, hospital visitation and other medical decision making privileges, spousal support, intestate succession, homestead protections, and many

other statutory protections. They claim the trial court erred in upholding the law on the basis that it reasonably served the State's interest in promoting the "link between procreation and child rearing." They argue that the large number of married couples without children, and the increasing incidence of same-sex couples with children, undermines the State's rationale. They note that Vermont law affirmatively guarantees the right to adopt and raise children regardless of the sex of the parents, see 15A V.S.A. §1-102, and challenge the logic of a legislative scheme that recognizes the rights of same-sex partners as parents, yet denies them—and their children— the same security as spouses.

In considering this issue, it is important to emphasize at the outset that it is the Common Benefits Clause of the Vermont Constitution we are construing, rather than its counterpart, the Equal Protection Clause of the Fourteenth Amendment to the United States Constitution. . . .

. . . "[O]ur constitution is not a mere reflection of the federal charter. Historically and textually, it differs from the United States Constitution. It predates the federal counterpart, it extends back to Vermont's days as an independent republic. It is an independent authority, and Vermont's fundamental law."

. . . [W]e turn to the question of whether the exclusion of same-sex couples from the benefits and protections incident to marriage under Vermont law contravenes Article 7. The first step in our analysis is to identify the nature of the statutory classification. As noted, the marriage statutes apply expressly to opposite-sex couples. Thus, the statutes exclude anyone who wishes to marry someone of the same sex.

Next, we must identify the governmental purpose or purposes to be served by the statutory classification. The principal purpose the State advances in support of the excluding of same-sex couples from the legal benefits of marriage is the government's interest in "furthering the link between procreation and child rearing". . . .

. . . [T]he reality today is that increasing numbers of same-sex couples are employing increasingly efficient assisted-reproductive techniques to conceive and raise children. . . . The Vermont Legislature has not only recognized this reality, but has acted affirmatively to remove legal barriers so that same-sex couples may legally adopt and rear the children conceived through such efforts. . . . The State has also acted to expand the domestic relations laws to safeguard the interests of same-sex parents and their children when such couples terminate their domestic relationship. . . .

. . . Therefore, to the extent that the State's purpose in licensing civil marriage was, and is, to legitimize children and provide for their security, the statues plainly exclude many same-sex couples who are no different from opposite-sex couples with respect to these objectives. If anything, the exclusion of same-sex couples from the legal protections incident to marriage exposes their children to the precise risks that the State argues the marriage laws are designed to secure against. In short, the marital exclusion treats persons who are similarly situated for purposes of the law, differently. . . .

. . . The question thus becomes whether the exclusion of a relatively small but significant number of otherwise qualified same-sex couples from the same legal benefits and protections afforded their opposite-sex counterparts contravene the mandates of Article 7. It is, of course, well settled that statutes are not necessarily unconstitutional because they fail to extend legal protection to all who are similarly situated. . . .

. . . While the laws relating to marriage have undergone many changes during the last century, largely toward the goal of equalizing the status of husbands and wives, the benefits of marriage have not diminished in value. On the contrary, the benefits and protections incident to a marriage license under Vermont law have never been greater. They include, for example, the right to receive a portion of the estate of a spouse who dies intestate and protection against disinheritance through elective share provisions, preference in being appointed as the personal representative of a spouse who dies intestate, the right to bring a lawsuit for the wrongful death of a spouse, the right to bring an action for loss of consortium, the right to workers' compensation survivor benefits, the right to spousal benefits statutorily guaranteed to public employees, including health, life, disability, and accident insurance, the opportunity to be covered as a spouse under group life insurance policies issued to an employee, the opportunity to be covered as the insured's spouse under an individual health insurance policy, the right to claim an evidentiary privilege for marital communications, homestead rights and protections, the presumption of joint ownership of property and the concomitant right of survivorship, hospital visitation and other rights incident to the medical treatment of a family member, and the right to receive, and the obligation to provide, spousal support, maintenance, and property division in the event of separation or divorce . . . (citations omitted).

. . . The legal benefits and protections flowing from a marriage license are of such significance that any statutory exclusion must necessarily be grounded on public concerns of sufficient weight, cogency, and authority that the justice of the deprivation cannot seriously be questioned. Considered in light of the extreme logical disjunction between the classification and the stated purposes of the law—protecting children

and "furthering the link between procreation and child rearing"—the exclusion falls substantially short of this standard. The laudable governmental goal of promoting a commitment between married couples to promote the security of their children and the community as a whole provides no reasonable basis for denying the legal benefits and protections of marriage to same-sex couples, who are no differently situated with respect to this goal than their opposite-sex counterparts. Promoting a link between procreation and child rearing similarly fails to support the exclusion. . . .

. . . Thus, viewed in the light of history, logic, and experience, we conclude that none of the interests asserted by the State provides a reasonable and just basis for the continued exclusion of same-sex couples from the benefits incident to a civil marriage license under Vermont law.;. . . .

. . . F. REMEDY

It is important to state clearly the parameters of today's ruling. Although plaintiffs sought injunctive and declaratory relief designed to secure a marriage license, their claims and arguments here have focused primarily upon the consequences of official exclusion from the statutory benefits, protections, and security incident to marriage under Vermont law. While some future case may attempt to establish that—notwithstanding equal benefits and protections under Vermont law—the denial of a marriage license operates per se to deny constitutionally-protected rights, that is not the claim we address today.

We hold only that plaintiffs are entitled under Chapter I, Article 7, of the Vermont Constitution to obtain the same benefits and protections afforded by Vermont law to married opposite-sex couples. We do not purport to infringe upon the prerogatives of the Legislature to craft an appropriate means of addressing this constitutional mandate, other than to note that the record here refers to a number of potentially constitutional statutory schemes from other jurisdictions. These include what are typically referred to as "domestic partnership" or "registered partnership" acts, which generally establish an alternative legal status to marriage for same-sex couples, impose similar formal requirements and limitations, create a parallel licensing or registration scheme, and extend all or most of the same rights and obligations provided by the law to married partners. . . .

. . . We hold that the current statutory scheme shall remain in effect for a reasonable period of time to enable the Legislature to consider and enact implementing legislation in an orderly and expeditious fashion. . . .

CIVIL UNIONS AND DOMESTIC PARTNERSHIPS

Civil unions grant state marriage rights to same-sex couples by creating a separate category of legal recognition. Vermont and Connecticut are the only two jurisdictions that currently recognize civil unions. On April 20, 2005, Connecticut became the first jurisdiction to voluntarily enact civil unions, as opposed to Vermont, which was forced by the courts to do so in the *Baker* case. Connecticut's civil union statute gives same-sex couples that choose to enter into a civil union the same legal rights and responsibilities given to married heterosexual couples. The Connecticut civil union statute, however, specifically defines marriage as "the union of one man and one woman." On March 21, 2006, eight couples challenged Connecticut's ban on same-sex marriage by filing suit against the state's Department of Public Health in New Haven Superior Court. The couples argued that civil unions create a separate status for gay couples and such a "separate but equal" distinction violates Connecticut's Constitution. The case is headed for the Connecticut Supreme Court regardless of who wins or loses at the lower court level.

A **domestic partnership** is a committed relationship between two persons of the same gender, who reside together and support each other, in a mutually exclusive partnership. Domestic partnership laws grant same-sex couples a way to formalize their relationship and gain certain rights and privileges under state law. The most significant difference between marriage and civil unions or domestic partnerships is that only married persons enjoy the more than 1,100 federal rights and privileges such as Social Security benefits, veterans' benefits, health insurance, Medicaid, hospital visitation, estate taxes, retirement savings, pensions, family leave, and immigration law. Because civil unions and domestic partnerships are not federally recognized, any benefits available at the state or local level are subject to federal taxation. For example, a man whose health insurance covers his male partner must pay federal taxes on the total employer cost for that insurance. Many opponents of civil unions and domestic partnerships claim that civil unions impose a second-class status on same-sex couples. Furthermore, same-sex couples who enter into a civil union or domestic partnership in one jurisdiction, then move to another state, risk the nonrecognition of their union.

Hawaii has enacted the **Reciprocal Beneficiaries Law**, which grants residents who are eighteen or older and not allowed to marry under state law the right to register for and benefit from hospital visitation rights, legal standing to sue in wrongful death cases, as well as property and inheritance rights. Maine has also enacted a domestic partnership law offering limited benefits to registered partners, including inheritance rights if a partner should die intestate or without a will and the right to make medical decisions should a partner become disabled. New Jersey's new domestic partner law, enacted in 2004, applies to both same-sex and heterosexual couples where one partner is age sixty-two or older. Benefits under this law are very limited and include the same rights as those for married couples regarding insurance coverage, medical decisions, and the filing of joint state tax returns.

Massachusetts: The First State to Legalize Same-Sex Marriage

The Massachusetts Supreme Court held in *Goodridge v. Department of Public Health* that a state law barring same-sex marriage was unconstitutional under the Massachusetts Constitution and that same-sex couples should have the right to enter into a civil marriage. The court reasoned that a civil union relegates same-sex couples to a different status, opposing the concept of "separate but equal."

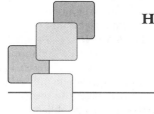
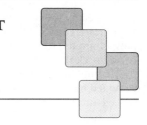

HILLARY GOODRIDGE vs. DEPARTMENT OF PUBLIC HEALTH

440 MASS. 309 (2003)

SUPREME JUDICIAL COURT OF MASSACHUSETTS

NOVEMBER 18, 2003

MARSHALL, C.J.

Marriage is a vital social institution. The exclusive commitment of two individuals to each other nurtures love and mutual support; it brings stability to our society. For those who choose to marry, and for their children, marriage provides an abundance of legal, financial, and social benefits. In return it imposes weighty legal, financial, and social obligations. The question before us is whether, consistent with the Massachusetts Constitution, the Commonwealth may deny the protections, benefits, and obligations conferred by civil marriage to two individuals of the same sex who wish to marry. We conclude that it may not. The Massachusetts Constitution affirms the dignity and equality of all individuals. It forbids the creation of second-class citizens. In reaching our conclusion we have given full deference to the arguments made by the Commonwealth. But it has failed to identify any constitutionally adequate reason for denying civil marriage to same-sex couples. . .

We are mindful that our decision marks a change in the history of our marriage law. Many people hold deep-seated religious, moral, and ethical convictions that marriage should be limited to the union of one man and one woman, and that homosexual conduct is immoral. Many hold equally strong religious, moral, and ethical convictions that same-sex couples are entitled to be married, and that homosexual persons should be treated no differently than their heterosexual neighbors. Neither view answers the question before us. Our concern is with the Massachusetts Constitution as a charter of governance for every person properly within its reach. "Our obligation is to define the liberty of all, not to mandate our own moral code." *Lawrence* v. *Texas*, 123 S.Ct. 2472, 2480 (2003) (*Lawrence*), quoting *Planned Parenthood of Southeastern Pa.* v. *Casey*, 505 U.S. 833, 850 (1992).

Whether the Commonwealth may use its formidable regulatory authority to bar same-sex couples from civil marriage is a question not previously addressed by a Massachusetts appellate court. It is a question the United States Supreme Court left open as a matter of Federal law in *Lawrence*, *supra* at 2484, where it was not an issue. There, the Court affirmed that the core concept of common human dignity protected by the Fourteenth Amendment to the United States Constitution precludes government intrusion into the deeply personal realms of consensual adult expressions of intimacy and one's choice of an intimate partner. The Court also reaffirmed the central role that decisions whether to marry or have children bear in shaping one's identity. *Id.* at 2481. The Massachusetts Constitution is, if anything, more protective of individual liberty and equality than the Federal Constitution; it may demand broader protection for fundamental rights; and it is less tolerant of government intrusion into the protected spheres of private life.

Barred access to the protections, benefits, and obligations of civil marriage, a person who enters into an intimate, exclusive union with another of the same sex is arbitrarily deprived of membership in one of our community's most rewarding and cherished institutions. That exclusion is incompatible with the constitutional principles of respect for individual autonomy and equality under law...

. . . The plaintiffs include business executives, lawyers, an investment banker, educators, therapists, and a computer engineer. Many are active in church, community, and school groups. They have employed such legal means as are available to them—for example, joint adoption, powers of attorney, and joint ownership of real property—to secure aspects of their relationships. Each plaintiff attests a desire to marry his or her partner in order to affirm publicly their commitment to each other and to secure the legal protections and benefits afforded to married couples and their children.

The Department of Public Health (department) is charged by statute with safeguarding public health. See G.L.c. 17. Among its responsibilities, the department oversees the registry of vital records and statistics (registry), which "enforce[s] all laws" relative to the issuance of marriage licenses and the keeping of marriage records, see G.L.c. 17, §4, and which promulgates policies and procedures for the issuance of marriage licenses by city and town clerks and registers. See, e.g., G.L.c. 207, §§ 20, 28A, and 37. The registry is headed by a registrar of vital records and statistics (registrar), appointed by the Commissioner of Public Health (commissioner) with the approval of the public health council and supervised by the commissioner. See G.L.c. 17, § 4.

In March and April, 2001, each of the plaintiff couples attempted to obtain a marriage license from a city or town clerk's office. As required under G.L.c. 207, they completed notices of intention to marry on forms provided by the registry, see G.L.c. 207, § 20, and presented these forms to a Massachusetts town or city clerk, together with the required health forms and marriage license fees. See G.L.c. 207, § 19. In each case, the clerk either refused to accept the notice of intention to marry or denied a marriage license to the couple on the ground that Massachusetts does not recognize same-sex marriage. Because obtaining a marriage license is a necessary prerequisite to civil marriage in Massachusetts, denying marriage licenses to the plaintiffs was tantamount to denying them access to civil marriage itself, with its appurtenant social and legal protections, benefits, and obligations....

. . . In short, for all the joy and solemnity that normally attend a marriage, G.L.c. 207, governing entrance to marriage, is a licensing law. The plaintiffs argue that because nothing in that licensing law specifically prohibits marriages between persons of the same sex, we may interpret the statute to permit "qualified same sex couples" to obtain marriage licenses, thereby avoiding the question whether the law is constitutional. See *School Comm. of Greenfield* v. *Greenfield Educ. Ass'n*, 385 Mass. 70, 79 (1982), and cases cited. This claim lacks merit . . .

...The larger question is whether, as the department claims, government action that bars same-sex couples from civil marriage constitutes a legitimate exercise of the State's authority to regulate conduct, or whether, as the plaintiffs claim, this categorical marriage exclusion violates the Massachusetts Constitution. We have recognized the long-standing statutory understanding, derived from the common law, that "marriage" means the lawful union of a woman and a man. But that history cannot and does not foreclose the constitutional question . . .

. . . We begin by considering the nature of civil marriage itself. Simply put, the government creates civil marriage. In Massachusetts, civil marriage is, and since pre-Colonial days have been, precisely what its name implies: a wholly secular institution. See *Commonwealth* v. *Munson*, 127 Mass. 459, 460-466 (1879) (noting that "[i]n Massachusetts, from very early times, the requisites of a valid marriage have been regulated by statutes of the Colony, Province, and Commonwealth," and surveying marriage statutes from 1639 through 1834). No religious ceremony has ever been required to validate a Massachusetts marriage. *Id.*

In a real sense, there are three partners to every civil marriage: two willing spouses and an approving State. See *DeMatteo* v. *DeMatteo*, 436 Mass.18, 31 (2002) ("Marriage is not a mere contract between two parties but a legal status from which certain rights and obligations arise"); *Smith* v. *Smith*, 171 Mass. 404, 409 (1898) (on marriage, the parties "assume[] new relations to each other and to the State"). See also *French* v. *McAnarney*, 290 Mass.544, 546 (1935). While only the parties can mutually assent to marriage, the terms of the marriage—who may marry and what obligations, benefits, and liabilities attach to civil marriage—are set by the Commonwealth. Conversely, while only the parties can agree to end the marriage (absent the death of one of them or a marriage void ab initio), the Commonwealth defines the exit terms. See G.L.c. 208 . . .

. . . Without question, civil marriage enhances the "welfare of the community." It is a "social institution of the highest importance." *French* v. *McAnarney, supra.* Civil marriage anchors an ordered society by encouraging stable relationships over transient ones. It is central to the way the Commonwealth identifies individuals, provides for the orderly distribution of property, ensures that children and adults are cared for and supported whenever possible from private rather than public funds, and tracks important epidemiological and demographic data.

Marriage also bestows enormous private and social advantages on those who choose to marry. Civil marriage is at once a deeply personal commitment to another human being and a highly public celebration of the ideals of mutuality, companionship, intimacy, fidelity, and family. "It is an association that promotes a way of life, not causes; a harmony in living, not political faiths; a bilateral loyalty, not commercial or social projects." *Griswold* v. *Connecticut*, 381 U.S. 479, 486 (1965). Because it fulfils yearnings for security, safe haven, and connection that express our common humanity, civil marriage is an esteemed institution, and the decision whether and whom to marry is among life's momentous acts of self-definition.

Tangible as well as intangible benefits flow from marriage. The marriage license grants valuable property rights to those who meet the entry requirements, and who agree to what might otherwise be a burdensome degree of government regulation of their activities. . .

... The benefits accessible only by way of a marriage license are enormous, touching nearly every aspect of life and death. The department states that "hundreds of statutes" are related to marriage and to marital benefits. . .

. . . Where a married couple has children, their children are also directly or indirectly, but no less auspiciously, the recipients of the special legal and economic protections obtained by civil marriage. Notwithstanding the Commonwealth's strong public policy to abolish legal distinctions between marital and nonmarital children in providing for the support and care of minors, see *Department of Revenue* v. *Mason M.*, 439 Mass. 665 (2003); *Woodward* v. *Commissioner of Social Sec.*, 435 Mass. 536, 546 (2002), the fact remains that marital children reap a measure of family stability and economic security based on their parents' legally privileged status that is largely inaccessible, or not as readily accessible, to nonmarital children. Some of these benefits are social, such as the enhanced approval that still attends the status of being a marital child. Others are material, such as the greater ease of access to family-based State and Federal benefits that attend the presumptions of one's parentage. . .

. . . It is undoubtedly for these concrete reasons, as well as for its intimately personal significance, that civil marriage has long been termed a "civil right." . . .

. . .The United States Supreme Court has described the right to marry as "of fundamental importance for all individuals" and as "part of the fundamental 'right of privacy' implicit in the Fourteenth Amendment's Due Process Clause." *Zablocki* v. *Redhail*, 434 U.S. 374, 384 (1978). See *Loving* v. *Virginia, supra* ("The freedom to marry has long been recognized as one of the vital personal rights essential to the orderly pursuit of happiness by free men").

Without the right to marry—or more properly, the right to choose to marry—one is excluded from the full range of human experience and denied full protection of the laws for one's "avowed commitment to an intimate and lasting human relationship." *Baker* v. *State, supra* at 229. Because civil marriage is central to the lives of individuals and the welfare of the community, our laws assiduously protect the individual's right to marry against undue government incursion. Laws may not "interfere directly and substantially with the right to marry." *Zablocki* v. *Redhail, supra* at 387. See *Perez* v. *Sharp*, 32 Cal. 2d 711, 714 (1948) ("There can be no prohibition of marriage except for an important social objective and reasonable means"). . .

. . .The Massachusetts Constitution protects matters of personal liberty against government incursion as zealously, and often more so, than does the Federal Constitution, even where both Constitutions employ essentially the same language. See *Planned Parenthood League of Mass., Inc.* v. *Attorney Gen.*, 424 Mass. 586, 590 (1997); *Corning Glass Works* v. *Ann & Hope, Inc. of Danvers*, 363 Mass. 409, 416 (1973). That the Massachusetts Constitution is in some instances more protective of individual liberty interests than is the Federal Constitution is not surprising. Fundamental to the vigor of our Federal system of government is that "state courts are absolutely free to interpret state constitutional provisions to accord greater protection to individual rights than do similar provisions of the United States Constitution." *Arizona* v. *Evans*, 514 U.S. 1, 8 (1995). . .

. . .The Massachusetts Constitution requires, at a minimum, that the exercise of the State's regulatory authority not be "arbitrary or capricious." *Commonwealth* v. *Henry's Drywall Co.*, 366 Mass. 539, 542 (1974). Under both the equality and liberty guarantees, egulatory authority must, at very least, serve "a legitimate purpose in a rational way"; a statute must "bear a reasonable relation to a permissible legislative objective." *Rushworth* v. *Registrar of Motor Vehicles*, 413 Mass. 265, 270 (1992). See, e.g., *Massachusetts Fed'n of Teachers* v. *Board of Educ.*, 436 Mass. 763, 778 (2002) (equal protection); *Coffee-Rich, Inc.* v. *Commissioner of Pub. Health*, 348 Mass. 414, 422 (1965) (due process). Any law failing to satisfy the basic standards of rationality is void.

The plaintiffs challenge the marriage statute on both equal protection and due process grounds. With respect to each such claim, we must first determine the appropriate standard of review. Where a statute implicates a fundamental right or uses a suspect classification, we employ "strict judicial scrutiny." . . .

. . . The department argues that no fundamental right or "suspect" class is at issue here, and rational basis is the appropriate standard of review. For the reasons we explain below, we conclude that the marriage ban does not meet the rational basis test for either due process or equal protection. Because the statute does not survive rational basis review, we do not consider the plaintiffs' arguments that this case merits strict judicial scrutiny.

The department posits three legislative rationales for prohibiting same-sex couples from marrying: (1) providing a "favorable setting for procreation"; (2) ensuring the optimal setting for child rearing, which the department defines as "a two-parent family with one parent of each sex"; and (3) preserving scarce State and private financial resources. We consider each in turn. . .

. . .The "marriage is procreation" argument singles out the one unbridgeable difference between same-sex and opposite-sex couples, and transforms that difference into the essence of legal marriage. Like "Amendment 2" to the Constitution of Colorado, which effectively denied homosexual persons equality under the law and full access to the political process, the marriage restriction impermissibly "identifies persons by a single trait and then denies them protection across the board." *Romer* v. *Evans*, 517 U.S. 620, 633 (1996). In so doing, the State's action confers an official stamp of approval on the destructive stereotype that same-sex relationships are inherently unstable and inferior to opposite-sex relationships and are not worthy of respect.

. . .The department's first stated rationale, equating marriage with unassisted heterosexual procreation, shades imperceptibly into its second: that confining marriage to opposite-sex couples ensures that children are raised in the "optimal" setting. Protecting the welfare of children is a paramount State policy. Restricting marriage to opposite-sex couples, however, cannot plausibly further this policy. "The demographic changes of the past century make it difficult to speak of an average American family. The composition of families varies greatly from household to household." *Troxel* v. *Granville*, 530 U.S. 57, 63 (2000). Massachusetts has responded supportively to "the changing realities of the American family," *Id.* at 64, and has moved vigorously to strengthen the modern family in its many variations. . .

. . .The department has offered no evidence that forbidding marriage to people of the same sex will increase the number of couples choosing to enter into opposite-sex marriages in order to have and raise children. There is thus no rational relationship between the marriage statute and the Commonwealth's proffered goal of protecting the "optimal" child rearing unit. Moreover, the department readily concedes that people in same-sex couples may be "excellent" parents. These couples (including four of the plaintiff couples) have children for the reasons others do—to love them, to care for them, to nurture them. But the task of child rearing for same-sex couples is made infinitely harder by their status as outliers to the marriage laws. While establishing the parentage of children as soon as possible is crucial to the safety and welfare of children, see *Culliton* v. *Beth Israel Deaconness Med. Ctr.*, 435 Mass. 285, 292 (2001), same-sex couples must undergo the sometimes lengthy and intrusive process of second-parent adoption to establish their joint parentage. While the enhanced income provided by marital benefits is an important source of security and stability for married couples and their children, those benefits are denied to families headed by same-sex couples. See, e.g., note 6, *supra*. While the laws of divorce provide clear and reasonably predictable guidelines for child support, child custody, and property division on dissolution of a marriage, same-sex couples who dissolve their relationships find themselves and their children in the highly unpredictable terrain of equity jurisdiction. See *E.N.O.* v. *L.M.M.*, *supra*. Given the wide range of public benefits reserved only for married couples, we do not credit the department's contention that the absence of access to civil marriage amounts to little more than an inconvenience to same-sex couples and their children. Excluding same-sex couples from civil marriage will not make children of opposite-sex marriages more secure, but it does prevent children of same-sex couples from enjoying the immeasurable advantages that flow from the assurance of "a stable family structure in which children will be reared, educated, and socialized." *Post* at 381 (Cordy, J., dissenting). . .

. . .In this case, we are confronted with an entire, sizeable class of parents raising children who have absolutely no access to civil marriage and its protections because they are forbidden from procuring a marriage license. It cannot be rational under our laws, and indeed it is not permitted, to penalize children by depriving them of State benefits because the State disapproves of their parents' sexual orientation.

The third rationale advanced by the department is that limiting marriage to opposite-sex couples furthers the Legislature's interest in conserving scarce State and private financial resources. The marriage restriction is rational, it argues, because the General Court logically could assume that same-sex couples are more financially independent than married couples and thus less needy of public marital benefits, such as tax advantages, or private marital benefits, such as employer—financed health plans that include spouses in their coverage.

An absolute statutory ban on same-sex marriage bears no rational relationship to the goal of economy. First, the department's conclusory generalization—that same-sex couples are less financially dependent on each other than opposite-sex couples—ignores that many same-sex couples, such as many of the plaintiffs in this case, have children and other dependents (here, aged parents) in their care. The department does not contend, nor could it, that these dependents are less needy or deserving than the dependents of married couples. Second, Massachusetts marriage laws do not condition receipt of public and private financial benefits to married individuals on a demonstration of financial dependence on each other; the benefits are available to married they mingle their finances or actually depend on each other for support.

The department suggests additional rationales for prohibiting same-sex couples from marrying, which are developed by some amici. It argues that broadening civil marriage to include same-sex couples will trivialize or destroy the institution of marriage as it has historically been fashioned. Certainly our decision today marks a significant change in the definition of marriage as it has been inherited from the common law, and understood by many societies for centuries. But it does not disturb the fundamental value of marriage in our society.

Here, the plaintiffs seek only to be married, not to undermine the institution of civil marriage. They do not want marriage abolished. They do not attack the binary nature of marriage, the consanguinity provisions, or any of the other gate—keeping provisions of the marriage licensing law. Recognizing the right of an individual to marry a person of the same sex will not diminish the validity or dignity of opposite-sex marriage, any more than recognizing the right of an individual to marry a person of a different race devalues the marriage of a person who marries someone of her own race. If anything, extending civil marriage to same-sex couples reinforces the importance of marriage to individuals and communities. That same-sex couples are willing to embrace marriage's solemn obligations of exclusivity, mutual support, and commitment to one another is a testament to the enduring place of marriage in our laws and in the human spirit.

It has been argued that, due to the State's strong interest in the institution of marriage as a stabilizing social structure, only the Legislature can control and define its boundaries. Accordingly, our elected representatives legitimately may choose to exclude same-sex couples from civil marriage in order to assure all citizens of the Commonwealth that (1) the benefits of our marriage laws are available explicitly to create and support a family setting that is, in the Legislature's view, optimal for child rearing, and (2) the State does not endorse gay and lesbian parenthood as the equivalent of being raised by one's married biological parents. These arguments miss the point. The Massachusetts Constitution requires that legislation meet certain criteria and not extend beyond certain limits. It is the function of courts to determine whether these criteria are met and whether these limits are exceeded. In most instances, these limits are defined by whether a rational basis exists to conclude that legislation will bring about a rational result. The Legislature in the first instance, and the courts in the last instance, must ascertain whether such a rational basis exists. To label the court's role as usurping that of the Legislature, see, e.g., *post* at 394–395 (Cordy, J., dissenting), is to misunderstand the nature and purpose of judicial review. We owe great deference to the Legislature to decide social and policy issues, but it is the traditional and settled role of courts to decide constitutional issues....

We also reject the argument suggested by the department, and elaborated by some amici, that expanding the institution of civil marriage in Massachusetts to include same-sex couples will lead to interstate conflict. We would not presume to dictate how another State should respond to today's decision. But neither should considerations of comity prevent us from according Massachusetts residents the full measure of protection available under the Massachusetts Constitution. The genius of our Federal system is that each State's Constitution has vitality specific to its own traditions, and that, subject to the minimum requirements of the Fourteenth Amendment, each State is free to address difficult issues of individual liberty in the manner its own Constitution demands....

...The department has had more than ample opportunity to articulate a constitutionally adequate justification for limiting civil marriage to opposite-sex unions. It has failed to do so. The department has offered purported justifications for the civil marriage restriction that are starkly at odds with the comprehensive network of vigorous, gender-neutral laws promoting stable families and the best interests of children. It has failed to identify any relevant characteristic that would justify shutting the door to civil marriage to a person who wishes to marry someone of the same sex.

The marriage ban works a deep and scarring hardship on a very real segment of the community for no rational reason. The absence of any reasonable relationship between, on the one hand, an absolute disqualification of same-sex couples who wish to enter into civil marriage and, on the other, protection of public health, safety, or general welfare, suggests that the marriage restriction is rooted in persistent prejudices against persons who are (or who are believed to be) homosexual. "The Constitution cannot control such prejudices but neither can it tolerate them. Private biases may be outside the reach of the law, but the law cannot, directly or indirectly, give them effect." *Palmore* v. *Sidoti*, 466 U.S. 429, 433 (1984) (construing Fourteenth Amendment). Limiting the protections, benefits, and obligations of civil marriage to opposite-sex couples violates the basic premises of individual liberty and equality under law protected by the Massachusetts Constitution....

OPPOSITION TO GAY MARRIAGE IN MASSACHUSETTS

In January of 2004, a number of state legislators determined that the ruling in *Goodridge* was ambiguous and suggested passage of a civil union bill. The State Supreme Judicial Court issued an advisory opinion calling the legislature's civil union proposal unconstitutional. In March of that year, the Massachusetts legislature proposed an amendment to the state constitution that would ban gay marriage, and instead offer same-sex couples civil union status and the same rights and responsibilities granted to heterosexual couples.

In September 2005, the Massachusetts legislature rejected the proposed change to the state constitution. The battle over gay marriage is not over yet. State legislators opposed to gay marriage and civil unions are preparing another proposed constitutional amendment through a ballot initiative that could be considered in

2008. To get the proposed amendment on the ballot, supporters must submit a petition with 65,000 signatures to the legislature.

CALIFORNIA'S BATTLE OVER SAME-SEX MARRIAGE

On March 7, 2000, the people of California voted on Proposition 22, a state version of the Defense of Marriage Act. The statute reads, "Only marriage between a man and a woman is valid or recognized in California." California did, however, pass the Domestic Partnership Act of 2003, which granted same-sex couples most of the rights enjoyed by heterosexual couples in the state.

California Domestic Partnership Act

California Family Code Section 297

   a. Domestic partners are two adults who have chosen to share one another's lives in an intimate and committed relationship of mutual caring.
   b. A domestic partnership shall be established in California when both persons file a Declaration of Domestic Partnership with the Secretary of State pursuant to this division, and, at the time of filing, all of the following requirements are met:

1. Both persons have a common residence.
2. Neither person is married to someone else or is a member of another domestic partnership with someone else that has not been terminated, dissolved, or adjudged a nullity.
3. The two persons are not related by blood in a way that would prevent them from being married to each other in this state.
4. Both persons are at least 18 years of age.
5. Either of the following:

   A. Both persons are members of the same sex.
   B. One or both of the persons meet the eligibility criteria under Title II of the Social Security Act as defined in 42 U.S.C. Section 402(a) for old-age insurance benefits or Title XVI of the Social Security Act as defined in 42 U.S.C. Section 1381 for aged individuals. Notwithstanding any other provision of this section, persons of opposite sexes may not constitute a domestic partnership unless one or both of the persons are over the age of 62.

6. Both persons are capable of consenting to the domestic partnership.
   c. "Have a common residence" means that both domestic partners share the same residence. It is not necessary that the legal right to possess the common residence be in both of their names. Two people have a common residence even if one or both have additional residences. Domestic partners do not cease to have a common residence if one leaves the common residence but intends to return.
   297.5. a. Registered domestic partners shall have the same rights, protections, and benefits, and shall be subject to the same responsibilities, obligations, and duties under law, whether they derive from statutes, administrative regulations, court rules, government policies, common law, or any other provisions or sources of law, as are granted to and imposed upon spouses.
   b. Former registered domestic partners shall have the same rights, protections, and benefits, and shall be subject to the same responsibilities,

obligations, and duties under law, whether they derive from statutes, administrative regulations, court rules, government policies, common law, or any other provisions or sources of law, as are granted to and imposed upon former spouses.

c. A surviving registered domestic partner, following the death of the other partner, shall have the same rights, protections, and benefits, and shall be subject to the same responsibilities, obligations, and duties under law, whether they derive from statutes, administrative regulations, court rules, government policies, common law, or any other provisions or sources of law, as are granted to and imposed upon a widow or a widower.

d. The rights and obligations of registered domestic partners with respect to a child of either of them shall be the same as those of spouses. The rights and obligations of former or surviving registered domestic partners with respect to a child of either of them shall be the same as those of former or surviving spouses.

e. To the extent that provisions of California law adopt, refer to, or rely upon, provisions of federal law in a way that otherwise would cause registered domestic partners to be treated differently than spouses, registered domestic partners shall be treated by California law as if federal law recognized a domestic partnership in the same manner as California law.

f. Registered domestic partners shall have the same rights regarding nondiscrimination as those provided to spouses.

g. Notwithstanding this section, in filing their state income tax returns, domestic partners shall use the same filing status as is used on their federal income tax returns, or that would have been used had they filed federal income tax returns. Earned income may not be treated as community property for state income tax purposes.

h. No public agency in this state may discriminate against any person or couple on the ground that the person is a registered domestic partner rather than a spouse or that the couple are registered domestic partners rather than spouses, except that nothing in this section applies to modify eligibility for long-term care plans pursuant to Chapter 15 (commencing with Section 21660) of Part 3 of Division 5 of Title 2 of the Government Code.

i. This act does not preclude any state or local agency from exercising its regulatory authority to implement statutes providing rights to, or imposing responsibilities upon, domestic partners.

j. This section does not amend or modify any provision of the California Constitution or any provision of any statute that was adopted by initiative.

k. This section does not amend or modify federal laws or the benefits, protections, and responsibilities provided by those laws.

l. Where necessary to implement the rights of registered domestic partners under this act, gender-specific terms referring to spouses shall be construed to include domestic partners.

m. (1)For purposes of the statutes, administrative regulations, court rules, government policies, common law, and any other provision or source of law governing the rights, protections, and benefits, and the responsibilities, obligations, and duties of registered domestic partners in this state, as effectuated by this section, with respect to community property, mutual responsibility for debts to third parties, the right in particular circumstances of either partner to seek financial support from the other following the dissolution of the partnership, and other rights and duties as between the partners concerning ownership of property, any reference to the date of a marriage shall be deemed to refer to the date of registration of a domestic partnership with the state.

2. Notwithstanding paragraph (1), for domestic partnerships registered with the state before January 1, 2005, an agreement between the domestic partners that the partners intend to be governed by the requirements set forth in Sections 1600 to 1620, inclusive, and which complies with those sections, except for the agreement's effective date, shall be enforceable as provided by Sections 1600 to 1620, inclusive, if that agreement was fully executed and in force as of June 30, 2005.

BY ORDER OF THE MAYOR OF SAN FRANCISCO

On February 12, 2004, San Francisco Mayor Gavin Newsome sent a letter to the San Francisco county clerk's office ordering the office to determine what changes should be made to forms issued by the city to couples applying for a marriage license. His objective was to gender-neutralize the language in these documents that limited marriage to being between a man and a woman. His reasoning was based on rulings handed down by supreme courts in other jurisdictions declaring that equal protection provisions in their state constitutions prohibit discrimination against gay men and lesbians. He explained that it was his belief that the California Constitution also prohibited similar discrimination against gays and lesbians.

In compliance with the mayor's order, the clerk's office revised the city's marriage license and marriage certificate applications. It eliminated the terms "bride," "groom," "unmarried man," and "unmarried woman" and replaced them with the terms "first applicant," "second applicant," and "unmarried individuals." The form also included a warning for couples to seek legal advice regarding the effect a marriage would have on already existing domestic partnerships and the possibility that the marriage status would not be recognized outside of San Francisco. Once the forms were revised, the clerk's office issued licenses to approximately 4,000 same-sex couples. The marriages that took place that day were voided by the California Supreme Court on August 12, 2004.

LOCKYER v. CITY AND COUNTY OF SAN FRANCISCO, 33 CAL.4TH 1055, 17

CAL.RPTR.3D 225, 95 P.3D 459 (2004)

SUPREME COURT OF CALIFORNIA

AUGUST 12, 2004

GEORGE, C.J.

We assumed jurisdiction in these original writ proceedings to address an important but relatively narrow legal issue—whether a local executive official who is charged with the ministerial duty of enforcing a state statute exceeds his or her authority when, without any court having determined that the statute is unconstitutional, the official deliberately declines to enforce the statute because he or she determines or is of the opinion that the statute is unconstitutional.

In the present case, this legal issue arises out of the refusal of local officials in the City and County of San Francisco to enforce the provisions of California's marriage statutes that limit the granting of a marriage license and marriage certificate only to a couple comprised of a man and a woman.

The same legal issue and the same applicable legal principles could come into play, however, in a multitude of situations. For example, we would face the same legal issue if the statute in question were among those that restrict the possession or require the registration of assault weapons, and a local official, charged with the ministerial duty of enforcing those statutes, refused to apply their provisions because of the official's view that they violate the Second Amendment of the federal Constitution. In like manner, the same legal issue would be presented if the statute were one of the environmental measures that impose restrictions upon a property owner's ability to obtain a building permit for a development that interferes with the public's access to the California coastline, and a local official, charged with the ministerial duty of issuing building permits, refused to apply the statutory limitations because of his or her belief that they effect an uncompensated "taking" of property in violation of the just compensation clause of the state or federal Constitution.

Indeed, another example might illustrate the point even more clearly: the same legal issue would arise if the statute at the center of the controversy were the recently enacted provision (operative January 1, 2005) that imposes a ministerial duty upon local officials to accord the same rights and benefits to registered domestic partners as are granted to spouses (see Fam. Code, § 297.5, added by Stats. 2003, ch. 421, § 4), and a local official—perhaps an officeholder in a locale where domestic partnership rights are unpopular—adopted a policy of refusing to recognize or accord to registered domestic partners the equal treatment mandated by statute, based solely upon the official's view (unsupported by any judicial determination) that the statutory provisions granting such rights to registered domestic partners are unconstitutional because they improperly amend or repeal the provisions of the voter-enacted initiative measure commonly known as Proposition 22, the California Defense of Marriage Act (Fam. Code, § 308.5) without a confirming vote of the electorate, in violation of article II, section 10, subdivision (c) of the California Constitution.

As these various examples demonstrate, although the present proceeding may be viewed by some as presenting primarily a question of the substantive legal rights of same-sex couples, in actuality the legal issue before us implicates the interest of all individuals in ensuring that public officials execute their official duties in a manner that respects the limits of the authority granted to them as officeholders. In short, the legal question at issue—the scope of the authority entrusted to our public officials—involves the determination of a fundamental question that lies at the heart of our political system: the role of the rule of law in a society that justly prides itself on being "a government of laws, and not of men" (or women).

As indicated above, that issue—phrased in the narrow terms presented by this case—is whether a local executive official, charged with the ministerial duty of enforcing a statute, has the authority to disregard the terms of the statute in the absence of a judicial determination that it is unconstitutional, based solely upon the official's opinion that the governing statute is unconstitutional. As we shall see, it is well established, both in California and elsewhere, that—subject to a few narrow exceptions that clearly are inapplicable here—a local executive official does *not* possess such authority.

(1) This conclusion is consistent with the classic understanding of the separation of powers doctrine—that the legislative power is the power to enact statutes, the executive power is the power to execute or enforce statutes, and the judicial power is the power to interpret statutes and to determine their constitutionality. It is true, of course, that the separation of powers doctrine does not create an absolute or rigid division of functions. (*Superior Court v. County of Mendocino* (1996) 13 Cal.4th 45, 52 [51 Cal.Rptr.2d 837, 913 P.2d 1046].) **(2)** Furthermore, legislators and executive officials may take into account constitutional considerations in making discretionary decisions within their authorized sphere of action—such as whether to enact or veto proposed legislation or exercise prosecutorial discretion. When, however, a duly enacted statute imposes a ministerial duty upon an executive official to follow the dictates of the statute in performing a mandated act, the official generally has no authority to disregard the statutory mandate based on the official's own determination that the statute is unconstitutional. (See, e.g., *Kendall v.United States* (1838) 37 U.S. 524, 613 [9 L.Ed. 1181] ["To contend, that the obligation imposed on the president to see the laws faithfully executed, implies a power to forbid their execution, is a novel construction of the constitution, and entirely inadmissible"].)

Accordingly, for the reasons that follow, we agree with petitioners that local officials in San Francisco exceeded their authority by taking official action in violation of applicable statutory provisions. We therefore shall issue a writ of mandate directing the officials to enforce those provisions unless and until they are judicially determined to be unconstitutional and to take all necessary remedial steps to undo the continuing effects of the officials' past unauthorized actions, including making appropriate corrections to all relevant official records and notifying all affected same-sex couples that the same-sex marriages authorized by the officials are void and of no legal effect.

(3) To avoid any misunderstanding, we emphasize that the substantive question of the constitutional validity of California's statutory provisions limiting marriage to a union between a man and a woman is not before our court in this proceeding, and our decision in this case is not intended, and should not be interpreted, to reflect any view on that issue. We hold only that in the absence of a judicial determination that such statutory provisions are unconstitutional, local executive officials lacked authority to issue marriage licenses to, solemnize marriages of, or register certificates of marriage for same-sex couples, and marriages conducted between same-sex couples in violation of the applicable statutes are void and of no legal effect. Should the applicable statutes be judicially determined to be unconstitutional in the future, same-sex couples then would be free to obtain valid marriage licenses and enter into valid marriages...

CALIFORNIA LEGISLATURE ATTEMPTS SAME-SEX MARRIAGE BILL

On September 6, 2005, the California Assembly became the first state legislative body to pass the **Religious Freedom and Civil Marriage Protection Act**—a law allowing same-sex couples to marry. Governor Arnold Schwarzenegger vetoed the bill on September 29, 2005.

NEW YORK AND NEW JERSEY HIGH COURT RULINGS

In July of 2006, the New York Court of Appeals, the State's highest court, rejected arguments by same-sex couples who claimed the state's ban on gay marriage violated the New York State Constitution. The court left the legal recognition of same-sex unions up to the Legislature. In October of 2006, New Jersey's state Supreme Court reached a different conclusion. While the Court did not follow in Massachusetts footsteps and legalize gay marriage, it declared that same-sex couples have the same rights as their heterosexual counterparts. The court gave the state legislature 180 days to revise its marriage statutes and either legalize gay marriage or provide for an alternative, such as civil unions.

FEDERAL AND STATE EFFORTS TO BAN SAME-SEX MARRIAGE

In addition to passage of the **Defense of Marriage Act**, other federal efforts included a proposed amendment to the United States Constitution that would ban same-sex marriage. Attempts to pass the **Federal Marriage Amendment** in 2005 were unsuccessful.

> *Marriage in the United States of America shall consist only of the union of a man and a woman.*
> *Neither this constitution or the constitution of any state, nor state or federal law, shall be construed to require that marital status or the legal incidents thereof be conferred upon unmarried couples or groups.*
> Proposed Federal Marriage Amendment

Most states ban same-sex marriage either by enactment of state statute or state constitutional amendments. In addition, most states refuse to recognize same-sex marriages legally created in other jurisdictions, either by state statute or constitutional amendment.

EXHIBIT 4–1 Sample Premarital Agreement (author unknown).

WHEREAS, the parties are contemplating a legal marriage under the laws of the State of Connecticut; and

WHEREAS, it is their mutual desire to enter into this Agreement whereby they will regulate their relationship toward each other with respect to the property each of them own and in which each of them has an interest;

NOW, therefore, it is agreed as follows:

1. That the properties of any kind or nature, real, personal or mixed, wherever the same may be found, which belong to each party, shall be and forever remain the separate estate of said party, including all interests, rents and profits which may accrue therefrom.

2. That each party shall have at all times the full right and authority, in all respects, the same as each would have if not married, to use, enjoy, mortgage, convey and encumber such property as may belong to him or her.

3. That each party may make such disposition of his or her property as the case may be, by gift or will during his or her lifetime, as each sees fit; and in the event of the decease of one of the parties, the survivor shall have no interest in the property of the estate of the other, either by way of inheritance, succession, family allowance or homestead.

4. That each party, in the event of a legal separation or dissolution of marriage, shall have no right as against the other by other by way of claims for support, alimony, property division, attorney's fees and costs.

5. This Prenuptial Agreement shall be construed under the laws of the State of Connecticut.

Dated this 10th day of May, 2001

_____
(Name)

_____
(Date)

_____
(Name)

_____
(Date)

_____
Witness

_____
Witness

END OF CHAPTER EXERCISES

Crossword Puzzle

Across

2. a model act drafted by the National Conference of Commissioners on Uniform State Laws that provides states with model legislation that addresses the issues necessary to create a valid premarital agreement

4. a proposed amendment to the United States Constitution that would ban same-sex— marriage. Attempts to pass the amendment in 2005 were unsuccessful

5. a separate category of legal recognition that grants same sex-couples marriage rights available to heterosexual couples, in the states of Vermont and Connecticut

6. landmark case decided by the Florida Supreme Court in 1970 which held that prenuptial agreements were not invalid *per se*

8. a Hawaii law that grants residents who are eighteen or older and not allowed to marry under state law, the right to register and benefit from hospital visitation rights, legal standing to sue in wrongful death cases, as well as property and inheritance rights

9. contractual obligations imposed by the courts to avoid unjust enrichment

10. a contract where the intention of the parties is inferred by their conduct

11. a lawsuit for support filed against a cohabitating partner

12. an express agreement between the parties delineating its specific terms

13. a contract entered into by parties who intend to marry

14. landmark cohabitation case decided by the California Supreme Court in 1976

Down

1. a proposed California bill allowing same-sex couples to marry that was vetoed by Governor Arnold Schwarzenegger on September 29, 2005

2. an agreement that is so unfair to one party that the court will refuse to enforce it

3. a committed relationship between two persons of the same gender, who reside together and support each other, in a mutually exclusive partnership

7. laws prohibiting interracial marriages

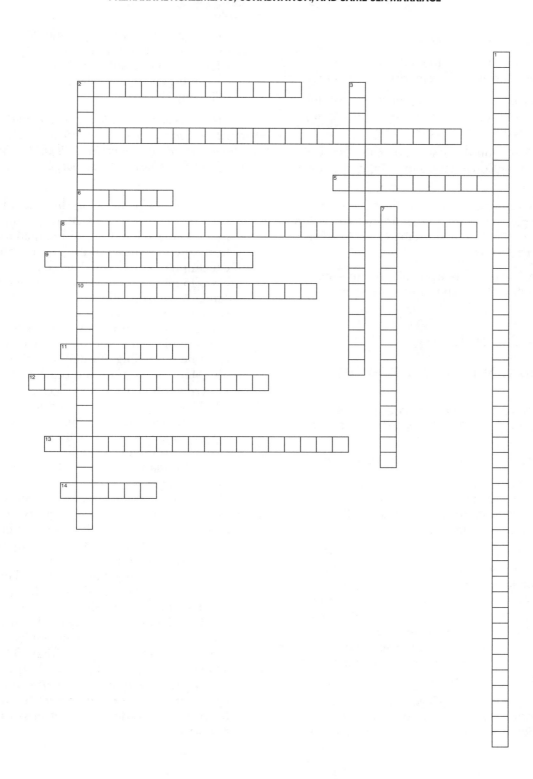

Review Questions

1. What are the requirements for drafting and executing a valid premarital agreement?

2. Why is the advice of independent counsel so important for the purpose of reviewing a premarital agreement?

3. Why do you think so many couples are choosing cohabitation instead of traditional marriage?

4. What remedies are available to cohabitating couples according to the landmark decision by the California Supreme Court in *Marvin v. Marvin*?

5. What options are available to same-sex couples who wish to formalize their relationships?

Cases for Briefing

Marvin v. Marvin, 557 P.2d 106 (1976)

Dornemann v. Dornemann, 48 Conn. Sup. 502, 850 A.2d 273 (2004)

Exploring the Workplace: Activities

1. Research your state's premarital agreement statute. Does your state follow the Uniform Premarital Agreement Act, a modified version, or a state version?

2. Research your state's marriage statute. In your jurisdiction, who may marry? Does your state ban same-sex marriage or any other alternative form of legal recognition for same-sex couples? If so, cite the statute or state constitutional amendment. Does your state recognize same-sex marriage, civil unions, or domestic partnerships? If so, cite the statute or case law.

3. You work as a paralegal for the law firm of Cocco, Cocco & Cocco in your state. Your supervisor, Attorney Rocco Cocco, asks you to review a premarital agreement drafted by the client, Frank Holloway, and to draft a letter on his behalf, which he will sign, explaining the enforceability of the following clause:

The parties agree not to have children. In the event the wife becomes pregnant, she shall terminate the pregnancy. If for any reason she shall fail to terminate the pregnancy, the husband shall not be liable for child support.

4. You work as a paralegal in the State of Connecticut for the Law Office of Emanuel Perez. Paula White has just retained the firm to represent her in the drafting and execution of a premarital agreement. She plans to marry her long-time boyfriend, James Meyerson, later this year. Both are residents of Branford, Connecticut. She lives at 121 Westway Drive and he lives at 231 Summit Place. Ms. White owns two apartment buildings located on 501 and 503 Main Street in Branford. Each building has twenty tenants in it and generates $750.00 per month per unit. Both properties were recently appraised at a fair market value of $1,000,000 each. These two properties have been in the White family for many years and Ms. White wants to keep it that way. She heard that a divorce court in the State of Connecticut may award any part of either party's estate in a divorce case regardless of whether it was acquired before or during the marriage. She is concerned that in the event of divorce, her husband may make a claim to this property. She would like to have a premarital agreement drafted to prevent this from happening. Using the following links, or any others you may find useful, draft a premarital agreement that will achieve Ms. White's objectives. **http://www.expertlaw.com/library/family_law/prenuptial_agreement_form.html http://www.deltabravo.net/custody/prenup.php**

CHAPTER 5

Alimony

KEY TERMS

adultery

alimony

alimony in gross

allowable deduction

arrearages

attorney's fees

Bankruptcy Abuse
Prevention and
Consumer Protection Act

bridge-the-gap alimony

canon law

church court

COBRA

cohabitation

contempt proceeding

cost of living clause

desertion

discretion of the court

divorce

divorce *a mensa et thoro*

divorce *a vinculo matrimonii*

domestic support obligations

ecclesiastical court

escalation clause

family support payments

front loading

gross income

habitual intemperance

incarceration in a penal
institution

incompatiblilty

institutionalization for
mental illness

irreconcilable differences

irremediable breakdown

irretrievable breakdown

IRS recapture rule

legal grounds

lump sum alimony

Married Women's Property Acts

mental cruelty

modification of alimony

net income

no-fault divorce laws

nominal alimony

pendente lite alimony

periodic alimony

permanent alimony

physical cruelty

rehabilitative alimony

reimbursement alimony

secular court

spousal maintenance

spousal support

wage execution

waiver of alimony

willful contempt

Alimony is the term given to a sum of money, or other property, paid by a former spouse to the other former spouse for financial support, pursuant to a court order, temporary or final, in a divorce proceeding. Terms such as **spousal support** or **spousal maintenance** are synonyms for alimony, and any one or all of these terms may be used by different jurisdictions in statutory or case law.

HISTORY OF ALIMONY

Historically, married women had no rights to property in their own name or independent of their husbands. They could not control their own income, enter into contracts, buy and sell land, or sue or be sued. Since the United States inherited its legal system from England, we must look to early English law to trace the history of alimony. In England, the ecclesiastical courts or church courts had the power to grant divorces.

ECCLESIASTICAL COURTS

For many centuries throughout Western Europe, **ecclesiastical courts** or **church courts** coexisted with **secular courts,** or courts administered by the state. In many European countries, there was an official state church and it was this church that controlled ecclesiastical courts. In England, eventually it was the Church of England or Anglican Church that administered the church courts. These courts had the jurisdiction to hear some matters that could also be heard in the general state courts. In certain areas, however, the ecclesiastical or church court was the exclusive forum for addressing disputes.

Ecclesiastical courts had exclusive jurisdiction over all family-related legal matters. In these matters, the church courts applied **canon law.** The term *canon law* refers to the Church's body of law or rules that determine man's moral obligations to man, to woman, and to God. In England, the Anglican Church retained much of the doctrine and dogma of the Roman Catholic Church, including the proscription against divorce as we know it and the status of matrimony as a sacrament. The "divorces" granted by these courts were not the divorces we are accustomed to today. Our definition of **divorce**, or **divorce *a vinculo matrimonii,*** is the complete severance of the marital relationship, allowing the parties to go their separate ways. This includes the right to remarry. The ecclesiastical courts only granted **divorce *a mensa et thoro,*** which means divorce from bed and board. The result of a divorce *a mensa et thoro* did not sever the marriage; it merely enabled the spouses to live separate and apart. In many religions, marriage is a sacrament not to be entered into lightly. In the eyes of God and the church, only the death of one of the two spouses ended a marriage. The church allowed only widowed persons to enter into new or second marriages.

The church also changed the status of individuals upon marriage in that they were viewed as one entity. This concept influenced the secular law regarding the economic positions of spouses at common law. Upon marriage, husband and wife merged into "one body," the "one" being the husband. By virtue of the marriage ceremony, the spouses entered into a marital contract that imposed the duty of support on the husband. In turn, the wife gave up her rights to control or possess property or earnings that belonged to her. Women did not work outside the home and upon marriage took on the traditional roles of homemaking and rearing the children. This enabled the husband to focus on his career and increase his earning capacity.

ORIGINS OF THE ALIMONY AWARD

Upon granting a divorce *a mensa et thoro,* the ecclesiastical courts ordered the husband to pay "alimony" or support to the wife. Not only was the husband obligated to support the wife during the marriage, this duty was ongoing, even through the separation period. The husband's duty to support the wife upon divorce was not absolute. The wife was entitled to alimony as long as she was an "innocent spouse." If she had caused the breakdown of the marriage, she would get nothing. This would leave the wife with no monetary support. If the husband were at fault for the breakup of the marriage, his punishment obligated him to pay for his fault. Historically, both the theoretical and practical basis for the creation of alimony was to provide compensation for the wife and punish the husband for his wrongdoing.

ALIMONY IN EARLY AMERICA

The English common law system was adopted by the settlers of America and along with it came the laws regarding the severing of a marriage and the legal disadvantages suffered by married women. The duty of husband to pay alimony upon divorce was codified in statutes of many American jurisdictions. In the late 1830s, American jurisdictions began passing the **Married Women's Property Acts**. These statutes eliminated the disadvantages of married women and gave them the right to control their own earnings, bring lawsuits, be sued, own their own property, enter into contracts, and function in a legal capacity. As time passed, societal attitudes toward women changed. Women were increasingly joining the workforce and gaining the ability to support themselves. Even though times were changing and more opportunities opened up to women, the American legal system still held on to the husband's duty to support his former wife.

When initiating a divorce action, the plaintiff spouse had to allege a legal reason or ground for requesting a divorce in the complaint or petition for dissolution of marriage. In the early 1970s many jurisdictions began passing **no-fault divorce**

FIGURE 5–1
In early times, a married couple was viewed as "one body" by the church, that one body being the husband.

laws. Prior to the passage of no-fault laws, a spouse seeking a divorce was required to have **legal grounds**—that is, facts proving that the other spouse was at fault. Some of the fault grounds included:

- **adultery,**
- **habitual intemperance,**
- **desertion,**
- **mental cruelty,**
- **physical cruelty,**
- **incarceration in a penal institution,** and
- **Institutionalization for mental illness.**

The plaintiff spouse was required to produce evidence to prove his case. If the wife was responsible for the breakdown of the marriage, she lost alimony and property. If the husband were at fault, he would probably have to pay alimony and give the wife a considerable portion of property. If the plaintiff spouse could not meet the burden of proof, no divorce would be granted. Parties seeking divorces colluded or conspired together to commit perjury in cases where no fault existed and the parties merely wished to go their separate ways and end an unhappy marriage. The frequency of this type of charade was one of many factors that prompted state legislatures to consider and eventually enact laws that made divorce easier in most circumstances. In 1969, California led the nation in the passage of this country's first no-fault divorce law.

ALIMONY AWARDS IN A NO-FAULT SETTING

Under our current system of no-fault divorce, the courts must first dissolve the marriage. After the marriage is dissolved, the court will then render orders regarding alimony, property division, child support, child custody, and attorney's fees. No-fault divorce means that in order for the court to dissolve a marriage, one of the parties only has to allege that the marriage has broken down and that there is no hope of reconciliation.

Depending on the jurisdiction, the no-fault ground may be referred to as one of the following:

- **irreconcilable differences,**
- **incompatibility,**
- **irretrievable breakdown,** and
- **irremediable breakdown.**

While all states have some form of no-fault divorce law, many jurisdictions also allow spouses to allege a fault ground in their divorce pleadings. Whether the issue of fault may be raised in determining alimony or property division depends on the jurisdiction.

CHEATING HUSBAND TRIES TO CHEAT WIFE!

In this case, the wife was awarded permanent alimony at the trial court level. On appeal, the court found that the husband was unable to meet his burden of proving that his wife was at fault for the breakdown of the marriage and not entitled to alimony. Both the husband and the wife represented themselves on the appeal as *pro per* parties.

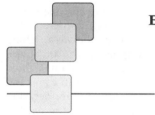

ETHEL RAE CORMIER THIBODEAUX V. EUGENE THIBODEAUX

454 S.2D 813 (1984)

COURT OF APPEAL OF LOUISIANA, THIRD CIRCUIT

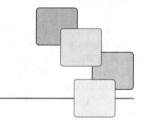

ETHEL C. THIBODEAUX, IN PRO PER.
EUGENE THIBODEAUX, IN PRO PER.

DOUCET, JUDGE.

Defendant, Eugene Thibodeaux, appeals from a judgment awarding plaintiff, Ethel Rae Cormier Thibodeaux, permanent periodic alimony at the rate of $150.00 per month. . . .

. . . On appeal defendant contends that the trial court erred in not finding that plaintiff was at fault in causing the dissolution of the marriage, thus precluding her from receiving permanent alimony. In the alternative, defendant asserts that the trial court erred in finding that the plaintiff did not have sufficient means for support such as would entitle her to an award of $150.00 per month in alimony.

Permanent periodic alimony may be awarded a spouse who had not been at fault and has not sufficient means for support. La.C.C. art. 160; *Lamb v. Lamb*, 460 So. 2d 634 (La. App. 3rd Cir. 1984); *Silas v. Silas*, 399 So. 2d 779 (La. App. 3rd Cir. 1981). The burden of proof is on the party seeking alimony to show that he or she is without fault in causing the dissolution of the marriage and that he or she is in necessitous circumstances and in need of support. *Lamb v. Lamb*, supra. A trial court's finding of fact on the issue of fault will not be disturbed on appeal unless it is clearly wrong. *Pearce v. Pearce*, 348 So. 2d 75 (La. App. 3rd Cir. 1977); *Boudreaux v. Boudreaux*, 460 So. 2d 722 (La. App. 3rd Cir. 1983). . . .

. . . Defendant bases his allegations of fault on (1) cruel treatment by his wife, C.C. art. 138(3); and/or (2) her public defamation of him, C.C. art.

138(4). C.C. art. 138(3) provides that cruel treatment by one of the spouses towards the other must be of such a nature as to render their living together insupportable. In addition, the jurisprudence holds that the fault sufficient to preclude a spouse from receiving permanent alimony must be a serious and independent contributory or proximate cause of the dissolution of the marriage. *Pearce v. Pearce,* supra; *Lamb v. Lamb,* supra.

Defendant cites as cruel treatment accusations by his wife that he was dating other women. The defendant testified that almost every week his wife would accuse him of seeing other women, usually when he "came home late from work." Defendant flatly denied dating or seeing other women. Plaintiff testified that she suspected defendant was seeing other women and that she accused him of this—but not every week. Plaintiff and her thirteen year-old daughter both testified that, as they were returning from church services one evening at approximately 10:00 p.m., they happened to see the defendant and a former girlfriend of his coming out of the front door of her residence. Defendant denied this allegation. Plaintiff also admitted that she had accused defendant of dating her brother's girlfriend.

The parties physically separated when plaintiff and her two children moved out of the family home. This step was taken approximately one week after defendant began hiding the household cookware so that plaintiff could not prepare meals. This was never specifically denied by defendant. There was evidence that shortly before plaintiff left, defendant disconnected the air conditioner—this was in the month of August. Defendant claimed that he only did this during the day when no one was home to save on his utility bill. However, plaintiff claims that defendant told her that he could not afford to support her and his girlfriend and that he wanted her out of the house. In other words, plaintiff claimed that defendant drove her out of the house. On a couple of occasions, plaintiff's son heard defendant tell his mother that he didn't want her in the home.

From this evidence the trial court concluded that the plaintiff was free from fault. The trial judge's reasons for this finding are not clear. However, from the evidence in the record before us we are unable to say that this conclusion of the trial court was clearly wrong. The record furnishes a basis for finding that the plaintiff's accusations of extra-marital activity were not totally unfounded and therefore would not constitute cruel treatment. A wife who observes her husband and his ex-girlfriend leaving her residence together at 10:00 p.m. is justified in having her suspicions aroused. More-over, it appears that the reason for the marital breakup rests on the shoulders of defendant who by his actions drove plaintiff from the family home. In addition, defendant testified at trial that he would welcome the plaintiff back but she refuses to return. Thus, by defendant's own testimony, the accusations made by his wife could not be considered a serious and independent contributory or proximate cause of the marital breakup.

Defendant next contends that the plaintiff publicly defamed him, and under La.C.C. art. 138(4), and the applicable jurisprudence, this constitutes fault sufficient to preclude her from receiving alimony. We will examine the issue of defamation even though, as we have discussed above with reference to alleged cruel treatment (accusations of infidelity), any public defamation could not, we feel, have been contributory or proximate cause of the marital breakup.

To establish a public defamation as contemplated in C.C. art. 138(4) it is necessary to prove the alleged defamatory statement was: (1) false; (2) made publicly to a person to whom the accuser has no legitimate excuse to talk about the subject of the accusation; (3) not made in good faith; and (4) made with malice (citation omitted).

As we have previously discussed, plaintiff's accusations were not totally unfounded and her suspicions were justifiably aroused. However, without regard to truth or falsity, there is no evidence that any statements made to others by the plaintiff were made with malice. Plaintiff, a beautician, apparently confided to her fellow beautician her belief that defendant was dating other women. There is nothing in the record to suggest that this was done with malice or was anything other than one person seeking sympathy or advice from another. A fellow employee of defendant testified that while he was working one day plaintiff came and asked him if "that woman" left. On another occasion as this same individual was walking past the parties' residence, plaintiff asked him "what woman Eugene was talking to." Again, we can discern no evidence of malice on the part of the plaintiff in making these vague inquiries and there is nothing to indicate that plaintiff acted other than in good faith. In view of these facts and circumstances and the applicable law and jurisprudence we find no error in the trial court's failure to find fault on the part of the plaintiff on the grounds of public defamation. . . .

. . . Considering the evidence as a whole we are unable to find any abuse of discretion in the trial court's awarding plaintiff permanent periodic alimony in the amount of $150 per month.

For the reasons assigned, we affirm the judgment of the trial court.

AFFIRMED.

The 1960s and 1970s also saw a change in society's view of men, women, and marriage. More opportunities were available to women so they could become economically self-sufficient. In addition, marriage was no longer viewed as a master/servant relationship, but rather an economic partnership, where the contributions of the wife as homemaker were also gaining a new respect.

The modern view of marriage is much like that of a business partnership, whereupon dissolution of the entity, the partners are entitled to a fair division of the marital assets. The courts prefer property division awards as opposed to alimony because the parties can make a "clean break" and go their separate ways, much like business partners. Alimony does not coincide with this modern view of marriage because there is still a legal tie between former spouses.

While most states gender-neutralized their alimony statutes on their own initiative, other states resisted until court intervention required such a change. For instance, the Supreme Court of the United States in *Orr v. Orr,* 440 U.S. 268 (1979), held that an Alabama statute imposing the obligation on the husband alone to pay alimony was unconstitutional in that it violated the Fourteenth Amendment's Equal Protection Clause. While the court may impose the duty to pay alimony on either spouse, the reality is that women are still earning less than men and comprise the majority of alimony recipients today. Spouses most likely to obtain alimony for a significant period of time are those who have been in long-term marriages (over ten years), have given up career opportunities to raise a family and care for the home, or those that are ill or have a disability and cannot work. Alimony may also be awarded to a spouse for a limited period of time, allowing the opportunity to become self-sufficient. Alimony is also appropriate if the parties do not have substantial assets and periodic payments would provide for the needs of a spouse. It is also crucial that the payor spouse be employed and have a stable work record. When substantial property is involved, property division is preferred for the purpose of allowing parties to make a clean break. From the ecclesiastical view to present, we have seen alimony evolve from a punishment to compensate a spouse for the bad acts of another, to a vehicle for providing economic support for a spouse.

Parties are free to negotiate an agreement regarding the amount of alimony to be paid. If the parties cannot agree, the court must make that decision. The determination of alimony is within the **discretion of the court.** This means that the court has the power to make the alimony decision and that an appellate court will not reverse that decision unless the judge somehow abused his discretion. The parties are also free to agree to a waiver, meaning that they will not seek an alimony award in the divorce case. Consider the following excerpt from *Lawsuits of the Rich and Famous:*

> But husbands are no longer the only ones being taken to the proverbial cleaners. *Good Morning America's* Joan Lunden irked some feminists in 1992 when she expressed ire over the $18,000 per month which she was told to hand over to Michael Krauss, 54, her husband of 14 years. A Westchester County judge also deemed that Ms. Lunden was also liable for the mortgage on the couple's 10-room house, as well as property taxes, fuel, electricity, cable TV bills, and payments on his life and health insurance. Hardcore women's libbers, who think that professional women should accept the spankings which sometimes come with professional territory, were miffed when the ordinarily good-natured hostess snarled, "This is a deplorable and shameful statement on how working women are treated."
>
> Feminist attorney Gloria Allred saw justice in the decision, telling *People* magazine, "If we want to make advances in women's rights, we can't deny men

their rights." But the National Organization for Women came to Lunden's defense, saying she was the victim of "the judicial version of 'Gotcha!'" Then, as if to pour salt on the wound, Lunden told *Redbook* magazine that she had sometimes superseded her ex-husband's ego, even on trivial matters; "Michael always wanted the reservations in his name. But with my name we would call at the last minute and still get a good table at a busy restaurant. . . ."

Ms. Lunden's remarks sparked responses from advocates for men's rights in the 1990's. Sidney Siller, founder and president of the National Organization for Men, a New York lawyer and the author of a men's rights column for *Penthouse* magazine, told the *San Francisco Chronicle*, "The peal of anguish that went up from women after the Joan Lunden case smacked of hypocrisy. There's not a level playing ground in the courts for men. . . . I've got one case on appeal, a man who is a disabled World War II veteran. His wife is working as an executive. For 40 years of marriage, she was always the main support, while he did work in houses they bought and sold. The judge denied him alimony because he had become an alcoholic. He would have been responsible for her, clearly, if the situation had been reversed."

If the Joan Lunden case constituted a reversal, then consider the $10 million which aerobics empress Jane Fonda has handed over to California Assemblyman Tom Hayden, even though Hayden himself reportedly only earns about $50,000 annually (Ms. Fonda, now married to cable entrepreneur and Atlanta Braves owner Ted Turner, is worth between $60 million and $100 million); or contemplate the $75,000 Goldie Hawn paid to get away from hubby Gus Trikonis in 1976, only to turn about five years later and relinquish half of her assets to spouse number two, Bill Hudson.

Or take the 1991 divorce case of Jane Seymour. In May of that year, the Santa Monica Superior Court awarded her husband, real estate developer David Flynn, $10,000 a month through 1994, plus coverage by Seymour of $500,000 in debts owed by Flynn's company and half the value of their $5 million Santa Barbara home, their furniture and their art.

Georgia beauty Kim Basinger is another wife caught up in the divorce courts' new-found sense of equity. In 1988, afraid that her ex-husband would go to the tabloids with tales of what he termed her "flamboyant affairs," she forked over to him $64,000 in support and the keys to their $700,000 Los Angeles home.

Likewise stung was designer Mary McFadden, 56, who in 1992 paid Kohle Yohannan, 26, her husband of a mere 22 months, $100,000 in alimony. According to *Parade Magazine*, things got nasty in that one when Yohannan claimed he had been "the victim of a much older, selfish alcoholic woman." She bit back, calling him a "spaced-out delinquent," a "known homosexual," and alleging that he was unable to consummate their marriage.

The mud began to fly, too, in the early rounds of divorce proceedings between Roseanne and Tom Arnold, in 1994. She renewed claims of spousal abuse by Tom and provided photographs of bruises she said were inflicted by her husband; she also resubmitted documents she said she had earlier withdrawn because she was afraid of Arnold. As for Arnold, he followed the lead of Flynn, Yohannan and others when he declared that he was unemployed and would need $100,000 per month in support. He also alleged that Roseanne had "plundered" his belongings and thrown his wardrobe into the pool at their Brentwood mansion.

Excerpt from *Lawsuits of the Rich and Famous* by W. Kelsea Wilbur Eckert and Jeff Trippe, pp. 34–36. Used with permission.

DETERMINING ALIMONY

State alimony statutes set forth a list of criteria to be weighed by the judge in evaluating whether or not an award of alimony is appropriate. Although the court considers each statutory factor, it does not have to give each factor equal weight. The court may focus on any number of factors depending on the circumstances of the case.

The California and Florida statutes presented next outline an example of statutory criteria considered by the family courts in determining whether an alimony award is appropriate.

STATUTES

WEST'S ANNOTATED CALIFORNIA CIVIL CODE

§ 4320. Determination of amount due for support; circumstances in ordering spousal support under this part, the court shall consider all of the following circumstances:

(a) The extent to which the earning capacity of each party is sufficient to maintain the standard of living established during the marriage, taking into account all of the following:

1. The marketable skills of the supported party and the job market for those skills; the time and expenses required for the supported party to acquire the appropriate education or training to develop those skills; and the possible need for retraining or education to acquire other, more marketable skills or employment.

2. The extent to which the supported party's present or future earning capacity is impaired by periods of unemployment that were incurred during the marriage to permit the supported party to devote time to domestic duties.

(b) The extent to which the supported party contributed to the attainment of an education, training, a career position, or a license by the supporting party.

(c) The ability to pay of the supporting party, taking into account the supporting party's earning capacity, earned and unearned income, assets, and standard of living.

(d) The needs of each party based on the standard of living established during the marriage.

(e) The obligations and assets, including the separate property of each party.

(f) The duration of the marriage.

(g) The ability of the supported party to engage in gainful employment without unduly interfering with the interests of dependent children in the custody of the party.

(h) The age and health of the parties.

(i) The immediate and specific tax consequences to each party.

(j) Any other factors the court determines are just and equitable.

FLORIDA STATUTES ANNOTATED (WEST)

61.08 Alimony

1. In a proceeding for dissolution of marriage, the court may grant alimony to either party, which alimony may be rehabilitative or permanent in nature. In any award of alimony, the court may order periodic payments or payments in lump sum or both. The court may consider the adultery of either spouse or the circumstances thereof in determining the amount of alimony, if any, to be awarded. In all dissolution actions, the court shall include findings of fact relative to the factors enumerated in subsection (2) supporting an award or denial of alimony.

2. In determining a proper award of alimony or maintenance, the court shall consider all relevant economic factors, including but not limited to:
   (a) The standard of living established during the marriage.
   (b) The duration of the marriage.
   (c) The age and the physical and emotional condition of each party.
   (d) The financial resources of each party, the nonmarital and the marital assets and liabilities distributed to each.
   (e) When applicable, the time necessary for either party to acquire sufficient education or training to enable such party to find appropriate employment.
   (f) The contribution of each party to the marriage, including, but not limited to, services rendered in homemaking, childcare, education, and career building of the other party.
   (g) All sources of income available to either party.
   The court may consider any other factor necessary to do equity and justice between the parties.

3. To the extent necessary to protect an award of alimony, the court may order any party who is ordered to pay alimony to purchase or maintain a life insurance policy or a bond, or to otherwise secure such alimony award with any other assets which may be suitable for that purpose. . . .

Statutory criteria are also important in negotiations. Lawyers will prepare with the statute in mind, looking at each factor in light of the facts within the particular client's case. If the jurisdiction's alimony statute does not enumerate criteria for determining alimony, it is important to check local case law. In considering an alimony award, the courts will examine the payor's ability to pay versus the recipient spouse's needs.

Balancing Need versus Ability to Pay

While Mr. Adkins, an attorney, clearly had the ability to pay, Mrs. Adkins failed to demonstrate her need for alimony to the court.

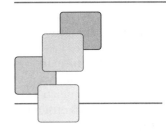

PAMELA S. ADKINS V. MILTON R. ADKINS

650 So.2d 61 (1994)

Florida District Court of Appeals, Third District

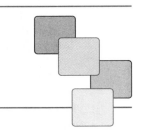

HUBBART, JUDGE.

This is an appeal by the wife, Pamela S. Adkins, and a cross-appeal by the husband, Milton R. Adkins, from an amended final judgment of marriage dissolution entered after a non-jury trial. For the reasons which follow, we affirm in part and reverse in part.

The wife on the main appeal raises a multitude of points which center around two general arguments containing a large number of related subpoints. . . . Second, it is urged that the trial court erred in failing to award the wife alimony and attorney's fees. . . .

. . . I. In the instant case, the parties married in 1978; it was the second marriage for both parties. There were no children borne of the marriage and the husband filed for dissolution of the marriage in 1987. The trial court made the following relevant findings in the amended final judgment under review:

. . . Each party entered this marriage with substantial assets. The Husband has estimated his net worth to approximate Five Hundred Thousand Dollars ($500,000.00), and the Wife has estimated hers to approximate Two Hundred Fifty Thousand Dollars ($250,000.00). Among the assets owned by the Husband was his home located at 3502 Alhambra Circle, Coral Gables, Florida, its furnishings, various investment properties, and a pension plan.

During the course of marriage, the parties, by agreement, maintained separate bank accounts, separate accounting records, and separate business interests. The Wife inherited from family members substantial assets consisting primarily of real estate and tillable farmland and having a net worth of approximately Two Million Dollars. During this marriage, the Wife managed her inherited property, churned her stock holdings profitably, and reinvested the profits of her labor in other property interests including income-producing property in North Carolina and a Shoney's Restaurant in South Carolina. At no time did the Wife share with her husband the fruits of her labor or the profits resulting therefrom. In fact, the Wife requested that the Husband reimburse her for any and all expenses she incurred from which the Husband and/or one of his assets may have derived a benefit.

The Husband worked diligently during this marriage to provide the Wife with a comfortable lifestyle. She was provided with a maid five days a week, a beautiful home, and an environment which included trips to Europe and elsewhere. In return for his labor, the Husband asked the Wife to abide by her premarital promise to provide a "nest," using the Wife's words, to be his companion and friend, and to be there when he returned from work. Instead, the Wife, for reasons unexplained, chose to lead a singular and self-gratifying lifestyle. For example, she would disappear from the home without notice or explanation for days, weeks, or even for months at a time. She hesitated to be a homemaker in any of the traditional senses. Although these responsibilities are not required by today's environment, they were the responsibilities that were

promised by the Wife to the Husband and they were the reasons that he was induced to marry her in the first instance. He had hoped to marry at last and forever and expressed to his wife his need for a warm, comfortable, and stable homeplace. The Wife argues that she redecorated the home and was responsible for the addition of a porch during the course of the marriage. The Husband does not deny that the Wife practiced her hobby of decorating, but does deny that such enhanced the value of his premarital asset or in any way provided a "substantial contribution" during the course of this marriage. The Court finds that the labors of the Wife were insubstantial and not the cause of any enhancement in the value of the Husband's home. As such, the Husband's home and contents were and shall remain an asset owned solely by him free of any claim or encumbrance in favor or the Wife. . . .

. . . With respect to the denial of Wife's request for alimony, the trial court made the following relevant findings in the amended final judgment:

"The Wife has advanced a claim for the award of temporary, permanent, rehabilitative, and/or lump-sum alimony, in this cause. In support of her request, she states that she has lost her job and is presently receiving unemployment compensation as a result. While receiving unemployment compensation, the Court finds that the Wife has a net worth in excess of Two Million Dollars. In fact, while completing the weekly form work required by the Bureau of Unemployment Compensation, the Wife has managed and maintained her stock portfolio, reinvested moneys received through the sale of a small portion of real estate, effected a tax-free exchange of her South Carolina assets for investment property in North Carolina, and has acquired an interest in a Shoney's Restaurant. In short, the Wife is gainfully employed at this time, managing her substantial estate. The Court finds that the Wife fails to demonstrate the need or entitlement to receive alimony from the Husband. In fact, at no time during the long pendency of this case did the Wife request and receive alimony or support from the Husband."

Given the substantial wealth and income-producing property of the Wife, the relatively high earning capacity of the Wife, and the relatively short-term nature of this marriage, we see no abuse of the trials court's discretion in denying the Wife's request for alimony. For the same reason, we see no abuse of discretion in the trial court's denial of attorney's fees for the Wife. At the very least, reasonable people may differ as to the propriety of the trial court's ruling in this respect (citations omitted).

RESOURCES FOR ALIMONY

Ability to pay involves an evaluation of the resources available to the payor spouse. The court looks at the following resources of a payor spouse:

- income from principal employment;
- income from any additional employment;
- income from rental property;
- investment income;
- income from royalties, copyrights, patents, and trademark rights; and
- pension income.

To determine the amount of resources available, the court looks at the payor spouse's **net income.** Taxes, debts, and allowable expenses must be deducted from the spouse's **gross income.** Gross income refers to sum of all available sources of income. Net income is the dollar amount remaining after **allowable deductions** have been subtracted. These amounts must be carefully scrutinized because manipulation of these figures may occur during the course of the dissolution action. Some spouses intentionally reduce their income during the pendency of the case. They may refrain from taking promotions or raises, purposely cut down hours, drastically reduce commissions, get rid of a part-time job, or seek employment where they are paid cash "under the table." The payor spouse may also negotiate more fringe benefits from an employer for the purpose of showing less monetary compensation. The challenge for the payee spouse is to produce enough evidence to prove that the reduction in income was intentionally manipulated for the purpose of showing a smaller income. In this situation, it is essential that the discovery materials be reviewed carefully to determine whether the payor is living far beyond his or her means. Debts and expenses should also be scrutinized. Transfers to third parties, such as loans to family members and relatives, should also be looked on with suspicion. The question that must be asked is, was this debt or expense acquired in good faith?

DETERMINING SPOUSAL NEED

A spouse is entitled to an alimony award sufficient enough to support him or her in the standard of living to which he or she had grown accustomed during the marriage. If the office represents the spouse seeking alimony, instruct the client to keep a log of attempts to find work. It may be very crucial to preserve that information for trial later. Has spouse had difficulty finding work due to lack of marketable skills or age discrimination?

The client should also keep a log of all expenses during the course of the divorce case. Later on, the paralegal may review and help clarify how much money the client needs to live. As stated earlier in this chapter, more and more frequently, women are perfectly able to reenter the workforce and become self-supporting. Family courts take this into consideration when making alimony awards. The trend is to award no alimony at all or alimony that is short in duration. The courts will also look at the property available for division between the spouses. If there is a sufficient amount of property to distribute, then the courts are less likely to award alimony.

Alimony may also be awarded where the payee spouse has custody of small children and cannot work full time. Because day care can be very expensive, it may make more economic sense for the courts to make an alimony award at least until the children have reached the age where they are in school full time. The custodial parent will then have more opportunities to seek employment outside the home.

An award of alimony is highly probable in the case of an older homemaker who lacks the skills to go into the workforce or in the case of a spouse who is in poor health. The courts want to prevent a spouse from becoming a "charge on the state," that is, from having to apply for welfare and be supported by the taxpayers.

BALANCING PROPERTY DIVISION, CHILD SUPPORT, AND ALIMONY

Courts do not make alimony awards in a vacuum. Judges balance property division, child support, and alimony in order to reach an adequate resolution given the resources of the parties and their particular circumstances. Property awards divide the marital assets. Child support awards provide money paid to the custodial spouse for the benefit of the children. When there is an adequate amount of property, a property award may be more attractive, especially if the payor spouse's income or employment is unstable. If a spouse is steadily employed and income is stable, alimony may be a better choice. Some jurisdictions have even codified consideration of the property award in their alimony statutes. A higher child support award may be preferable in certain cases because the custodial parent does not have to declare child support payments as income for tax purposes. On the other hand, child support terminates when the child reaches the age of majority. The spouse is then left only with the more modest alimony payment.

TYPES OF ALIMONY

The court may order alimony during the pendency of the divorce action and at the time that it renders its final orders at the divorce trial or other judgment. At the time of making the final orders, the court may award or the parties may agree to either permanent, rehabilitative, or reimbursement alimony. This section describes the different types of alimony with which the paralegal should become familiar.

PENDENTE LITE ALIMONY

Pendente lite **alimony awards,** or temporary alimony awards, are payments made during the pendency of the divorce with the purpose of providing temporary financial support for the spouse. In order for a court to make a temporary alimony award, the payor spouse must be served with notice, be physically present in court, and be given the opportunity to be heard and present his or her side of the case.

The Florida, Massachusetts, and Alabama statutes cited next are examples of the family courts' statutory power to provide temporary support for spouses.

FIGURE 5–2
A court may reduce an alimony award once a payee spouse has entered the workforce and is gainfully employed.

STATUTES

FLORIDA STATUTES ANNOTATED (WEST)

61.71. *Alimony pendente lite; suit money*
In every proceeding for dissolution of the marriage, a party may claim alimony and suit money in the petition or by motion, and if the petition is well founded, the court shall allow a reasonable sum therefor. If a party in any proceeding for dissolution of marriage claims alimony or suit money in his or her answer or by motion, and the answer or motion is well founded, the court shall allow a reasonable sum therefor.

MASSACHUSETTS GENERAL LAW'S ANNOTATED (WEST)

§ 17. *Pendency of action; allowance; alimony*
The court may require either party to pay into court for the use of the other party during the pendency or the action an amount to enable him to maintain or defend the action, and to pay to him alimony during the pendency of the action. When the court makes an order for alimony on behalf of a party, and such party is not a member of a private group health insurance plan, the court shall include in such order for alimony a provision relating to health insurance, which provision shall be in accordance with section thirty-four.

CODE OF ALABAMA

§ 30-2-50. *Allowance for support during pendency of action.*
Pending an action for divorce, the court may make an allowance for the support of either spouse out of the estate of the other spouse, suitable to the spouse's estate and the condition in life of the parties, for a period of time not longer than necessary for the prosecution of the complaint for divorce.

FINAL ORDERS

WAIVER OF ALIMONY

On the day of the final divorce hearing, one or both of the spouses may wish to waive or relinquish their right to ask for alimony. If alimony is not awarded in the original divorce decree, the parties may not return to court to seek a modification later should the need arise. The same is true if the judgment is silent on the issue of alimony. Judges often canvass each spouse during the final divorce trial to determine if they have full knowledge of the **waiver of alimony** and its consequences. Lawyers should also advise clients of the effect of a waiver, making sure that they understand the legal implications, long before going in front of a judge.

NOMINAL ALIMONY

Instead of waiving alimony, a spouse may ask for **nominal alimony** in the amount of $1.00 per year. The purpose of nominal alimony is to allow the spouse to preserve his or her right to return to court in the event there is a change in circumstances and obtain alimony at a future date, even though it was not necessary at the time the original decree was entered. Obtaining an order of nominal alimony will ensure that the court has continuing jurisdiction to make modifications in the future.

A PICTURE IS WORTH $1.00

A husband's midlife-crisis decision to abandon his job in sales in exchange for an uncertain career in photography did not elicit sympathy from the court when it came to supporting his ex-wife. The District Court of Appeal of Florida reversed the trial court's decision refusing to award the wife $1 in permanent periodic alimony in the event husband's new career didn't pay off. This case also refers to **bridge-the-gap alimony,** which is defined as short-term, lump-sum alimony awarded to a spouse for the purpose of transitioning from married to single status. It is awarded based on the traditional concepts of alimony—need versus ability to pay—and does not terminate upon death or remarriage. It is designed to pay for short-term, one-time expenses such as a rental security deposit, moving expenses, buying a car to get to and from work, or deposits for utilities, which may be necessary when the spouse does not have credit.

ROBERTA C. BLANCHARD V. MARAN L.BLANCHARD

793 SO.2D 989 (FLA.APP. 2 DIST. 2001)

—— DISTRICT COURT OF APPEAL OF FLORIDA, SECOND DISTRICT ——

ALTENBERND, JUDGE.

Roberta C. Blanchard, the wife, appeals a final judgment dissolving her marriage to Maran L. Blanchard, the husband. We reverse the judgment to the extent that it required the wife to pay to the husband bridge-the-gap alimony because the evidence did not support the award. In addition, we conclude that the trial court abused its discretion when it failed to award the wife

$1 in permanent periodic alimony to reserve her future right to alimony in light of the husband's work history during this long-term marriage. We affirm the remaining provisions of the final judgment.

The Blanchards were married over thirty years, during which time they raised three children to adulthood. The wife worked as a teacher throughout the marriage. For most of this marriage, the husband sold recreational vehicles and earned significantly more income than his wife.

In 1997, the husband believed his sales position was in jeopardy. Rather than seek reemployment in the same industry, he decided to leave that field and develop a career in photography. This was a rather high-risk decision in light of the parties' modest standard of living and the husband's limited experience with photography.

The parties discussed this career change before the husband embarked on the venture. At trial, however, they disagreed about the wife's level of support for her husband's proposed career change. The wife admitted that she did not initially object to the plan, and that she permitted the investment of approximately $12,000 in marital funds to start the business. Although the husband perceived that the wife eagerly supported his decision, she testified that she privately hoped the husband would soon give up and return to his prior sales career. In essence, she believed that she was supporting her husband through a temporary mid-life crisis.

Both parties testified that they discussed the length of time the husband would pursue his new career to determine whether it would be profitable. The wife alleged that this "trial period" was three to six months, whereas the husband asserted that the parties talked about a time frame of a year. From May 1997, until the time of trial in September 1998, the wife financially supported the couple while they continued to live in the marital home. At the time of trial, the husband had been in the photography business for sixteen months, but still was not making any significant profit from the business. He testified that while his wife paid the household expenses, he was supporting himself on only a $100-per-week "draw" from the business account.

The trial court acknowledged that if the parties had divorced before 1997, the wife would have been entitled to permanent periodic alimony because of the length of the marriage, the historical incomes of the parties, and the other factors set forth in section 61.08, Florida Statutes (1999). Nevertheless, the trial court found that the wife acquiesced in the husband's decision to change careers, making this a marital decision that she could not, thereafter, unilaterally retract. As a result, the trial court granted the husband's request for "bridge-the-gap" alimony and required the wife pay him $500 per month

for one year. The trial court did not grant the wife any amount of permanent periodic alimony because her current income far exceeded the husband's. In the final judgment, however, the trial court acknowledged that the husband might need to reconsider his options if his photography business did not soon become profitable.

Although we concur with much of the trial court's reasoning, we cannot affirm the trial court's decisions regarding the alimony requested by each party. Based upon the evidence presented, the trial court erred in awarding the husband bridge-the-gap alimony. In addition, the trial court abused its discretion by failing to reserve jurisdiction to potentially award the wife permanent alimony in the future.

In *Borchard v. Borchard,* 730 So.2d 748 (Fla. 2d DCA 1999), this court recognized that a trial court has the authority to fashion an award of permanent, lump-sum alimony, paid over a set period, to ease a party's transition from married life to single life. We cautioned, however, that "bridge-the-gap alimony is not a tool to compromise adversarial positions but to assist a spouse with any legitimate, identifiable, short-term need under circumstances where a lump sum award is reasonable and when the other spouse has the ability to pay the award. . . . It is a useful tool in a relatively small category of divorces." *Id.* at 753.

In *Borchard,* we envisioned a scenario in which a spouse was unable, through his or her own best efforts, to provide for the essentials of a transition from married life to single life. We emphasized that in some cases, a spouse may be unable to afford "basic living requirements" because of a divorce, particularly when there is a "meager" distribution of assets. *See id.* at 752-53. Here, there was no evidence that the husband lacked his basic needs. He received over $60,000 in marital assets, and these assets happened to be the more liquid of the parties' holdings. The trial court's equitable distribution scheme relieved him of all responsibility for the parties' marital debts. In truth, the husband is trying to receive rehabilitative alimony, disguised as bridge-the-gap alimony, to assist him in a risky, new business venture when he already has considerable experience and skill in another field. An award of rehabilitative alimony, however, generally requires a rehabilitative plan that will result in an increase in the party's income. *See Ingram v. Ingram,* 750 So.2d 130 (Fla. 2d DCA 2000). We decline to extend the purpose of bridge-the-gap alimony to meet the "needs" the husband pursues in this case.

We recognize that the wife participated, even if by acquiescence, in this career change. In addition, although she asserted the husband could become immediately reemployed in the recreational vehicle sales field, she offered no competent, substantial evidence sufficient to support imputing income to the husband.

As a result, the trial court was correct in finding that no income should be imputed to the husband at this time, and that an award of any significant amount of permanent alimony to the wife was not appropriate. *See Gildea v. Gildea*, 593 So.2d 1212 (Fla. 2d DCA 1992).

Nevertheless, the trial court acknowledged that the husband's venture was likely either to become successful or to force him into a more profitable career sometime in the next few years. Because the business was new and the parties' circumstances were evolving, there was no means by which the trial court could judge the future viability of the wife's permanent periodic alimony claim. The historic incomes of the parties, the length of the marriage, the moderate marital assets,

and the wife's needs, however, required an award of a nominal amount of permanent alimony to permit the wife to pursue a future increase should the husband's full earning potential materialize. *See Wing v. Wing*, 429 So.2d 782 (Fla. 3d DCA 1983); *Moore v. Moore*, 401 So.2d 841 (Fla. 5th DCA 1981). *See also Stock v. Stock*, 693 So.2d 1080 (Fla. 2d DCA 1997). Under these circumstances, the trial court abused its discretion in failing to award the wife a nominal amount of permanent periodic alimony, thus reserving jurisdiction to revisit this claim as the parties' new lives develop. *See Strahan v. Strahan*, 605 So.2d 1316 (Fla. 4th DCA 1992). *See also Fusco v. Fusco*, 616 So.2d 86 (Fla. 4th DCA 1993).

PERMANENT ALIMONY

Permanent alimony is the term applied to court-ordered payments that are to be made to a spouse on a regular and periodic basis and that terminate only upon the death, remarriage, or cohabitation of the other spouse or upon court order. Permanent alimony is awarded with less frequency today. Women have increasingly joined the workforce and developed marketable employment skills to help them become self-sufficient. If you recall the historical discussion regarding the extension of the husband's duty to support after awarding divorce *a mensa et thoro*, you will see that the expanded role of women in the workplace has made permanent alimony a rare disposition in today's divorce courts. Spouses who are more likely to receive permanent alimony awards are those who have been in long-term marriages, those unable to acquire marketable skills, and those who are ill or have a disability. It is highly unlikely for spouses in these cases to be able to go to work and earn enough to adequately support themselves.

UNCERTAIN FUTURE

In cases where a client's medical condition involves periods of remission, it is important to remember that a relapse may occur that may result in periods of disability and inability to earn a living. In this case, a wife's diagnosis of Crohn's disease gave the court cause to be concerned for her future and affirmed the trial court's ruling in favor of permanent alimony.

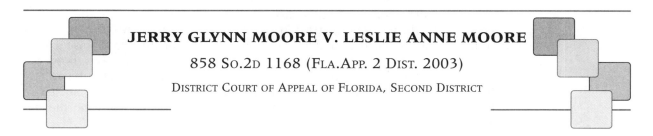

JERRY GLYNN MOORE V. LESLIE ANNE MOORE

858 So.2d 1168 (Fla.App. 2 Dist. 2003)

District Court of Appeal of Florida, Second District

CASANUEVA, JUDGE.

Jerry Glynn Moore, the Husband, appeals the final judgment of dissolution of marriage that awarded

Leslie Anne Moore, the Wife, $750 per month permanent alimony and made equitable distribution of the marital assets and liabilities. The Husband contends that the trial court erred in making the permanent alimony award by considering a future or anticipated event and by using the wrong income figure from the Wife's financial affidavits. We disagree and affirm the trial court's ruling.

The Moore's were married 9.7 years. At the time of trial, the Husband was 43 years old and the Wife was 32, with no children from the marriage. Two years prior to being married, the Wife was diagnosed with a debilitating disorder, Crohn's disease. Her condition worsened during the marriage, and she suffered periods of disability and inability to work. Because of her Crohn's disease, she had a number of surgeries and other treatments. However, at the time of trial the Wife was in remission, the duration of which could not be predicted with any certainty. Despite her illness, she was employed full-time as an administrative assistant at the time of the dissolution.

In making its determination to award the Wife permanent periodic alimony, the trial court found that the Wife had a gross income of $1542 per month, $533 monthly disability benefits scheduled to be suspended if she continued employment for roughly another month, and expenses of $2281 per month. The Husband was employed as a lineman for the power company. His gross monthly income was $6107 and net income was $3991. The trial court assessed the parties' relative financial resources and found a permanent alimony award of $750 per month reasonable. As a factor in making this award, the trial court said that it gave "major consideration to the Wife's debilitating illness and the testimony that she will undoubtedly suffer periods of remission and exacerbation of her illness which will, more than likely, result in her inability to fully support herself."

The Husband argues that the trial court's consideration of any potential progression of the disease violated the "well-settled rule" that the court could not consider future or anticipated events because of their speculative nature. *See Mallard v. Mallard,* 771 So.2d 1138, 1141 (Fla. 2000). Whether the trial court violated this "future event" rule of law is a legal issue and this court's review is de novo. *See Canakaris v. Canakaris,* 382 So.2d 1197, 1202 (Fla. 1980). As for the trial court's decision to award permanent alimony and the amount, this court's review is for abuse of discretion. *See Lowman v. Lowman,* 724 So.2d 648, 649 (Fla. 2d DCA 1999); *Murray v. Murray,* 598 So.2d 310, 312 (Fla. 2d DCA 1992).

It is clear that the trial court made its decision to award permanent alimony based on the statutory framework of section 61.08, Florida Statutes (2001), and not upon the occurrence of a future event. The court enumerated the factors and associated factual findings it considered, including the duration of the marriage, the couple's lifestyle, each party's physical and emotional health, and their respective financial resources, among others. Although the court's reference to the progressive nature of the Wife's Crohn's disease may have been misleading, her present medical condition was appropriately considered in accordance periodic alimony . . .

Affirmed.

Rehabilitative Alimony

The frequency of **rehabilitative alimony** awards reflects the current legal trend of providing short-term financial support to a former spouse. Rehabilitative alimony is awarded for a limited period of time to give the spouse the opportunity to become self-sufficient. In determining whether this type of alimony is appropriate, the crucial question to be answered is whether this spouse has the *ability* to become self-sufficient. For the traditional housewife who finds herself divorced after many years of marriage, and has never worked outside the home, this may not be possible; nor is it feasible for a disabled or ill spouse. In many cases, however, the spouse either has marketable skills or has the ability to obtain them within a reasonable period of time. Under these circumstances an award of rehabilitative alimony would provide the spouse with some financial assistance while she gets back on her feet.

Tennis Wife Gets Rehabilitative Alimony

The wife worked on more than her backhand in this marriage! In the end, Mrs. Evans had to join the workforce and establish a plan to become self-sufficient.

FIGURE 5-3
Judges can exercise their discretion when awarding rehabitative alimony while the payee spouse gets back on his or her feet.

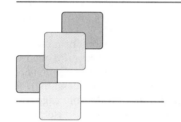

EDWIN E. EVANS v. CYNTHIA S. EVANS

559 N.W. 2D 240 (S.D. 1997)

SOUTH DAKOTA SUPREME COURT

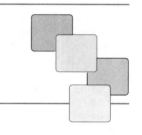

GILBERTSON, JUSTICE.

FACTS AND PROCEDURE

Ed and Cyndy were married in June 1973, following completion of Ed's first year of law school. Cyndy had completed her college degree and worked full time from the beginning of the marriage until the parties moved to Sioux Falls in June 1997. At that time Cyndy was expecting her first child. She did not return to the work force.

The parties' lifestyle was such that they belonged to a country club, had household help, and dined out frequently. They generally took two family vacations a year. The record reflects Ed worked many hours, including evenings and some weekends, and was often required to be out of town for days to weeks at a time. Cyndy volunteered her time in community, church, and school-related activities.

The parties have two children, Ashley and Kelsey, who were ages 17 and 14, respectively, at the time of the divorce trial. They attend parochial school and participate in many school and extracurricular activities. They drive late model cars and wear the best brand-named clothing. Cyndy has largely been responsible for coordinating the children's activities. While Ed was not available as much as Cyndy, he too took an interest in their children, assisting them with their homework and driving them to out-of-town functions.

In 1990, the parties began construction of a new home in Sioux Falls which ultimately cost considerably more money than had been originally planned. Around this time, Cyndy discontinued her volunteer activities and devoted her time instead to tennis and other personal interests. The parties admit they had problems with communication; the marriage began to deteriorate. In 1993, Cyndy invited a twenty-seven year old male tennis friend to move into the family's residence without discussing it with Ed and without his knowledge. When Ed learned of his wife's houseguest, he left home for a few days but returned at the childrens' request. He attempted to improve his relationship with Cyndy, but she showed little interest in attempts and spent evenings out with her friends, returning home in the early morning hours. Ed moved into a separate bedroom to show his displeasure, but the couple did not discuss their problems. By the summer of 1994, Cyndy had ceased attending family vacations, preferring instead to spend time with her friends at Lake Okoboji, while Ed and the children took family vacations without her. In the fall of 1994, Ed learned Cyndy was having an affair with a man who owned a home in Lake Okoboji. Although Cyndy initially denied the affair, she eventually admitted it was true. Upon learning this, Ed moved out of the parties' home.

Ed and Cyndy attempted a reconciliation, Cyndy promising to discontinue the affair and Ed promising to spend less time at work and more time with Cyndy and the children. Ed returned home, bought Cyndy a new car that she wanted, planned a family vacation in Jamaica for Thanksgiving, and purchased tickets for a concert Cyndy wanted to attend in Minneapolis. Within four days of Ed's return home, Cyndy announced she did not intend to stop seeing other men. Ed left home for the last time.

He continued spending time with Cyndy, however, and the family went on the planned vacation and to the concert and shopping trips in Minneapolis. Ed continued to provide spending money and paid the household expenses. He reduced his hours at work. Ed sought counseling and encouraged Cyndy to attend counseling sessions with him, or alone. She refused. Ed eventually gave up trying to reconcile the marriage.

During this period of separation, Ed paid Cyndy $10,000 per month to support her and their children. She stated they could not live on this amount. Ed suggested she sell the house. Cyndy refused and Ed filed the divorce action.

The trial court heard the matter over a four-day period, October 30–31, 1995, and on December 12–13, 1995. The trial court determined issues involving child support, property division, alimony award, and attorney fees. On February 16, 1996, the trial court awarded Ed a divorce on grounds of adultery and dismissed Cyndy's counterclaim. Both parties appealed the judgment of the trial court.

Cyndy raises . . . issues as follows. . . .

ANALYSIS AND DECISION

. . . 3. Whether the trial court erred in determining the amount of alimony awarded?

The trial court awarded Cyndy rehabilitative alimony of $2,500 per month for six months, and $1,000 per month for five years thereafter. Cyndy's vocational expert opined, and the trial court found, that she would be able to earn $25,000 per year within three to five years, after retraining and reentering the work force. Cyndy appeals this award, arguing she is entitled to substantially more alimony. She bases her argument on her years of service to the marriage as a wife and homemaker and the vast discrepancy between earning capabilities of the parties.

Our standard of review of challenges to a trial court's award of alimony is well established. *Dussart v. Dussart*, 1996 S.D. 41, 546 NW2d 109, 111; *DeVries v. DeVries*, 519 N.W.2d 73, 77 (S.D. 1994).

A trial court is vested with discretion in awarding alimony and its decision will not be disturbed unless it clearly appears the trial court abused its discretion. Trial courts must consider the following factors when setting an alimony award: (1) the length of the marriage; (2) the parties' respective ages and health; (3) the earning capacity of each party; (4) their financial situations after the property division; (5) their station in life or social standing; and (6) the relative fault in the termination of the marriage. A trial court's findings on these factors must support its legal conclusions. As often stated, an abuse of discretion exists only where discretion has been "exercised to an end or purpose not justified by, and clearly against, reason and evidence."

Additional factors must be considered when the trial court makes an award of rehabilitative alimony. *Saint Pierre v. Saint Pierre*, 357 N.W.2d 250, 252 (S.D. 1984). In awarding rehabilitative or reimbursement alimony, the trial court should be guided by "the amount of supporting spouse's contributions, his or her foregone [sic] opportunities to enhance or improve professional or vocational skills, and the duration of the marriage following completion of the nonsupporting spouse's professional education." *Id.* An award of rehabilitative alimony must be designed to meet an educational need or plan of action whose existence finds some support in the record. *Radigan*, 465 N.W.2d at 486; *Ryken v. Ryken*, 440 N.W.2d 300, 303 (S.D. 1989) (*Ryken I*). "[T]he decision to award 'reimbursement' or 'rehabilitative' alimony, and, if so, in what amount and for what length of time, is committed to the sound discretion of the trial court. The purpose of rehabilitative alimony is to put the supporting spouse in a position to likewise upgrade their own economic marketability." *Studt v. Studt*, 443 N.W.2d 639, 643 (S.D. 1989) (internal citations omitted).

A review of the record in this case demonstrates the trial court's consideration of all the necessary factors, including Cyndy's traditional role of homemaker {4} and the parties discrepancy in earning capabilities. {5} The trial court also considered Cyndy's financial situation after the property division and her fault in the dissolution of the parties' marriage and lack of cooperation in Ed's efforts to save the marriage. In granting a divorce in favor of Ed on the basis of adultery, the trial court had before it numerous examples of uncontested marital misconduct by Cyndy upon which to base its finding of fault:

1. Moving into the family home a twenty-seven year old male tennis friend without Ed's prior knowledge or consent;

2. Refusing to attend family vacations as in the past, but rather vacationing at Lake Okoboji with friends;

3. Having an affair with a man who owned a home at Lake Okoboji;

4. Refusing to stop seeing other men after Ed found out about the affair, and when Ed attempted reconciliation, and

5. Refusing to attend when Ed sought counseling and encouraged Cyndy to attend either with him or alone.

The trial court properly concluded that Cyndy's fault was a factor to be taken into account in deciding alimony.

Following division of the marital property, Cyndy leaves the marriage with over one million dollars in assets. Approximately $400,000 of these assets are in the form of cash payments to be paid to Cyndy by Ed either immediately or over a period of the next five years at 7% interest on the unpaid balance. The trial court found that, through conservative investment, Cyndy's liquid assets would provide annual income to her of $40,792, or 3,399 per month, without invading the principal. Following three to five years of wage-earning, this monthly income would rise to $4,782 per month. The trial court specifically noted that Cyndy would not be able to live in the luxurious lifestyle she enjoyed while married to Ed but, at the same time, should not be able to demand excessive long-term support from the husband to whom she did not wish to be married. The

trial court concluded Cyndy should be able to live comfortably on the amount awarded. The court acknowledged Cyndy's contribution to the family's accumulation of wealth and her husband's success, and further noted the award was justified due to Cyndy's forgone employment opportunities during the parties' twenty-two year marriage. We cannot say the trial court's award was against reason and the evidence.

Regarding "educational need or plan of action" that must be evidenced from the record for an award of rehabilitative alimony, *Radigan,* 465 N.W.2d at 486, Cyndy presented herself for evaluation by the vocational rehabilitation specialist who testified on her behalf. Following his evaluation, which included a personal interview with Cyndy, taking her educational and work history, and submitting her to various vocational and personality-type testing, this expert concluded Cyndy's best course of action for reentering the work force would be to complete approximately six months of select computer courses at a vocational school and begin work in an entry-level position in the banking field. Cyndy had worked in banking before the parties moved to Sioux Falls in 1977 and her test scores in the vocational evaluation demonstrated a high interest and ability in this area. Her test scores also were high in the fields of business and sales. Although Cyndy did not express to this specialist any specific plans for employment or retraining during their interview, it was noted by the expert at trial that this is not unusual for a person who had not been career-minded during a long marriage and is presently going through a divorce. The vocational rehabilitation specialist testified he and Cyndy discussed assistance with her career development after the divorce.

We affirm on this issue. . . .

REIMBURSEMENT ALIMONY

As the following chapter illustrates, some jurisdictions have categorized a professional or advanced degree acquired during the marriage as marital property. This categorization has enabled the courts to put a monetary value on the degree and to award the nondegreed spouse either money or other property for his or her contributions made during the marriage that enabled the other spouse to obtain the degree. Many jurisdictions, however, do not categorize a degree as property. This would leave the nondegreed spouse uncompensated for the sacrifices endured in hopes that their family would have a better future. Courts, however, have responded to this injustice by creating the **reimbursement alimony** award. Here, the nondegreed spouse may be "reimbursed" for his or her contribution to the student spouse's attainment of the advanced degree, which results in an enhanced earning capacity. The nondegreed spouse may have helped pay the student spouse's tuition, supported the family while the student spouse was in school, or relocated or put off pursuing his or her own education in hopes that these sacrifices would later pay off in an increased standard of living. In these jurisdictions, the nondegreed spouse is reimbursed for the monetary and nonmonetary efforts that enhanced the other spouse's earning capacity. Reimbursement alimony awards are generally non-modifiable and nonterminable so as to fully compensate the nondegreed spouse.

ADVANCED DEGREE DILEMMA

In a case of first impression, the Vermont Supreme Court determines how to compensate a spouse who has sacrificed her career goals in order to advance her husband's aspirations. The injustice occurs when, upon receiving his degree, the student spouse files for divorce long before the wife had a chance to enjoy the fruits of *her* labor.

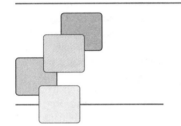

KEVIN A. DOWNS V. SUSAN A. DOWNS

154 VT. 161, 574 A.2D 156 (1990)

SUPREME COURT OF VERMONT

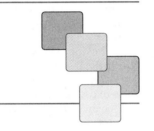

GIBSON, J.

Plaintiff and defendant both appeal from a provision in their divorce decree that sought to compensate defendant Susan Downs for funds contributed during the marriage toward plaintiff Kevin Downs' attainment of a medical degree. We reverse and remand the case for further proceedings consistent with the views expressed herein.

I

Kevin and Susan were married in August of 1976. At that time, Kevin, who had just graduated from college, and Susan, who had completed three years of university study, agreed that she would leave school and work while he attended medical school. Susan worked as a clerk at a department store from the fall of 1976 until March of 1980, a month before the birth of the parties' first child. Most of her salary was used to pay for living expenses while Kevin attended school; Kevin borrowed money through various loans to pay for his school expenses. Susan did not work outside the home after the birth of the parties' first child, and a second child was born in 1982, at which time Kevin was in the midst of a four-year medical residency at the Medical Center Hospital of Vermont. In August of 1983, Kevin moved out of the family home, and later that year, moved in with

another woman and her two children. Shortly thereafter, he filed for divorce. After finishing his residency in 1984, he began working as an obstetrician and gynecologist in practice with another doctor at an initial salary of approximately $60,000 a year, with an expectation of earning up to $200,000 a year in the near future.

After a hearing in July of 1984, the court granted Kevin a divorce and awarded custody of the children to Susan. The court also awarded her $1000 worth of home furnishings and a partially paid family car, and ordered that Kevin pay (1) $500 a month to Susan in rehabilitative maintenance for five years, (2) $500 a month per child in child support, (3) the children's health insurance, plus all reasonable medical, dental and hospital expenses not covered by insurance, (4) all reasonable expenses for higher education for the children, and (5) $50,590 to Susan within five years, a sum representing the total salary earned by her during the years she worked while Kevin attended medical school, plus interest at the rate of ten percent compounded annually.

In reaching the $50,590 figure, the court reasoned that an educational degree is not property, but that "the increased earning potential made possible by the degree is an asset to be distributed by the court." The court then proceeded to make its disposition of Kevin's enhanced earning potential under the property settlement statute,

15 V.S.A. § 751. The court considered itself unable, however, to award Susan any portion of the increase in Kevin's earning potential resulting from his medical degree because, while there was expert testimony that he could expect future earnings with a discounted present value of three million dollars, there was no testimony regarding the differential in earning capacity between a person with a four-year college degree and a person with a medical degree. Because of this, the court felt confined to making an award based on restitution, which it determined to be $50,590.

Following Susan's motion to alter or amend the order and for a partial new trial, the court held a second hearing and issued a revised order, awarding her $125,000 for Kevin's enhanced earning capacity and $77,281 for her nonmonetary contributions to the marriage. Kevin appealed the revised order, and we reversed the judgment, reinstating the original order because the revised order had not been issued until after the expiration of the nisi period. *Downs v. Downs,* 150 Vt. 647, 549 A.2d 1382 (1988) (mem.). Susan now appeals the original order, seeking a property division or maintenance award that reflects Kevin's increased earning potential resulting from his degree and her nonmonetary contributions to the marriage. In his cross-appeal, Kevin claims that the court erred in making its property disposition, arguing that, since he did not have the ability to pay the restitution amount at the time of the divorce, the order amounted to an improper award of property not acquired during the marriage.

II

In a case of first impression in Vermont, we consider the "diploma dilemma." The issue is what remuneration is available to a spouse who sacrifices career opportunities in order to further the other spouse's attainment of a professional degree, only to see his or her expectations of future financial security undermined when the student spouse, upon receiving the degree, shortly thereafter seeks a divorce. Although the trial court retains wide discretion in fashioning property and maintenance awards, *Buttura v. Buttura,* 143 Vt. 95, 99, 463 A.2d 229, 231 (1983), any award must fall within the flexible confines of Vermont's statutory guidelines. See 15 V.S.A. §§ 751, 752 . . .

Before addressing Vermont's relevant statutory provisions, we review how other jurisdictions have handled this issue. A few courts have held that a professional degree or the enhanced earning potential that it represents is a marital asset subject to distribution upon divorce of the parties. See, e.g., *In re Marriage of Horstmann,* 263 N.W.2d 885, 891 (Iowa 1978);

Woodworth v. Woodworth, 126 Mich. App. 258, 261, 337 N.W.2d 332, 334 (1983); *O'Brien v. O'Brien,* 66 N.Y.2d 576, 586–88, 489 N.E.2d 712, 717–18, 498 N.Y.S.2d 743, 748–49 (1985). In *O'Brien,* the court stated that a professional license constituted marital property, but based its decision on the state's Equitable Distribution Law, in which the court found a clear legislative mandate to include an interest in a professional license as marital property. *O'Brien,* 66 N.Y.2d at 583–84, 489 N.E.2d at 715, 498 N.Y.S.2d at 746.

Some courts have held that a professional degree is not an asset to be divided, but that the supporting spouse is entitled to compensation for the amount of his or her investment in the student spouse's education. See, e.g., *DeLa Rosa v. DeLa Rosa,* 309 N.W.2d 755, 759 (Minn. 1981) (supporting spouse awarded lump sum equalling monies she spent toward student spouse's living and educational expenses); *Hubbard v. Hubbard,* 603 P.2d 747, 751–52 (Okla. 1979) (supporting spouse entitled to lump-sum award in lieu of property to prevent unjust enrichment). Under certain circumstances, for instance where there is insufficient property to divide, other courts have provided "reimbursement alimony" or "rehabilitative alimony" awards rather than lump-sum awards. See, e.g., *Saint-Pierre v. Saint-Pierre,* 357 N.W.2d 250, 253 (S.D. 1984) (court should award reimbursement alimony in proper case); cf. *Mahoney v. Mahoney,* 91 N.J. 488, 501–05, 453 A.2d 527, 534–36 (1982) (only issue at trial was reimbursement claim, but degree holder's earning capacity was held to be a factor in determining permanent alimony, which could be adjusted in future if actual earnings diverged greatly from court's estimate). These courts point out that a professional degree, unlike a vested pension whose value can be readily computed, provides nothing more than the possibility of enhanced earnings that may never be realized. See *id.* at 496–97, 453 A.2d at 531–32.

The majority of courts have found fertile, neutral ground between the approaches described above. These courts hold that a professional degree is not an asset subject to property distribution upon divorce, but, in the interest of justice and equity, fashion a maintenance award using the increased earning potential of the spouse with the degree as a relevant factor in determining an appropriate award. See, e.g., *In re Marriage of Olar,* 747 P.2d 676, 680–81 (Colo. 1987) (en banc); *Drapek v. Drapek,* 399 Mass. 240, 246, 503 N.E.2d 946, 950 (1987); *Stevens v. Stevens,* 23 Ohio St.3d 115, 120, 492 N.E.2d 131, 135 (1986); *DeWitt v. DeWitt,* 98 Wis.2d 44, 60–61, 296 N.W.2d 761, 769 (1980); cf. *Washburn v. Washburn,* 101 Wn.2d 168, 176–79, 677 P.2d 152, 157–58 (1984) (en banc) (increased earning potential is a relevant factor in making maintenance award; no need to address "metaphysical" question of whether professional degree is property). According to these courts, an award of a lump sum would be based on speculative future earnings of the degree holder and amount to an improper attempt to apportion after-acquired property. See, e.g., *DeWitt*, 98 Wis.2d at 58–59, 296 N.W.2d at 768. Further, because a maintenance award is subject to later modification, in contrast to a property award, which may not be modified, such an award could be adjusted as a result of the effect of future events on the earning capacity of the spouse holding the degree. See, e.g., *Drapek*, 399 Mass. at 244, 503 N.E.2d at 949. This approach accords with existing Vermont law. 15 V.S.A. § 758; *Ellis v. Ellis*, 135 Vt. 83, 85, 370 A.2d 200, 201–02 (1977).

We agree with the majority reasoning and hold that increased earning capacity is not property subject to distribution under 15 V.S.A. § 751. Thus, the trial court erred in treating Kevin's increased earning potential as an asset to be disposed of under the property settlement statute. Indeed, under § 751 "the contribution by one spouse to the education, training, or increased earning power of the other" is one of the factors to be considered in making a property settlement, 15 V.S.A. § 751(b)(5); hence, it is logical to conclude that increased earning power itself is not marital property. See *Hodge v. Hodge*, 337 Pa. Super. 151, 156, 486 A.2d 951, 953 (1984) (court reached similar conclusion under similar statute). Of course, as provided in § 751(b)(5) and depending upon the circumstances, contributions to increased earning power could be a significant factor in determining a fair distribution of marital property. See *Mahoney*, 91 N.J. at 504, 453 A.2d at 535–36.

In situations as in the instant case, however, where there is not enough property to fairly compensate the supporting spouse for contributions toward the other spouse's attainment of a degree, Vermont's maintenance statute, 15 V.S.AO § 752, is sufficiently flexible to permit the court's consideration of the future earning prospects of the student spouse. Under § 752(a), a court may order permanent or rehabilitative maintenance payments if it finds that the spouse seeking maintenance (1) lacks sufficient income, property, or

both, "to provide for his or her reasonable needs," and (2) cannot support himself or herself "through appropriate employment at the standard of living established during the marriage or is the custodian of a child of the parties." We agree with the Colorado Supreme Court in *Olar*, which construed similar statutory language in a case addressing the same issue that is now before us. That court stressed the word "reasonable" in the phrase "reasonable needs" and "appropriate" in the phrase "appropriate employment," emphasizing that maintenance can be a tool to balance equities whenever the financial contributions of one spouse enable the other spouse to enhance his or her future earning capacity. *Olar*, 747 P.2d at 681–82. Thus, "reasonable needs" can mean more than mere sustenance and "appropriate employment" more than the ability to find work. *Id.* "[M]aintenance is not just a means of providing bare necessities, but rather a flexible tool by which the parties' standard of living may be equalized for an appropriate period of time." *Washburn*, 101 Wn. 2d at 179, 677 P.2d at 158.

Once the threshold criteria of § 752(a) have been met, the court shall award maintenance "in such amounts and for such periods of time *as the court deems just*, after considering *all relevant factors* including, *but not limited to*" such components as the financial resources of the party seeking maintenance, the property settlement awarded to that party, the party's ability to meet his or her needs independently, and the time and expense necessary for the party seeking maintenance to acquire an education so that he or she can find appropriate employment. § 752(b)(1) and (2) (emphasis added).

The scope of the statute is clearly broad enough to permit courts to consider the increased earning capacity engendered by a professional degree in determining an award of maintenance. Accordingly, we hold that, when one spouse obtains a professional degree during the marriage, but the marriage ends before the benefits of the degree can be realized, the future value of the professional degree is a relevant factor to be considered in reaching a just and equitable maintenance award . . .

MODES OF ALIMONY PAYMENT

Alimony payments may be made on a **periodic** basis (i.e., weekly), or they may be made in one single payment, known as **lump sum alimony** or **alimony in gross.** Once a spouse receives an award of lump sum alimony, his or her interest has vested. This means that he or she is entitled to the entire amount. This amount may be made in installments, if agreed upon by the parties or ordered by the court.

MODIFICATION OF ALIMONY

Modification of alimony addresses the issue of whether alimony may be either increased or decreased after the original order has been entered. To change or "modify" an alimony award, the party seeking the modification must go back to court and request that the court modify the original order. The moving party must prove that a substantial change of circumstances occurred since the date of the original order and that the change was involuntary. Because the court made the original order, only the court can change the obligations of the parties. For example, *pendente lite* orders may be modified during the *pendente lite* phase as long as the moving party can satisfy his or her burden of proof.

EXAMPLE

> John, who is employed at a factory, files for divorce. His wife Mary files a motion for pendente lite or temporary alimony. Based on her need and John's ability to pay, she is awarded $100 a week. John loses his job and does not pay Mary for ten weeks. John owes Mary $1,000 in alimony **arrearages** or "back alimony."

Upon losing his job, John should have immediately filed a motion for modification with the court. He would then be able to get the original $100 order modified because of a substantial change in circumstances, that is, the loss of his job. Once Mary stops receiving payments, she has the right to the arrearage, or amounts due by court order but unpaid. Mary may seek to enforce the original order by returning to court.

Final orders may also be modified upon a showing of a substantial change in circumstances. A party may request an order of one dollar of alimony per year. Obviously, this is only a nominal alimony amount; however, a request for such an award is necessary so the party may seek a modification after the entering of a final judgment. If no alimony is awarded to the spouse at the time the divorce decree is entered, he or she will be prohibited from coming back to court and seeking an alimony award in the future, because no basis exists for modifying it. The reason for the one dollar award is so that a nominal amount of alimony will leave the issue of alimony modifiable in the future in the event of a substantial change in circumstances.

Remember that an alimony award may be achieved in one of two ways: by agreement of the parties or by order of the court. When the parties are drafting an agreement, the modifiability of the alimony award must be addressed in the settlement agreement. While the parties may have agreed to the nonmodifiability of alimony and included such a clause in the separation agreement, the court may not enforce such a provision if a spouse would have to go on public assistance and be supported at taxpayers' expense.

Permanent alimony may be modified if there is a substantial change in circumstances. Remarriage automatically terminates permanent alimony in some jurisdictions, and in others, the party seeking the modification must do so through the court. When a former spouse remarries, the new spouse is legally obligated to provide spousal support. **Cohabitation,** which means unmarried parties living together, may also terminate alimony. While cohabiting parties do not have a legal obligation to support each other, sharing expenses may improve the financial position of the divorced spouse; in other cases, it may not. The court must look at requests for modification on a case-by-case basis.

ESCALATION CLAUSES AND COST-OF-LIVING INCREASE CLAUSES

In drafting settlement agreement provisions regarding alimony, the parties may include an **escalation clause** or **cost of living clause.** An escalation clause provides for increases in the alimony payments due to the increase of payor's income and an increase in the cost of living. The escalation clause obviates the need for the parties to go back to court for modifications, which will save parties time and money.

MEDICAL INSURANCE

Because alimony involves the support of a former spouse, this chapter would not be complete without a brief discussion of medical insurance. The **Consolidated Omnibus Budget Reconciliation Act (COBRA),** 26 U.S.C. sec. 4980B(f), is a federal law that enables a nonemployee spouse to continue his health insurance coverage provided by his spouse's employer, for a period of three years after the divorce, as long as the nonemployee spouse pays the premium. The children of the marriage may also be covered under COBRA during their dependency on their parents. Either one parent or both will be responsible for providing medical insurance coverage for the children.

State laws also have an impact on medical insurance coverage. Some jurisdictions require a divorced spouse to provide coverage for former spouses who are not able to provide coverage for themselves.

Sometimes the COBRA payments are too high and a spouse may seek health insurance through their employer or other resource.

MASSACHUSETTS GENERAL LAWS ANNOTATED (WEST)

§ 34. *Alimony or assignment of estate; determination of amount; health insurance.*
. . . When the court makes an order for alimony on behalf of a spouse, and such spouse is not covered by a private group health insurance plan, said court shall determine whether the obligor under such order has health insurance on a group plan available to him through an employer or organization that may be extended to cover the spouse for whom support is ordered. When said court has determined that the obligor has such insurance, said court shall include in the support order a requirement that the obligor exercise the option of additional coverage in favor of such spouse.

ATTORNEY'S FEES

It is the responsibility of the respective parties to pay their **attorney's fees.** A common myth still held by many women is that the husband is required to pay her attorney's fees. The case of *Orr v. Orr*, 440 U.S. 268 (1979) declared this statutory requirement unconstitutional. Either party, however, may seek attorney's fees from the other spouse. The standard the court applies in determining attorney's fees is the need of one spouse and the ability to pay of the other spouse.

Most attorneys require clients to pay a retainer before taking on their divorce case and will later seek an award of attorney's fees to reimburse their client. For those who cannot afford a retainer, some attorneys may motion the court at the beginning of the proceedings for an advance award of legal fees to represent the needy spouse. In these cases, it is advisable that the representation of the spouse be contingent upon the granting of the motion for attorney's fees by the court and the receipt of payment. The rules of ethics require that an attorney's fee must be *reasonable*. It is within the court's discretion to determine what is reasonable. When defending the moving party's motion for attorney's fees, it is essential that an itemized bill be requested and that the charges be reviewed.

TERMINATION OF ALIMONY

REMARRIAGE

Alimony usually terminates on remarriage. The underlying policy is that upon remarriage, the new spouse has a duty to support. It would be unfair to allow a divorced spouse, who now has remarried, to receive support from two sources. In some states alimony automatically terminates upon remarriage and the payor spouse simply ceases payments. In other states, the parties petition the court for termination of alimony.

NO DOUBLE DIPPING

In this case, the Court of Appeals of Iowa affirms the trial court's decision to terminate wife's alimony due to her remarriage based on the rationale that an ex-wife (or ex-husband, for that matter) should not be allowed to receive support from both her current *and* former spouse.

IN RE THE MARRIAGE OF GILBERT J. BAKER AND SUSAN D. BAKER

2-209/01-1203 (IOWA APP. 5-15-2002)

COURT OF APPEALS OF IOWA

MAHAN, P.J.

Susan Klaes appeals the district court decision terminating her alimony award due to remarriage. Susan claims her alimony should continue despite her remarriage. She also asks for attorney fees for this appeal. We affirm.

Susan and Gilbert Baker were married for thirty years. A dissolution decree was entered for the parties on February 22, 1999. At the time of the decree, Susan was fifty-one years old, and Gilbert was fifty-two. Gilbert was employed by his family's business and earned nearly $200,000 per year. Susan worked as a teacher during the early years of the marriage, but quit to have children. She had not worked outside the home throughout most of the marriage, but was currently working part-time as a substitute teacher.

The decree divided the marital assets equally, awarding each party $255,399. In addition, an inheritance of $24,629 was set aside to Susan, and an inheritance of $182,871 was set aside to Gilbert. Gilbert was ordered to pay Susan alimony of $4000 per month until August 2000, and then $2000 per month to terminate on the death of either party, or when Susan becomes sixty-five years old, whichever occurs first. The court noted Susan could earn $24,000 annually if she renewed her teaching certificate and became a full-time teacher.

Susan never renewed her teaching license. She obtained employment for thirteen weeks each year as a costumer for the Clinton Area Showboat Theatre, where she earns $3250 for the season. Susan also does substitute teaching and works in a fabric store. In 2000 Susan had total gross income of $7225.

On October 14, 2000, Susan married Charles Klaes, a retired police officer. Charles receives $23,000 annually, tax-free, from a disability pension. Charles operates a private investigation and security firm, which gave him income of $4150, plus he has a radio show, from which he earned $2238 in 2000. Charles's total annual income for 2000 was $29,388.

After the dissolution Gilbert sold his interest in the family business and moved to Michigan. He renewed his teaching license, but was unable to find full-time employment as a teacher, and became a substitute teacher. In October 1999, he married Robin, a kindergarten teacher.

Due to Susan's remarriage, Gilbert filed an application on February 2, 2001, to terminate his alimony obligation. The district court determined Susan had been awarded a combination of rehabilitative alimony, which ended in August 2000, and traditional alimony. The court concluded Susan had failed to show extraordinary circumstances to continue the award of alimony after her remarriage and terminated Gilbert's alimony obligation. Susan appealed...

...II. ALIMONY

Susan contends she should continue to receive alimony from Gilbert, despite her marriage to Charles. She asserts the alimony she was awarded past August 2000, was actually reimbursement alimony, not traditional alimony. She states this alimony is to reimburse her for the years she stayed at home instead of pursuing a career. She points out that her earnings do not meet her expenses and claims Charles is not able to contribute much to her support.

The parties' dissolution decree did not specifically state that alimony would terminate on remarriage. When a provision for alimony is silent on the issue of payment of alimony to a former spouse after his or her remarriage, the burden is on the former spouse contending the alimony should continue to show extraordinary circumstances warrant continuing the alimony. *In re Marriage of Phares*, 500 N.W.2d 76, 79 (Iowa Ct. App. 1993). The rationale behind this rule is it would be contrary to public policy to allow a party to receive support from both a prior and a current spouse. *In re Marriage of Bell*, 576 N.W.2d 618, 622 (Iowa Ct. App. 1998). Generally, whether remarriage terminates alimony depends on the purpose behind the award. *In re Marriage of Wendell*, 581 N.W.2d 197, 200 (Iowa Ct. App. 1998).

Rehabilitative and reimbursement alimony are often unaffected by remarriage. *Id.* Susan claims she was awarded reimbursement alimony. Reimbursement alimony is based upon economic sacrifices made by one spouse during the marriage that directly enhance the future earning capacity of the other spouse. *In re Marriage of Ales*, 592 N.W.2d 698, 704 (Iowa Ct. App. 1999). On the other hand, traditional or permanent alimony is usually payable for life or for so long as the dependent spouse is incapable of self-support. *In re Marriage of Francis*, 442 N.W.2d 59, 62 (Iowa 1989); *In re Marriage of Hettinga*, N.W.2d 920, 922 (Iowa Ct. App. 1997).

We agree with the district court's conclusion that Susan was awarded a combination of rehabilitative alimony, which ended prior to her remarriage, and traditional or permanent alimony. The dissolution decree in fact terms this alimony "permanent alimony" and states it is subject to future modification. Reimbursement alimony is not subject to modification. *Francis*, 442 N.W.2d at 64.

Susan's traditional alimony may be terminated upon her remarriage unless she shows extraordinary circumstances for continuing it. *See Phares*, 500 N.W.2d at 79. We find Susan has failed to show extraordinary circumstances under the facts in this case. Although Susan states she is unable to meet her expenses without support, this is due largely to the fact Susan is working far below her earning capacity. Susan admitted she had not looked for full-time employment. We affirm the district court's decision terminating Gilbert's alimony obligation...

Cohabitation

In some states, alimony may be modified when a recipient cohabits with a member of the opposite sex. The problem with cohabitation as opposed to remarriage is that a cohabitant has no legal duty to support. It is important when drafting the settlement agreement to specifically indicate what type of conduct gives rise to a modification.

Cohabitation Terminates Alimony Award

The Supreme Court of Connecticut upheld the trial court's termination of the wife's alimony award. The husband was able to prove that the wife's circumstances substantially changed when she moved in with the handyman.

Rehabilitative alimony is generally nonmodifiable; however, some courts retain jurisdiction for the purpose of modification. Lump sum alimony awards are generally not modifiable. This means that the lump sum alimony award is not affected by remarriage or cohabitation and at the death of the payor spouse, the payee spouse may sue the payor's estate for any payments due. Because reimbursement alimony is awarded on the basis of the amount contributed by the nondegreed spouse, it is commonly nonmodifiable.

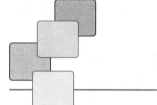

RITA A. LUPIEN V. HERVEY A. LUPIEN

192 CONN. 443, 472 A.2D 18 (CONN. 1984)

SUPREME COURT OF CONNECTICUT

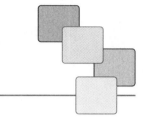

SPEZIALE, CHIEF JUSTICE.

The plaintiff appeals from the judgment to the trial court terminating her award of alimony. Because we hold that the trial court was not clearly erroneous in finding that the plaintiff was living with another person under circumstances that caused such a change of circumstances as to alter her financial needs, there is no error.

The parties were divorced on September 22, 1967, and the defendant was ordered to pay the plaintiff $150 per week periodic alimony. In 1980, the defendant moved to "modify the Judgment by reducing, suspending or terminating the alimony." The defendant claimed, inter alia, that the plaintiff was living with another man under circumstances that caused a change in her financial needs.[1]

Following a hearing on the motion, the trial court found that the plaintiff "is living openly with another man [and] receives support from this other man. . . ." The trial court modified the judgment of 1967 and

ordered alimony terminated. The plaintiff appealed and alleges that there was insufficient evidence to find either that the plaintiff was living with another person or that her living arrangements had caused a change in her financial circumstances. We disagree.

To modify an award of alimony pursuant to General Statute § 46b-86(b), the trial court must find "that the party receiving the periodic alimony is living with another person under circumstances which the court finds should result in the modification, suspension or termination of alimony because the living arrangements cause such a change of circumstances as to alter the financial needs of that party." (Footnote omitted). See *Kaplan v. Kaplan*, 185 Conn. 42, 440 A.2d 252 (1981). The trial court so found but the plaintiff argues that its finding was "clearly erroneous."

The evidence before the court showed that Gilbert Poirier had been living in a room in the plaintiff's home for two years. The plaintiff was paid $30 weekly for food by Poirier and he performed numerous handyman chores for her.[2] These chores included roofing the

---

[1]The defendant also claimed that the plaintiff's employment by Gilbert Poirier had caused a change in the plaintiff's financial circumstances.

[2]The plaintiff's twenty year old son also resided in the house and paid $30 weekly to the plaintiff.

garage, reconstruction of cubicles remaining from the defendant's dental practice, repair and maintenance of a swimming pool, and installation in the plaintiff's house of a wood stove owned by Poirier. Because of lack of finances, the plaintiff had not previously been able to "fix up" the house. Poirier and the plaintiff are "going steady" and "occasionally" have "marital relations." The plaintiff would like to marry him. After finding that the plaintiff and Poirier were "cohabitating" and that "the living arrangements . . . have caused such a change of circumstances as to alter materially

her financial needs," the trial court terminated the alimony award (footnote omitted). . . .

. . . There was evidence in this case to indicate both the plaintiff was living with another person and that this living arrangement caused such change in circumstances as to alter her financial needs. While termination of alimony is a harsh result, we are unable to say that the trial court's findings were clearly erroneous (footnote omitted). . . .

. . . There is no error.

DEATH

Alimony terminates on the death of either party unless otherwise stated in the settlement agreement or the divorce decree. If support is to be extended beyond death, it can be accomplished by an irrevocable insurance policy on the payor's life, naming payee spouse as beneficiary. Lump sum alimony paid in installments and property division awards do not terminate on the death of the payor spouse.

No Support beyond the Grave

The duty to pay alimony dies with the payor spouse unless he or she expressly obligates the estate to continue payments. In this case, the District Court of Appeal of Florida determined that Mr. O'Malley's intent to bind his estate was not implied in the language of the couple's separation agreement.

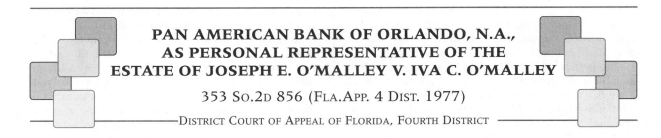

PAN AMERICAN BANK OF ORLANDO, N.A., AS PERSONAL REPRESENTATIVE OF THE ESTATE OF JOSEPH E. O'MALLEY V. IVA C. O'MALLEY

353 So.2d 856 (Fla. App. 4 Dist. 1977)

District Court of Appeal of Florida, Fourth District

ALDERMAN, CHIEF JUDGE.

The determinative issue in this appeal is whether a written separation agreement between Joseph E. O'Malley and Iva C. O'Malley, his former wife, is sufficient to obligate Mr. O'Malley's estate to continue alimony payments after his death. The trial court concluded that the agreement was sufficient and held Mr. O'Malley's estate liable for continued alimony payments. We reach a contrary conclusion and reverse.

When Mr. and Mrs. O'Malley were divorced, the judgment incorporated by reference their written separation agreement. The agreement provided: "Husband agrees to pay unto Wife as and for permanent alimony the sum of eight hundred fifty and no/100 dollars ($850.00) per month beginning March 1, 1972, and monthly thereafter until Wife becomes remarried or deceased." Mr. O'Malley subsequently died, survived by Mrs. O'Malley, who has not remarried. She filed a claim against his estate for continued alimony.

When the estate denied her claim she began a proceeding to enforce her claim, resulting in the judgments which are the subject of this appeal.

The trial court specifically found, and we agree, that the periodic payments called for in the agreement are alimony and not an integral part of a settlement of property rights between the parties. That is to say, the word "alimony" in the agreement is used in its technical sense to refer to the "nourishment" or "sustenance" which a husband may be compelled to pay his wife for her maintenance when he is living apart from her or when they are divorced. *Aldrich v. Aldrich,* 163 So.2d 276 (Fla. 1964).

An obligation to pay alimony ordinarily dies with the person who has the obligation, but he may agree to bind his estate to continue alimony payments after his death. *Allen v. Allen,* 111 Fla.733, 150 So.237 (1933). In the present case, the trial court found that Mr. O'Malley's intent to bind his estate, although not expressed, was implied in the language of the separation agreement quoted above. We disagree. If Mr. O'Malley had intended to obligate his estate for alimony payments after his death, it would have been a simple matter for him to have expressly said so...

...Turning now to the merits of the present case, we hold that the property settlement agreement between Mr. and Mrs. O'Malley is not sufficiently specific to obligate Mr. O'Malley's estate to continue alimony payments after his death. The language in question is similar to that commonly used in separation agreements and divorce judgments to indicate that the alimony is permanent, rather than temporary. We conclude that, absent an express agreement that the estate be so bound, the trial court had no authority to order Mr. O'Malley's estate to continue payments of alimony after his death. Such an agreement may not be implied from a provision which simply recites that alimony will be paid to Mrs. O'Malley until she "becomes remarried or deceased." Without doubt, it was within the power of the parties to contract for alimony after the husband's death; they needed only state their agreement with sufficient definiteness. They did not do so, and Mrs. O'Malley cannot now rely upon the court to imply what she and her husband might have agreed to.

Having reached this conclusion we need not discuss the other issues raised by appellant and by appellee on her cross-appeal.

REVERSED and REMANDED.

TAX CONSEQUENCES OF ALIMONY

Alimony payments to a spouse are considered a form of income to the spouse. Therefore, alimony is taxable to the recipient and deductible to the payor. The deductibility of alimony is advantageous to a payor spouse with high earnings. It is very important to obtain the Social Security number of the payor or recipient spouse so your client will have that information available at tax time. If your office is representing the recipient spouse, the attorney may encourage that spouse to pay quarterly estimated taxes to avoid a hefty tax burden at the end of the year.

The IRS Recapture Rule

In 1986, the Internal Revenue Service defined alimony as a payment made in cash or its equivalent pursuant to a court-ordered divorce agreement that terminates on death. In the past, lawyers would label property division as alimony for the purpose of deducting property distribution payments.

Property settlements are not deductible and by labeling these settlements as alimony, the payor spouse would deduct these payments from his income taxes. The IRS redefined alimony and limited the amount of alimony that can be deducted in the first three years after the divorce. If alimony payments total $15,000 or less per year, they are deductible. If they exceed $15,000, the payor must satisfy complex tax rules for this deduction. If the parties do not wish to have alimony taxed as income or deducted, then it should be indicated in the settlement agreement. This is known as the **IRS recapture rule.** The majority of property settlements in a divorce case are made in the first three years after the divorce. This is known as

front loading. Lawyers were structuring property settlements by classifying them as "alimony." By calling a property settlement "alimony" the payor client could deduct the amount from income taxes. The IRS monitors alimony payments for front loading. If the majority of payments are made in a period of years, at the year 3 mark, this will indicate that front loading has occurred. The IRS will then seek to *recapture* the tax deduction. To be safe, payments in year 1 should not exceed payments made in year 2 or year 3 by more than 15 percent.

Family Support Payments Versus Separate Payments of Alimony and Child Support

Family support payments is the term given to regular, periodic payments a payor spouse makes to the other spouse for the financial maintenance of both the ex-spouse and children. This amount is not delineated into a portion that comprises spousal alimony and a portion for child support, but rather one sum deemed "family support." Care should be taken so that a reduction of the amount of the family support payment does not occur upon the happening of a child-support-related event such as emancipation, employment, or the end of schooling.

The problem lies in determining what is alimony and what is child support. The IRS watches unallocated family support payments carefully. If the unallocated support payment is reduced due to changes in a child's age or needs, the IRS will be able to determine how much has been allocated for alimony and how much has been allocated for child support. If, previously, the payor spouse was deducting as alimony payments is an amount greater than the IRS subsequent determination of what constituted alimony, the payor spouse will have to pay a back tax and possibly a fine. If a payee spouse claimed as income a lesser amount of the family support payment than was actually allocated for alimony, the payee spouse will owe the IRS back taxes and also probably be subject to a fine.

Effects of Bankruptcy Law on Alimony, Child Support, and Property Distribution Settlements

On April 20, 2005, President Bush signed the **Bankruptcy Abuse Prevention and Consumer Protection Act**, enacting significant changes impacting divorce litigation. Most provisions took effect on October 17, 2005. Here are some of the highlights of interest to family law practitioners and their clients:

- The act replaced the terms *alimony, child support,* and *property settlements* with the phrase **domestic support obligations,** or DSOs. DSO includes "any obligation owed to or recoverable by a spouse, former spouse or child of a debtor, child's parent, legal guardian or responsible relative, or any governmental unit involved in the collection or enforcement of support obligations." This includes domestic support obligations ordered by a court either before or after the debtor filed a bankruptcy petition.

- Bankruptcy trustees are required to give written notice to anyone holding a claim for a domestic support obligation (for example, a spouse with an alimony, child support, or property settlement order) and any state child support, enforcement agency involved in the case.

- Property settlement awards are no longer dischargeable in bankruptcy. Prior to changes in the law, property settlements were dischargeable if the debtor could prove to the bankruptcy court that the true nature of the settlement was related to property rather than support.

- Child support and alimony payments are raised to first-priority position under the classification of unsecured creditors. Secured creditors take priority in bankruptcy proceedings—for example, a lender who holds a mortgage on real property.
- Automatic stays do not apply to domestic support obligations. Debtors may not obtain debt relief from the bankruptcy court unless they are current on postpetition obligations.
- The failure of a debtor to remain current on domestic support obligations is grounds for conversion (for example, amending the bankruptcy proceeding from a Chapter 7 Liquidation to a Chapter 13 Reorganization) or dismissal of the case.

SECURING ALIMONY PAYMENTS WITH LIFE INSURANCE

A recipient spouse may request, and a payor spouse may be ordered to obtain, life insurance to secure alimony or child support payments for the duration of the support obligation, in the event of the payor spouse's death. If the recipient spouse is receiving permanent alimony and the duration of the obligation cannot be determined because it terminates upon death, remarriage, or cohabitation, the parties will agree to, or the courts will set, a specific amount. The payor spouse names the recipient spouse as beneficiary under the policy.

It is also important for the recipient spouse to obtain verification that the policy is in force and that premiums have been paid. The recipient spouse should request, either in court or pursuant to a separation agreement, the payor spouse's consent to receive notification from the insurance company if the payor fails to pay the premium. If this occurs, the recipient spouse may pay the premium and file a motion for contempt with the court to recover the unpaid premium and possibly attorney's fees. If the premium is not paid and the payor spouse dies, the recipient spouse may file a claim against his or her estate.

In *Parley v. Parley*, the Connecticut Appellate Court held that when making orders to obtain life insurance, a court should consider the cost and availability of such coverage as well as the spouse's ability to pay in light of other financial obligations.

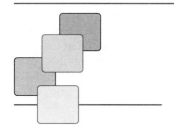

GAIL A. PARLEY V. JON A. PARLEY

72 CONN. APP. 742, 807 A.2D 982 (2002)

APPELLATE COURT OF CONNECTICUT

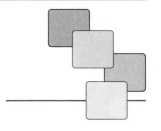

MIHALAKOS, J.

The defendant, Jon A. Parley, appeals from the judgment of the trial court dissolving the parties' marriage. On appeal, the defendant claims that the court improperly (1) ordered him to obtain life insurance to secure the court's alimony order . . .

. . . We reverse the judgment of the trial court as to its financial orders only and remand the matter to that court for a new trial as to the financial matters.

The following facts and procedural history are relevant to our consideration of the defendant's claims on appeal. The parties were married on August 10, 1979.

Five children were born to the marriage, two of whom reached the age of majority prior to the dissolution action. On April 20, 1999, the plaintiff, Gail A. Parley, brought an action seeking dissolution of the marriage, claiming that it had irretrievably broken down.

The court entered orders regarding property distribution, alimony, child support and other miscellaneous matters. As part of the dissolution decree, the court ordered the defendant to pay to the plaintiff alimony in the amount of $50 per week. At the time of the dissolution, the defendant held a life insurance policy. To secure the alimony payment, the court ordered the defendant to obtain additional life insurance....

...This appeal followed....

...The defendant first claims that the court improperly ordered him to obtain additional life insurance to secure his alimony obligation. Specifically, he argues that the court failed to inquire regarding the cost and availability of such insurance, and, therefore, improperly ordered him to obtain the insurance. We agree and vacate the order of the court regarding the additional insurance to secure the alimony payments.

"The ordering of security for alimony by a trial court is discretionary under [General Statutes § 46b-82]." *Cordone* v. *Cordone*, supra, 51 Conn. App. 534; General Statutes § 46B-82. The court's discretion, however, is not without limits. This court has held that the trial court must delve into certain matters before ordering a party to obtain life insurance to secure the payment of alimony. See *Michel* v. *Michel*, 31 Conn.App.338, 341, 624 A.2d 914 (1993). Specifically, the court must engage in a search and inquiry into the cost and availability of such insurance. *Id.*; see also *Lake* v. *Lake*, 49 Conn. App. 89, 92, 712 A.2d 989, cert. denied, 246 Conn.902, 719 A.2d 1166 (1998).

In the present case, the defendant held a life insurance policy at the time of the dissolution. The court ordered him to obtain additional life insurance to secure his alimony payments without inquiring into the cost or availability of the additional insurance. As in *Michel*, the court in the present case "has entered . . . financial orders that may be inappropriate, that is, too high or too low depending on the funds required to obtain such [additional] insurance." *Michel* v. *Michel*, supra, 31 Conn. App. 341. Although the charged party in *Michel* held no insurance at the time of the dissolution; *id.*, 340; we conclude that the same analysis is necessary in cases in which a party is ordered to obtain additional insurance. Because the court did not inquire as to the cost and availability of the additional life insurance, the court's order lacks a reasonable basis in the facts, and, therefore, constitutes an abuse of the court's discretion.

Although every improper financial order in a dissolution of marriage action does not necessarily merit a reconsideration of all of the court's financial orders; see, e.g., *Smith* v. *Smith*, 249 Conn. 265, 277, 752 A.2d 1023 (1999); in this case, the court's order that the defendant obtain additional life insurance is interdependent with its other financial orders and may not be severed from them. We must, therefore, remand the case to the trial court on all financial matters...

PRACTICAL TIPS FOR CLIENTS

- **Never make alimony or child support payments in cash.** The family attorney and/or the paralegal who has been working with the client should emphasize to the client that it is essential that alimony and child support obligations be paid with either check or money order to preserve proof that payments were actually made. If your client must use cash, tell the client that it is important to get a receipt. Receipt booklets may be purchased at any stationery store. The recipient client may receive alimony payments by being paid directly by the payor or through a **wage execution** where the alimony payment is deducted from the payor spouse's paycheck, or an automatic transfer from payor's bank account occurs.

- **Keep accurate and complete records of payments.** Clients should be told of the importance of record keeping. Both the payor spouse and the recipient spouse should keep good records for tax purposes, and may want to photocopy checks, money orders, or, if cash is tendered, request a copy of the receipt. The IRS can and may dispute deduction amounts or income received; therefore, adequate record keeping is essential.

FIGURE 5–4
If the IRS decides to dispute alimony allocations, adequate record keeping becomes essential.

■ **Recognize the need for lifestyle changes.** The financial reality for the recipient spouse is that alimony may not be enough to live on. It is important for the attorney or the paralegal to review a client's financial information with the client to determine how much he or she will need to live on and whether adjustments need to be made to their lifestyles after the divorce. The client may have to sell assets or find part-time work in order to supplement income. The client may have to go on a budget or cut up credit cards and cancel them with the credit card company in order not to incur any further debt. Consumer credit counseling services may be a good resource for clients who are in over their heads. Displaced homemaker groups may also provide support and budget counseling to help the traditional homemaker through the transition.

ENFORCEMENT OF COURT-ORDERED PAYMENTS

When a party entitled to alimony payments pursuant to a court order is not paid, that party may commence a civil **contempt proceeding** to force the payor spouse to comply with the court's order. This process begins with the recipient spouse filing the appropriate paperwork within that jurisdiction (e.g., a motion for contempt or a citation with an order to show cause). In the proper document, the recipient will state what was awarded in the original order, that the payor spouse has not paid since a specific date, and include a request that the delinquent spouse be found in contempt of court. These documents are served on the payor and filed in the court where the original alimony award was entered. A contempt is an extension of the divorce matter; therefore it is unnecessary to assert personal jurisdiction over the payor spouse. The only requirement is service, notice of the proceedings, and the opportunity to be heard.

Once the parties are in court, it is the payor spouse's burden to prove that she has, in fact, kept up the alimony payments and has the canceled checks or receipts to prove it. If the payor spouse cannot provide such proof, the court will order the payor spouse to pay the arrearage. If the arrearage cannot be paid in a lump sum, the court will make the arrearage payable in installments. The payor will then find herself obligated to make weekly payments on the arrearage in addition to the weekly payments authorized by the original court order.

The filing of a contempt action by the recipient spouse or payee spouse will often precipitate the filing of a modification motion by the payor spouse. This is especially true in cases where the payor spouse has failed to discharge his or her alimony or child support obligation because of unfavorably changed financial circumstances.

EXAMPLE

> On August 1, John is ordered by the court to pay $100 per week as alimony to his wife Linda. On October 1, John loses his job due to a layoff at the plant where he works. Four weeks pass and Linda is not paid her court-ordered alimony award. Linda files a contempt action. John is properly served. He meets with his lawyer who immediately files a modification on the basis that there has been a significant change in John's circumstances since the entering of the original alimony order— that is, John's being laid off.

In this scenario, John will probably not be able to modify his obligation for the arrearage because in most jurisdictions, past alimony amounts due may not be increased or decreased retroactively. Some states *do* allow for retroactive modifications of arrearages, but they are the exception not the rule. Most courts, however, can always modify an alimony order for prospective payments. In John's case, his substantiated showing of his changed circumstances and its negative financial consequences should be sufficient good cause for the court to lower his alimony obligation.

ATTORNEY'S FEES IN CONTEMPT ACTIONS

The recipient spouse who is forced to bring a contempt action may also demand attorney's fees from the delinquent spouse. The recipient spouse will prevail if the payor is found to be in **willful contempt.** The court is likely to find willful contempt if the recipient spouse proves that the payor spouse has the means to make the payments but purposefully and deliberately fails to do so. The court may also find willful contempt if the recipient spouse demonstrates that although financial problems now prevent the payor from complying with the court-ordered alimony obligation, the payor, himself or herself, caused the financial setback either by spending too much, voluntarily leaving his or her employment, defrauding the recipient spouse, or engaging in some other type of irresponsible conduct.

END OF CHAPTER EXERCISES

Crossword Puzzle

Across

4. short-term, lump-sum alimony awarded to a spouse for the purpose of transitioning from married to single status.

5. one or both of the spouses may wish to waive or relinquish their right to ask for alimony

7. temporary alimony

8. church rules that determine moral obligations

9. divorce from bed and board

11. unmarried parties living together

12. alimony awarded for a limited period of time to give a spouse the opportunity to become self-sufficient

Down

1. new federal bankruptcy law passed on April 20, 2005 (with most provisions effective October 17, 2005) that legislated significant changes impacting divorce litigation

2. United States Supreme Court case decided in 1979 declaring an Alabama statute imposing the obligation to pay alimony solely on the husband unconstitutional

3. alimony in the amount of $1.00 per year

6. an alimony order that terminates upon death, remarriage, or cohabitation

10. payments made to a spouse for his or her contributions toward the attainment of an advanced degree by a student spouse

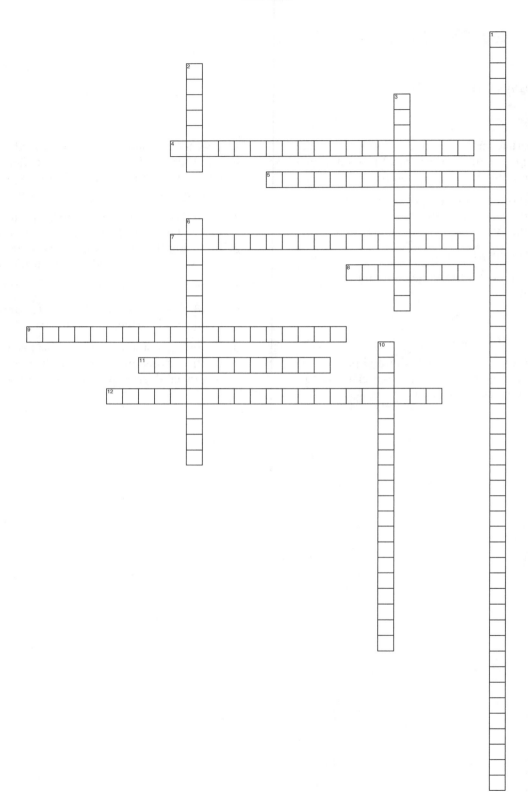

Review Questions

1 Define alimony.

2 What are the two interests the court must balance before awarding alimony to a spouse?

3 Briefly describe the different types of alimony discussed in the chapter.

4 Explain the effect of the Bankruptcy Abuse Prevention and Consumer Protection Act on alimony awards.

5 What are the tax consequences of alimony?

Cases for Briefing

Kean v. Commissioner, 407 F 3d 186 (3rd Cir. 2005)

Thiebault v. Thiebault, 421 N.W.2d 747 (Minn.Ct.App. 1988)

Exploring the Workplace: Activities

1. Go to **http://www.divorcenet.com/**. Find and read your state laws on alimony.

2. Review IRS Publication 504, Divorced or Separated Individuals at **http://www.irs.gov/ pub/irs-pdf/p504.pdf** and learn how to determine and label alimony amounts.

3. Read "Separation Agreements" at **http://www.divorcelawinfo.com/VA/Separation/maritalt.htm** and list the questions that should be asked when drafting the spousal support/alimony and life insurance provisions in a separation agreement.

4. Find the modification of alimony statute in your jurisdiction. Explain the criteria that must be met before the court modifies an alimony award.

5. You work as a paralegal for the law firm of Silva & Silva. Your supervisor, Adelia Silva, asks you to research a postjudgment modification issue on behalf of your client, Joseph Black. Mr. Black was divorced a year ago. Another law firm handled his divorce, but he wants your firm to handle the postjudgment matter. Under the terms of the divorce decree, Mr. Black was awarded rehabilitative alimony. The clause reads as follows:

Wife agrees to pay to Husband rehabilitative alimony in the amount of $300.00 per week for twenty-four (24) months, due and payable in hand or postmarked on the 10th day of each month beginning December 10, 2006. Said payments shall terminate at the conclusion of the twenty-four (24) month term and shall be taxable to Husband and deductible by Wife.

Mr. Black has informed your supervisor that he intends to remarry. He would like to know the effect of remarriage on his alimony award and whether he should postpone his wedding. The agreement is silent on the issue of remarriage. Apply the law of your state and prepare a client opinion letter that will be reviewed and signed by Attorney Silva, advising the client on this issue. Make sure you check both state statutory and case law.

CHAPTER

6

Property and Debt Distribution

KEY TERMS

antenuptial agreement

appreciation buyout

civil code

commingling

marital and separate property

concurrent ownership

creditor

debt

debtor

disclosure

dissipation

equitable distribution

Employee Retirement Income Security Act (ERISA)

equity

fair market value

goodwill

hold harmless clause

joint ownership

joint tenancy

marital assets

marital debts

marital property

necessaries

nonvested

offset

partnership pension

personal property

premarital agreement

prenuptial agreement

Qualified Domestic Relations Order (QDRO)

quasi-community

real property

Retirement Equity Act (REA)

right of survivorship

separate property

separation agreement

settlement agreement

sole ownership　　　　transmutation

tax deferred　　　　unity of spouses

tenancy by the entirety　　　　valuated

tenancy in common　　　　value

title　　　　vested

tracing

W hile the goal of alimony is to provide a needy spouse with support or "maintenance," the goal of property and debt distribution is to fairly distribute the marital assets and debts between the spouses. Property and debt division is one of the most contested issues in modern divorce cases, second only to custody disputes. Spouses generally accumulate a myriad of assets and debts during a marriage, which may take center stage at a divorce hearing where the central issue is "who gets what?" While asset accumulation is one of the goals of the married couple—especially the fulfilling of the American dream of home ownership—debts are unfortunately also part of the equation. In some marriages, distribution of debt may be the only financial issue to resolve.

This chapter focuses on the issue of property and debts and how they are divided at the time of divorce; therefore, an understanding of basic property principles is essential before proceeding any further.

BASIC PRINCIPLES OF PROPERTY

Property can be classified as either *real* or *personal*. **Real property** is land and anything affixed to it (examples: house, garage, barn, condominium). **Personal property** is anything other than real property that can be touched and is movable (examples: cash, automobiles, bank accounts, jewelry, furniture, clothing, stocks, bonds).

Property can be owned by an individual alone; this is known as **sole ownership**. Property also can be held by two or more persons together; this is known as **concurrent ownership** or **joint ownership.** A sole owner has the right to give, sell, will, encumber, and lease her property. In other words, a sole owner can do anything legal with her property without another's approval. Concurrent owners have rights and responsibilities vis-à-vis each other that differ from jurisdiction to jurisdiction. The most common forms of concurrent or joint ownership are as follows:

- tenancy in common,
- joint tenancy with right of survivorship,
- tenancy by the entirety, and
- community property.

Tenancy in Common

Tenants in common each own an undivided interest in the property, have equal rights to use and enjoyment, and may dispose of their share by gift, will, or sale. At the time of a co-owner's death, his share passes to his beneficiaries, if he left a will, or to his heirs under the intestacy succession laws of his state if he dies without a will.

Tenancy in Common as a form of joint ownership is frequently used by individuals who are not related to one another. It may be used by persons joining together to purchase real property as a business investment, or as the following example shows, it may be used by friends who buy a property to live in together.

> *Joe and Marty were college roommates. After graduation, they bought a three-bedroom beach house together in an up-and-coming shore community. Each man contributed half of the down payment and agreed to pay one-half of the mortgage payment, taxes, insurance, monthly utilities, and all repair or maintenance expenses. They took title to the property as tenants in common, with each having a 50 percent undivided interest in the property. The housing market in their area is booming, and the fair market value of their home has grown or appreciated considerably. Marty has recently become engaged to Gwen. He wishes to sell his interest in the beach house and buy something with Gwen. As a tenant in common, Marty has the right to sell his interest to anyone at any time. He does not need Joe's permission. He may sell the property to a stranger who could actually move in with Joe or charge Joe rent to live there alone. There are other options. Joe may decide that he wishes to sell his interest also. The men can put the property on the market, and when it sells divide the proceeds equally. If Joe wishes to stay in the house or at least keep the property, he may attempt to buy out Marty's interest at the current fair market value, or see if he can find a friend to buy out Marty; the new co-owner would then become a tenant in common with Joe.*

Joint Tenancy

Joint tenants own equal interests in property and at the death of one of the joint tenants, her interest automatically passes to the remaining joint tenant through what is known as the **right of survivorship.** A joint tenant also has the right to sell her interest in the jointly owned property. The sale of one co-owner's interest destroys the right of survivorship; the new co-owner and the remaining tenant now hold the property as tenants in common.

Joint tenancy is chosen as a form of ownership most often when the parties are married, are related, or are friends who have a very close relationship. This is probably so because joint tenancy includes the right of survivorship, and, as the following example shows, also allows a tenant to sell her interest without obtaining the other tenant's permission.

> *If Marty and Gwen do buy a home, they may decide to take title as joint tenants. If so, they will own equal interests in the property, regardless of any disparity in their respective monetary contributions. If either Marty or Gwen dies, the survivor will automatically become the owner of the entire piece of property. In order to take title as joint tenants, Marty and Gwen must buy the property at the same time from the same source. They may elect to use this form of ownership even though they have not yet married. Being a joint tenant does not deprive either person from selling their interest. For instance, if Gwen breaks her engagement to Marty, she may wish to sell her interest. The person whom she sells to will take title as a tenant, in common,*

and Marty's co-ownership status will automatically change to that of a tenant in common.

TENANCY BY THE ENTIRETY

Tenancy by the entirety is a form of co-ownership that can only exist between a husband and wife. It is similar to joint tenancy in that it carries with it the right of survivorship. The main difference, however, is that one tenant may not sever a tenancy by the entirety without the permission of the other co-tenant.

Tenancy by the entirety affords both spouses a greater say in whether or not the tenancy will continue. It protects a spouse from the consequences of the other spouse selling his or her interest without any discussion or notice.

Marty and Gwen may hold property together in tenancy in the entirety if they wait until they are married before buying a home. Just as is the case with joint tenancy, if either Marty or Gwen dies, the surviving spouse will become the sole owner. Unlike joint tenancy, both spouses have an undivided interest in the entire property, which cannot be broken into individual interests that may be sold at will. If during their marriage Marty decides to sell the property, he may not do so without Gwen's consent.

If Gwen brings a dissolution of marriage action, when the dissolution is granted, the court may order the property sold. Until that sale, the now divorced parties will hold the property as co-tenants.

COMMUNITY PROPERTY

In **community property** states, all property and income acquired during the marriage is deemed to be owned equally by both spouses, subject to certain exceptions. Community property is discussed in more detail later in this chapter.

Community property states have statutes providing that real estate purchased during the marriage is to be held by the spouses as community property. Exceptions to this rule are recognized when the real estate was purchased solely with funds that one of the spouses possessed prior to the marriage or had received as a gift or an inheritance.

If Marty and Gwen are married and reside in a community property state when they buy a home; unless one or more of the previously mentioned exceptions apply, they will each own a one-half interest in their home. Should they divorce, each spouse will be entitled to one-half of the proceeds of the sale of the house. However, if to purchase the home, Marty uses only the proceeds from the sale of his interest in the home he owned with Joe prior to marriage, this piece of property may fall outside of the community property estate and Gwen will not be entitled to half of it. Of course, in the real world, most people cannot buy their homes outright but must finance a considerable portion of the sale price. If Marty used his prior sale proceeds as a down payment and then during the course of the marriage, the mortgage payment, taxes, and other related expenses of homeownership came from income received by either or both Marty and Gwen, then, in a dissolution action, at least part of the value of the house will be community property. Further, if Marty's funds were kept in a joint bank account with Gwen's, and both parties contributed to and used these funds, then, as will be more fully discussed next, these funds may have lost their separate identity and become community property, so that Gwen will be entitled to half their value.

PROPERTY AND DEBT DISTRIBUTION UPON MARITAL DISSOLUTION

It is the responsibility of each party's attorney to determine the extent and value of the property owned and what the client should be entitled to at the time of divorce. This process begins with the task of determining what property the client and his spouse own, either solely or jointly, regardless of how the property is titled. **Title** indicates a party's ownership interest in property—that is, " whose name is the property in?" A list of property can be developed from information obtained from the client interview and through the formal discovery devices. The term **marital assets** refers to property acquired during a marriage. Here are some examples:

antiques	appliances	artwork
automobiles	bank accounts	boats
bonds	business interests	cash
clothing	collectibles (stamps, coins, etc.)	condominiums
copyrights	credit union accounts	goodwill
heirlooms	household furnishings	insurance
jewelry	judgments	lottery winnings
marital gifts	marital home	mutual funds
pending lawsuits	pension plans (401K, SEP, IRA)	pets
professional degrees	profit-sharing plans	silverware
stocks	tax refunds	time shares
trademarks	trailers	vacation homes

The next two cases presented in this chapter illustrate that marital property is not limited to traditional assets such as the marital home, bank accounts, and automobiles. Marital assets exist in many surprising forms. All it takes is a good legal eye to spot them and a good legal argument to toss them into the marital property pot. In *Campbell*, the court affirmed a long-standing rule defining lottery winnings as marital assets. In *Bennett*, the court determines the legal status of the family dog.

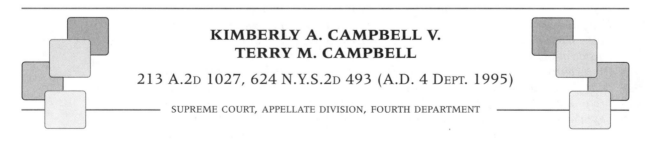

KIMBERLY A. CAMPBELL V.
TERRY M. CAMPBELL

213 A.2D 1027, 624 N.Y.S.2D 493 (A.D. 4 DEPT. 1995)

SUPREME COURT, APPELLATE DIVISION, FOURTH DEPARTMENT

MEMORANDUM:

Plaintiff and 10 co-workers agreed that they would take turns purchasing a lottery ticket and that, if any one of them purchased a winning ticket, the proceeds would be shared in 11 equal shares. Plaintiff purchased a lottery ticket on at least one prior occasion, but it was not a winner. A co-worker purchased a winning lottery ticket on October 7, 1992. The jackpot prize was

$4.5 million. Because of the policy of the New York State Lotto Commission to recognize only one winner per ticket, the co-worker obtained a Federal taxpayer identification number in the name of a trust and prepared a trust agreement for the disbursement of the lottery proceeds to all 11 co-workers. The trust agreement acknowledges the prior agreement of the parties, and all 11 co-workers executed the trust agreement.

Plaintiff commenced this action for divorce in 1993. Defendant counterclaimed for divorce and moved for an order enjoining and restraining plaintiff from spending or transferring her interest in the lottery proceeds. Defendant maintained that the lottery proceeds were marital property subject to equitable distribution. Supreme Court determined that the co-worker who purchased the winning lottery ticket was under no legal duty to share the proceeds with her co-workers, that the agreement to disburse a share of the proceeds to plaintiff constituted a gift, and that gift constituted plaintiff's separate property.

An agreement to share the proceeds of a lottery is a valid and enforceable agreement (citations omitted). An oral agreement to share proceeds that will be paid over a period of several years does not contravene the Statute of Frauds (citations omitted). The oral agreement to the co-workers was sufficiently definite to be enforced (citation omitted), and the court erred in concluding that the co-worker who purchased the winning ticket was under no legal duty to share the proceeds. Moreover, there is no evidence in the record of donative intent. It is undisputed that the co-worker acted pursuant to the oral agreement.

Domestic Relations Law §236(B)(1)(c) defines marital property as "all property acquired by either or both spouses during the marriage and before . . . commencement of a matrimonial action, regardless of the form in which title is held." Thus, property acquired during the marriage is presumptively marital property, and plaintiff had the burden of showing that it was separate property (citations omitted). Courts have universally held that the proceeds of a winning lottery ticket acquired by a spouse during the marriage constitute marital property (citations omitted). That principle applies to instances where one spouse contributed with third persons to a pool of funds used to purchase lottery tickets and one of the tickets was a winner (citations omitted). The agreement of the co-workers constituted a pooling arrangement, and plaintiff's share of the proceeds constitutes marital property (citations omitted). Thus, we modify the order on appeal by vacating that part denying defendant's motion and by determining that plaintiff's share of the lottery proceeds constitutes marital property.

Because the court determined that the proceeds were separate property, it did not consider whether plaintiff should be enjoined from transferring or otherwise disposing of the proceeds and whether the proceeds should be placed in escrow pending the distribution of marital property. We remit this matter to Supreme Court for determination of defendant's motion.

Order unanimously modified on the law and as modified affirmed without costs and matter remitted to Supreme Court for further proceedings.

DOG VISITATION?

Enforcement and supervision of pet visitation clauses would open the floodgates to litigation over pet-related problems. Traditionally, the courts have held that pets are personal property and will award the pet to either spouse at the time of the dissolution.

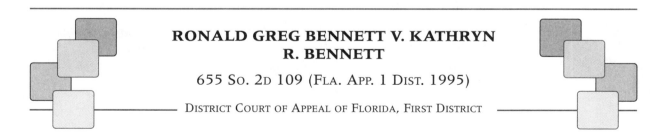

RONALD GREG BENNETT V. KATHRYN R. BENNETT

655 SO. 2D 109 (FLA. APP. 1 DIST. 1995)

DISTRICT COURT OF APPEAL OF FLORIDA, FIRST DISTRICT

WOLF, JUDGE.

Husband, Ronald Greg Bennett, appeals from a final judgment of dissolution of marriage which, among other things, awarded custody of the parties' dog, "Roddy." The husband asserts that (1) the trial court erred in awarding the former wife visitation with the parties' dog, and (2) the trial court erred in modifying the final judgment to increase the former wife's visitation rights with the dog. We find that the trial court lacked authority to order visitation with personal property; the dog would properly be dealt with through the equitable distribution process.

A brief recitation of the procedural history will demonstrate the morass a trial court may find itself in by extending the right of visitation to personal property. The parties stipulated to all issues in the final judgment of dissolution of marriage except which party would receive possession of the parties' dog, "Roddy." After a hearing, the trial court found that the husband should have possession of the dog and that the wife should be able to take the dog for visitation every other weekend and every other Christmas.

The former husband contested this decision and filed a motion for rehearing alleging that the dog was a premarital asset. He also filed a motion for relief from final judgment and an amended motion for rehearing. The wife replied and filed a motion to strike former husband's amended motion for rehearing and a motion for contempt. The former wife requested that the trial court transfer custody of the dog because the former husband was refusing to comply with the trial court's order concerning visitation with the dog.

A hearing on these motions was held on September 27, 1993. The wife's counsel filed an ore tenus motion requesting the trial court to change custody, or in the alternative, change visitation. The trial court denied the former husband's motion for rehearing and granted the former wife's ore tenus motion to change visitation. Thus, the trial court's ruling on visitation now reads:

7. *Dog, Roddy:* The former husband, RONALD GREGORY BENNETT, shall have custody of the parties' dog "Roddy" and the former wife, KATHRYN R. BENNETT n/k/a KATHRYN R. ROGERS, shall have visitation every other month beginning October 1, 1993. The visitation shall begin on the first day of the month and end on the last day of the month.

Based on the history of this case, there is every reason to believe that there will be continued squabbling between the parties concerning the dog.

While a dog may be considered by many to be a member of the family, under Florida law, animals are considered to be personal property. *County of Pasco v. Riehl,* 620 So. 2d 229 (Fla.2d DCA 1993), and *Levine v. Knowles,* 197 So. 2d 329 (Fla.3d DCA 1967). There is no authority which provides for a trial court to grant custody or visitation pertaining to personal property. §61.075, Fla.Stat. (1993).

While several states have given family pets special status within dissolution proceedings (for example, *see Arrington v. Arrington,* 613 S.W.2d 565 (Tex. Civ. App. 1981)), we think such a course is unwise. Determinations as to custody and visitation lead to continuing enforcement and supervision problems (as evidenced by the proceedings in the instant case). Our courts are overwhelmed with the supervision of custody, visitation, and support matters related to the protection of our children. We cannot undertake the same responsibility as to animals.

While the trial judge was endeavoring to reach a fair solution under difficult circumstances, we must reverse the order relating to the custody of "Roddy," and remand for the trial court to award the animal pursuant to the dictates or the equitable distribution statute.

WEBSTER and MICKLE, J.J., concur.

Debts are also part of the marital acquisition equation and must be identified as well as assets. **Marital debts** are the liabilities incurred by either spouse during the marriage. Examples of marital debts are as follows:

assessments	court judgments	credit card balances
loans	mortgages	tuitions
unpaid taxes	unreimbursed medical expenses	

Credit Card Crazy

In *Szesny,* the husband incurred debt of $82,000 as a result of his out-of-control spending. The Appellate Court of Illinois found no error with the lower court's ruling imposing the entire debt to the husband.

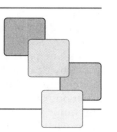

JAMES A. SZESNY V. TARYN SZESNY

197 ILL. APP. 3D 966, 145 ILL. DEC. 452, 557 N.E.2D 222
(ILL. APP. 1 DIST. 1990)

APPELLATE COURT OF ILLINOIS, FIRST DISTRICT, SIXTH DIVISION

PRESIDING JUSTICE LAPORTA DELIVERED THE OPINION OF THE COURT:

Respondent appeals from a Judgment of Dissolution of Marriage, claiming that the trial court abused its discretion in imposing almost the entire marital debt of over $82,000 upon him. . . . We affirm as to the distribution of the marital debt. . . .

. . . The parties were married on November 1, 1980 in Chicago Heights, Illinois. From the time of their marriage until late in 1984, they lived with Respondent's mother, paying no rent and making no monetary contributions to the household. In 1984 the couple purchased a house, borrowing the money needed for earnest money deposit ($5,000) and for a down payment ($20,000) from the bank where Respondent worked. The loans were secured by one-year lump-sum notes and liens on the cars of Respondent's mother and sister. The remaining $70,000 of the purchase price came in the form of a purchase money mortgage against the house, also held by the bank where Respondent worked.

Petitioner testified that after they purchased the house, their standard of living went down; they did not go out as often and went to "cheap places." Petitioner testified that she told Respondent that their credit cards should be destroyed and she destroyed several of them herself. Respondent testified that he opened new charge accounts and took the cash advances to pay off other charge accounts. Petitioner testified that she did not sign for these credit cards although some of them bore her name.

Respondent testified that their standard of living did not abate, and in fact their living expenses increased dramatically. Their consumer debt jumped from nothing to $40,000 in 1984, with $20,000 owed on charge cards at the end of 1985, $43,000 owed at the end of 1986, and over $70,000 owed at the end of 1987. The current debt is approximately $82,000. Respondent testified that various loans were taken out in an effort to retire some of the debt. He also admitted to "playing the field" with their joint checking account, by hoping that deposits would arrive in time to cancel overdrafts.

Petitioner testified that she would attempt to "force the balance" of their checking account registers at the end of each month, but this was difficult because Respondent would not record all transactions, would use counter checks instead of those provided for their account, and would not report deposits. When Petitioner questioned Respondent about the entries, they would argue and he would beat her. Respondent admitted that he did not always tell Petitioner about a deposit but testified that he always made a notation in the check register, and that Petitioner would ask him about them when reconciling the checkbook. . . .

. . . Respondent's first argument is that the trial court inequitably distributed the marital assets and debts by granting all assets to Petitioner and assessing all debts against Respondent. The trial judge found no appreciable marital assets, that Petitioner possessed only a triply-refinanced 1984 Mazda and a vanity which had been a gift from Respondent, and that Respondent retained what little marital property remained. Respondent argues that this decision is arbitrary and an abuse of the trial court's discretion. . . .

. . . However, in the case here the trial court specifically found that Respondent was solely responsible for the over $82,000 in debt. There was testimony that after they purchased the marital home, Petitioner drastically reduced her expenditures while Respondent maintained or increased his. The trial court noted that Respondent would go out at night without his wife and child; that he belonged to a health club; that Respondent opened charge accounts without Petitioner's knowledge or permission; that Respondent spent money on clothing for himself and at fine restaurants; that he gave money to his mother; that Respondent borrowed money but did not use it to reduce the marital debt; and that he "in effect kited his account in consumer debts." The trial court also found that Petitioner spent minimal amounts on clothing, ate in fast food restaurants, and in one year was responsible for less than one-twelfth of their total expenses.

Dissipation can occur prior to dissolution. (*Partyka*, 158 Ill. App. 3d at 549, 110 Ill. Dec. at 503, 511 N.E.2d at 680.) The key is whether one spouse uses marital property for his or her own benefit for a purpose unrelated to the marriage. (*Malters,* 133 Ill. App. 3d at 181–182, 88 Ill. Dec. at 469, 478 N.E.2d at 1077.) When one party is charged with dissipation, he must prove by clear and convincing evidence that the questioned expenditures were made for a marital purpose (citations omitted). . . . Unsupported statements that the funds were used for marital purposes are insufficient (citation omitted).

The trial court here noted that Respondent claimed to have spent the money for family expenses but that he could produce only a few credit card statements for insignificant amounts. The court also noted that Respon-

dent opened credit card accounts without Petitioner's permission, even though her name was used, and that Respondent retained total control of these accounts, having the statements sent to his mother's house. Where one spouse has sole access to funds or incurs debt without the knowledge of the other, that spouse can be held to have dissipated marital assets and can be held responsible for the entire debt (citations omitted). Here Respondent had sole access to the credit cards used to incur the debt, and for that reason the trial court properly found that he alone would be held responsible. . . .

. . . We affirm the distribution of marital debt as ordered by the trial court. . . .

THE DISTINCTION BETWEEN SEPARATE AND MARITAL PROPERTY

Once a list of a client's property and debts has been prepared, the next step is to divide the property into two categories: separate property and marital property. **Separate property** is property acquired by a spouse *prior* to the marriage or after the marriage by a gift, inheritance, or will, designated to that particular spouse alone. **Marital property** can be defined as property and/or income acquired during the marriage.

HEY . . . THAT'S MY PARENTS' MONEY

A common struggle in many divorce cases involves the down payment on the marital home. Kind parents who sometimes give money for the purchase of the home may find themselves in the middle of the separate versus marital property dilemma.

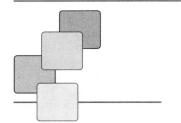 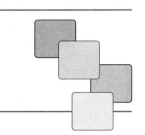

SHIRLEY R. COHEN V. HAROLD L. COHEN

474 P.2D 792 (1970)

SUPREME COURT OF COLORADO

GROVES, JUSTICE.

This proceeding arises out of a divorce action brought by the wife. The parties appear here in the same order as in the trial court and are referred to as plaintiff and defendant. The alleged error relates to the division of property and the award of alimony and attorney's fees to the plaintiff. We affirm. . . .

. . . The plaintiff's principal contention is that the court erred in finding that a monetary gift made by the defendant's parents was a gift to the defendant rather than to the plaintiff. Prior to the marriage the

defendant's father executed two checks payable to the plaintiff in the respective amounts of $6,000 and $5,000. The defendant's parents specified that the proceeds were to be applied towards the purchase of a home to be occupied by the parties, and the money was so applied. After executing the checks the father gave them to the defendant, who presented them to the plaintiff. The plaintiff endorsed the checks to the defendant and returned them to him. The defendant's father testified that he made the checks payable to the plaintiff on the advice of his accountant, who apparently thought this might cause a saving of gift tax. (The gift tax of $11,000 was later declared to the taxing authorities as having been made to the defendant.)

The court found that this was a gift by the defendant's parents to the defendant and that the plaintiff was not entitled to any portion of the $11,000 in the property division. The testimony was in conflict, but there is ample evidence to support the finding of the trial court as to the intent with respect to the gifts, and we should not and will not disturb that finding . . . .

Judgment affirmed.

HODGES, KELLEY and LEE, JJ., concur.

Remember that the definition of marital property excludes separate property. The issue of title or "whose name is property in" is unimportant. For instance, if the marital home was purchased during the marriage but title is solely in the wife's name as evidenced by the deed, it is still considered marital property. Both wife *and* husband have an interest in the home, regardless of whose name is on the deed. The family courts have statutory power to award property in a divorce matter regardless of the title interest.

The underlying policy behind the judicial authority statutes is that marriage is a **partnership.** In a business partnership, the partners pool their expertise, efforts, and resources to make the business operative and profitable. Similarly, during a marriage, the efforts and personal and financial resources of the parties are pooled for the benefit of the marital partnership. When the marriage has ended, each spouse has an interest in whatever has accumulated during the course of this partnership.

The task of defining separate and marital is an important part of the divorce process. The court will award separate property to the spouse entitled to its ownership. Once the separate property is parceled out to respective spouses, the marital property becomes one of the focal points of the divorce litigation. Whatever goes into the marital property pot is up for grabs. In some states, such as Connecticut, the court may award *any* of the spouses' property, separate or marital, in the course of the divorce proceedings to either spouse, regardless of whether the property is separate or marital.

STATUTES

Relief is also provided in jurisdictions that make distinctions between separate and marital property, if doing so would result in an unjust or unfair result.

Connecticut General Statutes Annotated (West)

§ 46b-81. (a) At the time of entering a decree of annulling or dissolving a marriage or for legal separation pursuant to a complaint under section 46b-45, the superior court may assign to either the husband or wife all or any part of the estate of the other. The court may pass title to real property to either party or to a third person or may order the sale of such real property, without any act by either the husband or the wife, when in the judgment of the court it is the proper mode to carry the decree into effect. . . .

(c) In fixing the nature and value of the property, if any, to be assigned, the court, after hearing the witnesses, if any, of each party, except as provided in subsection (a) of section 46b-51, shall consider the length of marriage, the causes for the annulment, dissolution of the marriage or legal separation, the age, health, station, occupation, amount and sources of income, vocational skills, employability, estate, liabilities and needs of each of the parties and the opportunity of each for future acquisition of capital assets and income. The court shall also consider the contribution of each of the parties in the acquisition, preservation or appreciation in value of their respective estates.

Frequently it is easy to determine what property belongs in the separate property category and what belongs in the marital property category; in other instances, the distinctions are not as clear. Separate property loses its separate classification and attains the marital property distinction when it is

- titled jointly,
- used for the purpose of supporting the marriage,
- becomes so commingled with marital property that its separate origin cannot be traced.

This transformation of separate property to marital property is known as **transmutation.** The process of determining when the asset was acquired by tracking its origin is called **tracing.** Tracing helps determine whether the property is separate or marital property. Tracing is not as easy as it sounds. The determination of what is separate or marital property may depend on whom your office is representing, and may ultimately have to be decided by the courts if the parties cannot agree.

Whenever separate property is transmuted, the attempts at making a solid distinction between separate and marital property become blurry and tracing will be problematic. Determining when a separate asset exactly makes the transition to marital property may be very difficult. When a couple marries, it is usually their intent to share their resources and work in unison for the benefit of the marital partnership. Marriages are not entered into with the intent of tracking and recording every penny or every hour of labor performed in the acquisition of those marital assets. Therefore, the issue of whether a questionable asset is classified as separate or marital property may have to be resolved by the family court.

THE PITFALLS OF COMMINGLING OF PROPERTY AND ASSETS

As mentioned, one reason why it may be hard to distinguish between separate property and marital property is that separate and marital property or the income from such property may be **commingled.**

For instance, when a husband inherits real property from a parent, that property is separate property. However, the property is rental property and the rental income goes into the spouse's checking account from which marital bills are paid.

After a few years, the husband wishes to mortgage the property to take out some funds to buy a vacation home for the family. Although the property is worth a lot (i.e., has a lot of equity), the husband cannot get the loan amount he needs because his income is not high enough. With his wife's income added in, however, together they can qualify for the mortgage they need. Since the wife is going on the mortgage, she wants to be on the deed also, so the husband quit claims a half interest to her. The couple pay cash for a vacation condo in another state with the proceeds from the mortgage on the rental property. They are both on the deed, having taken title in tenancy by the entirety. Six years later, the wife files for divorce and as part of her property settlement proposal, asks for money equal to one-half the market value of the vacation home, the rental property, and the parties' principal residence.

All of the bills for all the properties and other household expenses have been paid out of the joint checking account. Both parties' paychecks go into this account as well as the rent payments from the rental property.

The husband agrees to sell the family home and split the sale proceeds, but he does not wish to share the vacation home with his wife because the cash payment for the vacation home came from the equity in the rental property. He sees both as separate property.

In this case the assets have been confusingly commingled. The wife argues that the property taxes for both the rental property and the condo have been paid out of the joint checking account and that the condo fee for the vacation condo also is paid from that account. She also notes that while both of these properties have been maintained through funds from the joint checking account, the properties both have appreciated considerably and that's she is entitled to a percentage of the **appreciation.**

To avoid this type of commingling, it would have been better if the husband had a second checking account into which he put the rental income and then used the rental income to pay for the property taxes for that piece of real estate and for other related expenses such as insurance, maintenance, and any utilities not paid by tenants. To avoid having the wife on the rental property mortgage, he could have taken a second mortgage on the primary residence and made up any deficiency by taking a smaller mortgage on the rental property, which he could pay himself. Both parties would own the vacation condo and pay the condo fee and property taxes from the marital joint account. Upon the dissolution of their marriage, each spouse would be entitled to half the net value of the marital residence and the vacation home. The husband would have all of his separate rental property. If he could demonstrate that the rental income covered all of the property's expenses and that no marital assets were used nor any spousal effort expended for the property's upkeep, then he might not have to share any of the appreciation with his wife. On the other hand, if his spouse helped with caring for the property and if sometimes the marital funds had to be used for shortfalls due to inadequate rental income, then she would be entitled to a share of the appreciation in accordance with the amount of marital funds and her personal resources dedicated to maintaining that property. As will be discussed shortly, this type of outcome can and may occur in either a community property state or in what is termed as an *equitable distribution jurisdiction*.

VALUATION OF ASSETS

Once the property has been classified as either separate or marital property, the next step is to determine its **value;** that is, what is the marital property worth? What is the property's fair market value? **Fair market value** is the price a buyer is willing to pay a seller in exchange for the property.

FIGURE 6–1
A family home is often part of the marital property and attorneys need to determine how much equity the parties have in it.

Several methods are available to determine the value of marital property. Sometimes the parties are in agreement with the value of an asset and will mutually agree to a monetary figure. This consensus is very common with automobiles and the marital home. While many family homes are owned outright, others have outstanding mortgages and taxes due. Here, it is important to determine how much *equity* the parties have in the property. **Equity** is the fair market value of the property minus any encumbrances (i.e., mortgages, taxes, and liens).

The paralegal can verify the equity portion of the property by obtaining a release from the client authorizing the office to obtain information from the client's bank. Bank records can also help determine the value of various bank accounts. The values of stock, bonds, mutual funds, and other investments can be obtained from reviewing the *Wall Street Journal* or other financial publications.

EXAMPLE

John and Mary are married and they own a four-bedroom house. The fair market value of the marital home is $250,000. The outstanding mortgage due is $125,000, and property taxes due are $5,000. The equity is determined as follows:

FMV	$250,000
(less) Outstanding Mortgage & Property Taxes	$130,000
Equity	$120,000

RETAINING EXPERTS FOR VALUATION OF PROPERTY

If the parties cannot agree or are unable to determine the value of a marital asset, an expert can be retained. A family practice should always keep at its disposal a list of experts commonly used in family matters. The paralegal may assume the responsibility of maintaining a file folder on each expert, which should include an up-to-date resumé, list of fees, and area of expertise. Experts include accountants, appraisers, actuaries, bank counselors, domestic violence counselors, financial planners, pension valuators, social workers, psychiatrists, and psychologists.

If an expert is needed, either spouse or both should file a motion for appointment of an expert with the court. If the parties are in agreement, they can present the agreement to the court and put it on the record.

If they are not in agreement, the court will decide. The court will order the appointment of a disinterested expert, identify the specific property to be assessed, determine who will pay the expert, and determine how the expert will be paid.

IN RE THE MARRIAGE OF MICHAEL H. KEEDY AND CAROL SUE KEEDY

813 P.2D 442 (MONT. 1991)

SUPREME COURT OF MONTANA

GRAY, JUSTICE.

The appellant, Michael Keedy, appeals from the property distribution of the Eleventh Judicial District Court, Flathead County, in this marital dissolution action. We affirm in part, reverse in part, and remand for further proceedings. . . .

. . . The appellant and the respondent, Carol Keedy, were married on May 27, 1973, in Lincoln, Nebraska. At the time of the marriage, Michael's education consisted of a bachelor's degree and a juris doctorate degree; Carol possessed a bachelor's degree in education. Two children were born to the marriage: a son, born on October 29, 1974, and a daughter, born on November 23, 1979.

Throughout the marriage, Michael has been employed as a lobbyist, attorney, legislator and for the past seven years, district court judge. During the marriage Carol worked primarily as a homemaker; she currently teaches at a private school.

The parties separated on April 1, 1989, and brought this matter before the District Court on April 30, 1990. The District Court entered its Amended Findings of Fact, Conclusions of Law, and Order on August 3, 1990. Michael appeals.

The first issue raised on appeal is whether the District Court erred in including the entire baseball card collection as a marital asset.

The baseball card collection consists of approximately 100,000 baseball cards. Michael testified that he began the collection as a boy in 1954 and continued to collect the cards up through 1963. He resumed his card collecting again in 1971 and continued collecting baseball cards after his marriage to Carol in 1973. At trial he introduced into evidence various lists of cards in an attempt to demonstrate which cards he had acquired prior to the marriage and which cards he had acquired after the marriage.

Carol hired an appraiser who estimated the value of the entire collection at $208,000. Michael testified that he believed the collection to be worth $100,000. After struggling with the evidence before it, the District Court abandoned its attempt to determine which cards were brought into the marriage or to place a value on the baseball cards. The court required Michael to divide the collection into two equal piles and allow Carol to select one pile of cards.

Michael argues, first, that the District Court erred in including in the marital estate those baseball cards he brought into the marriage. He also contends that the current value of such cards is not a product of contribution from the marital effort and should be excluded from the marital estate as his separate property.

This Court has repeatedly held that distribution of marital assets by a district court, where based upon substantial credible evidence, will not be overturned absent a clear abuse of discretion (citation omitted).

Section 40-4-202(1), MCA, requires the courts to, [e]quitably apportion between the parties the property and assets belonging to either or both, however and whenever acquired. . . . In dividing property acquired prior to the marriage; . . . property acquired in exchange for property acquired before the marriage. . . ; [and] *the increased value of property acquired prior to marriage; . . . the court shall consider those contributions of the other spouse to the marriage, including:*

(a) the nonmonetary contribution of a homemaker;

(b) the *extent to which such contributions have facilitated the maintenance of this property;* and

(c) whether or not the property division serves as an alternative to maintenance arrangements. (Emphasis supplied)

The District Court properly determined that the baseball card collection was a marital asset, however, it erred in not crediting Michael with the value, at the time of the marriage, of the cards he brought into the marriage.

The value of the premarital cards at the *time of the marriage* was undisputed between the parties. Michael testified that the value of the collection at the time of the marriage, or shortly thereafter, was approximately $5,000. Carol herself proposed in her Trial Memorandum, that in order "to equitably divide the property, the [District] Court should award $5,000.00 to the Petitioner to represent the value of the baseball card collection that he brought into the marriage."

In considering the factors presented in § 40-4-202(1), MCA, it becomes apparent that the value of the premarital cards is not properly a part of the marital estate. The undisputed amount of $5,000 could not have been contributed to in any way by Carol.

However, the appreciation in value of the cards, including the premarital cards, properly could be included in the marital estate under §40-4-202(1), MCA, if the evidence supported spousal contribution to that appreciated value. Michael argues that the increase in value of the premarital baseball cards was not related to any marital contribution from Carol. We disagree.

In the present case, substantial credible evidence exists to support the finding that Carol contributed to the maintenance and growth of the collection. Evidence shows that she encouraged Michael to collect the cards, participated in the collection by buying foods associated with particular cards, and on at least one occasion, protected the cards from a flood while Michael was away from home. Testimony also indicated that Michael's card purchases strained the family budget at times, with the family sacrificing other items in order to build the collection.

It was not erroneous, under these circumstances, for the District Court to find that Carol contributed to the maintenance and growth of the card collection and, therefore, that she is entitled to share in the postmarital appreciation in value.

Thus, we hold that it was proper to include the baseball card collection as part of the marital estate, but that the District Court erred in failing to credit Michael with the undisputed value of $5,000 for the baseball cards he brought into the marriage. . . .

. . . Affirmed in part, reversed in part, and remanded to the District Court for further proceedings consistent with this opinion.

TURNAGE, C.J. and HARRISON, HUNT, McDONOUGH, and WEBER, JJ., concur.

TRIEWEILLER, Justice, concurring in part and dissenting in part.

EFFECT OF PREMARITAL AGREEMENTS ON PROPERTY DISTRIBUTION

Prior to marriage, the parties may have determined their respective property rights in a written document called a **prenuptial, premarital,** or **antenuptial agreement** (see Chapter 4). This is a contract entered into by the prospective spouses regarding their rights during the marriage and in the event of a divorce. It is essential to determine whether a client has entered into one of these agreements and to obtain a copy. Most courts will enforce these agreements provided that certain conditions existed at the time of their execution and circumstances have not substantially changed since the signing of the agreement. Premarital agreements must be in writing. There must be a full **disclosure** of all assets. This means that the parties must disclose the full extent and current values of all assets. The parties must also have an adequate opportunity to seek independent counsel before signing a premarital agreement.

In the absence of a premarital or prenuptial agreement, divorcing spouses are free to negotiate between themselves how property is to be distributed, and then enter into a mutually consensual agreement regarding the division of their marital assets and marital debts, as well as child custody and support, alimony, visitation, and attorney's fees. If the parties are unwilling to negotiate, or if negotiation on some or all aspects of the marital dissolution fails, the court will decide the outcome of the unresolved issues.

RESOLVING THE ISSUE OF PROPERTY DISTRIBUTION: CONTESTED OR UNCONTESTED

When the parties are able to negotiate a plan they find mutually acceptable, a **settlement agreement** or **separation agreement** is drafted and signed by both parties, thus obviating the need for a long court battle. Courts prefer agreements because the parties are more likely to be content with a settlement they have voluntarily negotiated and crafted. The court will not change or question an agreement unless it appears to be unfair or against public policy. The court will generally approve the agreement upon determining that it was entered into voluntarily and that it is fair and equitable. Courts also prefer agreements because it keeps the court docket moving by disposing of cases without protracted judicial proceedings and thus conserves judicial resources.

When the parties are unable to reach an agreement, it is up to the court to resolve the property dispute. Trial courts have great discretion in their decision-making powers. A trial court is in the best position to observe the demeanor of the parties. A trial court's decision will not be reversed on appeal unless the appellant can convince the higher court that the trial court abused its discretion by either misapplying the law or by making erroneous rulings regarding the admission of evidence.

When resolving disputes over the division of property, the courts will first make an award of separate property to the owner spouse. The definition of separate versus marital property may be one of the first areas of contention in the trial. Once the marital property pot has been defined, the court will divide the property according to the jurisdiction's property distribution statute. Family law paralegals must become familiar with their jurisdictions' statutes and the case law interpreting those statutes.

JURISDICTIONAL APPROACHES TO PROPERTY DISTRIBUTION

In the United States, two systems are used to dictate the division of marital property upon the dissolution of marriage: *equitable distribution* and *community property distribution*.

EQUITABLE DISTRIBUTION

As mentioned in earlier sections of this book, our system of jurisprudence is based on the English common law. The English common law system was also the approach used to determine the division of marital property upon dissolution of a marriage. Upon marriage, a husband and wife merged into a single legal entity—the husband. This was known as the **unity of spouses.** At common law, married women had no separate legal identity. A married woman could not own or manage her own property, she could not sue or be sued, nor could she control her wages. As time passed, and attitudes toward married women changed, state legislatures in the United States, toward the end of the 1800's, enacted the Married Women's Property Acts. These statutes removed the common law strictures that prevented married women from owning and managing their own resources.

Although these statutes made it possible for women to own their own property, the divorce law did not change along with the new status of married women. Property acquired during the marriage was divided on the basis of who supplied the funds to purchase the property and possessed title. Traditionally, married women did not work outside the home. Husbands bought the property, retained title and ownership, and upon divorce, walked away with the lion's share of the assets. While jointly held property was divided between the spouses, the courts had no power to award property solely owned by one spouse to the nontitle spouse. States legislatures eventually saw the inequity and harshness of this method of property division and enacted statutes allowing family courts to distribute property acquired during marriage on the basis of equity or fairness, as opposed to ownership. This is known as the **equitable distribution** system of dividing marital property. Family courts in equitable distribution states, in determining how property is to be divided between a divorcing couple, must evaluate each spouse's interest in the marital property on an individual or case-by-case basis. Equitable distribution state statutes enumerate statutory factors that the courts must consider in the division of marital assets and debts. These factors commonly include: the length of the marriage, the work history and job prospects of each spouse, the physical and mental health of each spouse, the source of particular assets, and the expenses of the children. Some of these factors are listed in the Connecticut statute. The courts, however, are not required to give equal weight to each factor, and have the discretion to make decisions based on the merits of the particular case before them.

Most jurisdictions in the United States follow the equitable distribution system of property division. However, several states, particularly those located in the American Southwest, and originally settled by Spanish and French colonists, adhere to the distribution system known as community property.

COMMUNITY PROPERTY

In community property jurisdictions, property acquired during the marriage belongs equally to each spouse, unless it has been excluded as separate property. California's property division statute provides that the court will "equally" divide the community estate of the parties.

STATUTES

CALIFORNIA CIVIL CODE ANNOTATED (WEST)

§ 2550. *Manner of Division of Community.*
Except upon the written agreement of the parties, or on oral stipulation of the parties in open court, or as otherwise provided in this division, in a proceeding for dissolution of marriage or for legal separation of the parties, the court shall, either in its judgment of dissolution of the marriage, in its judgment of legal separation of the parties, or at a later time if it expressly reserves jurisdiction to make such a property division, divide the community estate of the parties equally.

The community property arrangement is based on Spanish and French concepts of marital property as codified in the *code civile* or **civil code,** the system of law existing on the European mainland, as opposed to the common law system of England.

The nine states that use the community property system are mostly situated in the West and Southwest region of the United States. The community property states are (see Figure 6–2):

Arizona	New Mexico
California	Texas
Idaho	Washington
Louisiana	Wisconsin
Nevada	

The community property system assumes that both husband and wife contribute to the accumulation of marital assets. This concept valued the work of the husband who traditionally worked outside the home as well as that of the stay-at-home spouse who took care of the home and the children. The husband, however, had the right to control the community property, until such statutory provisions were found to violate the Equal Protection Clause of the U.S. Constitution. Upon acquisition of any asset or income during the marriage, both spouses acquire an equal interest in the property, regardless of who supplied the funds for its acquisition. Because each spouse is deemed to have contributed to the acquisition of the marital assets (and also the marital debts), the assets and debts are divided on a 50/50 basis upon divorce. The various community property states allow for deviations or application of the equitable distribution system after the property has been divided on a 50/50 basis.

FIGURE 6–2
Most of the
community property
states are located in
the West and
Southwest.

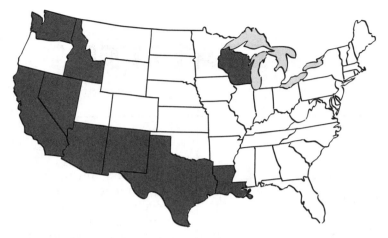

Community Property States: Arizona, Nevada, California, Washington,
Wisconsin, Idaho, Louisiana, New Mexico, Texas

STATUTES

Arizona and California also recognize what is known as **quasi-community.** If a married couple acquires property in a noncommunity property state and then moves to a community property jurisdiction, upon divorce, the property is considered community property. Therefore, community property carries its distinctiveness over state lines.

NEVADA REVISED STATUTES ANNOTATED

ALIMONY AND ADJUDICATION OF PROPERTY RIGHTS; AWARD OF ATTORNEY'S FEE; Except as otherwise provided in NRS 125, 155 and unless the action is contrary to a premarital agreement between the parties which is enforceable pursuant to chapter 123A of NRSl

1. In granting a divorce, the court: . . . (b) Shall, to the extent practicable, make an equal disposition of the community property of the parties, except that the court may make an unequal disposition of the community property in such proportions as it deems just if the court finds a compelling reason to do so and sets forth in writing the reasons for making the unequal disposition.

2. Except as otherwise provided in this subsection, in granting a divorce, the court shall dispose of any property held in joint tenancy in the manner set forth in subsection 1 for the disposition of community property. If a party has made a contribution of separate property to the acquisition or improvement of property held in joint tenancy, the court may provide for the

reimbursement of that party for his contribution. The amount of reimbursement must not exceed the amount of the contribution of separate property that can be traced to the acquisition or improvement of property held in joint tenancy, without interest of any adjustment because of an increase in the value of the property held in joint tenancy. The amount of the reimbursement must not exceed the value, at the time of the disposition of the property held in joint tenancy for which the contribution of separate property was made. In determining whether to provide for the reimbursement, in whole or in part, of a party who has contributed separate property, the court shall consider:

(a) The intention of the parties in placing the property in joint tenancy;

(b) The length of the marriage;

(c) Any other factor which the court deems relevant in making a just and equitable disposition of that property.

As used in this subsection, "contribution" includes a down payment, a payment for the acquisition or improvement of property, and a payment reducing the principal of a loan used to finance the purchase or improvement of property. The term does not include a payment of interest on a loan used to finance the purchase or improvement of property, or a payment made for maintenance, insurance or taxes on property.

3. Whether or not application for suit money has been made under the provisions of NRS 125.040, the court may award a reasonable attorney's fee to either party to an action for divorce if those fees are in issue under the pleadings.

4. In granting a divorce, the court may also set apart such portion of the husband's separate property for the wife's support, the wife's separate property for the husband's support or the separate property of either spouses for the support of their children as is deemed just and equitable. . . .

If you are a practicing paralegal in a community property state, it is essential that you become familiar with the intricacies of the community property laws in your state, as they differ from jurisdiction to jurisdiction.

COMMUNITY PROPERTY RULES AND EXCEPTIONS

The general rule is that anything a married couple accumulates during marriage is community property. Both spouses own an undivided share of the whole. There are some exceptions to this rule. Property owned by a spouse before marriage or property acquired during the marriage through a gift or an inheritance remains the separate property of that spouse. However, if the separate property is commingled with community property, such as when a cash gift to one spouse is deposited into a joint checking account, that money may be transmuted into property of the community's estate.

Although the general rule and the exceptions seem clear and straightforward, many issues can arise in a dissolution action that must be decided by more complicated rules. For instance, if a couple resides in a community property state, and one spouse buys a piece of real estate in a equitable distribution state and puts title in his name only, how do the courts of the community property state treat this asset in a dissolution proceeding?

Similarly, when a couple are married and reside in a community property state for several years, then move to a equitable distribution state and subsequently decide to divorce, how do the courts in equitable distribution states treat property acquired during the marriage while the couple were living in the community property state?

Issues also arise on the death of one spouse. In a community property state, again the general rule is that upon the death of one spouse, one-half of the community property becomes the deceased person's (decedent's) estate and it passes through devise (will) or descent (state inheritance statutes) to the heirs. The other half of the community property estate is retained by the surviving spouse. In an equitable distribution state, if, for instance, a married couple owned a home as tenants by the entirety arrangement, when one spouse died a full interest in the house would automatically pass to the surviving spouse and the heirs would have no claim to that part of the decedent's estate.

If a couple whose primary residence was in a community property state bought a second home in an equitable distribution state and took the property as tenancy in the entirety or joint tenancy with the right of survivorship, a court in a community property state will most likely deny any challenge to the survivorship status. The court should hold that the form of ownership assumed in the other state was allowable under the laws of the equitable distribution state and that the equitable distribution state had jurisdiction; hence the survivorship right remained.

CALCULATION OF THE COMMUNITY PROPERTY MARITAL ESTATE

Most community property states determine the value of the community estate by ascertaining the fair market value of the community assets minus the joint debts and other obligations of the parties. The figure obtained is the net community estate. Unless the parties agree otherwise and the court allows it, each spouse must receive one-half of the net community estate. This does not require the spouses to divide every asset in half; rather, the net value of the assets received by each spouse must be equal.

CHARACTERIZATION OF COMMUNITY DEBTS

In a community property state, all debts incurred from the beginning of the marriage to the date the parties separate are community debts. Each spouse is equally responsible for these debts regardless of which party incurred the debt and regardless if it was with or without the other spouse's knowledge.

During the marriage, each spouse is responsible for 100 percent of the debt, and upon dissolution, the law is that each spouse will assume one-half of the liabilities owed.

EXCEPTIONS TO THE COMMUNITY PROPERTY RULES

Even though the community property states are well known for their rule of an equal division of all marital assets and no division of separate assets, there are instances were these rules are modified to prevent unfairness or injustice.

Several community property states have enacted legislation to authorize a deviation from the community property strictures and spell out under what circumstances such a deviation may occur.

For instance, in Arizona, while the general practice is to equally distribute the community assets, if one spouse has dissipated the assets of the community estate through gambling, drugs, frivolous spending, or has hidden community property from the other spouse, the court will address this inequity by awarding the other spouse more of the community estate.

If an attorney feels that the circumstances of his or her client's marriage contain aspects that would qualify under one of these conditions, then the attorney will present these circumstances in a manner that most effectively makes the situation fit the condition. Louisiana is a community property state; however, state law allows prospective spouses to opt for the same separate property status they had as single persons. This alternative allows spouses to claim all assets, including retirement benefits, as separate property without accounting to the other spouse regarding the accrual, treatment, or disposal of assets. However, any contributions to a retirement plan made during the marriage will be considered community property and subject to division.

In Texas, as will soon be discussed more fully, when a married couple moves to Texas from an equitable distribution state, the status of property deeded or titled to only one spouse does not change. However, in a dissolution proceeding, if the parties cannot agree on how assets are to be divided, the court will step in and in this instance can and may divide property acquired while living outside the state in a manner that is fair and equitable. This could mean that such property be divided equally regardless of which spouse's name the title is vested in, or it could mean that a percentage of the property be allocated to the other spouse.

In Nevada, community property is divided equally between divorcing spouses unless a court determines that such division is unjust. In that case, the court will divide property in a manner it deems equitable. Two of the factors the court will consider include the length of the marriage and the contribution either spouse made from separate property in acquiring or maintaining such property.

In California, the law requires that the community estate be divided equally if there is no written agreement to the contrary. Spouses may enter into an agreement where they can modify the division of assets, and if the agreement is entered into freely and knowingly, the court will allow it.

In California, equal ownership of assets does not depend on the quality or quantity of a spouse's contribution. Spouses are considered equal partners in the marriage. Each spouse shares the marital property regardless of whether the assets were earned by one or the other.

In a dissolution proceeding in California, the court may allocate assets of comparable value to the former husband and wife to make the overall division equal. Every asset does not have to be divided.

PROBATE ISSUES IN COMMUNITY PROPERTY STATES AND EQUITABLE DISTRIBUTION STATES

Spouses in a community property state receive one-half of the community estate upon the death of the other spouse. A spouse may leave separate property to anyone. A spouse may change this division by will but may not leave less than one-half of the marital estate to the other spouse unless both parties sign an agreement that makes all or some of the community property separate property. In that instance, the spouse may devise the separate property as he or she wishes.

Several community property states have statutes that allow married couples to hold title to assets such as their home or investment accounts as "community property with the right of survivorship." Under this arrangement, when one spouse dies, the other spouse receives all of the assets held this way and these assets are not subject to probate proceedings.

In an equitable distribution state, each spouse owns what their name is on, whether it be a deed, automobile or boat registration document, stock certificate, or other paper conferring title. In an equitable distribution jurisdiction, a husband or wife may leave whatever property he or she owns to whomever he or she wishes provided the other spouse receives at least what the state legislature or state common law has determined is the minimal spousal share.

In an equitable jurisdiction state, there are statutes of succession to ensure that a nonworking spouse will have at the minimum a fixed percentage of their deceased spouse's estate so that upon his death they will not be divested of all property acquired during marriage. California, because of the community property system of marital property ownership, does not have these types of statutes. Therefore, the quasi-community property system remedies the situation. Other states—Texas, for example—do not change the status of property that was acquired while living elsewhere. When a married couple moves to Texas, the status of property acquired elsewhere does not change. Texas does not have laws providing each spouse with a statutory share of the other's assets. Hence the nonworking spouse who would be entitled to one-half or one-third of her husband's estate despite his testamentary disposition in an equitable distribution state is out in the cold in Texas, where she has no statutory right to her husband's estate and may be disinherited under his will.

States with quasi-community property systems differ in various aspects. For instance, some states disagree about whether the nonworking spouse is entitled to one-half of the quasi-community property or to one-half of each asset.

MOVING FROM A COMMUNITY PROPERTY STATE TO AN EQUITABLE DISTRIBUTION STATE

In general, equitable distribution states treat property acquired during marriage in a community property state as jointly held property in which each spouse has an undivided one-half interest. However, to the extent the common law states also have an elective or forced statutory share in a surviving spouse, that right is usually not extended to the undivided one-half interest owned by the deceased spouse. That one-half interest will fall outside the estate.

DISTINCTIONS BETWEEN SEPARATE AND MARITAL PROPERTY IN COMMUNITY PROPERTY STATES AS COMPARED WITH DISTINCTIONS IN EQUITABLE DISTRIBUTION STATES

In community property states as in equitable distribution states, the courts make a distinction between separate property and marital property. As mentioned, property that one spouse already owned at the time of the marriage or received during the marriage through gift or inheritance is considered separate property.

In a community property state, a spouse's separate property is not included in the community estate before the estate is divided. Therefore, the spouse owning that property will leave the marriage with one-half of the community property and all of his or her separate property.

In an equitable distribution state, where the goal is equitable or fair division of the marital estate, one spouse's separate property may or may not be included in the marital estate. For instance, if either or both of the parties purchased cars during the marriage and each spouse has title to one car, these assets will be considered part of the marital estate. This will be especially beneficial to a spouse who purchased a car several years ago. That car will be included in the marital estate. If the other spouse recently purchased an expensive new car during the marital partnership, that will also be included in the marital estate. The assets of the marital estate will be totaled up and then divided in a manner that the court deems equitable. This division need not be 50/50 to be equitable. If the court finds that both parties contributed significantly to the economic partnership, the assets may be equally divided. However, if the court finds or if the parties agree that one spouse's effort was far greater than the other's effort, the property division will reflect that situation. If for instance, for several years a woman holds down a very demanding job that is the only source of income to the household, and she also provides all of the care for the couple's three children and does the housework, while the husband does not work and assumes no household or child-care responsibilities, the court may distribute the bulk of the marital estate to the woman, especially if she has physical custody of the children. On the other hand, if the nonworking husband was a stay-at-home dad and took care of the household chores, including meals, laundry, and cleaning and also functioned as the children's primary caregiver, the division would more likely be equal distribution, or close to it.

TREATMENT OF THE APPRECIATION OF SEPARATE PROPERTY DURING THE MARRIAGE

In many states, where a spouse owns an asset at the time of marriage, the spouse will be entitled to an amount equal to the entire value of that asset at the time of the marriage. If the asset has appreciated, the other spouse may be entitled to an amount that can be as much as one-half of the value of the appreciation. The court may look at the contributions the other spouse made to the marital partnership and how these contributions facilitated the maintenance of this asset.

For instance, when Marty became engaged to Gwen he may have decided to keep his interest in the beach house and rent his half interest to a friend of Joe's who would move in. Over the years, he would enjoy rental income that would help to pay the taxes on the house and his share of the insurance repairs and maintenance. At the time Gwen brings a dissolution, the house has tripled in value and Gwen wants 50 percent of Marty's share of the appreciation.

As the *Keedy* case demonstrates, there is a good chance that Gwen will get exactly what she is requesting. The court may look at whether Gwen made a contribution to the appreciation. If it finds that she helped Marty with any cleaning and repairs or yard work at the beach house, she had a role in maintaining the property. Similarly, when the property taxes were due, if paying them strained the family budget, Gwen's forbearance also helps to maintain the asset.

There are instances where a spouse who has an investment fund at the time of the marriage lets it sit and neither contributes more to it nor makes any withdrawals from it. During the marriage, the value appreciates considerably and there was little or no maintenance needed while this asset grew. In such a case, this asset remains separate property and is not figured into the marital estate.

There are other times when a spouse will share in the appreciation of an investment product. If Marty brings to the marriage a 401K plan worth $15,000, and during the course of the marriage makes contributions from his earnings, which increase the amount of the fund, Gwen will be entitled to a share of the appreciation of the portion of the fund made up of Marty's postmarriage contributions.

After ten years the fund is worth $75,000. Over those ten years, Marty put in $3,000 per year for a total of $30,000. Total pre- and postmarital contributions equal $45,000, so that the total appreciation is $30,000. Since twice as much money was put into the fund after the marriage, the marital contribution was twice as much as the amount in the fund prior to marriage.

Thus, twice as much of the appreciation amount should be counted in the marital estate. Therefore, $20,000 of appreciation plus the $30,000 Marty contributed during the marriage are part of the marital estate and Gwen should get half, or $25,000.

THE NOT-SO-OBVIOUS ASSETS OF MARRIAGE—GOODWILL, PENSIONS, AND PROFESSIONAL DEGREES

INTRODUCTION

It is important that all marital assets be identified. The client must inform his or her attorney regarding all actual or potential assets so that the client's attorney can determine what rights, if any, the client may have in the asset. Some marital assets are not so obvious because they are not present in tangible form, that is, something we can see and touch. These intangible assets, however, may have substantial value and it would be considered legal malpractice not to identify, valuate, and seek a fair division for the client. Some of the major intangible marital assets include goodwill, pension, and the professional degree.

GOODWILL

Goodwill is a term used to describe the ability of a business or professional to attract future customers and repeat business due to a good reputation in the community. A dollar value on goodwill can be determined by an expert. Many states identify goodwill as marital property if a business or career has been enhanced during the marriage. A spouse who assists the other spouse in achieving that reputation may be entitled to share in the enhanced earning capacity that reputation will bring. Even where a spouse has stayed at home as a traditional homemaker, her contribution to the marital partnership has enabled her husband to pursue his business endeavors and create the goodwill that has enhanced his business reputation in the community. Therefore, in many states, she is entitled to a portion of the goodwill value of the business.

In calculating goodwill, it is essential that an expert be obtained to valuate this asset. Exhibit 6–1 illustrates a letter from an accounting firm enlisted to calculate the celebrity goodwill of comedian Jim Carrey. The letter details the documents necessary to make such a calculation. Other states are not as willing to define goodwill as marital property because reputation is not an "asset."

THE GOODWILL OF BETHANY FOOT CLINIC

In this case of first impression, the Supreme Court of Oklahoma held that the goodwill of a medical sole proprietorship was a marital asset and its value subject to division by the family courts.

ROBERT J. TRACZYK V. KATHLEEN M. TRACZYK

891 P.2D 1277 (OKLA. 1995)

SUPREME COURT OF OKLAHOMA

SIMMS, JUSTICE.

Husband first takes issue with the trial court considering the goodwill of his medical practice as marital property. He testified that there was no goodwill because he was the reason the patients came to the Bethany Foot Clinic and "not very many" of the patients would stay at the Bethany Foot Clinic with a new doctor if Husband sold it.

The professional practice of one spouse is an appropriate element of the marital property to be divided between the parties where it is jointly-acquired property. *Ford v. Ford,* 766 P.2d 950 (Okla. 1988); *Carpenter v. Carpenter,* 657 P.2d 646 (Okla. 1983). The issue before us is whether goodwill of Husband's podiatry practice may be considered in determining the value of the practice. . . .

. . . Pursuant to 60 O.S.1991, §§315 and 316, goodwill of a business is defined as "the expectation of continued public patronage," and is considered property transferable like any other property. *See also Freeling v. Wood,* 361 P.2d 1061, 1063 (Okla. 1961). ("The 'good will' value of any business is the value that results from the *probability that old customers will continue to trade with an established concern*. . . . [Such] good will of a business may be sold.") (Emphasis supplied); *Travis v. Travis,* 795 P.2d 96, 97 (Okla. 1990) (quoting *Freeling); Mocnik v. Mocnik,* 838 P.2d 500, 504 (Okla. 1992) (quoting *Travis). . . .*

In determining the value of the Bethany Foot Clinic, the expert witness consulted the Goodwill Registry, "an accumulation of information concerning sales of medical related practices by experts." From this publication, the expert determined that of the most recent purchases of podiatry clinics, an average of thirty-two percent (32%) of the podiatry patients stay with the clinic after it is sold to a new doctor. The range from which he obtained the average was 21% to 44% of clients staying. Noting that the traditional method used in valuing a medical practice is the previous year's gross income, the expert then took the previous year's gross income at the clinic ($324,201.51) and multiplied it by the 32% figure to arrive at a goodwill value of $103,744.00. Adding this to the value of the remaining business assets, the expert found the total

value of the Bethany Foot Clinic to be $152,605.44. The trial court accepted this valuation and used it in determining how much alimony in lieu of property division to award.

We find that the trial court did not err in considering the goodwill of the Bethany Foot Clinic as a factor in determining the value of the clinic as marital property. The goodwill of the Bethany Foot Clinic is distinct from the personal reputation of Dr. Traczyk. Although many of Dr. Traczyk's patients would not continue to patronize the Bethany Foot Clinic were Dr. Traczyk to sell to another podiatrist, competent evidence indicates that many would stay. Indeed, Dr. Traczyk may use the goodwill as a selling point to potential purchasers.

"If goodwill is to be divided as an asset, its value should be determined either by an agreement or *by its fair market value.* Both of these methods are widely accepted for valuing goodwill. *See* annotation, 78 A.L.R.4th 853, 860–71 (1987). *Mocnik,* 838 P.2d at 505.". . .

. . . Husband further argues that by both allowing goodwill to be divided as marital property and awarding support alimony, the trial court has charged him twice for his future income. We first reiterate that the goodwill of the Bethany Foot Clinic is not properly characterized as future income. Rather, it is an asset of the clinic.

Husband, though, disagrees with the distinction between future income and assets. He asserts two cases cited in *Travis* resolve the issue of "double-dipping" into his future income. However, we find these cases, *Holbrook v. Holbrook,* 103 Wis. 2d 327, 309 N.W.2d 343 (1981) and *Beasley v. Beasley,* 359 Pa. Super. 20, 518 A.2d 545 (1986), *allocatur denied,* 516 Pa. 631, 533 A.2d 90 (1987), unpersuasive because, as *Travis* indicates, they both concerned the goodwill of law practices where such goodwill was related to the reputation of the lawyer. In other words, *Holbrook* and *Beasley* are distinguishable because they did not involve a professional practice with transferable goodwill as the case at bar did.

The goodwill of the Bethany Foot Clinic was valued as an asset and was a factor in determining the total value of the business for property division purposes. This goodwill was part of the property which should be divided between the parties; Wife had a right to receive her share of the property. 43 O.S.1991, §121. On the other hand, the award of *support alimony* was a separate determination based upon Husband's ability to pay and Wife's demonstrated need. *Johnson v. Johnson,* 674 P.2d 539 (Okla. 1983). Although the property division is permanent and irrevocable, the award of support alimony is subject to modification upon a showing of substantial change in circumstances, i.e. Husband's ability and/or Wife's demonstrated need. 43 O.S.1991, §134; *Clifton v. Clifton,* 801 P.2d 693 (Okla. 1990).

"[S]upport alimony is not alimony in lieu of a division. Support alimony is exactly what its name implies, alimony for support and maintenance. Alimony *in lieu*

of a division is given for satisfaction of a property division obligation. These are distinct obligations and the acceptance of one does not by implication waive the right of the other." *Greer v. Greer,* 807 P.2d 791, 794 (Okla. 1991) (Emphasis in original). By awarding support alimony and including goodwill in the value of the business for property division purposes, the trial court did not "double dip" into Husband's future income. Both awards, one for support alimony and one for alimony in lieu of property division were proper and distinct from the other. We find no error in the trial court's valuation of the marital property and award of alimony in lieu of property division. . . .

PENSIONS

Next to the marital home, a **pension** may very often be the largest asset available for distribution upon divorce. A pension is a retirement benefit acquired by an employee. At the time of retirement, the employee is entitled to receive the pension funds, either by periodic payments or in a lump sum. Pension may be funded either through contributions from the employer, employee, or a combination of both. A spouse seeking a portion of the employee spouse's pension is only entitled to the portion of the pension acquired during the marriage.

A pension is either **vested** or **nonvested.** While an employee is entitled to walk away from her job with the contribution made by her during her period of employment, she will only be entitled to the funds contributed by the employer if her pension has vested. A vested pension entitles the employee to the employer's contribution portion provided that the employee has worked for the employer for an enumerated number of years. Once the employee has reached the specific benchmark, her right to the employer contribution attaches and she is entitled to the pension. If she leaves her employment with an unvested pension, the right to the employer portion of the funds has not yet attached. In a divorce case, a vested pension should be considered marital property. An unvested pension represents a future expectancy interest. If an unvested employee leaves her employer before the vesting period, a divorcing spouse may only be entitled to a portion of the employee spouse's contributions.

Whether your office is representing the employee spouse or the nonemployee spouse, it is necessary to obtain the following information, either through discovery or the client interview:

1. Name, address, and telephone number of the plan administrator,
2. Copy of the pension plan, and
3. A computer printout of monies paid into the plan by the client.

A pension must be **valuated.** This means that the value or worth of the pension must be determined. Valuation will provide the attorney with a dollar amount attached to the pension so that the client's interests in marital property can be adequately protected. Numerous pension valuation services are available to family law attorneys. Many advertise in professional publications directed at the family bar. These services employ experts trained at valuing pensions and determining their fair market value. If the parties wish to forego the valuation of the pension because of the added expense, a clause in the settlement agreement indicating that the valuation was waived is essential to protect the attorney from a malpractice claim.

Once a pension has been valuated, the attorneys for the parties must determine how this asset will be divided. This will depend on what other types of marital assets are available for distribution. If there is very little cash or other assets to distribute, the parties may seek to obtain a **Qualified Domestic Relations Order (QDRO).** This is a court order served on the pension administrator ordering the plan to distribute a specified portion of the pension funds to the nonemployee spouse. Appendix B includes two QDROs prepared in the divorce of comedian Jim Carrey and his wife, Melissa.

While state law dictates property division, federal law controls retirement benefits. When addressing the distribution of pension funds, employers must comply with the **Employee Retirement Income Security Act (ERISA).** ERISA is a federal statute passed in 1974 to protect employees and their pensions in case an employer declares bankruptcy or goes out of business. This law governs retirement pay and pension benefits. ERISA was amended by the **Retirement Equity Act (REA)** of 1984. This federal statute determines the manner in which states may divide a pension at the time of divorce, and its requirements must be complied with in order for the QDRO to be valid. If the QDRO is invalid, the plan will not release any funds.

Pensions, either through an employer or self-directed (i.e., an IRA a spouse may have started on his own at a local bank), are **tax deferred.** This means that taxes on the income produced by the pension will not be paid until the monies are withdrawn at the time of retirement. If these funds are withdrawn prior to retirement, tax penalties will be imposed. An accountant should be consulted to determine the tax liability of liquidating any deferred compensation plan. The tax liability should be determined in advance so as to negotiate a payment of taxes due between the spouses. If the tax consequences are overlooked, the employee spouse could be in for a big surprise come tax time.

An employee spouse may not wish to have her pension distributed. If there are ample funds, the parties may agree to a **buyout.** In this scenario, the pension will be valuated, and the employee spouse will give cash to the nonemployee spouse in exchange for any interest he may have in her pension. This would allow the employee spouse's pension to remain untouched. The parties may also agree to **offset** the pension with other assets. For example, the employee spouse may agree to transfer her interest in the marital home or other marital assets in exchange for the full ownership of her pension benefits.

Federal law requires that the employee spouse name the nonemployee spouse as a beneficiary of his retirement benefits. Once the marriage has been severed by a court, the client should be advised to change the beneficiary designation immediately. A certified copy of the judgment or certificate of dissolution complete with a court seal should be filed with the pension plan along with any necessary form required by the particular plan.

PENSIONS AND OTHER DEFERRED COMPENSATION PLANS AS A PART OF PROPERTY DISTRIBUTION

Under the federal Employment Retirement Income Security Act (ERISA), a spouse must be named as a beneficiary on the other spouse's pension. When the parties divorce, each spouse will have an interest in the other spouse's holdings if the pension increased during the marriage through the spouse's employment.

If prior to marriage a spouse works for an employer for several years and becomes vested in a pension, then leaves that employer, and makes no more contribution to that pension but will receive the value of the pension at retirement, that pension is the spouse's separate property.

Similarly, if before marriage a person contributes to a pension, 401K plan, or other type of retirement plan, the amount in that plan at the time of marriage is the person's separate property. During the marital partnership, if the person continues to make payments and the amount in the plan grows, the other spouse at the time of dissolution is entitled to one-half the amount by which the account has grown since the date of the marriage.

Sometimes, if there are other assets of the marriage in addition to the pensions, a spouse may choose not to disrupt the other spouse's pension plan but may take another asset of the marriage that equals what would be his or her share of the pension. If both spouses have pension plans, a property distribution scheme may be worked out whereby each spouse keeps his or her own pension and if one spouse's pension is greater than the other, the spouse with the lesser pension will get another asset to offset the disparity. This type of arrangement can be implemented in both community property states and equitable distribution states. Theoretically, in a community property state each pension should be divided down the middle, but if the parties agree that an alternate plan will keep both pensions intact and still facilitate an equal division of the marital community property, the court will not object.

THE GARBAGE MAN'S DISABILITY PENSION

In 1991, the New York Court of Appeals held that a portion of a Department of Sanitation worker's disability pension was marital property and thus subject to equitable distribution.

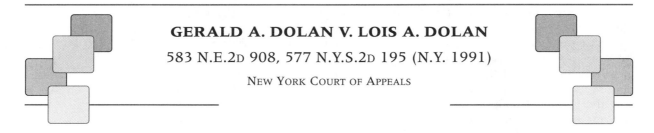

GERALD A. DOLAN V. LOIS A. DOLAN

583 N.E.2D 908, 577 N.Y.S.2D 195 (N.Y. 1991)

NEW YORK COURT OF APPEALS

ALEXANDER, J.

On this appeal, plaintiff-husband challenges the Appellate Division's affirmance of Supreme Court's determination that a portion of his ordinary disability pension received from the New York City Employee's Retirement System is marital property and thus subject to equitable distribution pursuant to Part B Section 236 of the Domestic Relations Law. We conclude that inasmuch as a portion of that ordinary disability pension represents deferred compensation related to length of employment occurring during the marriage, it constitutes marital property subject to equitable distribution. Thus, there should be an affirmance.

The parties to this litigation were married on July 23, 1966. Three children were born of the union. In 1969,

plaintiff became employed by the New York City Department of Sanitation. Nine years later he injured his back when he fell from a sanitation truck. He could not work at all for approximately five weeks and was unable to perform his normal work routine when he returned to work. Eventually, he was retired on an ordinary disability pension pursuant to Section 13-167 of New York City Administrative Code, effective April 17, 1980. At the time of his retirement, he had accumulated approximately eleven years of service with the Department of Sanitation, thus entitling him to pension benefits of $811.84 per month from the New York City Employee's Retirement System. He subsequently became employed by Marist College where he then enrolled as a full-time student.

. . . The court concluded that 47.62% of plaintiff's ordinary disability pension was marital property subject to equitable distribution and that the remaining 52.38% was disability payment, and thus, was separate property not subject to equitable distribution.

In order to determine the allocation between retirement benefits and disability benefits, the court compared the pension benefit plaintiff would have received had he retired normally with the allowance plaintiff received under the ordinary disability retirement provision. If plaintiff had fifteen years of service, he would have had vested regular pension benefits (see, NYS Admin Code §13-173.1) computed under the formula for determining normal retirement allowances, and his pension would have been considerably less—it would have equaled 47.62% of what he received under the ordinary disability plan. Supreme Court concluded that 47.62% of the ordinary disability was pure pension, and thus was marital property of which defendant was entitled to 50%. The court also determined that defendant was entitled to 23.81% of any future increase in the monthly pension payment as well as retroactive pension payments from the date of the commencement of the action.

The Appellate Division affirmed Supreme Court's determination in all respects concluding that because the ordinary disability pension benefits plaintiff was receiving has a ten-year service requirement, such benefits were not solely compensation for injuries but were, in part, an award for length of service. It also concluded that the method used by Supreme Court to determine defendant's award was proper (—AD2d—). For reasons set forth below, we affirm.

The New York Legislature has determined that marital property shall include "all property acquired by either or both spouses during the marriage and before the execution of a separate agreement or the commencement of a matrimonial action" (Domestic Relations Law §236 [B][1][d]). This Court has previously determined that pension benefits or vested rights to those benefits, except to the extent that they are earned or acquired before marriage or after commencement of a matrimonial action, constitute marital property (see, *Majauskas v. Majauskas*, 61 NY2d 481, 490). That determination was consistent with the intent of the Legislature as embodied in DRL §236(B)(5)(d)(4) and accords with our understanding that a pension benefit is, in essence, a form of deferred compensation derived from employment and an asset of the marriage that both spouses expect to enjoy at a future date (*Damiano v. Damiano*, 94 AD2d 132, 137). Allowing one spouse to share the pension benefit the other obtains through employment and considering such benefits to be marital property is also consistent with the concept of equitable distribution which rests largely on the view that marriage is, among other things, an economic partnership to which each party has made a contribution (id. at 138).

However, any compensation a spouse receives for personal injuries is not considered marital property and is not subject to equitable distribution (DRL §236 [B][1][d][2]). Thus a number of courts in this state have distinguished a "retirement pension" from a pure "disability pension" noting that the former is subject to equitable distribution whereas the latter, received as compensation for personal injuries, is not (see *Mylette v. Mylette*, 163 AD2d 43m revg, 140 Misc 2d 607; *West v. West*, 101 AD2d 834, after remittur, 115 AD2d 601; *Newell v. Newell*, 121 Misc 2d 586).

Plaintiff argues that his disability pension should not be subject to equitable distribution. He points to the fact that he was not eligible to receive a normal retirement pension because he had not been employed a sufficient number of years to be vested. Thus, had he retired without a disability in April 1980, he would have received no pension benefit. He contends that the pension benefits he receives are based merely upon his disability and should not be considered Marital property. These arguments are unavailing.

Plaintiff was retired pursuant to the retirement for ordinary disability provision of Section 13-167 of the New York City Administrative Code, which entitles a member of the city civil service to receive an ordinary disability pension if he or she "is physically or mentally incapacitated for the performance of duty and ought to be retired," provided he or she "has had ten or more years of duty-service and was a member or otherwise in city-service in each of the ten years next preceding his or her retirement" (NYC Admin Code §13-167 [a][1]). Thus, an employee may receive an ordinary disability pension even if the disability was not the result of a job-related accident, provided the employee satisfies the length of service requirement.

By contrast, a civil service member qualifying for a pension for "accident disability" does not have to satisfy a length of service requirement. Rather, the only requirement for entitlement to an "accident disability" pension is that the employee be "physically or mentally incapacitated for the performance of city-service, as a natural and proximate result of such city-service," and that the "disability was not the result of willful negligence" on the part of the employee (NYC Admin Code §113-168). Thus, the statutory scheme distinguishes between eligibility for "regular," "ordinary disability" and "accidental disability" pensions on the basis of length of service; entitlement to a "regular" pension vests upon 15 years of service (NYC Admin Code §13-173.1) and an "ordinary disability" pension upon 10 years of service (NYC Admin Code §13-167[a][1]), while there exists no length of service requirement for an "accidental disability" pension.

As indicated previously, it is firmly established in our jurisprudence that an employee's interest in " 'pension rights', the rights commonly accorded an employee and his or her spouse in a pension plan,. . . except to the extent that [that interest] is earned before marriage or after commencement of a matrimonial action, is marital property" (*Majauskas v. Majauskas,* 61 NY2d 481, 490, supra), the pension benefits constituting a form of deferred compensation derived from employment (*West v. West,* 101 AD2d 834, supra). In the typical pension plan, the employees' rights are incremental in that for each month or year of service, the employee receives credit which will enter into the computation of what the pension plan will pay to the employee (*Majauskas v. Majauskas,* supra at 490).

It is clear from the length of service requirement for the ordinary disability pension at issue here that plaintiff is being compensated for his length of service to the Department of Sanitation in addition to being compensated for the injuries he sustained. Indeed, implicit in the service requirement for this ordinary disability pension is the desire to provide employees whose injuries have prevented them from working until normal retirement age with some form of compensation for their injuries while also awarding them a portion of the deferred compensation to which they would have been entitled but for the injuries (see e.g. *Mylette v. Mylette,* 163 AD2d 463, 465 supra). Thus, to the extent plaintiff's ordinary disability pension represents deferred compensation, it is indistinguishable from a retirement pension and therefore, to that extent, is subject to equitable distribution (see e.g. *Mylette v. Mylette,* 163 AD2d 463, 463 supra; *West v. West,* 101 AD2d 834, supra; *Newell v. Newell,* 121 Misc 2d 586, supra; see generally, Annotation, Pension or Retirement Benefits as Subject to Award or Division by Court in Settlement of Property Rights Between Spouses, 94 ALR3d 176 §13).

Accordingly, the order of the Appellate Division should be affirmed, with costs.

Order affirmed with costs. Opinion by Judge Alexander. Chief Judge Wachtler and Judges Simons, Kaye, Titone, Hancock, and Bellacosa concur.

PROFESSIONAL DEGREE

In a marital partnership, spouses often make sacrifices of time, energy, and financial resources for the future good of the partnership. One of the sacrifices often made is putting a spouse through school. Many spouses who make the decision to seek a professional degree or license do so with the commitment and support of the other spouse. This decision may require moving to another city or town or sometimes another country. It also can involve the decision of the nonstudent spouse to give up, either permanently or temporarily, his or her own professional goals while the student spouse pursues his or her goals. It can involve the nonstudent spouse working as the sole breadwinner in order to allow the student spouse time to focus on scholastic endeavors. It can also involve a drastic change in lifestyle in which the student spouse devotes a majority of his or her time on studies at the expense of spending quality time with the family. It can also involve financial sacrifices in terms of money needed for books, tuition, and debt incurred for academic loans. These sacrifices are made in hopes that a professional or advanced degree will provide the family unit with a more prosperous future in which homes and other assets may be purchased, children educated, and retirement plans funded.

Despite these high hopes and dreams of a higher standard of living, many nonstudent spouses upon graduation have found themselves served with divorce papers while the student spouse embarks on a new career, with newfound friends and, sometimes, new romantic love interests! Some states have classified a professional degree as marital property if it was obtained during the marriage. In these jurisdictions, a nonstudent spouse who makes monetary and nonmonetary contributions that enhance the other spouse's earning potential may claim a portion of the value of the professional degree as marital property. An expert can provide

FIGURE 6–3
Some jurisdictions consider an advanced degree to be marital property if it was obtained during the marriage.

a monetary figure representing the value of a professional degree. The court will then award a portion of the value to the nonstudent spouse pursuant to the state's property division laws. Other jurisdictions have refused to recognize the professional degree as a marital asset. Courts have even extended the professional degree as property theory to any artistic or athletic skill developed during the marriage that enhances the participant spouse's earning capacity. To compensate the nonstudent spouse, however, some states have awarded reimbursement alimony to the nonstudent spouse for his or her efforts and contributions toward the attainment of the spouse's enhanced earning capacity.

WIFE'S SLAM DUNK

In *Marriage of Anderson,* the court held that an NBA player's contract signed by the husband for the 1988–1989 season was marital property and subject to equitable distribution.

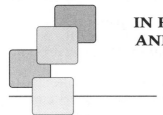

IN RE THE MARRIAGE OF BERNADETTE K. ANDERSON AND RICHARD A. ANDERSON

811 P.2D 419 (COLO.APP. 1990)

COLORADO COURT OF APPEALS, DIV. II.

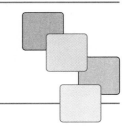

OPINION BY JUDGE ROTHENBERG.

In this dissolution of marriage action, Bernadette K. Anderson (wife) appeals from permanent orders entered relating to distribution of property and maintenance. We reverse and remand with directions.

The principal issue on appeal is whether husband's player contract with a professional basketball team constitutes marital property subject to division.

At the time of the decree on March 1, 1989, husband was currently under a three-year contract with the Portland Trail Blazers for the 1988–89, 1989–90 and 1990–91 seasons. According to the contract, he was to receive three yearly lump-sum payments totaling 1.5 million dollars. On October 5, 1988 and December 1, 1988, he received the first payment which totaled $267,000 after taxes. Remaining payments of

$475,000 and $575,000 were payable December 1989 and December 1990, respectively.

The NBA player contract in issue was never made part of the trial court record, but testimony of both husband and his attorney-agent indicated that the contract guaranteed payment: (1) if he died; (2) if he sustained injury during an NBA game or an official practice session; (3) if he had a mental breakdown or disability; (4) if he was terminated for lack of skill; or (5) if he were traded or waived by the team. Payment was not guaranteed if he sustained a physical disability from an injury unrelated to an NBA game or practice, or if he failed to pass a physical exam at the beginning of each season.

Husband testified that he used part of the $267,000 received to pay marital debts, child support maintenance and mortgage payments on the parties' townhouse. At the time of the permanent orders, however, he still had $150,000 in treasury securities and $14,000 in his checking account.

The trial court ruled that husband's NBA contract including the $267,000 payment already received by husband was not marital property, but was income belonging to the husband for husband's future services. On appeal, wife argues that husband's NBA contract is marital property, and she relies heavily on cases holding that a spouse's compensation which is deferred until after the dissolution, but fully earned during the marriage, is marital property (citations omitted). . . .

. . . In our view, the money already received by husband during the marriage is not future income. It is cash on hand and therefore marital property subject to division. Accordingly, we hold that the money paid under the contract for the 1988–89 season and not expended for marital purposes as of the date of the dissolution *is* marital property subject to equitable distribution, and the trial court erred in ruling otherwise.

However, as to the final two years of husband's contract, we hold that those payments to be received for the 1989–90 and 1990–91 seasons do not constitute property; rather, they constitute future income. *See In re Marriage of Faulkner, supra.*

Section 14-10-113, C.R.S. (1987 Rel.Vol.6B) requires a trial court to consider three separate issues regarding the equitable distribution of assets in a dissolution: (1) It must characterize the asset and determine whether it is property; (2) it must then allocate the asset as separate property of one spouse or as marital property; and (3) finally, it must distribute the property equitably (citation omitted). . . .

On remand, the court should consider all relevant factors in distributing the marital property here including the contribution of each spouse during the marriage, the fact of their separation, and any dissipation of marital property (citation omitted). . . .

. . . The judgment as to maintenance and division of property is reversed, and the cause is remanded to the trial court for further proceedings not inconsistent with the views expressed herein.

TURSI and HUME, J.J., concur.

DISTRIBUTION OF THE MARITAL DEBTS

Division of the marital debts is as important as division of the marital assets. Many failed marriages have no assets, but only debts to parcel out between the parties. A **debt** is a sum of money owed to a party called a **creditor.** The party responsible for the debt is called a **debtor.**

Debts must be identified and classified as either separate or marital debt. Then the obligation to pay is imposed on the respective spouses according to state law. Like separate property, debts incurred by a spouse prior to marriage belong to that spouse. A creditor in this case may only attach separate property to satisfy a debt incurred before the marriage. If no separate property exists, the creditor may then seek to attach marital property for satisfaction of the debt.

Debts incurred during the course of the marriage are considered marital debts. Just as spouses are jointly entitled to share in the fruits of the marriage, they will also be jointly responsible for the debts incurred during the marriage, regardless of whether the debt was incurred by one spouse or both. During the course of the marriage, couples will incur debts for **necessaries** such as food, clothing, shelter, and medical care. As long as a debt for necessaries is incurred during the marriage, both spouses are responsible for the debt. This obligation to provide for the necessaries of the family was historically imposed on the husband. Today, both husbands and wives are mutually responsible for providing the essentials to their families. A creditor due an obligation regarding a necessary may seek an attachment of marital property. Note that in the *Szesny* case, illustrated earlier in this chapter, the husband was held responsible for debts incurred during the marriage that were not classified as necessaries. Husband had dissipated the marital assets and it would have been unfair for the court to hold the wife responsible for the husband's wrongdoing.

During the divorce process, the parties are free to negotiate regarding which spouse will assume a particular debt. If there is no dispute, a separation agreement will be drafted and the debt clauses will specify the debts to be assumed by the respective parties. The debt section should also include a **hold harmless clause.** A hold harmless clause indicates that a particular spouse will be responsible for a debt incurred during the marriage, that he will be solely responsible for its payment, and that the other spouse shall be free and clear of any obligation regarding that debt. This agreement, however, is not binding on a creditor. A creditor who is due a debt incurred during the marriage may sue one or both spouses regardless of what the separation agreement indicates. The hold harmless clause allows the spouse who got "stuck" paying the debt to turn around and seek repayment from the spouse initially obligated under the separation agreement. Remember also that although the creditor may only sue the spouse who incurred the debt during marriage, if judgment is granted in favor of the creditor, the creditor may seek to enforce the judgment against the marital assets of the marriage, assets in which the other spouse has an interest. After a divorce, a creditor can still seek to satisfy the debt by pursuing the spouse most able to pay the debt.

If the court must determine the allocation of debts, the spouse's ability to pay and assets available will be considered.

DISSIPATION OF MARITAL ASSETS

Just as each spouse during the period of a marriage may contribute to the acquisition, enhancement, preservation, and appreciation of the marital estate, so either or both spouses may *dissipate* or waste away marital assets. **Dissipation** or depletion of the marital assets can occur in one or more of the following ways:

- overspending during the course of an intact marriage.
- overspending in contemplation of divorce.
- overspending upon formal or informal notice of impending divorce.
- destroying, giving away, or selling a spouse's property.

Activities that constitute dissipation include running up credit card debt, depleting or closing out joint checking and savings accounts, making suspicious loans to relatives, purchasing "big ticket" items with cash, gambling, and making high-risk or highly speculative investments.

When making property distribution awards in a dissolution proceeding, the court will take into consideration each spouse's role in and responsibility for the dissipation of marital assets. The court may punish the wrongdoing spouse by requiring the spouse to compensate the other spouse for the waste. This may be accomplished either by awarding the innocent spouse a larger percentage of the marital property or by ordering the wrongdoing spouse to pay to the other spouse an amount of cash equal to the monetary value of the assets depleted.

MOTORCYCLE MADNESS

Let's discuss the *Click* case. In defiance of a court order, Mr. Click took the Clicks' Gold Wing motorcycle and had an accident, which left him comatose. The Gold Wing was destroyed in the accident, leaving Mrs. Click to argue that her husband had dissipated a marital asset.

 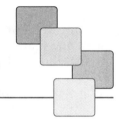

IN RE MARRIAGE OF WANDA CLICK AND ROBERT CLICK

169 ILL. APP. 3D 48, 119 ILL. DEC. 701, 523 N.E.2D 169
(ILL. APP. 2 DIST. 1988)

APPELLATE COURT OF ILLINOIS, SECOND DISTRICT

JUSTICE UNVERZAGT DELIVERED THE OPINION OF THE COURT.

Petitioner, Wanda Click, appeals from the property distribution portion of an order entered by the circuit court of Kane County dissolving her marriage to Robert Click. While petitioner's action was pending, Robert was critically injured in a motorcycle accident. He has been in a coma since May 4, 1986. The trial court consolidated the dissolution action with an action by Robert's mother, Jacquelyn Click, to have Robert adjudicated a disabled adult and to have a guardian appointed for him. Jacquelyn was subsequently appointed guardian of Robert's person and estate, and she participated in the property division portion of the dissolution proceeding on his behalf.

Wanda initially sought to enforce a settlement agreement which she alleged the parties had reached before Robert's accident. The court rejected that claim, however, concluding that Wanda had not sufficiently established the terms of the alleged agreement to allow it to be enforced. On March 19,1987, the court entered an order dissolving the marriage and dividing the marital property. The court noted that, according to Wanda, Robert was a professional thief who had only occasionally been "gainfully employed" during the marriage. Wanda worked only part-time during the marriage. The court found the testimony regarding the parties' earnings to be incredible as the evidence demonstrated that they had acquired assets far in excess of their reported income. The property division

portion of the order directed the sale of the marital residence, in which Wanda was residing, and an equal distribution of the proceeds between the parties. It awarded Robert the proceeds of a worker's compensation claim involving an employment related injury he had received, the proceeds of a pending action concerning his motorcycle accident, the salvage value of the Gold Wing motorcycle on which he was injured, a motorcycle trailer, and a number of personal items. It awarded Wanda a 1983 automobile, a smaller motorcycle, an aluminum boat, and some personal items. Wanda was additionally required to reimburse Robert for some of his furnishings which she sold after his accident, and for some charges she made to his credit cards. The court also ordered the equal division of any property contained in a safe deposit box and an equal division of the sale proceeds of a speedboat "if it is ever located," which Wanda claimed Robert had bought. The court directed the guardian to sell all of the assets assigned to Robert and to use the proceeds for his care. The court reserved the issue of future maintenance for Robert.

On appeal, Wanda alleges that: . . . (2) the evidence demonstrated that Robert had dissipated a marital asset by destroying the Gold Wing motorcycle. . . .

. . . Petitioner next contends that the court erred in rejecting her claim that Robert dissipated a marital asset when he took the Gold Wing motorcycle in contravention of a court order and then destroyed it in the accident that left him comatose. Dissipation of marital assets is generally defined as "the use of marital property for the sole benefit of one of the spouses for a purpose unrelated to the marriage at a time that the marriage is undergoing an irreconcilable breakdown" (citations omitted). While petitioner correctly asserts that courts have occasionally found a dissipation of assets where the dissipating spouse has derived no personal benefit from his or her actions (see, *e.g., In re Marriage of Siegel* (1984), 123 Ill. App. 3d 710, 719, 79 Ill. Dec. 219, 463 N.E.2d 773), we know of no authority, nor has petitioner cited any, which would permit a party to be held accountable for a dissipation which is not only detrimental to both parties, but purely unintentional as well. Robert violated a court

order in taking the motorcycle—conduct which would ordinarily have resulted in the court's imposition of contempt sanctions against him. (See generally *In re G.B.* (1981), 88 Ill. 2d 36, 41, 58 Ill. Dec. 845, 420 N.E.2d 1096 (regarding a court's inherent contempt power).) There was no evidence to suggest that his injury and the destruction of the motorcycle were anything other than accidental, however, and we therefore conclude that the court correctly found that he did not dissipate a marital asset. . .

. . . Judgment affirmed.

NASH and REINHARD, JJ., concur.

During the pendency of a divorce or dissolution action, each spouse may have some access to the marital assets. During that period, each spouse has the right to use some portion of marital funds to pay for legitimate expense including the payment of reasonable legal fees in conjunction with the divorce action. Divorcing spouses may also use marital funds to pay certain personal expenses that they always paid from the funds during the course of the marriage. Such expenses may include individual property tax bills for each spouse's automobile, automobile insurance and health insurance premiums, expenses for unexpected or emergency home repairs, dental work, reasonable expenses of the minor children, and, of course, reasonable expenditures for necessaries such as food, clothing, and shelter.

TAX ISSUES IN DISSOLUTION MATTERS

TAX CONSEQUENCES IN A COMMUNITY PROPERTY STATE

In a community property state if spouses are filing separately, with a few exceptions, each person must declare as income one-half of the total of both incomes, no matter how much more or less they actually realized in income. This way, tax refunds should be equal. When parties divorce, the tax refunds for the final marital year will be equal. The parties, however, may agree that one party will give all or part of their refund check over to the other party. Additionally, even in community property states, if a court finds that one party is more at fault or has been secreting funds away, the court may award both refunds or a sum equal to both refunds to the other spouse.

TAX CONSEQUENCES IN AN EQUITABLE DISTRIBUTION STATE

In many equitable distribution states, if a couple is in the process of getting divorced but has not divorced by December 31, they must file jointly or however they filed in previous years of their marriage. If they do file jointly, they will receive a joint income tax refund and it will be made out to the both of them. Sometimes one of the spouses will refuse to sign the check because he or she does not believe the other spouse should receive any of the refund. In this situation, this check should be held in escrow until the parties or their lawyers can agree on who gets what and how much of what. Again, this may all go to one party to offset the value of some other asset given to the other party.

THE INTERNAL REVENUE SERVICE AND PROPERTY DIVISION

1. THE INCOME TAX ADVANTAGES OF A MONETARY LUMP SUM CHARACTERIZED AS PROPERTY RATHER THAN ALIMONY

In the case of a monetary lump sum that is characterized as property, there is no tax liability such as that which is described next concerning alimony. Divorce has many tax consequences. A spouse paying periodic alimony may deduct this from his income on his tax return. The spouse receiving the alimony must declare the alimony as income and pay tax on it. If a spouse agrees to pay the other spouse a one-time lump sum alimony payment, in the year in which he makes the payment, the spouse may claim that payment as a deduction and the payee spouse must claim the lump sum as income and pay tax on it. The large tax bite on a lump sum provides a rationale for a payee spouse to agree to take lump sum alimony spread over two or possibly three tax years. The payor may also desire this as it will provide a deduction spread over two or three tax years. This is fine as long as the payee spouse knows that the payor spouse has healthy financial status and sufficient assets that will not be depleted or wasted within the given time frame.

2. THE TAX CONSEQUENCES OF THE SALE OF REAL PROPERTY THAT DOES NOT CONSITUTE THE PRIMARY OR MARITAL RESIDENCE

Sometimes when spouses divorce, it is necessary for them to sell some of their real property in order to actualize the property distribution. When such a division results in the necessity to sell a piece of real property, including vacation homes or rental property, the issue of the division of responsibility for the capital gains taxes must be addressed. It is important that the parties consult a tax attorney and/or a certified public accountant for guidance in this area.

THE EFFECT OF BANKRUPTCY ON A PROPERTY SETTLEMENT

When all marital assets are distributed at the time of the dissolution, and one spouse files for bankruptcy afterward, the other spouse will suffer no ill effects.

On the other hand, if as part of the property settlement one spouse agrees to pay the other spouse a certain amount of money payable in three installments over a two-year period, should the payor spouse declare bankruptcy before making all three payments, that spouse will declare the unpaid portion of the monetary settlement as an unsecured debt and the other spouse may receive a mere percentage or nothing at all if debts taking higher priority consume most or all of the assets of the debtor's estate.

Therefore, if a spouse knows or suspects that the other spouse is in serious financial trouble, that spouse should attempt to get all of the monetary settlement at the time the divorce occurs.

Sometimes, a spouse will seek a lump sum alimony payment as part of the dissolution proceeding. If the spouse agrees to take the lump sum in two or three installments and the other spouse declares bankruptcy before completing payment, this debt will not be dischargeable in bankruptcy providing the payee spouse can produce the legal documents identifying this debt as alimony. After the bankruptcy is over, the payor spouse will still owe the remainder of the alimony obligation and the payee spouse may file a motion for contempt and request that the court order the payor to pay up, issue a wage execution, or approve the payee spouse's application for a judgment lien on any real estate, stocks, bonds, or other like assets that the payor spouse has acquired.

TORT AWARDS AND OTHER JUDGMENTS AS MARITAL PROPERTY

If during the course of the marriage one party seeks relief through an administrative agency (e.g., a claim for workers' compensation or a discrimination claim that is settled or adjudicated at the level of the Commission on Human Rights and Opportunity/Equal Employment Opportunities Commission) or the courts due to the tortious or statutory misconduct of a third party, any settlement, award, or judgment shall be deemed an asset of the marriage. This is based upon the theory that had the parties remained married, the family unit would have enjoyed the benefits of the settlement, award, or judgment and that the family unit, which includes the former or soon-to-be-former spouse, suffered economic losses or emotional distress as a result of the third party's misconduct. Despite the fact that all or a portion of any settlement, award, or judgment may be taxable as income to the injured spouse, any portion of any award that is given, by judgment of the court presiding over the dissolution of marriage or pursuant to the terms of the parties' settlement agreement, to the uninjured spouse is deemed as property settlement and is therefore nontaxable.

EXHIBIT 6–1 Calculating goodwill.

IRA W. BRODSKY, C.P.A.
EDWARD J. LIEBERMAN, C.P.A.
PHOEBE H. SHAW, C.P.A.
JOSEPH S. SWEENEY, C.P.A.
RICHARD S. TAYLOR, C.P.A.

TAYLOR AND LIEBERMAN
AN ACCOUNTANCY CORPORATION
10880 WILSHIRE BOULEVARD · SUITE 1100
LOS ANGELES, CALIFORNIA 90024

TELEPHONE
(310) 476-9930

TELECOPIER
(310) 474-2733

June 30, 1994

Brenda A. Beswick, Attorney at Law
Trope and Trope
12121 Wilshire Boulevard
Suite 801
Los Angeles, CA 90025

Re: Marriage of Carrey

Dear Brenda:

The following is a list of the initial documents and information which we will need to begin our work regarding the calculation of goodwill for the above-stated matter:

JAMES CARREY

1. Cash flow and income tax projections for 1994.

2. All contracts, agreements, and related amendments in effect from the date of marriage through the most current date available, except those previously provided, as follows:
   a. "Night Life"
   b. "Peggy Sue Got Married"
   c. "Earth Girls are Easy"
   d. "Jim Carrey Special"
   e. "Doing Time on Maple"
   f. "Ace Ventura"
   g. "The Mask"
   h. "In Living Color"
   i. "Dumb and Dumber"
   j. United Talent Agency contract dated March 12, 1993

3. Listing of all written, published, produced and/or performed works including date written and/or started, date completed and compensation received beginning August 29, 1984 through the most current date available.

JIMMY-GENE, INC.

3. Corporate tax returns for the period beginning August 29, 1984 through August 31, 1989.

4. Financial statements for the period beginning September 1, 1993 through the most current date available.

EXHIBIT _3_

EXHIBIT 6–1 Continued

Brenda Beswick, Attorney at Law
June 30, 1994
Page 2

5. All contracts, agreements, and related amendments in effect
    from August 29, 1984 through the most current date
    available, except those previously listed in #2 above.

PIT BULL PRODUCTIONS, INC.

6. Financial statements for the period beginning January 1,
    1994, through the most current date available.

7. All contracts, agreements, and related amendments in effect
    from December 13, 1993, through the most current date
    available, except those previously listed in #2 above.

AGENTS

8. Schedule of all meetings or telephone discussions regarding
    television, film or other projects whether or not offered or
    accepted. The schedule should include dates and terms of
    compensation beginning March 28, 1987 through the most
    current date available.

    This request is not intended to be an all inclusive list of
documents necessary to perform our work. Review of the above
information may reveal items which warrant further inquiries and
documentation in order to complete our assignment.

    Please contact me with any questions you may have.

                                  Sincerely,

                                  Phoebe H. Shaw

                                  Phoebe H. Shaw

PHS:tgw:L063094

END-OF-CHAPTER EXERCISES

Crossword Puzzle

Across

1. Form of ownership existing only between husband and wife

3. Person to whom a debt is owed

5. Property owned equally by both spouses

6. Right to co-owner's share of property upon his death

7. Professional degree

9. Tracking an asset's origin

10. Merging of husband and wife into one legal entity

11. Combining marital property and separate property

12. Liabilities incurred by either spouse during marriage

13. Price a seller will pay for property

15. Property a spouse inherits during the marriage

16. Stocks and bonds

17. Cash payment for relinquishing an interest in another's asset

18. Result of a business's good reputation

19. Concurrent owner

20. Wasting assets

Down

2. An increase in a property's value

4. Court order regarding distribution of pension funds

8. System of marital property division based on fairness and equity more than ownership or title

14. Land and anything affixed to it

Review Questions

1. Define marital property and separate property, and identify the factors used to place property into one category or the other.

2. When is a spouse's pension a marital asset, when is it not, and why?

3. What is the relationship between the Employment Retirement Income Security Act and a Qualified Domestic Relations Order and how do they protect the financial position of the nonpensioner spouse when the other spouse has a pension?

4. In a community property state, what property is considered community property and what property is considered separate property?

5. If a couple is getting divorced in a community property state, what are the factors or circumstances that could result in one party getting a greater share of the marital estate than the other party?

6. A woman is injured in a car accident and brings a lawsuit. Two years later and six months after her husband has begun dissolution proceedings, the case is settled and the woman receives a check for $75,000. Is this settlement money part of the marital estate in either an equitable distribution state or a community property state? If so, how would this property be distributed under each distribution system?

Cases for Briefing

Brief and compare the following cases:

Krafick V. Krafick, 234 Conn. 783 (1995)

Krafick V. Krafick, 34 Conn. App. 930 (1994)

Exploring the Workplace: Activities

1. As part of your duties in the family law division of a medium-size firm, you have to research issues pertaining to separate property and marital property. Your firm's client is a stay-at-home mom and full-time homemaker who for the last twenty years has belonged to a stock club with four other women. She always used what she referred to as her own money to invest with the club. She got her own money from gifts from her husband and, earlier in her life, from her parents. Over the years, the stock club has made money, lost money, and made money again. Currently in the club fund there is $250,000.

The client's husband claims that he is entitled to one-half of his wife's share, which is approximately $50,000. Your client does not think he is entitled to any of this because she used her own money to invest and never used any joint assets to buy stocks. You are in a community property state. Your supervisor wants you to find a case in your state or, if there is nothing on point, in one of the other community property states that will be helpful to the client. Brief this case—apply the facts and present your conclusions to your supervising attorney in an interoffice memorandum.

Go to Family Law Courts at **http://www.familymatters.com. Etc** for assistance with this activity.

CHAPTER 7

Child Custody, Visitation, and Rights Of Third Parties

KEY TERMS

artificial insemination

best interest of the child

best interest standard

Child Abuse Prevention and Treatment Act (CAPTA)

custodial parent

custody evaluations

expert witness

family relations unit

family services division

fixed schedule

home state

in vitro fertilization

joint custody

legal custody

mandatory parenting education programs

noncustodial parent

parens patriae

parental alienation

Parental Alienation Syndrome (PAS)

parenting plan

patria potestas

physical custody

primary caretaker

psychological parent

reasonable rights of visitation

Sexual Allegations in Divorce (SAID)

shared physical custody

sole custody

split custody

standing

supervised visitation

surrogate mother
tender years doctrine
third-party intervenor
Uniform Child Custody
Jurisdiction and Enforcement
Act (UCCJEA)

unsupervised visitation
visitation rights
virtual visitation

When a family unit is intact, the children reside with the parents in the family home and both parents share the right to make decisions regarding their children's health, education, and welfare. If the family unit dissolves, and husband and wife begin living separately, formal arrangements must be made for the care and custody of the children either through a stipulated agreement by the parents that is approved of by the court and made an order, or through a determination made and ordered by the court, when a mutually agreed-on arrangement is not possible. In either case, court orders will be entered and will address the issues of where the children will reside and who will be responsible for making decisions regarding their health, education, and welfare.

Throughout history, society's legal systems have used various methods to decide child custody issues. At times, societies and their legal systems have had very 'cut and dry' and inflexible rules for awarding the guardianship and/or legal and physical custody of children to one parent or the other when the marital unit was dissolved.

A HISTORICAL PERSPECTIVE ON CUSTODY

THE AGE OF PATERNAL DOMINANCE

In ancient civilizations, fathers possessed absolute right to the possession of their children. This right was known as **patria potestas.** Centuries later, at English common law, the father's right of possession still prevailed. In both England and the United States, until the early nineteenth century, according to traditional concepts of property law and the law of child custody, children were chattels, the private property of the estate of their fathers. The father had complete authority over his children and controlled their education, discipline, and upbringing. If the parent's marriage broke down, upon its dissolution, the father had a superior right to custody. In a few present-day patriarchal societies, the right of *patria potestas* prevails; however, most contemporary societies have long discarded this custom.

THE SHIFT TO MATERNAL CONTROL

By the end of the nineteenth century many societal changes had occurred that shifted the preference from father to mother in custody determinations. The Industrial Revolution played a significant role in this shift. When families lived on and operated the family farm as an economic enterprise, the father of the family occupied the leadership role and made decisions that affected every aspect and detail of the lives of the other family members. In addition, the father was almost always physically with the children. He was able to direct and supervise their upbringing since his place of work was also the family's home. With the coming of the factory system and people's migration to urban areas, the father began to work out of the home and the mother became the manager of the household and children.

It was during this time period that the traditional roles of father as breadwinner and mother as homemaker emerged. With the mother dominant at home and responsible for meeting the children's needs throughout the day, the viewpoint developed that a mother's continuing presence was indispensable for the physical and emotional well-being of the minor children. For many years, the courts routinely awarded custody to the mother even if the father opposed this choice, unless the father or another relative seeking custody could prove that the mother was unfit to care for the child. The theoretical justification for the placing of children with their mother was known as the "tender years" doctrine.

THE TENDER YEARS DOCTRINE

The **tender years doctrine** was based on the assumption that young children needed to be and were better off being cared for by their mothers than by anyone else. Fathers were not viewed as being equipped to deal with the care of infants and young children. Children of tender years included children ages twelve and under. However, custody of children between age twelve and the age of majority was also almost always awarded to their mothers. Occasionally, custody of an older son might be awarded to his father, either because the mother could not control the child, the son wished to live with the father, or the mother and father agreed that the father would have custody of the older child.

The practice of routinely granting custody to the mother continued until the early 1970s, a decade that witnessed a great increase in the incidence of awarding custody to the father and also heralded the advent of joint custody and split custody as alternatives to **sole custody** by either parent. This change occurred as the primacy of the tender years doctrine declined and was replaced by the gender-neutral **best interest of the child** standard. The **"best interest" standard** opened the contest for custody not only to fathers but to other potential caregivers when the child's well-being or interests could be best served by such a custody determination.

THE TRANSITION FROM "TENDER YEARS" TO "BEST INTEREST"

As noted earlier, the 1960s and 1970s brought many societal changes including an increase in the number of mothers who worked outside the home during marriage and/or upon marital dissolution.

Prior to these decades, when a marriage broke up, the mother was most often a nonworking spouse who in many instances had never had a paying job. The father worked outside of the home, and was the family's only source of economic support. Upon dissolution of the marriage, the court usually awarded the nonworking spouse alimony, intending, among other things, to provide the wife with the unearned income she would need to maintain the household and remain at home to raise the children to adulthood. Giving custody to fathers generally was not a viable option, because fathers had to work to support themselves, their former spouses, and the children.

FIGURE 7–1
Until the 1970s, custody was traditionally awarded to mothers as a result of the tender years doctrine.

With the advent of greater and better-paying job opportunities for women, many mothers went to work. Therefore, in situations where both husband and wife were considered fit parents, the wife was no longer the undisputed choice for custody, especially if she worked outside of the home. Courts had adhered to the belief that children of "tender years" always belonged with their mothers because young children needed personal care throughout the day and stay-at-home mothers were available to provide this case.

Once mothers went to work and left the child care to a nanny, an older sibling, other relative, or a day care center, they no longer presented a more favorable choice than the working father who could also engage similar resources to care for the child. The child's well-being or interests were no longer necessarily best served by awarding sole custody to the mother. Fathers who desired custody and who were keenly aware of these changed conditions could now present arguments to the court that were very logical, persuasive, and, above all, successfully resulted in an award of custody to fathers.

Frequently, at the heart of the successful father's argument was the contention that the children would be better off with the father. Many fathers' attorneys, phrasing this concept in a more intellectually sophisticated manner, reminded the court that the "best interests of the child" should determine the custody disposition and that the interests of their client's child would be best served by placing the child with his or her father. Courts, for many years, had been able to routinely apply the tender years doctrine with such conviction because the courts believed that maternal custody promoted the children's best interest. That is no longer true.

FIGURE 7–2
After the shift from the tender years doctrine to the best interest standard, fathers began to be awarded custody more often than in the past.

By the end of the 1970s, the best interest of the child had become a very significant factor that most jurisdictions considered. This trend continued and by the 1990s, virtually all jurisdictions had abandoned the blanket or automatic tender years presumption of maternal custody in favor of identifying what determination would promote the child's best interests.

DETERMINING CHILD'S BEST INTEREST

While the best interest of the children remains the preferred standard today, legal and psychological experts differ on the factor or factors to apply in determining "best interest."

The discipline of child development and child psychology grew tremendously during the 1960s and 1970s. The knowledge gained from these fields and the criteria that emerged were applied to the making of custodial decisions on a regular basis. Courts increasingly referred the issue of custody to the court's **family relations unit** or **family services division.** In this unit, trained social workers and mental health professionals conducted studies and applied child development and child psychology concepts to make custody and visitation recommendations. Further, working parents frequently employed their own psychologists and psychiatrists to evaluate their children and testify on their behalf in court as **expert witnesses.**

The gender-neutral best interest standard may be difficult to define. Some courts have used the primary caretaker rule, or psychological parent, while other jurisdictions have enacted specific factors to be considered when determining best interest in custody cases.

STATUTORY FACTORS

State statutory schemes articulate the factors used by family court judges in determining the preferable placement of a child in a disputed custody action. An excerpt of Arizona's custody statute illustrates the factors considered in determining the best interest of the child.

ARIZONA REVISED STATUTES ANNOTATED (WEST)

25.403. **Custody; Best Interest of Child.** . . .

A. The court shall determine custody, either originally or upon petition for modification, in accordance with the best interests of the child. The court shall consider all relevant factors, including:

1. The wishes of the child's parent or parents as to custody.
2. The wishes of the child as to the custodian.
3. The interaction and interrelationship of the child with the child's parent or parents, the child's siblings and any other person who may significantly affect the child's best interest.
4. The child's adjustment to home, school and community.
5. The mental and physical health of all individuals involved.
6. Which parent is more likely to allow the child frequent and meaningful continuing contact with the other parent.
7. If one parent, both parents, or neither parent has provided primary care of the child.
8. The nature and extent of coercion or duress used by a parent in obtaining an agreement regarding custody.
9. Whether a parent has complied with Chapter 3 article 5 of this title. . . .

Family court judges have broad discretion in resolving issues of child custody and visitation. The court must not only assess a parent's ability to provide a child with the necessities of life such as food, clothing, and shelter, but also with nurturance, love, and affection. Certain factors have emerged as essential indicators of whether a certain custodial disposition is in the child's best interest.

PSYCHOLOGICAL PARENT

Where both parties are equally fit, a court may order a custody study to ascertain which parent is the child's **psychological parent.** Often, the parent who has had the child since the child's birth and/or who has spent the most meaningful time with the child, has bonded most fully with the child, and who has provided the most psychological nurturance to the child is considered the psychological parent. Custody is frequently awarded to the psychological parent because it is considered harmful to wrest the child away from the individual whom the child considers his psychological parent, the one with whom he has the strongest bonds.

PRIMARY CARETAKER

Courts frequently decide that custody should be awarded to the child's **primary caretaker.** The primary caretaker is the individual who has done most of the significant parenting of the child since birth or for the several preceding years. The primary caretaker is usually the child's psychological parent. The primary caretaker standard is in effect similar, if not identical, to the psychological parent concept.

THE PRIMARY CARETAKER RULE

An excerpt from the following case illustrates the factors used by courts in identifying a child's "primary caretaker."

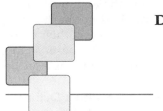

DEBRA PASCALE V. JAMES PASCALE

660 A.2D 485 (N.J. 1995)

SUPREME COURT OF NEW JERSEY

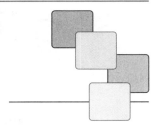

... In cases of only joint legal custody, the roles that both parents play in their children's lives differ depending on their custodial functions. In common parlance, a parent who does not have physical custody over her child is the "non-custodial parent" and the one with sole residential or physical custody is the "custodial parent." Because those terms fail to describe custodial functions accurately, we adopt today the term "primary caretaker" to refer to the "custodial parent" and the term "secondary caretaker" to refer to the "non-custodial parent." Although both roles create responsibility over children of divorce, the primary caretaker has the greater physical and emotional role. Because the role of "primary caretaker" can be filled by men or women, the concept has gained widespread acceptance in custody determination. . . . Indeed, many state courts often determine custody based on the concept of "primary caretaker." E.g. *Burchard v. Garay,* 724 P.2d 486 (Cal. 1986);

Maureen F. G. v. George W. G., 445 A.2d 934 (Del. 1982); *Agudo v. Agudo,* 411 So. 2d 249 (Fla. Dist. Ct. App. 1982); *Rolde v. Rolde,* 425 N.E.2d 388 (Mass. App. Ct. 1981); *Maxfield v. Maxfield,* 452 N.W.2d 219 (Minn. 1990); *Riaz v. Riaz,* 789 S.W.2d 224 (Mo. App. Ct. 1990); *Burleigh v. Burleigh,* 650 P.2d 753 (Mont. 1982); *Crum v. Crum,* 505 N.Y.S.2d 656 (App. Div. 1986); *Moore v. Moore,* 574 A.2d 105 (Pa.Super. Ct. 1990); *Pusey v. Pusey,* 728 P.2d 117 (Utah 1986); *Harris v. Harris,* 546 A.2d 208 (Vt. 1988); *Garska v. McCoy,* 278 S.E.2d 357 (W. Va. 1981).

In one of the earliest cases using the concept of "primary caretaker," the Supreme Court of Appeals of West Virginia articulated the many tasks that make one parent the primary, rather than secondary, caretaker: preparing and planning of meals; bathing, grooming, and dressing; purchasing, cleaning and caring for clothes; medical care, including nursing and general trips to physicians; arranging for social interaction among peers; arranging alternative care, i.e., babysitting or daycare; putting child to bed at night, attending to child in the middle of the night and waking the child in the morning; disciplining; and educating the child in a religious or cultural manner. *Garska, supra,* 278 S.E.2d at 363. . . .

Once the tender years doctrine lost favor and the shift away from always awarding sole custody to the mother occurred, there was another shift, as well, from always awarding custody to only one parent. When both parents worked, sometimes courts believed that both parents should be jointly responsible for the children's financial maintenance and for the children's physical and emotional care, and the joint custody practice began to emerge.

Parents having **joint custody** are jointly or equally responsible for the financial, emotional, educational, and health-related needs of their children. They have an equal responsibility and an equal degree of say in deciding how to meet the various needs of their children. Joint custody will only be successful if the parents can communicate effectively, put aside personal feelings when dealing with issues relating to the children, be flexible enough to compromise when each party has a different view on how to handle some aspect of the child's upbringing, and be able to negotiate to arrive at an adequate solution when conflicts arise.

All jurisdictions now prefer the belief or presume that joint or shared custody is in the best interest of the children. This preference rests on the presumption that despite the breakdown of the parents' marriage, both parents play a significant role in the well-being of the children.

The trend toward a presumption in favor of joint custody raised concerns among advocates for victims of domestic violence regarding the appropriateness of this arrangement. Under these circumstances, joint custody is not in the children's best interest as it may have an extremely detrimental effect on their emotional and physical health and well-being. States have responded by enacting statutes requiring the court to consider evidence of domestic violence as a factor in custody or visitation disputes.

Evidence of violence inflicted by one parent over another is also a factor for the court to consider in a custody or visitation dispute. Some states have even legislated consideration of domestic violence in custody or visitation cases, as illustrated by the following Arizona statute.

STATUTES

ARIZONA REVISED STATUTES ANNOTATED (WEST)

`25-403 (B)` . . . The court shall consider evidence of domestic violence being contrary to the best interests of the child. If the court finds that domestic violence has occurred, the court shall make arrangements for visitation that best protects the child and the abused spouse from further harm. The person who has committed an act of domestic violence has the burden of proving that visitation will not endanger the child or significantly impair the child's emotional development. . . .

The Battle over Sydney and Justin Simpson

While O. J. Simpson was acquitted in criminal court of murdering his ex-wife, Nicole Brown Simpson, the California Court of Appeals held that the family court judge who awarded Simpson custody of his children on his release from prison should have waited for the verdict in the wrongful death suit before making a custody decision. On November 10, 1998, the appellate court reversed the family court's decision on the grounds that evidence of Nicole's murder should have been considered, and thus remanded the case for a new custody hearing.

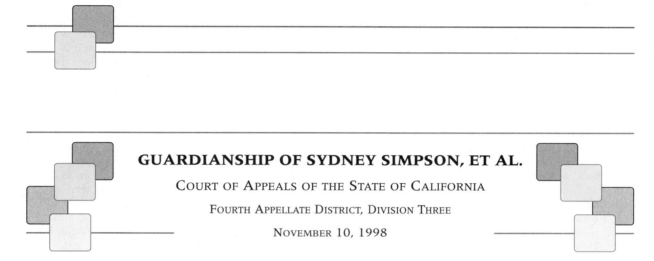

GUARDIANSHIP OF SYDNEY SIMPSON, ET AL.

COURT OF APPEALS OF THE STATE OF CALIFORNIA

FOURTH APPELLATE DISTRICT, DIVISION THREE

NOVEMBER 10, 1998

Appeal from a judgment of the Superior Court of Orange County, Nancy Wieben Stock, Judge. Reversed and remanded. . . .

I. INTRODUCTION

A guardianship was established for Sydney and Justin Simpson after their father, O.J. Simpson, was jailed on the charge of murdering Nicole Brown Simpson, their mother, and another victim, Ron Goldman. We need not go into the details of the killings, but certain, basic well-reported—and undisputed—facts about them are unavoidably relevant to the proceeding before us now; Nicole's throat had been slit, and she had been left in a pool of blood at her own doorstep while her children, Sydney and Justin, lay sleeping in the house. It was only a happenstance that the neighbors discovered the body first, sparing the children the horror of finding their dead mother. Whoever committed this crime must have acted in extreme rage and anger and been oblivious to the possibility that the victim's children might discover the body.

After his acquittal in a criminal trial, Simpson requested termination of the guardianship. At the hearing on the termination, the guardians sought to introduce evidence regarding the circumstances of Nicole Simpson's murder. The trial court refused to consider any of it holding that the guardians had waived the issue by not listing any "murder witnesses" on their witness list.

At the time of this guardianship proceeding, the father also faced a *civil* trial in which the plaintiffs sought to establish his liability for the death of the mother. The guardians' attorneys apparently hoped the civil case would conclude in time for the court to take note of its results, which would not only spare their clients great expense, but also save the court the necessity of a prolonged examination of the murder evidence. The court, however, did not wait for the conclusion of the civil case (which, as is common knowledge, ended with a judgment of the father's liability), explaining in its written order that the civil case could not have thrown any light on the guardianship termination anyway, because, in its opinion, the civil case entailed a lower standard of proof than the one involved in the guardianship proceeding. In any event, that case is itself not yet final for issue preclusion purposes, so the trial court could not take judicial notice of its *result.*

While we understand the incredible pressure the court was under, the fact remains that it made a number of errors. These errors require reversal of the order terminating the guardianship.

First and foremost, the grisly circumstances of the murder itself simply could not be ignored, even if consideration of them would have taken some time. We acknowledge, of course, that consideration of the "murder issue" (as it is sometimes, rather understatedly, referred to in the briefs) would have necessitated a longer trial. However, because the court sat as a court of *equity*, dealing with the *interests of children*, not a court of criminal law in which the standard is guilt beyond a reasonable doubt, there was no need for reenactment of the so-called trial of the century. Consideration of the murder issue would have been conducted by a judge in a well-secured courthouse with the actual proceedings barred to the public, with the power to control the presentation of evidence and prevent unnecessary distraction and delay. With the cooperation of the parties at least, much of the evidence could easily have been presented by way of excerpts from the transcripts in the criminal and civil cases. Had the court considered the murder issue, there would have been no jury, no endless sidebar conferences, and no media distractions. Judges cannot avoid the single most important and relevant issue in a case—particularly a case involving children and the possibility of violence—just because trying that issue will take time. The standard is whether the consumption of time is "undue." (Evid. Code, §352.). . . .

II. THE HISTORY OF THE GUARDIANSHIP

Sydney and Justin's mother, Nicole, and Ronald Goldman were murdered on June 12, 1994. Five days later Simpson was arrested for the crime. On the day of his arrest Simpson signed a document giving temporary care of Sydney and Justin to their maternal grandparents, Louis and Juditha Brown; later, on July 27, 1994, the Browns petitioned the trial court to be appointed guardians of Sydney and Justin. Several months later, on October 7, 1994, the court made a formal order appointing the Browns as the children's guardians.

Simpson's incarceration lasted some 17 months. When released he promptly filed a petition to terminate the guardianship pursuant to section 1601 of the Probate Code, asserting that in light of his release there was "no further need" for the guardianship. . . .

III. DISCUSSION

A. THE EVIDENCE BEARING ON "THE MURDER ISSUE"

1. The Relevance of the Evidence

Let us get right to the point. The murder of Sydney and Justin's mother was an extraordinarily violent act showing callous disregard for them. *If* Simpson committed the crime, that information was highly relevant to whether the children should be returned to him. . . .

. . . It may reasonably be inferred from the almost universally known circumstances of the killing that the crime evidenced great violence and rage. We by no means must conclude that Simpson committed the crime to say that *if* he did, that fact was certainly relevant to show a *propensity toward violence* on his part.

As a matter of case law, as well as common sense, the question of whether one parent has actually murdered the other is about as relevant as it is possible to imagine in any case involving whether the surviving parent should be allowed any form of child custody. *In re Sarah H.* (1980) 106 Cal. App. 3d 326 is particularly instructive in this regard. There, the father was a "hard-drinking ranch hand" who "had been a good father to all his children." (*Id.* at pp. 331–332 (conc. opn. of Reynoso, J.).) However, he had a tendency to become violent when drunk; indeed, as the court put it. "alcohol-induced violence was consistent with the father's character." (*Id.* at p. 330.) He beat the mother to death in one of his drunken rages (he was later found guilty of voluntary manslaughter after a no contest plea), and his tendency to such violence was held to constitute substantial evidence justifying not only the establishment of a guardianship—much less its continuation—but also the actual *termination* of *all* parental rights in a dependency proceeding because detriment beyond a reasonable doubt had been shown. (*Id.* at pp. 328–329.). . . .

. . . Finally, the analogous case of *Guardianship of Smith* (1957) 147 Cal. App. 2d 686 is also instructive. There the mother was tried and, like Simpson, acquitted of the murder of the other parent arising out of his death in a car bomb planted by the mother's paramour. Despite the acquittal, the trial judge allowed the entire record of a murder trial to be admitted into evidence, and the evidence contained in that record formed the basis of a decision to maintain the guardianship, which was then upheld on appeal. (See *id.* at p. 699.)

It is clear, then, that evidence of whether Simpson killed Sydney and Justin's mother was not only relevant to the termination of the guardianship, it was so relevant that it could not be reasonably ignored. . . .

TRADITIONAL CUSTODY ARRANGEMENTS

Parents who reside together enjoy the right to **physical custody** of their children. This right, sometimes referred to as *residential* or *domiciliary custody*, means that the children live with the parents. The parents also have **legal custody** of the children, which means they have the right to make major decisions on behalf of their children regarding health, education, and religious upbringing. When the marital relationship breaks down, the parents no longer enjoy these rights simultaneously. Crafting a custody arrangement involves structuring the rights of the parents in arrangements that are in the children's best interest.

If the parties cannot reach an agreement on custody, the court will decide what is in the children's best interest based on the testimony of the parties, lay witnesses, and experts such as mental health counselors who perform **custody evaluations.** A custody evaluation is conducted by either a psychologist or psychiatrist who will interview both parties and the children and make a recommendation regarding what type of custody arrangement is in the children's best interest. The following custody arrangements address a combination of these rights. The court may award a custody evaluation or the parties may request one by filing a motion with the court. Typically, both parents share the cost of the evaluation.

If cost is an issue for the clients, most family courts have state-employed counselors available to conduct such evaluations, the cost of which is paid by the taxpayers. They are often referred to a family relations, family services, or other equivalent counselor used in a particular jurisdiction. They conduct custody and visitation evaluations and make them available to the court and the parties once they are completed. Very often, cases are resolved after reviewing the evaluations. If there is no resolution, the evaluation is admitted into evidence at trial; the family services officer is called to the witness stand and is subject to questioning by the parties.

In cases involving child custody, the court may appoint or the parties may request the appointment of an attorney for the minor children or a guardian ad litem. The attorney for the children represents their wishes and the guardian ad litem represents what is in the children's best interest. When a guardian ad litem has not been appointed, the attorney for the children represents not only the children's wishes but also their best interests. When these two roles conflict, the attorney must ask for the appointment of a guardian ad litem, or guardian for the legal proceedings, to represent the children's best interest. An example would be a child's attorney representing an abused child who wished to live with the abusive parent. In this case, the lawyer must advocate the child's wishes, but ask for a guardian ad litem to advance the best interest of the child.

JOINT LEGAL CUSTODY

Joint legal custody is presumed to be in the best interest of the children because both parents are involved in their lives. When parents have joint legal custody, they both share in making the major decisions in the lives of the children. This is especially important for fathers. Mothers are often awarded custody of the children and fathers often feel left out of the decision-making process. While both parents share in making decisions regarding the children's upbringing, the child resides with one parent. The noncustodial parent has visitation or access, frequently during the week as well as summer and school vacations. Nevertheless, the children's primary residence is with the custodial parent. In this instance, because the custodial parent has expenses for the children's daily needs, the joint but noncustodial parent will be ordered to pay child support to the custodial parent for the financial maintenance of the children.

Joint Legal and Physical Custody (Shared Custody)

In *joint legal and physical custody* (sometimes referred to as **shared physical custody**), both parents make the major decisions regarding the children's upbringing and they share residential custody. This means that the children reside with each parent approximately half of the time. This arrangement succeeds most often when each parent resides geographically close to each other and close to the children's school, church, doctor, and site of children's residential activities. Under shared custody arrangements, the children reside with one parent for a certain amount of days per week and a certain number of days with the other. Typically, neither parent pays the other parent child support because both parents share expenses. When one parent's income is significantly higher than the other's, however, the more affluent parent gives the other parent money to cover the children's needs.

Sole Legal and Physical Custody

Parents with sole custody, or **custodial parents,** have the right to make all major decisions regarding the children's health, education, and religious upbringing as well as have the children living in the home with them. **Noncustodial** parents have visitation or access rights as well as the ability to make day-to-day decisions when the children are in their care.

As stated earlier, all states presume that a joint custody arrangement is in the best interest of the children. A parent who can present strong evidence to the court that joint custody is not in the children's best interest may rebut this presumption. If there is child abuse, substance abuse, or parents' harboring great animosity toward each other, making every decision a struggle, joint custody will not serve the children's best interest. In these types of situations, the best interest of the children will be better served by awarding one parent sole custody and the other parent visitation or access, provided that the custodial parent's authority will not thwart or impair the noncustodial parent's relationship with the children.

Split Custody

A split custodial arrangement is less frequently used than other types of custody dispositions. Under the practice of **split custody,** one parent has sole custody of the child for a part of the calendar year, each year, and the other parent has sole custody for the remaining portion of the year. Sometimes under a split custody arrangement, the split will be equal; each parent will have custody of the child for six months. During that time period, the parent will have sole custody of the child and complete physical custody of the child.

Sometimes split custody means that one parent has sole custody and physical custody of the child during the school year and the other parent has sole and physical custody of the child for the summer months. Each parent has full authority to make decisions regarding the child's health, education, discipline, recreation, and welfare. This arrangement differs from joint custody with shared physical custody in that parents with joint custody with shared physical custody must consult the other custodial parent regarding at least major decisions regarding health, education, and welfare. For instance, if while a child residing for the school year with the mother under joint custody physical or otherwise decided to have the child undergo elective surgery for removal of tonsils and adenoids, if the father who had joint custody did not agree that such removal was the best medically appropriate alternative, then the parents would have to reach some type of agreement before surgery could be performed. Under a split custodial arrangement, the parent enjoying physical custody time could have the child undergo elective surgery without the legal consent of the other parent.

Split custody was actually a compromise before the 1970s. For several decades during the first half of the twentieth century, courts entered orders for a split custodial arrangement in instances either where both parents requested it or where the court felt that such a "Solomon" type of disposition was the fairest under the circumstances. In the 1960s and 1970s the arrangement occurred mainly when parents lived in different parts of the country or in different countries. Split custody can be very disruptive and undermine the child's need for continuity and stability in his or her relationships and environment. This type of arrangement is used very little today. Today, most, if not all, courts apply the "best interest of the child" standard to decisions regarding custody, and the current prevailing view is that split custody is detrimental to a child's best interest.

Another type of split custody arrangement may involve the splitting of siblings. One parent would be awarded custody of one or more children, and the other parent would have custody of the others. Courts generally frown on splitting up siblings. Keeping brothers and sisters together provides the children with some level of stability at a time when the breakup of their parents is traumatic for them to handle. There are some instances, however, where splitting the siblings may actually be in the best interest of the children, as one parent may be better able to control, discipline, or care for a particular child.

FIGURE 7–3
Courts prefer not to break up siblings when a marriage dissolves, because keeping brothers and sisters together provides children with some level of stability during this rough period.

VISITATION RIGHTS

A noncustodial parent has the right to frequently spend time with the child unless the court finds that visitation in some way endangers the child's emotional, mental, moral, or physical health. Family courts will award **visitation rights** to a parent in this position. The parties may agree to a visitation schedule or it may be determined by the courts if the parties reach a stalemate.

There are two types of visitation schedules: **reasonable rights of visitation** or a **fixed schedule.** Reasonable visitation is a very flexible arrangement that requires the parties to work out their own schedule. This works best when the parties can reasonably coordinate visitation between themselves. This requires the ability to communicate and the willingness to put aside their differences for the benefit of the children. Some divorce decrees will include this provision, and as soon as the ink dries the parties are back in court. Sometimes the custodial parent will set up obstacles to the noncustodial parent's visitation rights. The noncustodial parent may also disrupt the "reasonable" visitation schedule by showing up at the custodial parent's home at inconvenient days and times (especially when the custodial parent becomes romantically involved with someone else!). At this point, one of the parties returns to court for the purpose of enforcing visitation or modifying the existing "reasonable" rights of visitation to a more definite schedule.

Fixed schedules are definite dates and time frames set aside for the purpose of allowing a noncustodial parent to visit with the child. Fixed schedules should spell out the days and hours on which a noncustodial parent may see the child. In addition, it is also a good idea to deal with holidays, birthdays, vacations, reasonable hours for phone calls, and other details so as to avoid conflict between the parties.

In some hostile divorces, the law office will often hear complaints from the client on the day following visitation. For example, custodial parents may call screaming about the noncustodial parent's failure to either pick up or return the child on time. In the latter scenario, some custodial parents will go so far as to call the police when the noncustodial parent is only delayed by several minutes! Custodial parents may also complain that the child looks dirty, has not eaten, or acts out after visitation. Some go further by making allegations regarding child sexual abuse. Noncustodial parents may raise similar concerns, in addition to complaints about the child not being available for visits because the custodial parent has taken it upon himself not to make the child available.

When a client calls with visitation complaints and the attorney is not available, the paralegal should take detailed notes regarding the client's concerns and inform the attorney. Remember not to give legal advice! Clients may be very agitated and may push the paralegal in a moment of desperation. Be polite and courteous, but do not give advice even if you know the answer. Let the attorney handle it.

A paralegal should also be familiar with the difference between unsupervised and supervised visitation. **Unsupervised visitation** permits a noncustodial parent to freely visit with the child without others present, wherever she reasonably wishes to take the child and engage in child-appropriate activities. **Supervised visitation** limits a parent's visitation rights in that it dictates restrictions surrounding the visits. Supervised visitation may be ordered in cases where a noncustodial parent has certain problems that question her ability to properly supervise the child. Parents who have substance abuse problems, mental or physical issues, a history of domestic violence, or are too immature to care for the child on their own may be required to have another person present during the visits at a designated time and place. This person can sometimes be the custodial parent unless there is a history of domestic violence or problems with the parents' interaction. In this case, a neutral third party would be the best solution.

VIRTUAL VISITATION

Utah was the first jurisdiction, and Wisconsin the second, to enact virtual visitation legislation. Other states are in the process of drafting or proposing similar legislation. **Virtual visitation** is a court order allowing a parent in a divorce to communicate and maintain a relationship with the children through the use of technologies such as Internet video conferencing, web cams, email, instant messaging or any other type of wired or wireless technology. In cases where the parents are divorced, it allows the noncustodial parent to maintain contact with the child between actual visits.

Virtual visitation is used as a supplement to live visitation and telephone contact. It is also not a justification for relocating a child to another state or for reducing the amount of live visitation with a noncustodial parent. Opponents feel that it will be used as a replacement for live visitation as technology becomes more popular. Virtual visitation is not for everyone, as it requires a certain amount of technological savvy. A family court that orders virtual visitation will also have to determine who will pay for the equipment and installation.

Governor Jim Doyle signed Wisconsin's virtual visitation statute into law on March 22, 2006. The Wisconsin statute includes a legislative preamble explaining the new statute, which reads as follows:

Wisconsin Senate Bill 244

Analysis by the Legislative Reference Bureau

Under current law, in a divorce or legal separation in which a minor child is involved, and in a paternity action, the court must grant sole legal custody of the child to one parent or joint legal custody to both parents together. In addition, the court must allocate between the parents periods of physical placement, which is the condition under which the child is physically placed with the parent and the parent has the right and responsibility during that time to care for, and make routine daily decisions concerning, the child. The court may deny parent periods of physical placement with the child only if being physically placed with the parent would endanger the child's physical, mental, or emotional health.

This bill provides that, if the court grants periods of physical placement to both parents, the court may grant to a parent a reasonable amount of electronic communication at reasonable hours during the other parent's periods of physical placement with the child. Electronic communication is defined as time during which a parent and his or her child communicate by using various types of communication tools, such as the telephone, electronic mail, instant messaging, and video conferencing or other wired or wireless technologies via the Internet. The basis for granting electronic communication is whether it is in the child's best interest and whether equipment for providing electronic communication is reasonably available to both parents. Electronic communication may be used only to supplement, and not as a substitute or replacement for, the physical placement that a parent has with the child.

The bill provides that a parenting plan that a party files with the court before a pretrial conference when legal custody or physical placement is contested must include any electronic communication a parent is requesting and must indicate whether equipment for providing electronic communication is reasonably available to both parents. The bill also provides that, if a parent is proposing to move with the child and the other parent objects to the move, the court may not use the availability of electronic communication as a factor in support of a modification of physical placement or a refusal to prohibit the parent from moving with the child.

The people of the state of Wisconsin, represented in senate and assembly, do enact as follows:

SECTION 1. 767.001 (1g) of the statutes is created to read:

767.001 **(1g)** "Electronic communication" means time during which a parent and his or her child communicate by using communication tools such as the telephone, electronic mail, instant messaging, video conferencing or other wired or wireless technologies via the Internet, or another medium of communication.

SECTION 2. 767.23 (1) (ap) of the statutes is created to read:

767.23 **(1)** (ap) Upon the request of a party, granting periods of electronic communication to a party in a manner consistent with s. 767.24. The court or circuit court commissioner shall make a determination under this paragraph within 30 days after the request for a temporary order regarding periods of electronic communication is filed.

SECTION 3. 767.24 (1m) (L) of the statutes is amended to read:

767.24 **(1m)** (L) Whether and how the child will be able to contact the other parent when the child has physical placement with the parent providing the parenting plan, and what electronic communication, if any, the parent is seeking.

SECTION 4. 767.24 (1m) (Lm) of the statutes is created to read:

767.24 **(1m)** (Lm) Whether equipment for providing electronic communication is reasonably available to both parents.

SECTION 5. 767.24 (4) (e) of the statutes is created to read:

767.24 **(4)** (e) If the court grants periods of physical placement to more than one parent, the court may grant to either or both parents a reasonable amount of electronic communication at reasonable hours during the other parent's periods of physical placement with the child. Electronic communication with the child may be used only to supplement a parent's periods of physical placement with the child. Electronic communication may not be used as a replacement or as a substitute for a parent's periods of physical placement with the child. Granting a parent electronic communication with the child during the other parent's periods of physical placement shall be based on whether it is in the child's best interest and whether equipment for providing electronic communication is reasonably available to both parents.

SECTION 6. 767.327 (5m) of the statutes is renumbered 767.327 (5m) (intro.) and amended to read:

767.327 **(5m)** DISCRETIONARY OTHER FACTORS TO CONSIDER. (intro.) In making a determination under sub. (3), the: (a) The court may consider the child's adjustment to the home, school, religion and community.

SECTION 7. 767.327 (5m) (b) of the statutes is created to read:

767.327 **(5m)** (b) The court may not use the availability of electronic communication as a factor in support of a modification of a physical placement order or in support of a refusal to prohibit a move.

SECTION 8. Initial applicability.

(1) PARENTING PLANS. The treatment of section 767.24 (1m) (Lm) of the statutes first applies to parenting plans filed with the court on the effective date of this subsection.

Parenting Plans

Studies from the mental health community conclude that the children of divorce benefit tremendously when the parents work together. Even though the parties can no longer live together as husband and wife, they still are in a co-parenting relationship if the marriage produced children. When parties share children in common, it will be impossible for them to go their separate ways unless it is a case of complete abandonment. The current trend in the United States is to encourage divorcing parents to work together in their children's best interest and focus their attention on the children's needs.

More states are requiring parents to submit parenting plans to the court. A **parenting plan** is an agreement created by both parents detailing how they will continue their parenting responsibilities towards their children after their marriage is dissolved. A parenting plan addresses the following:

1. **Decision Making.** This section delineates which parent will make the major decisions in the lives of the children. States are beginning to use the term *decision-making responsibility* in place of the word *custody* and the terms *access* or *parenting time* in place of the term *visitation*. Parenting plans reflect this new language, so it is important to become familiar with these terms.

2. **Children's Schedule.** In this section, the parents structure the children's schedule, defining how, where, and with whom the children will spend their week, including weekends, vacations, and holidays. This section may also include details as to pick-up and drop-off responsibilities, telephone access, notifying the other parent when changes need to be made in the schedule, giving the other parent right of first refusal when a babysitter is needed, and provisions on dealing with school cancellations, teacher conferences, or illness.

3. **Resolving Future Disputes.** The answer to custody and visitation disputes has often been to resolve them in a court of law. States that have adopted parenting plans discourage litigation and encourage mediation or counseling before intervening in a postjudgment dispute. In this section of the plan, the parties must outline how they will resolve future disputes regarding custody and visitation as well as who will assist them in the process. Will they seek a mediator, mental health counselor, minister, or other third party to help them resolve their differences amicably? Litigation is looked at as a last resort.

4. **Modification and Periodic Review.** Children's needs change as they age. A parenting plan that addresses the needs of an infant will be inadequate for a teenager. The parties may wish to build in provisions for periodic review of the plan to accommodate the changing needs of growing children. The parties should also address how they will deal with changes in life circumstances such as remarriage, cohabitation, relocation, and child-related issues. The plan may also include a general statement of cooperation and mutual respect between the parents.

Once the parenting plan is complete and signed by the parties, the court reviews it to determine if it is in the best interest of the children. While courts are in favor of parties reaching an agreement by their own accord, any provisions dealing with the welfare of the children must pass court scrutiny.

In 2005, the State of Connecticut enacted a law requiring a parenting plan in custody cases. Here is an example of the requirements of the plan:

Connecticut General Statutes Section 46b-56

- d) In any proceeding before the Superior Court involving a dispute between the parents of a minor child with respect to the custody, care, education and upbringing of such child, the parents shall file with the court, at such time and in such form as provided by rule of court, a proposed parental responsibility plan that shall include, at a minimum, the following: (1) A schedule of the physical residence of the child during the year; (2) provisions allocating decision-making authority to one or both parents regarding the child's health, education and religious upbringing; (3) provisions for the resolution of future disputes between the parents, including, where appropriate, the involvement of a mental health professional or other parties to assist the parents in reaching a developmentally appropriate resolution to such disputes; (4) provisions for dealing with the parents' failure to honor their responsibilities under the plan; (5) provisions for dealing with the child's changing needs as the child grows and matures; and (6) provisions for minimizing the child's exposure to harmful parental conflict, encouraging the parents in appropriate circumstances to meet their responsibilities through agreements, and protecting the best interests of the child.

- (e) The objectives of a parental responsibility plan under this section are to provide for the child's physical care and emotional stability, to provide for the child's changing needs as the child grows and to set forth the authority and responsibility of each parent with respect to the child.

- (f) If both parents consent to a parental responsibility plan under this section, such plan shall be approved by the court as the custodial and access orders of the court pursuant to section 46b-56, as amended by this act, unless the court finds that such plan as submitted and agreed to is not in the best interests of the child.

MANDATORY PARENTING EDUCATION PROGRAMS

Most states require divorcing parents with minor children to attend **mandatory parenting education programs.** They generally consist of several group sessions with a mental health professional approved by the state, who mandates attendance by the parents in divorce cases. The goal of the program is to educate parents on the effects of divorce on the children. They also focus on the children's emotional well-being and how the parents promote the children's emotional health by reassuring them that the divorce was not their fault and that their parents still love them. Parents are also educated on how to help the children through the transition and how to avoid hurtful or negative behaviors that may scar the children emotionally by keeping children out of their conflicts. Following is an example of Minnesota's parenting education program statute.

Minnesota Statutes 518.157—Parent Education Program in Proceedings Involving Children

- **Subdivision 1.** Implementation; administration. By January 1, 1998, the chief judge of each judicial district or a designee shall implement one or more parent education programs within the judicial district for the purpose of educating parents about the impact that divorce, the restructuring of families, and judicial proceedings have upon children and families; methods for preventing parenting time conflicts; and dispute resolution options. The chief judge of each judicial district or a designee may require that children attend a separate education program designed to deal with the impact of divorce upon children as part of the parent education program. Each parent education program must enable persons to have timely and reasonable access to education sessions.

■ **Subd. 2.** Minimum standards; plan. The Minnesota Supreme Court should promulgate minimum standards for the implementation and administration of a parent education program. The chief judge of each judicial district or a designee shall submit a plan to the Minnesota conference of chief judges for their approval that is designed to implement and administer a parent education program in the judicial district. The plan must be consistent with the minimum standards promulgated by the Minnesota Supreme Court.

■ **Subd. 3.** Attendance. In a proceeding under this chapter where custody or parenting time is contested, the parents of a minor child shall attend a minimum of eight hours in an orientation and education program that meets the minimum standards promulgated by the Minnesota Supreme Court. In all other proceedings involving custody, support, or parenting time the court may order the parents of a minor child to attend a parent education program. The program shall provide the court with names of persons who fail to attend the parent education program as ordered by the court. Persons who are separated or contemplating involvement in a dissolution, paternity, custody, or parenting time proceeding may attend a parent education program without a court order. Unless otherwise ordered by the court, participation in a parent education program must begin within 30 days after the first filing with the court or as soon as practicable after that time based on the reasonable availability of classes for the program for the parent. Parent education programs must offer an opportunity to participate at all phases of a pending or postdecree proceeding. Upon request of a party and a showing of good cause, the court may excuse the party from attending the program. If past or present domestic abuse, as defined in chapter 518B, is alleged, the court shall not require the parties to attend the same parent education sessions and shall enter an order setting forth the manner in which the parties may safely participate in the program.

■ **Subd. 4.** Sanctions. The court may impose sanctions upon a parent for failure to attend or complete a parent education program as ordered.

■ **Subd. 5.** Confidentiality. Unless all parties agree in writing, statements made by a party during participation in a parent education program are inadmissible as evidence for any purpose, including impeachment. No record may be made regarding a party's participation in a parent education program, except a record of attendance at and completion of the program as required under this section. Instructors shall not disclose information regarding an individual participant obtained as a result of participation in a parent education program. Parent education instructors may not be subpoenaed or called as witnesses in court proceedings.

■ **Subd. 6.** Fee. Except as provided in this subdivision, each person who attends a parent education program shall pay a fee to defray the cost of the program. A party who qualifies for waiver of filing fees under section 563.01 is exempt from paying the parent education program fee and the court shall waive the fee or direct its payment under section 563.01. Program providers shall implement a sliding fee scale.

CHILD'S PREFERENCE

Some parents have the mistaken belief that a child's preference is the determining factor in a custody dispute. Courts are well aware that parents may pressure children, shower them with gifts, or avoid disciplining them in an effort to win their favor in a custody fight. While courts will consider the child's wishes as to whom she would prefer as a custodian, this is only one factor in a list of many that must be balanced in the best interest equation. States vary in terms of the age at which they will consider the child's wishes or the maturity level necessary for the child to form an intelligent decision.

THE RIGHT TO DECIDE

The *Harbin* case illustrates Georgia's child preference statute, which allows a child of fourteen years of age the right to decide his custodian, unless that custodian is deemed to be unfit.

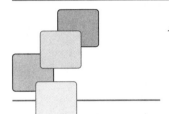

ALICE JACKSON HARBIN V. ALLEN THOMAS HARBIN

238 GA. 109, 230 S.E.2D 889 (GA. 1976)

SUPREME COURT OF GEORGIA

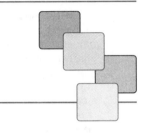

PER CURIAM.

This is an appeal from the denial of a petition to change custody. It was brought by the appellant-mother against the appellee-father who had been granted custody in a divorce action in 1972. There are three sons aged 15, 14 and 12 years. This appeal involves only the elder two children who have elected to live with the appellant. . . . In the divorce action the mother was found to be unfit to have custody. A previous petition to change custody was denied in 1974 with a finding that there was no evidence of the mother's rehabilitation. . . .

Appellant contends that since her children over 14 years of age had elected to live with her, the trial court erred in ruling that she had the burden of persuasion as to her fitness to have custody. Appellant concedes that absent such an election by a child over 14 years of age, the moving party has the burden of showing a change of conditions materially affecting the welfare of the child. However, it is argued that once a 14-year-old child makes an election to live with one parent, the other parent has the burden of showing the selected parent is unfit to have custody. Appellant relies on Code Ann. §74-107 which provides, ". . . where the child has reached the age of 14 years, such child shall have the right to select the parent with whom such child desires to live and such selection shall be controlling unless the parent so selected is determined not to be a fit and proper person to have the custody of said child." Code Ann. §30-127 contains the same provision. . . .

. . . The mother who was the parent selected by the children presented evidence of her fitness to have custody. The father who has custody of the children presented evidence of the mother's unfitness by introducing the record of their 1972 divorce action and the 1974 judgment finding no evidence of rehabilitation. In our opinion the critical issue here is whether the 1972 divorce record and the later 1974 decree are, as contended in enumeration of error #3, inadmissible as evidence of the mother's unfitness. If this evidence is inadmissible then there is no evidence of the mother's unfitness and she is entitled to custody under Code Ann.§74-107 and Code Ann.§30-127.

In *Adams v. Adams*, supra, it is stated, "It is not a new or novel concept that a minor child may well be capable of making a wise selection. . . . Under the Act of 1962 (Ga.L.1962, pp. 713–715) [Amendment to Code Ann. §74-107 and Code Ann. §30-127] no parental right of custody by judgment or decree can defeat the right of a child reaching 14 years of age 'to select the parent with whom such child desires to live.' " This case together with a careful reading of the 1962 Act, which is now incorporated into Code Ann. §30-127, persuades us that a child of 14 years or more was mature enough to select the parent with whom he desired to live and that this right of selection was controlling despite previous adjudications of unfitness. Therefore, it is our conclusion that such child's right of selection can only be defeated by a showing of present unfitness. . . . Accordingly, there is no evidence of the present unfitness of the appellant-mother to have custody. The judgment of the trial court must be reversed. The case is remanded for further hearing to permit the appellee to present evidence of appellant's present unfitness to have custody of her two children over 14 years of age.

Judgment reversed.

PARENTAL MISCONDUCT

Parental fault or misconduct is not a factor in deciding custody unless the parent's behavior effects the best interest of the children. The court looks at the parent's conduct and determines if such conduct is a danger to the health and welfare of the children. For example:

■ A parent's religious beliefs are not a basis for granting or denying custody unless religious practices such as excessive corporal punishment, prolonged prayer or meditation services, excessive door-to-door solicitation, or avoidance of medical treatment are involved.

■ An adulterous parent may not be a very good spouse, but the act of adultery alone is not enough to deny a parent custody or visitation.

■ A particular mental or physical health problem does not automatically render a parent unfit. The court will focus on how the parent's particular condition affects his or her ability to provide the necessary care and supervision for the child. In cases of a parent coping with mental health issues, it is not enough to claim that a parent is unfit because he or she takes medication or sees a therapist. The opposing parent must prove that the emotional and psychiatric disorder affects the best interest of the children. An allegation that a parent is unfit because they take medication or see a therapist may backfire; the court may view this as a responsible act on behalf of a parent dealing with mental health issues.

■ Cohabitation, remarriage, or a parent's dating may not be grounds for terminating custody or visitation unless the parent's new partner abuses the child or the parent, or engages in other behavior that puts the child at risk.

■ A parent's consumption of drugs, alcohol, or other addictive substances may result in loss of custody if the behavior presents a danger to the children. In the case of *DeMatteo v. DeMatteo*, 194 Misc.2d 640, 749 N.Y.S.2d 671 (2002), a 14-year-old child requested that his mother be prohibited from exposing him to cigarette smoking during her court-order visitation. The issue before the court was:

Should the court take judicial notice: (1) that environmental tobacco smoke is a carcinogen; (2) that environmental tobacco smoke causes respiratory infections in children; (3) that environmental tobacco smoke causes asthma; (4) that environmental tobacco smoke causes coronary heart disease; and (5) that childhood exposure to environmental tobacco smoke causes increased risk of lung cancer. *(DeMatteo, 641)*

The New York Supreme Court held:
    (1) The court takes judicial notice that environmental tobacco smoke is a carcinogen and causes lung cancer in otherwise healthy nonsmokers and that the children of smoking parents suffer a higher incidence of respiratory infections and smaller rates of increases in lung functions. The court declines to take judicial notice of any other questions presented.

(2) The plaintiff or any other party may introduce evidence to refute this holding at a hearing or trial. Any party seeking to refute the matter judicially noticed will have the burden of proof. Each party will have the burden of proof regarding any proposed visitation scheme that they propound.

(3) Pending a hearing or trial the defendant's house where the child spends the majority of his time will remain a smoke-free home. The plaintiff will not smoke in her home 24 hours prior to scheduled visitations. There shall be no smoking in either parties' residence or automobile in Nicholas' presence. All parties shall have 30 days to request a hearing/trial; if no such request is received, this further decision/second interim order shall become final. *(DeMatteo, 642)*

■ A parent's sexual preference may impact a court's decision regarding custody depending on the jurisdiction and the personal views of the presiding judge as well as attorneys involved in the case. Many gay parents all over the country have lost custody of their children due to their sexual preference, on the basis that their sexual preference in and of itself is contrary to the best interest of the children. Denying gay parents custody still takes place even in states that do not condone such discriminatory standards. Many courts, however, focus on whether the parent's conduct has a detrimental impact on the children.

MOTHER'S SEXUAL PREFERENCE

In the *Charpentier* case, although the mother did not contest a decree granting custody to the father, she did dispute the financial orders entered by the trial court, claiming that the lower court was unduly influenced by her lifestyle. This case illustrates the trial court's concern with the effect of the mother's lifestyle and her same-sex partner's mental illness on the children.

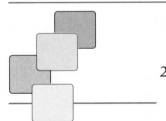
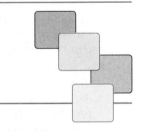

REAL J. F. CHARPENTIER V. CATHY A. CHARPENTIER

206 CONN. 150, 536 A.2D 948 (CONN. 1998)

SUPREME COURT OF CONNECTICUT

SHEA, J.

. . . The parties were married on October 2, 1967. During the marriage five children were born, ranging in age from five to twelve at the time of judgment. The marriage was dissolved on August 22, 1986 by the Honorable Joseph Bogdanski, state trial referee, acting as the trial court. The trial court awarded the plaintiff husband, Real J. F. Charpentier, custody of the five children, and granted a right of reasonable visitation to the defendant wife. The defendant has not contested the custody decree. . . .

. . . A major contention of the defendant is that the trial court's financial orders were impermissibly influenced by her admitted lesbian sexual preference. We conclude that the trial court's financial orders were not so premised, but instead reasonably reflected the economic burden imposed on the plaintiff by the custody decree as the parent primarily responsible for raising five young children.

The defendant does not dispute engaging in an adulterous relationship with another woman, M, before the parties' separation. In December, 1984, while the plaintiff was hospitalized for seven days for viral pneumonia, the defendant moved M into the family home to live there amidst the five children. When the plaintiff returned home to recuperate, the defendant would leave each night to spend time with M. In February, 1985, the plaintiff moved out of the house. Within one day, the defendant had invited M again to live in the house with her and the children.

There is some indication in the record that the trial court might have been influenced by the defendant's lesbian sexual preference when it awarded custody of the children to their father, although the trial court was also much concerned with the abusive behavior of M toward the children. The trial court stated: "In spite of the dissolution action, there does not appear to be hostility or anger displayed by the parties to each other, and it is apparent that both parents deeply love their children. It further appears that both parents are capable of raising five children alone. The problem here is the presence in the homestead of a third party [M]. The children all blame her for the breakup of their parent's marriage. They feel they are second best to her, and feel that their mother prefers to spend more time with her than with them. They have spoken of their concerns regarding the open display of affection between two lesbian women in the home and their desire not to have this done in front of their friends. As the children grow older they will have to struggle with a home life that is quite different from those of their peers. [M] has displayed difficulty in dealing with stress by impulsively attempting suicide or requesting in-patient hospitalization. The children have complained of her yelling at them and slapping them. It is not clear at this time how much stress and tension she can tolerate, and a household of five children can produce a chaotic environment."

We construe the references in the memorandum of decision to the defendant's lesbian relationship as indicating concern of the trial court not with her sexual orientation per se but with its effect upon the children, who had observed in the home inappropriate displays of physical affection between their mother and M, who had twice been institutionalized for mental problems, had been diagnosed as a schizophrenic, and had a history of suicide attempts, to continue to reside in the home with the children, especially when left alone to care for them. In awarding custody, the trial court ordered that M not be present during the defendant's visitation. . . .

- Behaviors such as speaking badly about the other parent in front of the child; discussing the reasons behind the breakdown of the marital relationship; false allegations of child, sexual, physical; and emotional abuse; blaming the other parent for the financial problems now encountered by the custodial parent; using the child to carry negative messages to the other parent, and asking the child to choose between parents is called **parental alienation.** A child's response to this psychological manipulation may destroy the child's once-positive relationship with that parent. The psychological literature refers to the child's response as **Parental Alienation Syndrome,** or **PAS.** If a custodial parent deliberately disparages and badmouths the noncustodial parent to the point where the child no longer wants to visit or spend time with that parent, the courts may intervene by awarding custody to the noncustodial parent. Diagnosis of PAS is made by a mental health professional who may be called into court as an expert witness. An expert opposing the diagnosis may also be called to the stand, resulting in a battle of the experts.

- In 1974, Congress passed the **Child Abuse Prevention and Treatment Act (CAPTA),** 42 U. S. C. A. Section 5101. Prior to the passage of this law, child abuse remained in the closet. The act required the states to adopt child abuse prevention laws or risk losing federal funding. Professionals who deal with children are mandated to report suspected child abuse and receive immunity for reports of suspected child abuse or neglect made in good faith. Mandated reporters include medical professionals, school personnel, police officers, mental health professionals, social workers, and members of the clergy. There is a lot of pressure on professionals to report suspected child abuse. Many feel that it is better to err on the side of caution rather than risk the possibility that their failure to report could result in a child's continued mistreatment or even death. Given this environment, a parent falsely alleging child abuse knows that such a claim will get an immediate reaction, not only from mandated reporters but also the court system. There are, unfortunately, many divorce litigants who falsely accuse their spouses of child sexual abuse. The mental health profession calls this **SAID,** which stands for **Sexual Allegations in Divorce.** SAID is a type of parental alienation syndrome and occurs when one parent uses psychological manipulation to encourage the child to fabricate allegations of child sexual abuse. States have passed legislation to punish false accusers; however, the small penalties associated with such activity pale in comparison to the consequences suffered by someone who is wrongly accused. Great damage is also done to true victims of child sexual abuse who may be looked upon with greater suspicion.

- A client who feels he or she is being falsely accused of child sexual abuse should retain counsel immediately. Generally, the state child protection department or police initiate an investigation. It is very important for clients to be represented at every stage of the case, including administrative intervention, no matter how benign it may look, especially if the parties are going through a divorce.

THE CASE OF BRIDGET MARKS, JOHN AYLSWORTH, AND THE TWINS

On June 1, 2004, the issue of parental alienation made national news in the case of Bridget Marks and John Aylsworth. Marks is an actress and former Playboy model who had an affair with a married casino executive named John Aylsworth. The affair resulted in Marks giving birth to twin daughters and a bitter custody fight. The trial court gave custody to Aylsworth on the basis that Marks sought to prevent the four-year-old twins from seeing their father by falsely accusing him of child sexual abuse, and that the mother had coached the children to make these allegations. The appellate court, however, returned custody of the children to Marks.

IN THE MATTER OF JOHN A. V. BRIDGET M.

791 N.Y.S.2D 421, 16 A.D.3D 324 (1ST DEPT 2005)

APPELLATE DIVISION OF THE SUPREME COURT OF NEW YORK, FIRST DEPARTMENT

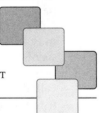

Saxe and Sullivan, JJ., concur in a memorandum by Sullivan, J., as follows:

This is an appeal from a Family Court order transferring custody of four-year-old twin girls, born out of wedlock, who had resided with their mother from birth, to the father on the basis of a finding, after an evidentiary hearing, that the mother had coached the children to make false accusations of sexual abuse

against the father and was thereby undermining his relationship with them. The evidence adduced at the hearing, which spanned 14 days and encompassed the testimony of 32 witnesses and 52 exhibits, is summarized as follows.

In 1998, petitioner John A. (the father), 48 years of age at the time, married and the father of four adult children, became romantically involved with respondent

Bridget M. (the mother), a 32-year-old actress/model, residing in Manhattan, whom he met on one of his business trips to New York. An executive of a corporation based in St. Louis, Missouri, the father has residences in Manhattan and St. Louis, as well as the marital home, which he shares with his wife, in Malibu, California.

In early 1999, the mother discovered that she was pregnant. The father's wife learned of the affair and of the mother's pregnancy in April of the same year and filed for divorce in California. It should be noted that while the California divorce petition has not been pursued, it has never been withdrawn. According to the mother, the father and his wife telephoned her on several occasions, urging her to abort the pregnancy and offering her money to do so. On September 8, 1999, the mother gave birth to twin daughters, Scarlett and Amber.

While the mother testified that the father was excited about the prospect of starting a family with her and that he intended to leave his wife, the father denied ever expressing such an intention. And, although the mother testified that she wanted to marry the father, it is undisputed that she had been carrying on a simultaneous sexual relationship with another man, to whom she was engaged at the time of the hearing. Although the father refused to sign an acknowledgment of paternity at the hospital, he was listed as the father on the children's birth certificates. DNA testing performed shortly thereafter confirmed his paternity.

Although, as noted, the testimony was conflicting as to the father's intentions, Family Court, relying on the testimony of the mother's therapist, which it found credible, rejected his "protestations that he did nothing to give the mother cause to believe that he would leave his wife and build a life with [her] and the twins." At an October 2000 session that the father attended, he indicated to the therapist that he planned to divorce his wife and have the mother and the twins move with him to St. Louis.

The father's wife testified that after the events of September 11, 2001, she and the father decided to remain together. Notwithstanding, the father continued his relationship with the mother, "although the testimony indicates that there was a marked deterioration . . . after the father failed to divorce his wife by the fall of 2001." According to the father, from September 1999 through October 2002, he made more than 70 trips to New York, usually for business purposes, staying with the mother and the children 90% of the time. During these visits, he would parent the children, play with them, read to them and take them out. He also provided monthly financial support. He testified that the mother sometimes evinced jealousy, complaining that he was not paying sufficient attention to her. The mother, on the other hand, testified that the father visited with the children only when it was convenient during his visits to New York and that it is she who raised, nurtured and cared for them since their birth. While the father continued to live in California and Missouri, she not only provided the twins' day-to-day care but made all the decisions regarding their emotional, physical, educational and religious development.

On September 30, 2002, after the parties' relationship had ended, the father filed a Family Court petition for an order of filiation, even though his paternity had been established at birth. The mother contested the petition and, questioning the reliability of the DNA test arranged by the father after the births, demanded that another DNA test be performed. The effect of the mother's actions was to leave the father, pending receipt of the results, without any legal right to see the children. Visitation was arranged only with the mother's permission.

On February 4, 2003, upon receipt of positive DNA results, the father filed a petition in Family Court for visitation. The mother requested that any visitation be supervised because, since their infancy, the father had been acting in a sexually inappropriate manner with the children, playing with them roughly, exposing his genitalia to them and making lewd comments to her about their genitalia. On the basis of these allegations, the court, pending investigation, ordered supervised visitation. The parties stipulated that Linda Ehrenfreund, a social worker, would act as supervisor and, on April 14, 2003, the court appointed Stephen Bates Billick, M.D., qualified as an expert in psychiatry, forensic child psychiatry and child sexual abuse, as the neutral forensic evaluator.

Between March 2003 and the commencement of the hearing on November 3, 2003, the father's visitation was supervised by three different social workers, Ehrenfreund for visits on March 29, April 19 and April 20 and Jewel Roberts for all visits beginning May 18, except for those on June 15, September 13 and 14 and October 11 and 12, when social worker Traci Shinabarger supervised visitation. The mother claimed that the father had molested Scarlett in the bathroom of his apartment either on April 19 or April 20, while Ehrenfreund was supervising visitation. She also claimed that the father had molested Amber during Roberts's watch, on a July 12 visit to Central Park, when he had taken Amber to the bathroom.

The mother testified that after the twins returned home from the April 20 visit, Scarlett called out to Pam S., a family friend/nanny, that she needed help and asked her to wipe her like Daddy did without using toilet paper. When instructed to tell her mother,

Scarlett told the mother that "Daddy touched my peepee and he didn't use toilet paper." Pam S. called the State Central Agency to report that both children had been touched; the Administration for Children's Services (ACS) was also notified and criminal investigations ensued. On May 14, 2003, at the mother's request, Family Court appointed Roberts to replace Ehrenfreund.

According to the mother, the twins had told her that Roberts was absent for periods during the visits she supervised, prompting the mother to hire a private investigator to follow and videotape the visitation. The mother testified that after the July 12, 2003 visit to an amusement park, Amber told her that the father had "touched her peepee in the bathroom." According to the mother, Scarlett told her that the father was in the bathroom with Amber "for a long time," while she was outside holding his wife's hand. According to the private investigator, Roberts could not see the bathroom from where she was sitting. Over the next few days, Amber began complaining about irritation in her vaginal area, which, on examination, was red and inflamed. The mother took both children to the Cornell Medical Center emergency room, where they were diagnosed with vaginitis, and, on referral, to a doctor at Cornell the next day. Based on this diagnosis and Amber's account of the bathroom incident, the mother moved to suspend the father's visitation pending an investigation. In turn, the father moved to amend his visitation petition to one seeking custody. The court granted the motion to amend but did not suspend visitation.

Aside from his own testimony and that of his wife, the father's case consisted of the testimony of his four adult children attesting to his uniformly appropriate behavior towards them, the social workers who had supervised his visitation, as well as the ACS Child Protective Specialist who investigated the complaint and found it "unfounded" and, most notably, the report and testimony of Dr. Billick. Distilled to its essence, the father's case was that: the sexual abuse allegations were unfounded; respondent had coached the children to make false statements about their father; the charges were either made maliciously to frustrate visitation or were the product of the mother's delusional thinking; the mother's inability or unwillingness to foster the father's relationship with the children made her unfit to be the custodial parent; she was incapable of placing the needs of the children above her own; the father would be the better custodial parent and, although the children would experience significant stress and anguish as a result of any change in custody, in the final analysis, they would benefit from such a change.

The mother called four expert witnesses, including Dr. Celia Blumenthal, a child psychiatrist who had five therapy sessions with the children at the time of the alleged abuse and found the complaints of sexual abuse to be reliable, and the therapist to whom the father expressed his intention to leave his wife for the mother and the twins. The mother also called an investigator in the Police Department's Manhattan special victims unit assigned to investigate the criminal allegations of sexual abuse, who testified that she was unable to determine whether the charges were true and that the investigation remained open. Dr. Blumenthal further testified that the trauma and psychological damage that the children would suffer from a change of custody would be long term because of their age and the strong bond they had developed with their mother. The mother also called numerous character witnesses, including the director of the nursery school attended by the twins since September of 2002, who testified that the mother's relationship with them was "warm, loving, caring, very appropriate." She found the children's development to be "very appropriate[,] [n]ormal, no issues."

The essence of the mother's evidence was that: she and the children were strongly bonded; she is an excellent parent who puts the children's needs ahead of her own; she did not interfere with the father's relationship with the children and has the capacity, as the custodial parent, to facilitate his relationship with them; and she is not delusional and did not make up the abuse allegations. She argued that even if the allegations were contrived, the appropriate remedy is not the loss of custody of the children but, rather, treatment and that it would be extremely detrimental to the children to remove them from the parent who had been, since birth, their primary caretaker. A major thrust of the mother's case was addressed to discrediting Dr. Billick's report and testimony recommending a change in custody.

The Law Guardian presented a case in support of the father consisting of the testimony of Lisa Lubell, a certified social worker from Lawyers for Children, who was qualified as an expert with a specialty in child sexual abuse. Lubell expressed the opinion "with a high degree of certainty [that] these children were not sexually abused by their father" and recommended that it was in the best interest of the children that custody be awarded to the father in New York with liberal visitation to the mother. Julie Dowling, also qualified as an expert in social work and employed by Lawyers for Children, concurred in Lubell's opinion.

At the conclusion of the Law Guardian's case, the father and his wife were recalled to testify that if the father were granted custody they would relocate to New York City. Thereafter, on April 27, 2004, the mother sought to reopen the hearing to present newly discovered evidence that, during the hearing, the father was involved in an affair with another woman. Although supported by an affidavit from the woman's former husband, the motion was denied.

In a May 21, 2004 original decision supplemented by a June 28, 2004 expanded decision, Family Court awarded custody of the twins to the father, conditioned on his living within 40 miles of the New York City metropolitan area, with supervised visitation to the mother, who was directed not to permit any contact between Pam S. and the children. Transfer of custody was deferred until June 1, 2004, the completion of the school year. In reaching its decision, Family Court relied primarily on the testimony of Dr. Billick, Lisa Lubell and Julie Dowling, all of whom recommended that the father be awarded custody. The court found that the testimony and recommendations of the mother's experts were "of little probative value" since none of them performed forensic evaluations of the father and mother or of the children.

The court supported its factual findings by application of the legal principle that a custodial parent's willful deprivation of the noncustodial parent's visitation rights constitutes "an act so inconsistent with the best interests of the children as to, per se, raise a strong probability that the [parent] is unfit to act as a custodial parent," quoting *Entwistle v. Entwistle* (61 AD2d 380, 384–385 [1978], *appeal dismissed* 44 NY2d 851 [1978]). It relied on *Matter of Karen B. v. Clyde M.* (151 Misc 2D 794 [1991], *affd sub nom. Matter of Karen PP. v. Clyde QQ.*, 197 AD2d 753 [1993]), for the proposition that two instances of false accusations will justify a change in custody. The court further found that the father was an experienced and caring parent, loved by the twins, and that he would be capable of fostering a relationship with their mother, while she was incapable of reciprocating. While the father's extramarital affairs impact on his ability to be a good husband, the court held, they do not affect his ability to be a proper custodial parent. The orders entered on both of these decisions are before us on appeal as is the order denying the motion to reopen the hearing to consider newly discovered evidence. I would modify and deny the father's petition for custody.

Despite disagreement with its ruling on custody, I acknowledge that Family Court correctly found that the sexual abuse allegations were false and that the children had been coached, a determination that turned, in large part, on the court's observation of demeanor and its assessment of the credibility of the witnesses and the character, temperament and sincerity of the parties involved (*see Eschbach v. Eschbach*, 56 NY2d 167, 173–174 [1982]; *Fanelli v. Fanelli*, 215 AD2d 718, 719 [1995]). That finding, however, does not lead inexorably to the conclusion that custody should be awarded to the father. The custody determination turned largely on the testimony and report of Dr. Billick, the neutral forensic evaluator and only witness at the hearing to advocate relocation of the children to California; a recommendation, ultimately rejected by the court, that borders on the punitive.

Notwithstanding Dr. Billick's conclusion that the mother had engaged in conduct undermining the father's relationship with the children, he found nonetheless that: the children functioned at an appropriate level; Amber had a positive relationship with the father; the children want to see the father, enjoy being with him, and are comfortable with him; they have a warm attachment to the father and showed no adverse behavior towards him and even have affection and fondness for the father's wife. Thus, despite the finding that the mother was attempting to undermine the relationship between the father and the children, the relationship was, in fact, a healthy one, one that even yielded affection and fondness between the children and the father's wife.

Moreover, Dr. Billick also found that the mother is a "good enough mother" who demonstrates general day-to-day competency in that regard. Ms. English, the director of the nursery school attended by the children, found the mother's relationship with the children to be "warm, loving, caring and very appropriate." She described the children as respectful to teachers, happy, able to relate well to the other children and having good social skills.

Thus, the hearing testimony established that the father had a good relationship with the children, unimpaired by the mother, that he visited with them prior to and throughout the proceeding and enjoyed daily telephone calls with them while they were in the mother's custody, and that the mother was a good mother, a fact tellingly demonstrated by the children's social skills and development. In such circumstances, it was not in the children's best interest to award the father custody and to subject them to the trauma of being separated from their primary caretaker since birth and removal from the only home they have ever known. The appropriate response to the mother's unacceptable conduct, that is, using the children as pawns in her battle with the father is, as Dr. Blumenthal opined, not removal from the mother's custody, but treatment of her condition.

In that regard, Family Court Act § 656 provides for the imposition of an order of probation with mandatory participation in programs of treatment, counseling and rehabilitation for her problem . . . The matter, after restoration of custody to the mother, should be remanded to Family Court to fashion the appropriate remedy.

Under the foregoing analysis, the appeal from the denial of the mother's motion to reopen the hearing to consider newly discovered evidence demonstrating that the father had engaged in another affair during the hearing is academic. It should be noted, however, that the proffered evidence, if credible, bore on the father's claims that he and his wife had decided to stay together and were relocating to New York, a subject he introduced. Indeed, the record is bare, other than the testimony as to the intention to relocate in New York, as to who will care for the children while the father travels on business. The facile claim, on oral argument, that the father will parent the children "24/7" rings hollow.

Finally, it seems apparent, in reviewing this record, that the ultimate decision as to the key issue in this case, i.e., whether to award custody to the father because of the mother's attempts to undermine his relationship with the children, was made on the basis of the experts' testimony. Courts should be ever mindful that, while the forensic expert may offer guidance and inform, the ultimate determination on any such issue is a judicial function, not one for the expert.

In this regard, it should be noted that there is an ongoing debate in both the legal community and the mental health profession as to the implications of expert psychological opinion in custody litigation, especially when the opinion is a conclusion as to the ultimate determination as to where to award custody so as to serve the child's best interest. . .

REPRODUCTIVE TECHNOLOGY AND CUSTODY DISPUTES

Traditionally, the children in the center of a custody battle were conceived through the sexual union of their parents. As if the courts did not have enough problems deciphering these cases, enter the world of creating families through reproductive technology. Issues involving in vitro fertilization, artificial insemination, and surrogacy are increasingly making their way into the family courts. The need to reproduce and create a family is not only an avenue sought by heterosexual couples who cannot conceive, but also by gay and lesbian couples who wish to have children but find procreation impossible due to biological impediments.

IN VITRO FERTILIZATION

In vitro fertilization is the process of conceiving a human embryo outside of the biological parents' physical bodies. Eggs or ova are removed from the female, sperm is taken from the father, and the two substances are joined together in a petri dish and then transplanted back into the mother's or surrogate mother's uterus to facilitate the natural development of the fetus. A nonmedical term used to describe a child conceived through in vitro fertilization is "test tube baby."

Sometimes, the embryos are frozen for later use. This practice can lead to problems later on. There are legal issues associated with in vitro fertilization, especially when the couple decides to divorce. While it is relatively easy to divide up fine china, furniture, and knickknacks, it is not so easy to divide the frozen embryos. If the mother chooses to have the embryos implanted in her uterus or the father chooses to have them implanted in a surrogate's uterus after the divorce, this will raise custody, visitation, and child support issues for all parties involved. If one parent wants the embryos destroyed, this raises ethical and religious concerns, especially among those whose faith views destruction of the embryos in the same manner as it views abortion.

The law regarding custody of frozen embryos varies from state to state, with some jurisdictions providing no statutory or judicial guidance on the subject. The parties involved in conceiving through in vitro fertilization sign a contract delineating what is to be done with the frozen embryos. While some states will uphold the agreement under contract law theory, the state of Louisiana forbids destruction of the frozen embryos regardless of any agreements entered into by the parties. There are three judicial rulings in the United States of importance regarding custody of frozen embryos:

- **Davis v. Davis, 842 S.W. 2d 588 (1992).** Mr. and Mrs. Davis were unable to have children, so they sought the services of a fertility clinic in Knoxville. With the clinic's assistance, they produced nine embryos. Two of the embryos were implanted in Mrs. Davis, but did not develop. The remaining seven were frozen in the clinic's cold-storage unit. The in vitro fertilization agreement signed by the parties did not include any provisions on what to do with any unused embryos. When Mr. Davis filed for divorce, there was a dispute over what to do with the frozen embryos and how to legally characterize them. Mr. Davis argued that the embryos were not alive and, as a result, the court had to apply the same principles it used to resolve issues over joint property. He wanted to have the embryos destroyed. The trial court declared that "life begins at conception" and the frozen embryos were children and not property. Once the court characterized the frozen embryos as children, it applied the best interest standard and awarded the seven remaining embryos to Mrs. Davis, who originally wanted to try to conceive a child. If Mrs. Davis did conceive and ultimately gave birth, the issues of child custody, support, and visitation would be decided at a later time. Mr. Davis's appeal had eventually reached the Tennessee Supreme Court. By this time, Mrs. Davis had remarried, moved out of state, and wished to donate the frozen embryos to a childless couple. The Tennessee Supreme Court ruled in favor of Mr. Davis since Mrs. Davis no longer wanted the frozen embryos and he wished to have them discarded. Justice Martha Craig Daughtrey summarized the court's ruling on how to resolve disputes over frozen embryos in the following paragraph:

  In summary, we hold that disputes involving the Disposition of preembryos produced by in vitro fertilization should be resolved, first, by looking to the preferences of the progenitors. If their wishes cannot be ascertained, or if there is dispute, then their prior agreement concerning Disposition should be carried out. If no prior agreement exists, then the relative interests of the parties in using or not using the preembryos must be weighed. Ordinarily, the party wishing to avoid procreation should prevail, assuming that the other party has a reasonable possibility of achieving parenthood by means other than use of the preembryos in question. If no other reasonable alternatives exist, then the argument in favor of using the preembryos to achieve pregnancy should be considered. However, if the party seeking control of the preembryos intends merely to donate them to another couple, the objecting party obviously has the greater interest and should prevail.(*Davis,* **604**)

- **Kass v. Kass, 91 N.Y. 2d 554, 696 N.E. 2d 174 (1998).** In this case, the couple divorced after nine unsuccessful attempts at in vitro fertilization and $75,000 dollars in fees. At the fertility clinic, the parties signed an agreement donating any unused eggs for research purposes by the clinic, which would then destroy them after their scientific use. The parties engaged in a custody battle when Mrs. Kass decided she wanted the frozen embryos for future implantation, a position opposed by her husband, who argued that the frozen embryos were property and that the contract signed by the parties was binding. The New York Court of Appeals agreed with Mr. Kass and enforced the contract.

- **A.Z v. B.Z, 431 Mass. 150, 725 N.E.2d 1051 (2000).** This case involved a custody battle over four frozen embryos that the wife wanted implanted, even though the parties were going through a divorce. The husband filed an injunction, asking the court to prevent her from proceeding with her plan. The parties had signed a consent agreeing that the embryos would be implanted even though the parties separated. The trial court judge held that the consent form was not binding because of the divorce, the father's unwillingness to become a parent, and the unfairness to the child, who would be unwanted by one of its parents. The Massachusetts Supreme Judicial Court agreed with the trial court and affirmed the lower court's decision on the basis that the consent forms were not enforceable against the father.

Artificial insemination is the technique of injecting a male's semen into a female's uterus through the use of artificial means. The goal of artificial insemination is to impregnate the woman without physical contact with the male. Heterosexual couples use this method when conceiving in the natural way is not possible due to a physical or mental health condition. Lesbian couples who wish to create families also use artificial insemination. Gay men or heterosexuals who cannot conceive also use artificial insemination when employing the services of a surrogate mother.

A **surrogate mother** is a woman who agrees by contract to bear a child for a couple or an individual who cannot conceive in exchange for a fee. The surrogate mother is either impregnated with a male's sperm or in vitro fertilization. A couple who cannot conceive through natural means may implant an embryo created in a petri dish into a surrogate's uterus for development when the wife is unable to carry a fetus. This is known as gestational surrogacy. As part of the contract, the surrogate mother agrees to bear the child in exchange for a fee that will cover her medical and any other expenses related to the pregnancy as well as an adoption fee for her services. As part of the contract, the surrogate mother agrees to terminate her parental rights and give the child up for adoption to the other party in the contract.

The law regarding surrogacy contracts varies from state to state. Some jurisdictions have declared these contracts to be illegal, unenforceable, and void against public policy. Other jurisdictions may prohibit the payment of a fee above and beyond the surrogate mother's birth-related expenses. A ban on such fees takes the profit motive out of the equation and may in some sense discourage women from going through the nine-month pregnancy without some sort of compensation above and beyond medically related expenses. Courts and legislatures confronted with this issue are particularly concerned with preventing baby selling and the exploitation of women. Many state surrogacy laws have been crafted by judges who creatively applied the principles of contract law, paternity law, family law, and criminal law and public policy considerations in forging a solution to disputes before them. The applicable law in a surrogacy case depends on the law of the state where the child is born.

Surrogacy agreements are potential landmines for custody disputes, especially when the surrogate mother changes her mind and refuses to give up custody of the child. A surrogacy contract that received nationwide publicity in the late 1980s was the case of Baby M. Mary Beth Whitehead, who was also the biological mother in this case, agreed to be a surrogate for William and Elizabeth Stern. Due to a diabetic condition, Mrs. Stern could not have children, so she and her husband agreed that Ms. Whitehead would be artificially inseminated with his sperm. Mrs. Stern would then adopt the child. Mrs. Whitehead changed her mind and sued for custody of the baby. The Sterns won custody of Baby M after a New Jersey court applied the best interest standard in the case. Mrs. Whitehead did, however, receive visitation rights with the child.

GRANDPARENTS' RIGHTS AND THE RIGHTS OF THIRD PARTIES

As a rule, a court may not enter an order permitting a third party legally enforceable visitation rights. As with most rules, however, exceptions exist.

In a divorce case, the husband and wife are the only legally recognizable parties to the action. When an individual who is neither mother nor father seeks to have visitation, if the family unit is intact, a third party has no standing to bring an action in court.

Standing is a legal term. It determines whether a party has a legal right to request an adjudication of the issues in a legal dispute. However, where the family unit is no longer intact, there are instances where a third party has standing to petition the court for custody or visitation. Every jurisdiction has enacted statutes permitting grandparents to intervene in divorce cases and request visitation or custody of the minor children. Once the court grants third parties a legal right to be heard in the proceedings, they are considered **third-party intervenors.**

PROTECTING THE INTACT FAMILY

The *Castagno* case outlines the common law and statutory changes that allowed grandparents into divorce court. The courts, however, will not intrude on an intact family and will allow parents to make the decision regarding the grandparents' access to the children. A court can order visitation for a man who cohabited with a woman for years and developed a bond as a psychological parent with the woman's child.

The general rule is that no third party may petition for visitation when the family is intact. This is a common law rule based on the presumption that parents have a constitutional right to raise their children as they see fit, free from the interference of third parties. This right, however, is not absolute. The state may intervene on behalf of abused and neglected children, and courts have the power to give visitation or custody to third parties when they deem it is in the child's best interest. This is known as the doctrine of **parens partriae**. *Parens patriae* is Latin term that

FIGURE 7–4
Every jurisdiction has enacted statutes that permit grandparents to seek visitation or custody rights with minor grandchildren, where the family unit is no longer intact.

describes the power of the state to protect and care for children when the parents are unwilling or unable to do so.

Grandparents may obtain visitation or custody rights under the following circumstances:

- Statutes and court procedures allowing grandparents to request visitation when the children's parents are getting divorced or when one of the parents dies.

- When there is a breakdown in the parent-child relationship, for example, removal of the children from the parents care by state social workers due to abuse and neglect and the grandparents' petition for custody or guardianship. There are many grandparents, as well as aunts and uncles, who have come to the rescue of children under these circumstances and provide them with a stable and loving environment.

- With the consent of the parents in cases where the biological parents can no longer care for the children.

- Through informal family arrangements where the parents voluntarily maintain contact with the grandparents despite death, divorce, or other breakdown in the parents' relationship.

From the early 1970s to the 1980s, every state enacted some type of statute giving grandparents visitation when the court determined that it was in the children's best interest. These statutes varied from state to state. In the late 1990s, many state courts invalidated third-party visitation statutes, claiming they violated a parent's constitutional right to raise their children without influence or interference from others. Courts thus were declaring that it was unconstitutional to intrude on an intact family.

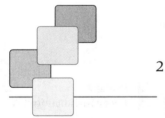

JEAN T. CASTAGNO, ET AL. V. TINA WHOLEAN, ET AL.

239 CONN. 336, 684 A.2D 1181 (CONN. 1996)

SUPREME COURT OF CONNECTICUT

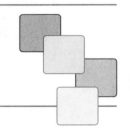

KATZ, J.

The sole issue in this appeal is whether, pursuant to General Statutes §46b-59,[1] the trial court had subject matter jurisdiction to entertain a petition by grandparents for visitation rights with their minor grandchildren when the grandchildren and their parents were

---

[1] General Statute §46b-59 provides: "the superior court may grant the right of visitation with respect to any minor child or children to any person, upon an application of such person. Such order shall be according to the court's best judgment upon the facts of the case and subject to such conditions and limitations as it deems equitable, provided the grant of such visitation rights shall not be contingent upon any order of financial support by the court. In making, modifying or terminating such an order, the court shall be guided by the best interest of the child, giving consideration to the wishes of such child if he is of sufficient age and capable of forming an intelligent opinion. Visitation rights granted in accordance with this section shall not be deemed to have created parental rights in the person or persons to whom such visitation rights are granted. The grant of such visitation rights shall not prevent any court of competent jurisdiction from thereafter acting upon the custody of such child, the parental rights with respect to such child or the adoption of such child and any such court may include in its decree an order terminating such visitation rights.

not involved in any case or controversy currently before the court and there was no claim that the family unit was no longer intact. We conclude that although §46b-59 lacks specific language imposing any threshold requirement, established rules of statutory construction, the context of the statute and its legislative history support the incorporation of a requirement that plaintiffs must demonstrate disruption of the family sufficient to justify state intervention. In the absence of any attempt by the plaintiffs here to satisfy this threshold requirement, we conclude that the trial court lacked jurisdiction to decide the issue of visitation and, therefore, properly dismissed the plaintiffs' action (footnote omitted). Accordingly, we affirm the judgment of the trial court. . . .

. . . The plaintiffs argue that the trial court misconstrued §46b-59 to contain threshold requirements not expressed in the plain language of the statute. Specifically, the plaintiffs claim that the application of §46b-59 is not limited by any threshold requirements, and that the sole criterion for application of the statute is the best interest of the child. Accordingly, the plaintiffs argue that any third party who seeks state intervention, in the form of a court's grant of visitation rights, may petition the court at any time, and need not present any allegations that the minor child's family is no longer intact. The plaintiffs further maintain that, because the language of §46b-59 is clear and unambiguous, it was inappropriate for the trial court to rely on the legislative history of the statute to establish any threshold requirements. We disagree.

We begin with the common law background against which the visitation statutes were enacted. At common law, grandparents, or third parties in general, have no right to visitation. Rather, the decision as to who may or may not have access to a minor child has been deemed an issue of parental prerogative (citations and footnote omitted). The common law reflects the belief that the family unit should be respected, and its autonomy and privacy invaded through court action only in the most pressing circumstances. "That right [of the parents to determine the care, custody, and control of their children] is recognized because it reflects a strong civilization, and because the parental role is now established beyond debate as an enduring American tradition" (citation and footnote omitted). All families may have, at one time or another, unhappy conflicts and disputes among adult relatives that might result in an absence of contact between those adults and their minor relatives—be they grandchildren, nieces or nephews, cousins, etc.—but longstanding tradition holds that, absent compelling circumstances justifying some state intervention in the form or a judicial order, the parents' decision, whether wise or not, prevails. . . .

. . . The right to family autonomy and privacy acknowledged in the common law has been recognized as so fundamental as to merit constitutional protection. Consequently, any legislation affecting it is strictly scrutinized (citation omitted). . . .

. . . The plaintiffs' construction of §46b-59 would allow the court to intrude upon an intact family that has not already opened itself to such intrusion. . . .

TROXEL V. GRANVILLE: U.S. SUPREME COURT SETS NEW STANDARD FOR THIRD-PARTY VISITATION

Grandparent visitation becomes problematic when parents refuse to maintain the children's relationship with the grandparents after a bitter divorce, breakup, or a parent's death. In the year 2000, the U.S. Supreme Court addressed the issue of the rights of third parties seeking visitation with children in the case of *Troxel v. Granville* (530 US 57, 120 S Ct. 2054,147 L.Ed 29 [2000]). The case began with a relationship between Tommie Granville and Brad Troxel, an unmarried couple who had two daughters. Their relationship ended in 1991. Brad Troxel moved out and went to live with his parents, Jenifer and Gary Troxel. During this time, the children visited their father on weekends, as well as spent time with their grandparents. Tragically, Brad Troxel committed suicide in 1993. After Brad's suicide, Tommie Granville informed the paternal grandparents that she wanted to reduce their visits with the children to once a month. Granville had since remarried and was in the process of rebuilding her family.

- ■ The Troxels petitioned for visitation under a Washington statute. The statute, Revised Code of Washington, Section 26.10.160 (3), at the time allowed "any person" to petition for visitation rights "at any time," whenever the court determined that such visitation was in the children's best interest. While Granville did not oppose the petition, she did not agree with the amount of time the Troxels were seeking for visitation. She argued that in the absence of a custody dispute or challenge regarding her fitness as a parent, she should have the right to decide issues involving her children. In 1995, the Washington Superior Court ruled in favor of the grandparents, giving them more visitation rights because, in the court's opinion, it was in the children's best interest. The Washington Court of Appeals reversed the decision and held that nonparents lacked standing to sue under the Washington law. The Washington Supreme Court affirmed, declaring the Washington statute unconstitutional because it interfered with her fourtheenth Amendment right to privacy and child-rearing authority. The grandparents disagreed and appealed their case to the U.S. Supreme Court.

■ The issue on appeal before the Supreme Court was whether the Washington statute, which allowed any person to petition for court-ordered visitation over a parent's objection if the visitation was in the child's best interest, interfered with a parent's constitutional right to raise his or her children. In a 6–3 decision written by Justice Sandra Day O'Connor, the Supreme Court held that the Washington statute was too broad and unconstitutional as applied. The Court held that it violated a parent's right under the Due Process Clause of the fourteenth Amendment to make decisions concerning the care of their children and went on to write that the "[t]he liberty interest at issue in this case—the interest of parents in the care, custody, and control of their children—is perhaps the oldest of the fundamental liberty interests recognized by this Court."

State Response to *Troxel*

After the *Troxel* decision, states either revised their visitation statute or waited for the courts to find their respective state statute unconstitutional under the *Troxel* decision. It is important to become familiar with your particular jurisdiction's response to *Troxel*, as each state may interpret the case differently, sending more cases to the Supreme Court in the future. State statutes or court decisions bringing their state law in line with the *Troxel* decision require a two-prong test:

1. A break in the parent-child relationship; and
2. Grandparents (or third party) must prove by clear and convincing evidence that visitation is in the child's best interest.

Some constitutional scholars argue that the *Troxel* decision may also require third parties to demonstrate that the child will suffer harm from the lack of visitation.

The decision in *Troxel* applies to any third party seeking time with a child. This not only includes grandparents, but also other relatives and unmarried partners.

State Application of *Troxel*

In *Roth v. Weston*, the Supreme Court of Connecticut interpreted the Connecticut visitation statue, one similar to that of the State of Washington, in light of the decision in *Troxel*. The decision creates a new standard for third parties seeking visitation as well as interesting discussion on the rights of parents and third parties in children's lives.

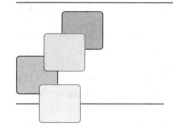

MINDY ROTH V. STAN WESTON

259 Conn. 202,789 A.2d 431 (2002)

Supreme Court of Connecticut

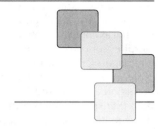

KATZ, J.

The defendant, Stan Weston, appeals from the judgment of the trial court granting an application for visitation with the defendant's two minor children to the plaintiffs, Mindy Roth and Donna Campbell, respectively the children's maternal grandmother and maternal aunt, pursuant to General Statutes § 46B-59. . .

. . .The defendant claims that, in light of the United States Supreme Court's recent decision in *Troxel* v. *Granville*, 530 U.S. 57, 120 S.Ct. 2054, 147 L.Ed.2d 49 (2000), § 46b-59 is either facially unconstitutional or unconstitutional as applied to the facts of the present case. We conclude that the statute is unconstitutional as applied to the extent that the trial court, pursuant to the statute, permitted third party visitation contrary to the desires of a fit parent and in the absence of any allegation and proof by clear and convincing evidence that the children would suffer actual, significant harm if deprived of the visitation. Accordingly, we reverse the judgment of the trial court ordering visitation.

The record discloses the following undisputed facts. The plaintiffs filed a complaint in the trial court seeking visitation with the defendant's children in March, 2000, three months after the defendant's wife had committed suicide. The defendant had refused to permit any contact between the plaintiffs and his children during the months following his wife's death. The plaintiffs' complaint alleged that the family unit had been disrupted by the death of the children's mother and therefore was no longer intact. The plaintiffs further alleged that visitation was in the best interest of the children. They did not, however contend that the defendant was in any way an unfit parent. . .

. . . in *Troxel* v. *Granville*, supra, 530 U.S.57, the United States Supreme Court reviewed a decision by the Washington Supreme Court holding its visitation statute facially unconstitutional. That statute provides that "[a]ny person may petition the court for visitation rights at any time including, but not limited to, custody proceedings. The court may order visitation rights for any person when visitation may serve the best interests of the child whether or not there has been any change of circumstances." Wash. Rev. Code

§ 26.10.160(3) (2000). The trial court in *Troxel* awarded visitation to the paternal grandparents after their son had committed suicide and the children's mother limited their access to the children. The Washington Supreme Court had held that a state constitutionally may interfere with the fundamental right of parents to rear their children only to prevent harm or potential harm to a child. *In re Custody of Smith*, 137 Wash.2d 1, 19–20, 969 P.2d 21 (1998), aff'd sub nom. *Troxel* v. *Granville*, 530 U.S.57, 120.S.Ct. 2054, 147 L.Ed.2d 49 (2000). Section 26.10.160(3) of the Washington Code failed to meet that standard because it required no threshold showing of harm. *In re Custody of Smith*, supra,15–20. Moreover, by allowing "'any person' to petition for forced visitation of a child at 'any time' with the only requirement being that the visitation serve the best interest of the child," according to the court, the visitation statute swept too broadly. Id., 20. Specifically, the statute authorized a contested visitation order at the behest *of any person at any time* subject only to a best interests of the child standard. Additionally, a parent's decision that visitation would not be in the child's best interest would be accorded no deference, and the best interest determination would rest solely in the discretion of the judge, whose assessment would necessarily prevail regardless of the parent's estimation of the child's best interests. Id., 21. Essentially, the decisional framework authorized by the statute and employed by the trial court directly contravened the traditional presumption that a fit parent acts in the best interest of his or her child. In conclusion, the Washington Supreme Court announced a categorical rule that third parties who seek visitation always must prove that the denial of visitation would harm the child. Id., 20. Short of preventing harm to the child, the best interests of the child were "insufficient to serve as a compelling state interest overruling a parent's fundamental rights." Id. The court reasoned that because the constitution permits interference with the fundamental rights of parents to rear children only to prevent harm or potential harm, the statute was facially unconstitutional. Id.

Following its grant of certification, a plurality of the United States Supreme Court, hesitant to conclude that a state statute addressing nonparental visitation was per se unconstitutional, held the statute unconstitutional as applied. *Troxel* v. *Granville*, supra, 530 U.S. 67. Despite concerns about the "breathtakingly broad" language of the statute, the plurality explained that "[b]ecause much state-court adjudication in this context occurs on a case-by-case basis, we would be hesitant to hold that specific nonparental visitation statutes violate the Due Process Clause as a per se matter." Id., 73. The court began with a discussion of the long recognized premise that a parent's interest in the nurture, upbringing, companionship, care, and custody of children are generally protected by the due process clause of the fourteenth amendment. . .

. . . The court decided, in essence, that "the Due Process Clause does not permit a State to infringe on the fundamental right of parents to make child rearing decisions simply because a state judge believes a 'better' decision could be made." Id., 72–73. Because neither the Washington nonparental visitation statute nor the trial court in that case required anything more, the plurality of the court held that the Washington statute, as applied in the case, was unconstitutional. Id., 73.

. . . We now consider, therefore, what statutory parameters would be consistent with both the constitutional interest at stake and our legislature's intent to limit the court's jurisdiction over nonparental visitation.

We begin with the standard of review applicable to this legislative intrusion. Despite its recognition of a parent's liberty interest in the care, custody and control of his or her children in general and in visitation matters in specific, the court in *Troxel* abstained from applying the strict standard of review typically utilized when a state action infringes on enjoyment of a fundamental right. Indeed, courts and commentators alike have noted that the *Troxel* plurality did not specify the appropriate level of scrutiny to apply to statutes that infringe on the parent-child relationship...

. . . Nevertheless, we conclude that, consistent with the court's determination that a parent's interest in the care, custody and control over his or her children is "perhaps one of the oldest of the fundamental liberty interests recognized by [the] Court"; *Troxel* v. *Granville*, supra, 530 U.S. 65; the application of the strict scrutiny test is required to any infringement it may suffer.

. . . We, therefore, consider what jurisdictional and substantive requirements would ensure that the statute is narrowly tailored to achieve a compelling interest.

We first examine the jurisdictional prerequisite of standing, that is, which persons may intrude upon a parent's autonomy. "Standing is . . . a practical concept designed to ensure that courts and parties are not vexed by suits brought to vindicate nonjusticiable interests and that judicial decisions which may affect the rights of others are forged in hot controversy, with each view fairly and vigorously represented. . . . These two objectives are ordinarily held to have been met when a complainant makes a colorable claim of direct injury [that the complainant] has suffered or is likely to suffer, in an individual or representative capacity. Such a personal stake in the outcome of the controversy . . . provides the requisite assurance of concrete adverseness and diligent advocacy." (Internal quotation marks omitted.) *Connecticut Associated Builders & Contractors* v. *Hartford*, 251 Conn. 169, 178, 740 A.2d 813 (1999). "If a party is found to lack standing, the court is without subject matter jurisdiction to determine the cause." (Internal quotation marks omitted.) *Weidenbacher* v. *Duclos*, 234 Conn. 51, 54 n. 4, 661 A.2d 988 (1995).

Where fundamental rights are implicated, such as in the present case, standing serves a function beyond a mere jurisdictional prerequisite. It also ensures that the statutory scheme is narrowly tailored so that a person's personal affairs are not needlessly intruded upon and interrupted by the trauma of litigation . . .

. . . We know from prior analysis that § 46b-59, as initially enacted; see Public Acts 1978, No. 78-69; permitted only grandparents to petition for visitation. *Castagno* v. *Wholean*, supra, 239 Conn. 347–48. In 1983, however, § 46b-59 was amended to its current form to allow "any person" to petition for visitation, like the Washington statute at issue in *Troxel*. See Public Acts 1983, No. 83-95. We view the 1983 amendment that extended standing to any third person as a reflection of the legislature's recognition that persons other than parents may have substantial relationships with children that warrant preservation. "Ours is by no means a tradition limited to respect for the bonds uniting the members of the nuclear family. The tradition of uncles, aunts, cousins, and especially grandparents sharing a household along with parents and children has roots equally venerable and equally deserving of constitutional recognition. . . . Even if conditions of modern society have brought about a decline in extended family households, they have not erased the accumulated wisdom of civilization, gained over the centuries and honored throughout our history that supports a larger conception of the family. . . . Decisions concerning child rearing, which *Yoder, Meyer, Pierce* and other cases have recognized as entitled to constitutional protection, long have been shared with grandparents or other relatives who occupy the same household—indeed who may take on major responsibility for the rearing of the children. Especially in times of adversity, such as the death of a spouse or economic need, the broader family has tended to come together for mutual sustenance and to maintain or rebuild a secure home life." *Moore* v. *East Cleveland*, 431 U.S. 494, 504–505, 97 S.Ct. 1932, 52 L.Ed.2d 531 (1977).

We recognize that, in many households, grandparents, as well as people who have no biological relationship with a child, undertake duties of a parental nature and that states have sought to ensure the welfare of children by protecting those relationships . . .

. . .Therefore, we acknowledge that a person *other than* a blood relation may have established a more significant connection with a child than the one established with a grandparent or some other relative. Conversely, we recognize that being a blood relation of a child does not always translate into that relative having significant emotional ties with that child. Indeed, as § 46b-59 implicitly recognizes, it is not necessarily the biological aspect of the relationship that provides the basis for a legally cognizable interest. Rather, it is the nature of the relationship that determines standing.

Consequently, we conclude that, in light of the presumption of parental fitness under *Troxel*, parents should not be faced with unjustified intrusions into their decision-making in the absence of specific allegations and proof of a relationship of the type contemplated herein...

We next address the second jurisdictional factor in this analysis, that is: what the third party must allege before intrusion by way of a third party visitation petition is justified . . .

. . . We are persuaded, therefore, that an allegation, along with proof thereof, that the parent's decision regarding visitation will cause the child to suffer real and substantial emotional harm likewise presents a compelling state interest that will permit interference with parental rights, provided the petitioner has established a parent-like relationship with the child . . .

. . . We recognize that some jurisdictions do not consider a showing of harm to the child to be constitutionally required before a third party will be afforded visitation over the parents' objections . . .

. . . We are not persuaded, however, by the reasoning of those jurisdictions. Indeed, although the plurality in *Troxel* avoided the issue, its prior decisions clearly reflect a tolerance for interference with parental decisions only when the health or safety of the child will be jeopardized or there exists the potential for significant social burdens . . .

. . .In setting forth this admittedly high hurdle, we recognize that there are often substantial benefits to a child in having close and sustained ties with extended family and those persons, while not related by blood, who take on caregiving roles. Grandparents, in particular, can serve an important role, especially after a parent dies . . .

. . . The last factor to be considered is what standard of proof must be required in order for the intrusion of this nature to be justified. When constitutional issues are at stake, a heightened evidentiary standard is warranted . . .

. . . Accordingly, several states apply a clear and convincing standard of review in visitation proceedings. . .

. . . We believe the stricter standard of proof is sounder because of the ease with which a petitioning party could otherwise intrude upon parental prerogative...we determine that a nonparent petitioning for visitation pursuant to § 46b-59 must prove the requisite relationship and harm, as we have previously articulated, by clear and convincing evidence.

. . . Implicit in the statute is, as we have stated, a rebuttable presumption that visitation that is opposed by a fit parent is not in a child's best interest. In sum, therefore, we conclude that there are two requirements that must be satisfied in order for a court: (1) to have jurisdiction over a petition for visitation contrary to the wishes of a fit parent; and (2) to grant such a petition.

First, the petition must contain specific, good faith allegations that the petitioner has a relationship with the child that is similar in nature to a parent-child relationship. The petition must also contain specific, good faith allegations that denial of the visitation will cause real and significant harm to the child. As we have stated, that degree of harm requires more than a determination that visitation would be in the child's best interest. It must be a degree of harm analogous to the kind of harm contemplated by §§ 46b-120 and 46b-129, namely, that the child is "neglected, uncared-for or dependent."

The degree of specificity of the allegations must be sufficient to justify requiring the fit parent to subject his or her parental judgment to unwanted litigation. Only if these specific, good faith allegations are made will a court have jurisdiction over the petition.

Second, once these high jurisdictional hurdles have been overcome, the petitioner must prove these allegations by clear and convincing evidence. Only if that enhanced burden of persuasion has been met may the court enter an order of visitation. These requirements thus serve as the constitutionally mandated safeguards against unwarranted intrusions into a parent's authority.

. . . We first address the requirement that the plaintiffs establish that they have had a parent-like relationship with the children. The plaintiffs' complaint alleges merely that they are the maternal grandmother and maternal aunt to the defendant's children. In addition to being close blood relations to the children, however, the record supports the trial court's conclusion that both Roth and Campbell had developed loving and responsible relationships with the children. In the two years preceding the death of the children's mother, both of the plaintiffs regularly visited with or telephoned the children, as much as several days per week. They participated in the children's birthday celebrations, took the children to parks, and played with the children at their home. Roth frequently stayed overnight at her daughter's house with the children and on occasion the children stayed at Roth's house when their parents were away. The defendant's oldest child, his daughter, occasionally slept overnight at Campbell's home.

Although these facts reflect that the plaintiffs were involved in an ongoing relationship with the children, we conclude that they fail to establish the type of relationship we have articulated herein. The plaintiffs have not shown that they have acted in a parental type of capacity to the children as required under § 46b-59.

With respect to the second jurisdictional requirement, the plaintiffs' complaint is silent as to the issue of whether the court's denial of visitation would result in actual, significant harm to the children. The trial court concluded that the plaintiffs had "met their burden of proof by clear and convincing evidence that it will be in the minor children's best interests to have unsupervised visitation with these plaintiffs. . . ."

. . . In the present case, the plaintiffs neither alleged that the children would be significantly harmed were the court to have denied visitation nor proved that fact by clear and convincing evidence. Therefore, we conclude that the trial court improperly applied the analytical framework set forth in this opinion and improperly granted visitation rights to the plaintiffs in violation of the defendant's due process rights under both the state and federal constitutions.

In the absence of the essential allegations and proof in support thereof, both of the nature of the relationship between the plaintiffs and the defendant's minor children as well as the harm that the children would suffer were visitation denied, the trial court did not have jurisdiction over the petition for visitation.

The judgment is reversed and the case is remanded with direction to dismiss the petition.

STATUS OF UNMARRIED PARENTS AND THEIR RIGHTS AND RESPONSIBILITIES

Unmarried parents have the same rights and responsibilities as married parents. When an unmarried couple is living together with their biological child, each parent is considered to be the legal guardian of the child. When an unmarried couple splits up, each parent is still considered to be the child's legal guardian unless one of the parents brings a legal action to obtain sole or joint legal custody. Most states have enacted statutes that authorize an unmarried parent to go into court and request that the court enter a custody order that both parents must honor. Usually the party bringing the action into court is the parent with whom the child is residing. That parent seeks to have the court invest him or her with either sole custody or joint legal custody with physical custody in that party. This petitioning party may also request that the court enter an order for payment of child support by the parent who does not reside with the child.

When a parent brings an action for custody and/or child support, the parent must arrange for legal service of the action on the other parent to give the parent notice that this action is taking place. When the other parent is served with legal process, that parent may obtain legal counsel to represent his or her interests, choose to represent himself or herself by entering a *pro se* appearance, or simply do nothing. Frequently, the parent served with a custody action, through counsel, will negotiate to have the petitioning parent agree to joint legal custody with physical custody in the petitioning parent. Sometimes the other parent will threaten to seek sole custody if the petitioning party does not agree to joint legal custody. Occasionally the other parent will seek sole custody not as a strategic tactic but because the other parent wants the child to reside with him or her.

If parents cannot come to an agreement regarding custody, the court will usually refer the matter to the family relations division of the court. Family relations officers will conduct an investigation or study to decide what custodial disposition will best promote the child's interests. Most states have statutes or case law providing that there is a presumption that joint legal custody best serves the child's interests. However, this presumption is rebuttable. If family relations officers conclude that the parents are unable to communicate productively to make joint decisions for their child's health, education, and welfare, the family relations division will recommend that one parent have sole custody and that the other parent have visitation in a manner consistent with the child's well-being.

If the court awards one parent sole custody or enters an order for joint legal custody with legal residence invested in one parent, the court, upon motion from the custodial parent, will also order the noncustodial parent to pay child support. In states that have established uniform child support guidelines, these guidelines will be applied in the same manner they are applied to determine child support for divorcing parents. Child support is discussed in more detail in Chapter 8.

THE ABSENT PARENT

When a parent bringing a custody and support action cannot locate the other parent, the requirement of providing that parent notice is met by publishing a legal notice of the action in a newspaper with a circulation in the geographical area in which the other parent was last known to reside. If the absent parent does not appear at the court proceeding, the court will usually enter an order of sole custody in favor of the petitioning parent. Depending on the rules of the jurisdiction, the court may or may not enter an order for child support. In those states that use uniform child support guidelines and apply a formula based on each parent's income to determine the amount of child support payments, the court will not make a child support order against a nonappearing or absent parent.

CHALLENGES TO CHILD SUPPORT ORDERS

When a child's mother seeks child support from a man whom she never married or a man who was not legally her husband when the child was born, the man whom she alleges is the child's father may deny that he is the child's biological father and demand a paternity test.

PATERNITY ISSUES

Before the advent of DNA tissue analysis, a test to determine paternity could only eliminate a man as a child's father. If the man was not eliminated, the court would look at other factors to decide whether or not he was the father.

Most states have common law holdings that there is a rebuttable presumption that a child born to a woman during the existence of a legally valid marriage is the child of the husband. This presumption may be overcome upon a showing that during the period of conception the husband had no access to the child's mother or was sterile at that time or otherwise medically incapable of fathering a child.

For an unmarried mother, the task of proving paternity was even harder. Frequently, the determination rested on the subjective opinion of the judge. With the advent of DNA testing, a near foolproof method of determining paternity has emerged.

A father contesting paternity may request a DNA test. This test uses several genetic markers to identity genetic similarities between the putative father and the child. If the test shows a likelihood of paternity of 91 percent or better, most courts make a determination that the putative father is the child's biological father. The father will be ordered to pay child support. He will also have the right to reasonable visitation with his child, and, if he wishes, he may seek legal custody of the child then or at any future time during the child's minority.

JURISDICTIONAL ISSUES IN CHILD CUSTODY AND VISITATION CASES

Before legislation was adopted addressing interstate jurisdiction over child custody and visitation matters, noncustodial parents would take children over state lines for the purpose of "forum shopping". This means that they looked for a court that would grant them custody of their children contrary to the one entered by the original court hearing the custody dispute. In response to this problem, the National Conference of Commissioners on Uniform State Laws drafted the Uniform Child Custody and Jurisdiction Act (UCCJA) to dissuade parents from kidnapping their own children. Every jurisdiction in the country passed a state version of the UCCJA by the year 1981. (See Appendix G for the Connecticut version of the act.) In that same year, Congress passed a federal law addressing the issue of interstate custody jurisdiction called the Parental Kidnapping Prevention Act (PKPA).

Problems quickly arose in the application of these two conflicting statutes. The UCCJA discouraged parents from running off to another jurisdiction with the child for the purpose of modifying an existing court order by establishing jurisdiction over child custody in one state alone and prohibiting modification of that order as long as the original state retains jurisdiction. The UCCJA did not give the child's home state priority in determining which state had jurisdiction to hear a custody case, in direct contradiction to the PKPA. The term **home state** is defined as the state where a child has resided for a period of six months. In addition to giving the child's home state priority in custody cases, it also stated that once a state exercised jurisdiction over a custody case, it had continuing jurisdiction until both parents and the children were no longer in that state. The UCCJA and PKPA also lacked enforcement of interstate custody and visitation orders.

Acknowledging these differences and the conflicts that arose, the Uniform Law Commissioners drafted the **Uniform Child Custody Jurisdiction and Enforcement Act (UCCJEA)** of 1997. The UCCJEA replaced the UCCJA by conforming the UCCJA to the PKPA, and added interstate enforcement of child custody and visitation orders. Following are some significant highlights of the UCCJEA. Lawyers and paralegals must not only read the UCCJEA, but also the case law interpreting the statute from jurisdiction to jurisdiction. The UCCJEA:

- Requires courts to honor the orders of the home state in determining which state has jurisdiction in interstate child custody and visitation cases. This is the most significant provision in the UCCJEA. A new state court may only modify another state's previous child custody or visitation order if the child resided in the new state for six months.

- Allows a state to retain continuing exclusive jurisdiction once it has taken jurisdiction over a case and retained such jurisdiction until all of the parties involved in the dispute moved out of the state. This prevents a parent from removing the child to another state and then seeking a more favorable custody order in the new state. In applying the UCCJEA, the new state is required to decline jurisdiction over the case.

- In cases where the child is abandoned, abused, or neglected and is present in a state other than the home state, the UCCJEA allows the new state to take temporary emergency jurisdiction over the case. While the new state may not have jurisdiction because it is not the home state of the child, it may make a temporary emergency order for the protection of the child until the appropriate jurisdiction may be determined. It is possible that the new state may retain continuing jurisdiction if no other state has the authority to continue jurisdiction or refuses continued jurisdiction.

- Prohibits simultaneous proceedings in cases where one parent files a custody or visitation in one state, while another is filed in a different jurisdiction.

- Requires states to enforce custody and visitation orders from states that conform to the UCCJEA, which currently includes all fifty states. The parent must register the domestic order in the new state, unless it is contested. If not contested, the court has the authority to enforce the order through its contempt powers.

END OF CHAPTER EXERCISES

Crossword Puzzle

Across

3. the process of conceiving a human embryo outside of the biological parents' physical bodies

6. the technique of injecting a male's semen into a female's uterus through the use of artificial means

8. a woman who agrees by contract to bear a child for a couple or an individual who cannot conceive in exchange for a fee

9. the right to make major decisions on behalf of their children regarding health, education, and religious upbringing

10. also referred to as residential or domiciliary custody; means that the children live with a parent

12. speaking badly about the other parent in front of the child; discussing the reasons behind the breakdown of the marital relationship; false allegations of child sexual, physical, and emotional abuse; blaming the other parent for the financial problems now encountered by the custodial parent; using the child to carry negative messages to the other parent; and asking the child to choose between parents

13. replaced the UCCJA by conforming the UCCJA to the PKPA, and added interstate enforcement of child custody and visitation orders

14. a type of parental alienation syndrome that occurs when one parent uses psychological manipulation to encourage the child to fabricate allegations of child sexual abuse

15. U.S. Supreme Court case decided in 2000 addressing the the rights of grandparents and third parties seeking visitation with children in the case of death or divorce

16. a court order allowing a parent in a divorce to communicate and maintain a relationship with the children through the use of technologies such as Internet video conferencing, web cams, email, instant messaging, or any other type of wired or wireless technology

Down

1. the state where a child has resided for a period of six months

2. a federal law requiring states to adopt child abuse prevention laws or risk losing federal funding

4. several group sessions with a mental health professional approved by the state and where attendance is mandatory; the goal of the program is to educate parents on the effects of divorce on the children

5. a Latin term that describes the power of the state to protect and care for children when the parents are unwilling or unable to do so

7. recommendations made by a mental health professional regarding what type of custody arrangement is in the children's best interest

10. the syndrome defined by mental health professionals describing a child's response to parental alienation that results in destroying the child's once-positive relationship with a parent

11. an agreement created by both parents detailing how they will continue their parenting responsibilities towards their children after their marriage is dissolved

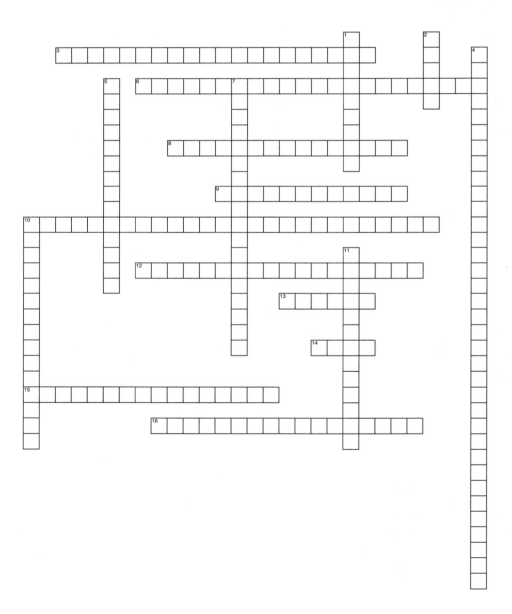

Review Questions

1. List and define the different types of custody arrangements discussed in this chapter.

2. Why do most courts presume that joint legal custody is in the best interest of the children?

3. When is a joint custody arrangement not in the best interest of the children?

4. What is the purpose of requiring divorcing parents to attend mandatory parenting education programs? What is a parenting plan, and what issues does it normally address?

5. What is the most significant feature of the Uniform Child Custody Jurisdiction and Enforcement Act, and why?

Case for Briefing

Conkel v. Conkel, 31 Ohio App.3d 169, 509 N.E.2d 983 (1987)

Exploring the Workplace: Activities

1. You work as a paralegal at the Law Office of Patricia H. Garner. She is a solo practitioner and extremely busy divorce attorney with absolutely no time to spend doing legal research. Mr. Hitendar Patel and his wife Lata have an appointment late this afternoon for advice regarding their rights as grandparents. Their son and his wife are going to file for divorce and they assume the wife will get custody of the two minor children, ages three and four. The Patels are very involved with the children. Their daughter-in-law is a science professor at the local community college and works Monday through Thursday from 8:00AM to 4:30PM, and on Tuesday and Thursday nights from 7:00PM to 9:15PM. The Patels care for the children on a daily basis and have done so since birth. The children are very close to their grandparents. Their son works a full forty-hour week as an engineer. They want to know their rights in the event their daughter-in-law refuses to let them see the children. As it stands now, they plan to continue caring for the children after the couple separates, but they don't want to take any chances. Attorney Garner asks you to research the status of grandparents' rights in your state. She heard some lawyers talking about the *Troxel* case, but she doesn't know much about it.

   Using the Internet or state-specific materials, determine the status of grandparents' rights in your state after the U.S. Supreme Court decision in *Troxel v. Granville*. Prepare an interoffice memorandum for your supervisor, citing any changes in your state statute and/or case law reflecting any changes.

2. You work as a paralegal for Raymond Jackson, a well-known father's rights advocate in the state of Wisconsin. Attorney Jackson represents client Frank Reed in a divorce case. Mr. Reed is a traveling salesman for a pharmaceutical company and is out of town at the company headquarters for several weeks of the year. You are in the process of completing the parenting plan and Attorney Jackson asks you to draft a virtual visitation clause in accordance with Wisconsin's statute to facilitate virtual visitation when Mr. Reed is away from home. In addition to drafting the clause, go to **http://www.internetvisitation.org/** and see if you can learn how to set this up. Draft a letter to the client explaining the process.

3. You work as a paralegal for the law firm of Schultz, Berkowitz, and Seeley in your state. The office represents Lucille Chen, who is in the midst of a bitter custody battle. Mr. Chen has threatened to "take the children away" from her because she is a "psycho." Mrs. Chen is taking medication for a chemical imbalance. She sees a therapist regularly and a psychiatrist to monitor her prescriptions. She has always taken good care of her children and has

been their primary caretaker. She sought help for her mental health issues voluntarily, getting help from the outpatient psychiatric clinic at the local hospital. Her condition was exacerbated when Mr. Chen started having an affair at work with the receptionist in his office building. She is worried about losing her children. What is your opinion regarding Mrs. Chen's concerns?

4. You work as a paralegal in the Law Office of Elaine Coker in the State of Oregon. Your office represents Jonathan Arthur, the petitioner in a divorce case against his wife, Renee. Mr. Arthur has had temporary custody of their seven-year-old son Justin (date of birth January 10, 2000), and has been his primary caretaker for all of Justin's life. Mrs. Arthur plans to be discharged from an inpatient drug rehabilitation program just before the divorce becomes final. She has been in the program for six months and is doing very well. She and Mr. Arthur are in agreement over all issues of the divorce. Mr. Arthur will have sole legal and residential custody of the child. Mrs. Arthur suggested unsupervised visits, but Mr. Arthur thinks it's too much too soon and he is not quite ready to leave her alone with the child. Mrs. Arthur agreed to supervised parenting time from 10:00AM to 5:00PM on Saturdays,

and her parents Nicholas and Catherine Bedell have agreed to supervise the visits at their home at 649 Ferris Lane in Elmira, Oregon. Mr. or Mrs. Bedell will transport the child to and from the visits and their car is equipped with a child safety seat. Mrs. Bedell may attend the child's baseball games and any school activities as long as she is sober. She cannot be intoxicated during visits or phone calls with her child and will attend outpatient treatment and support groups to maintain her sobriety. There are no firearms in the Bedell household and her parents have assured Mr. Arthur that alcohol and drugs are not on the premises. They have also agreed not to allow her into the home if she is "high" and will immediately contact Mr. Arthur. Mrs. Arthur may call the child on any day and at any time before 7:30PM as long as she is sober.

Go to Family Law Oregon Courts,

http://www.ojd.state.or.us/osca/cpsd/ courtimprovement/familylaw/parenting plan.htm, and read about safety-focused parenting plans. On this website, find the safety-focused parenting plan for supervised visits and draft an agreement on behalf of Mr. Arthur using this form as guide.

CHAPTER 8

Child Support

KEY TERMS

administrative enforcement

arrearage

Bureau of Support Enforcement (IV-D agency)

capias

Child Support Enforcement and Establishment of Paternity Act

child support guidelines

combined net income

contempt hearing

deviation from the guidelines

doctrine of equitable estoppel

Family Support Act of 1988

motion for contempt

motion for modification of child support

National Conference of Commissioners on Uniform State Laws

parent locator services

postmajority support agreement

Revised Uniform Reciprocal Enforcement of Support Act (RURESA)

total net income

Uniform Desertion and Non-Support Act

Uniform Interstate Family Support Act (UIFSA)

Uniform Reciprocal Enforcement of Support Act (URESA)

The marital obligation to financially support and maintain minor children who are issue of a marriage does not cease for either parent upon dissolution of the marriage. Both parents are expected to provide economic support for their children. The dissolution decree will include an order for financial support of each child until such child reaches age eighteen, the age of majority.

Traditionally, when parents divorced, the father was usually the primary or sole breadwinner. Sole custody was awarded to the mother while support came from the noncustodial parent, usually the father. Today, the noncustodial parent continues to have an obligation for child support. In addition, even where parents have joint custody, courts will order the parent with whom the child does not make his or her primary residence to make child support payments to the parent with whom the child resides.

CHILD SUPPORT GUIDELINES: FEDERALLY MANDATED REQUIREMENTS

In the mid-1980s the federal government through its appropriate agencies studied court-ordered child support awards made in various jurisdictions throughout the country. In response to this problem, Congress passed the **Family Support Act of 1988.** This federal law requires every state to adopt numerical child support guidelines based on the income of the parties. The act mandates that the guidelines establish a rebuttable presumption in favor of a numerical computation of the child support obligation—in essence, taking it out of the trial judge's discretion. The states may establish their own deviation criteria after showing that application of the guideline figure would create an injustice or would be inappropriate under the circumstances. The federal study revealed that the amounts that many, if not most, courts ordered noncustodial parents to pay toward the support of their children were far too low to keep up with then-spiraling inflation and too little to meet the children's needs. Absent any uniform and rational guidelines, the amounts set for child support rested on the judge's discretion. Many judges set arbitrary amounts that were usually too low to make much of a difference in the custodial parent's ability to financially maintain the children in the family. Many judges ordered minimal child support payments because of their belief that the noncustodial parent would not pay anything substantial.

As a result of this practice, many single-parent homes existed at or below the poverty line. Single parents, usually single mothers, were forced to rely on government assistance for survival. The federal government, by mandating each state to adopt uniform and rational child support guidelines, sought to return the child support obligation back where it belonged, namely, with both parents—noncustodial as well as custodial. States were required to base child support awards on numerical guidelines rather than judicial whims. State legislatures enacted laws to require a uniform method of determining child support, and formula tables and child support guideline worksheets were created by each jurisdiction to execute these legislative enactments.

Today many courts apply statutorily enacted formulas to determine the amount the noncustodial parent must pay for the support of each child. These are known as **child support guidelines.** Appendix C of this book contains an example of Massachusetts's child support and arrearage guidelines. Statutes establishing these guidelines were passed by state legislatures as a result of federal mandates to do so.

This Arizona statute legislates the state's child support guidelines and sets forth the criteria for establishing those guidelines.

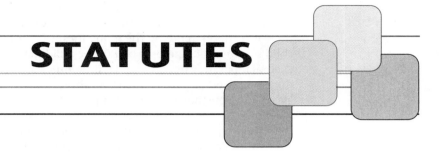

STATUTES

ARIZONA REVISED STATUTES ANNOTATED (WEST)

25-320 The supreme court shall establish guidelines for determining the amount of child support. The amount resulting from the application of these guidelines shall be the amount of child support ordered unless a written finding is made, based on criteria approved by the supreme court, that application of the guidelines would be inappropriate or unjust in a particular case. The supreme court shall review the guidelines at least once every four years to ensure that their application results in the determination of appropriate child support amounts. The guidelines and criteria for deviation from them shall be based on all relevant factors, including:

1. The financial resources and needs of the child.

2. The financial resources and needs of the custodial parent.

3. The standard of living the child would have enjoyed had the marriage not been dissolved.

4. The physical and emotional condition of the child, and the child's educational needs.

5. The financial resources and needs of the noncustodial parent.

6. Excessive or abnormal expenditures, destruction, concealment or fraudulent disposition of community, joint tenancy and other property held in common.

7. The duration of visitation and related expenses. . . .

DETERMINING EACH PARENT'S OBLIGATION FOR CHILD SUPPORT

Most jurisdictions in the United States have complied with the federal mandate and have a system for determining the exact amount a noncustodial parent must pay, given that parent's financial circumstances and the financial circumstances of the custodial parent. In addition, the states complying with the federal mandate have developed child support worksheets that assist parties in the calculation of this obligation. Exhibit 8–1 illustrates Connecticut's worksheet and Exhibit 8–2 gives samples of New York's worksheet. Each parent's income is a factor, as is the cost of living in the geographical area and the age and needs of each child. Each parent's net income is added together to arrive at a **combined** or **total net income** figure. A preset percentage is applied to this figure to establish how much of this combined income should be allocated for the financial maintenance of the child or for each of the children. The amount arrived at is often termed the *child maintenance figure.*

Then, *a formula is applied to determine how much of this amount must be paid by the noncustodial parent.* For instance, if each parent has the same amount of net income, the court, upon applying the guidelines, will order the noncustodial parent to pay child support equal to one-half of the child maintenance figure. Similarly, if a non-custodial parent's net income is three times as high as that of the custodial parent, the noncustodial parent must pay three-fourths of the child maintenance figure, leaving the custodial parent to supply the other one-fourth needed.

Some states consider each parent's gross income as a starting point, rather than net income. Some states also consider other factors in addition to income to determine child support obligations. For instance, Massachusetts also considers each parent's assets and other resources, the number of children in a household, and the age of each child for whom support is to be ordered.

DETERMINING A PARENT'S INCOME

The *Rosenbloom* case involves a father's appeal of the trial court's increase in his child support obligation pursuant to the mother's postjudgment motion to modify. After the divorce, the mother remarried. The Louisiana Court of Appeal held that, under Louisiana law, a court may consider the benefits a parent derives from remarriage in determining the combined monthly income of the parties in arriving at the child support obligation.

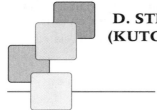

D. STEPHEN ROSENBLOOM V. RENEE BAUCHET (KUTCHER), WIFE OF D. STEPHEN ROSENBLOOM

654 SO. 2D 877 (LA. APP. 4 CIR. 1995)

COURT OF APPEAL OF LOUISIANA, FOURTH DISTRICT

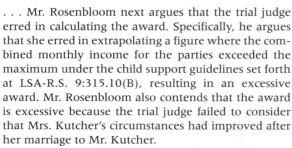

. . . Mr. Rosenbloom next argues that the trial judge erred in calculating the award. Specifically, he argues that she erred in extrapolating a figure where the combined monthly income for the parties exceeded the maximum under the child support guidelines set forth at LSA-R.S. 9:315.10(B), resulting in an excessive award. Mr. Rosenbloom also contends that the award is excessive because the trial judge failed to consider that Mrs. Kutcher's circumstances had improved after her marriage to Mr. Kutcher.

With regard to the children of the marriage, both the father and the mother have the obligation to support. Support is to be granted considering the needs of the person to whom it is due, and the circumstances of those who are obligated to pay it (citation omitted). The court may consider as income the benefits a party derives from remarriage, expense-sharing, or other sources. LSA-R.S. 9:315(6)(c). In arriving at an award, the totality of relevant circumstances must by considered (citation omitted).

LSA-R.S. 9:315.10(B) provides:

If the combined adjusted gross income of the parties exceeds the highest level specified in the schedule contained in R.S. 9:315.14, the court shall use its discretion in setting the amount of the basic child support obligation, but in no event shall it be less than the highest amount set forth in the schedule.

Under the clear provisions of LSA-R.S. 9:315.10(B), the trial court has discretion in setting the amount of child support when the combined adjusted gross income of the parties exceeds the highest figure provided in the schedule, and its judgment in such matters will not be disturbed in the absence of a showing of an abuse of that discretion (citation omitted).

In the instant case, the trial court used the combined monthly income of the parties in calculating the award. The trial judge determined that Mr. Rosenbloom's monthly income was $39,891.50, by dividing his 1993 gross income of $478,698.00 by 12. As to Mrs. Kutcher's monthly income, the trial judge correctly considered the living expenses incident to her second marriage. The trial judge stated:

[t]he Court notes that in the case of Mrs. Kutcher that she has no single source of income of her own other than approximately 5,000 dollars a year that she earns. The bulk of her income comes from (A) what the Court will describe as an expense sharing that she receives the benefits from her current spouse, Robert Kutcher. And under R.S. 9:315(6)(c)—the law tells us that the Court can only consider as income the benefits a party derives from expense sharing or other sources. However, in determining the benefits of expense sharing the Court shall not consider the income of another spouse regardless of the remarriage existence except to

the extent that such income is used directly to reduce the costs of a party's actual expenses.

So, consequently, to determine what Mrs. Kutcher's income is, the Court has to make a determination as to the benefits she receives from Mr. Kutcher. And that part of the statute also says, with regard to the party's actual expenses, his contribution to her actual expenses would not come from his gross income but from his net income.

The judge then correctly determined that Mrs. Kutcher's monthly income was $9,040.12.

BY AGREEMENT OR BY COURT ORDER

A divorcing couple may wish to avoid a trial and enter an agreement on the amount of support to be paid by the noncustodial parent to the custodial parent for the support of the minor children. While family court judges prefer agreements to litigating domestic issues, the court will examine the amount agreed upon by the parties and compare it to the amount the custodial parent would have received under the state's child support guidelines. If the amount is less than the guidelines, the parties must convince the judge that awarding this figure would be in the best interest of the children. The court has the final say in the amount of child support and can override the agreement of the parties. The judge must enter the reasons for deviating from the guidelines on the court record.

If the parties cannot agree on the amount of child support to be paid by the noncustodial parent, the court will issue a figure based on the guidelines and will incorporate this figure into the court's order. The order typically requires the noncustodial parent to pay a sum to the custodial parent on a monthly or weekly basis and that the duty to pay support shall continue until the child reaches the age of majority or becomes emancipated by a court of law.

UTILIZING COMPUTER SOFTWARE

Most states that have adopted child support guidelines use worksheets and legislated criteria to determine the exact amount of child support due. The family services units of many states also assist the parties in determining the figures. Computer programs have emerged in many states where the calculation of child support is complex. The use of software saves time and money when calculating child support obligations in a busy law office. The user collects the data from the client and spouse and inputs the information into the system.

The California guidelines, for example, are calculated using a complicated algebraic formula. To ensure the accuracy of the calculations, computer programs are used. The most commonly used program in this jurisdiction is called DissoMaster©. The paralegal inputs information such as the custody arrangement, income of the parties, mandatory payroll deductions, child-care expenses, and so on, and the software generates a child support figure. A paralegal working in the state of California, for instance, would learn how to use DissoMaster© by attending training sessions or by accessing the tutorial available on the company's website, **http://www.dissomasterinfo.com/tutorials.html.**

It is important for paralegals practicing in the field of family law to become familiar with the computer software most used by law firms in their state and to seek classes or tutorials that provide training in the software.

DEVIATION CRITERIA

In jurisdictions where child support guidelines are applied, statutory maximum and minimum limits usually exist for contributions by each parent. However, if the parties agree between themselves that one party or the other will pay more or less of the statutorily determined amount, frequently courts will allow this **deviation from the guidelines** providing that the parties present the court with a good reason for the departure and providing that allowing the deviation does not appear to financially deprive the child.

The parties may not always agree on a deviation from the guidelines. In these cases, the parties are allowed to argue their reasons for and against the proposed amount of child support. Here are some of the factors a court may take into consideration when deciding whether or not to deviate from the guidelines:

- The extraordinary expenses incurred for the care of a physically or mentally disabled child;
- The noncustodial parent's obligation to pay child support to dependents from a previous marriage or relationship;
- The earning capacity of a parent—a parent who has a license to practice medicine and decides to work as a medical assistant may be deemed to be underemployed by the court;
- Whether other assets are available to the parent, but do not appear on the calculation under the child support guidelines;
- Extraordinary expenses incurred by the parents in traveling a significant distance to visit with the children or legitimate expenses associated with the parent's employment, business, or medical expenses;
- Shared custody arrangements where both parents have physical custody of the children for equal time; and
- The noncustodial parent is highly compensated and such compensation exceeds the state's child support guidelines.

TENNIS, ANYONE?

In this section, we revisit the *Evans* case illustrated earlier in Chapter 5. This excerpt deals with determining child support obligation when the income of the parents exceeds the state's child support guidelines.

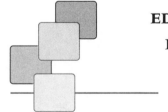

EDWIN E. EVANS V. CYNTHIA S. EVANS

1997 S.D. 16, 559 N.W.2D 240 (S.D. 1997)

SUPREME COURT OF SOUTH DAKOTA

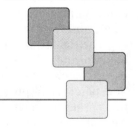

. . . ANALYSIS AND DECISION

1 Whether the trial court abused its discretion in failing to consider the children's actual needs and standard of living in setting child support?

SDCL 25-7-6.2 provides guidelines that trial courts must follow in setting child support amounts. However, where the parties' income exceeds the statutory guidelines, SDCL 25-7-6.9 provides the child support obligation "shall be established at an appropriate level, taking into account the actual needs and standard of living of the child" (citation omitted). . . .

. . . Cyndy sought $5,000 per month in child support, however, she produced an exhibit which listed expenses of $4,410 per month. Itemized, this figure included:

$400	for food
580	for vehicle expenses
110	per month for medical expenses
550	per month for educational expenses
500	per month for vacations
100	per month for dining out
550	for entertainment and allowances
200	for clothing purchases
1,300	for tennis expenses (Kelsey only) (clothes, supplies, lessons, tournament travel)
60	for piano lessons
25	for beauty shop expenses
25	for cosmetics expenses
10	for newspapers and subscriptions
$4,410	

The trial court ruled at an interim hearing that $1,300 per month for tennis expenses was clearly excessive and Ed would not be required to pay this expense. . . .

. . . Subtracting the $1,300 per month tennis expense from Cyndy's itemized living expenses for the children leaves a balance of $2,185 per month. The trial court ordered Ed to pay child support in this amount, plus pay $500 per month in allowances directly to the children, and $600 per month for their tuition at parochial school, and provide health insurance for each child, for a total child support obligation of $3,505 per month.[1] The trial court noted that Ed had agreed to pay the children's allowances, parochial school tuition, medical insurance, and college expenses. The trial court noted this child support award still provided a "luxurious lifestyle" for the two girls.[2]

On appeal, Cyndy notes the amount of Ed's child support obligation, as determined by the trial court, is approximately 12% of his $25,000 net monthly income. Cyndy argues the trial court made two errors: 1) it applied the wrong legal standard by focusing on the children's needs rather than their standard of living; and 2) it substituted its personal judgment of what the children's standard of living should be, for the standard set by the parties themselves during their marriage.

In the trial court's memorandum decision, it cited "the needs of the children and the father's ability to pay" as the standard for determining child support obligations above the statutory guidelines. It then stated that because the father's ability to pay was not at issue in this case, the only consideration need be the "reasonable needs of the children." This solitary consideration does not reflect the standard set by statute and prior case law. As noted above, the trial court's inquiry is to take into account the actual needs and standard of living of the children. However, the record reflects the trial court did not apply only the reasonable needs of the children and that it did consider their standard of living in making its determination. A trial court is not required to accept either party's claimed expenses. To do so would remove the trial court's discretion in setting child support obligations where the parties' income exceeds the guidelines set forth in SDCL 25-7-6.2. Cyndy has the burden of proving her claimed expenses reflect the children's needs and standard of living (citation omitted).

Cyndy's claim of $1,300 per month ($15,600 annually) for tennis expenses is a projected expense for only one of the couple's daughters, which includes Cyndy's traveling expenses to accompany her daughter. Ed points out, which Cyndy does not dispute, that this projected expense is $6,760 per year more than was spent in 1995 for Kelsey to travel and participate in tournaments in several states. Ed also notes, which Cyndy does not dispute, that this projection is based in part on daughter Ashley's involvement with tennis, which she severely curtailed after her sixteenth birthday. At the time of this appeal, Kelsey is fifteen years old. As such, Cyndy has failed to prove the $1,300 per month is reflective of Kelsey's standard of living prior to the couple's divorce. (citation omitted). . . . The trial court did not abuse its discretion in ordering support in an amount that will adequately care for the children's actual needs and permit them to enjoy a standard of living commensurate with that prior to their parents' divorce (citation omitted). . . .

---

[1] We note several of these items the trial court ordered Ed to pay *in addition to* the $2,185 total amount were already included in the $2,185 total in Cyndy's list of expenses. Therefore, the amount actually awarded is closer to the amount requested by Cyndy than she argues in her appeal to this Court.

[2] Supplemental information in Ed's brief to this Court notes his older daughter graduated from high school in May 1996 and is currently enrolled in a private college in Minnesota. Ed continues to pay Cyndy the amount ordered by the trial court for two children and has not moved for a reduction of that amount.

MODIFICATION OF CHILD SUPPORT ORDERS

The order for child support entered at the time of dissolution can be modified if there is a substantial change in the financial circumstances of either party. If the paying party suffers a downward shift in income, that party may file a motion with the court to modify the child support to reflect his or her decreased ability to pay. Sometimes a court will not decrease the amount and direct the financially strapped party to economize in other areas of life. This is frequently the case where the custodial parent's income was not substantial at the time of dissolution and has not increased or has in fact decreased. On the other hand, if the custodial parent's income has increased or was substantial to begin with, the court may grant the noncustodial parent's request for a lowering of the amount of periodic child support payments.

In the states where statutory guidelines are used, and a formula is applied to determine each parent's contribution toward the dollar amount needed for the support of the child, if the noncustodial parent's income has dropped, then the court may decide that a greater proportion of the custodial parent's income shall be dedicated to child support and that the noncustodial parent's financial obligation will decrease. Conversely, if the noncustodial parent's income has risen substantially, the custodial spouse may bring a **motion for modification of child support** requesting the court to order the noncustodial parent to pay higher periodic child support payments, so that less of the custodial parent's income will be needed for the child. The court will grant this motion if the custodial parent demonstrates the need for additional support. Even if the children are being adequately provided for under the prevailing order, if the noncustodial parent's income has risen dramatically and includes many discretionary income dollars, the court may see fit to order a higher support obligation providing the court is given proper information on how this extra money will be put to use for the child's benefit.

The noncustodial parent may also have a substantial increase in income upon the death of a relative who has left him or her a large inheritance or has been lucky enough to win the lottery.

A noncustodial parent may seek a reduction in his or her child support obligations due to a loss of employment, illness, disability, or unforeseen economic circumstances. A noncustodial parent employed in the area of lower Manhattan when the Twin Towers came down or running a business in New Orleans after Hurricane Katrina would argue that these unforeseen occurrences created a substantial change in circumstances that required a change in the original support order.

The court may also order a change in the amount of child support when there are substantial changes in circumstances involving the children. This may include providing for the needs of a growing child who now needs more food, more expensive clothing, unreimbursed medical or dental expenses, and costs associated with school such as class trips, yearbook and class ring expenses, and the school prom.

Informal Agreements

Sometimes parents who have had a substantial change in circumstances attempt to work out informal agreements regarding the payment of child support. While the parties believe they are saving money on legal fees by resorting to self-help, the agreement is not enforceable in a court of law. Furthermore, there may be a misunderstanding of the terms of the modification between the parties that may create a "he said, she said" scenario that may result in costly litigation. Parties who agree to a modification should put the terms in writing and ask the court to enter an order on the terms. Under these circumstances, the order may be enforced in the event that one of the parties fails to fulfill his or her obligations.

CHILD SUPPORT ENFORCEMENT

A child support order is an enforceable judgment. A custodial parent who has a court order for child support and is not receiving funds from the noncustodial parent must resort to the legal system.

The process of enforcement can be quite frustrating for a custodial parent who is in need of money to support the children and must resort to the courts for help. A custodial parent who has access to enough funds to hire a private attorney and pursue the matter through civil enforcement of the order in the family courts may be at a greater advantage than a custodial parent who must rely on the overburdened administrative enforcement system.

Every jurisdiction has an administrative enforcement system in the form of a child support enforcement agency that assists custodial parents with collecting child support. These agencies collect child support on behalf of the state when the taxpayers provide the children with support in the form of public assistance.

When applying for state welfare, a custodial parent agrees to assist the state in identifying and locating the noncustodial parent, as well as assigning to the state rights of collection. The custodial parent is also required to pursue the collection of child support, and any monies collected are taken by the state as reimbursement for state welfare payments.

Custodial parents who are not receiving state welfare may also apply for administrative enforcement assistance for a small fee.

CIVIL ENFORCEMENT

If a noncustodial parent fails to pay all or part of the child support obligation, the custodial parent may file a **motion for contempt.** This motion will alert the court to the other party's failure to comply with the court's earlier support order and will request that the court provide relief by ordering the other party to pay the back child support owed as well as the attorney's fees the custodial parent has expended to bring the deficiency to the court's attention. If the noncustodial parent does not appear at the **contempt hearing,** the court may order what is known as a **capias.** A capias is a document empowering a sheriff to arrest the nonappearing, noncustodial parent and bring him or her to jail and to court. However, if the noncustodial parent cannot be located by a sheriff or other court officer, the custodial parent may turn to administrative enforcement. Administrative enforcement also comes into the picture when the custodial parent is receiving government assistance or when the noncustodial parent has left the jurisdiction.

ADMINISTRATIVE ENFORCEMENT

The term **administrative enforcement** refers to action by a state or federal agency. Many states have **Bureaus of Support Enforcement** or **IV-D agencies**

FIGURE 8–1
If a parent
continually neglects
to pay child support,
administrative
enforcement may
become the only
solution.

(pronounced "four-d agencies"). These agencies are state agencies mandated by federal law, pursuant to the **Child Support Enforcement and Establishment of Paternity Act** passed by Congress in 1974. Their purpose is to facilitate the entry and enforcement of child support orders on a state-by-state basis. These agencies provide four services: (1) location of noncustodial parents through **parent locator services,** which are statutorily empowered to search the records of state and federal agencies such as the state's department of motor vehicles, or department of revenue services and/or the federal government's Social Security Administration and the Internal Revenue Service; (2) establishment of the paternity of children through testing of putative fathers; (3) facilitation of the entry of support orders following the location of the noncustodial parent or following the establishment of paternity; and (4) the enforcement of existing orders.

MEANS OF ENFORCEMENT

Most jurisdictions allow for a variety of enforcement means when enforcing child support orders. They include:

- Wage garnishment—deducting payments from the noncustodial parent's paycheck. In order to obtain a wage garnishment, the custodial parent must obtain a court order for child support, which is then served on the noncustodial parent's employer. The employer is then obligated to deduct the child support payments from the noncustodial parent's check and send a check to the custodial parent.
- Filing a negative report with a credit-reporting agency. This tactic interferes with the noncustodial parent's ability to obtain credit.

- Intercepting federal and state tax refunds and unemployment compensation—for example, if a noncustodial parent owes child support, his or her state or federal tax refund or unemployment compensation may be intercepted to pay for the amounts owed.

- Denial of U.S. passport if the noncustodial parent owes more than $5,000 in child support.

- Obtaining a writ of execution—the custodial parent may enforce a child support order by obtaining a judgment and attaching the noncustodial parent's property, such as bank accounts, real estate, motor vehicles, and so on.

- Cash bond—a court order requiring the noncustodial parent to post a cash bond to secure the support payments.

- Denial or revocation of state-issued occupational and motor vehicle licenses.

- Obtaining a contempt order from the court that results in the incarceration of the noncustodial parent. If a noncustodial parent willfully fails to abide by a court order, he or she may be incarcerated on the grounds of civil contempt. The contempt petition is filed by the custodial parent, scheduled for a court hearing, and served on the noncustodial parent by a sheriff. During the hearing, the noncustodial parent must explain why he or she is in contempt. Very often, the filing of a contempt petition triggers the filing of a modification petition on behalf of the noncustodial parent. The noncustodial parent may have a legitimate reason for failing to make child support payments, such as loss of employment or illness. These two actions are often heard during the same hearing. If the noncustodial parent is found in contempt of court, the judge has the power to incarcerate the individual and not release the individual until a payment has been made. The noncustodial parent usually contacts a friend or relative to bring money for his or her release. In some cases, the threat of incarceration may be enough to motivate child support payments.

- Criminal prosecution—every jurisdiction has the statutory power to punish noncustodial parents who do not pay child support orders. In these cases, the noncustodial parent may be incarcerated or placed on probation as long as the child support is paid as scheduled. Indigent noncustodial parents facing incarceration under a contempt petition or criminal prosecution are entitled to a court-appointed attorney.

- Parent locator services—noncustodial parents who wish to avoid paying child support may leave the city or state or obtain jobs where they are paid "under the table." A custodial parent may have no other choice but to go on public assistance and have the taxpayers support the children. The federal and state governments have created parent locator services, whereby a search of IRS, Social Security, motor vehicle, and other records may be accessed for information on the noncustodial parent. Once the information is obtained, it can be used to help enforce pending orders.

INTERSTATE ENFORCEMENT OF CHILD SUPPORT ORDERS

One of the biggest problems facing custodial parents trying to enforce child support orders is doing so when the noncustodial parent has moved out of the state. Noncustodial parents may move to another jurisdiction under the mistaken belief that the original order cannot be enforced or that they may obtain a more favorable modification in another jurisdiction. For example, the child support guidelines in the state granting the original order may be much higher than the guideline amount in another state. This discrepancy in figures might encourage a parent to "forum shop" for a better deal.

The Full Faith and Credit Clause of the U.S. Constitution, however, mandates that each state honor final court orders entered by judges in other states and apply that particular state's laws. This mandate, however, does not include orders of a temporary nature. The Constitution requires the new state to apply the law of the jurisdiction where the original order was entered in order to determine whether the judgment is modifiable. This includes both **arrearages** (past-due payments) and any future payments.

A series of uniform acts passed by the states have been enacted to provide remedies to custodial parents seeking to enforce orders across state lines. The **Uniform Desertion and Non-Support Act** was published by the **National Conference of Commissioners on Uniform State Laws (NCCUSL)** in 1910 and made deserting or refusing to provide support to a spouse or child under the age of sixteen a punishable offense. The one major flaw of this act was that it did not allow for interstate enforcement of state support orders. Noncustodial parents who wished to avoid court orders simply left the state. Extredition of the offending parent was a long and often fruitless process. This left the state welfare departments with the expense of supporting children.

To remedy the flaws in the Uniform Desertion and Non-Support Act, NCCUSL drafted the **Uniform Reciprocal Enforcement of Support Act (URESA).** The purpose of URESA was to improve enforcement of orders across state lines. URESA included both criminal and civil enforcement provisions. Criminal enforcement was accomplished by the obligee state (the state where the custodial parent resides) demanding that the obligor state (the state where the noncustodial parent resides) extradite the noncustodial parent to the obligee state or, in the alternative, that the noncustodial parent submit himself or herself to the obligee state's jurisdiction.

A custodial parent who chose civil enforcement of the child support order would bring an action in his or her state, and this jurisdiction would decide if noncustodial parent had a duty to support the children. If the answer was in the affirmative, the court would enter an order of support and would then forward that order to the court in the noncustodial parent's state of residence. This state would now have jurisdiction over the noncustodial parent and have the authority to notify the noncustodial parent and conduct a hearing. The order could then be enforced in the noncustodial parent's state.

URESA was amended in 1958, resulting in the **Revised Uniform Reciprocal Enforcement of Support Act (RURESA).** There were two very important changes to URESA. The first was to facilitate the exchange of evidence from the obligee's state to the obligor's state. The purpose behind URESA was being defeated because the obligor's state did not have the necessary evidence to enforce orders against the obligor, who very often walked out of court a winner. RURESA now required the obligee's state to send any evidence available along with the obligee's file.

The second change in RURESA was the ability of the obligee to take the initiative to register the court order in a court located in the obligor's state and bring the initial proceeding in that court. While this new provision enabled custodial parents to take more aggressive action against the noncustodial parent, the problem of multiple state orders emerged. For example, if a noncustodial parent moved from New York to Connecticut to New Hampshire and the custodial parent sought an order in each court, there would be three different state laws and original and modified orders to decipher.

In 1992, NCCUSL replaced URESA and RURESA with the **Uniform Interstate Family Support Act (UIFSA)** and has since been adopted by every state in the United States. (See Appendix D for Florida's version of UIFSA.) UIFSA is divided into five parts:

1. General Provisions
2. Establishing a Support Order
3. Enforcing a Support Order
4. Modifying a Support Order
5. Parentage

UIFSA addressed the problem of multiple orders by allowing a child support order to be modified based on the law of the state with original jurisdiction. This is called *continuing exclusive jurisdiction*. So in the previous example, the Connecticut and New Hampshire courts could only modifiy the original order based on the law of the State of New York. Under UIFSA, the noncustodial parent's state must honor the original support order and may not enter a new order or modify the existing order to conform to its guidelines for determining the amount of support. Only the custodial parent's state may modify its own order, unless the parties agree to the modification in writing or both parties have moved to the new state, thus giving the new state jurisdiction over the matter.

A custodial parent seeking relief under UIFSA would file a petition in his or her own jurisdiction. The original court files the petition in a court where the obligor resides, where a hearing is held on the matter. An attorney employed by the state will represent the interest of the custodial parent at the hearing held in the obligor's state, unless the custodial parent has enough money to hire a private attorney to represent his or her interests and prosecute the petition. While state child support enforcement systems throughout the country are well intentioned, they are overwhelmed with a large volume of work. This makes the system frustrating for custodial parents trying to collect unpaid child support.

CHILD SUPPORT ORDER AND THE RIGHT TO VISITATION

Just as a noncustodial parent has an obligation to support her minor children, so must the custodial parent comply with the court's order giving the noncustodial parent reasonable visitation.

These obligations are separate obligations, independent of one another, and the default on one obligation by one parent will not excuse the default of the other parent on his obligation. If a noncustodial parent ceases to pay child support, the custodial parent may not withhold visitation; and if a custodial parent refuses to make the minor children available for visitation, the noncustodial parent is not excused from paying child support. A minority of states allow a noncustodial parent who is refused visitation to petition the court to temporarily cease child support payments.

Each party may seek to remedy the respective default by filing a motion for contempt of a court order. The injured party may request that the offending party be held in contempt of court and be ordered to resume her obligation. As mentioned, frequently the party bringing the motion for contempt will request and receive an order from the court that the offending party pay the costs and reasonable attorney's fees of the injured party. An attorney's fee award is made on the rationale that the party bringing the action would not have incurred the expense of representation had the other party fulfilled his legal obligation.

ADDITIONAL SUPPORT ORDERS

Sometimes support orders contain obligations beyond a periodic monetary payment. For instance, a judge may order a noncustodial parent to provide medical coverage to all children until they reach the age of majority. Also, when parties negotiate an agreement that one party shall pay private school tuition for all children during minority, this provision will be incorporated into the separation agreement. If the parent refuses to pay for tuition during minority, the other party may file a motion for contempt to enforce this agreed-to obligation. If the offending party counters this motion for contempt with a motion to modify the obligation for tuition because of changed financial circumstance, the court will not even consider a modification unless the separation agreement provided an accommodation for the event of changed circumstances. Further, the court will always order the party to pay the past-due amount. As noted, a past-due amount is termed an arrearage.

SUPPORTING A SECOND FAMILY

Noncustodial parents often create new families to support by either remarrying, cohabitating with a domestic partner, or engaging in intimate relations and choosing not to live with the other biological parent. In the past, family courts enforced the "first family first" rule; child support payments to the first family could not be reduced based on the argument that the noncustodial parent now had a second family to support. While some jurisdictions still adhere to this rule, the majority of states allow for some type of readjustment based on the best interest of the child theory. Though a noncustodial parent's obligation to support the first family is not diminished by the creation of a second family, a custodial parent who is receiving child support and remarries is still entitled to child support unless the new spouse adopts the child.

NEW SPOUSE OR DOMESTIC PARTNER'S INCOME

What effect does a new spouse or domestic partner's income have on child support payments? While state child support guidelines do not consider a new spouse or domestic partner's income in calculating child support payments, their respective contributions to the family finances may effect child support payments in the form of a deviation from the child support guidelines. Remarriage or cohabitation may be considered a "substantial change in circumstances" that warrants another visit to family court for an adjustment in the amount of support paid.

If the obligor has remarried and has new children to support, he or she will inevitably file for a modification on the grounds that there is a change in circumstances because there are now more mouths to feed. The recipient spouse, on the other hand, may find that his or her child support payments will be reduced because the obligor has created a second family. The court makes the reduction because it must take into account the best interest of the children and must reallocate the income in order to cover both families.

If the recipient spouse has remarried or is cohabitating with a domestic partner who is making contributions to the household, including gifts to the children, the recipient spouse may find his or her child support reduced.

A Tale of Domestic Partner's Income

In *Unkelbach v. McNary,* the Connecticut Supreme Court held that while a new spouse or domestic partner's income is not included in the child support calculations, any contributions made by the new spouse or domestic partner toward living expenses could be taken into consideration and treated as gifts.

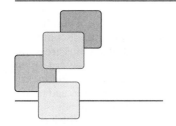
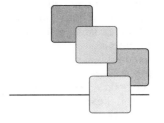

LINDA JOYCE UNKELBACH V. JOHN THOMAS McNARY

244 CONN. 350, 710 A. 2D 717 (1998)

SUPREME COURT OF CONNECTICUT

KATZ, J.

The issues to be decided in this appeal are whether: (1) in modifying the defendant's child support obligation, the trial court properly considered contributions made by the defendant's domestic partner toward their shared living expenses as an element of the defendant's gross income under the Child Support and Arrearage Guidelines. . .

. . .The facts that are relevant to this appeal are not disputed. The parties' marriage was dissolved on February 1, 1988. The separation agreement ordered into effect by the court on that date awarded primary physical custody of the parties' two minor children to the plaintiff, and ordered the defendant to pay child support in the amount of $375 per week. At the time of dissolution, the defendant earned a gross weekly wage of $1778.85, and the plaintiff earned a gross weekly wage of $74.40.

As of January 1, 1995, the defendant unilaterally ceased making his court ordered child support payments and, instead, began to make payments that were smaller in amount and sporadic in occurrence. On February 23, 1995, the plaintiff filed a motion for contempt based upon the defendant's failure to pay the child support as ordered. Shortly thereafter, on March 1, 1995, the defendant filed a motion for modification of his child support obligation. The court issued an

interim order reducing the defendant's child support to $108 per week, and the parties, with the approval of the court, agreed that any permanent modification of child support would date back to March 1, 1995.

In the fifteen months prior to the time when the defendant ceased making the initial court-ordered child support payments, a number of changes in his circumstances occurred. In October, 1993, his employment was terminated as a result of company downsizing, and he was provided with fifty weeks of severance pay at his full salary rate. He received his last severance check in October, 1994. From approximately October, 1994, through May, 1995, he experienced health problems for which he was twice hospitalized and underwent two surgeries. In July, 1995, the defendant applied for and subsequently received twenty-six weeks of unemployment compensation. Eventually, in April, 1996, he began to receive pension distributions from his former employer in the gross amount of $311 per week.

Following the termination of his employment, the defendant formed a business known as Construction Consultants and Managers, Inc. (Construction Consultants). In 1995, he transferred his interest in the business to Joan Shoham, his domestic companion, for the purpose of obtaining minority-owned business status in order to enhance the company's ability to obtain contract work. Both the defendant and his companion receive compensation from Construction Consultants, although limited in amount. As of October, 1996, the defendant was receiving $202 per week in gross compensation from Construction Consultants, and Shoham had received a total of $7200 for the year to that date. The trial court found that there was insufficient evidence to determine accurately how much compensation, if any, would redound to the defendant from Construction Consultants in the future, but noted that the success of the business had thus far been limited.

The defendant and Shoham, who have lived together in the defendant's home for approximately the past eight years, commingle their personal incomes to a certain extent and use a joint bank account to pay for household expenses. The trial court found that since October, 1995, Shoham's personal funds have been the source of all monthly mortgage payments on the defendant's home, all monthly payments on the defendant's home equity loan, all monthly loan payments on the defendant's automobile, and all periodic payments for home electricity, cable service, natural gas service, telephone service, property taxes on the residence, groundskeeping, and groceries. Shoham testified that she makes these payments as gifts to the defendant and does not expect to be reimbursed by him.

Since the dissolution of the parties' marriage, the plaintiff has been employed on a full-time basis. From November, 1994, until November, 1995, she was employed as a branch director and supervisor for a home nursing care provider, at a salary of approximately $60,000 per year. The plaintiff voluntarily left that employment because it involved long hours that she felt interfered with her responsibilities as the primary caretaker of the parties' minor children. Thereafter, she obtained employment requiring her to work only between the hours of 8:30 a.m. and 4 p.m. at a salary of approximately $41,000 per year, or a gross income of $800 per week.

In considering the defendant's motion for modification of his child support obligation, the trial court concluded that a substantial change in circumstances had occurred affecting the ability of each of the parties to provide support for their minor children. The court concluded that the defendant had established his inability to comply with the original child support order due to changes in his health and employment. Although the court found that the defendant's capacity to earn income in the future had not diminished, it did not, as a result, deviate from the guidelines in setting the amount of his child support obligation. Instead, in accordance with its finding of a substantial change in circumstances, the court modified the defendant's child support obligation from $375 per week to $252 per week. The court also ordered the defendant to pay $1000 per month in child support arrearage payments, and awarded the plaintiff attorney's fees in the amount of $1000. Subsequently, the court awarded an additional $3250 in attorney's fees to the plaintiff for the purpose of defending the appeal.

In deciding upon the modified amount of child support to be ordered, the court considered the defendant's present ability to pay. In that regard, it found that the defendant's gross income included amounts contributed by Shoham toward their household expenses. Recognizing that Shoham shared in the value of most of her contributions toward the household expenses, the court found the value of Shoham's contributions to the defendant to be $514 per week, or one half of their actual value, with the exception of the amount paid toward the defendant's automobile loan, which the court included in full in its calculations.

The defendant first claims that the trial court incorrectly interpreted the definition of gross income set forth in the guidelines when it included in his gross income contributions made by Shoham toward their shared living expenses. According to the defendant, the definition of gross income should not be read to include such contributions because the guidelines preclude consideration of the income of a subsequent spouse or domestic partner in calculating child support, and the inclusion of the contributions leads, in effect, to consideration of Shoham's income. The plaintiff argues, conversely, that including the contributions in the defendant's gross income is not the same as including Shoham's actual income, but only amounts to consideration of specific gifts regularly made by her and, therefore, does not contravene the guidelines. In that regard, the plaintiff contends that inclusion of the contributions in income is in accord with the existing law of this state, which recognizes that gifts received on a regular and consistent basis, regardless of their source, are includible in income in the context of dissolution proceedings where financial orders are being determined. We agree with the plaintiff. . . .

. . .We begin with a brief overview of the guidelines. The guidelines are predicated upon the concept that children should receive the same proportion of parental income that they would have received had the family remained intact. Child Support and Arrearage Guidelines, Preamble, § (c), pp. ii–iii. Toward that end, the guidelines are income driven, rather than expense driven. At each income level, the guidelines allocate a certain percentage of parental income to child support. The percentage allocations contained in the guidelines aim to reflect the average proportions of income spent on children in households of various income and family sizes, and contain a built-in self-support reserve for the obligor. Id., §§ (c) and (d), pp. ii-iii. The result is that the guidelines incorporate an allocation of resources between parents and children that the legislature has decided is the appropriate allocation. Consequently, our interpretation of the guidelines must seek to preserve this allocation.

The definition of gross income set forth in the guidelines does not address explicitly contributions or gifts given by a subsequent spouse, domestic partner, or any other third party, to a parent whose child support obligation is being determined. Section 46b-215a-1 (11) of the Regulations of Connecticut State Agencies defines gross income as "the average weekly income before deductions." That section further identifies twelve specific elements of gross income and provides that "[g]ross income includes, but is not limited to" those items. Regs., Conn. State Agencies § 46b-215a-1 (11) (A). In addition, that regulation expressly excludes two items from the definition of gross income, namely, child support received on behalf of a child living with the parent for whom the support obligation is being determined, and federal, state and local public assistance grants. Regs., Conn. State Agencies § 46b-215a-1 (11) (B). Although this definition does not specifically identify contributions or gifts received from a subsequent spouse, domestic partner, or other third party as an item expressly included in gross income, the definition does provide that the items expressly enumerated do not comprise an exhaustive list. Regs., Conn. State Agencies § 46b-215a-1 (11) (A). Gifts are also not mentioned in the list of items that are expressly excluded from gross income under subsection (11) (B) of the regulation. Therefore, while the issue of whether gifts are includible in income is not resolved by reference to the definition of gross income alone, it is clear that, by its plain language, the definition does not preclude their inclusion.

The guidelines are preceded by a preamble that "is intended to assist users of the child support and arrearage guidelines but is not part of the official regulations." Child Support and Arrearage Guidelines, Preamble, § (a), p. i. The preamble explains the concept of gross income contained in the guidelines, but, like the definition, does not address contributions or gifts made by third parties to parents. The preamble addresses the actual *income* of a subsequent spouse or domestic partner, and makes clear that such income is not included in the definition of gross income. Child Support and Arrearage Guidelines, Preamble, § (f)(1)(F), p. ix. It does not, however, indicate expressly that contributions or gifts from a subsequent spouse, domestic partner, or other third party, are intended to be excluded from gross income under the guidelines.

We have previously interpreted broadly the definition of gross income contained in the guidelines to include items that, in effect, increase the amount of a parent's income that is available for child support purposes. In *Jenkins* v. *Jenkins*, 243 Conn. 584, 704 A.2d 231 (1998), we held that social security dependency benefits received directly by the children of a noncustodial parent on account of that parent's disability must be included in the noncustodial parent's income for purposes of determining the parent's child support obligation. We reasoned that, because the guidelines provide for a credit against the child support obligation in the amount of the benefits paid directly to the children, the noncustodial parent benefits by having an obligation discharged, thereby enabling him to retain more income for himself. We also reasoned in part that the failure to include the social security dependency benefits in the noncustodial parent's gross income would lead to a result that is inconsistent with the public policy underlying the guidelines—namely, the policy, when determining child support obligations, of accounting for all income that would have been available to support the children had the family remained intact. Therefore, we required that the benefits be included in gross income under the guidelines.

Similarly, in other proceedings emanating from the dissolution of a marriage, our approach has been to interpret the concept of income broadly so as to include in income items that increase the amount of resources available for support purposes. In cases concerning alimony, we have indicated that regularly and consistently received gifts, whether in the form of contributions to expenses or otherwise, are properly considered in determining alimony awards to the extent that they increase the amount of income available for support purposes. . . .

. . .To the extent that they are indicative of the approach we have adopted in the past—interpreting gross income broadly so as to include items that increase the amount of income available for support purposes—our prior cases addressing child support and alimony are significant, because the same effect that compelled those decisions is present in this case. Here, the regular contributions made by Shoham increase the amount of the defendant's income that is available for support purposes.

The defendant relies primarily upon the public policy embodied in the preamble to the guidelines for his argument that the contributions should not be included in gross income. The preamble provides that the commission for child support guidelines (commission), which promulgated the guidelines, decided not to include the income of a subsequent spouse or domestic partner in the definition of gross income contained in the guidelines because the inclusion of such income "inevitably leads to extremely complex calculations, especially if the spouse or partner has his or her own child support obligations," and because "there is under Connecticut law no legal basis for imputing support liabilities to such a [third party]." Child Support and Arrearage Guidelines, Preamble, § (f)(1)(F), p. ix. The defendant argues that this policy is contravened when contributions toward a parent's living expenses made by a parent's domestic partner are included in the parent's income because the domestic partner in effect becomes a source of support for the children of the parent's prior marriage. We disagree.

The inclusion of regularly received gifts in a parent's income differs significantly from the inclusion of the income of a subsequent spouse or domestic partner. First, including the value of gifts received from a subsequent spouse or domestic partner does not have the effect of imputing liability to that individual. A domestic partner whose own actual income is at issue has only two options if he or she seeks to have that income excluded from the parent's gross income. He or she must choose between terminating the income generating activity or altering the relationship with the parent in order to prevent the inclusion of his or her income in the parent's gross income. In this situation, however, no such problem is presented. A donor is entitled to cease making gifts at any time and, at such time as that occurs, the parent may seek a modification of the child support obligation based upon the resulting reduction in income, without penalty to either the parent or the donor. Therefore, no liability may be imputed to a third party donor based upon the inclusion of the gifts made by the donor in the recipient's gross income.

Second, the inclusion of regularly and consistently received gifts does not lead to the extremely complex calculations that the commission sought to avoid when it decided against including a subsequent spouse's or domestic partner's income in the definition of gross income. As this court stated in *Rubin*, "evidence of past gratuities does not inevitably entail the necessity of probing into the personal financial affairs of persons who have no other involvement in the marital dispute before the court than their relationship to one of the parties." *Rubin* v. *Rubin*, supra, 204 Conn. 239.

Third, the inclusion of contributions and other gifts in gross income is not likely to result in a diversion of the donor's resources from the donor's own obligations or dependents. We logically may presume, based upon the fact that the donor has *chosen* to make the gifts, that the donor is financially able to do so. Conversely, if the resources used to make the gifts were needed to provide for the third party's own needs or the needs of the

third party's dependents, we may presume that the gifts would not have been made.

Finally, the fact that the commission decided to make clear in the preamble that gross income does not include the income of a subsequent spouse or domestic partner, but did not discuss any other exemptions from gross income, indicates that regularly and consistently received gifts were not intended to be excluded from gross income. The guidelines, both in the preamble and in the definition section, § 46b-215a-1 of the Regulations of Connecticut State Agencies, contain express exclusions from an otherwise broad definition of gross income. Therefore, there is no basis for reading the exclusion contained in the preamble broadly. In fact, to do so would be inconsistent with our established policy of reading broadly the definition of gross income. If the commission had intended to exclude gifts from gross income, it could have done so expressly. The fact that it did not supports our interpretation.

The legislative policy underlying the guidelines further supports an interpretation of gross income that includes gifts that are regularly and consistently received. As we have already noted, the guidelines are predicated upon the concept that children should receive the same proportion of parental income that they would have received had the family remained intact. Child Support and Arrearage Guidelines, Preamble, § (c), pp. ii–iii. At each income level, they allocate a certain percentage of parental income to child support. The allocations are intended to reflect the average proportion of income that, theoretically, would be spent on children in intact families, and contain built-in self-support reserves for obligors. Id., §§ (c) and (d), pp. ii–iii. In situations like the present one, the failure to include the contributions of the parent's domestic partner leads to an allocation between parent and child that is proportionately at odds with the allocation contemplated by the guidelines. Here, the defendant, rather than being required to spend a certain proportion of his weekly income on his own support needs, instead has nearly all of his income available for other purposes. The guidelines, however, being income driven, do not contain an expense category wherein the benefit received by the defendant may be reflected. As a result, the only way in which to reflect the economic reality of the defendant's situation, and thereby arrive at an allocation of resources between parent and child that is consistent with the guidelines, is to include the contributions in income for child support determination purposes.

For all of the above reasons, we conclude that the trial court properly included in the defendant's gross income the contributions made by his domestic partner toward his living expenses when it determined his child support obligation under the guidelines. . . .

Nonbiological Parent's Duty to Support: The Doctrine of Equitable Estoppel

Courts across the United States have ordered nonbiological parents to pay child support on the basis of their relationship with the child. The problem usually arises when the relationship between the biological parent and friend, spouse, or lover terminates. This individual may have provided the child with financial support and may have interacted with a child as if the child were his or her own. The biological parent brings an action in the courts for child support relying on the **doctrine of equitable estoppel.** Under the doctrine of equitable estoppel, a court may hold that because the individual voluntarily assumed some type of parental role in the child's life and the child relied on this role, the individual is now obligated to provide the child with financial support.

Nice Guys Finish Last

When a nonbiological parent voluntarily promises to provide financial support to a child, he may be barred from avoiding any future obligation if he stops paying, based on the theory that the child has now relied on his promise.

NYGARD V. NYGARD

156 Mich. App. 94, 401 N.W.2d 323 (1986)

Michigan Court of Appeals

T.M. Burns, P.J.

Defendant Dudley Neil Nygard appeals as of right from the provisions of a divorce judgment requiring defendant to contribute to the support and maintenance of Shuntelle Lee Nygard, a minor child.

Plaintiff Michael Ann Nygard met the defendant, Dudley Nygard, in July of 1982, and began to spend a good deal of time with him thereafter. By October of 1982, a strong relationship had developed between the two. In October of 1982, plaintiff discovered that she was pregnant. It is undisputed that the pregnancy was not a result of plaintiff's relationship with defendant. Rather, plaintiff's pregnancy resulted from a short relationship with a man named "Tim" whom she had met in May of 1982 during a stay in Florida. Plaintiff was shocked and upset when she discovered that she was pregnant and did not know how she would support a child.

In late October or early November of 1982, plaintiff advised defendant that she was pregnant and that the child was not his. She told him that she planned to go to Alaska, where her brother lived, and give the baby up for adoption. Defendant asked plaintiff not to go to Alaska and stated that he did not want to lose her.

Defendant wanted to marry plaintiff and thought that the mother and baby would be a "package deal." Defendant agreed to raise the child as his own. When he agreed to treat the baby as his own, he meant that he would buy her things, feed her, and house her.

Plaintiff decided not to go to Alaska and give the child up for adoption. She stressed that one of the main reasons she did not do so was because of defendant's statements.

On December 4, 1982, the parties were married. Defendant indicated that they married before the child was born so that the child would have defendant's name and so that no one would know that he had not fathered the child.

Shuntelle was born on February 14, 1983. Defendant was present in the delivery room during birth. He acknowledged to hospital personnel that he was the child's father and his name was placed on the birth certificate. Defendant treated Shuntelle as his own child during the marriage and encouraged her to call him "Papa."

The couple separated in May of 1984. On June 6, 1984, plaintiff filed a complaint for divorce against defendant in Schoolcraft Circuit Court. On June 22, 1984, a temporary order of child support was entered by the circuit court. On October 11, 1984, defendant filed a motion to "remove the minor child from the divorce complaint and to discontinue child support" on the ground that he was not the biological father of the minor child. The circuit court denied defendant's motion. Defendant thereafter filed for leave to appeal, which this Court denied. On September 26, 1985, a judgment of divorce was entered. The judgment included provisions requiring defendant to contribute to the support and maintenance of the minor child. Because defendant was sick at the time, the judgment indicated that once defendant returned to work on a full-time basis, he was to pay support and maintenance of $99 per week. Defendant now appeals as of right. We believe that the trial court properly concluded that defendant could be held responsible for child support payments.

Defendant argues that the trial court erred in finding defendant estopped to deny parentage of the child and estopped to deny his obligation to support the child. We find that, under the facts of this case, defendant has an obligation to contribute to the support of this child.

It is generally recognized that the biological parents are obligated by law to maintain and support their children. The duty to support arises both from common law and from statutory law. . . .

. . .In this case, there is no biological relationship from which a support obligation can arise. In most cases in which there is no biological relationship between the child and the adult, the adult is not required to support the child. . . .However, there are exceptional situations in which an adult who is not a biological parent of a child may be required to make payments to be used to support the child.

One such exceptional situation was refereed to by this Court in *Johnson v. Johnson*, 93 Mich. App. 415; 286 N.W.2d 886 (1979). In that case, the plaintiff was a man who married the defendant knowing that she was carrying a child for whom he was only possibly the biological father. Plaintiff thereafter held himself out as the father and supporter of the child for several years. In *Johnson*, this Court stated:

> Even if plaintiff were not the biological father of the child, by marrying defendant he forecloses any action by her to seek support from the child's biological father. Actions under the paternity act are authorized only where the woman was unmarried from the conception to the date of birth of the child. MCL 722.711(a) and (b), 722.714(b); MSA 25.491(a) and (b), MSA 25.494(b). As the Ohio court observed in *Burse v. Burse*, 48 Ohio App.2d 244 248; 356 N.E.2d 755 (1976), "the man at the time he marries the woman, knowing the woman is pregnant by another man, should be cognizant that he is foreclosing the chance of the unborn child being

legitimized by its natural father and is barring a bastardy action by the mother against the natural father.

Plaintiff assumed the status of father of this child when the child was born and continued as such for ten years until he amended his divorce complaint at trial. As the child was born during the marriage while the parties lived together as husband and wife, it was not necessary for plaintiff to go through adoption proceedings. Conversely, after plaintiff has represented himself as the father of this child for nine to ten years, he may not now say that he was not.

On the facts of this case the Court is compelled to hold that plaintiff is estopped by his conduct to deny paternity of this child. [93 Mich. App. 419-420.]

While the situation was present in *Johnson* is somewhat different from the situation here, the policies and rationale of *Johnson* are sound and applicable in this case. We agree with *Johnson* that under certain circumstances a person other than a biological parent may be held responsible for child support. Such a concept is not novel or extraordinary. In this case, we find it equitable to hold defendant responsible for child support payments.

In addition, we believe that traditional notions of estoppel may provide a basis for plaintiff's requested relief. The facts of this case suggest either that plaintiff and defendant entered into an enforceable contract whereby defendant agreed to support the child, or, if the statute of frauds prevents the contract from being enforceable, that defendant may be held responsible under the doctrine of "equitable estoppel" or "promissory estoppel.". . .

. . .The elements of equitable or promissory estoppel are: (1) a promise; (2) that the promisor should reasonably have expected to induce action of a definite and substantial character on the part of the promisee; (3) which in fact produced reliance or forbearance of that nature; and (4) in circumstances such that the promise must be enforced if injustice is to be avoided. . . .

. . .Each of these elements is clearly present in this case. The circumstances of this case are such that the promise must be enforced if injustice is to be avoided. Because of defendant's promise an obligation arose both to plaintiff and to the child. We believe that this promise can be enforced by the circuit court in this divorce proceeding.

However, our de novo review leads us to the conclusion that payments of $99 per week may be inappropriate under the circumstances of this case. We remand to the circuit court for reconsideration of this amount. The circuit court may consider the fact that defendant is not the natural father of the child and may reduce defendant's required payments if the circumstances so indicate. Remanded. We do not retain jurisdiction. No costs.

On March 9, 2006, the National Center for Men filed a lawsuit in federal court on behalf of Matt Dubay, who challenged a court order requiring him to pay the sum of $500 per month in child support. Dubay alleged that he relied on his girlfriend's representations that due to a health problem, she was unable to get pregnant. Dubay also alleged that he made it clear to her that he did not want to father any children at this time in his life. As a result of their sexual relationship, the girlfriend gave birth to a daughter.

Dubay fought the court's child support order on the grounds that it was unconstitutional and violated his reproductive rights. He argued that the support order violated his right to equal protection under the Fourteenth Amendment of the U.S. Constitution by discriminating against him on the basis of gender. As a legal basis for his argument, Dubay cites *Roe v. Wade,* claiming that while women have the right to avoid procreating by having an abortion, men do not have equal rights in relieving themselves of fatherhood. He stated that the Michigan paternity laws were unconstitutional because they required fathers to pay child support for unwanted children. On July 19, 2006, the federal court dismissed Dubay's lawsuit, calling it frivolous, and awarded the state attorney's fees for defending the action.

POSTMAJORITY CHILD SUPPORT

A parent's obligation to support a child typically terminates when the child dies, reaches the age of majority, or becomes emancipated by a court of law.

Prior to 1970, the age of majority in most states was twenty-one. When parties agreed or when a judge ordered a parent to pay children's college costs, failure to do so constituted contempt as long as the child was under the age of twenty-one. This enabled courts to enforce at least two and often three years of college tuition.

In 1970, many states lowered the age of majority to eighteen. Family courts charged with adjudicating disputes on payments for the minor child no longer had jurisdiction to enforce a provision in a separation agreement that obligated a non-custodial parent to pay college tuition for a child who had reached the age of eighteen. Because most children do not even start college until they are over the age of eighteen, this change wreaked havoc in splintered families where agreements long counted on were no longer worth the legal paper on which they were written.

To remedy this situation, eventually a number of state legislatures passed laws that provided henceforth—but not retroactively—that (1) divorcing parties could include a provision in their separation agreement for the postmajority support of children and (2) request that this provision along with the rest of the agreement be enacted into the divorce decree. The new statutes provided that if such a provision was enacted into the order of divorce or dissolution, then the family court had jurisdiction to enforce the clause.

Postmajority support agreements frequently address payment for college tuition or other postsecondary education, payment for the maintenance of postmajority adult children with special needs, and the payment of medical and dental insurance coverage on dependent adult children while they are students or when they are newly employed but not yet eligible for coverage at work. These

FIGURE 8–2
Postmajority support
agreements for
college expenses
came about as a
result of the age of
majority being
lowered from
twenty-one to
eighteen during the
1970s.

types of postmajority support provisions are realistic in our current society because young adults frequently continue to have the need for some form of financial support from their family of origin. In instances where both the custodial and the non-custodial parent shared the support obligation during the child's minority, both parents should be required to continue with this obligation if they previously agreed to do so in their separation agreement.

POSTMAJORITY EDUCATIONAL SUPPORT ORDERS

There are a small number of jurisdictions that grant the family court judge the authority to order parents to pay a child's postsecondary educational expenses past the age of majority. In the State of New York, for example, the court may order parents to pay for such costs after considering the best interest of the children and the parents' circumstances.

The State of Connecticut passed a statute in 2002 requiring the family courts to address the issue of postmajority educational support after considering a list of statutory factors. Parents in Connecticut may be required to pay such costs until the child's twenty-third birthday.

Connecticut Public Act No. 02-128
An Act Concerning Educational Support Orders
Be it enacted by the Senate and House of Representatives in General Assembly convened:

Section 1. (NEW) (*Effective October 1, 2002*) (a) For purposes of this section, an educational support order is an order entered by a court requiring a parent to provide support for a child or children to attend for up to a total of four full academic years an institution of higher education or a private occupational school for the purpose of attaining a bachelor's or other undergraduate degree, or other appropriate vocational instruction. An educational support order may be entered with respect to any child who has not attained twenty-three years of age and shall terminate not later than the date on which the child attains twenty-three years of age.

(b) (1) On motion or petition of a parent, the court may enter an educational support order at the time of entry of a decree of dissolution, legal separation or annulment, and no educational support order may be entered thereafter unless the decree explicitly provides that a motion or petition for an educational support order may be filed by either parent at a subsequent date. If no educational support order is entered at the time of entry of a decree of dissolution, legal separation or annulment, and the parents have a child who has not attained twenty-three years of age, the court shall inform the parents that no educational support order may be entered thereafter. The court may accept a parent's waiver of the right to file a motion or petition for an educational support order upon a finding that the parent fully understands the consequences of such waiver.

(2) On motion or petition of a parent, the court may enter an educational support order at the time of entry of an order for support pendente lite pursuant to section 46b-83 of the general statutes.

(3) On motion or petition of a parent, the court may enter an educational support order at the time of entering an order of support pursuant to section 46b-61 or 46b-171 or similar section of the general statutes, or at any time thereafter.

(4) On motion or petition of a parent, the court may enter an educational support order at the time of entering an order pursuant to any other provision of the general statutes authorizing the court to make an order of support for a child, subject to the provisions of sections 46b-212 to 46b-213v, inclusive, of the general statutes, as amended.

(c) The court may not enter an educational support order pursuant to this section unless the court finds as a matter of fact that it is more likely than not that the parents would have provided support to the child for higher education or private occupational school if the family were intact. After making such finding, the court, in determining whether to enter an educational support order, shall consider all relevant circumstances, including: (1) The parents' income, assets and other obligations, including obligations to other dependents; (2) the child's need for support to attend an institution of higher education or private occupational school considering the child's assets and the child's ability to earn income; (3) the availability of financial aid from other sources, including grants and loans; (4) the reasonableness of the higher education to be funded considering the child's academic record and the financial resources available; (5) the child's preparation for, aptitude for and commitment to higher education; and (6) evidence, if any, of the institution of higher education or private occupational school the child would attend.

(d) At the appropriate time, both parents shall participate in, and agree upon, the decision as to which institution of higher education or private occupational school the child will attend. The court may make an order resolving the matter if the parents fail to reach an agreement.

(e) To qualify for payments due under an educational support order, the child must (1) enroll in an accredited institution of higher education or private occupational school, as defined in section 10a-22a of the general statutes, (2) actively pursue a course of study commensurate with the child's vocational goals that constitutes at least one-half the course load determined by that institution or school to constitute full-time enrollment, (3) maintain good academic standing in accordance with the rules of the institution or school, and (4) make available all academic records to both parents during the term of the order. The order shall be suspended after any academic period during which the child fails to comply with these conditions.

(f) The educational support order may include support for any necessary educational expense, including room, board, dues, tuition, fees, registration and application costs, but such expenses shall not be more than the amount charged by The University of Connecticut for a full-time in-state student at the time the child for whom educational support is being ordered matriculates, except this limit may be exceeded by agreement of the parents. An educational support order may also include the cost of books and medical insurance for such child.

(g) The court may direct that payments under an educational support order be made (1) to a parent to be forwarded to the institution of higher education or private occupational school, (2) directly to the institution or school, or (3) otherwise as the court determines to be appropriate.

(h) On motion or petition of a parent, an educational support order may be modified or enforced in the same manner as is provided by law for any support order.

(i) This section does not create a right of action by a child for parental support for higher education.

(j) An educational support order under this section does not include support for graduate or post-graduate education beyond a bachelor's degree.

(k) The provisions of this section shall apply only in cases when the initial order for parental support of the child is entered on or after the effective date of this section.

Approved June 7, 2002

TAX CONSEQUENCES OF CHILD SUPPORT

While alimony is treated as income to the recipient spouse for tax purposes and deductible to the payor, the payment of child support is a tax-neutral event. Child support cannot be deducted from the payor's income taxes, nor must it be included as income on the recipient's tax return. A parent who pays more than 50 percent of the actual costs of child support may claim the child as a dependent on his or her tax return. It is advisable that clients deal with this matter at the time of the divorce and reach some type of agreement as to who will claim the child. Both parents claiming the child as a dependent is sure to trigger a red flag at the Internal Revenue Service and possibly subject the client to an audit.

EXHIBIT 8–1 Sample child support worksheet: Connecticut.

CONNECTICUT CHILD SUPPORT AND ARREARAGE GUIDELINES
WORKSHEET A – Page 1

MOTHER	FATHER	NAME OF CUSTODIAN

COURT _____ D.N./CASE NO. _____ NUMBER OF CHILDREN ____

CHILD'S NAME	DATE OF BIRTH	CHILD'S NAME	DATE OF BIRTH

	MOTHER	FATHER
I. Net Income Computation (Weekly amounts)		
1. Gross income (attach verification)	$_____	$_____
2. Number of exemptions for tax purposes	_____	_____
3. Federal income tax	$_____	$_____
4. State and local income tax	$_____	$_____
5. Social security tax or mandatory retirement	$_____	$_____
6. Health insurance premiums (other than child)	$_____	$_____
7. Union dues or fees	$_____	$_____
8. Unreimbursed work-related day care	$_____	$_____
9. Other alimony and child support orders	$_____	$_____
10. Sum of lines 3 - 9	$_____	$_____
11. Net income (line 1 minus line 10)	$_____	$_____
II. Current Support Determination		
12. Combined net weekly income (nearest $10.00)	$_____	
13. Basic obligation (from schedule)	$_____	
14. Check here if noncustodial parent is a low-income obligor (see instructions)	_____	
15. Child's health insurance premium	$_____	$_____
16. Total obligation (Line 13 minus noncustodial parent's line 15 amount if line 14 is checked; line 13 plus line 15 total for all other cases)	$_____	
17. Each parent's decimal share of line 12 (If line 14 is checked, skip this line and line 19, and enter the line 16 amount in the noncustodial parent's column on line 18.)		
18. Each parent's share of the total obligation (Line 17 times line 16 for each parent)	_____	_____
19. Health insurance premium adjustment	$_____	$_____
20. Social security benefits adjustment	$_____	$_____
21. Sum of lines 19 and 20 (for each parent)	$_____	$_____
22. Recommended support amounts (Line 18 minus line 21)	$_____	$_____
23. Current support order (Noncustodial parent(s) only. If different from line 22 amount, explain in section VI.)	$_____	$_____

GO TO THE NEXT PAGE

EXHIBIT 8–1 Continued

CONNECTICUT CHILD SUPPORT AND ARREARAGE GUIDELINES
WORKSHEET A – Page 2

III. Total Arrearage Determination

24. Delinquencies on current support orders $ _____

25. Unpaid court-ordered arrearages $ _____

26. Past-due support (not court-ordered) $ _____

27. Total arrearage (sum of lines 24 through 26) $ _____

IV. Arrearage Payment Determination

28. Current support order from line 23 (or imputed
support obligation for IV-D arrearages owed to
the state or if child living with obligor) $ _____

29. Twenty percent (20%) of line 28
(or fifty percent (50%) of line 28 if
there is no child under age 18) $ _____

30. Noncustodial parent's line 11 amount $ _____

31. Fifty-five percent (55%) of line 30 $ _____

32. Line 31 minus line 28 $ _____

33. Line 28 plus $145 $ _____

34. Line 30 minus line 33 $ _____

35. Recommended arrearage payment $ _____

   (Smallest of lines 29, 32, and 34; or $5.00/month if child living with
   obligor and obligor's gross income is not more than 250% of poverty level;
   or the lesser of $5.00/week or line 34 for low-income obligor. If arrear-
   ages are owed to the state and the family, $5.00/month of this amount is
   allocated to the state, and the balance to the family.)

36. Arrearage payment order (At least $5.00/month
unless line 34 is less than $1.00. If different
from line 35, explain in section VI.) $ _____

V. Order Summary

37. Current support order $ _____

38. Arrearage payment order $ _____ $ _____
       to state   to family

39. Total arrearage $ _____ $ _____
       to state   to family

40. Total weekly support order
(Line 37 plus line 38 total) $ _____

VI. Deviation Criteria Applied

41. Reasons for deviation from current support and/or arrearage guidelines:

   _____

   _____

   _____

   _____

   _____   _____   _____
   Prepared by   Title   Date

EXHIBIT 8–2 Sample child support worksheet: New York.

SUPREME COURT OF THE STATE OF NEW YORK

1 COUNTY OF _____
--X

2

3

                                              Index No.: _____

                              Plaintiff,

                                          CHILD SUPPORT
     -- against --   **WORKSHEET**

4

                              Defendant
--X

This worksheet is submitted by Plaintiff who is the *custodial/noncustodial* parent in the above captioned action. All numbers used are YEARLY figures; weekly or monthly amounts have been converted to annualized numbers. [References are to DRL Section 240(1-b)].

                                                    FATHER   MOTHER

5 **STEP 1** MANDATORY PARENTAL INCOME

1. Gross (total) income (as reported on most recent Federal tax return, or as computed in accordance with Internal Revenue Code and regulations) [(b)(5)(i)]:   _____ _____

    The following items MUST be added if not already included in Line 1:
2. Investment income [(b)(5)(ii)]:   _____ _____
3. Workers' compensation [(b)(5)(iii)(A)]:   _____ _____
4. Disability benefits [(b)(5)(iii)(B)]:   _____ _____
5. Unemployment insurance benefits [(b)(5)(iii)(C)]:   _____ _____
6. Social Security benefits [(b)(5)(iii)(D)]:   _____ _____
7. Veterans' benefits [(b)(5)(iii)(E)]:   _____ _____
8. Pension/retirement income [(b)(5)(iii)(F)]:   _____ _____
9. Fellowships and stipends [(b)(5)(iii)(G)]:   _____ _____
10. Annuity payments [(b)(5)(iii)(H)]:   _____ _____
11. If self-employed, depreciation greater than straight-line depreciation used in determining business income or investment credit: (b)(5)(vi)(A):   _____ _____
12. If self-employed, entertainment and travel allowances deducted from business income to the extent the allowances reduce personal expenditures [(b)(5)(vi)(B)]:   _____ _____
13. Former income voluntarily reduced to avoid child support [(b)(5)(v)]:   _____ _____
14. Income voluntarily deferred [(b)(5)(iii)]:   _____ _____

List how you obtained the defendant's income for these calculations:_____
_____

    A. TOTAL MANDATORY INCOME: _____ _____

(Form UD-8)

EXHIBIT 8–2 Continued

6   **STEP 2** NON-MANDATORY PARENTAL INCOME

15. Income attributable to non-income producing assets [(b)(5)(iv)(A)]:   _____ _____
16. Employment benefits that confer personal economic benefits
(such as meals, lodging, memberships, autos, etc.) [(b)(5)(iv)(B)]:   _____ _____
17. Fringe benefits of employment [(b)(5)(iv)(C)]:   _____ _____
18. Money, goods and services provided by relatives and
friends: (b)(5)(iv)(D)]:   _____ _____

     B. TOTAL NON-MANDATORY INCOME: _____ _____

7   **C. TOTAL INCOME** (add Line A + Line B):   ========= =========

8   **STEP 3** DEDUCTIONS

19. Expenses of investment income listed on line 2 [(b)(5)(ii)]:   _____ _____
20. Unreimbursed business expenses that do not reduce personal
expenditures [(b)(5)(vii)(A)]:   _____ _____
21. Alimony or maintenance actually paid to
a former spouse: [(b)(5)(vii)(B)]:   _____ _____
22. Alimony or maintenance paid to the other parent but only
if child support will increase when alimony stops [(b)(5)(vii)(C)]:   _____ _____
23. Child support actually paid to other children the parent
is legally obligated to support [(b)(5)(vii)(D)]:   _____ _____
24. Public assistance [(b)(5)(vii)(E)]:   _____ _____
25. Supplemental security income [(b)(5)(vii)(F)]:   _____ _____
26. New York City or Yonkers income or earnings taxes actually paid
[(b)(5)(vii)(G)]:   _____ _____
27. Social Security taxes (FICA) actually paid [(b)(5)(vii)(H)]:   _____ _____

9   **D. TOTAL DEDUCTIONS**:   _____ _____

10   **E. FATHER'S INCOME** (Line C minus Line D):   _____

11   **F. MOTHER'S INCOME** (Line C minus Line D):   _____

     STEP 4 [(b)(4)]

12   **G. COMBINED PARENTAL INCOME** (Line E + Line F):   ========

(Form UD-8)

EXHIBIT 8–2 Continued

STEP 5 [(b)(3) and (c)(2)]

MULTIPLY Line G (up to $80,000) by the proper percentage (17% for 1 child, 25% for 2 children, 29% for 3 children, 31% for 4 children, or 35% (minimum) for 5 or more children) and insert in Line H.

13   **H. COMBINED CHILD SUPPORT:** . . . .   ========

14   **STEP 6** [(c)(2)]

    I. DIVIDE the noncustodial parent's amount on Line E or Line F: _____
    by the amount of Line G: _____
    to obtain the percentage allocated to **the noncustodial parent:**   _____%

    STEP 7 [(c)(2)]

15   **J. MULTIPLY line H by Line I:**   _____

    STEP 8 [(c)(3)]

16   **K. DECIDE the amount of child support to be paid
on any combined parental income exceeding $80,000
per year using the percentages in STEP 5 or the
factors in STEP 11-C or both:**   _____

17   **L. ADD Line J and Line K:**   _____

    This is the amount of child support to be paid by the noncustodial parent to the custodial parent for all costs of the children, except for child care expenses, health care expenses, and college, post-secondary, private, special or enriched education.

    STEP 9 SPECIAL NUMERICAL FACTORS

18   CHILD CARE EXPENSES

    M. Cost of child care resulting from custodial parent's:
    __working; __attending elementary education; __attending secondary education; __attending higher education; __attending vocational training leading to employment: [(c)(4)] __seeking work [(c)(6)]:   _____

(Form UD-8)

EXHIBIT 8–2 Continued

---

19   **N. MULTIPLY Line M by Line I**:   _____

This is the amount the noncustodial parent must contribute to the custodial parent for child care.

HEALTH EXPENSES [(c)(5)]

20   **O. Reasonable future health care expenses
         not covered by insurance**:   _____

21   **P. MULTIPLY Line O by Line I**:   _____

This is the amount the noncustodial parent must contribute to the custodial parent for health care or pay directly to the health care provider.

22   **Q. EDUCATIONAL EXPENSE**
         If appropriate, see STEP 11(b) [(c)(7)]   _____

23   **STEP 10** LOW INCOME EXEMPTIONS [(d)]

         R. Insert amount of noncustodial parent's income from Line E or Line F: _____

         S. Add amounts on Lines L, N, P and Q
         (This total is "basic child support"):   _____

         T. SUBTRACT Line S from Line R: =========

                 If Line T is more than the self-support reserve for this current year, then the low income exemptions do not apply and child support remains as determined in STEPS 8 and 9. If so, go to STEP 11. The self-support reserve is 135% of the official Federal poverty level for a single person household as promulgated by the U.S. Dept. of Health and Human Services and modified on April 1st of each year.

                 If Line T is less than the Federal poverty level for this current year, then complete Lines U, V and W.

24   **U. Insert amount of non-custodial parent's income from Line E or Line F**:   _____

25   **V. Self-support reserve**   _____

26   **W. Subtract Line V from Line U**:   =========

(Form UD-8)

EXHIBIT 8–2 Continued

If Line W is more than $300 per year, the Line W is the amount of basic child support. If Line W is less than $300 per year, then basic child support must be a minimum of $300 per year. The defendant may attempt to show that he/she cannot pay this minimum amount.

If Line T is greater than Federal poverty level for 1997, but is less than the self-support reserve, then complete Lines X, Y and Z.

27   **X. Insert amount of noncustodial parent's income from Line E or Line F:** _____

28   **Y. Self-support reserve:** _____

29   **Z. SUBTRACT Line Y from Line X:** _____

If Line Z is more than $600 per year, then Line Z is the amount of basic child support. If Line Z is less than $600 per year, then basic child support must be a minimum of $600 per year. The defendant may attempt to show that he/she cannot pay the minimum amount.

30   **STEP 11** NON-NUMERICAL FACTORS

(a) NON-RECURRING INCOME [(e)]

A portion of non-recurring income, such as life insurance proceeds, gifts and inheritances or lottery winnings, may be allocated to child support. The law does not mention a specific percentage for such non-recurring income. Such support is not modified by the low income exemptions. Enter any relevant information:

(b) EDUCATIONAL EXPENSES [(c)(7)]

New York's child support law does not contain a specific percentage method to determine how parents should share the cost of education of their children. Traditionally, the courts have considered both parents' complete financial circumstances in deciding who pays how much. The most important elements of financial circumstances are income, reasonable expenses, and financial resources such as savings and investments. Enter any relevant information:

(c) ADDITIONAL FACTORS [(f)]

Section 240(1-b) of the Domestic Relations Law lists 10 factors that should be considered in deciding on the amount of child support for (i) combined incomes of more than $80,000 per year or (ii) to vary the numerical result of these steps because the result is "unjust or inappropriate."

(Form UD-8)

EXHIBIT 8–2 Continued

These factors are:

1. The financial resources of the parents and the child.
2. The physical and emotional health of the child and his/her special needs and aptitudes.
3. The standard of living the child would have enjoyed if the marriage or household was not dissolved.
4. The tax consequences to the parents.
5. The non-monetary contributions the parents will make toward the care and well-being of the child.
6. The educational needs of the parents.
7. The fact that the gross income of one parent is substantially less than the gross income of the other parent.
8. The needs of the other children of the noncustodial parent for whom the noncustodial parent is providing support, but only (a) if Line 22 is not deducted; (b) after considering the financial resources of any other person obligated to support the other children; and (c) if the resources available to support the other children are less then the resources available to support the children involved in this matter.
9. If a child is not on public assistance, the amount of extraordinary costs of visitation (such as out-of-state travel) or extended visits (other than the usual two to four week summer visits), but only if the custodial parent's expenses are substantially reduced by the visitation involved.
10. Any other factor the court decides is relevant.

Enter any relevant information:_____

_____

_____

NON-JUDICIAL DETERMINATION OF CHILD SUPPORT [(h)]

Outside of court, parents are free to agree to any amount of support, so long as they sign a statement that they have been advised of the provisions of Section 240(1-b) of the Domestic Relations Law. However, the court cannot approve agreements of less than $300 per year. This minimum is not per child, meaning that the minimum for three (3) children is $300 per year, not $900 per year. In addition, the courts retain discretion over awards of child support.

The foregoing have been carefully read by the undersigned, who states that they are true and correct.

31

                              _____
                              Plaintiff

(Form UD-8)

EXHIBIT 8–2 Continued

STATE OF NEW YORK, COUNTY OF _____, ss.:

32   I, _____, being duly sworn, depose and say that: I am the Plaintiff in this action; I have read this Child Support Worksheet and I know its contents; they are true to my own knowledge, except as to the matters stated to be upon information and belief, and as to those I believe them to be true.

                                        _____

                                        Plaintiff

Sworn to before me on
_____, 19___

(Form UD-8)

END-OF-CHAPTER EXERCISES

Crossword Puzzle

Across

3. a motion filed when a parent fails to pay his or her child support obligations

4. a document empowering a sheriff to arrest the noncustodial parent

6. statutorily enacted formulas to determine the amount the noncustodial parent must pay for the support of each child

8. amount of past-due child support

Down

1. Uniform Interstate Family Support Act

2. a departure from the child support guidelines

5. a commission that drafts model child support enforcement acts

4. Uniform Reciprocal Enforcement of Support Act

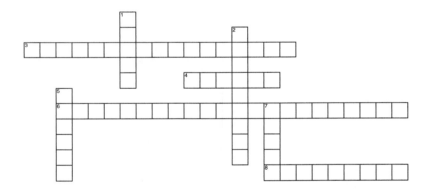

Review Questions

1. What are child support guidelines?

2. What is meant by deviation from the child support guidelines?

3. Under what circumstances may a child support order be modified?

4. What is the Uniform Interstate Family Support Act? How does this act differ from the Uniform Reciprocal Enforcement of Support Act in the type of remedies it provides?

5. What is postmajority child support?

Case for Briefing

BURSE V. BURSE, 48 Ohio App. 2d 244, 356 N.E.2d 755 (1976)

Exploring the Workplace: Activities

1. Research your state's child support guidelines at **http://www.supportguidelines.com/ links.html** and prepare a one-page summary on the highlights of your state law.

2. Using the Internet as your guide, find your state's child support guidelines and list the deviation criteria available in your jurisdiction.

3. You work as a paralegal in your state for the Law Office of Colton & Cuello. Your client, Alba Rivera, is currently receiving child support for her two minor sons from her former husband, Carlos. She plans on remarrying within the next few months and wants to know what effect, if any, her remarriage will have on her child support payments. Ms. Rivera plans on quitting her full-time job as a receptionist once she is married. Her fiancé is quite well off and has stated to her that she no longer has to work if she chooses not to. Draft an interoffice memo directed to your supervisor, Sandra Colton, regarding the effect of a new spouse's income on child support.

4. Using the Internet, find the computer software programs used in your jurisdiction to calculate the amount of child support due under your state's guidelines. (e.g., What is the software program called? Are classes or online tutorials available for training legal professionals in how to use the software?)

5. Using the Internet, find the agency in your state responsible for enforcing child support orders. What is the name of this agency and what services are available for custodial parents who wish to enforce a child support order against a noncustodial parent who has left the state?

6. Using the Internet, research the law in your state regarding postmajority support. How does your state deal with the issue?

CHAPTER

9

Initial and Responsive Pleadings

KEY TERMS

abode service

affidavit

affidavit of publication

answer

appearance

application for a
prejudgment remedy

body

caption

complaint

contempt

court-entry fee

cross-complaint

default judgment

defendant

defendant spouse

dissipation

domicile

filing fee

in personam jurisdiction

in rem jurisdiction

juris number

jurisdiction

motion for disclosure
of assets

notice to appear for a
deposition to disclose assets

order to show cause

pendente lite motion

personal service

petition

petitioner

plaintiff

plaintiff spouse

pleading

prayer for relief

pre-return date relief

request for an order
attaching known assets

residency   subject matter jurisdiction

respondent   subscription

return date   summons

rules of court   temporary restraining order

service by publication   venue

service of process   verification

sheriff's return

Following the client interview and the signing of the retainer letter, the supervising attorney on the file will delegate to an appropriate staff member the responsibility of preparing the documents that must be filed with the court to initiate the divorce proceeding or other desired family-related suit.

PROCESSING THE DISSOLUTION ACTION

Every jurisdiction has its own rules for the processing of a dissolution or divorce action. The paralegal must become thoroughly familiar with the jurisdictional procedural rules that govern the preparation and filing of dissolution documents, including the prescribed format for these papers as well as the time frames specified for initiating and responding to each document. This information can be found in the jurisdiction's official publications containing the procedural rules of the jurisdiction, commonly known as the **rules of court.** Additional or supplemental information can also frequently be found in the state's official statutory code.

A dissolution is a civil action. As with all civil lawsuits, the action is commenced when the opposing party is served with a document known as either the **complaint** or the **petition.** Whether this document is called a complaint or a petition depends on the jurisdiction's preference for one term or the other. In the state of Connecticut, the initial document in a family action is called the complaint, whereas in New York the same document is called a petition. In jurisdictions where the term *complaint* is used, the party commencing the action is called the **plaintiff** and the party against whom the action is brought is called the **defendant.** In jurisdictions where the term *petition* is used, the commencing party is called the **petitioner** and the party against whom the action is being brought is called the **respondent.**

DIVORCE JURISDICTION

The term **jurisdiction** is used to describe the court's control or power over a specific geographic territory. It also refers to the power of the courts to hear and resolve a dispute. State courts have jurisdiction or the power to hear and resolve divorce cases. Three types of jurisdictional issues are relevant to divorce cases: subject matter, in personam, and in rem.

SUBJECT MATTER JURISDICTION

When representing the plaintiff spouse, the first step in the divorce process is to determine whether the client meets the state's residency requirements. This will give the state court **subject matter jurisdiction** over the divorce. This is the court's power to actually hear a divorce case. If the state does not have subject matter jurisdiction over the divorce, any orders entered dissolving the marriage, as well as any other issues, will be void. In Connecticut, for example, either spouse must fulfill one of the statutory **residency** requirements for a Connecticut court to have jurisdiction over the case. The term *residency* refers to the **domicile** of the parties. *Domicile* is defined as residing in a state with the intent to permanently remain. The court has jurisdiction to hear the divorce case as long as one of the spouses meets the residency requirements. Residency requirements vary from state to state, so it is important for paralegals to become familiar with their state's laws.

Connecticut General Statutes Section 46b-44 Residency Requirement

(a) A complaint for dissolution of a marriage or for legal separation may be filed at any time after either party has established residence in this state.

(b) Temporary relief pursuant to the complaint may be granted in accordance with sections 46b-56 and 46b-83 at any time after either party has established residence in this state.

(c) A decree dissolving a marriage or granting a legal separation may be entered if: (1) One of the parties to the marriage has been a resident of this state for at least the twelve months next preceding the date of the filing of the complaint or next preceding the date of the decree; or (2) one of the parties was domiciled in this state at the time of the marriage and returned to this state with the intention of permanently remaining before the filing of the complaint; or (3) the cause for the dissolution of the marriage arose after either party moved into this state.

(d) For the purposes of this section, any person who has served or is serving with the armed forces, as defined by section 27-103, or the merchant marine, and who was a resident of this state at the time of his or her entry shall be deemed to have continuously resided in this state during the time he or she has served or is serving with the armed forces or merchant marine.

IN PERSONAM JURISDICTION/RESIDENT DEFENDANT

All jurisdictions require that the defendant to a divorce action, even if he or she is not in the state, be given notice of the proceedings by service of the pleadings and an opportunity to be heard. **In personam jurisdiction** means that once the defendant is served with the initial pleadings, the court may enter orders and enforce judgments against that individual. In personam jurisdiction is obtained by **service of process** on the defendant.

Typically, service of process, or formal delivery of the initial pleadings, is easy when the defendant resides in the state. The initial pleadings are served on the defendant by a sheriff, marshal, process server, constable, or indifferent person. Service of process may be obtained by serving the defendant in hand. This is called **personal service.** The defendant may also be served by **abode service,** which means leaving a copy of the pleadings at his or her home. If the plaintiff does not know the defendant's current address, but the last known address is in the same state where the plaintiff resides, the plaintiff may seek permission from the court to serve the defendant through **service by publication.** Service by publication is accomplished by publishing a legal notice in a newspaper circulated in the city or town of the defendant's last known address, informing the defendant of the proceedings. Once the court has in personam jurisdiction over the defendant, the judge may enter orders on alimony, child support, and property distribution, which may be enforced against the defendant. If it is determined that the defendant spouse was not properly served, the court may not have jurisdiction and any orders entered may be subject to jurisdictional attack by the defendant's legal counsel.

In Personam Jurisdiction/Nonresident Defendant

When the defendant spouse resides out of state, state procedural rules must be followed for the court to obtain in personam jurisdiction over a nonresident defendant. In personam jurisdiction is necessary for the court to enter orders against a nonresident defendant. If the plaintiff knows where the nonresident defendant lives, the plaintiff may have to obtain permission from the court to serve the defendant at his or her residence in accordance with the laws of that particular jurisdiction. Service of process over a nonresident defendant may take the form of actual in-hand service of process in another state by an authorized person or through certified or registered mail. Service by registered and certified mail can present problems if the nonresident defendant does not sign for the documents or fails to enter an appearance in the divorce case. Under this scenario, the court may have limited power to enter certain orders against a nonresident defendant. Once the defendant files an appearance in the case, the court has in personam jurisdiction over that individual. In either case, obtaining actual notice is crucial to enable the court in the plaintiff's state to exercise jurisdiction and enter orders against the nonresident defendant. If the plaintiff does not have an address for a nonresident defendant but knows the jurisdiction of his or her last known address, the defendant may receive notice by service through publication.

Proper Venue

Once the residency requirement is fulfilled, the next step is to choose the proper divorce court within the state in which to file the initial pleadings. This is known as the proper **venue.** There may be a number of divorce courts situated in any given counties or districts within a state. Generally, the proper venue in which to file an action is the county district where either one of the spouses resides. If both live in the same district, there is no problem. If both reside in separate districts, then it is a "race to the courthouse." If an improper venue is chosen—for instance, the district where the plaintiff is employed—as a matter of convenience, the defendant may move to dismiss the divorce action on the basis of improper venue.

In Rem Jurisdiction

Another type of jurisdiction commonly encountered in divorce cases is **in rem jurisdiction.** In rem jurisdiction is the power of the courts to actually dissolve the marriage. In order for the state court to have in rem jurisdiction, either one of the spouses must be domiciled in that jurisdiction. Lack of in rem jurisdiction prohibits a court from dissolving the marriage.

It is important to note that in personam jurisdiction is not needed for the plaintiff to obtain a divorce. As long as the court has in rem jurisdiction, it has the authority to dissolve the marriage. The court, however, must have in personam jurisdiction over the defendant in order to enter financial orders such as alimony, property distribution, child custody and support, and visitation.

INITIAL PLEADINGS IN A DISSOLUTION ACTION

THE PLEADINGS

The documents that state the plaintiff's claims giving rise to the dissolution action and the defendant's responses or defenses to such claims are documents known as **pleadings.** The pleadings in any litigation matter include a *summons* and *complaint* or *petition;* and an *answer, special defenses, counterclaims,* and *cross-claims.*

THE COMPLAINT

The initial pleading filed in a dissolution matter is the *complaint.* As mentioned, sometimes the initial pleading is called the *petition.* However, because the more commonly used term is *complaint,* that term will be used here. A document known as a **summons** usually accompanies the complaint. In most jurisdictions, the summons is a one-page preprinted form on which the names and addresses of parties and the name and address of the court are inserted (see Exhibit 9–1). The summons directs the defendant to appear in court and answer the allegations in the complaint. The spouse bringing the dissolution of marriage action is designated as the **plaintiff spouse.** The spouse against whom the dissolution proceeding is brought is designated as the **defendant spouse.** The plaintiff spouse will initiate the legal proceeding.

The law firm representing the plaintiff spouse will file the pleading known as the complaint. In this document, the plaintiff spouse will allege that grounds exist for a divorce, recite these grounds, and request that the court grant a divorce and enter orders regarding the distribution of marital property and, when appropriate, orders relating to child custody, alimony, and child support and orders addressing any other form of relief the spouse has requested.

FORM OF THE DISSOLUTION COMPLAINT

A dissolution or divorce complaint has distinct sections. They are the *caption,* the *body,* the *prayer,* and the *subscription* (some jurisdictions also require a *verification*).

THE CAPTION

The **caption** refers to the initial section of the complaint, which contains the names of the parties, the name and division of the court, the return date of the action, and the date the complaint was drawn up. The **return date** is a date in the near future by which the complaint must be returned to the court clerk's office and filed with the court, along with a check for whatever filing fee the jurisdiction requires to process the complaint. A heading is also included to indicate that the document being drafted is a "complaint."

RETURN DATE: August 15, 2005	:	SUPERIOR COURT
RODNEY BRONSON	:	JUDICIAL DISTRICT OF NEW HAVEN
v.	:	AT NEW HAVEN
EVELYN BRONSON	:	July 15, 2005

THE BODY

The **body** of the complaint contains the necessary factual information that establishes the jurisdiction of the court and identifies the grounds on which the divorce is being sought. In addition, other mandatory information in the body of the complaint includes the names and addresses of the parties, their date and place of marriage, and the names of all minor children born during the period of the marriage.

Complaint

1. The parties intermarried on March 28, 1996, at Woodbridge, Connecticut.
2. The wife's maiden name was EVELYN CONNER.
3. One of the parties has resided in the state of Connecticut for at least twelve months preceding the filing of the complaint.
4. The marriage of the parties has broken down irretrievably and there is no hope of reconciliation.
5. The parties have two minor children born issue of this marriage:
   Marlise Bronson   D.O.B. June 7, 1997
   Sydney Bronson   D.O.B. August 6, 1998
6. No other minor children have been born to the wife since the date of the marriage.
7. Neither party has been the recipient of any form of public assistance.

PRAYER FOR RELIEF

The **prayer for relief** section of the complaint contains the plaintiff's request for a dissolution and for court orders, when appropriate, regarding property distribution, alimony, child custody, support of the minor children, and the wife's request for restoration of her maiden name. Certain jurisdictions require very specific detail regarding the nature and extent of relief sought while others require a more general statement. In either case, however, it is always a good idea to include a "catc hall" phrase such as "and such other relief as the court deems fair and equitable."

WHEREFORE, the plaintiff claims,

1. A dissolution of marriage

2. Custody of the minor children

3. Child support

4. Alimony

5. An equitable distribution of the marital assets, debts, and liabilities

6. Attorney's fees

7. Such other relief as the court deems fair and equitable.

THE SUBSCRIPTION AND VERIFICATION

The **subscription** and/or **verification** section of the complaint is included to confirm the truth and accuracy of the allegations and to confirm the veracity of the party making these allegations. The subscription contains the signature of the attorney filing the complaint, along with the attorney's address, phone number, and license number, known in some jurisdictions as the **juris number.** When an attorney signs a complaint, the attorney is representing or *subscribing* that to the best of the attorney's knowledge, the facts contained within are true and accurate. In some jurisdictions, the plaintiff bringing the action is also required to sign the complaint and to attest to its veracity. In these instances, the plaintiff will sign a sworn statement, under oath, that the facts contained in the allegations are true. By so doing, the plaintiff is that the information is accurate and true. Hence the plaintiff's swearing and signing is termed the verification. A verified complaint used in the state of New York is illustrated in Exhibit 9–2.

THE PLAINTIFF,
RODNEY BRONSON

BY:_____
    Justine F. Miller, Esq.
    His Attorney
    22 Park Place
    New Haven, CT 06511
    (203) 555-4444
    Juries No. 313133

Exhibit 9–3 includes the complaint for dissolution of marriage filed by Lucille Ball against Desi Arnaz on March 3, 1960, in Los Angeles, California.

PREPRINTED COMPLAINT FORM

The computer age has revolutionized the court record-keeping system. Entire court case files are now being kept on disk. This phenomenon has given rise to the creation and use of many preprinted forms in lieu of manuscripted or individually drafted documents. Many jurisdictions are beginning to require that attorneys fit their pleading information into blank portions of uniform preprinted forms that can easily be scanned into the computerized case files in the courthouse. Therefore, the complaint, which is computer compatible now, will contain all of the sections just listed, but these sections will be compressed into the sections of the preprinted complaint form. An example of a preprinted form appears in Exhibit 9–4, which illustrates a complaint for dissolution of marriage in the case of actor Kevin Costner and his former wife Cynthia.

PRE-RETURN DATE RELIEF

Sometimes, a plaintiff spouse needs and may seek immediate relief or court intervention known as **pre-return date relief.** The plaintiff spouse may have serious and real concerns that the act of serving the dissolution complaint on the defendant spouse may cause the defendant spouse to take certain immediate initiatives that will either damage the plaintiff spouse economically or harm the plaintiff physically and/or emotionally.

For instance, when the plaintiff spouse serves a dissolution complaint in which that spouse seeks, as part of the dissolution action, a division of the marital assets and/or alimony and child support, the defendant spouse may attempt to move, hide, or dispose of assets that would be considered assets of the marital union to avoid having to share them or "split" their value with the plaintiff spouse.

There may also be assets acquired during the marriage where title rests completely with one partner or the other. For example, title to each family car will usually be in the name of only one spouse. In many jurisdictions, inheritances bequeathed to one spouse or gifts given solely to one spouse are not marital assets. However, practically every other possession acquired during the marriage is a joint asset. The plaintiff spouse may have concerns that the defendant spouse will dispose of bona fide joint property that is not legally registered to both parties. For instance, the defendant spouse may sell an expensive car purchased with marital funds and pocket or bury the money. The defendant spouse who has equal signing power or a joint checking account, joint savings account, joint CD certificates, or joint stock accounts may attempt to withdraw the contents of these accounts upon being served with divorce papers. To avoid this **dissipation** or squandering of assets, the plaintiff spouse may file along with the dissolution complaint an **application for a prejudgment remedy** to attach marital assets during the period pending litigation.

In many jurisdictions, a plaintiff spouse may apply for an attachment of known joint assets. Sometimes the court will grant a temporary attachment until there is a hearing on the matter; at other times the hearing must occur before even a temporary or *pendente lite* order is issued.

Sometimes a defendant spouse owns a business that the plaintiff spouse has had little hands-on involvement with, and hence the plaintiff spouse does not know the actual value of the business. The plaintiff spouse may also serve on the defendant, along with a **request for an order attaching known assets,** a **motion for disclosure of assets** to be made under oath. If the plaintiff is not satisfied with the disclosure, later in the discovery phase of the dissolution suit, the plaintiff may serve the defendant with a **notice to appear for a deposition to disclose assets.** In this deposition, the defendant spouse will be questioned, under oath, on the previous disclosure to determine whether it completely reveals all of the defendant's assets.

The format, language, and other requirements for drafting attachment documents vary from jurisdiction to jurisdiction. A paralegal must check local court rules to ensure that the proper format is complied with. Sometimes the local rules or the local practice book has an annotated edition that contains sample forms. Otherwise, litigation form books may be available for the particular state family court system where the action is to be filed. These form books will enable the paralegal to tailor the documents to fit the jurisdiction.

TEMPORARY RESTRAINING ORDER

Sometimes when a plaintiff spouse has decided to file a dissolution action, the plaintiff spouse fears that notice of this action will trigger a response in the defendant spouse that includes being physically and verbally abusive to the plaintiff and possibly to the children as well. A plaintiff spouse may be afraid to return to the family home while the defendant continues to reside there.

Under these circumstances, if the fear is justified, the plaintiff may seek pre-return date relief in the form of a court-ordered **temporary restraining order** to restrain the defendant spouse from entering the family home for a significant number of days. In the application for such a restraining order, the plaintiff spouse will include a signed, sworn statement known as an **affidavit** that certain prior events have occurred and support the plaintiff spouse's belief that a restraining order is needed to keep the spouse safe from grave harm the defendant would otherwise inflict. A set of specific legal documents must be filed with the court in order for the court to consider the plaintiff's request for a restraining order. A paralegal must know what documents are included in this set and be especially careful to include everything needed and to make sure each document is factually and procedurally correct.

Exhibit 9–5 contains a sample set of documents for requesting a temporary restraining order. In addition, Appendix E includes a sample restraining order and affidavit filed by comedienne Roseanne against her former husband Tom Arnold. Again, students should seek model documents from their own jurisdictions to ensure procedural compliance.

SERVICE OF PROCESS OF THE DIVORCE COMPLAINT

Once the law office has prepared the divorce or dissolution summons and complaint, the paralegal may be responsible for seeing that these documents are properly served on the defendant. In most jurisdictions, the divorce complaint, just like the complaint in a regular civil lawsuit, must be served on the defendant named in the action by a statutorily authorized process server.

A paralegal will contact the office of the sheriff or process server to confirm that the person is available and willing to handle the matter. The paralegal will mail or hand-deliver the papers to be served, or the sheriff, constable, or process server will come to the law office and pick up the papers. If the case involves service on a nonresident defendant or an in-state defendant whose whereabouts are unknown, the paralegal may have to prepare motions to seek a court order to serve such persons through certified mail on publication.

The process server must locate the party to be served and complete service either by delivering the true and attested copies of the initial pleadings. Once service is completed, the sheriff or process server will mail or hand-deliver to the law office the original of the summons and complaint along with his written **sheriff's return** in which he affirms that on a specified date, he served the defendant by leaving with the defendant in his hands, at his abode or by mail, a true and attested copy of the summons and complaint. Exhibit 9–6 illustrates California's Proof of Service of Summons in the Costner divorce. The sheriff's or server's bill for services rendered normally accompanies the return.

After the sheriff or process server returns the summons and complaint to the law office, these documents must be brought to the court and filed, along with a fee, known in most jurisdictions as a **filing fee** or a **court-entry fee.** In addition, an increasing number of jurisdictions now require that accompanying documents be filed at the same time as the complaint. These accompanying documents may include a financial affidavit, a custody affidavit, and stipulations regarding the irretrievable breakdown of the marriage.

Once a complaint has been filed, the clerk will assign the case a docket number. This number will be used on all further communications from the court. In addition, the parties should now replace the return date category with the case number in the caption section of all future documents filed with the court in this matter.

RESPONSIVE PLEADINGS TO THE DISSOLUTION COMPLAINT

When a spouse is served with divorce or dissolution papers, the spouse must decide what type of responsive action to take or whether to respond at all. The dissolution summons will command the defendant spouse to appear before the court on or before a certain date, and to do so not by appearing in person, but by filing a written appearance form or by having the defendant spouse's attorney file a written **appearance** on his or her behalf.

If the defendant spouse fails to file an appearance, depending on the court rules of the particular jurisdiction, the judicial system will handle this failure in one of two or three different ways. In many states, the defendant spouse's failure to file an appearance can result ultimately in a **default judgment** being entered against that person. This means that the plaintiff spouse will "win" the dissolution or divorce suit by default; that is, the plaintiff spouse will be granted a divorce. In addition, if the court has personal jurisdiction over the defendant spouse, the court, even in the absence of the defendant, may order both spousal support and child support. In this event, the defendant will be notified by mail of the court's orders. If the defendant does not make the court-ordered payments and is still within the jurisdiction, the plaintiff spouse may serve the defendant with additional legal papers. These papers, often collectively called an **order to show cause,** will require the defendant to appear under penalty of civil arrest and to show cause or offer a good reason why the defendant should not be penalized or held in **contempt** for not making the courtordered payments. In this instance, if the defendant spouse again fails to appear in court, the court may and usually will order a *capias,* which is actually an arrest warrant for committing a civil violation, in this case, a violation of a court order.

If a plaintiff spouse seeks a divorce from a spouse who has fled the jurisdiction or who may still be in the jurisdiction but is "whereabouts unknown" as far as a place of abode or place of employment, then the plaintiff spouse may have a sheriff or process server serve the defendant by publication. The sheriff will put a legal notice in the legal notices section of a newspaper in the city, town, or general area where the defendant was last known to reside or where the defendant is thought to be residing. This legal notice will, in fact, be a printing of the test of the divorce or dissolution complaint. Once the notice is published and the newspaper sends the sheriff its **affidavit of publication**, the sheriff will make a return noting the service by publication and return the complaint to the law firm for filing in court. Under these circumstances, after the appropriate waiting period, the plaintiff may seek to have the court formally dissolve the marriage. The plaintiff will appear on a certain date; the court will note that the defendant, served by publication, has failed to appear. The defendant spouse will be defaulted and the divorce or dissolution will be granted. However, the court will not have the authority to enter orders for alimony or child support because the court has no personal jurisdiction over the defendant spouse.

The case of the nonappearing spouse is the exception rather than the rule. Most often, the defendant spouse obtains the services of an attorney who files a written appearance on behalf of the defendant spouse, and who also files responsive pleadings to the dissolution complaint. Naturally, the defendant spouse must contact an attorney or a law firm and have an initial interview with the attorney or firm's officer. The client interview of the defendant spouse will proceed in a manner that is similar to the interview process described for the plaintiff spouse in Chapter 3. If an agreement is reached regarding representation, the defendant spouse will sign a retainer letter with the law office, pay a retainer fee, and the office will begin to draft the responsive pleadings. This task will be delegated to the family law paralegal.

THE APPEARANCE AND THE ANSWER

As mentioned, the attorney or firm representing the defendant spouse must file an appearance. This appearance is a one-page form that lists the name of the case, the return date, the name of the party being represented, the fact that the party is the defendant in the action, and the name, address, phone number, and juris number of the attorney or law firm. A sample of a typical appearance form is provided in Exhibit 9–7.

The next document to be filed is the **answer.** The answer, like the complaint, will have a caption containing the name of the case and the return date. It will also have a body where each of the allegations contained in the numbered paragraphs in the complaint is responded to. The defendant spouse will either admit or deny each allegation or, in appropriate instances, will state that he or she lacks the necessary information or knowledge on which to form a response. Exhibit 9–8 illustrates a preprinted answer form.

The next section of the answer is the prayer section. In this section, the defendant spouse will make known his or her requests regarding alimony, child support, child custody, and/or visitation. For instance, a defendant spouse may admit that the marriage has broken down irretrievably in the response to the allegations section. However, in the prayer section, the defendant may signal his or her opposition to the plaintiff spouse's requests by requesting full custody of the minor child or children and by requesting child support and alimony. On the other hand, if the defendant spouse does not object to the plaintiff spouse's request for custody, the defendant spouse will request reasonable visitation rights. If the defendant spouse does not wish any alimony, the defendant will remain silent on this issue and deal with the question of the plaintiff spouse's requests for alimony and child support at a later time in the proceedings. The defendant spouse should always request an equitable division of marital property and should request such other relief as the court deems fair and equitable.

The answer, like the complaint, has a subscription section, which lists the defendant spouse's attorney's name and other identifying information. In some jurisdictions, the defendant spouse, like the plaintiff spouse in the complaint, may have to provide a signed and sworn-to verification of the answer.

THE CROSS-COMPLAINT

In most jurisdictions, the defendant-spouse has the right to file an additional pleading called a **cross-complaint.** In the cross-complaint, the defendant spouse assumes the role of a plaintiff by bringing a cross-action or countersuit for dissolution in which the party makes allegations and asks the court to grant him or her the relief of a dissolution or divorce and orders regarding custody, child support, alimony, and property division. Since the advent of no-fault divorce and the fault-neutral ground of irretrievable marital breakdown, cross-complaints have been rarities. Previously, when divorces were granted only on allegation and proof of a fault-based ground or grounds, the spouse sued for divorce on the grounds of mental cruelty or adultery or another negative ground and was frequently countersued by his or her spouse, who alleged a ground of equally negative conduct. This practice has virtually disappeared except in instances where the divorce is very bitter and where either the marital property is extensive or where the custody of the children is hotly contested. A sample cross-complaint appears in Exhibit 9–9. This form serves the purpose for both complaints and cross-complaints in that it contains virtually the same information. If a cross-complaint is filed, then the original plaintiff spouse must file an answer to this pleading that responds to all allegations and contains its own request for relief.

Once all of the previously mentioned documents have been filed with the court, the pleadings are closed, and the pleading phase of the dissolution process is over. Even if the parties have no areas of disagreement, there will be a statutory waiting period before the divorce is granted. In the meantime, whether the parties are in agreement or not, there will be hearings to provide for temporary relief to the parties while the divorce is pending. During this pendency period, the court will entertain motions regarding alimony, child support, child custody, and other pertinent issues. These motions are known as *pendente lite* **motions** and are discussed in the next chapter.

EXHIBIT 9–1 Sample summons.

1   **SUPREME COURT OF THE STATE OF NEW YORK**   Index No.:_____
2 3   **COUNTY OF** _____   Date Summons filed:_____
4   --X   Plaintiff designates _____
5   County as the place of trial
                                                            The basis of venue is:
6   _____
                                    Plaintiff,
                -against-   **SUMMONS WITH NOTICE**
                                                            Plaintiff/Defendant resides at:
7   _____
8   _____
                                    Defendant.   _____
        --X

ACTION FOR A DIVORCE

To the above named Defendant:

9   **YOU ARE HEREBY SUMMONED** to serve a notice of appearance on the ❏ *Plaintiff*
OR ❏ *Plaintiff's Attorney(s)* within twenty (20) days after the service of this summons, exclusive
of the day of service (or within thirty (30) days after the service is complete if this summons is not
personally delivered to you within the State of New York); and in case of your failure to appear,
judgment will be taken against you by default for the relief demanded in the notice set forth below.

10, 11 Dated _____   ❏ *Plaintiff*
                                                       ❏ *Attorney(s) for Plaintiff*
12   Address:

                                                       Phone No.:

13   **NOTICE:**   The nature of this action is to dissolve the marriage between the parties, on the
                       grounds: **DRL §170 subd._____ - _____
                                                        _____

        The relief sought is a judgment of absolute divorce in favor of the Plaintiff dissolving the marriage
        between the parties in this action. The nature of any ancillary or additional relief demanded is:
14   _____
        _____
        _____
        _____
        _____

        **Insert the grounds for the divorce:
        DRL §170(1) - cruel and inhuman treatment   DRL §170(4) - adultery
        DRL §170(2) - abandonment   DRL §170(5) - living apart one year after separation decree or judgment of separation
        DRL §170(3) - confinement in prison   DRL §170(6) - living apart one year after execution of a separation agreement

(Form UD-1 - Rev. 5/99)

EXHIBIT 9–2 Sample of a verified complaint.

1

SUPREME COURT OF THE STATE OF NEW YORK
COUNTY OF _____

--X

23

                      Plaintiff,

    -against-

Index No.:

VERIFIED COMPLAINT

ACTION FOR DIVORCE

4

                     Defendant.

--X

5   **FIRST:**

Plaintiff *herein / by* _____, complaining of the Defendant, alleges that the parties are over the age of 18 years and;

6   **SECOND:**

❑ The Plaintiff has resided in New York State for a continuous period in excess of two years immediately preceding the commencement of this action.
                          OR
❑ The Defendant has resided in New York State for a continuous period in excess of two years immediately preceding the commencement of this action.
                          OR
❑ The Plaintiff has resided in New York State for a continuous period in excess of one year immediately preceding the commencement of this action, and:

    a. ❑ the parties were married in New York State.
    b. ❑ the Plaintiff has lived as husband or wife in New York State with the Defendant.
    c. ❑ the cause of action occurred in New York State.
                          OR
❑ The Defendant has resided in New York State for a continuous period in excess of one year immediately preceding the commencement of this action, and:

    a. ❑ the parties were married in New York State.
    b. ❑ the Defendant has lived as husband or wife in New York State with the Plaintiff.
    c. ❑ the cause of action occurred in New York State.
                          OR
❑ The cause of action occurred in New York State and both parties were residents thereof at the time of the commencement of this action.

7   **THIRD:** The Plaintiff and the Defendant were married on _____ in (city, town or village; and state or country) _____.

EXHIBIT 9–2 Continued

8   The marriage was   *not*   performed by a clergyman, minister or by a leader of the Society for Ethical Culture.

(If the word "not" is deleted above check the appropriate box below).

❑   *To the best of my knowledge I have taken all steps solely within my power to remove any barrier to the Defendant's remarriage.*   **OR**

❑   *I will take prior to the entry of final judgment all steps solely within my power to the best of my knowledge to remove any barrier to the Defendant's remarriage.*   **OR**

❑   *The Defendant has waived in writing the requirements of DRL §253 (Barriers to Remarriage).*

9   **FOURTH:**   ❑ There are no children of the marriage.   **OR**

            ❑ There *is (are)* _____ child(ren) of the marriage, namely:

<u>Name</u>	<u>Date of Birth</u>	<u>Address</u>
_____	_____	_____
_____	_____	_____
_____	_____	_____
_____	_____	_____
_____	_____	_____

10   The Plaintiff resides at _____ .

The Defendant resides at _____ .

11   The parties are covered by the following group health plans:

<u>Plaintiff</u>   **<u>Defendant</u>**

Group Health Plan:_____   Group Health Plan:_____
Address:_____   Address:_____
Identification Number:_____   Identification Number:_____
Plan Administrator:_____   Plan Administrator:_____
Type of Coverage:_____   Type of Coverage:_____

12   **FIFTH:**   The grounds for divorce that are alleged as follows:

<u>Cruel and Inhuman Treatment (DRL §170(1))</u>:

❑   At the following times, none of which are earlier than (5) years prior to commencement of this action, the Defendant engaged in conduct that so endangered the mental and physical well-being of the Plaintiff, so as to render it unsafe or improper for the parties to cohabit (live together) as husband and wife.

       (State the facts that demonstrate cruel and inhuman conduct giving dates, places and specific acts. Conduct may include physical, verbal, sexual or emotional behavior.)

_____
_____
_____
_____

EXHIBIT 9–2 Continued

_____
_____
_____
_____

(Attach an additional sheet, if necessary).

Abandonment (DRL 170(2)):

❑   That commencing on or about _____, and continuing for a period of more than one (1) year immediately prior to commencement of this action, the Defendant left the marital residence of the parties located at _____, and did not return. Such absence was without cause or justification, and was without Plaintiff's consent.

❑   That commencing on or about _____, and continuing for a period of more than one (1) year immediately prior to commencement of this action, the Defendant refused to have sexual relations with the Plaintiff despite Plaintiff's repeated requests to resume such relations. Defendant does not suffer from any disability which would prevent   _her / him_   from engaging in such sexual relations with Plaintiff. The refusal to engage in sexual relations was without good cause or justification and occurred at the marital residence located at _____.

❑   That commencing on or about _____, and continuing for a period of more than one (1) year immediately prior to commencement of this action, the Defendant willfully and without cause or justification abandoned the Plaintiff, who had been a faithful and dutiful _husband / wife_ by depriving Plaintiff of access to the marital residence located at _____.
This deprivation of access was without the consent of the Plaintiff and continued for a period of greater than one year.

Confinement to Prison (DRL §170(3)):

❑   (a)   That after the marriage of Plaintiff and Defendant, Defendant was confined in prison for a period of three or more consecutive years, to wit: that Defendant was confined in _____ _____ prison on _____, and has remained confined to this date; and

   (b)   not more that five (5) years has elapsed between the end of the third year of imprisonment and the date of commencement of this action.

Adultery (DRL §170(4)):

❑   (a)   That on _____, at the premises located at _____, the Defendant engaged in sexual intercourse with _____, without the procurement nor the connivance of the Plaintiff, and the Plaintiff ceased to cohabit (live) with the Defendant upon the discovery of the adultery; and

   (b)   not more than five (5) years elapsed between the date of said adultery and the date of commencement of this action.

(Attach a corroborating affidavit of a third party witness or other additional proof).

EXHIBIT 9–2 Continued

<u>**Living Separate and Apart Pursuant to a Separation Decree or Judgment of Separation (DRL §170(5)):**</u>

❑　　(a)　　That the _____ Court, _____ County, _____ (Country or State) rendered a decree or judgment of separation on _____, under Index Number _____; and

　　　　(b)　　that the parties have lived separate and apart for a period of one year or longer after the granting of such decree; and

　　　　(c)　　that the Plaintiff has substantially complied with all the terms and conditions of such decree or judgment.

<u>**Living Separate and Apart Pursuant to a Separation Agreement (DRL §170(6)):**</u>

❑　　(a)　　That the Plaintiff and Defendant entered into a written agreement of separation, which they subscribed and acknowledged on _____, in the form required to entitle a deed to be recorded; and

　　　　(b)　　that the *agreement / memorandum of said agreement* was filed on _____ in the Office of the Clerk of the County of _____, wherein *Plaintiff / Defendant* resided; and

　　　　(c)　　that the parties have lived separate and apart for a period of one year or longer after the execution of said agreement; and

　　　　(d)　　that the Plaintiff has substantially complied with all terms and conditions of such agreement.

13　　**SIXTH:**　　There is no judgment in any court for a divorce and no other matrimonial action between the parties pending in this court or in any other court of competent jurisdiction.

14　　　　　　**WHEREFORE** , Plaintiff demands judgment against the Defendant as follows: A judgment dissolving the marriage between the parties and

❑　　_____

　　　_____

　　　_____

　　　_____

AND

❑　equitable distribution of marital property;

OR

❑　marital property to be distributed pursuant to the annexed separation agreement / stipulation;

OR

❑　I waive equitable distribution of marital property;

and any other relief the court deems fitting and proper.

15　　　　Dated:_____

16　　　　　　　　　　　　　　　　　　　　　　　❑　*Plaintiff*
　　　　　　　　　　　　　　　　　　　　　　　　❑　*Attorney(s) for Plaintiff*
　　　　　　　　　　　　　　　　　　　　　　　　　Address:

　　　　　　　　　　　　　　　　　　　　　　　　　Phone No.:

EXHIBIT 9–2 Continued

17   STATE OF NEW YORK, COUNTY OF _____ ss:

               I _____ (Print Name), am the Plaintiff in the within action for

a   divorce. I have read the foregoing complaint and know the contents thereof. The contents are true to my own knowledge except as to matters therein stated to be alleged upon information and belief, and as to those matters I believe them to be true.

Subscribed and Sworn to
before me on

_____

_____
                    Plaintiff's Signature

_____
    NOTARY PUBLIC

(Form UD-2 - Rev. 5/99)

EXHIBIT 9–3 Sample complaint for dissoltuion.

1 GANG, TYRE, RUDIN & BROWN
   6400 Sunset Building
2 Los Angeles 28, California
   HOllywood 3-4863
3
   Attorneys for Plaintiff
4

5

6

7

8   IN THE SUPERIOR COURT OF THE STATE OF CALIFORNIA

9   IN AND FOR THE COUNTY OF LOS ANGELES

10

11 LUCILLE BALL ARNAZ,

              Plaintiff,   SMD. No._____

12   COMPLAINT FOR DIVORCE
          -vs.-
13   (Extreme Cruelty)
    DESIDERIO ALBERTO ARNAZ, III,
14
              Defendant.
15 _____

16   Plaintiff complains of defendant and alleges:

17   I.

18   Plaintiff and defendant were intermarried in

19 Greenwich, Connecticut on November 30, 1940.

20   II.

21   Plaintiff alleges that she has been a resident of

22 the County of Los Angeles for more than three years, and of

23 the State of California for more than one year next preceding

24 the filing of this complaint.

25   III.

26   Plaintiff alleges the following facts as required

27 by Section 426(a) of the Code of Civil Procedure of the State

28 of California:

29   1. The parties were intermarried in Greenwich,

30 Connecticut.

31   2. The date of said marriage was November 30, 1940.

32   3. The date of separation was February 26, 1960.

318

EXHIBIT 9–3 Continued

1   4. The time elapsing between the date of marriage

2 and the date of separation is nineteen years and three months.

3   5. There are two children the issue of said

4 marriage, to-wit, Lucie Desiree Arnaz, age 8-1/2 years, and

5 Desiderio Alberto Arnaz, IV, age 7 years.

6   IV.

7   Defendant has been guilty of extreme cruelty to

8 plaintiff. As a direct result of such cruelty and conduct

9 of defendant, defendant has wrongfully inflicted grievous

10 mental suffering upon plaintiff.

11   V.

12   Plaintiff and defendant are owners of community

13 property and there is certain separate property owned by both

14 plaintiff and defendant. Plaintiff and defendant have ne-

15 gotiated, except in certain minor particulars, a Property

16 Settlement Agreement with respect to their property rights

17 and interests and their marital rights and obligations. If

18 said Property Settlement Agreement is executed by the parties

19 prior to the trial of the within action, plaintiff believes

20 the same will be fair, just and equitable and will submit the

21 same to the Court for approval.

22   VI.

23   Plaintiff is a fit and proper person to have the

24 care and custody of minor children of the parties, subject to

25 the right of reasonable visitation of said children by de-

26 fendant. The Property Settlement Agreement which the parties

27 have negotiated, as hereinabove alleged, will contain pro-

28 visions with respect to the support, maintenance and education

29 of said minor children which plaintiff believes will be fair,

30 just and reasonable, but which provisions shall be subject

31 to modification by further order of this Court.

32   WHEREFORE, plaintiff prays judgment as follows:

EXHIBIT 9–3 Continued

1.   That the bonds of matrimony now existing between plaintiff and defendant be dissolved.

2.   That the custody of said minor children be awarded to plaintiff, subject to the right of reasonable visitation by defendant.

3.   That the Property Settlement Agreement, to be executed by the parties prior to the trial of this action, be approved, confirmed and ratified by the Court and that the parties be ordered to comply with the executory terms and provisions of such agreement.

4.   That the defendant be directed to pay the plaintiff for the support, maintenance and education of the children of plaintiff and defendant such sum as the parties may agree upon in such Property Settlement Agreement, until further order of the Court.

5.   For such other and further relief as the Court may deem equitable in the premises.

GANG, TYRE, RUDIN & BROWN

By _____
Attorneys for Plaintiff

EXHIBIT 9–4 Sample preprinted from illustrating a complaint for dissolution of marriage.

ATTORNEY OR PARTY WITHOUT ATTORNEY *(Name and ...g Address):*	TELEPHONE NO.: (310) 477-5450	FOR COURT USE ONLY
GERALD L. FRIEDMAN PROFESSIONAL CORPORAT State Bar No. 033401 11400 W. Olympic Boulevard, Ninth Floor Los Angeles, California 90064-1565 ATTORNEY FOR *(Name):* PETITIONER		

ATTORNEY FOR *(Name):* PETITIONER

SUPERIOR COURT OF CALIFORNIA, COUNTY OF LOS ANGELES
STREET ADDRESS: 111 North Hill Street
MAILING ADDRESS: 111 North Hill Street
CITY AND ZIP CODE: Los Angeles, California 90012
BRANCH NAME: Central District

FILED
LOS ANGELES ... PT
NOV - 4 1994
EDWAHU m. ... K
BY G. MENDIZABAL, DEPUTY

MARRIAGE OF
PETITIONER: CYNTHIA R. COSTNER

RESPONDENT: KEVIN M. COSTNER

PETITION FOR
[X] Dissolution of Marriage   [X] And Declaration Under Uniform
[ ] Legal Separation   Child Custody Jurisdiction Act
[ ] Nullity of Marriage

CASE NUMBER:
BD203807

1. RESIDENCE (Dissolution only) [X] Petitioner   [ ] Respondent   has been a resident of this state for at least six months and of this county for at least three months immediately preceding the filing of this Petition for Dissolution of Marriage.

2. STATISTICAL FACTS
   a. Date of Marriage: February 11, 1978
   c. Period between marriage and separation
      Years: 16   Months: 4
   b. Date of Separation: June 23, 1994
   d. Petitioner's Social Security No.: To Be Furnished
   e. Respondent's Social Security No.: To Be Furnished

3. DECLARATION REGARDING MINOR CHILDREN OF THIS MARRIAGE FOR WHOM SUPPORT MAY BE ORDERED OR WHO MAY BE SUBJECT TO CUSTODY OR VISITATION ORDERS
   a. [ ] There are no minor children.   b. [X] The minor children are:

Child's name	Birthdate	Age	Sex
Anne C. Costner	4/15/84	10	F
Lily M. Costner	8/4/86	8	F
Joe T. Costner	1/31/88	6	M

   c. IF THERE ARE MINOR CHILDREN, COMPLETE EITHER (1) OR (2)
      (1) [X] Each child named in 3b is currently living with [X] petitioner [ ] respondent
          in the following county *(specify):*   Los Angeles
          During the last five years each child has lived in no state other than California and with no person other than petitioner or respondent or both. Petitioner has not participated in any capacity in any litigation or proceeding in any state concerning custody of any minor child of this marriage. Petitioner has no information of any pending custody proceeding or of any person not a party to this proceeding who has physical custody or claims to have custody or or visitation rights concerning any minor child of this marriage.
      (2) [ ] A completed Declaration Under Uniform Child Custody Jurisdiction Act is attached.

4. [X] Petitioner requests confirmation as separate assets and obligations the items listed
   [ ] in Attachment 4   [X] below:

Item	Confirm to
Per Agreement of the parties	Each of the parties

(Continued on reverse)

Form Adopted by Rule 1281
Judicial Council of California
1281 (Rev. January 1, 1994)

PETITION
(Family Law)

Family Code, §§ 2330, 3409
Cal. Rules of Court, rule 1215

ORIGINAL

321

EXHIBIT 9–4 Continued

MARRIAGE OF (last name, first name of parties):	CASE NUMBER:
COSTNER, CYNTHIA R. and KEVIN M.	ORIGINAL

5. DECLARATION REGARDING COMMUNITY AND QUASI-COMMUNITY ASSETS AND OBLIGATIONS AS CURRENTLY KNOWN

    a. ☐ There are no such assets or obligations subject to disposition by the court in this proceeding.

    b. ☒ All such assets and obligations have been disposed of by written agreement.

    c. ☐ All such assets and obligations are listed ☐ in Attachment 5 ☐ below (specify):

6. Petitioner requests

    a. ☒ Dissolution of the marriage based on
        (1) ☒ irreconcilable differences. FC 2310(a)
        (2) ☐ incurable insanity. FC 2310(b)

    b. ☐ Legal separation of the parties based on
        (1) ☐ irreconcilable differences. FC 2310(a)
        (2) ☐ incurable insanity. FC 2310(b)

    c. ☐ Nullity of void marriage based on
        (1) ☐ incestuous marriage. FC 2200
        (2) ☐ bigamous marriage. FC 2201

    d. ☐ Nullity of voidable marriage based on
        (1) ☐ petitioner's age at time of marriage. FC 2210(a)
        (2) ☐ prior existing marriage. FC 2210(b)
        (3) ☐ unsound mind. FC 2210(c)
        (4) ☐ fraud. FC 2210(d)
        (5) ☐ force. FC 2210(e)
        (6) ☐ physical incapacity. FC 2210(f)

7. Petitioner requests that the court grant the above relief and make injunctive (including restraining) and other orders as follows:

		Petitioner	Respondent	Joint	Other
a.	Legal custody of children to *Per Agreement of the parties*	☐	☐	☒	☐
b.	Physical custody of children to *Per Agreement of the parties*	☐	☐	☒	☐
c.	Child visitation be granted to *Per Agreement of the parties*	☐	☐	☐	☐
	☐ supervised as to (specify):				
d.	Spousal support payable by (wage assignment will be issued)	☐	☐		
e.	Attorney fees and costs payable by *Per Agreement of parties*	☐	☐		
f.	☐ Terminate the court's jurisdiction (ability) to award spousal support to respondent.				
g.	☒ Property rights be determined. Per Agreement of the parties				
h.	☐ Wife's former name be restored (specify):				
i.	☐ Other (specify):				

8. If there are minor children of this marriage, the court will make orders for the support of the children without further notice to either party. A wage assignment will be issued.

9. ' I have read the restraining orders on the back of the Summons, and I understand that they apply to me when this petition is filed.

    I declare under penalty of perjury under the laws of the State of California that the foregoing is true and correct.

Date: October 25, 1994

            ▶ ✓ *Cynthia R. Cost*
                  (SIGNATURE OF PETITIONER)
            CYNTHIA R. COSTNER

GERALD L. FRIEDMAN
....
(TYPE OR PRINT NAME OF ATTORNEY)
            ▶ *Gerald L. Friedman*
                  (SIGNATURE OF ATTORNEY FOR PETITIONER)

NOTICE: Please review your will, insurance policies, retirement benefit plans, credit cards, other credit accounts and credit reports, and other matters you may want to change in view of the dissolution or annulment of your marriage, or your legal separation. However, some changes may require the agreement of your spouse or a court order (see Family Code sections 231-235).

1281 (Rev. January 1, 1994)   **PETITION**   Page two
                            (Family Law)

EXHIBIT 9-5 Sample documents requesting a temporary restarting order.

Procedures for

Relief From Abuse Process

STATE OF CONNECTICUT SUPERIOR COURT

Domestic Violence Programs and Counseling Services

Statewide Hotline   **888-774-2900**

ANSONIA
  The Umbrella Program   203-736-9944
BRIDGEPORT
  Center for Women and Families of
  Eastern Fairfield County   203-384-9559
DANBURY
  Women's Center of Greater
  Danbury, Inc.   203-731-5206
DANIELSON
  Domestic Violence Program
  United Services, Inc.   860-774-8648
ENFIELD
  Network Against Domestic
  Abuse of North Central CT   860-763-4542
GREENWICH
  Domestic Abuse Services
  of Greenwich   203-622-0003
HARTFORD
  Hartford Interval House   860-527-0550
MANCHESTER
  Interval House   860-645-4033
MERIDEN
  Meriden-Wallingford Chrysalis   203-238-1501
MIDDLETOWN
  New Horizons   860-347-3044
NEW BRITAIN
  Prudence Crandall Center   203-225-0357
NEW HAVEN
  Domestic Violence Services of
  Greater New Haven   203-789-8104
NEW LONDON
  Women's Center of S.E. Connecticut
NORWALK
  Domestic Violence
  Crisis Center   860-701-6000
SHARON/FALLS VILLAGE
  Women's Support Services   203-852-1980
STAMFORD
  Stamford Domestic Violence
  Crisis Center   860-364-1900
TORRINGTON
  Susan B. Anthony Project   203-357-8162
WATERBURY
  Safe Haven   860-482-7133
WILLIMANTIC
  Domestic Violence Program   203-575-0036
  United Services, Inc.   860-456-9476

JDP-FM-142
Rev. 12/03

Extending the Restraining Order

If the Applicant wants the restraining order to extend beyond the period ordered by the court, that person must submit a Motion to Extend to the clerk's office. To help prevent the order from lapsing, the motion should be submitted at least two to three weeks before the restraining order expires. After the motion is submitted, the clerk will schedule a hearing, and return the motion to the Applicant for service on the Respondent. On the hearing date the same court procedures apply as those described in "The Court Hearing" section of this brochure.

Disclaimer: These procedures have been compiled by the Judicial Branch as a public service and pursuant to the provisions of C.G.S. § 46b-15b. They are based upon the Connecticut General Statutes in effect at the time of Publication. This information is not intended as a substitute for obtaining legal advice from a Connecticut attorney. You are solely responsible for any actions you take on your own behalf. The clerk's office may assist you with procedural questions, however, the staff cannot act as your attorney or give you legal advice and are not responsible for any errors or omissions in these procedures. If you feel you need more information or assistance, you should either consult an attorney or read the appropriate sections of the Connecticut General Statutes and the Connecticut Practice Book.

EXHIBIT 9–5 Continued

Procedures for Filing an Application

The person who prepares the Application for Relief From Abuse is called the "Applicant" in the restraining order process. The person against whom the Application is filed is called the "Respondent."

Forms Needed to Apply

Complete an Application for Relief From Abuse (JD-FM-137), and an Affidavit (JD-FM-138), following the instructions printed on the top of each form. If you are seeking temporary custody of children, you must also complete an Affidavit Concerning Children (JD-FM-164).

Fees

There are no court fees charged for the filing of the initial Application or for any motion to modify or extend the order. The fee for service of the Application and any ex parte order will be paid for by the Judicial Branch.

Application Procedures

The Applicant must submit the completed forms to the clerk. The Application and Affidavit(s) must be signed in the presence of a clerk, notary public or Commissioner of the Superior Court.

The Application and Affidavit(s) will be reviewed by a Judge. The Applicant may be required to testify in court when the Judge reviews the Application.

Next Steps

After the Judge Rules on the Application

If the Application for Relief From Abuse is granted, the clerk's office will process the papers and return to the Applicant two (2) certified copies of any ex parte Restraining Order Relief From Abuse (JD-FM-139) and the original Application, Affidavit(s) and Order. The clerk will send a copy of the order or the information contained therein to law enforcement within forty-eight hours.

Service of Process on the Respondent

The Applicant should immediately bring the original Application (JD-FM-137), Affidavit(s) (JD-FM-138 and, if applicable, JD-FM-164), and Restraining Order Relief From Abuse (JD-FM-139) or Order and Notice of Court Hearing (JD-FM-140) to a State Marshal or any proper officer for service. A current list of State Marshals may be obtained from the Judicial Branch web site at www.jud.state.ct.us or from the clerk's office. At certain court locations, a State Marshal will be at the courthouse at established times during the day to help facilitate service. The State Marshal or other proper officer must serve a copy of these papers on the Respondent at least five days before the hearing date to notify that person of the ex parte order, if any, and hearing date.

If ex parte relief was ordered, the Applicant should keep one of the certified copies of the Restraining Order Relief From Abuse (JD-FM-139) with her or him at all times and the other in a safe place.

After the State Marshal has served the papers, the original papers must be returned to the clerk's office so that the clerk can perform all necessary administrative and clerical tasks required before the scheduled court hearing date. It is recommended that the papers be returned to the clerk's office at least two (2) full working days before the scheduled hearing date.

Firearm Restrictions

Firearm restrictions apply to individuals subject to restraining or protective orders. A notice of the firearm restrictions is printed on the Restraining Order Relief From Abuse and Order and Notice of Court Hearing Relief From Abuse forms.

The Court Hearing

Court Procedure

The Applicant must be present in court at the time and date scheduled for the hearing if she or he wants the court to enter or continue a restraining order. If the Respondent wishes to be heard concerning the Application, that person must also appear at the time and date scheduled.

At the hearing, the Applicant will be able to present to the Judge the reasons for seeking or continuing the restraining order and the Respondent will have the opportunity to be heard. Witnesses or evidence that will support the Applicant's claims or the Respondent's defense should be brought to court.

After the Hearing

After the hearing, if the restraining order is granted by the Judge, the Applicant will receive two (2) certified copies of a new Restraining Order Relief From Abuse (JD-FM-139) form. A copy will be given or mailed to the Respondent. The clerk will send a copy of the order or the information contained therein to law enforcement within forty-eight hours.

The Applicant should keep one of the certified copies of the Restraining Order Relief From Abuse (JD-FM-139) with her or him at all times and the other in a safe place.

Effective Period of the Restraining Order

The orders after hearing are effective for six months unless a different period is ordered by the court. The Applicant should contact the police department immediately and file a complaint if the Respondent violates any order issued.

Duration of the Order

EXHIBIT 9–5 Continued

**APPLICATION FOR
RELIEF FROM ABUSE**

JD-FM-137 Rev. 12-03 C.G.S. §§ 29-28, 29-32, 29-33, 29-36k,
29-36i, 46b-15, 52-231a, 53a-217c.

**STATE OF CONNECTICUT
SUPERIOR COURT**

www.jud.state.ct.us

**INSTRUCTIONS
TO APPLICANT**
{
1. Use a typewriter or print clearly in ink. You must also complete an Affidavit, form JD-FM-138. Give both forms to the Clerk of Court.
2. After your Application and Affidavit are processed, the clerk will give you the proper papers to have served on the Respondent.
3. Make sure the originals are returned to court after service.

**INSTRUCTIONS
TO CLERK**
{
1. If Ex Parte relief is ordered, prepare Restraining Order - Relief From Abuse, form JD-FM-139; be sure to check the Ex Parte Restraining Order box on page 1 and complete the Order and Notice of Court Hearing on page 2.
2. If Ex Parte relief is NOT ordered, prepare Order and Notice of Court Hearing - Relief From Abuse, form JD-FM-140.
3. Provide the Applicant with the original and one copy of the Application and Affidavit. Retain copies of each for court file.
4. Provide the Applicant with the Procedures For Relief From Abuse Process brochure JD-FM-142P for further information.

JUDICIAL DISTRICT OF	COURT LOCATION (No., street, town and zip code)	DOCKET NO. (For court use only)

NAME OF APPLICANT (Your name)	DATE OF BIRTH (mm/dd/yyyy)	SEX (M/F)	RACE

ADDRESS TO WHICH APPLICANT'S MAIL IS TO BE SENT (No., street)	(Town)	(State)	(Zip Code)

APPLICANT'S TOWN OF EMPLOYMENT (If employed)	(State)	(Zip Code)

NAME OF YOUR ATTORNEY (If any)	ATTORNEY'S TEL. NO.

NAME OF RESPONDENT (Person against whom application is filed)	DATE OF BIRTH (mm/dd/yyyy)	SEX (M/F)	RACE

ADDRESS OF RESPONDENT (No., street)	(Town)	(State)	(Zip Code)

RESPONDENT IS ("X" all that apply)

☐ MY SPOUSE ☐ MY CHILD ☐ MY PARENT ☐ A PERSON 18 OR OVER RELATED TO ME BY BLOOD OR MARRIAGE
☐ MY FORMER SPOUSE ☐ A PERSON 16 OR OVER WITH WHOM I RESIDE OR WITH WHOM I HAVE RESIDED
☐ PARENT OF MY CHILD ☐ A CARETAKER WHO IS PROVIDING SHELTER IN HIS OR HER RESIDENCE TO A PERSON 60 YEARS OF AGE OR OLDER
☐ A PERSON WITH WHOM I HAVE (OR RECENTLY HAD) A DATING RELATIONSHIP

☐ "X" here if a Protective Order/Restraining Order exists affecting any party to this Application (Enter Docket No.and Court Location)	DOCKET NO.	COURT LOCATION
☐ "X" here if a dissolution of marriage (divorce), custody or visitation action exists involving the same parties. (Enter Docket No.and Court Location)	DOCKET NO.	COURT LOCATION

APPLICATION FOR RELIEF FROM ABUSE

I have been subjected to a continuous threat of present physical pain or physical injury by the Respondent named above as stated more fully in my attached Affidavit. I request that the court: ("X" all that apply)

☐ 1. ORDER THAT THE RESPONDENT NAMED ABOVE:
   ☐ Refrain from imposing any restraint on me.   ☐ Refrain from entering the family dwelling or my dwelling.
   ☐ Refrain from threatening, harassing, assaulting, molesting, sexually assaulting or attacking me.

(NOTE: The address provided here will be included on any orders entered by the court. If you do not wish to provide your address, do not complete this box. However, failure to disclose your location information may limit the protection you can receive by the restraining order. If you believe that disclosure of location information would jeopardize you and/or your child(ren)'s health, safety or liberty, you may file a Request For Nondisclosure of Location Information with the Clerk of

ADDRESS OF DWELLING (No., street, town, state, zip code)

☐ 2. AWARD ME TEMPORARY CUSTODY OF THE FOLLOWING MINOR CHILD(REN) WHO IS (ARE) ALSO
   THE CHILD(REN) OF THE RESPONDENT:

NAME (First, Middle Initial, Last)	SEX (M/F)	DATE OF BIRTH (MM/DD/YYYY)		NAME (First, Middle Initial, Last)	SEX (M/F)	DATE OF BIRTH (MM/DD/YYYY)
1			4			
2			5			
3			6			

☐ 3. ORDER THAT THE RELIEF REQUESTED ABOVE IN NUMBER 1 EXTEND TO:
   ☐ The child(ren) named in Number 2 above.
   ☐ Other persons (Specify name(s) and relationship(s) to you)

☐ 4. FURTHER ORDER:

REQUEST FOR EX PARTE (IMMEDIATE) RELIEF ("X" if applicable)

☐ 5. I REQUEST THAT THE COURT ORDER EX PARTE (IMMEDIATE) RELIEF BECAUSE I BELIEVE THERE IS
   AN IMMEDIATE AND PRESENT PHYSICAL DANGER TO ME AND/OR MY MINOR CHILDREN.

SIGNED (Applicant) X	Subscribed and sworn to before me:	SIGNED (Clerk, Notary, Comm. Sup. Ct.)	DATE SIGNED

OPTIONAL TO APPLICANT (If you choose to answer "X" the appropriate boxes below)
1. Does the respondent hold a permit to carry a pistol or revolver?.................. ☐ YES ☐ NO ☐ UNKNOWN
2. Does the respondent possess one or more firearms?................................... ☐ YES ☐ NO ☐ UNKNOWN

EXHIBIT 9–5 Continued

**AFFIDAVIT -
RELIEF FROM ABUSE**

JD-FM-138 Rev. 6-03
C.G.S. §§ 46b-15, 52-231a, P.B. § 25-57

**STATE OF CONNECTICUT
SUPERIOR COURT**

www.jud.state.ct.us

INSTRUCTIONS TO APPLICANT *(Affiant)*

This affidavit must be completed and given to the clerk along with your completed Application for Relief From Abuse, form JD-FM-137. Your affidavit must include a statement of the conditions from which you seek relief and must be made under oath (you must swear that your statement is true and sign it in front of a court clerk, a notary public, or an attorney who will also sign and date the affidavit). The statement must be true to the best of your knowledge. **Give recent, specific examples along with dates** *and state if any arrest was made related to the incidents outlined in this statement.*

If you seek temporary custody of your minor child(ren), you must also complete an Affidavit Concerning Children, form JD-FM-164.

NAME OF APPLICANT *(Your name)*	NAME OF RESPONDENT *(Person against whom application is filed)*	DOCKET NO. *(For court use only)*

STATEMENT OF CONDITIONS FROM WHICH YOU SEEK RELIEF

I, the undersigned, duly depose and say that I am the Applicant in this matter and state as follows:

STATEMENT CONCERNING TEMPORARY CUSTODY OF CHILDREN

"X" one of the following:

☐ I am not seeking temporary custody of any minor child(ren) in this matter.

☐ I am seeking temporary custody of my minor child(ren) in this matter.
(Complete an Affidavit Concerning Children, form JD-FM-164, and bring it to the clerk along with this form and your completed Application For Relief From Abuse, form JD-FM-137.)

I hereby certify that the foregoing statements are true to the best of my knowledge and belief.	SIGNATURE	PRINT NAME OF PERSON SIGNING	
SUBSCRIBED AND SWORN TO BEFORE ME *(Asst. Clerk, Comm. of Superior Court, Notary Public)*			DATE SIGNED

EXHIBIT 9–6 Sample proof of service document.

MARRIAGE OF (last name, first name of parties): — COSTNER, Cynthia R. and Kevin M.	CASE NUMBER: BD 203 807

Serve a copy of the documents on the person to be served. Complete the proof of service. Attach it to the original documents. File them with the court.

PROOF OF SERVICE OF SUMMONS (Family Law)

1. I served the Summons with Standard Restraining Orders (Family Law), blank Response, and Petition (Family Law) on respondent *(name)*: **Kevin M. Costner**

   a. with (1) [XX] blank Confidential Counseling Statement   (4) [XX] ~~completed and~~ blank Income and
           (2) [ ] Order to Show Cause and Application   Expense Declarations
           (3) [ ] blank Responsive Declaration   (5) [ ] completed and blank Property Declarations
                                                            (6) [XX] Other *(specify)*: **Certificate of Assignment**

   b. [ ] By leaving copies with *(name and title or relationship to person served)*:

   c. [ ] By delivery at [ ] home [ ] business
           (1) Date of: (3) Address:
           (2) Time of:

   d. [XX] By mailing (1) Date of: **11/7/94**   (2) Place of: **Los Angeles, CA**

2. Manner of service: *(Check proper box)*
   a. [ ] Personal service. By personally delivering copies to the person served. (CCP 415.10)
   b. [ ] Substituted service on natural person, minor, incompetent. By leaving copies at the dwelling house, usual place of abode, or usual place of business of the person served in the presence of a competent member of the household or a person apparently in charge of the office or place of business, at least 18 years of age, who was informed of the general nature of the papers, and thereafter mailing (by first-class mail, postage prepaid) copies to the person served at the place where the copies were left. (CCP 415.20(b)) (Attach separate declaration stating acts relied on to establish reasonable diligence in first attempting personal service.)
   c. [XX] Mail and acknowledge service. By mailing (by first-class mail or airmail) copies to the person served, together with two copies of the form of notice and acknowledgment and a return envelope, postage prepaid, addressed to the sender. (CCP 415.30) (Attach completed acknowledgment of receipt.)
   d. [ ] Certified or registered mail service. By mailing to address outside California (by registered or certified airmail with return receipt requested) copies to the person served. (CCP 415.40) (Attach signed return receipt or other evidence of actual delivery to the person served.)
   e. [ ] Other *(specify code section)*:
       [ ] Additional page is attached.

3. The NOTICE TO THE PERSON SERVED on the summons was completed as follows (CCP 412.30, 415.10, and 474):
   a. [XX] as an individual
   b. [ ] on behalf of Respondent
       under [ ] CCP 416.90 (Individual)   [ ] CCP 416.70 (Ward or Conservatee)   [ ] CCP 416.60 (Minor)
                  [ ] Other *(specify)*:
   c. [ ] by personal delivery on *(date)*:

4. At the time of service I was at least 18 years of age and not a party to this action.
5. Fee for service: $ –0–
6. Person serving:
   a. [XX] Not a registered California process server.   e. [ ] California sheriff, marshal, or constable.
   b. [ ] Registered California process server.   f. Name, address, and telephone number and, if
   c. [ ] Employee or independent contractor of a   applicable, county of registration and number:
       registered California process server.   **Gerald L. Friedman**
   d. [ ] Exempt from registration under Bus. & Prof.   **11400 W. Olympic Blvd., 9th Fl.**
       Code section 22350(b).   **Los Angeles, CA 90064-1565**
                                                  (310) 477-5450

I declare under penalty of perjury under the laws of the State   (For California sheriff, marshal, or constable use only)
of California that the foregoing is true and correct.   I certify that the foregoing is true and correct.
Date: 4-26-95   Date:

▶ *Gerald L. Friedman*   ▶
       (SIGNATURE)   (SIGNATURE)

Form Adopted by Rule 1283.5   **PROOF OF SERVICE OF SUMMONS**
Judicial Council of California   **(Family Law)**
1283.5 (New January 1, 1991)   **1283.5**
                                                              BD108

EXHIBIT 9–7 Sample appearance form.

APPEARANCE
JD-CL-12 Rev. 10-04
Pr. Bk. §§ 3-1 thru 3-6, 3-8

NOTICE TO PRO SE PARTIES
A pro se party is a person who represents himself or herself. It is your responsibility to inform the Clerk's Office if you have a change of address.

STATE OF CONNECTICUT
SUPERIOR COURT
www.jud.state.ct.us

INSTRUCTIONS

1. Type or print legibly.
2. **Judicial District Court Locations:** In any action returnable to a Judicial District court location, file only the original with the clerk. In criminal actions see instruction #4.
3. **Geographical Area Locations:** In any action returnable to a Geographical Area court location, except criminal actions, file original and sufficient copies for each party to the action with the clerk. In criminal actions see instruction #4.
4. **In Criminal and Motor Vehicle Actions** (Pr. Bk. Secs. 3-4, 3-5): Mail or deliver a copy of the appearance to the prosecuting authority, complete the certification at bottom and file original with the clerk.
5. **In Summary Process Actions:** In addition to instruction #2 or #3 above, mail a copy to the attorney for the plaintiff, or if there is no such attorney, to the plaintiff and complete the certification below.
6. **In Small Claims Matters:** File the original with the Small Claims area or Housing Session location. Mail or deliver a copy to the attorney or pro se party and complete the certification below.
7. **For "In-lieu-of" Appearances** (Pr. Bk. Sec. 3-8): Complete the certification below.
8. Pursuant to Pr. Bk. Sec. 17-20, if a party who has been defaulted for failure to appear files an appearance prior to the entry of judgment after default, the default shall automatically be set aside by the clerk.
9. **In Juvenile Matters:** Do not use this form. Use form JD-JM-13 Appearance, Juvenile Matters.

DOCKET NO.
RETURN DATE
SCHEDULED COURT DATE *(Criminal/Motor Vehicle Matters)*

NAME OF CASE *(FIRST-NAMED PLAINTIFF VS. FIRST- NAMED DEFENDANT)*

☐ Judicial District	☐ Housing Session	☐ G.A. No. _____	ADDRESS OF COURT *(No., street, town and zip code)*

▼ **PLEASE ENTER THE APPEARANCE OF** ▼

NAME OF PRO SE PARTY *(See "Notice to Pro Se Parties" at top)*, OR NAME OF OFFICIAL, FIRM, PROFESSIONAL CORPORATION, OR INDIVIDUAL ATTORNEY	JURIS NO. OF ATTY. OR FIRM

MAILING ADDRESS *(No., street, P.O. Box)*	TELEPHONE NO. *(Area code first)*

CITY/TOWN	STATE	ZIP CODE	FAX NO. *(Area code first)*	E-MAIL ADDRESS

in the above-entitled case for: *("X" one of the following)*

☐ The Plaintiff.
☐ All Plaintiffs
☐ The following Plaintiff(s) only: _____
☐ The Defendant.
☐ The Defendant for the purpose of the bail hearing only *(in criminal and motor vehicle cases only)*.
☐ All Defendants.
☐ The following Defendant(s) only: _____
☐ Other *(Specify)* _____

Note: If other counsel or a pro se party have already appeared for the party or parties indicated above, state whether this appearance is:

☐ In lieu of appearance of attorney or firm or pro se party *(Name)* already on file (P.B. Sec. 3-8) **OR**   _____   *(Name and Juris No.)*
☐ In addition to appearance already on file.

SIGNED *(Individual attorney or pro se party)* X	NAME OF PERSON SIGNING AT LEFT *(Print or type)*	DATE SIGNED

CERTIFICATION	*FOR COURT USE ONLY*

This certification must be completed in summary process cases (Pr. Bk. Sec. 3-5(a)); for "in lieu of" appearances (Pr. Bk. Sec. 3-8); in criminal cases (Pr. Bk. Sec. 3-5(d)); and in small claims matters.

I hereby certify that a copy of the above was mailed/delivered to:

☐ All counsel and pro se parties of record as listed below and on additional sheet. *(For summary process, criminal actions and small claims matters)*
☐ Counsel or the party whose appearance is to be replaced as listed below and on additional sheet. *(For "in lieu of" appearances)*

SIGNED *(Individual attorney or pro se party)* X	DATE COPY(IES) MAILED OR DELIVERED

NAME OF EACH PARTY SERVED *	ADDRESS AT WHICH SERVICE WAS MADE

* If necessary, attach additional sheet with names of each party served and the address at which service was made.

APPEARANCE

EXHIBIT 9–8 Sample preprinted answer form.

DISSOLUTION ANSWER
JD-FM-160 Rev. 10-05
P.B. § 25-9, P.A. 05-10

STATE OF CONNECTICUT
SUPERIOR COURT
www.jud.state.ct.us

COURT USE ONLY
ANSWER

INSTRUCTIONS
Complete the form below and file it with the Court Clerk. If you are the defendant, you must also file an Appearance form (JD-CL-12). You may also file a Dissolution of Marriage Cross-Complaint (JD-FM-159) or Dissolution of Civil Union Cross-Complaint (JD-FM-159A) to tell the Court what you want the judge to order.

☐ **Answer to Divorce (Dissolution of Marriage) Complaint**
☐ **Answer to Dissolution of Civil Union Complaint**
☐ **Answer to Divorce (Dissolution of Marriage) Cross-Complaint**
☐ **Answer to Dissolution of Civil Union Cross-Complaint**

JUDICIAL DISTRICT OF	AT *(Town)*	RETURN DATE *(Mo., day, yr.)*
PLAINTIFF'S NAME *(Last, First, Middle Initial)*	DEFENDANT'S NAME *(Last, First, Middle Initial)*	DOCKET NO.

Number each line in the chart below to match the numbered paragraphs in the <u>Complaint</u> or <u>Cross-Complaint</u> (example: 1, 2, 3, 4, 5a, 5b). Use as many lines as you need. For each paragraph, mark an "X" for Agree, Disagree, or Do Not Know.

PARAGRAPH NO.	AGREE	DISAGREE	DO NOT KNOW

I certify that a copy of the above was mailed/delivered to all counsel and pro se parties of record on:

DATE MAILED/DELIVERED	SIGNED *(Attorney or pro se party)* X	PRINTED NAME
ADDRESS *(No., street, town or city, zip code)*		

NAME AND ADDRESS OF EACH PERSON TO WHOM A COPY WAS MAILED OR DELIVERED*

If necessary, attach additional sheet with name of each party served and the address at which service was made.

EXHIBIT 9–9 Sample cross-complaint.

DIVORCE COMPLAINT (DISSOLUTION OF MARRIAGE)	STATE OF CONNECTICUT SUPERIOR COURT	CROSS COMPLAINT CODE ONLY
JD-FM-159 Rev. 6-03 C.G.S. § 46b-40, et seq., P.B. § 25-2, et seq.	*www.jud.state.ct.us*	**CRSCMP**

☐ **Complaint:** Complete this form. Attach a completed Summons (JD-FM-3) and Notice of Automatic Court Orders (JD-FM-158).
☐ **Amended Complaint.**
☐ **Cross Complaint:** Complete this form and attach to the Answer (JD-FM-160) unless it is already filed.

JUDICIAL DISTRICT OF	AT *(Town)*	RETURN DATE *(Month, day, year)*	DOCKET NO.
PLAINTIFF'S NAME *(Last, First, Middle Initial)*		DEFENDANT'S NAME *(Last, First, Middle Initial)*	

1. WIFE'S BIRTH NAME *(First, Middle Initial, Last)*

2. DATE OF MARRIAGE	3. TOWN AND STATE, OR COUNTRY WHERE MARRIAGE TOOK PLACE

4. *(Check all that apply)*

☐ The husband or the wife has lived in Connecticut for at least twelve months before the filing of this divorce complaint or before the divorce will become final.
☐ The husband or the wife lived in Connecticut at the time of the marriage, moved away, and then returned to Connecticut, planning to live here permanently.
☐ The marriage broke down after the wife or the husband moved to Connecticut.

5. A divorce is being sought because: *(Check all that apply)*

☐ This marriage has broken down irretrievably and there is no possibility of getting back together. **(No fault divorce)**
☐ Other *(must be reason(s) listed in Connecticut General Statute § 46b-40(c)):*

_____
_____
_____

Check and complete all that apply for items 6-13. Attach additional sheets if needed.

6. ☐ No children were born to the wife after the date of this marriage.
7. ☐ There are no minor children of this marriage.
8. ☐ The following children have been born to the wife or have been adopted before, on or after the date of this marriage and the husband is the father/adoptive father. *(List only children who have not yet reached the age of 23.)*

NAME OF CHILD *(First, Middle Initial, Last)*	DATE OF BIRTH *(Month, day, year)*

9. ☐ The following children were born to the wife **after** the date of the marriage and the husband **is not the father.** *(List only children who have not yet reached the age of 23.)*

NAME OF CHILD *(First, Middle Initial, Last)*	DATE OF BIRTH *(Month, day, year)*

(Continued...)

EXHIBIT 9–9 Continued

10. ☐ The wife is pregnant with a child due to be born on *(date)* _____

   The father of this unborn child is *(check one)* ☐ the husband ☐ not the husband ☐ unknown.

11. If there is a court order about any child listed above, name the child(ren) below and the person or agency awarded custody or providing support:

CHILD'S NAME	NAME OF PERSON OR AGENCY
CHILD'S NAME	NAME OF PERSON OR AGENCY
CHILD'S NAME	NAME OF PERSON OR AGENCY

12. The husband, the wife, or any of the child(ren) listed above has received financial support from the State of Connecticut. *(Check one)* ☐ Yes ☐ No ☐ Do not know
   If yes, send a copy of the Summons, Complaint, Notice of Automatic Court Orders and any other documents filed with this Complaint to the Assistant Attorney General, 55 Elm Street, Hartford, CT 06106, and file the Certification of Notice *(JD-FM-175)* with the court clerk.

13. The husband, the wife, or any of the child(ren) listed above has received financial support from a city or town in Connecticut. *(Check one)* ☐ Yes *(State city or town: _____)* ☐ No ☐ Do not know
   If yes, send a copy of the Summons, Complaint, Notice of Automatic Court Orders and any other documents filed with this Complaint to the City Clerk of the town providing assistance and file the Certification of Notice *(JD-FM-175)* with the court clerk.

The Court is asked to order: *(Check all that apply)*

☐ A divorce (dissolution of marriage).

☐ A fair division of property and debts.

☐ Alimony.

☐ Child Support.

☐ An order for the post-majority educational support of the child(ren) pursuant to C.G.S. § 46b-56c.

☐ Visitation.

☐ Name change to: _____

☐ Sole custody.

☐ Joint legal custody, Primary residence with:

_____

And anything else the Court thinks is fair.

SIGNATURE	PRINT NAME OF PERSON SIGNING		DATE SIGNED
ADDRESS		JURIS NO. *(If applicable)*	TELEPHONE (Area code first)

> • *If this is a Complaint, attach a copy of the Automatic Court Orders before serving a copy on the Defendant.*
>
> • *If this is an Amended Complaint or a Cross Complaint, you must mail or deliver a copy to anyone who has filed an appearance and you must complete the certification below.*

I certify that a copy of the above was mailed/delivered to all counsel and pro se parties of record on:

.DATE MAILED OR DELIVERED	SIGNED *(Attorney or pro se party)*
NAME OF EACH PERSON SERVED*	ADDRESS WHERE SERVICE WAS MADE *(No., street, town, zip code)**

*If necessary, attach additional sheet with name of each party served and the address at which service was made.

JD-FM-159 *(Back)* Rev. 6-03

END OF CHAPTER EXERCISES

Crossword Puzzle

Across

2. service by publication of a legal notice in a newspaper circulated in the city or town of the defendant's last known address, informing the defendant of the proceedings

4. personal service over the defendant; it means that once the defendant is served with the initial pleadings, the court may enter orders and enforce judgments against that individual

5. service on a defendant by leaving a copy of the pleadings at his or her home

6. document accompanying a complaint or petition in a divorce case

8. describes the court's control or power over a specific geographic territory; also refers to the power of the courts to hear and resolve a dispute

10. initial pleading filed in a dissolution matter

11. residing in a state with the intent to permanently remain

12. party against whom the divorce action is brought

Down

1. the court's power to actually hear a divorce case

2. formal delivery of the initial pleadings

3. the power of the courts to actually dissolve the marriage

5. sworn statement

7. the domicile of the parties

9. party commencing a divorce action

Review Questions

1 Why is obtaining in personam jurisdiction over the defendant important in a divorce case?

2 What does the family law attorney represent to the court when he or she signs the complaint or petition? What is the signing called and where does it occur in the document?

3 What are the paralegal's responsibilities for arranging service of the divorce or dissolution complaint?

4 What is service by publication and when is this form of service used in a divorce or dissolution action?

5 Describe the responsive pleadings filed by the defendant.

Case for Briefing

Zwerling v. Zwerling, 167 Misc.2d 782, 636 N.Y.S.2d 595 (1995)

Exploring the Workplace: Activities

1. Following the links on the website **http://www.divorcesource.com/tables/tables.shtml** entitled "Divorce Law Reference Table," Table 1, look up your state and find the residency requirements in your jurisdiction.

2. Go to **http://www.courtinfo.ca.gov/forms/fillable/fl100.pdf,** where you will find a California Petition for Dissolution of Marriage. Summarize the nine declarations in this petition.

3. Go to **http://www.courtinfo.ca.gov/forms/fillable/fl110.pdf**, where you will find a California Summons for a divorce case. Summarize the notice to the respondent.

4. Using the Internet or state-specific resources, find the procedure and forms necessary in your state to file the initial and responsive pleadings in a divorce action.

5. If you were going to file for divorce in your state, in which county or district would you file your case? Determine the proper venue.

CHAPTER

Pendente Lite Motions and Orders

KEY TERMS

body

caption

certification

child support guidelines

cooling-off period

court calendar

custody affidavit

deny

docket control system

ex parte

ex parte proceeding

grant

motion day

motion for alimony, *pendente lite*

motion for child support, *pendente lite*

motion for contempt

motion for counsel fees

motion for custody, *pendente lite*

motion for exclusive possession of the marital residence, *pendente lite*

motion for modification

motion for payment of mortgage payments and insurance premiums, *pendente lite*

motion for use of motor vehicle, *pendente lite*

motion for visitation

motion to freeze marital assets

motion to restrain party from entering marital residence

moving party

order	restraining order
pendente lite motion	short calendar
pro per	signature (subscription)
pro se	

In the United States, there is no such thing as an instant divorce. Every jurisdiction has some type of **cooling-off period** or waiting requirement that must elapse before a final divorce decree may be entered. The term *cooling-off period* refers to the statutorily mandated time period following the initiation of divorce proceedings during which no final decree may be entered. This period usually runs for a number of months depending on the jurisdiction.

In many instances, the divorce decree is not issued immediately after the cooling-off period has expired. This is so because divorce presents many complex issues that the parties must resolve or the court must resolve for them. In addition, the parties' respective attorneys' calendars must be accommodated and the court calendar must be considered. The judicial system provides vehicles through which the parties may seek and obtain court orders to determine how the obligations of the marriage partnership may be fulfilled during the time frame. One spouse or the other may use such vehicles to obtain relief on the issues of spousal support, maintenance and custody of the minor children, use of the family residence, protection from an abusive or violent spouse, and arrangements for paying bills to creditors for obligations the marital unit incurred.

The paralegal working in a family law practice plays an important role in facilitating relief for his or her client. Specific documents must be prepared and filed with the court to provide temporary relief for the client seeking such assistance. These documents are called *pendente lite* **motions.**

PENDENTE LITE MOTIONS

Pendente lite is a Latin term meaning "during the litigation." The term *temporary* is also used interchangeably when describing *pendente lite* motions. While a divorce action is pending, the court, upon a party's motion, will consider entering certain orders with which the parties must comply from the time the order is entered until the entry of final orders at the time of the divorce decree.

ANATOMY OF A MOTION

The family law division of every U.S. jurisdiction has certain requirements regarding the form and manner in which motions should be filed. The local rules of practice provide guidelines and sometimes sample forms to follow. In addition, law libraries have many types of form books, which display typical motions, and law offices typically have forms on disk and hardcopy, which can be modified for use in specific cases.

Although specifics vary from jurisdiction to jurisdiction and from case to case, motions have general features common to all jurisdictions: All motions have a *caption*, a *body* and a *signature* or *subscription* section; further, most state court systems require a separate *order* page and a *certification* page.

CAPTION

The **caption** section of a motion must have the docket number, the names of the parties, the name of the court, its geographical location, and the date the motion was filed. This information is arranged either in a block form or modified block form. The action will also contain the title or heading of the motion. The title will appear a few spaces down from the other information and usually will be centered and either underlined, printed in bold, or both.

EXAMPLE

DOCKET NO. FA 96-123456	:	SUPERIOR COURT
BRONSON, RODNEY HAVEN	:	JUDICIAL DISTRICT OF NEW
V.	:	AT NEW HAVEN
BRONSON, EVELYN	:	AUGUST 15, 2005

MOTION FOR RETURN OF PERSONAL PROPERTY

BODY

The **body** of the motion identifies the party filing the motion, the relief specifically requested, and the grounds or basis on which relief is requested.

EXAMPLE

The plaintiff-husband respectfully moves for an order requiring the defendant-wife to turn over to the plaintiff-husband and permit him to retrieve from the marital house, the following items of personal property:

1. Golf clubs
2. Grandmother's rocking chair

SUBSCRIPTION

The **signature** or **subscription** section lists in block form the designation given to the party in the lawsuit, namely, whether the party is the plaintiff or defendant in the action, the actual name of the party, and then a signature line, the name of the attorney acting on the party's behalf, followed by the attorney's address, license number, and usually her phone number.

If a party is bringing the action himself or herself without benefit of counsel, the party is said to be acting ***pro se*** or ***pro per.*** In such a case, the words *pro se* appear underneath the party's name and then the party's own address and phone number are listed.

EXAMPLE

THE PLAINTIFF, RODNEY BRONSON

BY _____

      JUSTINE F. MILLER, ESQ.
      HIS ATTORNEY
      22 PARK PLACE
      NEW HAVEN, CT 06511
      (203) 861-4444
      JURIS NO. 3131333

ORDER

An **order** is a statement that sets forth the judge's decision on a particular motion before the court. When drafting a motion, an order is included for convenience of the court and may even be required in many jurisdictions.

In many areas of law, the order page of a motion simply contains the title "ORDER" and the following language: "The foregoing motion having been heard, it is hereby ORDERED: GRANTED/DENIED." In family law, the order page frequently contains more specific and more elaborate directives. For instance, the order page accompanying a motion for alimony may contain the statement that the defendant pay to plaintiff spouse the sum of a specific dollar amount at a specific interval, such as $100 a week. The order for child support is usually similarly specific.

Motions for visitation frequently set the number of times for visiting each week and the house where such visits will take place. This is done if the parties have concerns about the duration, frequency, and location of visits, and have not been able to work out these arrangements informally. Where parties have no differences on the issue, an order for reasonable visitation will suffice.

EXAMPLE

ORDER

The foregoing motion having been heard, it is hereby ORDERED:

    GRANTED/DENIED

      THE COURT

        By: _____

            Judge

ORDER

The foregoing motion having been heard, it is hereby ORDERED:

    That the plaintiff-husband pay to the defendant-wife the sum of $ _____ per _____ as alimony pendente lite. *This order shall commence on _____ 20 _____.*

    THE COURT

        By: _____

            Judge

CERTIFICATION

All parties must receive notice of every motion filed with the court. Court systems recognize the need for efficient and economic service upon parties. Unlike the complaint in a lawsuit, courts do not require most motions to be served by a sheriff or other process server. The typical mode of serving a motion is to file the original of the motion with the clerk of the court either by hand-delivering it or mailing it to the clerk's court address and, on the same day, mailing a copy of the motion to the attorneys appearing for the other parties or to the *pro se* litigant.

The **certification** page of the motion states that a copy of the foregoing (motion and order) was sent on a specific date to all counsel of record and *pro se* appearing parties (if any). This page is signed by the moving party's attorney or by the party, if acting *pro se.* Some local practice rules require that the attorney for the moving party recite the names and addresses of all parties to whom the motion was sent.

EXAMPLE

CERTIFICATION

This is to certify that a true copy of the foregoing motion was mailed, postage prepaid, on this date to all counsel and pro se parties of record on this _____ day of _____, 2005 as follows:

Grace A. Luppino, Esq.
555 Main Avenue
New Haven, CT 06511

Justine F. Miller, Esq.
Commissioner of the Superior Court

Certain motions have additional requirements. On rare occasions, a motion must be served by a process server. However, this usually does not occur during the pendency of the proceeding. Some motions must be filed with an accompanying financial affidavit or an affidavit stating other facts. Other motions will not be accepted by the court for filing without an accompanying memorandum of law setting forth a legal argument for the granting of the motion. Some motions require descriptions of real and personal property when the ownership and location of such property is relevant.

MOST FREQUENTLY USED FAMILY LAW MOTIONS

A number of *pendente lite* or temporary motions are commonly used in family law practice and the paralegal should be familiar with them. They are as follows:

- motion for alimony,
- motion for custody of minor children,
- motion for child support,
- motion for visitation,
- motion for counsel fees,

- motion for exclusive possession of the marital residence,
- motion for use of motor vehicle,
- motion for payment of mortgage payments and insurance premiums,
- motion to restrain party from entering the marital residence (restraining order), and
- motion to freeze marital assets.

In most family court jurisdictions, the motion practice rules are so flexible that a moving party can create motions to ask the court for an order on various items particular to the party's circumstances. For instance, one party may file a motion for payment of children's secondary school tuition or a motion for joint use of the parties' sailboat.

MOTION FOR ALIMONY

A **motion for alimony** seeks the court to order one spouse to make payments of support to the other spouse. Temporary support payments enable the requesting spouse to meet his or her financial obligations during the pendency of the divorce. Motions for alimony are most common when one spouse has stayed in the home or has earned much less than the other spouse during the marriage (see Exhibit 10–1).

The following case illustrates a dispute over a motion for pendente lite relief.

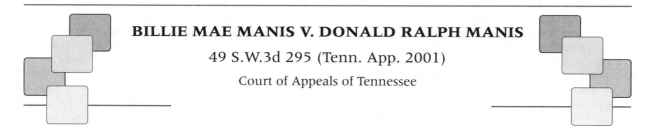

BILLIE MAE MANIS V. DONALD RALPH MANIS

49 S.W.3d 295 (Tenn. App. 2001)

Court of Appeals of Tennessee

D. MICHAEL SWINEY, JUDGE

BACKGROUND

Ms. Billie Mae Manis (Appellee, hereinafter "Wife") and Mr. Donald Ralph Manis (Appellant, hereinafter "Husband") had been married for 41 years when Wife filed for divorce on the grounds of inappropriate marital conduct. Husband and Wife both are 68 years old. Wife has worked outside the home for less than two years during her married life, at stores such as K-Mart, and in Mr. Manis' businesses. Husband has owned and managed various businesses in Sevier and surrounding counties, including pawnshops and horseback riding enterprises, throughout the marriage. He testified that he retired from salaried work in those businesses during the course of this litigation. The record shows, however, that he still controls these businesses and receives income from them. . . .

. . . the Special Master found that Wife is in need of alimony and Husband has the ability to pay. He opined that, although public policy and the legislative intent in Tennessee favors alimony in solido or rehabilitative alimony, Wife's lack of earning ability, Husband's high earning ability, Husband's fault, the 45 year marriage, and Wife's need preponderate in favor of periodic alimony in this case, payable until death or remarriage of Wife or death of Husband. The Special Master found that Husband had been required to pay $1,000 per month in excessive alimony from his first payment under the Court's *pendente lite* award, and awarded Husband a credit for this excess against any accrued alimony arrearage or against future alimony payments. He ordered Husband to pay $2,327.67 in base alimony per month, plus $744.77 to extinguish the mortgage on the marital residence and to pay, as alimony, the cost of two life insurance policies upon his life. Husband also was ordered to make a payment on March 1 of every year to offset Wife's tax liability for the alimony, to maintain health insurance for Wife, and to pay Wife's unreimbursed medical and medication expenses. Wife was awarded reasonable attorney fees, and fees of the Special Master were taxed 2/3 to Husband and 1/3 to Wife. The Special Master ordered that "any further issues for which the parties desire an explicit finding of fact or ruling may be raised within 15 days of this opinion."

Both parties filed numerous Objections to the Special Master's Report. Husband objected to the amount of alimony awarded. Husband argued that the Special Master was appointed in January 1998 but did not file his report until November 30, 1998, and in that interim, Husband had retired, so that he no longer had an income sufficient to pay the amount of alimony ordered.

Further, Husband argued that he had voluntarily given Wife $8,000 each month from July 1995 through October 1, 1998 for her support, for a total of more than $300,000, and that the Special Master should have considered these payments as part of Wife's share of the marital estate or as excess alimony. He sought credit against future alimony for those voluntary payments. Husband further alleged that the Special Master had erred on virtually all of the findings of fact and conclusions of law as to the valuation of marital property. . .

. . . Husband appeals, raising ten issues concerning the . . . amount of temporary alimony . . .

. . . 2. Whether the Trial Court erred in the amount of alimony *pendente lite* or the amount of periodic alimony awarded or in requiring Husband to pay Wife an additional sum for her federal income tax obligation arising from alimony?

. . . Husband's issues concerning alimony are: (1) the amount of temporary alimony; (2) the amount of periodic alimony; (3) the failure of the Trial Court to offset from alimony vested social security benefits due to Wife; and (4) the Trial Court's order that Husband make an annual payment to Wife representing the amount Wife pays as federal income tax on her alimony. We first note that the Trial Court did grant Husband a credit toward his obligation to reimburse Wife for her tax liability for any amount of Social Security benefits Wife received the prior year.

There are no hard and fast rules for spousal support decisions. *Kinard v. Kinard*, 986 S.W.2d, 220. 234 (Tenn.Ct.App. 1998). Trial judges have broad discretion

to determine whether spousal support is needed and, if so, its nature, amount and duration. *Garfinkel*, 945 S.W.2d at 748. Appellate courts are generally disinclined to second-guess a trial judge's spousal support decision unless it is not supported by the evidence or is contrary to the public policies reflected in the applicable statutes. *Kinard*, 986 S.W.2d at 234. The purpose of long-term spousal support is to provide support to a disadvantaged spouse who is unable to achieve some degree of self-sufficiency. *Id.*

Spousal support decisions hinge on the unique facts of the case and require a careful balancing of the factors in Tenn Code Ann. § 36-5-101 (d)(1). In virtually every case, the two most important factors are the demonstrated need of the disadvantaged spouse and the obligor's spouse's ability to pay. *Kinard*, 986 S.W.2d at 235.

Wife is 68 years old and has an eleventh grade education. The Special Master found that she has health problems, including high blood pressure, a hiatal hernia, stomach and thyroid ailments. He further found that she has no savings account, no retirement account, no money market accounts. She virtually has never worked outside the home during the parties' 45-year marriage. She has no source of income or support aside from her Husband, who owns a number of successful business enterprises and remains well able to accommodate his personal income needs despite his recent decision to retire from salaried employment in those businesses. The Special Master carefully reviewed Wife's affidavit of income and expense, allowing some of the items and disallowing others. He ordered that $744.77 of Wife's monthly alimony payments would cease when the mortgage payment in that amount on the marital home was extinguished, either by monthly payments or by Husband's paying off the mortgage. He also ordered Husband to make an annual alimony payment on March 1st to reimburse Wife for the income tax liability she will incur as a result of receipt of her monthly alimony payments. It appears the Special Master awarded Wife a monthly alimony amount that closely tracks her reasonable monthly expenses, and therefore the annual payment for her income tax liability is necessary as she will not be able to accumulate income from which to pay this expense. Considering the familiar factors set forth in Tenn Code Ann. § 36-5-101(d)(1), we find the Trial Court did not err in the amount of alimony awarded to Wife . . .

MOTION FOR CUSTODY OF MINOR CHILDREN

A **motion for custody** requests the court to order that one parent have the primary obligation for care and custody of the minor children and the authority to make decisions concerning how the care and maintenance of the children is to be administered. This motion must be taken very seriously by the party who wishes permanent custody of the children. If the pendency period is lengthy, the likelihood of a change in the custody from one parent to the other is very slight because courts do not make changes in the child's living arrangements after the child has adjusted to being primarily with one parent and is accustomed to that parent's style of parenting. Because the outcome of this motion is so significant, many attorneys pursue this phase of the divorce proceeding with meticulous care and great vigor (see Exhibit 10–2). Whenever a party seeks to obtain custody of a child through a court proceeding, they may be required by state law to file a custody affidavit along with their motion for custody. In this document, signed under oath, the moving party swears that there are no other custody proceedings pending regarding the minor child or children in question.

MOTION FOR CHILD SUPPORT

The party filing a motion for custody frequently also files a **motion for child support,** which seeks an order from the court that the other parent—that is, the noncustodial parent—contribute to the financial support of the children. The court will order the noncustodial parent to pay a specific amount for each child. The court will determine this amount by referring to state-enacted **child support guidelines,** which impose a duty on a noncustodial parent for an amount based on his or her income and the age and number of the minor children. A more detailed discussion of the child support guidelines appears in Chapter 6. State guidelines typically establish an amount for the noncustodial parent to pay after also considering the custodial parent's income and ability to provide for the financial needs of the children (see Exhibit 10–3).

The following case illustrates an appeal of the trial court's award of temporary child support.

FIGURE 10–1
Courts do not like to change a child's living arrangements once the child has gotten used to living with one parent.

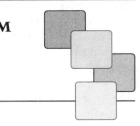

DONNA EISENBAUM V. ALAN EISENBAUM

44 Conn. App. 605, 691 A.2d 25(1997)

Appellate Court of Connecticut

HENNESSY, J.

The defendant appeals from the trial court's pendente lite order of child support. On appeal, the defendant claims that the trial court improperly (1) exceeded its jurisdiction in ordering the defendant to make payments other than child support, (2) awarded the plaintiff counsel fees and (3) changed the effect of its order in its response to the plaintiff's motion for clarification.

The facts relevant to this appeal are as follows. The parties' marriage was dissolved in 1980. They later resumed living together and, in 1983, the parties had a child. They had a second child in 1986. The defendant has acknowledged paternity of both children. From November, 1983, to September, 1993, the parties lived together as husband and wife, although they were not legally married. Throughout the ten year period, the plaintiff has not worked outside the home, by mutual agreement of the parties. She has, instead, attended to the children's needs and to household matters. The defendant, who terms himself an investor, has had an income averaging approximately $250,000 per year over the past five years.

The parties separated in September, 1993. After the separation, the defendant moved out of the house but continued to pay household expenses, credit card bills, gas charges and expenses for the children, such as clothes, gymnastics and soccer.

The plaintiff subsequently brought an action seeking, inter alia, support for the children. After a hearing on February 14, 1995, the trial court temporarily ordered the defendant to pay as child support, $1000 per week and to continue to pay the household expenses and the outstanding credit card balance. In its March 28, 1995 memorandum of decision and its May 4, 1995 response to the plaintiff's motion for clarification, the trial court stated that its prior temporary order would continue as the permanent pendente lite order.

On May 17, 1995, the defendant filed an appeal from the trial court's order regarding his obligation to pay the household and credit card expenses. On July 19, 1995, the trial court granted the plaintiff's motion to terminate the stay and awarded her $10,000 in counsel fees. Upon the defendant's motion for review, this court reinstated the appellate stay. On November 2, 1995, the trial court responded to the plaintiff's motion for clarification indicating that its March, 1995 order was a "combination child support order of cash and in kind necessary to maintain the family home for the benefit of the children." The defendant amended his appeal to include the issues regarding the trial court's award of counsel fees and its November 1995 response to the motion for clarification.

The defendant first claims that the trial court exceeded its jurisdiction by making a pendente lite order other than child support. He argues that the portion of the trial court's order requiring him to pay the household expenses and the credit card bill is a disguised alimony order and, therefore, the order was outside the court's jurisdiction.

General Statutes § 46b-61 allows the trial court to make any order as to the "custody, care, education, visitation and support of any minor child of the parties" in all cases in which the parents of the minor child live separately. "To determine the amount of support required by minor children, the court considers the needs of the children and the respective abilities of the parents to maintain them." *Whitney v. Whitney*, 171 Conn. 23, 29, 368A.2d 96 29, 368 A.2d 96 (1976); see also General Statutes § 46b-84(c).

"'In determining whether a trial court has abused its broad discretion in domestic relations matters, [the reviewing court allows] every reasonable presumption in favor of the correctness of [the trial court's] action.'" *Ashton* v. *Ashton*, 31 Conn. App. 736, 742, 627 A.2d 943 (1993), cert. denied, 228 Conn. 901, 634 A.2d 295 (1994).

We conclude that the trial court did not abuse its discretion in ordering the defendant to pay the household expenses. We also conclude, however, that the court improperly ordered the defendant to pay the credit card balance.

In the plaintiff's financial affidavit, she listed her total weekly expenses for herself and her two children as approximately $1843. We conclude that the trial court properly ordered the defendant to pay the household expenses in addition to $1000 per week based on the needs of the children and the parties' ability to pay. The trial court, however, had no authority to order the defendant to pay the credit card debt as part of pendente lite child support. "Child support orders must be based on the statutory criteria enumerated in General Statutes § 46b-84 of which one of the most important is the needs of the child." *Brown* v. *Brown*, 190 Conn. 345, 349, 460 A.2d 1287 (1983). Here, the record contains no evidence that the payment of the credit card balance was necessary for the maintenance of the children.

This part of the support order was, therefore, improper. . . .

MOTION FOR VISITATION

The noncustodial parent has a right to visitation (or access) with the children. Upon motion, the court will address the noncustodial parent's desire for visitation and will tailor the provision in the visitation order to the best interests of the child. It is not unusual for a noncustodial parent's **motion for visitation** to request that the court enter an order for "reasonable visitation" without specifying the breadth or limits of this visitation. An order for "reasonable rights of visitation" leaves much to the discretion of the parties and its success depends on the ability of the soon-to-be ex-spouses to communicate and negotiate a visitation schedule between themselves. When the parties are unable to do this, a more definite visitation schedule becomes necessary that spells out frequency and duration of visitation, with dates and times of pickup and return specified. Upon a motion for visitation with a detailed schedule, if the court finds that good cause exists, it will order such an arrangement (see Exhibit 10–4).

MOTION FOR COUNSEL FEES

The court has the power, upon **motion for counsel fees** of one of the parties, to order the spouse to pay the reasonable attorney's fees of the moving party. If the court orders reasonable counsel fees, the court will usually specify a dollar amount it deems reasonable. This amount may or may not reflect the actual amount the party will have to pay his or her attorney. Often the court's estimate of "reasonable" falls far below what the client is actually charged.

Sometimes courts choose to deny a motion for counsel fees *pendente lite* and instead indicate that a decision on counsel fees will only be made at the final hearing. Further, when both parties have ample funds or other assets in their own right, the court will not order one party to pay for the other party's legal fees associated with the divorce (see Exhibit 10–5).

The following case discusses the issue of awarding counsel fees in a domestic relations case.

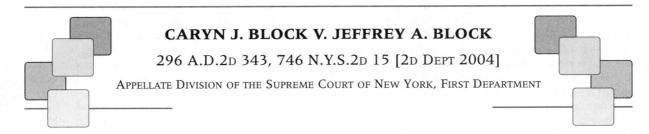

CARYN J. BLOCK V. JEFFREY A. BLOCK

296 A.D.2D 343, 746 N.Y.S.2D 15 [2D DEPT 2004]

APPELLATE DIVISION OF THE SUPREME COURT OF NEW YORK, FIRST DEPARTMENT

BEFORE: NARDELLI, J.P., SAXE, BUCKLEY, SULLIVAN, GONZALEZ, JJ.

In awarding unallocated interim counsel and expert fees in the amount of $35,000 to assist the wife in preparing for the forthcoming trial to determine the value of the fees due the husband, an attorney, for his representation of clients in personal injury cases, the IAS court properly took into consideration the relative financial circumstances of the parties (*see, Charpié* v. *Charpié*, 271 A. D. 2d 169) as well as the nature and extent of the issues to be litigated, as to which the court was uniquely positioned to assess.

The same, however, cannot be said with respect to the award of interim counsel fees in defending the appeal of the interim $35,000 award. There can be no dispute that a spouse, on a proper showing, is entitled under Domestic Relations Law § 237(a) to counsel fees for representation during the appellate process (*see*, *Anostario* v. *Anostario*, 252 A. D. 2d 895). We find, however, no justification, either on the basis of need or fairness, for the award of $15,000 in interim fees to defend against the appeal of the earlier $35,000 award. The wife earns a substantial income, approximately $100,000 annually, receives $49,000 yearly in child support and expenses, has assets of $142,000, has previously been awarded $87,750 in legal fees, aside from the $35,000 awarded in the September 20, 2001 order under review, which we are affirming, as well as $31,081.43 in expert fees, and has already received $216,000 in equitable distribution to be supplemented by a further distribution after resolution of the valuation of the contingency fee cases. In the absence of financial hardship and any showing as to the estimated value and extent of the legal services contemplated, neither of which is demonstrated here, a trial court should not award interim attorneys' fees prospectively for an appeal. It is not, as the dissent suggests, the lack of "an exact breakdown" as to the "expected cost of the appeal" which we find troubling, but rather the total absence of any showing whatever as to the anticipated cost or value of the services contemplated in connection with the appeal. Surely, if counsel is able to estimate the cost of the appeal at $25,000 it is not asking too much to require him to make some showing as to the contemplated services justifying such an award.

Moreover, a trial court should strive to avoid the appearance that it is punishing a litigant for pursuing his or her right to appeal. The fact that, in appealing from the award of $35,000 in interim counsel fees, the husband might be viewed as pursuing a "scorched earth" tactic, as charged by the wife, does not justify an award that serves, in effect, as a sanction for taking an appeal. Moreover, although that is not the case here since the husband perfected his appeal, courts should take pains to assure that an award of an additional fee to defend against an appeal of an award of a fee does not act as a deterrent to the review of the original award.

Finally, we are asked to affirm the award of a $15,000 fee, granted after a request for $25,000, for which no showing as to the extent of the services to be rendered or hours expended has been made. While an appellate court, concededly, has the authority, and is in a better position than a trial court, to assess the extent of the legal services and their reasonable value in connection with the appeal it has heard, all that we have before us is an 11-page respondent's brief in an appeal that was submitted, not argued. Small wonder that there is such widespread criticism of the high cost of matrimonial litigation. (*See*, *Charpi* v. *Charpi*, supra, 271 A.D.2d at 170-171; *see also*, "Defusing the M.D., NYLJ 3/9/93, p. 2; "Reflections on Matrimonial Lawyers, Judges and Practice, Part I," David B. Saxe, NYLJ, 1/8/93, p. 2.)

On any future application for fees and on a proper showing, the IAS court may, of course, consider the reasonable services rendered herein as part of the continuum of services required in representing the wife.

With respect to the alarmist tone of the dissent, we would merely point out that we have left open the opportunity for the payment of counsel fees in the defense of this appeal and have set forth the standard for the award of a prospective fee in such a case. As we have noted, no showing was made here. We believe, moreover, that vacatur, not pruning, is the only appropriate response to an award of $15,000 granted solely on the following submission by plaintiff on the motion: "Plaintiff should be awarded $25,000 counsel fees to defend against defendant's appeal to the Appellate Division. She cannot possibly afford to fund that effort herself, and of course defendant knows it."

All concur except Saxe and Gonzalez, JJ. who dissent in part in a memorandum by Saxe, J. as follows:
SAXE, J. (dissenting in part)

Although nominally taking issue solely with the fee awarded to pay for the *appeal* of the pendente lite counsel fee award, the majority today, in less than four full pages, has begun an assault upon the developing case law intended to "make sure that marital litigation is shaped not by the power of the bankroll but by the power of the evidence" (Scheinkman, Practice Commentaries, McKinneys Cons Laws of NY, Book 14, Domestic Relations Law C237:1, at 6, citing *O'Shea* v. *O'Shea*, 93 N. Y.2d 187). Its decision encourages a resurrection of the law's previous approach, under which a less affluent wife in divorce proceedings typically found herself in a weaker bargaining position, unable to pay for legal representation at a level her wealthier spouse was able to obtain, and having to virtually impoverish herself before she could receive any relief from the court.

In *Charpié* v. *Charpié* (271 A.D.2d 169), we had the opportunity to observe that even among the affluent, a large disparity between divorcing spouses' assets and earning power often results in an inequity in the context of divorce litigation by which "a spouse with Lawyer Conduct in Matrimonial Actions recommended that "the better practice is for judges to award adequate pendente lite counsel fees early in the action, and to make appropriate adjustments when necessary" (Report, Committee to Examine Lawyer Conduct in Matrimonial Actions, May 4, 1993, at 37). Indeed, the intransigence of the problem of non-monied spouses not being awarded sufficient interim counsel fees was addressed again in the 1996 report of the New York Judicial Committee on Women in the Courts, in which it was stated that the "common practice of routinely denying or deferring such applications [for interim fees] . . . does not seem to have improved in any significant degree" (Report, New York Judicial Committee on Women in the Courts, May 1996, at 20).

Here, appropriately, the majority does not take issue with the $35,000 interim counsel and expert fee award challenged by the defendant husband, despite the wife's annual income of $100,000, assets of $142,000, and distributive award of $216,000. Rather, although it acknowledges the right to an award of counsel fees for an appeal (*see*, Domestic Relations Law § 237[b]; *Borakove v. Borakove*, 116 A.D.2d 683), the majority asserts that *"[i]n the absence of financial hardship* and any showing as to the estimated value and extent of the legal services contemplated, neither of which is demonstrated here, a trial court should not award interim attorneys' fees prospectively for an appeal" (emphasis added).

As a practical matter, the experienced matrimonial trial judge, like this Court, has sufficient knowledge to assess with some accuracy the amount of time it should realistically take to handle an appeal such as this one. Therefore, the lack of information in an attorney's affidavit attesting to an exact breakdown of the expected cost of the appeal should not invalidate the fee application, particularly since such an assertion is necessarily an estimate of contemplated work. Indeed, while an application for interim counsel fees must be supported by an affidavit from counsel (22 NYCRR 202 16[k][3]), as a general rule such an affidavit does not and cannot contain a realistic breakdown of how the lawyer anticipates the contemplated litigation to proceed. It is the IAS judge who has the best objective understanding and appreciation of the case, including the extent of the record, the issues involved, and the approach to be expected of the appealing party, and we ought to give full deference to her evaluation of the situation.

In view of the limited value of a submission from the attorney applying for fees, that in effect guesses at the estimated extent of the legal services contemplated, the majority's ruling amounts to a pronouncement that the matrimonial court should not make a prospective interim fee award for an appeal in the absence of financial hardship. This runs counter to the developing rule intended to ensure a level playing field, and would propel the law back to the older rule of *Kann v. Kann*

(38 A. D. 2d 545), by which courts were not permitted to award counsel fees wherever the spouse seeking the award possessed assets sufficient to pay those fees.

The majority also appears to take the position that the court's award of interim appellate counsel fees amounts to an improper sanction, by which the monied spouse was being punished for pursuing his right to appeal from the interim fee award. This view fails to recognize that by bonding an eminently reasonable pendente lite counsel fee award and taking an appeal, the monied spouse was demonstrating exactly how a substantially wealthier spouse can use his resources against the less powerful spouse to obtain leverage in the litigation.

In the vast majority of cases, this Court has rejected, with good reason, challenges to pendente lite fee awards. We have reiterated the well-established rule that the appropriate remedy lies in a prompt trial in which the facts may be examined (*see, e.g., Halperin v. Halperin*, 234 A.D.2d 59). Therefore, the taking of an appeal to challenge a fee award which could be adjusted at the close of the case represents the type of unnecessary litigation that puts a non-monied spouse who must pay for the costs of the appeal into a weaker bargaining position. To require the non-monied spouse to use up a portion of her finite resources to defend against such an appeal, without awarding her fees to cover the additional cost arising from the appeal, further skews the playing field we are trying to level.

Here, defendant husband's income for 1999, the last year for which he produced tax returns, was nearly $1,000,000, while plaintiff wife now earns $110,000. While her distributive award combined with her net assets may leave her with the apparently substantial sum of approximately $300,000, those funds will only remain substantial if they are not consumed by the extraordinary expense of contested matrimonial litigation, particularly the type of repeated interlocutory appeals and motions we see here. This court has previously noted that defendant had engaged in "obstructive tactics" (*see, Block v. Block*, 258 A.D.2d 324, 326); importantly, we have already seen three prior appeals in this action (*see*, 245 A.D.2d 153; 258 A.D.2d 324; 277 A.D.2d 87). Clearly, interim appellate fees are no less necessary in this case than the interim counsel fees awarded for counsel's pre-trial and trial work.

The majority misjudges the nature and quality of counsel's work by implying that his relatively short 11-page brief reflects that his efforts on the appeal were limited. The value of appellate work should not be judged solely on the basis of how many trees were felled to produce a brief. Indeed, appellate justices regularly exhort counsel to limit the size of their briefs, and we often note that it takes extra time, effort, and skill to streamline and shorten a brief; a well-researched and well-written 11-page brief, responsive to appellant's contentions, may require as much time and attention as a carelessly drafted 20-page brief. Notably, the brief in question effectively responded to all the contentions raised in appellant's brief. In addition, beyond counsel's efforts on the brief, he was forced to expend additional time opposing defendant's applications to this Court for an interim stay and then for a stay pending appeal.

Finally, even assuming that a reasonable counsel fee for the present appeal may be less than the $15,000 awarded, this Court's reversal of the award and outright denial of the motion is an inappropriate response. Since it is undisputed that the agreed-upon hourly rate of plaintiff's well-respected counsel is $400, a reasonable number of hours for careful preparation of the brief, time spent on the stay motions, in addition to printing and clerical costs, could easily bring the cost of even this straightforward appeal to something close to the amount awarded. Any inequity is better addressed by an adjustment in the context of the final judgment, based upon counsel's affidavit attesting to the actual services rendered. It is unseemly and unnecessary to deprive defendant wife of the whole sum because a small fraction of it is perhaps unearned at this time.

Moreover, the majority fails to consider that its ruling is likely to lead matrimonial trial judges to conclude that they may not approximate and award prospective interim counsel fees for appeals (*but see, LeRoy v. LeRoy,* 276 A.D.2d 442). The likely result is that judges will find it necessary to refer the issue of appellate counsel fees to Special Referees for fact-finding, a process that consumes additional hours of court time and months of delay for hearings and the follow-up motions to confirm or disaffirm the Referee's recommendations (*see,* CPLR 4403). This is exactly the type of ancillary, sideshow litigation that our court administrators have been trying to eliminate in matrimonial litigation (*see,* Silbermann, *An Assessment of the First Three Years of the 'New' Matrimonial Practice Rules,* NYLJ, Dec 30, 1996, at 1). Moreover, the additional cost of such a procedure would be far greater than any possible difference between the $15,000 awarded here and the amount actually needed to successfully perform the work.

In my view, the $15,000 awarded for interim appellate counsel fees should be affirmed. In any event, since the trial court has the authority to make adjustments in fee awards in the final judgment, the issue of whether defendant is entitled to recoup a portion of that payment may be addressed by the trial court in that context, when counsel will be able to submit exact information as to the extent and value of the appellate work performed. . . .

MOTION FOR EXCLUSIVE POSSESSION OF THE MARITAL RESIDENCE

The court has the power upon **motion for exclusive possession of the marital residence** by either spouse to order temporary possession of the marital home to the moving spouse. While most couples who own a house own it jointly, the motion is just for possession during the pendency of the lawsuit. This motion determines which of the spouses will live in the family residence until the final divorce decree is entered. At the time of the final decree, the court will recognize each spouse's interest in the property and make equitable orders for the disposition to the residence. Courts are reluctant to order either spouse to leave the family home during the pendency period because of the financial burden it imposes on the spouse having to leave. However, the court will make such an order if the spouses are in agreement as to one spouse leaving or if there are issues of family violence (see Exhibit 10–6).

MOTION FOR USE OF MOTOR VEHICLE

Sometimes household automobiles are titled jointly or in the name of one spouse only. Therefore, the spouse without legal title or sharing title may find it necessary to motion the court to order that one of the family automobiles be designated for his or her use. This motion, a **motion for use of motor vehicle,** like the others, typically has an order page attached and is presented to the court usually at the same time other *pendente lite* motions for alimony, child support, use of the family home, custody, and visitation are addressed (see Exhibit 10–7).

Motion for Payment of Mortgage Payments and Insurance Premiums

One spouse may make a **motion for payment of mortgage payments and insurance premiums**, which asks the court to order the other spouse to make all or part of the mortgage payment on the family home and also to pay all or part of the insurance premiums needed to keep in effect policies that insure family assets or policies that provide medical or life insurance coverage for the spouses and minor children (see Exhibit 10–8).

Restraining Orders

Many judicial systems permit spouses to file a legal document, called a **restraining order,** that requests that the court order the other party to refrain from certain actions or types of conduct or behavior. These orders include a **motion to freeze marital assets,** that is, a restraining order not to deplete the family assets, sell the family home, or any of the family motor vehicles, boats, or other significant articles of personal property; a restraining order freezing the savings or checking account so that neither party may subsequently race to the bank and empty such joint accounts of funds; and a restraining order preventing one party or the other from entering the family home (a **motion to restrain party from entering marital residence**) or harassing or assaulting the other spouse (see Exhibit 10–9).

Ex Parte Proceedings

The U.S. Constitution and its state counterparts protect defendants from someone walking into a court without their knowledge, accusing them of some wrongdoing, and obtaining a court order. The general rule is that defendants have a right to procedural due process. This is the right to notice of the proceedings as well as the opportunity to be heard. *Ex parte* proceedings are an exception to this rule. **Ex parte** is a Latin term meaning "by one party" or "for one party." An **ex parte proceeding** is a court hearing conducted in response to a moving party's *ex parte* motion or petition. The opposing party is not present during an *ex parte* proceeding because these documents are generally filed in an emergency situation. The most common type of *ex parte* order is a restraining order in a domestic violence case. For example, an abused spouse who feels that she is in imminent physical danger may file an *ex parte* motion to order her husband out of the marital home. Another example would be learning that a spouse is preparing to leave the country or move to another state and take the minor children with her. The father in this case would file an *ex parte* motion to restrain her actions. *Ex parte* motions are also filed to prevent the transfer or hiding of assets.

Ex parte orders are temporary in nature because the defendant has not had an opportunity to be heard. The moving party must file an application for *ex parte* relief as well as an affidavit supporting the reasons for the action. If the moving party is aware that the defendant has an attorney, defendant's counsel should be contacted. The moving party goes to court without the other party present and the judge hears only one side of the story. While the court may grant an *ex parte* order immediately upon determining that there is good cause to do so, a hearing is scheduled within a matter of days to allow the defendant to appear and be heard by the court. Notice of this second proceeding will be sent to the defendant informing him or her of the opportunity to be heard on that date. At the second hearing, the defendant will have the opportunity to present his or her own evidence. The moving party may also present further evidence. At the close of this hearing, the judge will continue, modify, or vacate the order.

The following case illustrates an "emergency motion" as well as issues involving military parents.

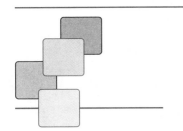
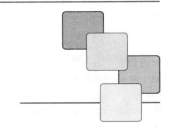

EX PARTE K.N.L.

872 So.2d 868 (Ala.Civ.App. 2003)

Court of Civil Appeals of Alabama

CRAWLEY, JUDGE

K.N.L., the mother of B.D.P., petitions this court for a writ of mandamus directing the Baldwin Juvenile Court to grant her motion to stay a pendente lite child custody proceeding. We deny the petition.

The mother is a member of a United States Army Reserve unit that was called to active duty on February 10, 2003, for deployment overseas as a part of "Operation Enduring Freedom." The mother sought a stay of the pendente lite child custody proceeding pursuant to the Soldiers' and Sailors' Civil Relief Act of 1940, 50 App. U.S.C. § 501 et seq. ("the Act").

K.N.L. ("the mother") and W.D.P. ("the father") are the parents of B.D.P. ("the child"), a 10-year-old girl. The parents have never been married. They lived together for the first six years of the child's life and then broke up in 1999, with the father taking up residence in Alabama and the mother taking up residence in Pennsylvania. For the next two years, the child, by agreement of the parties, lived with the father in Alabama during the school year and with the mother in Pennsylvania during the summer. In May 2000, the mother executed a power of attorney in favor of the father, allowing him to assume and maintain guardianship of the child during a time when the mother's reserve unit had been activated.

On May 2, 2002, the father filed in the Baldwin Juvenile Court a petition seeking sole physical custody of the child and requesting child support from the mother. The mother alleges that she was not served with the father's petition until nearly two months after the petition was filed. On May 20, 2002, as the parties had previously agreed, the child left for summer visitation with the mother in Pennsylvania. On July 28, 2002, the mother filed a motion for a 30-day extension of time to answer the father's petition. Three days later, the mother filed an appearance for the limited purpose of filing a motion to dismiss the father's petition based upon her belief that the Alabama court had no personal jurisdiction over her. The mother did not return the child to the father at the end of the summer visitation.

On November 7, 2002, following a hearing, the juvenile court denied the mother's motion to dismiss. On November 14, 2002, the mother filed a "Contest of Paternity," alleging that W.D.P. was not the child's biological father and requesting that the court order paternity testing. On December 13, 2002, the father, alleging that the mother had failed to return the child at the beginning of the school year and had denied him any physical contact with the child, filed a petition for pendente lite custody of the child, or, in the alternative, for visitation with the child pending a final hearing on his custody and support petition.

On January 17, 2003, the juvenile court determined, based on an affidavit of paternity signed by the parties, that the issue of paternity was precluded by the doctrine of res judicata; therefore, the court denied the mother's request for paternity testing. The juvenile court set the father's custody and child-support petition for a hearing on April 14, 2003.

On February 26, 2003, the father filed an emergency motion for pendente lite custody of the child, alleging that the mother had filed a number of baseless motions in an attempt to delay the custody proceedings; that the mother had failed to return the child at the beginning of the school year according to the parties' agreement; that he had reason to believe that the mother's military unit had recently been activated; that the mother had given legal guardianship of the child to the maternal grandmother in Florida; and that the mother had set up a child-support allotment payable to the maternal grandmother. The juvenile court set the father's emergency motion for pendente lite custody for a hearing on March 19, 2003. On the morning set for the hearing, the mother moved to stay the proceedings, alleging that, because of her military orders, it was impossible for her to attend any custody hearing—final or pendente lite—and seeking a postponement under the Act until she returned from her overseas assignment. The mother attached to her motion a letter from her commanding officer and a copy of her activation orders, dated February 10, 2003, from the Department of the Army. The father filed an affidavit on April 21, 2003, stating that he had been informed by the child that, one week before the scheduled March 19, 2003, hearing, the mother's new husband had traveled to the home of the maternal grandmother in Florida to retrieve the child and to take her back to Pennsylvania to live with him while the mother was on active duty.

In *Ex parte Integon Corp.*, 672 So.2d 497 (Ala. 1995), our supreme court reiterated what a petitioner must establish in order to be entitled to the issuance of a writ of mandamus.

> Mandamus is a drastic and extraordinary writ, to be issued only where there is (1) a clear legal right in the petitioner to the order sought; (2) an imperative duty upon the respondent to perform, accompanied by a refusal to do so; (3) the lack of another adequate remedy; and (4) properly invoked jurisdiction of the court.

672 So.2d at 499. The applicable portion of the Act provides:

> At any stage thereof any action or proceeding in any court in which a person in military service is involved, either as plaintiff or defendant, during the period of such service or within sixty days thereafter may, in the discretion of the court in which it is pending, on its own motion, and shall, on application to it by such person or some person on his behalf, be stayed as provided in this Act [Sections 501 to 591 of this Appendix], unless, in the opinion of the court, the ability of the plaintiff to prosecute the action or the defendant to conduct his defense is not materially affected by reason of his military service. 50 App. U.S.C. § 521.

In *Richardson v. First National Bank of Columbus*, 46 Ala.App. 366. 242 So.2d 676 (Ala.Civ.App. 1970), this court explained the purpose of the Act:

> 'The Soldiers' and Sailors' Civil Relief Act of 1940 (in like manner with all similar previous acts in our history)

was prompted by at least two considerations, first, the maintenance in the armed forces of a reasonable measure of that unbothered serenity and security in respect of personal responsibilities which effectively promotes military efficiency and the national defense; and secondly, the assurance that in the field of individual justice no advantage in judicial proceedings by or against a soldier or sailor will result from his absorption in his country's defense.'. . .

. . . The Act "places upon the trial judge a wide discretion; and, in determining whether a service [member] is entitled to relief, each case must stand upon its own merits." 247 Ala. at 315, 24 So.2d at 222. "Whether to grant a continuance or stay pursuant to the act is a matter which rests in the sound discretion of the trial court and will not be disturbed on appeal absent an abuse of that discretion.". . .

. . . Decisions construing the Act indicate that when a military parent seeks a stay of a child-custody or visitation proceeding, the trial judge should consider the impact of such a stay on the other parent's right to visit and communicate with the children. *See, e.g., Henneke v. Young*, 145 Ohio App.3d 111, 115, 761 N.E.2d 1140, 1143 (2001). In *Henneke*, the divorce judgment awarded the father, who was stationed in Korea, custody of the parties' three children and gave the mother "'[v]isitation . . . as agreed upon between the parties.'" 145 Ohio App.3d at 112, 761 N.E.2d at 1141. In response to the mother's motion to set a specific visitation schedule, the trial court awarded the mother one week of visitation in August. When the father indicated his inability to comply with the visitation order, the mother filed a petition seeking to hold the father in contempt. The father moved to have the contempt proceeding stayed until he was "relieved from his current assignment in Korea." 145 Ohio App.3d at 113, 761 N.E.2d at 1141. The trial court granted the stay, the mother appealed, and the Ohio appellate court reversed. The court stated:

> [W]hen exercising its discretion in this matter, the trial court should have considered the nature of the civil action at issue here. The dispute between the parties involves their children—the oldest of whom was nine years old at the time the proceedings were stayed—and the right of their natural mother to visit and communicate with them. Under the trial court's ruling, [the father] could prevent [the mother] from seeing her children for a substantial period of time while he is serving in Korea, without [the mother's] being able to do anything to vindicate her right, pursuant to the orders of the trial court, to visit and to communicate with her children. Under these circumstances, we conclude that the trial court acted unreasonably by suspending the proceedings in this matter, during the entire time that [the father] will serve in Korea, pursuant to the Soldiers' and Sailors' Civil Relief Act. 145 Ohio App.3d at 115, 761 N.E.2d at 1143.

. . . The juvenile court would have been well within its discretion in determining that the mother had intentionally delayed the custody proceedings and had used her active-duty orders in an eleventh-hour attempt to effect a long-term denial of the father's rights to visitation and custody. The Act "'is not to be employed as a vehicle of oppression or abuse. . . .' Such statutes were enacted . . . for the protection of the service [member's] rights and remedies, but not to be unjustly taken advantage of.". . .

. . . The juvenile court would also have been within its discretion in deciding that the best interests of the child would be served by having her reside, pending a final hearing on the merits of the custody issue, with her natural father rather than with a third party such as the maternal grandmother or the mother's new husband.

Finding that the mother had no clear legal right to a stay and that the juvenile court did not abuse its discretion in denying the stay, we conclude that the petition for the writ of mandamus is due to be denied.

THE PARALEGAL'S ROLE IN FACILITATING *PENDENTE LITE* MATTERS

The paralegal in a family law practice will perform many of the steps needed to bring *pendente lite* motions before the court. Frequently, the paralegal will draft all *pendente lite* motions for review by the attorney handling the file and any other documents that must accompany the motions in their respective jurisdiction.

After such review and any possible editing, the paralegal finalizes the motions for filing and makes sure that the appropriate number of copies are created. The paralegal ensures that the motions are filed with the proper court and copies are properly mailed to all necessary parties. The paralegal must make sure that he or she sends the motion to the right court and to the proper division of the court handling family matters.

After the motion is filed with the court, the court clerk will assign the motion date for a court hearing. The clerk will send a **court calendar** to each attorney or *pro se* party. The court calendar is a small printed booklet or a set of pages that shows a number of cases listed according to parties and docket number (see Exhibit 10–10). Each case has a number, which indicates the order in which cases will be heard. However, the court calendar lists only a starting time for the court day, not for each case, so all attorneys must be there for the call of cases at that starting time even if their case is one of the last to be heard. In many jurisdictions, courts set aside one or two specific days of the week to hear motions brought before the court. Some court systems refer to these times as **motion days,** while other jurisdictions call the designated times a **short calendar.**

In every law office at least one staff person has the responsibility of keeping track of when each attorney must be in court. Often this function is delegated to the paralegal. The need to keep track of or docket all court dates is obvious. Failure to appear at a hearing may seriously disadvantage a client, drag out proceedings, and sometimes subject an attorney to a malpractice suit. The need for a **docket control system** is imperative.

DOCKET CONTROL SYSTEM

Dates for motions, trials, and other types of hearings come from different sources. In a law office where general litigation is practiced as well as family law, the attorneys may receive calendars from both state and federal courts throughout the state. They may also receive calendars from arbitration bodies and notices of hearings before various commissions and administrative agencies such as the Workers' Compensation Commission, the Commission on Human Rights and Opportunities, and the Unemployment Commission. Calendaring these dates immediately is essential. As soon as these notices arrive, the paralegal must make sure that these hearing dates are entered on the docket control system.

Every law office has a master calendar. In addition, every attorney has his or her own calendar that reflects dates for out-of-court appointments as well as court commitments. The paralegal should enter the court date on the master calendar at once. After this is done, the paralegal should check the responsible attorney's desk calendar to see if there is a conflict and also to enter the date on that attorney's specific calendar. As mentioned previously, the person bringing the motion is known as the **moving party.** The moving party will decide whether to go forward with the motion, that is, appear to argue the motion on the date the court has scheduled. On receipt of a court calendar, the paralegal must first determine whether the motion was brought by an attorney in the firm or by an opposing party. If the motion originated in the paralegal's firm, the paralegal should ask the attorney who brought the motion whether he or she plans to proceed with the motion on the date assigned. If the motion came from an opposing party, the paralegal must find out if the attorney handling the matter for the firm is available to appear at the motion hearing and whether he or she wishes to be there on that date.

If the attorney in the paralegal's firm brought the motion and plans to argue it on the date assigned, the paralegal should call the client to confirm the party's availability for court on that date if the client is needed at the hearing. A letter should be sent to the client confirming the date of the hearing and the necessity of his presence. Then the paralegal must call the office of opposing counsel to notify that attorney that the motion will go forward. If the moving party is the opposing party, the opposing party will notify the paralegal's firm of her intention to go forward or postpone the hearing and the paralegal will communicate this information to necessary individuals.

If the motion is going forward, the paralegal should locate the file prior to the hearing date and make sure that all recently received documents and other pieces of correspondence are appropriately filed. The file should be reviewed and updated on the day before the hearing and the motion should be placed in the front of the court documents section of the file so it will be readily available to the attorney. In addition, the paralegal should confer with the attorney to ensure that other supporting documentation needed at the hearing is put with the file in a manner that is readily available to the attorney at the hearing. The paralegal should prepare the file so that the attorney may review it before the proceeding.

If the parties can reach an agreement on the *pendente lite* motions, they will prepare an agreement, or stipulation, outlining the terms and present it to the court. Exhibit 10–11 illustrates a stipulation regarding *pendente lite* support in the divorce of comedian Jim Carrey and his former wife Melissa.

If the parties cannot agree, they may be required to meet with the court's family services division to assist them in arriving at an agreement. If this is unsuccessful, the court will hold a hearing on the motion. At the hearing the judge will either **grant** or **deny** the motion. If the motion is granted, the court will enter the appropriate orders. The parties are now required to follow the court's order. When the attorney returns from court, the paralegal should review the file to make sure that the motion with orders filled in is properly replaced in the file in the appropriate section.

MOTIONS FOR CONTEMPT AND MODIFICATION

CONTEMPT

When either party does not comply with a court order made in response to a previous motion, the opposing party may seek to have the party comply by filing what is known as a **motion for contempt** (see Exhibit 10–12). The moving party must prove that the noncompliant party willfully violated the court's order. For example, suppose that upon the filing of Mrs. Bronson's motion for visitation, the court enters an order granting Mrs. Bronson reasonable rights of visitation with her minor children. A problem arises when Mrs. Bronson attempts to exercise her rights pursuant to the order and Mr. Bronson refuses to allow her access to the children. Mrs. Bronson's recourse at this stage will be the motion for contempt.

Before drafting the motion for contempt, the paralegal must review the file in order to determine the court's original orders regarding Mrs. Bronson's motion for visitation. The motion for contempt must recite the court's original orders, when they were entered, the judge who entered such orders, and that the noncompliant party is willfully in violation of such order. The motion for contempt must also specify the type of relief sought, which may include a finding of contempt, payment of counsel fees and costs, and possible incarceration. If the motion for contempt addresses financial matters, the paralegal must also include a request for payment of any arrearages due by the spouse in contempt.

MODIFICATION

Sometimes *pendente lite* orders entered by the court are changed when a substantial change in the parties' circumstances occurs from the time the original order was entered. The legal vehicle for making such changes during the *pendente lite* phase is known as the **motion for modification** (see Exhibit 10–13).

For example, suppose that on August 15, 2005, the court grants Mr. Bronson his motion for alimony *pendente lite* and orders Mrs. Bronson to pay him $275 per week. Mrs. Bronson makes weekly payments up to August 22, 2005. On August 25, 2005, Mrs. Bronson loses her job and is not employed again until September 20, 2005. At her new job, Mrs. Bronson earns far less than she did at her previous job. To change the existing order, Mrs. Bronson must file a motion for modification.

Note that while Mrs. Bronson was in the process of job hunting, Mr. Bronson was probably on the phone to his attorney and that office has responded with a motion for contempt against Mrs. Bronson. It is very common for motions for modification and motions for contempt to be filed and addressed simultaneously before the court by the respective parties.

The following case illustrates a motion for modification of child custody.

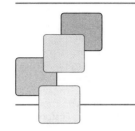
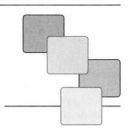

KELVIN DALE WALKER V. ELIZABETH ASHLEY WALKER

26559 (MO.APP.S.D. 2006)

MISSOURI COURT OF APPEALS, SOUTHERN DISTRICT, DIVISION TWO

PHILLIP R. GARRISON, JUDGE

Kelvin Dale Walker ("Father") appeals the trial court's judgment denying his motion to modify custody regarding his three minor children, contending that substantial and significant changes of circumstances had occurred, that modification was in the children's best interest, and that the trial court failed to make specific factual findings. We affirm.

On December 28, 2001, the marriage between Husband and Elizabeth Ashley Walker ("Mother") was dissolved and they were granted joint legal custody of their three minor children, K.W., born July 25, 1989, L.W., born June 16, 1993, and K.D.W., born May 19, 1995. Mother was granted primary physical custody with Father receiving specific periods of custody, including one weekend per month during the school year, holiday visitation and the entire summer vacation when the children were out of school.

On June 10, 2002, Father filed a "Motion for Family Access Order" stating that Mother had denied him visitation and telephone contact with the minor children from January 1, 2002, through June 10, 2002. Following a hearing on Father's motion, the court found that Mother had violated the judgment by denying Father specific visitation and telephone contact. The court ordered that the children be in the custody of Father from July 16, 2002, until August 17, 2002, at which time he was to return the children to Mother.

On May 27, 2004, Father filed a motion to modify the dissolution decree, and a motion for emergency relief and temporary custody of the three minor children alleging that substantial changes of circumstances had occurred with the minor children in that K.W. had been taken into juvenile custody in Prairie County, Arkansas, and Father had not been notified of this action. He sought legal and physical custody of all three minor children with Mother to have reasonable visitation.

A hearing was held on the motion for emergency relief and temporary custody. The court entered a temporary order affirming the visitation schedule ordered in the dissolution decree and directed that Mother's summer visitation be exercised only in the State of Missouri. Father was awarded temporary custody of K.W. upon his release from the juvenile authorities in Prairie County, Arkansas.

On Mother's motion, a guardian ad litem, Amy L. Boxx ("Boxx"), was appointed and a hearing was held on Father's motion to modify. In its judgment the court found that Father had failed to establish a substantial and significant change of circumstances, or that the best interests of the children required modification of the prior custody order. The trial court denied Father's motion to modify and ordered that the court's dissolution judgment, with regard to custody and visitation, remain in full force and effect. This appeal followed.

Appellate courts will affirm the trial court's judgment in custody modification cases if it is supported by substantial evidence, is not against the weight of the evidence, and does not erroneously declare or apply the law. . . .

. . . In Point I, Father contends that the trial court erred in denying his motion because there was substantial and competent evidence of a change in the circumstances of Mother and/or the minor children, and that modification of custody was in the best interests of the children. He alleges that a substantial change in circumstances had occurred in that 1) minor child K.W. was taken into juvenile custody without Mother informing Father; 2) Mother did not abide by the joint custody plan, in that she interfered with his visitation rights; 3) Mother did not notify Father of the children's health, education and welfare; 4) Mother's home environment was not suitable for the children; and 5) Mother did not properly supervise the children, *e.g.* K.W. was allowed to consume alcohol while in her custody.

At the outset we note that Father fails to direct us to any case that holds that a trial court erred in denying a modification motion under these, or similar circumstances. Child custody modification is governed by Section 452.410.1. This statute requires that the trial court "shall *not*" modify an existing custody arrangement unless it finds a change in circumstances of the minor children or the custodian and that such a modification is in the best interests of the minor children. Section 452.410.1 (emphasis added). The burden is on the moving party to prove a substantial change has occurred and that a modification of custody is in the best interests of the minor children. *McCreary v. Mc-Creary*, 954 S.W.2d 433, 439 (Mo.App.W.D. 1997). A change in circumstances must be significant before a custody decree can be modified. *McCubbin v. Taylor*, 5 S.W.3d 202, 207 (Mo.App.W.D. 1999). An evidentiary basis to support a finding of changed circumstances must be present in order for the trial court to have jurisdiction to consider making a change in custody. *Id.* When a trial court does not find a substantial change of circumstances, it never reaches the best interests issue. *Wood v. Wood*, 94 S.W.3d 397, 405 (Mo.App.W.D. 2003).

In this case the trial court found that Father did not meet this burden stating in pertinent part:

> The credible evidence shows that certain changes have occurred since the original Dissolution Judgment. For example, both [Father] and [Mother] have violated the terms of that judgment by cohabiting with unrelated adults of the opposite sex while the minor children have been in their custody. However, the Court finds that none of these changes meet the statutory requirement of a substantial or significant change of circumstances, which would mandate a modification of the Court's prior judgment regarding custody and visitation. Both parties continue to contribute to the numerous difficulties surrounding their relationship and their visitation with the minor children. It is also obvious from the testimony and demeanor of the parties that the acrimony which has characterized their past relationship continues to exist. This fact not only prevents the establishment of a positive and productive relationship between the parties, but it adversely affects the best interests of the minor children. There was no credible evidence that a change in custody would eliminate the animosity between the parties. . .

. . . in this case the trial court denied Father's modification motion without reaching the best interest issue, finding that no substantial change in circumstances had occurred. When a moving party has failed to establish a substantial change of circumstances, the trial court does not even consider whether a change in custody would have been in the best interests of the child. It would make little sense to hold that the trial court must make written findings as to an issue it is not required to consider. Therefore, written findings as to the best interests prong are not required unless the trial court first finds movant has established a substantial change of circumstances of the children or their custodian. . . .

The judgment is affirmed.

EXHIBIT 10–1 Sample motion for alimony.

DOCKET NO. FA 96-123456	:	SUPERIOR COURT
BRONSON, RODNEY	:	JUDICIAL DISTRICT OF NEW HAVEN
V.	:	AT NEW HAVEN
BRONSON, EVELYN	:	AUGUST 15, 2005

MOTION FOR ALIMONY PENDENTE LITE

The plaintiff-husband in the above-captioned matter respectfully requests that this Court order the defendant-wife to pay to him a reasonable sum for his support during the pendency of this action.

THE PLAINTIFF,
RODNEY BRONSON

BY:_____

JUSTINE F. MILLER, ESQ.
HIS ATTORNEY
22 PARK PLACE
NEW HAVEN, CT 06511
(203) 861-4444
JURIS NO. 313133

ORDER

The foregoing motion having been heard, it is hereby ORDERED:

That the defendant-wife pay to the plaintiff-husband the sum of $_____

per _____ as alimony pendente lite.

This order shall commence on _____, 20_____.

The Court

By:_____
Judge

CERTIFICATION

This is to certify that a true copy of the foregoing motion was mailed, postage prepaid, on this date to all counsel and pro se parties of record on this _____ day of _____, 2005 as follows:

Grace A. Luppino, Esq.
555 Main Avenue
New Haven, CT 06511

_____
Justine F. Miller, Esq.
Commissioner of the Superior Court

EXHIBIT 10–2 Sample motion for child custody.

DOCKET NO. FA 96-123456	:	SUPERIOR COURT
BRONSON, RODNEY	:	JUDICIAL DISTRICT OF NEW HAVEN
V.	:	AT NEW HAVEN
BRONSON, EVELYN	:	AUGUST 15, 2005

MOTION FOR CHILD CUSTODY PENDENTE LITE

The plaintiff-husband in the above-entitled action respectfully requests that he be awarded sole custody pendente lite of the minor children of the parties with reasonable rights of visitation to the defendant-wife.

THE PLAINTIFF,
RODNEY BRONSON

BY: _____
JUSTINE F. MILLER, ESQ.
HIS ATTORNEY
22 PARK PLACE
NEW HAVEN, CT 06511
(203) 861-4444
JURIS NO. 313133

ORDER

The foregoing motion having been heard, it is hereby ORDERED that sole custody of the minor children be awarded pendente lite to the plaintiff-husband, with reasonable rights of visitation to the defendant-wife.

That these orders shall commence on _____, 20_____.

The Court

By: _____
JUDGE

CERTIFICATION

This is to certify that a true copy of the foregoing motion was mailed, postage prepaid, on this date to all counsel and pro se parties of record on this _____ day of _____, 2005 , as follows:

Grace A. Luppino, Esq.
555 Main Avenue
New Haven, CT 06511

_____
Justine F. Miller, Esq.
Commissioner of the Superior Court

EXHIBIT 10–3 Sample motion for child support.

DOCKET NO. FA 96-123456   :   SUPERIOR COURT

BRONSON, RODNEY   :   JUDICIAL DISTRICT OF NEW HAVEN

V.   :   AT NEW HAVEN

BRONSON, EVELYN   :   AUGUST 15, 2005

MOTION FOR CHILD SUPPORT PENDENTE LITE

The plaintiff-husband in the above-referenced matter hereby moves that the Court order the defendant-wife to pay to him a reasonable sum for the care, maintenance, and support of the minor children, pendente lite.

THE PLAINTIFF,
RODNEY BRONSON

BY: _____

JUSTINE F. MILLER, ESQ.
HIS ATTORNEY
22 PARK PLACE
NEW HAVEN, CT 06511
(203) 861-4444
JURIS NO. 313133

ORDER

The foregoing motion having been heard, it is hereby ORDERED:

That the defendant-wife pay to the plaintiff-husband the sum of $_____ per _____ as child support, pendente lite.

That this order shall commence on _____, 20_____.

THE COURT

BY: _____
JUDGE

CERTIFICATION

This is to certify that a true copy of the foregoing motion was mailed, postage prepaid, on this date to all counsel and pro se parties of record on this _____ day of _____, 2005, as follows:

Grace A. Luppino, Esq.
555 Main Avenue
New Haven, CT 06511

_____
Justine F. Miller, Esq.
Commissioner of the Superior Court

EXHIBIT 10–4 Sample motion for visitation.

DOCKET NO. FA 96-123456	:	SUPERIOR COURT
BRONSON, RODNEY	:	JUDICIAL DISTRICT OF NEW HAVEN
V.	:	AT NEW HAVEN
BRONSON, EVELYN	:	AUGUST 15, 2005

MOTION FOR VISITATION

The defendant-wife in the above-entitled matter respectfully requests that she be granted reasonable rights of visitation with the minor children of the parties.

THE DEFENDANT,
EVELYN BRONSON

BY: _____
GRACE A. LUPPINO, ESQ.
HER ATTORNEY
555 MAIN AVENUE
NEW HAVEN, CT 06511
(203) 333-3333
JURIS NO. 160000

ORDER

The foregoing motion having been heard, it is hereby ORDERED:

That the defendant-wife shall have reasonable rights of visitation with the minor children of the parties.

That this order shall commence on _____, 20_____.

THE COURT

BY: _____
              JUDGE

CERTIFICATION

This is to certify that a true copy of the foregoing motion was mailed, postage prepaid, on this date to all counsel and pro se parties of record on this _____ day of _____, 2005, as follows:

Justine F. Miller
22 Park Place
New Haven, CT 06511

_____
Grace A. Luppino, Esq.
Commissioner of the Superior Court

EXHIBIT 10–5 Sample motion for payment of counsel fees.

DOCKET NO. FA 96-123456	:	SUPERIOR COURT
BRONSON, RODNEY	:	JUDICIAL DISTRICT OF NEW HAVEN
V.	:	AT NEW HAVEN
BRONSON, EVELYN	:	AUGUST 15, 2005

MOTION FOR COUNSEL FEES PENDENTE LITE

The defendant-wife in the above-captioned matter hereby moves that the Court order the plaintiff-husband to pay a reasonable sum toward the defendant-wife's counsel fees.

THE DEFENDANT,
EVELYN BRONSON

BY: _____
GRACE A. LUPPINO, ESQ.
HER ATTORNEY
555 MAIN AVENUE
NEW HAVEN, CT 06511
(203) 333-3333
JURIS NO. 160000

ORDER

The foregoing motion having been heard, it is hereby ORDERED:

That the plaintiff-husband pay to the defendant-wife the sum of $_____ as counsel fees, pendente lite.

That these orders shall commence on _____, 20_____.

THE COURT

BY: _____
JUDGE

CERTIFICATION

This is to certify that a true copy of the foregoing motion was mailed, postage prepaid, on this date to all counsel and pro se parties of record on this _____ day of _____, 2005, as follows:

Justine F. Miller
22 Park Place
New Haven, CT 06511

_____
Grace A. Luppino, Esq.
Commissioner of the Superior Court

EXHIBIT 10–6 Sample motion for exclusive possession of marital residence.

DOCKET NO. FA 96-123456	:	SUPERIOR COURT
BRONSON, RODNEY	:	JUDICIAL DISTRICT OF NEW HAVEN
V.	:	AT NEW HAVEN
BRONSON, EVELYN	:	AUGUST 15, 2005

MOTION FOR EXCLUSIVE POSSESSION OF THE MARITAL RESIDENCE

The plaintiff-husband hereby moves that this Court award exclusive possession and use of the family residence at 328 Sycamore Street, New Haven, CT, to the plaintiff-husband.

THE PLAINTIFF,
RODNEY BRONSON

BY: _____
JUSTINE F. MILLER, ESQ.
HIS ATTORNEY
22 PARK PLACE
NEW HAVEN, CT 06511
(203) 861-4444
JURIS NO. 313133

ORDER

The foregoing motion having been heard, it is hereby ORDERED:

GRANTED/DENIED
THE COURT

BY: _____
JUDGE

CERTIFICATION

This is to certify that a true copy of the foregoing motion was mailed, postage prepaid, on this date to all counsel and pro se parties of record on this _____ day of _____, 2005, as follows:

Grace A. Luppino, Esq.
555 Main Avenue
New Haven, CT 06511

_____
Justine F. Miller, Esq.
Commissioner of the Superior Court

EXHIBIT 10–7 Sample motion for use of motor vehicle.

DOCKET NO. FA 96-123456	:	SUPERIOR COURT
BRONSON, RODNEY	:	JUDICIAL DISTRICT OF NEW HAVEN
V.	:	AT NEW HAVEN
BRONSON, EVELYN	:	AUGUST 15, 2005

MOTION FOR USE OF JOINTLY OWNED MOTOR VEHICLE

The defendant-wife in the above-referenced matter respectfully requests that this Court order the plaintiff-husband to make available to her the use of the jointly owned Buick Skylark, which is not being used presently by either party.

THE DEFENDANT,
EVELYN BRONSON

BY: _____
GRACE A. LUPPINO, ESQ.
HER ATTORNEY
555 MAIN AVENUE
NEW HAVEN, CT 06511
(203) 333-3333
JURIS NO. 160000

ORDER

The foregoing motion having been heard, it is hereby ORDERED:

GRANTED/DENIED
THE COURT

BY: _____
JUDGE

CERTIFICATION

This is to certify that a true copy of the foregoing motion was mailed, postage prepaid, on this date to all counsel and pro se parties of record on this _____ day of _____, 2005, as follows:

Justine F. Miller
22 Park Place
New Haven, CT 06511

_____
Grace A. Luppino, Esq.
Commissioner of the Superior Court

EXHIBIT 10–8 Sample motion for payment of mortgage and insurance premiums.

DOCKET NO. FA 96-123456	:	SUPERIOR COURT
BRONSON, RODNEY	:	JUDICIAL DISTRICT OF NEW HAVEN
V.	:	AT NEW HAVEN
BRONSON, EVELYN	:	AUGUST 15, 2005

<u>**MOTION FOR PAYMENT OF MORTGAGE**</u>
<u>**AND HEALTH INSURANCE PREMIUMS, PENDENTE LITE**</u>

The plaintiff-husband in the above-referenced matter respectfully requests that the Court enter an order pendente lite that the defendant-wife make monthly mortgage payments on the family home and make monthly payments for health insurance premiums for the plaintiff-husband and minor children.

In support hereof, the plaintiff-husband represents as follows:

1. Prior to the institution of this action, the defendant-wife made monthly payments on the family home located at 328 Sycamore Street, New Haven, Connecticut.

2. The plaintiff-husband and the minor children continue to reside at the above-mentioned premises and intend to remain there while this matter is pending.

3. The plaintiff-husband lacks adequate financial resources to pay the monthly mortgage payment at this time; and if the defendant-wife fails to pay the mortgage, the parties will lose this jointly owned asset of the marriage, and the plaintiff-husband and the minor children will be without housing.

4. Prior to the institution of this action, the defendant-wife paid monthly health insurance premiums for a health plan covering herself, the plaintiff-husband and the minor children.

5. The plaintiff-husband lacks adequate financial resources to pay monthly health insurance premiums for himself and the minor children; if the defendant-wife fails to pay monthly health premiums, the plaintiff-husband and minor children will lack health insurance during the pendency of this action.

WHEREFORE, the plaintiff requests that the Court order the defendant-wife to continue to make the monthly mortgage payments on the family home and continue to pay monthly health insurance premiums for the plaintiff-husband and minor children throughout the pendency of this action.

THE PLAINTIFF,
RODNEY BRONSON

BY: _____
JUSTINE F. MILLER, ESQ.
HIS ATTORNEY
22 PARK PLACE
NEW HAVEN, CT 06511
(203) 861-4444
JURIS NO. 313133

EXHIBIT 10–8 Continued

ORDER

The foregoing motion having been heard, it is hereby ORDERED:

GRANTED/DENIED

THE COURT

BY: _____

JUDGE

CERTIFICATION

This is to certify that a true copy of the foregoing motion was mailed, postage prepaid, on this date to all counsel and pro se parties of record on this _____ day of _____, 2005, as follows:

Grace A. Luppino, Esq.
555 Main Avenue
New Haven, CT 06511

_____
Justine F. Miller, Esq.
Commissioner of the Superior Court

EXHIBIT 10–9 Sample restraining order.

DOCKET NO. FA 96-123456	:	SUPERIOR COURT
BRONSON, RODNEY	:	JUDICIAL DISTRICT OF NEW HAVEN
V.	:	AT NEW HAVEN
BRONSON, EVELYN	:	AUGUST 15, 2005

<u>**MOTION TO RESTRAIN**</u>

   The defendant-wife in the above-entitled action respectfully represents what the plaintiff-husband has, within his control, significant cash and property assets of the marriage. The defendant-wife desires to secure all assets of the marriage so they will be available for a decree of equitable distribution pursuant to applicable state law.

   WHEREFORE, the defendant-wife moves for an order restraining the plaintiff-husband from removing, sequestering, hiding, transferring, disposing of and/or selling, encumbering, liening, mortgaging, or otherwise disposing of any assets during the course of this action.

THE DEFENDANT,
EVELYN BRONSON

BY: _____
GRACE A. LUPPINO, ESQ.
HER ATTORNEY
555 MAIN AVENUE
NEW HAVEN, CT 06511
(203) 333-3333
JURIS NO. 160000

<u>**ORDER**</u>

The foregoing motion having been heard, it is hereby ORDERED:

GRANTED/DENIED
THE COURT

BY: _____
JUDGE

<u>**CERTIFICATION**</u>

   This is to certify that a true copy of the foregoing motion was mailed, postage prepaid, on this date to all counsel and pro se parties of record on this _____ day of _____, 2005, as follows:

Justine F. Miller
22 Park Place
New Haven, CT 06522

_____
Grace A. Luppino, Esq.
Commissioner of the Superior Court

EXHIBIT 10–10 Sample court calendar.

NNH$$$sh2

**Judicial District of New Haven
SUPERIOR COURT**

Short Calendar

**235 Church Street—New Haven
9:30 A.M.**

NOTICE — MARKING CASES

IN ORDER FOR A CASE TO BE ASSIGNED TO A JUDGE, COUN-SEL/PRO SE PARTIES MUST TELEPHONE THE SHORT CALENDAR MARKING LINE AT (203) 789-7648 AND MARK THE CASE "READY". The marking line is open from 9:30 a.m. Wednesday to 11:00 a.m. Friday of the week prior to every calendar. In the event a state holiday falls on the Friday immediately preceding the calen-dar, the marking line will close at 11:00 a.m. Thursday of the week prior to the calendar. Movants must indicate on the marking line whether the case being marked is on Short Calendar No. 2 or Short Calendar No. 5.

Counsel/pro se parties must give timely notice to each other of all markings. In addition, notice must be given to the Attorney General's Office at (860) 808-5150 if any party is receiving or has received Public Assistance. Failure to do so will result in the matter not being heard. If conflicting markings are made, the last one

(Notice Continued on Last Column)

**TABLE OF CONTENTS
SHORT CAL. NO. 2**

FAMILY
  QUESTIONS OF LAW ARG.   11/30/98 09.30
  DISCLOSURES ARG.   11/30/98 09.30
  DORMANCY BY COURT ORDER 11/30/98 09.30
  MISCELLANEOUS ARG.   11/30/98 09.30

11/30/98 09.30
FAMILY
QUESTIONS OF LAW ARG.

0246821 S   MOAN-SOMMERS,LOUISE
FA-86   V.   SOMMERS,JOHN S
                 (1)
J. CHIARELLI   PRO SE
                         R.K. WALSH
 ARG   126.50 MOT OPEN/MODIFY JUDGMENT
 ARG   127.00 MOT PROTECTIVE ORDER
 ARG   128.00 MOT RESTRAINING ORDER
 ARG × 129.00 MOTION TO STRIKE

0416827 S   WALKER,MILTON L
FA-98   V.   WALKER,DENEEDA
PRO SE   CT.L.S.WATERBURY
 ARG   102.00 MOTION TO DISMISS

0415891 S   SANDORA,DEBORAH I
FA-98   V.   SANDORA,EDMOND H
                 (3)
NOYES & M PC   DEY S & A LLC
 ARG   103.00 MOTION FOR COUNSEL FEES
 ARG   104.00 MOTION FOR SANCTIONS
 ARG   105.00 MOTION FOR STAY
 ARG × 106.00 MOTION TO DISMISS

GA× 0415498 S BOND,GILBERT I
FA-98   V.   BOND,ANITA L
                 (4)
PECK & PECK   RW CALLAHAN
 ARG × 117.00 MOTION TO DISMISS
 ARG   118.00 MOTION FOR STAY
 ARG   120.00 MOTION FOR ORDER

11/30/98 09.30
FAMILY
DISCLOSURES ARG.

0419070 S   BIATOWAS,JANE
FA-98   V.   BIATOWAS,STANLEY
                 (5)
ESPOSITO J J PC   KOLB C & E PC
 ARG   104.00 MOT EXTEND TIME-DSCOVERY

0416274 S   POTTS,CAROLYN
FA-98   V.   POTTS,PHILIP
                 (6)
G. H. KAHN   NOYES & M PC
 ARG   103.00 MOT EXTEND TIME-DSCOVERY

11/30/98 09.30
FAMILY - DORMANCY
DORMANCY BY COURT ORDER

0414106 S   ESPOSITO,MICHAEL A
FA-98   V.   ESPOSITO,LAURA C
                 (7)
GREAVES & S LLC   BERNBLUM & GREEN
 110.00 MOT OPEN DISMISSAL JDGHT

0413732 S   LONERGAN,JENNIFER
FA-98   V.   LONERGAN,CHRISTOPHER
                 (8)
GENTILE C & N LL   PRO SE
 103.00 MOT OPEN DISMISSAL JDGHT

0414139 S   HELLER,ERICK
FA-98   V.   HELLER,CHERIE
                 (9)
R.TIETJEN   PRO SE
 102.00 MOT OPEN DISMISSAL JDGHT

0414743 S   HOLLAND,MARY C
FA-98   V.   HOLLAND,THIMUEL
                 (10)
PRO SE   PRO SE
AAG GG WILLIAMS
 103.00 MOT OPEN DISMISSAL JDGHT

0412747 S   DUBE,KATHRYN M
FA-98   V.   DUDE,HENRY G
                 (11)
PRO SE   HEFFERNAN & F LL
 105.00 MOT OPEN DISMISSAL JDGHT

11/30/98 09.30
FAMILY
MISCELLANEOUS ARG.

0418500 S   TORRES,ESTHER
FA-98   V.   TEJEDA,RAMON
                 (12)
MOSCOWITZ C & K   NO APPEARANCE
 ARG × 101.00 MOT CUSTODY-PD LITE
 ARG   102.00 MOT FOR SUPPORT-PD LITE

0414301 S   GOLUB, BETH A
FA-98   V.   GOLUB, ERIC
                 (13)
BROZDOWSKI P L L
 ARG × 105.00 MOTION FOR ORDER
 ARG   106.00 MOTION FOR ORDER
 ARG   107.00 MOTION FOR COUNSEL FEES

0419602 S   BENEVENTO,ELLEN L
FA-98   V.   BENEVENTO,VINCENT J
                 (14)
T.R.BAINER   NO APPEARANCE
 ARG × 101.00 MOT FOR ALIMONY-PD LITE
 ARG   102.00 MOT CUSTODY-PD LITE
 ARG   103.00 MOT FOR SUPPORT-PD LITE
 ARG   104.00 MOTION FOR POSSESSION
 ARG   105.00 MOTION FOR COUNSEL FEES

0415503 S   CARABETTA,LINDA S
FA-98   V.   CARABETTA,GARY LYNN
                 (15)
D.POLAN   BUDLONG & ASSOCI
 ARG   109.00 OBJECTION TO MOTION

0345804 S   DUBE,RACHEL
FA-93   V.   FREDERICKS,ROBERT
                 (16)
GESMONDE P S & P   PRO SE
G. H. KAHN   J. CHIARELLI
 ARG   189.00 MOT DETERMINE ARREARAGE

0287705 S   PICCOLO,KEVIN M
FA-89   V.   PICCOLO,DEBRA A
                 (17)
PRO SE   PRO SE
                         MF VOLPE
 ARG   180.00 MOT REFER TO FRD

0395706 S   BURRIS, ROBERT
FA-97   V.   BURRIS, MAUREEN
                 (18)
PRO SE   PRO SE
JW AUGER   LEGAL CLINIC
                         JE HUDSON
                         SUPPORT ENF UNIT
 ARG   128.00 MOTION FOR COUNSEL FEES

0273107 S   WALTER,TERRI
FA-88   V.   WALTER,NOEL DAVIS
                 (19)
W.J. NULSEN   PRO SE
 ARG   138.00 MOT OPEN/MODIFY JUDGMENT

0405610 S   LANE, REGINA E.
FA-95   V.   LANE, KENNETH H.
                 (20)
PRO SE   PRO SE
L. PARLEY
J. H. KELLEY
L.J. COSTANTINI
 ARG   580.00 MOT WITHDRAW APPEARANCE

0373911 S   WILLIAMS,FELICIA
FA-95   V.   WILLIAMS,ROBERT J
                 (21)
M.I. OLMER   ADELMAN L OFFICE
 ARG   148.00 MOT PERMISSION WD APPRNC

0402512 S   MUELLER,STEVEN K
FA-97   V.   MUELLER,CHARISSE G
                 (22)
R.S. FRIEDMAN   E.J. DOLAN
 ARG   107.00 MOTION FOR VISITATION

0412912 S   VANWILGEN,STEPHANIJA
FA-98   V.   VANWILGEN,AART III
                 (23)
MURPHY MAUREEN   ULLMAN P & SKLAV
AA WALLACE
 ARG   112.00 MOT CUSTODY-PD LITE

0390614 S   COX, SHAWN D.
FA-96   V.   COX, STEVEN P.
                 (24)
H.D.MURPHY   E.J. DOLAN
 ARG   117.50 MOT OPEN/MODIFY JUDGMENT

0365115 S   GLENN,BARBARA
FA-94   V.   GLENN,JOSEPH K
                 (25)
PRO SE   GJ SACHS
CHILD SPT ENF A   M.F. BRUNSWICK
 ARG   125.00 MOT OPEN/MODIFY JUDGMENT

0415615 S   GOULET, RAYMOND III
FA-98   V.   REYNOLDS, WENDY
                 (26)
DIANA C T & COMO   H.A.LAWRENCE
                         L. PARLEY
 ARG   120.00 MOTION FOR MODIFICATION

0385316 S   KUNTZ, SUSAN
FA-96   V.   KUNTZ, THOMAS
                 (27)
GOLDBLATT G & R   V. MCMANUS, JR.
 ARG   110.50 MOT OPEN/MODIFY JUDGMENT

0418422 S   DICICCO,JANICE
FA-98   V.   DICICCO,MARVIN J
                 (28)
J. CHIARELLI   J. E. SPODNICK
 ARG × 101.00 MOTION FOR POSSESSION
 ARG   102.00 MOTION FOR INJUNCTION
 ARG   103.00 MOT FOR TRANSPORTATION
 ARG   104.00 MOTION FOR ORDER
 ARG   106.00 MOT FOR ALIMONY-PD LITE

NEW HAVEN   COLUMN 1
                         SHORT CAL NO. 2   COLUMN 2   COLUMN 3

EXHIBIT 10–10 Continued

```
0419223 S      GOLD,INGRID
FA-98      V. GOLD,LOUIS
                     ( 29)
S.O.LEBAS            F. L. CIRILLO
ARG * 101.01 MOT FOR SUPPORT-PD LITE
ARG   101.02 MOT FOR ALIMONY-PD LITE
-----------------------------------
0406424 S      EDWARDS,MARK R    ET AL
FA-97      V. EDWARDS,BONNIE
                     ( 30)
ADELMAN L OFFICE        D.R. DANIELS
                        AAG AS GUIDO
                        WALLACE & O LLC
ARG * 147.00 MOTION FOR MODIFICATION
ARG   148.00 MOTION FOR ORDER
ARG   149.00 MOT FOR SUPPORT-PD LITE
ARG   150.00 MOTION FOR ORDER
-----------------------------------
0416924 S      JEFFERSON,LOUIS
FA-98      V. JEFFERSON,KIMBERLY L
                     ( 31)
PRO SE               PRO SE
ARG * 102.00 MOT FOR ORDER PEND LITE
ARG   103.00 MOT FOR ORDER PEND LITE
-----------------------------------
0418524 S      SARGENT,DOREEN
FA-98      V. SARGENT,ERNEST
                     (' 32)
F. M. GLYNN          NO APPEARANCE
ARG * 101.01 MOT CUSTODY-PD LITE
ARG   101.02 MOT FOR SUPPORT-PD LITE
ARG   102.00 MOT FOR ALIMONY-PD LITE
-----------------------------------
0365225 S      KASSHEIMER,MICHAEL
FA-94      V. KASSHEIMER,SUSAN A
                     ( 33)
DUMARK & LINDSAY     SOUSA R C & ASSO
ARG   121.00 MOTION FOR MODIFICATION
-----------------------------------
0414527 S      HERNANDEZ,OTTO R
FA-98      V. IRIZARRY,MARIA
                     ( 34)
D. L. DENVIR         M.DOODY
                     AAG GM BARTO
ARG * 112.00 MOT MOD SUPPORT P/L
ARG   112.50 MOT MOD VIS P/L
-----------------------------------
0418127 S      D'AMICO,LYNNE L
FA-98      V. D'AMICO,SALVATORE G
                     ( 35)
N.M. LEGINSKY        PRO SE
ARG * 101.00 MOT FOR ORDER PEND LITE
-----------------------------------
0418527 S      MAZZELLA,ANNA MARIA
FA-98      V. MAZZELLA,WILLIAM
                     ( 36)
CANTOR F R & G P     NO APPEARANCE
ARG * 101.00 MOT FOR ALIMONY-PD LITE
ARG   102.01 MOT CUSTODY-PD LITE
ARG   102.02 MOT FOR SUPPORT-PD LITE
ARG   103.00 MOTION FOR POSSESSION
-----------------------------------
0412728 S      SPEARMAN,PATTI
FA-98      V. WILLIAMS,CHRISTOPHER
                     ( 37)
PRO SE               NO APPEARANCE
C.E.FRONTIS
ARG   106.00 MOTION FOR CONTINUANCE
-----------------------------------
0419329 S      GUISTINELLO,SUSAN
FA-98      V. GUISTINELLO,ANTHONY
                     ( 38)
NOYES & M PC         AA WALLACE
ARG * 103.00 MOT IMMEDIATE HEARING
ARG   105.01 MOT CUSTODY-PD LITE
ARG   105.02 MOT JOINT CUSTODY
ARG   106.00 MOTION FOR POSSESSION
ARG   107.00 MOT FOR ALIMONY-PD LITE
ARG   108.00 MOT FOR SUPPORT-PD LITE
ARG   109.00 MOTION FOR ORDER
ARG   110.00 MOTION FOR POSSESSION
ARG   111.00 MOT APPT GUARDIAN AD LIT
-----------------------------------
0387930 S      CLOSE,MEAD A
FA-96      V. CLOSE,JOYCE
                     ( 39)
JACOBS G B & D P        PRO SE
                        WINNICK R & C LL
                        AAG AS GUIDO
ARG * 119.00 MOT OPEN/MODIFY JUDGMENT
ARG   121.00 MOTION FOR ORDER
-----------------------------------
```

```
NYx 0416631 S  BONITO,SUSAN Z
FA-98      V. ZISEK,MICHAEL
                     ( 40)
AMENDOLA &N.         PRO SE
ARG   109.00 MOT FOR SUPPORT-PD LITE
-----------------------------------
0418431 S      PELLERIN,CAROL
FA-98      V. PELLERIN,DAVID J
                     ( 41)
D. L. DENVIR         P. E. RICCIARDI
ARG * 102.01 MOT CUSTODY-PD LITE
ARG   102.02 MOT FOR SUPPORT-PD LITE
ARG   102.50 MOTION FOR ORDER
-----------------------------------
0419432 S      MATTEO,GINA
FA-98      V. MATTEO,JOHN
                     ( 42)
JACOBS G B & D P     NO APPEARANCE
ARG * 101.00 MOT FOR SUPPORT-PD LITE
ARG   102.01 MOT CUSTODY-PD LITE
ARG   102.02 MOTION FOR VISITATION
ARG   103.00 MOTION FOR POSSESSION
-----------------------------------
0419533 S      DAY,LISA
FA-98      V. DAY,DAVID JR
                     ( 43)
FARRELL & LESLIE     NO APPEARANCE
ARG   101.00 MOTION FOR ORDER
-----------------------------------
0385434 S      PICHE, DONALD
FA-96      V. PICHE, ROSE
                     ( 44)
R.M.KESSLER          PRO SE
                     MA WIELER
ARG   107.00 MOT OPEN/MODIFY JUDGMENT
-----------------------------------
0372136 S      ALLISON,ROBERT J
FA-95      V. ALLISON,KATHLEEN T
                     ( 45)
G. BATTISTOLI        PRO SE
                     SUSMAN D & S PC
ARG   121.00 MOT OPEN/MODIFY JUDGMENT
-----------------------------------
0265836 S      CONSIGLIO, BARBARA A
FA-87      V. CONSIGLIO, VINCENT J
                     ( 46)
SCHETTINO & T.       ADELMAN L OFFICE
SUPPORT ENF UNIT
ARG * 139.00 OBJECTION TO MOTION
ARG   140.00 MOT OPEN/MODIFY JUDGMENT
-----------------------------------
0321937 S      KAUFFMAN,JANET ANN
FA-91      V. KAUFFMAN,BRUCE B
                     ( 47)
PRO SE               MCNAMARA & GOODM
N.R.NESI
J. L. WELTY
ARG   134.00 MOT OPEN/MODIFY JUDGMENT
-----------------------------------
0409338 S      ROCZYNSKI,LYDIA
FA-98      V. ROCZYNSKI,DARREN J
                     ( 48)
RM STUTMAN           ADELMAN L OFFICE
ARG   133.00 MOT PERMISSION WD APPRNC
-----------------------------------
0419040 S      MCDANIEL,RAUN M
FA-98      V. MCDANIEL,DONALD G
                     ( 49)
C NEWMAN             GESMONDE P S & P
ARG   107.00 MOT JOINT CUSTODY
ARG   108.00 MOTION FOR ACCOUNTING
-----------------------------------
0363542 S      GAMM, JOHN
FA-94      V. GAMM, INGRID
                     ( 50)
GOLDBLATT G & R
                     WEINSTEIN & W PC
                     ULLMAN P & SKLAV
                     VOTRE A A PC
ARG   172.00 MOTION FOR COUNSEL FEES
-----------------------------------
0397542 S      SAVAGE,MARY ELLEN
FA-97      V. ELLIOTT, E.DONALD
                     ( 51)
RUBIN & E.           AMENDOLA & A LLC
ARG * 124.00 MOT APPOINT ATTORNEY
ARG   126.00 MOT RETURN PERSONAL ITEM
-----------------------------------
0415643 S      CORNING,TERRI
FA-98      V. OWENS,KENNETH
                     ( 52)
HARRINGTON & FOR     PRO SE
                     B.H. COX
                     ---CONTINUED
```

```
ARG * 103.01 MOT CUSTODY-PD LITE
ARG   103.02 MOT FOR SUPPORT-PD LITE
-----------------------------------
0388143 S      BALDWIN,ALISA
FA-96      V. CLARK,STERLING
                     ( 53)
M KOSSAR             PRO SE
ARG   103.00 RULE OPEN/MODIFY JDGMENT
-----------------------------------
0417444 S      HOGFELDT,SHARON A
FA-98      V. HOGFELDT,KARL
                     ( 54)
GOULD & G PC         NO APPEARANCE
ARG   103.00 MOTION FOR ORDER
-----------------------------------
0417544 S      WILDER,GAYLE
FA-98      V. WILDER,REGINALD
                     ( 55)
LEVY & S LLC         PRO SE
                     PARRETT P P & C
ARG   113.00 MOTION FOR MODIFICATION
-----------------------------------
0419245 S      BUCCI,CYNTHIA
FA-98      V. BUCCI,JOSEPH
                     ( 56)
NOYES & M PC         NO APPEARANCE
ARG * 101.00 MOT ALIMNY-CUSTDY-SUPPRT
ARG   102.00 MOTION FOR ORDER
ARG   103.00 MOTION FOR COUNSEL FEES
-----------------------------------
0416846 S      GALLI,DANIELLA
FA-98      V. SOEHNLEIN,PAUL
                     ( 57)
BROZDOWSKI P L L     PRO SE
ARG   102.00 MOT APPOINT CONCILIATOR
-----------------------------------
0415149 S      SANTARPIA,ROBERT
FA-98      V. SANTARPIA,VALERIE
                     ( 58)
RUBIN & E.           PRO SE
ARG   110.00 MOTION TO SEAL FILE
-----------------------------------
0381451 S      ROBLES, LISA J.
FA-95      V. ROBLES, WILSON
                     ( 59)
MF VOLPE             CASHMAN W H & AS
ARG   128.00 MOTION FOR ORDER
-----------------------------------
0399752 S      ERRANTE, STEVEN
FA-97      V. ERRANTE, NANCY
                     ( 60)
LYNCH T K & E PC        G. H. KAHN
COUGHLIN Z M.
ARG   135.00 MOT PROTECTIVE ORDER
ARG   136.00 MOT PROTECTIVE ORDER
ARG * 137.00 MOTION FOR ORDER
-----------------------------------
0416953 S      MOCCIO,SHERI
FA-98      V. MOCCIO,ROBERT
                     ( 61)
J. CHIARELLI         PARRETT P P & C
ARG * 101.00 MOTION FOR POSSESSION
ARG   102.00 MOT RETURN PERSONAL ITEM
ARG   103.00 MOT FOR ALIMONY-PD LITE
ARG   104.00 MOTION FOR ORDER
ARG   105.00 MOTION FOR COUNSEL FEES
ARG   106.00 MOT FOR TRANSPORTATION
ARG   107.00 MOTION FOR INJUNCTION
ARG   109.00 MOTION FOR POSSESSION
ARG   110.00 MOT EXTEND TIME-DSCOVERY
-----------------------------------
0416554 S      FITZGERALD,JOHN D
FA-98      V. FITZGERALD,SUZANNE
                     ( 62)
KOLB C & E PC        NOYES & M PC
ARG * 101.00 MOT ALIMNY-CUSTDY-SUPPRT
ARG   102.00 MOTION FOR COUNSEL FEES
ARG   103.00 MOTION FOR ORDER
ARG   104.00 MOTION FOR POSSESSION
ARG   105.00 REQUEST FOR CONCILIATION
-----------------------------------
0399254 S      LEETE, LINDA
FA-97      V. LEETE, BRADFORD
                     ( 63)
R.TIETJEN            J. A. KEYES
AAG AS GUIDO         HARRINGTON & FOR
ARG * 124.00 MOT FOR SUPPORT-PD LITE
ARG   125.00 MOTION FOR ORDER
-----------------------------------
0415655 S      SMITH,DION H
FA-98      V. SMITH,MICHELE L
                     ( 64)
                     ---CONTINUED
```

EXHIBIT 10-10 Continued

Column 7

D. L. DENVIR   CELLA M & WILLIA
ARG   112.00 MOTION FOR MODIFICATION

0261057 S   MURRAY,TERESA A
FA-87   V. MURRAY,THOMAS W SR
           (65)
J. CHIARELLI   PARRETT P P & C
ARG ✗ 139.00 MOTION FOR SANCTIONS
ARG   140.00 MOTION FOR SANCTIONS

    0404657 S   KARATZAS,TINA
FA-97   V. KARATZAS,DINO
           (66)
TYLER, C. & A.   COHEN G I L O OF
ARG   111.00 MOTION FOR SANCTIONS

0414757 S   BRACERO,MELISSA
FA-98   V. BRACERO,MARIO J
           (67)
ADELMAN L OFFICE   DL WRIGHT
ARG   113.00 MOTION FOR MODIFICATION

0350459 S   SASSO,WARREN
FA-93   V. SASSO,SUSAN B
           (68)
M.F. BRUNSWICK   M.H.LERNER
PERELMUTTER & P.   WEIGAND M & A PC
ARG   212.00 MOTION FOR MODIFICATION

0390959 S   MAGNAN, EILENE
FA-96   V. MAGNAN, LEONARD J.
           (69)
CANTOR F R & G P   D.POLAN
COHEN & THOMAS
YOLEN & P LLC
ARG   157.00 MOT PERMISSION WD APPRNC

0403360 S   LAFASCIANO,TRACY
FA-97   V. LAFASCIANO,JASON
           (70)
PRO SE   GESMONDE P S & P
ANNUNZIATA A PC
AAG AS GUIDO
ARG   125.00 MOT OPEN/MODIFY JUDGMENT

0419360 S   BASCOM,MICHELE
FA-98   V. BASCOM,DAVID M
           (71)
FARRELL & LESLIE   NO APPEARANCE
ARG ✗ 101.00 MOT FOR SUPPORT-PD LITE
ARG   102.00 MOT FOR ALIMONY-PD LITE

0419661 S   SPERANDEO,RALPH A JR
FA-98   V. SPERANDEO,MARGARET R
           (72)
WE SKIPTUNAS   NO APPEARANCE
ARG   101.00 MOT CUSTODY-PD LITE

0416262 S   LABANARA,PATRICIA A
FA-98   V. LABANARA,ROBERT L
           (73)
CANTOR F R & G P   DH BROWN
ARG ✗ 101.00 MOT FOR ALIMONY-PD LITE
ARG   102.00 MOTION FOR POSSESSION

0397662 S   CLARK,JENNIFER (CT)
FA-97   V. NOONAN, MICHAEL
           (74)
PRO SE   T.R.BAINER
H.I.MENDELSOHN
CADDEN I & IVERS
AAG AS GUIDO
CHILD SPT ENF A
ARG ✗ 118.00 RULE OPEN/MODIFY JDGMENT
ARG   119.00 MOT PERMISSION WD APPRNC

0257962 S   CONSOLATORE, DAWN
FA-87   V. CONSOLATORE, ROBERT
           (75)
PRO SE   PARRETT P P & C
ANTOLLINO,A & S.
ARG   124.00 MOTION FOR ORDER

0377965 S   QUIELLO,OLIVIA
FA-95   V. QUIELLO,MICHAEL J
           (76)
BERDON Y & M PC   E.J. DOLAN
           JACOBS G B & D P
           KOLB C & E PC
ARG   119.00 MOT OPEN/MODIFY JUDGMENT

Column 8

0418464 S   DOSTIE,LISA
FA-98   V. HURTEAU,THOMAS W
           (77)
PRO SE   NIRTO K & B PC
ARG   106.00 MOT OPEN/MODIFY JUDGMENT

0418465 S   VACCARO,PAUL D
FA-98   V. VACCARO,ANN T
           (78)
KOLB C & E PC   O'DONNELL J L OF
ARG ✗ 111.00 MOT EXTEND TIME
ARG   112.00 MOTION FOR MODIFICATION

    0404266 S   SAUERBRUNN,PAULA
FA-97   V. SAUERBRUNN,FREDERICK
           (79)
D.W.CELOTTO,JR.   LASALA, W. & W.
N.EISENHANDLER
ARG ✗ 122.00 MOT JOINT CUSTODY
ARG   123.00 MOTION FOR POSSESSION
ARG   124.00 MOTION FOR ORDER

0359266 S   RICHMOND,WILLIAM M
FA-94   V. RICHMOND,NORMAJEAN
           (80)
J. CHIARELLI   BERNBLUM & GREEN
ARG   138.00 MOTION FOR ORDER

0280467 S   HARMS,SHEILA
FA-89   V. HARMS,EDWARD
           (81)
JACOBS G B & D P   TYLER, C. & A.
ARG   126.00 MOT OPEN/MODIFY JUDGMENT

0417667 S   MEHTA,VARSHA
FA-98   V. MEHTA,PRASHANT
           (82)
GESMONDE P S & P   COUGHLIN & M.
ARG ✗ 101.00 MOT FOR SUPPORT-PD LITE
ARG   102.00 MOT FOR ALIMONY-PD LITE
ARG   103.00 MOT JOINT CUSTODY

0389467 S   LAZROVE,STEVEN
FA-96   V. LAZROVE,ANNE
           (83)
COHEN G I L O OF   TYLER, C. & A.
ARG   152.00 MOT REFER TO FRD

0405168 S   BARNETT,SCOTT
FA-97   V. BARNETT,PAMELA
           (84)
SCHEIRER & GELLE   BERSHTEIN B & B
ARG   130.00 MOT PERMISSION WD APPRNC

0367268 S   TEODOSIO,ROBIN L
FA-94   V. TEODOSIO,FRANK V
           (85)
V LILBURN   SOLOMON K & W PC
ARG ✗ 122.00 MOTION FOR COUNSEL FEES
ARG   123.00 MOT REFER TO FRD
ARG   124.00 MOT OPEN/MODIFY JUDGMENT
ARG   125.00 MOT OPEN/MODIFY JUDGMENT

0415369 S   WADE,MICHAEL G
FA-98   V. FORD-WADE,ANNIE E
           (86)
LS DRESSLER   NO APPEARANCE
ARG   101.00 MOT FOR RECONCILIATION

0391871 S   CLUKEY, GENEVIEVE S.
FA-96   V. CLUKEY, THOMAS F.
           (87)
RUBIN & E.   GOLDBLATT G & R
JACOBS G B & D P   PARRETT P P & C
ARG ✗ 235.01 MOT FOR ALIMONY-PD LITE
ARG   235.02 MOT FOR SUPPORT-PD LITE
ARG   236.00 OBJECTION TO MOTION
ARG   237.00 MOTION FOR COUNSEL FEES

0418671 S   FOSTER,LINDA L
FA-98   V. FOSTER,GLENN P
           (88)
L.L. LEVY   M.BELLEZZA
ARG ✗ 101.01 MOT FOR ALIMONY-PD LITE
ARG   101.02 MOTION FOR ALLOWANCE

PA✗ 0402673 S   MILLER,PAMELA ROBYN
FA-97   V. MILLER,PAUL BRIAN
           (89)
ADELMAN L OFFICE   CANTOR F R & G P
ARG   112.00 MOTION FOR COUNSEL FEES

Column 9

0419273 S   COLEMAN,DAWN
FA-98   V. COLEMAN,WILLIAM L
           (90)
PRO SE   NO APPEARANCE
ARG   101.00 MOT FOR ORDER PEND LITE

0419573 S   SPARANO,DEBRA
FA-98   V. SPARANO,DANIEL SR
           (91)
NOYES & M PC   NO APPEARANCE
ARG   001.06 MOTION FOR COUNSEL FEES

0418675 S   GUIMARES,ALBERT
FA-98   V. SMITH,LYDIA A
           (92)
VISHNO R & V PC   RR KLASKIN
ARG ✗ 102.01 MOT FOR ALIMONY-PD LITE
ARG   102.02 MOT FOR COUNSEL FEES

0412676 S   FRECKELTON,ERICKA A
FA-98   V. FRECKELTON,LEONARD
           (93)
LAMBOLEY L FIRM   NO APPEARANCE
L.MARLOW
ARG ✗ 108.00 MOTION FOR COUNSEL FEES
ARG   109.00 MOTION FOR GENETIC TEST

0394176 S   CRISCUOLO, KIMBERLY
FA-96   V. CRISCUOLO, MARK
           (94)
BERDON Y & M PC   J. F. CIRILLO
           JC DELANEY
ARG   131.00 MOT OPEN/MODIFY JUDGMENT

0401377 S   PURPORA,SUZANNE
FA-97   V. PURPORA,DAVID P
           (95)
LYNCH T K & E PC   PRO SE
           ANDROSKI A & AND
           R.A. VOLO
ARG   158.00 MOTION FOR ORDER

0329780 S   ARNEILL, BONNIE B.
FA-92   V. ARNEILL, BRUCE P.
           (96)
SUSMAN D & S PC   J. L. WELTY
ARG   131.00 MOT PERMISSION WD APPRNC

0400181 S   CLARK, DEBORAH A.
FA-97   V. PERRY, JOHN C.III
           (97)
PRO SE   PRO SE
JACOBS G B & D P   PT GIORDANO
AAG GM BARTO
GESMONDE P S & P
ARG   131.00 MOT PERMISSION WD APPRNC

0385281 S   CORVI, PETER A.
FA-96   V. CORVI, PAMELA R.
           (98)
CONN L L S FUND   PRO SE
           MCMAHON ELIZABET
ARG   114.00 MOTION FOR MODIFICATION

0419381 S   TUCKER,SUZANNE M
FA-98   V. TUCKER,ALAN R
           (99)
VAVRA N J L OFFI   NO APPEARANCE
ARG ✗ 101.01 MOT JOINT CUSTODY
ARG   101.02 MOT CUSTODY-PD LITE
ARG   101.03 MOT FOR SUPPORT-PD LITE
ARG   101.04 MOT FOR ALIMONY-PD LITE

0393482 S   THOMPSON, WILLIAM
FA-96   V. THOMPSON, ELIZABETH
           (100)
R. GEE, JR.   A.S.DIBENEDETTO
           AAG GM BARTO
           AAG GG WILLIAMS
ARG ✗ 111.00 MOT RETURN PERSONAL ITEM
ARG   112.00 MOTION FOR ORDER

0385982 S   RUETTGER,LOUIS M
FA-96   V. RUETTGER,KARY M
           (101)
PRO SE   PRO SE
J. MIRSKY   DS GROGINS
           YOLEN & P LLC
ARG   121.00 MOTION FOR COUNSEL FEES

EXHIBIT 10–10 Continued

```
0418083 S      ROSEN,JO-ANN
FA-98      V. ROSEN,JAMES
                  ( 102)
RUTKIN & O PC          J. L. WELTY
ARG * 101.01 MOT FOR ALIMONY-PD LITE
ARG   101.02 MOT MEDICAL EXPENSES
ARG   101.03 MOTION FOR COUNSEL FEES
ARG   102.00 MOTION FOR ORDER
-----------------------------------------
0412284 S      RYAN,BERNADETTE D
FA-98      V. RYAN,EDWARD JOSEPH
                  ( 103)
O'DONNELL J L OF       LYNCH T K & E PC
ARG * 113.00 MOTION FOR ORDER
ARG   114.00 MOTION FOR ORDER
-----------------------------------------
0280386 S      RICHITELLI,DAWN
FA-89      V. RICHITELLI,MICHAEL
                  ( 104)
PHILPOT W M J L      PRO SE
                     MIRTO K & B PC
ARG   136.00 MOT OPEN/MODIFY JUDGMENT
-----------------------------------------
0418186 S      PRINDLE,JAQUELINE C
FA-98      V. PRINDLE,BRUCE D
                  ( 105)
CELLA M & WILLIA       NO APPEARANCE
ARG   101.00 MOT FOR SUPPORT-PD LITE
-----------------------------------------
0419186 S      HUBYK,GREGORY
FA-98      V. HUBYK,PATRICIA
                  ( 106)
DINAN & D            PRO SE
                    N.EISENHANDLER
ARG * 101.01 MOT CUSTODY-PD LITE
ARG   101.02 MOT FOR SUPPORT-PD LITE
ARG   101.03 MOT FOR ALIMONY-PD LITE
ARG   101.04 MOTION FOR COUNSEL FEES
ARG   102.01 MOTION FOR POSSESSION
ARG   102.02 MOTION FOR COUNSEL FEES
ARG   105.01 MOT CUSTODY-PD LITE
ARG   105.02 MOT FOR SUPPORT-PD LITE
ARG   105.03 MOTION FOR VISITATION
ARG   105.04 MOT FOR ALIMONY-PD LITE
ARG   106.00 MOTION FOR POSSESSION
ARG   107.00 MOTION FOR COUNSEL FEES
-----------------------------------------
0414089 S      GERBE,BARBARA
FA-98      V. BERBE,RAYMOND
                  ( 107)
M.SULLIVAN          P. E. RICCIARDI
ARG   106.00 MOTION FOR ORDER
-----------------------------------------
0417790 S      KENNEY,CHRISTY
FA-98      V. KENNEY,JOHN
                  ( 108)
C.J.RIETHER            NO APPEARANCE
ARG * 101.01 MOT FOR ALIMONY-PD LITE
ARG   101.02 MOTION FOR COUNSEL FEES
-----------------------------------------
0419390 S      GUZMAN,SAMUEL
FA-98      V. GUZMAN,MIRIAM
                  ( 109)
KINNEY & SECOLA        NO APPEARANCE
ARG   101.00 MOTION FOR VISITATION
-----------------------------------------
0417591 S      ANDERSON,THERESA
FA-98      V. ANDERSON,DENIS
                  ( 110)
GREENBERG H & C      PRO SE
ARG * 101.00 MOT FOR ALIMONY-PD LITE
ARG   102.01 MOT CUSTODY-PD LITE
ARG   102.02 MOT FOR SUPPORT-PD LITE
ARG   103.00 MOTION FOR POSSESSION
-----------------------------------------
0411392 S      CARRANO,ARTHUR T
FA-98      V. CARRANO,HEATHER A
                  ( 111)
SOLOMON K & W PC       BOGDANOFF & C LL
ARG   129.00 MOTION FOR MODIFICATION
-----------------------------------------
0415692 S      GARTMAN,KENDRA
FA-98      V. GARTMAN,DONALD P III
                  ( 112)
G. H. KAHN             KOLESNIK & NORRI
ARG   108.00 OBJECTION TO MOTION
-----------------------------------------
0412394 S      NOSAL,MICHELE H
FA-98      V. NOSAL,ANDREW JOHN
                  ( 113)
SOLOMON K & W PC       B.A.CHAPLIN
ARG   136.00 MOTION FOR ORDER
-----------------------------------------
```

```
0345594 S      HARRIS, DARIN
FA-93      V. HARRIS, ANTHONY
                  ( 114)
PRO SE               PRO SE
ARG   108.00 RULE OPEN/MODIFY JDGMENT
-----------------------------------------
0411995 S      LARKIN,DOROTHY
FA-98      V. LARKIN,WILLIAM
                  ( 115)
ENGELMAN & WELCH       COHEN G I L O OF
ARG   106.00 MOTION TO COMPEL
-----------------------------------------
0416996 S      SWANSON,KAREN
FA-98      V. MCNERNEY,DENNIS
                  ( 116)
M.H.LERNER             NO APPEARANCE
ARG   101.00 MOT REFER TO FRD
-----------------------------------------
0351197 S      BEAMON, CLAUDETTE J.
FA-93      V. BEAMON, KEVIN E.
                  ( 117)
PRO SE               PRO SE
                     NUGENT & BRYANT
ARG   147.00 MOT OPEN/MODIFY JUDGMENT
-----------------------------------------
FPT 0401197 S  ROSEMAN,SHELLEY
FA-97      V. ROSEMAN,MARK
                  ( 118)
LEVY & S LLC         PRO SE
S.O.LEBAS              G. H. KAHN
ARG   155.80 MOT OPEN/MODIFY JUDGMENT
-----------------------------------------
0418697 S      BISHOP,JONATHAN B
FA-98      V. BISHOP,DIANE P
                  ( 119)
H.D.MURPHY             G. BATTISTOLI
ARG * 102.00 MOT FOR ALIMONY-PD LITE
ARG   103.00 MOT RETURN PERSONAL ITEM
-----------------------------------------
0383998 S      WILLIAMS,MARCELLE A.
FA-96      V. WILLIAMS,STANLEY A.
                  ( 120)
M.H.LERNER           PRO SE
ALBIS & PELLEGRI       E.J. DOLAN
ARG * 149.00 MOTION FOR ORDER
ARG   150.00 MOTION FOR ORDER
-----------------------------------------
0598598 S      KACANICH, GARY
FA-97      V. KACANICH, LORRAINE
                  ( 121)
COHEN & W PC           G. BATTISTOLI
                       L. PARLEY
ARG   123.00 MOT PERMISSION WD APPRNC
-----------------------------------------
0248099 S      CONTESSA,KATHLEEN
FA-86      V. CONTESSA,DOMINIC
                  ( 122)
E.J. DOLAN             JACOBS G B & D P
ARG   127.00 MOTION FOR ORDER
-----------------------------------------

CHIEF CLERK
```

NOTICE (continued from Column 1)

recorded controls. There is no marking to a later time or separate assignment.

A list of cases marked "Ready" and the judges and courtrooms to whom these cases are assigned, will be posted on the FIRST FLOOR, THIRD FLOOR, AND OUTSIDE THE CLERK'S OFFICE, the preceding Friday afternoon.

FAMILY RELATIONS

Parties must discuss their matter with a counselor from Family Relations when they arrive for their hearing. A Family Relations sign-up sheet is posted on the wall outside of Courtroom 3E for this purpose. Counselors will also be available to discuss pending motions prior to the assigned short calendar date. Call (203) 789-7903 for an appointment.

```
          COLUMN 10                    COLUMN 11
NEW HAVEN        SHORT CAL NO. 2
```

EXHIBIT 10–11 Sample stipulation regarding temporary support in a divorce case.

SIMKE, CHODOS, SILBERFELD & ANTEAU, INC.
6300 Wilshire Boulevard
Suite 9000
Los Angeles, California 90048-5202
(213) 653-0211

FILED

Los Angeles Superior Court

JAN 2 1 1994

EDWARD M. KRITZMAN, CLERK

BY H. HINAGA, DEPUTY

Attorneys for Respondent,
    MELISSA JANE CARREY

SUPERIOR COURT OF THE STATE OF CALIFORNIA

FOR THE COUNTY OF LOS ANGELES

In re the Marriage of:)   CASE NO. BD 135 499
)
)
Petitioner: JAMES EUGENE CARREY   )   STIPULATION RE: PENDENTE
)   LITE SUPPORT
            and   )
)
Respondent: MELISSA JANE CARREY   )
)
_____)

WHEREAS, due to the uncertainty of Petitioner's employment that will exist until approximately March 1, 1994; and

WHEREAS, the parties are desirous of entering into a stipulation relative to spousal and child support for income tax purposes; and

WHEREAS, the parties are desirous of establishing some certainty as to spousal and child support for the months of January, February and March of 1994; and

WHEREAS, the parties are agreeable to any such agreement being without prejudice to the contentions of either party,

NOW, THEREFORE, IT IS HEREBY STIPULATED by and between the parties hereto, and joined in by their respective counsel as

10145\stpbl293.car   1

EXHIBIT 10–11 Continued

1
2
3
4
5
6
7
8
9
10
11
12
13
14
15
16
17
18
19
20
21
22
23
24
25
26
27
28

<u>In re Marriage of Carrey</u>   L.A.S.C. Case No. BD 135 499

follows:

    1.   That for the months of January, February and March of 1994, Petitioner shall pay to Respondent, as and for spousal support, the sum of $20,600.00 (Twenty-Thousand, Six-Hundred Dollars) per month, payable one-half (1/2) on the first and one-half (1/2) on the fifteenth days of each month, commencing January 1, 1994, and continuing thereafter through March 15, 1994.

    The spousal support paid by Petitioner to Respondent shall be reportable as income by Respondent and deductible by Petitioner for income tax purposes.

    2.   That Petitioner shall pay to Respondent, as and for child support of the minor child of the parties, the sum of $5,300.00 (Five-Thousand, Three-Hundred Dollars) per month, payable one-half (1/2) on the first and one-half (1/2) on the fifteenth days of each month, commencing January 1, 1994 and continuing thereafter through the payment on March 15, 1994.

    3.   Petitioner shall continue to pay and maintain the existing policies of medical and life insurance for the benefit of Respondent and the minor child.

    4.   That with respect to the minor child, the parties shall share equally any non-insurance covered expenses, which shall include at the commencement of 1994, the deductible portions.

    5.   Respondent shall be responsible for all of the living expenses of herself and the minor child while in her custody, including but not limited to mortgage payments and real property taxes on the family residence, household expenses and private school expenses for the minor child. Additionally, Respondent

10145\stpbl293.car   2

EXHIBIT 10–11 Continued

In re Marriage of Carrey   L.A.S.C. Case No. BD 135 499

shall be responsible for any credit card charges incurred by her
after January 1, 1994, and at such time as she receives credit
cards which have been issued in her name alone, she will surrender
the joint credit cards in her possession.

 6.   The aforesaid spousal and child support shall be without
prejudice to either party's position, and in the event either
party hereafter files an Order to Show Cause proceeding for
pendente lite spousal and child support, same shall be retroactive
to January 1, 1994, with Petitioner receiving credit for the
payments hereinabove set forth.

DATED: ~~December____, 1993~~
       JANUARY 14, 1994   _____
                           JAMES EUGENE CARREY, Petitioner

DATED: December _6_, 1993 _____
                           MELISSA JANE CARREY, Respondent

APPROVED AS TO FORM AND CONTENT:

                           _____
                           NORMAN M. DOLIN, Attorney for
                           Petitioner, JAMES EUGENE CARREY

SIMKE, CHODOS, SILBERFELD & ANTEAU, INC.

By_____
    RONALD W. ANTEAU, Attorneys for
    Respondent, MELISSA JANE CARREY

EXHIBIT 10–12 Sample motion for contempt.

DOCKET NO. FA 96-123456	:	SUPERIOR COURT
BRONSON, RODNEY	:	JUDICIAL DISTRICT OF NEW HAVEN
V.	:	AT NEW HAVEN
BRONSON, EVELYN	:	SEPTEMBER 21, 2005

MOTION FOR CONTEMPT

The plaintiff in the above-referenced matter respectfully requests that the court find the defendant in contempt of court for failing to pay plaintiff court-ordered alimony payments. In support hereof, the plaintiff represents as follows:

1. On August 15, 2005, the court ordered the defendant to make weekly pendente lite alimony payments to the plaintiff in the amount of $275.

2. The defendant has failed to make weekly pendente lite alimony payments in any amount since August 29, 2005.

3. The defendant currently owes the plaintiff back pendente lite alimony in the amount of FIVE HUNDRED AND FIFTY DOLLARS ($550).

WHEREFORE, the plaintiff asks that the court find the defendant in contempt of the Court's order of August 15, 2005, and exercises its power to compel defendant to abide by said court order.

THE PLAINTIFF,
RODNEY BRONSON

BY: _____
JUSTINE F. MILLER, ESQ.
HIS ATTORNEY
22 PARK PLACE
NEW HAVEN, CT 06511
(203) 861-4444
JURIS NO. 313133

ORDER

The foregoing motion having been heard, it is hereby ORDERED:

GRANTED/DENIED
THE COURT

BY: _____
JUDGE

EXHIBIT 10–12 Continued

<u>CERTIFICATION</u>

This is to certify that a true copy of the foregoing motion was mailed, postage prepaid, on this date to all counsel and pro se parties of record on this _____ day of _____, 2005, as follows:

Grace A. Luppino
555 Main Avenue
New Haven, CT 06511

_____
Justine F. Miller, Esq.
Commissioner of the Superior Court

EXHIBIT 10–13 Sample motion for modification.

DOCKET NO. FA 96-123456	:	SUPERIOR COURT
BRONSON, RODNEY	:	JUDICIAL DISTRICT OF NEW HAVEN
V.	:	AT NEW HAVEN
BRONSON, EVELYN	:	SEPTEMBER 21, 2005

MOTION FOR MODIFICATION OF ALIMONY

The defendant in the above-referenced matter respectfully requests that the Court modify its order for alimony to reflect the defendant's changed financial circumstances.

In support hereof, the defendant represents as follows:

1. On August 15, 2005, this honorable court ordered the defendant to make weekly alimony payments pendente lite to the plaintiff in the amount of $275.

2. The defendant complied with the court's order from the date of its entry through August 22, 2000.

3. On or about August 25, 2005, defendant's employment was terminated and defendant has remained without employment until September 20, 2005.

4. Defendant's income from her present employment is considerably lower than income from defendant's previous position.

5. Defendant is unable to pay plaintiff the weekly amount of $275.

WHEREFORE, the defendant requests that the Court modify its alimony order of August 15, 2005 to reflect the defendant's adversely changed financial circumstances.

THE DEFENDANT,
EVELYN BRONSON

BY: _____
JUSTINE F. MILLER, ESQ.
HIS ATTORNEY
22 PARK PLACE
NEW HAVEN, CT 06511
(203) 861-4444

ORDER

The foregoing motion having been heard, it is hereby ORDERED:

GRANTED/DENIED
THE COURT

BY: _____
JUDGE

EXHIBIT 10–13 Continued

<u>CERTIFICATION</u>

This is to certify that a true copy of the foregoing motion was mailed, postage prepaid, on this date to all counsel and pro se parties of record on this _____ day of _____, 2005, as follows:

Grace A. Luppino
555 Main Avenue
New Haven, CT 06511

_____
Justine F. Miller, Esq.
Commissioner of the Superior Court

END OF CHAPTER EXERCISES

Crossword Puzzle

Across

3. the day set aside in family courts for motion hearings

5. a Latin term meaning "by one party" or "for one party"

8. section of the motion containing a description of the relief specifically requested by the client

10. self-representation

11. the party bringing or filing the motion

12. statutory cooling-off period

13. section of the motion included for the convenience of the court

14. section of the motion containing the case docket number, names of the parties, and name of the court

15. the process of keeping track of important court dates

Down

1. a request for temporary spousal support

2. a motion filed when either party does not comply with a court order

4. a motion filed when either party seeks to change an original court order

6. documents filed with the court to provide temporary relief for a client

7. a motion filed by a noncustodial parent whose ex-spouse refuses to allow him to see the children

9. a motion requesting that the court order the other party to refrain from certain actions

Review Questions

1 What is a statutory waiting requirement in a divorce case?

2 Explain the purpose of a *pendente lite* motion.

3 What is the paralegal's role in facilitating *pendente lite* motions?

4 Explain the purpose of motion days or a short calendar.

5 What is a docket control system? What is the importance of maintaining a docket control system in a law office?

Case for Briefing

Graf v. Graf, 208 N.J. Super. 240, 505 A.2d 207(1985)

Exploring the Workplace: Activities

1. Go to **http://www.flcourts.org/gen_public/family/forms_rules/index.shtml** and find the Florida motions for Motion for Temporary Support with Dependent or Minor Children and Temporary Order of Support with Dependent or Minor Children.

2. You work as a paralegal for the Law Office of Barbra Naughton in your state. Merrill Van, a client, informs Attorney Naughton that he needs an emergency divorce from his wife who lives in the same state. Go to **http://www.cyberstation.net/paralegal/** and find the mandatory waiting requirement in your jurisdiction.

   a) Draft a letter to Mr. Van, on behalf of Attorney Naughton, advising him of the mandatory waiting period in your state.

   b) Are there any other possible solutions for Mr. Van? A coworker heard that you could get a "quickie" divorce in the Dominican Republic. Are there any other alternatives? Using the Internet, determine if this is at all possible and draft an interoffice memo informing Attorney Van of your findings.

3. You work as a paralegal for the law firm Zullo, Kretsch, and Barinsky in your state. Your office represents Anthony Guttmann as the defendant in a divorce action against his wife, Lori Guttmann. He and his wife have been living separate and apart for over a month. During this time, Mrs. Guttmann was very cooperative in arranging visitation with Mr. Guttmann and their two children, Gunter and Alisa. Once the initial pleadings were served on Mr. Guttmann, Mrs. Guttmann would not let him see the children. There are currently no pending orders in this case. Using forms found on the Internet or state-specific resources, draft the appropriate *pendente lite* motion and order in response on behalf of Mr. Guttmann.

4. You work as a paralegal for the Law Office of Melissa M. Fae in your state. Attorney Fae represents Twanetta Gibbs as the plaintiff in a divorce action against her husband, Erik Gibbs. She recently filed for divorce. Upon being served with the initial pleadings, Mr. Gibbs moved out of the marital home into his sister's basement. Mrs. Gibbs works full time but cannot make ends meet on her salary. Mr. Gibbs is also employed full time, but refuses to give her any money to help support the children and pay the bills on the marital home. Using forms found on the Internet or state-specific resources, draft the appropriate *pendente lite* motion and order in response on behalf of Mrs. Gibbs.

5. Using the Internet as a guide, research the law in your state regarding *ex parte* restraining orders in domestic violence cases. What is the procedure for obtaining temporary emergency relief in your jurisdiction? How soon after the *ex parte* hearing will the opposing party have to appear and present its side of the case? You can start your research by going to **http://www.aardvarc.org/dv/orders.shtml.**

CHAPTER

The Discovery Process in Family Law

KEY TERMS

affidavit of fees and costs

capias

confidential

confidentiality agreement

cross-examination

deponent

deposition

direct examination

discovery

discovery tool

duplicative

financial affidavit

interrogatories

irrelevant

joint stipulation

malpractice

memorandum of law

motion for disclosure
of assets

motion for protective order

motion to approve
confidentiality agreement

motion to compel
answers to interrogatories

motion to compel discovery

motion to compel
examination

notice of deposition

notice of filing
of interrogatories

notice of responding
to and/or objecting
to interrogatories

objection

overbroad

privilege

redirect

request

request for admission

request for physical
or mental examination

request for production
of documents

requesting party

responding party

subpoena

subpoena duces tecum

The discovery process is an important part of any type of civil suit. **Discovery** is the term used to describe the process or stage in a civil litigation matter during which information is gathered by each party for use in their case against the other party. There are set procedures known as **discovery tools** that the court allows the parties to employ while conducting discovery. The court, upon a motion from one of the parties, may hold the other party in contempt and/or compel the other party to release information held back unless the reluctant party has asserted a valid *objection* or *privilege*.

In a dissolution action, discovery is used to acquire essential information that will lead to an equitable distribution of marital property and to accurately determine each party's income in order to set alimony and child support payments. Finally, discovery can provide the information needed to make wise decisions about what type of custody the court will award and what visitation arrangements are in the child's best interests.

DISCOVERY TOOLS

In any type of lawsuit each party has the right to use any or all of the following discovery vehicles:

- interrogatories,
- requests for the production of documents,
- requests for physical and mental examination,
- requests for admission, and
- depositions.

In litigation involving family law matters, most and sometimes all of these general discovery tools are used. Frequently, family law attorneys also employ additional discovery-oriented procedures designed to elicit specific information essential to the resolution of the particular issues involved in a family law matter. Examples include the motion for disclosure of assets and the parties' respective financial affidavits.

What follows is a description of both the general discovery tools common to all types of litigation and the subsidiary discovery vehicles commonly used in family matters. Accompanying each of these descriptions is a summary of the family law paralegal's role and duties in facilitating effective use of each discovery tool and procedure.

INTERROGATORIES

Interrogatories are written questions that one party in a lawsuit serves on any opposing party or parties. The party on whom the interrogatories are served must answer the interrogatories under oath. A party may object to having to answer an interrogatory. **Objections** can be asserted on the grounds that the information sought is **irrelevant, overbroad,** or **duplicative.** A party may also refuse to answer by asserting a privilege. A **privilege** is a court-conferred right permitting parties in a lawsuit to keep confidential any information exchanged between themselves and another person in instances where there was a special type of relationship between themselves and the other person that generated an expectation of trust, confidentiality, and privacy. For instance, the court recognizes

- spousal privilege,
- attorney/client privilege,
- physician/patient (therapist/client) privilege, and
- priest/penitent (clergy/parishioner) privilege.

Interrogatories in a family law proceeding may seek to have the other party identify all banks accounts, stock accounts, and real property held by that party jointly or in his or her name, solely. Interrogatories may contain questions about a spouse's current employment, earned income, bonuses, and health insurance and life insurance coverage. The purpose of these types of interrogatories is to uncover all of the opposing party's assets and sources of earned and unearned income, as well as forms of nonmonetary employment compensation.

Interrogatories may also seek to have the opposing party spouse reveal the names of parties residing with the spouse, the names and addresses of doctors who have treated the spouse or who have treated the minor children when in that spouse's care, and the names of day care providers or other child care workers who have cared for the child or children. Interrogatories must be answered in writing, under oath, and by the party on whom they have been served.

PREPARATION OF INTERROGATORIES

The paralegal in a family law practice will often have the task of drafting interrogatories to be served on the opposing party. The paralegal should begin this process by reviewing the client's file and making a list of all areas where information will be needed from the opposing spouse. Then the paralegal, with the supervising attorney's approval, should schedule a meeting with the client.

Prior to the meeting the paralegal prepares a rough draft of the interrogatories or questions to be posed and answered. At the meeting, the client and paralegal review these questions, correct any inaccurate information, and add and delete questions they agree are appropriate. Following the initial meeting, the paralegal revises the draft of the interrogatories and presents this revised draft to the supervising attorney for review and further revision, if necessary.

Once the supervising attorney completes any needed revisions and signs off on the document, the paralegal prepares the final form of the interrogatories and returns the completed document to the supervising attorney for final review and signature. Once signed, the paralegal ensures that the document is sent to the opposing party's attorney. In most jurisdictions, interrogatories and responses are not filed with the court. Many states, however, require that parties file with the court a **notice of filing of interrogatories** and a **notice of responding to and/or**

objecting to interrogatories. The paralegal should learn the jurisdiction's requirements for filing any documents related to interrogatories and responses and time limitations on such filings.

The paralegal may also have the responsibility of monitoring the opposing party's compliance in response to the interrogatories. In many jurisdictions, the rules of court provide that interrogatories must be answered or objected to within thirty days of receipt. It is not unusual for a party's attorney to file a motion for extension of time in which to reply or object to the interrogatories or to informally have an agreement with the opposing party's counsel to provide the responses within a reasonable amount of time after the thirty-day period. However, an informal agreement allowing for additional time does not exempt the responding party from the obligation of filing any objections to any of the interrogatories within the original thirty-day period.

Sometimes, the thirty-day period will pass without any communication from the party served. The paralegal will have the compliance date marked or her calendar. If the answers to the interrogatories do not arrive at the office by the date due or shortly thereafter, the paralegal will notify her supervising attorney and learn from the attorney whether she should prepare a **motion to compel discovery** for filing with the court. In some family law practices, the office will have a procedure whereby upon the expiration of the thirty-day period, the paralegal will automatically prepare a motion to compel for the attorney's signature and filing with the court. Frequently, simply receiving a motion to compel will be enough to hasten the opposing party's provision of responses, and the motion will not have to be heard by the court. Again, though, because the thirty-day period has passed, the responding party will have lost their opportunity to object to any of the questions and must answer all of the interrogatories.

If objections to any of the interrogatories are filed timely, and if the parties' attorneys have conferred and are unable to resolve the issue of objections, the paralegal will prepare a **motion to compel answers to interrogatories,** which will address the objections, dispute their validity, and request that the court overrule them. A hearing will take place, and after hearing oral argument from the parties' respective attorneys, the court will decide whether any of the interrogatories objected to must be answered and whether any of the objections fall within the allowed exceptions for not complying.

Once all the required interrogatory responses are received by the office, the paralegal will review the document. If any of the answers reveal the need to request certain documents, previously not known of, the paralegal will relay this information to the supervising attorney and inquire whether such documents should be added to any forthcoming production requests that the paralegal will prepare.

PREPARATION OF RESPONSES TO INTERROGATORIES

As mentioned, a party served with interrogatories must answer the interrogatories in writing and under oath, and within a specific time frame. In the oath, the party must state that his answers or responses are true and accurate to the best of his knowledge. This obligation to answer truthfully and accurately does not preclude the law firm from providing a client with assistance in forming and articulating accurate responses or from providing technical assistance in the manuscripting or transcribing of the answers or objections.

When a law firm receives a set of interrogatories for a particular client to answer, frequently the family law paralegal will see to it that the client provides the required responses within the appropriate time frame. The paralegal often copies the interrogatory papers and sends a copy to the client with a cover letter explaining that the client should try to provide answers to all questions as best she can. In this letter the paralegal will also tell the client to mail back her responses as soon as possible. After the client has sent the responses to the law firm, the paralegal reviews the information and then, with the approval of the supervising attorney, calls the client and sets a date for the client to come to the office and meet with the paralegal to discuss and finalize the responses.

At this meeting, the paralegal assists the client in reformulating any answers that are incomplete or that do not really answer the question asked. In addition, the paralegal helps the client delete any information in answers that should be objected to or that is privileged. The paralegal also helps the client delete any information that has not been requested, especially information that, if left in the response, would, in fact, help the other side with their case and hurt the client.

The paralegal may also be extremely helpful to the client by telling the client how to go about getting some information sought that is not in the client's possession but that only the client can obtain. There may be an interrogatory that asks for details about the client's health plan, such as whether it covers children who are over eighteen but full-time students. Another interrogatory may ask whether any life insurance or disability income is available through employment. Another interrogatory may ask for the name of the plan administrator for the client's pension plan. Some clients may not have the know-how or patience to negotiate the various bureaucratic procedures required to obtain such information. An experienced family law paralegal, one who has been confronted with this type of situation before, will be able to help clients cut through the "red tape," find the individuals they need to speak to, and obtain the necessary information. Sometimes, the paralegal will encourage the client to make telephone calls to the proper entities while the client is in the law office so that the paralegal can intervene if necessary to explain more precisely what information is needed.

After the client and paralegal have finalized the responses, the paralegal prepares a final document that is reviewed by the supervising attorney. If the supervising attorney has questions or concerns regarding any part of the document, these issues are discussed and resolved. The paralegal then revises the document as needed, and the attorney reviews the revised document.

If everything is in order, the paralegal again arranges for the client to come to the office, review the final document, and then, subject to any final revisions, the client signs the responses under oath in the presence of two witnesses, and a notary public or officer of the court acknowledges her oath. Once finalized, the paralegal sends the responsive document to the opposing party's counsel and files notice with the court, if such notice is required. A sample set of interrogatories is provided in Exhibit 11–1.

REQUESTS FOR PRODUCTION

Parties may request production and inspection, and often copying, of documents that are relevant to a dissolution action (see Exhibit 11–2). For instance, by means of a **request for production of documents,** one party can request inspection of the other party's federal and state tax returns, canceled checks, bills for the minor children's summer camp or private school, copies of health insurance plans, insurance policies, copies of driver's licenses, pay stubs, and titles to cars, boats, or other recreational vehicles. The party asking to see and, most likely, copy these documents is called the **requesting party.** The party who must produce these documents is known as the **responding party.**

The responding party must produce all documents requested unless he has a valid objection or the documents are privileged, or **confidential,** or the responding party does not have what has been requested and has no idea of where these documents are. Sometimes, a responding party may withhold a document on the grounds that it is confidential. In a family law matter, this issue might arise when the requesting party seeks information relating to the respondent's business, profession, or employment. For the respondent to produce this information, the respondent might be divulging a trade secret, classified work-related data, or even information about an invention for which the respondent is seeking a patent, or about an artistic work the respondent wishes to have copyrighted before revealing it to the public. In instances like this, either or both parties may draft and file with the court a **motion for protective order** and a **confidentiality agreement.** These documents will ensure that although certain confidential information will be disclosed to the opposing party, that party, under penalty of law, must limit disclosure of this information to the court and the parties only and must affirmatively act to protect the confidentiality of the material provided.

PREPARATION OF REQUESTS FOR PRODUCTION

The family law paralegal is often the person who prepares the preliminary draft of production requests that the client or the supervising attorney wishes to make. The steps in this process are similar to the steps utilized for preparing interrogatories. The paralegal reviews the file, consults with the attorney and with the client, and also draws on models of production requests from previous similar types of family law actions.

When the opposing party remits documents in response to the request, the paralegal checks off these documents, catalogs them, and prepares a list of documents not produced so that the supervising attorney will know of and can respond to the opposing party's noncompliance.

Sometimes when documents are produced and the paralegal catalogs them, the paralegal will recognize that some of the documents suggest the presence of other documents that should be produced. For instance, cancelled checks from a spouse's separate personal or business checking account may include checks written monthly to pay a bill on an unknown credit card. The paralegal may want to ask the supervising attorney whether there should be an second request for production asking for copies of the last twelve months of receipts for this credit card and for copies of the last twelve months' receipts from any other credit card the responding party may possess. If the responding party has not kept all of the receipts, copies can obtained from the credit card companies. Once all of these receipts have been provided to the law office, the paralegal will have the task of organizing them both chronologically and according to category of expenditure (entertainment, recreation, food, clothing, gifts, gasoline, etc.). The paralegal may also add up the expenditures in each category and come up with a total of all charges. Breaking the receipts down in this fashion and providing a summary of the pattern of spending to the supervising attorney will help greatly when the supervising attorney questions the spouse in a deposition.

PREPARATION OF RESPONSES TO REQUESTS FOR PRODUCTION

The family law paralegal may also be responsible for orchestrating a client's response to the opposing side's production requests. When the law firm receives a request for the production of documents, the paralegal sends a copy to the client just as the paralegal has sent the client a copy of interrogatories served. Because there is only a thirty-day time limit in which to respond to both interrogatories and production requests, the paralegal follows up the letter with a phone call to the client in which the paralegal offers assistance in helping the client to identify and find the requested documents. The paralegal should also meet with the supervising attorney to discuss which documents the attorney wishes to withhold as privileged, which documents the attorney objects to producing, and which documents, if any, the attorney wishes to be shielded by a protective order and confidentiality agreement.

If the attorney is seeking either a protective order or a confidentiality agreement, the paralegal may have the responsibility of drafting a motion for protective order or a **motion to approve confidentiality agreement.** Some jurisdictions require the filing of a memorandum of law in support of this type of request. If the paralegal has been adequately trained to do legal research, the supervising attorney may delegate to the paralegal the task of doing the legal research necessary for identifying and articulating the legal standard that must be met for the granting of a protective order or a confidentiality agreement.

REQUEST FOR PHYSICAL OR PSYCHIATRIC EXAMINATION

In a dissolution action, one party may request that the other party submit to a physical examination and/or a psychiatric evaluation (see Exhibit 11–3). This may occur when the requesting party believes and alleges that the other party's physical or mental status should preclude awarding child custody or unsupervised visitation to the other party.

A party may also file a **request for physical or mental examination** if the opposing party has requested a high amount of alimony on the basis that she is physically unable to work or too emotionally unstable to work, or where the party on her financial affidavit reflects high weekly costs for mental health counseling or therapy.

Finally, in dissolutions involving minor children, the children's mother may request a physical examination of the male spouse to establish paternity of the child for purposes of support, custody, and visitation. The husband/spouse may also request a paternity test if he doubts that he is the natural father of one or more of the children born during the marriage.

PREPARATION OF A REQUEST FOR A MEDICAL EXAMINATION

When a family law paralegal has an initial informational interview with a client, as discussed in an earlier section, the paralegal asks the client to complete a questionnaire that addresses many aspects of the client's marital history and each spouse's individual family background, educational attainments, and medical history. After reviewing the client's responses, the paralegal may immediately recognize the existence of one of the previously mentioned circumstances that gives rise to the need for a physical or mental examination of the opposing party. The paralegal should bring this to the attention of the supervising attorney. If the supervising attorney agrees with the paralegal's analysis, she will direct the paralegal to prepare the document for filing in court.

In most jurisdictions, the party desiring such an examination must file a document with the court known as a **request** rather than a motion. A request differs from a motion in that it is automatically granted by the court thirty days after filing, absent the opposing party's objection. The family paralegal files the original of the request document with the court and makes sure that proper service is made on the opposing party's counsel. If no objection is filed within the prescribed time limit and the time limit expires, the paralegal prepares a letter to opposing counsel requesting dates on which to schedule the requested examination or examinations. Absent the timely filing of an objection, the opposing party must submit to the examination within a reasonable amount of time. If the party refuses to do so, the paralegal must alert the supervising attorney of this failure and, with the supervising attorney's approval, file a **motion to compel examination.**

Frequently, an opposing party may object to an examination completely, or object unless there is agreement as to the choice of examiner, agreement as to the extent, nature, and exact purpose of the exam, or the use to which the requesting party will allocate the results. When an objection is filed, the opposing attorneys may be willing to negotiate a compromise and avoid litigating the issue in open court.

If no agreement is reached, the matter is scheduled for a hearing and the paralegal keeps a watchful eye for the court calendar that will be sent to the law firm indicating the date of the hearing. When it arrives, the paralegal will docket the hearing on the calendar. If the scheduled date conflicts with other obligations of the attorney handling the case, the paralegal apprises the supervising attorney, who then decides whether to send another of the firm's attorneys to the hearing or to have the paralegal attempt to reschedule the matter. The paralegal is also responsible for notifying the client of the need to be in court on the hearing date. If the supervising attorney believes that the client will need to offer testimony, the paralegal may schedule a meeting with the client prior to the hearing to review the matter and prepare the client for his appearance on the witness stand.

PREPARATION OF A RESPONSE TO A REQUEST FOR A MEDICAL EXAMINATION

When the family law firm receives a request that a client be subjected to a physical examination or mental or psychological evaluation, the attorney handling the file may direct the paralegal to communicate the request to the party and arrange for an office conference to discuss the request. After this meeting, the supervising attorney may decide to object to the request or negotiate with opposing counsel to allow the examination subject to agreed-on parameters such as the ones previously mentioned.

Usually, a party's attorney will not allow a blanket assent to an examination and the uses to which the results will be applied unless the examination is limited by its own nature and/or unless the client insists on no limitations. The family law paralegal may have the task of drafting a letter to the opposing counsel memorializing the limiting terms parties have agreed to. If no agreement is reached, the paralegal will, within the thirty-day period, draft and see to the finalization of an objection or objections that must be filed with the court. Once filed, the paralegal will make sure that the court's notice of a hearing on the objections is noted, and docketed on the firm's calendar, and that any need for a continuance is requested in a timely manner.

If a client must submit to a medical examination or mental or psychological evaluation, the paralegal may be the staff person who arranges for the client's appointment, notifies the client of this appointment, and telephones the client a day or two before the appointment to remind the client of this obligation. After the examination, the paralegal should make sure that the firm receives a copy of the examining physician's report and/or a copy of the results of any laboratory tests.

If there has been a request for a client to submit to a paternity test, the supervising attorney will probably suggest to the client that he not oppose the request because, absent a compelling reason, the court will overrule his objection, especially since the test now consists merely of taking DNA from saliva through a quick swab of the interior of the mouth. If there are compelling circumstances to oppose a determination of paternity at this time, the client should bring the situation before the court. For instance, a child or children who are older and who have had the client as their psychological father for their entire lives would undoubtedly be devastated to learn that at the same time that their parents are divorcing, their father is really not their biological parent. In this situation, especially if the client desires to continue with his parental obligations, a judge might decide that it is not in the children's best interest for such a determination to be made at the same time as the divorce.

If a paternity test is to be done on the client, the paralegal may have the responsibility for setting it up. In most communities, there are public and quasi-public health organizations that offer such testing periodically at a low cost. The paralegal may wish to keep a listing of these agencies available so that she can schedule a test at a facility offering testing immediately, within the following week or two.

REQUEST FOR ADMISSION

Sometimes either party in a dissolution action may file a **request for admission** of certain facts or events (see Exhibit 11–4). In civil suits, one party may request formally that an opposing party admit the truth of some fact or event that will inevitably be proved at trial. For instance, one party may request that the other party admit that although the other party receives child support for three minor children, the oldest child resides with the noncustodial parent. If one party files a request for admission with the court, and the other party does not object to this request within thirty days after it is filed, the facts or events requested to be admitted are deemed admitted. If the other party does file an objection, then the parties may negotiate a compromise of admissions or, if no compromise is reached, the parties' attorneys will argue their respective positions before the court.

PREPARATION OF A REQUEST FOR ADMISSIONS

The family law paralegal is responsible for recognizing any circumstances listed on the client questionnaire that may necessitate the filing of a request for admission from the opposing party. The paralegal should apprise the supervising attorney of such circumstances and if the supervising attorney agrees that a request for admission of certain facts is in order, then the paralegal may prepare the document, present it to the attorney for review and signing, and see that it is filed properly with the court and that a copy is mailed to the opposing counsel in a timely manner.

Once such a document is filed, the paralegal should watch the calendar to ensure that any objections received from opposing counsel are filed within the thirty-day time limit. If objections are filed timely and the parties' attorneys reach a compromise, the paralegal prepares, for court filing, either a revised request for admissions negotiated and agreed to by both parties, which will be automatically granted after thirty days, or a **joint stipulation** in which the opposing party withdraws its objections subject to the modification of some aspect of the requested admissions.

PREPARATION OF A RESPONSE TO A REQUEST FOR ADMISSION

Frequently, when an attorney receives a request for admission from opposing counsel, the attorney will ask the paralegal to contact the client, explain the purpose of a request for admission, describe the nature of the admissions sought, and inquire whether the facts the opposing counsel seeks to have admitted are true and accurate. The paralegal discusses the outcome of this conversation with the supervising attorney, who will decide how to respond to the request. If the paralegal feels that the client needs further explanation or clarification of the request for admissions, the paralegal should convey this to the attorney, who may wish to speak to the client personally before proceeding further. The attorney may direct the paralegal to send the client a copy of the request for admission and a cover letter that requests the client to call the office and set up a time for an office meeting or telephone conference with the attorney to discuss how to proceed.

The paralegal must also monitor the running of the thirty-day objection deadline so that before the time period expires, the attorney confers with opposing counsel and decides whether to allow the admissions or have the paralegal prepare a stipulation, or prepare objections to the request for admission to be heard by the court. If objections are filed and the court schedules a hearing, the paralegal will be responsible for docketing the date and notifying the client. If a scheduling conflict exists, the paralegal may have to notify the office of opposing counsel of this conflict and also notify the court by requesting a continuance for the hearing.

If the client was informed of the hearing date scheduled by the court before the conflict became apparent, the paralegal should also call the client to let the client know that the matter will have to be rescheduled. At that time, it will be beneficial for the paralegal to determine the client's availability for the purposes of rescheduling the hearing. Similarly, the paralegal should attempt to obtain some available dates from the office of opposing counsel. Some courts require the filing of a motion for continuance and require moving counsel to indicate a future date or dates upon which all counsel and parties will be available. The paralegal should notify the court as soon as the conflict is discovered so that the respective dates of the parties' availability do not change before rescheduling of the hearing.

DEPOSITIONS

The need for depositions does not arise in every dissolution case. Depositions are employed primarily when there is a need to identify all of the opposing spouse's assets or when documentation is needed to support one parent's claim that the child's interest will be best served by investing sole custody in that parent, or when a parent wishes to establish the need to severely restrict the other party's visitation rights.

A **deposition** is a procedure in which one party's attorney orally questions an opposing party or a nonparty witness who has sworn under oath to answer all questions truthfully and accurately to the best of his or her knowledge and ability. The person being deposed is known as the **deponent.** The format of a deposition includes the initial questioning by the deposing party's attorney.

This questioning is termed **direct examination**. After the deposing attorney conducts the direct examination, the opposing party's lawyer has the opportunity to cross-examine his or her client. After this **cross-examination,** the deposing attorney may question the deponent on any subject covered in the cross-examination testimony. This questioning is known as **redirect** questioning.

The following individuals must be present at a deposition: the deposing attorney, the opposing party, and the court reporter. The attorney for the opposing party *should* also be present. The deposing party's client may be present and, for practical reasons, should be present. If, however, the deposing party's client in a dissolution suit is terrified of the opposing party, and the deposing lawyer decides that the risks to his or her client's well-being outweigh the value of the client's presence at the deposition, the attorney may choose to depose the opposing party outside the client's presence. The deposing attorney may also decide to have his or her paralegal present to take notes or retrieve documents for direct questioning or cross-examination.

At the deposition of a nonparty witness, all parties must be invited but their presence is not mandatory. Usually the opposing party's lawyer will attend and want the client also to attend. The court reporter must always be present at a deposition.

DEPOSITION EXPENSES

Depositions are expensive. Therefore, the need for a deposition must be great enough to justify the expense. An attorney will apprise a client of the availability of the deposition as a discovery tool and may strongly recommend deposing the opposing party or a witness or witnesses. However, the decision to depose ultimately rests with the client, who must pay the attorney for time spent preparing for and appearing at the deposition and who must pay the court reporter for transcription services at the deposition and for the typed transcript of the deposition.

Early in a client's representation the attorney should make the client aware of the possible need for depositions and the anticipated costs. An attorney should also tell his client that the opposing spouse's attorney may require that she be deposed. A client may refuse to appear at a deposition once she is noticed. Exhibit 11–5 provides a sample **notice of deposition,** which is served on a party to a lawsuit by sending the notice via first-class mail to the party's lawyer.

Once a party has been served, the party through his or her attorney has the following options:

1. Appear at the deposition at the noticed time and place,
2. Negotiate to reschedule the deposition to a time and/or place mutually agreeable to the deposing party and the party being deposed, or
3. Request to have the other party cancel the deposition by offering to negotiate or informally resolve the issue that has given rise to the noticing of a deposition.

If a deposing party's purpose for the deposition is to uncover the opposing party's hidden assets or hidden and ongoing source of income, the party noticed for deposition may decide to amend her financial affidavit to reflect these amounts, thus obviating the need, time, and expense of a deposition, or the party may simply decide to give the opposing spouse a higher property settlement or agree to a higher amount of alimony or child support or both.

Sometimes the simple act of noticing a party for a deposition will produce one or another of these results. Doing so is considered an act of strategy!

THE PARALEGAL'S ROLE IN THE DEPOSITION

At a minimum, the paralegal in a family law practice is responsible for preparing the notice of deposition, determining the client's availability, and sending copies to all counsel and *pro se* parties. Because a deposition is usually held at the law offices of the deposing attorney, the paralegal must check the availability of the conference room, or in a larger firm, the availability of one of the conference rooms.

Sometimes, either the attorney or the paralegal will call the opposing attorney or their paralegal to agree and reserve in advance the date or dates for the deposition. These dates then appear on the notice of deposition, which must nevertheless be served even if the respective attorneys have agreed to the fact of the deposition and its place, time, and date.

The paralegal must also make arrangements for a court reporter to be present at the deposition to take the deponent's testimony. The paralegal may contact a court reporting agency or an individual court reporter whom the firm has worked with previously. Sometimes when calling an agency or business that employs several court reporters, the agency contact person may request that the paralegal mail or fax to that person a copy of the notice of deposition sent to opposing counsel. This practice helps the agency provide accurate information to the attending court reporter regarding time, place, and the names of the parties and attorneys. It also serves as documentation for billing purposes that the deposition was ordered. If for some reason the deposition is cancelled or must be rescheduled, the paralegal should notify the individual court reporter or agency as soon as she knows of the change to avoid any charge to the client or firm, and to reserve a court reporter for the new date if that date is known.

NOTICING OF NONPARTY WITNESSES

The paralegal is also often responsible for preparing the paperwork needed to bring a nonparty witness to a deposition.

To require a nonparty witness to appear at a deposition to be deposed, the deposing lawyer must serve a subpoena on the witness ordering his or her appearance. A **subpoena** is a legal document signed by an officer of the court that requires the person receiving it to appear under penalty of law at the time, date, and place indicated on the document (see Exhibit 11–6). A sheriff or other indifferent person serves the subpoena on the nonparty witness. In many jurisdictions, the statute requires the sheriff to give the nonparty witness cash or a check to reimburse the nonparty for a percentage of his travel expenses from his home to the site of the deposition. A **subpoena duces tecum** is a subpoena commanding a party or witness, who has in his or her possession documents that are relevant to a case, to produce them at a deposition, motion hearing or trial.

Typically, the paralegal prepares the subpoena and arranges for the sheriff to pick up the subpoena and serve the witness. The paralegal is responsible for giving the sheriff the proper address for the witness and possibly a physical description of the witness. Also, the paralegal should later check with the sheriff to determine if service has indeed been made.

A subpoena must be served at least eighteen hours before the scheduled proceeding. Usually the subpoena is served earlier because most jurisdictions require the party issuing the deposition subpoena to give notice to the opposing party's counsel of the date and time of the deposition and invite the opposing counsel and opposing party to attend. Eighteen hours is not reasonable notice for the other counsel. On the other hand, the deposing party's attorney does not wish to give the witness too much time to either prepare or engage in a lengthy consultation with the opposing party's attorney. The paralegal will be responsible for sending opposing counsel a *notice of intent to depose nonparty witness,* as well as for contacting a person authorized to serve the subpoena on the nonparty witness.

MOTION FOR DISCLOSURE OF ASSETS

Frequently, in conjunction with the taking of a party's deposition, the deposing attorney will file with the court a **motion for disclosure of assets** (see Exhibit 11–7). In this motion, the moving attorney requests the court to order the opposing party to bring to the deposition detailed information on all existing assets and acceptable documentation to substantiate the extent and/or limits of the party's assets. The opposing attorney may object to the granting of this motion, in which case the court hears arguments from both sides and either grants or denies the motion. If the motion is granted, the party must under penalty of law bring such materials to the deposition. There, the opposing counsel examines the documents and questions the party on various aspects of the information. Naturally, the deponent's attorney will have an opportunity for cross-examination and the deposing attorney may conduct redirect examination on the cross-examination.

If a party's attorney is not deposing the opposing party, the party's attorney may still file a motion for disclosure of assets. If the motion is granted, the opposing party's attorney must see that a written disclosure is made, that it is accompanied by requested documentation, and that the disclosure is made within the court-ordered time frame. If a party fails to fully disclose his or her assets, the opposing counsel may file a motion to hold the party in contempt of a court order. If contempt is proven, the court may order immediate and full disclosure that, if not complied with, may result in the court issuing a **capias,** which is a civil arrest warrant served by a sheriff ordering that officer to take physical custody of the party and bring him or her to the appropriate corrections facility, that is, *jail,* where they will remain incarcerated until they make arrangements to comply with the court's order for disclosure.

A motion for disclosure of assets in a family law matter typically requests disclosure of all real and personal property owned by a spouse either in her own name or owned jointly with the spouse or with another person or entity. Examples of such assets include bank accounts, certificates of deposit, mutual funds, stocks, boats, cars, and parcels of real estate. The motion for disclosure of assets and the assets it involves is discussed extensively in Chapter 6, which covers property distribution.

PREPARATION OF A MOTION FOR DISCLOSURE OF ASSETS

The family law paralegal is often given the task of drafting the motion for disclosure of assets. The paralegal should review the client intake sheet on which the client has listed assets he believes the other spouse owns. In addition, the paralegal should confer with the client over the phone or in person to review the assets listed and determine whether other categories of assets should also be requested to be disclosed. After the conference, the paralegal drafts the motion and submits it to the supervising attorney for review and possible revision.

Once the final draft of the motion is approved and signed by the supervising attorney, the paralegal files the motion. The court schedules the motion for a hearing that the paralegal then dockets or, if necessary, reschedules through a continuance. If the motion is granted, the paralegal monitors the compliance with the motion and drafts a motion for contempt if disclosure is not made or if disclosure is not complete.

When the paralegal drafts the contempt motion, the supervising attorney may also have the paralegal file a motion for sanctions and costs, providing the jurisdiction allows for such a motion. If so, the supervising attorney will prepare a listing of the number of hours he spent preparing the motion for sanctions and costs and the motion for contempt. He will also list what tasks he performed during these hours of preparation and give this information to the paralegal, who will prepare a formal **affidavit of fees and costs** that will detail the activities the attorney undertook to prepare the motions and total up his hours, his hourly rate, the fee for each task, and the total amount he must charge his client unless the court orders that the opposing party and/or his counsel pay the amount since the work was required to facilitate the opposition's compliance with the disclosures sought.

PREPARATION OF A RESPONSE TO A MOTION FOR DISCLOSURE OF ASSETS

If the opposing party serves the firm's client with a motion for disclosure of assets, the supervising attorney may decide to file with a court a written objection to the motion for disclosure of assets, and may direct the paralegal to draft such an objection and possibly draft a **memorandum of law** supporting the objection. After the supervising attorney reviews and finalizes these documents, the paralegal prepares them in final form, obtains the attorney's signature on them, and sees that the originals of the documents are filed with the court and that copies are properly noticed on opposing counsel.

If the court orders a client to disclose the enumerated assets, the paralegal may be given the task of helping the client list all of the assets and compile, assemble, and organize the substantiating documentation. Once this is done, the paralegal drafts the document containing the disclosed information and documentation, submits it for review and signing to the attorney, transmits the information to opposing counsel, and formally notices the court of the client's compliance.

THE FINANCIAL AFFIDAVIT

Certainly most, if not all, jurisdictions require that both parties in a dissolution or divorce proceeding file a financial affidavit with the court within a specified period of time after the commencement of the proceeding. A **financial affidavit** is a sworn statement that enumerates the party's sources of income, earned and unearned; the party's expenses, necessary and optional; and all of the party's assets and liabilities. As mentioned, assets include real and personal property, such as cash on hand, cars, furniture, stocks and bonds, rental property, vacation homes, and the interest, if any, in one's primary residence. Liabilities include debts such as credit card balances, student loans, court judgments, mortgages, and balances owed on any and all other secured and unsecured loans.

The party completing the affidavit must provide either a weekly or monthly breakdown of income, expenses, and payments on debts. Whereas in years past the financial affidavit was drafted by a party's attorney, most jurisdictions now provide a preprinted, two-sided "fill-in-the blanks" form (see Exhibit 11–8). Most family law courts require the filing of this document before resolving any matters of any nature, financial or otherwise, in the pending proceeding. Financial affidavits must always be filed not only in dissolution matters, but also in any subsequent matters involving a change in alimony and child support orders.

PREPARATION OF A FINANCIAL AFFIDAVIT

The family law office paralegal frequently assists the client in preparation of the financial affidavit. The amount of assistance needed will vary depending on the individual client's level of financial sophistication, her recordkeeping and organizational skills, the quantity and nature of the assets and liabilities involved, and the complexity or simplicity involved in calculating sources of income and essential and nonessential expenses. At the very least, the paralegal will transmit a copy of the financial affidavit form to the client together with a cover letter instructing the client to complete and return the form to the law office together with copies of applicable substantiating documentation such as bills, bank statements, cancelled checks, rental or mortgage payment receipts, pay stubs, and tax returns. When the paralegal receives this information, he may have to see that the amounts reported are broken down into the periodic increments the court requires. For instance, if a client forwards pay stubs that report gross income, deductions, and net income on a bimonthly basis and the jurisdiction requires a weekly breakdown or a monthly breakdown on the affidavit, the paralegal will have to apply arithmetic skills to arrive at and furnish the appropriate figures sought.

In instances where the parties in a dissolution proceeding each earn a moderate income from only one or two sources—for instance, employment compensation and bank account interest—the completion of the financial affidavit is fairly simple. However, when one or both of the divorcing parties have a very high earned income as well as considerable unearned income from several sources, and where the parties, together or separately, have accumulated valuable assets, both tangible and intangible, the completion of a financial affidavit in a manner that accurately and fully reflects each party's financial status is extremely complex. Arriving at proper figures may entail consulting with the client's accountant, financial advisor, and/or investment broker and retaining independent experts to evaluate pension assets and equity in business entities or to appraise tangible personal property such as antiques, expensive household furniture, artwork, and other valuable collectibles.

It is extremely important that the financial information obtained be complete and accurate. The paralegal assigned to the file must perform her duties in a very thorough, responsible, and competent manner. Failure to do so could expose the client to allegations of fraud because the financial affidavit is signed under oath. The injured client who has provided honest and full disclosure to the firm handling the matter could seek redress against the firm through an action for professional malpractice and/or breach of fiduciary duty.

The paralegal may also have responsibilities involving the review of the financial affidavit submitted by an opposing party. The paralegal may have to meet with the client to review the other party's affidavit. If the client believes that the opposing spouse has not fully disclosed all assets or sources and amounts of income, or has misrepresented her financial position, the paralegal must report this to the supervising attorney immediately with a summary of the reasons the client has given to support his belief. Subsequently, the attorney may assign the paralegal various tasks designed to properly uncover the opposing party's hidden or undervalued assets and unreported or underreported sources of income.

Again, we cannot stress too strongly that the paralegal must handle these assignments with the utmost care and professionalism. Failure to do so can mislead the supervising attorney, who may honestly "miss" identifying and locating all of the opposing party's assets and sources of income. If divorcing parties agree to a financial settlement based on wrong data, the party injured by lack of the right information can and may bring suit against his attorney for negligent legal representation, more commonly known as **malpractice.** The supervising attorney is ultimately responsible for the negligent actions of the law office staff persons assigned to the file, and this attorney as well as the entire firm will suffer the consequences. If the attorney has instructed the paralegal in a clear and understandable manner to perform relatively standard procedures for obtaining the additional information sought and the paralegal performs this work in a slipshod or incomplete way, yet leads the supervising attorney to believe that the work has been done in a responsible manner, the paralegal should and most likely will be terminated and may have difficulty obtaining employment in any other law firm.

On the other hand, if an attorney assigns a paralegal work well beyond the paralegal's area of knowledge, training, and expertise and, further, if the attorney fails to review the paralegal's work product before sending it out of the office or relies on the work product to make decisions on the case, the paralegal is blameless. The attorney has committed malpractice and should be dismissed from the firm, but the paralegal should not be held responsible if she completed the assigned work to the best of her training and ability and the supervising attorney failed to review the work before relying on it.

Sometimes an attorney will in good faith assign a paralegal work that is beyond her reach. In this instance, the paralegal and attorney are best served if the paralegal honestly reports her concerns about being able to complete the assignment adequately. The attorney is then put on notice and can either modify the parameters of the assignment or tell the paralegal to complete the assignment as given to the best of her ability, knowing that the results cannot be relied on as a finished product.

EXHIBIT 11–1 Sample interrogatory.

DOCKET NO. FA 96-123456   : SUPERIOR COURT

BRONSON, RODNEY   : JUDICIAL DISTRICT OF NEW HAVEN

V.   : AT NEW HAVEN

BRONSON, EVELYN   : SEPTEMBER 14, 2000

INTERROGATORIES

The plaintiff requests that the defendant answer under oath the following interrogatories within thirty days of the service hereof by serving the same upon counsel for the defendant of this action and that they can be provided by the defendant with substantially greater facility than they can otherwise be obtained by the plaintiff.

1. State whether or not you have any present or future interest in any pension plan, retirement plan, profit sharing plan, stock option plan, deferred income plan, or other similar type of plan, annuity, or fund.

2. If the answer to Interrogatory 1 is yes, please answer the following:

   a. The type of plan, annuity, or fund:

   b. Name of the plan, annuity, or fund:

   c. Account number of the plan, annuity, or fund:

   d. Name and address of the plan administrator, trustee, or custodian:

   e. Age of eligibility for each plan, annuity, or fund:

   f. Date when each plan, fund, or annuity will vest:

EXHIBIT 11–1 Continued

g.   Present value of each plan, fund, or annuity:

h.   Projected value of plan, fund, or annuity at eligibility age:

i.   Date of withdrawal for each plan, fund, or annuity:

j.   Amount of benefits upon retirement for each plan, fund, or annuity:

THE PLAINTIFF,
RODNEY BRONSON

BY: _____

JUSTINE F. MILLER, ESQ.
HIS ATTORNEY
22 PARK PLACE
NEW HAVEN, CT 06511
(203) 861-4444
JURIS NO. 313133

The foregoing answers are true to the best of my knowledge and belief.

_____

Rodney Bronson

Subscribed and sworn to me this _____ day of _____, 20__.

_____

Notary Public/
Commissioner of the Superior Court

EXHIBIT 11–1 Continued

<u>ORDER</u>

The foregoing motion having been heard, it is hereby ORDERED:

GRANTED/DENIED

THE COURT

BY: _____

JUDGE

<u>CERTIFICATION</u>

This is to certify that a true copy of the foregoing motion was mailed, postage prepaid, on this date to all counsel and pro se parties of record on this _____ day of _____, 2000, as follows:

Grace A. Luppino, Esq.
555 Main Avenue
New Haven, CT 06511

_____
Justine F. Miller, Esq.
Commissioner of the Superior Court

EXHIBIT 11–2 Sample request for production.

DOCKET NO. FA 96-123456 : SUPERIOR COURT

BRONSON, RODNEY : JUDICIAL DISTRICT OF NEW HAVEN

V. : AT NEW HAVEN

BRONSON, EVELYN : SEPTEMBER 14, 2000

REQUEST FOR PRODUCTION

The plaintiff represents that certain documents material to the pending action, which are not privileged or within the possession of the plaintiff, whose production would be of assistance in the prosecution of the action, can be provided by the defendant with substantially greater facility than they could otherwise be obtained by the plaintiff and therefore requests that the defendant produce for inspection and copying the following:

1. Copies of any pension plan, retirement plan, profit sharing plan, stock option plan, deferred income plan, or other similar type plan, annuity, or fund.

2. Copies of all statements of accounts for the year 20___ through the present date which indicates the amount to your interest and contributions to all said plans, annuities, or funds.

THE PLAINTIFF,
RODNEY BRONSON

BY: _____
JUSTINE F. MILLER, ESQ.
HIS ATTORNEY
22 PARK PLACE
NEW HAVEN, CT 06511
(203) 861-4444
JURIS NO. 313133

ORDER

The foregoing motion having been heard, it is hereby ORDERED:

GRANTED/DENIED
THE COURT

BY: _____
JUDGE

CERTIFICATION

This is to certify that a true copy of the foregoing motion was mailed, postage prepaid, on this date to all counsel and pro se parties of record on this ____ day of _____, 2000, as follows:

Grace A. Luppino, Esq.
555 Main Avenue
New Haven, CT 06511

_____
Justine F. Miller, Esq.
Commissioner of the Superior Court

EXHIBIT 11–3 Sample request for medical examination.

DOCKET NO. FA 96-123456   : SUPERIOR COURT

BRONSON, RODNEY   : JUDICIAL DISTRICT OF NEW HAVEN

V.   : AT NEW HAVEN

BRONSON, EVELYN   : SEPTEMBER 14, 2000

REQUEST FOR PSYCHIATRIC EXAMINATION

The plaintiff, Rodney Bronson, requests the Court to order a psychiatric evaluation of the defendant, Evelyn Bronson. The plaintiff contends that the mother's ability to care for the children is at issue.

THE PLAINTIFF,
RODNEY BRONSON

BY: _____

JUSTINE F. MILLER, ESQ.
HIS ATTORNEY
22 PARK PLACE
NEW HAVEN, CT 06511
(203) 861-4444
JURIS NO. 313133

ORDER

The foregoing motion having been heard, it is hereby ORDERED:

GRANTED/DENIED
THE COURT

BY: _____
JUDGE

CERTIFICATION

This is to certify that a true copy of the foregoing motion was mailed, postage prepaid, on this date to all counsel and pro se parties of record on this _____ day of _____, 2000, as follows:

Grace A. Luppino, Esq.
555 Main Avenue
New Haven, CT 06511

_____
Justine F. Miller, Esq.
Commissioner of the Superior Court

EXHIBIT 11–4 Sample request for admission.

DOCKET NO. FA 96-123456 : SUPERIOR COURT

BRONSON, RODNEY : JUDICIAL DISTRICT OF NEW HAVEN

V. : AT NEW HAVEN

BRONSON, EVELYN : SEPTEMBER 14, 2000

REQUEST FOR ADMISSION

The plaintiff hereby requests the defendant to admit the truth of the following statements:

That the defendant's employer provides health insurance coverage for all biological or adopted minor children of the insured employee, regardless of their place of residence.

THE PLAINTIFF,
RODNEY BRONSON

BY: _____
JUSTINE F. MILLER, ESQ.
HIS ATTORNEY
22 PARK PLACE
NEW HAVEN, CT 06511
(203) 861-4444
JURIS NO. 313133

ORDER

The foregoing motion having been heard, it is hereby ORDERED:

GRANTED/DENIED
THE COURT

BY: _____
JUDGE

CERTIFICATION

This is to certify that a true copy of the foregoing motion was mailed, postage prepaid, on this date to all counsel and pro se parties of record on this _____ day of _____, 2000, as follows:

Grace A. Luppino, Esq.
555 Main Avenue
New Haven, CT 06511

_____
Justine F. Miller, Esq.
Commissioner of the Superior Court

EXHIBIT 11–5 Sample notice of deposition.

DOCKET NO. FA 96-123456   : SUPERIOR COURT

BRONSON, RODNEY   : JUDICIAL DISTRICT OF NEW HAVEN

V.   : AT NEW HAVEN

BRONSON, EVELYN   : SEPTEMBER 14, 2000

NOTICE OF DEPOSITION

The plaintiff, Rodney Bronson, hereby gives notice that his attorney intends to take the deposition of the defendant, Evelyn Bronson, regarding her knowledge of the above-captioned matter on October 22, 2000, at 11:30 a.m., before court reporters at the law office of the plaintiff's counsel located at 22 Park Place, New Haven, CT.

THE PLAINTIFF,
RODNEY BRONSON

BY: _____
    JUSTINE F. MILLER, ESQ.
    HIS ATTORNEY
    22 PARK PLACE
    NEW HAVEN, CT 06511
    (203) 861-4444
    JURIS NO. 313133

CERTIFICATION

This is to certify that a true copy of the foregoing motion was mailed, postage prepaid, on this date to all counsel and pro se parties of record on this ____ day of _____, 2000, as follows:

Grace A. Luppino, Esq.
555 Main Avenue
New Haven, CT 06511

_____
Justine F. Miller, Esq.
Commissioner of the Superior Court

EXHIBIT 11–6 Sample subpoena.

STATE OF CONNECTICUT
SUPERIOR COURT

SUBPOENA FAMILY/JUVENILE
JD-FM-126   Rev. 4-89 (Old SJC-11A)
C.G.S. 52-143, 52-144, 52-260

INSTRUCTIONS

To be used only if the witness is being subpoenaed by the state in family or juvenile matters, including those subpoenas issued by the attorney general, or an assistant attorney general, or by any public defender or assistant public defender acting in his/her official capacity. (For example, in family matters, use in conjunction with form JD-FM-124.)

NAME OF CASE | DOCKET NO.

NAME AND ADDRESS OF COURT (No., street and town)

TO

DATE AND TIME YOU ARE TO APPEAR

BY AUTHORITY OF THE STATE OF CONNECTICUT, you are hereby commanded to appear before the Superior Court in session at the above address on the date indicated above or to such day thereafter and within sixty days hereof on which the action named above is legally to be tried, to testify what you know in said action pending in the court.

YOU ARE FURTHER COMMANDED TO BRING WITH YOU AND PRODUCE:

HEREOF FAIL NOT, UNDER PENALTY OF THE LAW.

To any proper officer or indifferent person to serve and return.

NAME OF STATE AGENT ISSUING SUBPOENA | TITLE

SIGNED (Clerk, Commissioner of Superior Court) | ON (Date) | AT (Town)

NOTICE TO THE PERSON SUMMONED

You must report to the court at the time and address shown above and remain until this case is disposed of and you are discharged by the court. Present this subpoena when you report. Your statutory fees as witness will be paid by the clerk of the court where you are summoned to appear, if you give the clerk this subpoena on the day you appear. If you do not appear in court on the day and at the time stated, or on the day and at the time to which your appearance may have been postponed or continued by order of an officer of the court, the court may order that you be arrested. In addition, if you fail to appear and testify, without reasonable excuse, you shall be fined not more than twenty-five dollars and pay all damages to the aggrieved party.

RETURN OF SERVICE

JUDICIAL DISTRICT OF | DATE

ss. , Connecticut

Then and there I made service of the within subpoena not less than eighteen hours prior to the time designated for the person summoned to appear, by reading the same in the presence and hearing/leaving a true and attested copy hereof in the hands/at the last usual place of abode of each of the within-named persons, viz:

FEES

COPY

ENDORSEMENT

SERVICE

TRAVEL (Show miles and amount)

The within is ☐ the original/ ☐ a true copy of the original subpoena.

ATTEST (Signature of proper officer or indifferent person) | TITLE (If applicable) | **TOTAL**

DISTRIBUTION: WHITE - Return to court after service   YELLOW - Witness   PINK - Retained by clerk

EXHIBIT 11–7 Sample motion for disclosure of assets.

DOCKET NO. FA 96-123456   : SUPERIOR COURT

BRONSON, RODNEY   : JUDICIAL DISTRICT OF NEW HAVEN

V.   : AT NEW HAVEN

BRONSON, EVELYN   : SEPTEMBER 14, 2000

MOTION FOR DISCLOSURE OF ASSETS

The plaintiff in the above-captioned matter hereby requests the Court to order the defendant to disclose her assets.

Wherefore, the plaintiff requests the Court to order the defendant to appear at the office of the undersigned on October 22, 2000, to disclose under oath during a deposition, all of her assets.

THE PLAINTIFF,
RODNEY BRONSON

BY: _____

JUSTINE F. MILLER, ESQ.
HIS ATTORNEY
22 PARK PLACE
NEW HAVEN, CT 06511
(203) 861-4444
JURIS NO. 313133

ORDER

The foregoing motion having been heard, it is hereby ORDERED:

GRANTED/DENIED
THE COURT

BY: _____
JUDGE

CERTIFICATION

This is to certify that a true copy of the foregoing motion was mailed, postage prepaid, on this date to all counsel and pro se parties of record on this ____ day of _____, 2000, as follows:

Grace A. Luppino, Esq.
555 Main Avenue
New Haven, CT 06511

_____
Justine F. Miller, Esq.
Commissioner of the Superior Court

EXHIBIT 11–8 Financial affidavit

FINANCIAL AFFIDAVIT JD-FM-6 Rev. 5-98 P.B. 25-30	**STATE OF CONNECTICUT** **SUPERIOR COURT**	COURT USE ONLY FINAFF	‖‖‖‖‖‖‖
		DOCKET NO.	

FOR THE JUDICIAL DISTRICT OF	AT *(Address of court)*	NAME OF AFFIANT *(person submitting this form)*
NAME OF CASE		☐ PLAINTIFF ☐ DEFENDANT
OCCUPATION	NAME OF EMPLOYER	
ADDRESS OF EMPLOYER		

A. WEEKLY INCOME FROM PRINCIPAL EMPLOYMENT *(Use weekly average not less than 13 weeks)*

	DEDUCTIONS	AMOUNT/WEEK		DEDUCTIONS *(Cont.)*	AMOUNT/WEEK		
1.		$	4.		$	GROSS WKLY WAGE FROM PRINCIPAL EMPLOYMENT →	$
2.		$	5.		$	TOTAL DEDUCTIONS →	$
3.		$	6.		$	NET WEEKLY WAGE →	$

B. ALL OTHER INCOME *(Include in-kind compensation, gratuities, rents, interest, dividends, pension, etc.)*

1. WEEKLY INCOME

SOURCE OF INCOME	GROSS AMT/WK	SOURCE OF INCOME	GROSS AMT/WK		
1.		2.		GROSS WEEKLY INCOME FROM OTHER SOURCES →	$
DEDUCTIONS / AMOUNT/WEEK	$	DEDUCTIONS / AMOUNT/WEEK	$	TOTAL DEDUCTIONS →	$
	$		$	NET WEEKLY INCOME FROM OTHER SOURCES →	$
	$		$		
	$		$	ADD "NET WEEKLY WAGE" FROM SECTION A, AND "NET WEEKLY INCOME" FROM SECTION B, AND ENTER TOTAL BELOW:	
	$		$		
	$		$	**A** TOTAL NET WEEKLY INCOME →	$

2. WEEKLY EXPENSES

1. RENT OR MORTGAGE	$			Gas/Oil	$	11. DAY CARE	$
2. REAL ESTATE TAXES	$	6. TRANSPORTATION		Repairs	$	12. OTHER *(specify below)*	
3. UTILITIES	Fuel	$		Auto Loan	$		$
	Electricity	$		Public Trans.	$		$
	Gas	$	7. INSURANCE PREMIUMS	Medical/Dental	$		$
	Water	$		Automobile	$		$
	Telephone	$		Home-owners	$		$
	Trash Collection	$		Life	$		$
	Cable T.V.	$	8. MEDICAL/DENTAL		$		$
4. FOOD		$	9. CHILD SUPPORT *(order of court)*		$		$
5. CLOTHING		$	10. ALIMONY *(order of court)*		$	**B.** TOTAL WEEKLY EXPENSES →	$

3. LIABILITIES

CREDITOR *(Do not include mortgages or loan balances that will be listed under assets.)*	AMOUNT OF DEBT	BALANCE DUE	DATE DEBT INCURRED	WEEKLY PAYMENT
	$	$		$
	$	$		$
	$	$		$
	$	$		$
	$	$		$
	$	$		$
C. TOTAL LIABILITIES *(Total Balance Due on Debts)* —	$		**D** TOTAL WEEKLY LIABILITY EXPENSE.	$

(continued)

EXHIBIT 11–8 Continued

4. ASSETS	**A. Real Estate**	Home	ADDRESS	VALUE *(Est.)* $	MORTGAGE $	EQUITY $
		Other:	ADDRESS	VALUE *(Est.)* $	MORTGAGE $	EQUITY $
		Other:	ADDRESS	VALUE *(Est.)* $	MORTGAGE $	EQUITY $

B. Motor Vehicles	Car 1:	YEAR	MAKE	MODEL	VALUE $	LOAN BALANCE $	EQUITY $
	Car 2:	YEAR	MAKE	MODEL	VALUE $	LOAN BALANCE $	EQUITY $

C. Other Personal Property	DESCRIBE AND STATE VALUE OF EACH ITEM	TOTAL VALUE
		$

D. Bank Accounts	BANK NAME, TYPE OF ACCOUNT, AND AMOUNT	TOTAL BANK ACCOUNTS
		$

E. Stocks, Bonds Mutual Funds	NAME OF COMPANY, NUMBER OF SHARES, AND VALUE	TOTAL VALUE
		$

F. Insurance *(exclude children)*	NAME OF INSURED	COMPANY	FACE AMOUNT $	CASH VALUE $	AMT. OF LOAN $	TOTAL VALUE
			$	$	$	
			$	$	$	$

G. Deferred Compensation Plans	NAME OF PLAN *(Individual I.R.A., 401K, Keogh, etc.)* AND APPROX. VALUE	TOTAL VALUE *(less loans)*
		$

H. All Other Assets		TOTAL VALUE
		$

I. Total	E. TOTAL CASH VALUE OF ALL ASSETS —	$

5. HEALTH INSURANCE	NAME AND ADDRESS OF HEALTH OR DENTAL INSURANCE CARRIER
	INSURANCE POLICY NO. NAME(S) OF PERSON(S) COVERED BY THE POLICY

SUMMARY
(Use the amounts shown in boxes A thru E of sections 1–4.)

TOTAL WEEKLY INCOME (A)	$	TOTAL CASH VALUE OF ASSETS (E)	$
TOTAL WEEKLY EXPENSES (B + D)	$	TOTAL LIABILITIES (C)	$

CERTIFICATION
I hereby certify that the foregoing statement is true and accurate to the best of my knowledge and belief.

SIGNED *(Affiant)*	Subscribed and sworn to before me on	DATE	SIGNED *(Notary, Comm. of Superior court)*

JD-FM-6 Rev. 5-98 (Back)

END OF CHAPTER EXERCISE

Crossword Puzzle

Across

3. the reason for an objection to a discovery request made on the basis that what is being asked or sought has already been asked or sought

5. the person who is being questioned at a deposition

7. a legal document requiring a person to appear for a proceeding under penalty of law

8. a sworn statement that enumerates the party's sources of income, earned and unearned; the party's expenses, necessary and optional; and all of the party's assets and liabilities

9. a proceeding at which a party's lawyer has the opportunity to question the opposing party under oath

10. devices that an attorney may use to gather information for the case against the other party

Down

1. A document that asks the court to take some type of action; it is automatically granted by the court, thirty days after filing, absent the opposing party's objection

2. the process or stage in a civil litigation matter during which information is gathered by each party for use in their case against the other party

4. information that is privileged; that is, not everyone is allowed access to it

6. a document empowering a sheriff to arrest a nonappearing, noncustodial parent and bring him or her to jail and to court

Review Questions

1. What is the purpose of the discovery process in a family law proceeding?

2. List and describe the five discovery tools and explain how each of these tools can be used in a family law proceeding.

3. What is the difference between an objection and a privilege raised in the discovery process?

4. List the privileges and objections that may be asserted to prevent disclosure of discovery information sought in a dissolution matter.

5. What types of interrogatories might be filed in a dissolution matter where the issue of child custody is contested?

6. What types of documents might either party request in a family law proceeding relating to a divorce matter for a modification of alimony, child support, or custody?

7. How may the paralegal assist in the preparation of interrogatories and production requests?

8. How may the paralegal assist in preparing responses to interrogatories and production requests?

9. If a party does not furnish adequate financial information and records in response to interrogatories and production requests, what other means may the opposing party employ to obtain this information?

10. What is the difference between a request and a motion?

11. Give one example of when a party's attorney in a family law proceeding might decide to file a request for admission.

12. What is the paralegal's role in assisting a party in complying with a request for admission?

13. What are the advantages and disadvantages of employing depositions as a discovery tool in a family law proceeding?

14. What is the paralegal's role at the deposition of the client and at the deposition of the opposing party?

15. Describe the paralegal's role in preparing a client's financial affidavit, and list the types of documentation the paralegal should request and obtain from the client to ensure that the information provided is complete and accurate.

Cases for Briefing

PARRY V. PARRY, 2D04-2109 (Fla.App. 2 Dist. 200)

LEVIN V. LIGON, A109477 (Cal.App. 2006)

IN RE MARRIAGE OF NELSON, *139 Cal.App.4th 1546* **(2006)**

Exploring the Workplace: Activities

1. Your firm represents Mrs. Church in her pending dissolution action, and the Court has already issued pendent lite orders relating to support and custody. Your supervising attorney informs you that Mrs. Church just called to tell him that she has lost her job and will lose her medical benefits for herself and her children within 30 days unless she elects to pay a hefty monthly premium under COBRA for the next 36 months. She also indicated that she cannot pay for health insurance or otherwise maintain the household without additional assistance from Mr. Church until she finds new employment. Your supervising attorney tells you to set up a meeting with Mrs. Church to obtain all information needed to bring the matter back to Court. He also tells you to draft for his review all the documents that must be filed with the Court to prepare for the modification hearing. Describe how you would go about completing this task and identify the information you would need from Mrs. Church and identify the documents you would be preparing for filing with the Court. What would you hope to be the outcome of the upcoming modification hearing?

2. When you meet with Mrs. Church, she tells you that she suspects that Mr. Church has additional sources of income which he did not disclose on his financial affidavit and that he keeps the income from these other sources hidden in a separate bank account. When you mention this to your superior, he tells you to research your local practice book and family law statutes to see what avenues exist to expose these assets, and to present your findings to him in an inter-office memorandum. Using your own jurisdiction's rules of family practice and family law statutes, determine what legal measures may be taken to discovery these additional sources of income. Present your findings in an inter-office memorandum and make recommendations on how to proceed.

FAMILY LAW AND DISCOVERY

Go to: www.paralegalgateway.com/ divorcediscovery.html

CHAPTER

12

Separation Agreements

KEY TERMS

boilerplate	proposal
compromise	proposal letter
hold harmless provision	separation agreement
merger	uncontested

O nce discovery has been exchanged, reviewed, and analyzed, a picture of the marital estate emerges. The next step is for the parties to draft and exchange proposals. **Proposals** are formal written indications, from one party to the opposing party, that communicate what the first party is seeking in terms of a divorce settlement. Proposals are drafted after the attorney has consulted with the client. A client who is fully informed regarding the extent of the marital estate may determine, with the assistance of the attorney, what type of settlement he will seek. The **proposal letter** will detail the client's position on the various legal issues to be resolved: property division, alimony, child custody, visitation and support, maintenance of health and life insurance, distribution of debts and other liabilities, and, of course, counsel fees. Remember, the client determines what he is seeking in a divorce settlement, so any formal offer of settlement must be approved by the client before it is submitted to the opposing party. Similarly, any proposal or counterproposal received by an attorney should always be forwarded to the attorney's client for review and written approval before acceptance.

Many divorces are settled without a trial. With the help of their attorneys or mediators, many clients are able to resolve their issues through negotiation and compromise. Attorneys on opposing sides confer with each other and propose resolutions through telephone calls, meetings, and correspondence. The attorney's office communicates proposals to the client and the parties often come to a resolution. Sometimes the parties agree on some issues, but reach a stalemate on others. If this happens, the court will decide the unresolved issues after a trial.

Once the parties have reached a resolution, one of the parties undertakes the responsibility of reducing the agreement to a writing known as a **separation agreement**. In some jurisdictions, this writing is referred to as a *property settlement, settlement agreement,* or *marital settlement agreement.* A separation agreement is a contract between spouses who are in the process of obtaining a divorce or a legal separation. This agreement resolves the various legal issues that arise when a marriage dissolves.

Traditionally, the public policy of the states has been to encourage and preserve marriage. Marriage and the family unit are the very foundation on which our society has been built. At one time courts were very reluctant to accept separation agreements in divorce cases since these agreements promoted the breakdown of the family. Even today, courts will validate separation agreements only when entered into after one of both parties have instituted legal proceedings for divorce or for a legal separation. If the marriage has deteriorated with no hope of reconciliation, the courts will be more likely to accept the separation agreement. If the parties to a failed marriage have amicably agreed to the terms of their dissolution, it is in the best interest of all parties involved for the court to accept the separation agreement rather than forcing an agonizing divorce trial. The parties must indicate in their agreement that their marriage has broken down, there is no hope of reconciliation, and the parties intend to live separate and apart.

An agreement avoids the need for a contested divorce trial. The case will proceed as an **uncontested** matter. When a matter is uncontested, this means that neither party objects to the court granting a divorce and entering an order of marital dissolution. However, even when a divorce action is uncontested, most jurisdictions require a formal court proceeding at which at least the petitioning spouse must appear. This proceeding is relatively short. The parties will arrive at court on the date of the uncontested hearing with the signed separation agreement. The document will be submitted to the court. The judge will review the agreement and determine if it is fair and equitable and if it has been entered into voluntarily.

MERGER OF SEPARATION AGREEMENT INTO THE COURT'S DECREE

As mentioned earlier, the separation agreement is a contract between the spouses. The language in the agreement will indicate if the parties want the agreement to *survive* as a contract or if the parties want it merged into the court's decree. If the agreement survives as a contract, the agreement cannot be modified unless both parties mutually consent. In the event that one of the parties fails to comply with the provisions of the agreement, the aggrieved party will be left with the traditional contractual remedies such as breach of contract and specific performance. If the agreement is instead merged into the court's decree, the **merger** is no longer a contract between the two parties, but rather a court order, which can be modified or enforced through contempt of court proceedings.

ADVANTAGES OF REACHING AN AGREEMENT

A successfully negotiated separation agreement reflects the best efforts of both parties and their respective attorneys. Legal professionals should encourage agreements for many reasons. Agreements are quicker, more economical, and the parties are not subjected to an adversarial system that may destroy the little civility remaining between them. The ability to have some input regarding the resolution of the divorce affords the parties more control than they would have if the judge were to decide the case. Reaching an agreement, however, involves compromise on the part of both parties. **Compromise** involves meeting someone halfway or giving up a position in exchange for something else. By its very definition, compromising parties are generally not 100 percent satisfied with a separation agreement. The degree of noncompliance with separation agreements is very high. Even the most carefully scripted and negotiated agreement may result in noncompliance even before the ink has dried.

PARALEGAL'S ROLE IN DRAFTING THE SEPARATION AGREEMENT

Paralegals may be assigned the task of drafting a separation agreement under the attorney's supervision. To begin drafting the separation agreement, the paralegal must have a copy of the finalized proposal and a good understanding of the agreement between the parties. This is an essential element before commencing the initial draft.

The paralegal must next obtain a model separation agreement or several models to use in constructing one for the client. Standardized or **boilerplate** separation agreement forms or clauses may be available in the particular jurisdiction's practice book. Forms and clauses may also be found in loose-leaf legal publications specializing in family law. Model separation agreements may also be available in the local law library or in the law office library. In addition, the law office may maintain its own file of standard separation agreements, either on computer or as hardcopies. Paralegals may also review closed divorce files that contain previously drafted separation agreements.

The paralegal may need to draw from several resources to obtain the necessary language to draft the agreement. Whenever using standardized forms or previously drafted separation agreements as models, the paralegal must proceed with a great deal of caution. The agreement should contain the particular provisions applicable to the underlying case—it should not be merely an exercise in filling in the blanks. The paralegal should also check local practice rules and statutory and case law, which may require the inclusion of some mandatory provisions or language in order to make the agreement legally effective.

The paralegal may also have responsibilities related to reviewing an agreement drafted by the opposing party. In this case, the paralegal, under the attorney's supervision, reviews the separation agreement to make certain it reflects the agreement of the parties. If the document appears to depart from what was agreed to, the paralegal will bring this departure to the attorney's attention, and may also wish to offer suggested revisions to cure the discrepancies.

Whether on the drafting side or reviewing side, several drafts may be necessary to script an agreement that accurately reflects the intent of the parties. Separation agreements should be drafted with great care, because the parties to it will have to live with this agreement long after they have left the courthouse. Agreements drafted too hastily, without adequate review and reflection, by both attorneys and clients, set the stage for unnecessary future battles. Each party will hold the other to every letter, syllable, and punctuation mark in their agreement. Therefore, it is necessary to draft them carefully, make them clear and readable, and spell out any definitions or terms that could later cause confusion.

FINALIZING THE SEPARATION AGREEMENT

Once the attorney has approved a final draft, an office appointment with the client should be scheduled. At this meeting the attorney carefully reviews the agreement with the client and thoroughly answers any and all questions the client poses. If the client approves the agreement and the opposing side does likewise, the case will proceed as an uncontested divorce matter. If the parties are still in dispute over various sections, renegotiation and revisions may be appropriate.

We cannot stress the importance of careful drafting. Sometimes when dissolution actions have been particularly draining, the attorneys and paralegals may hurriedly draft an agreement with very little thought or reflection. The trap is that this agreement may continue to haunt both client and attorney as various sections become disputed in postjudgment battles.

BASIC CLAUSES AND STRUCTURE OF THE SEPARATION AGREEMENT

The paralegal should delineate the various subjects covered by the separation agreement by dividing them into "articles" or "sections" and using roman numerals or cardinal numbers in numerical sequence. It is important to organize the agreement in this manner for quick reference and logical sequence.

HEADING

Every agreement should have a heading. As mentioned earlier, various headings can be used depending on your supervisor's wishes or the accepted local preference: *SEPARATION AGREEMENT, PROPERTY SETTLEMENT, PROPERTY SETTLEMENT AGREEMENT, MARITAL SETTLEMENT, MARITAL SETTLEMENT AGREEMENT,* or *AGREEMENT.*

IDENTIFICATION

The identification clause identifies the parties, their respective residences, and the respective label that will be used to refer to each spouse throughout the agreement, avoiding the need to spell out full names each time one is used. It also indicates the date on which the agreement was executed.

EXAMPLE

SEPARATION AGREEMENT[1]

THIS AGREEMENT, made and entered into this 6th day October, 2006, by and between RENEE ANDREWS of Guilford, Connecticut (hereinafter referred to as "Wife") and JOHN ANDREWS of New Haven, Connecticut (hereinafter referred to as "Husband"): I

RECITALS

The recitals section indicates the date and place of the marriage, names and ages of the minor children, grounds for the dissolution, a declaration that the parties are living separate and apart, the pendency of an action for dissolution, and the intent to settle the spouses' rights and obligations pursuant to this action. Each sentence is often preceded by the word "WHEREAS."

EXAMPLE

WITNESSETH:

WHEREAS, the parties married each other on August 17, 1990 at New Haven, Connecticut; and
Whereas, said parties have three minor children born issue of this marriage:

David Andrews, born June 22, 1992

Bruce Andrews, born November 9, 1993

Denise Andrews, born April 23, 1996

No other minor children have been born to the Wife since the date of the marriage;
WHEREAS, irreconcilable differences have arisen between the parties as a result of which the marriage of the parties has broken down irretrievably and they are now and have been living separate and apart; and
WHEREAS, the Wife has instituted an action against the Husband a dissolution of marriage, and further relief, which case is currently pending in the Superior Court for the Judicial District of New Haven at New Haven.
WHEREAS, the parties wish to enter into an agreement under which they will continue living separate and apart and under which fair and reasonable provisions will be made for the support of each other and the minor children and for the settlement, adjustment and compromise of all property rights and obligations resulting from the marriage.
NOW THEREFORE, in consideration of the premises and the mutual promises and undertaking therein set forth and for other good and valuable consideration paid over by each party to the other, the receipt and sufficiency of which is hereby acknowledged, it is covenanted and agreed as follows:

---

[1] The text of the separation agreement illustrated in this chapter has been constructed from provisions and portions of provisions of separation agreements that the authors of this book have accumulated during their years of practice and as such reflects the work of anonymous authors.

IRRETRIEVABLE BREAKDOWN

This clause indicates that the marriage has broken down and there is no hope of the parties reconciling.

EXAMPLE

ARTICLE I

Irretrievable Breakdown

The marriage of the parties has broken down irretrievably, and there is no prospect of reconciliation.

SEPARATION OF THE PARTIES

This clause indicates that the parties intend to live separate and apart and will not interfere with each other. In addition, each one is free to dispose of his or her property upon death as he or she sees fit.

EXAMPLE

ARTICLE II

Separation of the Parties

2.1 *The parties may and shall at all times hereafter live separate and apart for the rest of their mutual lives. Each shall be free from interference, authority or control, direct or indirect, by the other as fully as if he or she were single and unmarried. Each may reside at such place or places as he or she may select. The parties shall not molest each other or compel or endeavor to compel the other to cohabit or dwell with him or her, by any legal or other proceedings for the restoration of conjugal rights or otherwise.*

2.2 *The Husband and Wife shall have the right to dispose of his or her property by will or otherwise in such manner as they may, in his or her uncontrolled discretion deem proper; and neither one will claim any interest in the estate of the other.*

ALIMONY

The alimony clause addresses the payment of alimony, maintenance, or spousal support. The agreement should clearly spell out the type of alimony, frequency and mode of payment, modifiability, and termination. If the parties are waiving alimony, it should be spelled out in the agreement.

ARTICLE III

Spousal Support

3.1 The Husband shall pay to the Wife as periodic alimony the sum of $600.00 per week commencing October 13, 2006 for a NONMODIFIABLE period of 416 weeks/8 years up to, but not including, the week ending October 13, 2014, unless terminated earlier as provided herein.

3.2 Alimony shall terminate prior to October 13, 2014 upon the occurrence of the first of the following events: a) death of either party; b) remarriage of the Wife; or c) cohabitation of the Wife with an unrelated male over the age of 18 years. Cohabitation shall have the meaning from time to time, as per applicable Connecticut Statutes.

3.3 Alimony may be modified as to amount upon mutual agreement of the parties or upon a showing by either party of a substantial change in the circumstances of either party which warrants such modification.

3.4 For federal and state income tax purposes, the spousal support payments shall be reportable as income by the Wife and deductible by the Husband.

REAL PROPERTY

The real property section deals with the parties' disposition of any real property owned. The most common asset to be dealt with is the marital home. The parties may agree to put the house up for sale and divide the proceeds after expenses have been paid. Another option is for one party to buy out the other party, or offset it with a pension. If the parties have minor children, the custodial parent may be allowed to live in the home until the emancipation of the children. Once the last child has reached age eighteen, the home can be sold.

ARTICLE IV

Real Property

4.1 The parties agree that the Wife shall have exclusive possession of the marital residence located at 14 Lantern Place, in Guilford, Connecticut, until such time as the youngest child graduates from high school or attains the age of 19 years, whichever occurs first. Within 30 days of the first of these occurrences, the Wife shall arrange for the parties to list the marital residence for sale with a mutually agreed-upon listing agent. The parties shall agree on the listing price. In the event that the parties cannot agree on the listing price, the property shall be listed at a price to be determined by the listing agent in accordance with the market values existing at that time. The parties agree to accept the first offer on the house that is at least 85% of the asking price.

4.2 When the house is sold, the parties agree that the Husband shall receive 1/3 of the net proceeds and the Wife shall receive 2/3 of the net proceeds. The parties shall contribute equally to the closing costs associated with the sale of the house.

4.3 While the Wife has exclusive possession of the marital residence, she shall be solely responsible for payment of the existing mortgage, property taxes, and homeowner's insurance as well as ordinary and necessary maintenance and repairs to the premises. The Wife shall have 100% of the tax deduction for mortgage interest and property taxes. If the Wife fails to fulfill the above-listed obligations, the Husband may seek relief from this court, including, but not limited to, an order for immediate sale of the property.

4.4 The Husband shall be responsible for 1/3 of any extraordinary and necessary maintenance, repair, or replacement costs associated with the marital residence, included but not limited to painting of the exterior of the residence, replacement of the heating system, and any major electrical or plumbing repairs.

Personal Property

In the personal property clause, the parties address the division of their personal property. This includes motor vehicles; bank, pension, and retirement accounts; household furnishings; and miscellaneous matters.

Example

Article V

Personal Property

5.1 Motor Vehicles
The Wife shall have sole title, possession, and ownership of the 2005 Nissan Pathfinder.
The Husband shall have sole title, possession, and ownership of the 2002 BMW Convertible.
From and after the date of this Agreement, each party shall be responsible for any and all costs associated with said respective vehicles, and shall indemnify and hold the other harmless for all said costs.
This shall include any and all property taxes now due and owing for these vehicles.

5.2 Bank Accounts, Investments, Pension, and Retirement Accounts
The Wife shall retain sole right, title, and interest in and to the following:
a) Northern Imperial Bank checking account number 005340 50591, approximate value $3,755.00
b) Hubbard Growth Fund, approximate value $7,590.00
c) Long River Bank IRA, approximate value $11,000

The Husband shall retain sole right, title, and interest in and to the following:
a) Northern Imperial Bank checking account number 00510066201, approximate value $2,350.00
b) Manhattan Merchant's Bank IRA, approximate value $16,150.00
c) Dominion Forklift, 330 shares (inherited from grandfather), approximate value $45,000.00

The Husband and Wife will equally divide the following jointly held investments:
a) Northern Imperial Money Market, approximate value $28,000.00
b) Aquitaine Fund, approximate value $6,650.00

The Husband and Wife shall divide the Husband's 401k plan as follows:
c) The Husband shall retain 100% of the amount existing in the plan at the time of the parties' marriage, approximate value $18,000
d) The parties shall equally divide the remaining amount in the plan, approximate value $46,000.00

5.3 Furnishings, Appliances, Tools, and Miscellaneous Items at the Marital Residence
The Wife shall retain all of the furnishings, appliances, tools, and miscellaneous items located at the martial residence with the exception of the following items of personal property which the Husband shall remove as soon as possible but in any event before November 6, 2006:
a) grape press
b) power drill
c) electric shrub clippers

(continued)

> c) *grandmother's sterling silver tea set*
> d) *espresso machine*
> e) *camcorder*
> f) *snow mobile*
> g) *grandfather's mahogany clothes tree*
> h) *burgundy leather recliner in the family room*
> i) *plasma t.v. in master bedroom*
> j) *all personal clothing, jewelry, and sports equipment*
>
> 5.4 *Proceeds from Personal Injury Claim*
> *The Husband waives any right, title interest in and to all proceeds, settlements, and judgments obtained by the Wife as a result of her personal injury suit arising from her 2005 automobile accident.*

Custody and Access

The issues considered in the custody and access section involve the type of custody (sole, joint, split) arrangement agreed to by the parties. Access is also addressed either by a "reasonable access" clause or by a more detailed schedule. In some situations, access to the child may be supervised. The success of a "reasonable access" arrangement will depend on how well the parties can arrange visits between themselves. A more detailed schedule may specify particular days, times, transportation, place of pickup and drop-off, holidays, summer vacations, and birthdays. A clause requiring the custodial parent to contact the noncustodial parent may also be included to cover certain situations such as medical emergencies.

The issue of relocation by the custodial parent should also be addressed in this section.

EXAMPLE

> ### Article VI
>
> #### Child Custody and Access
>
> 6.1 *The parties shall have joint legal custody; primary residence shall be with the Wife.*
>
> 6.2 *The Husband shall have reasonable periods of parental access as mutually agreed upon by the parties.*
>
> 6.3 *Periods of parental access during holidays and school vacations shall be mutually agreed upon by the parties.*
>
> 6.4 *In the event of a dispute, the parties hereby agree to submit the matter to the Family Relations division of the court for mediation.*

Child Support

The child support section should specify the amount of child support due and the date on which it is payable. It is very important to include the date on which the payments are to commence so as to avoid confusion.

Other matters that may be addressed in this section are whether support payments will extend beyond a child's majority. Some parties will agree to pay for a child's college education, which should be clearly expressed in the agreement and include any restrictions or conditions the parents may have regarding the choice of location or cost of the school.

This section should also address which parent will declare the children as dependants for federal and state income tax purposes.

EXAMPLE

ARTICLE VII

Child Support, Qualified Child-Care Expenses, and Costs of Extracurricular Activities

7.1 *Commencing on Friday, October 6, 2006, the Husband shall pay to the Wife the sum of $610.00 per week as child support in accordance with the Child Support Guidelines. The Court may adjust this amount upward or downward in accordance with the guidelines until all of the children have reached their majority subject to any postmajority obligations either party may have under subsection 7.4 of this article.*

7.2 *The parties shall share the qualified child-care costs in accordance with the percentages established in the Child Support Guidelines. This provision shall include the cost of any summer camp fees that are incurred as summer child-care.*

7.3 *The parties agree to be equally responsible for the costs of the agreed-upon extracurricular activities of the children.*

7.4 *The parties hereby agree that the Superior Court shall retain jurisdiction over issues of Post-Majority Educational Support pursuant to Conn. Gen. Stat. §46b-56c.*

7.5 *The Husband shall claim David Andrews and Bruce Andrews as dependants on his state and federal income tax returns.*

7.6 *The Wife shall claim Denise Andrews as a dependant on her state and federal income tax returns.*

LIFE INSURANCE

Frequently parties agree that during the minority of the children, the parent who does not have physical custody of the children will carry life insurance for their benefit so that if he or she dies before the children reach their majority, the benefit will help the surviving parent to offset the loss of child support payments.

EXAMPLE

ARTICLE VIII

Life Insurance

8.1 *The Husband agrees to maintain the existing life insurance policy on his life in the amount of $500,000 until the youngest child graduates from high school or attains the age of 19 years, whichever occurs sooner.*

8.2 *The Husband agrees that the Wife shall remain as the beneficiary of this life insurance policy until the youngest child graduates from high school or attains the age of 19 years, whichever occurs sooner.*

8.3 *On or about November 1 of each year, the Husband shall provide the Wife with verification that said life insurance policy is still in force in the amount of $500,000, and that the Wife is still the beneficiary of said life insurance policy.*

HEALTH INSURANCE

Many parties have health insurance coverage that is provided as a fringe benefit by their employer. Self-employed parties may carry their own health insurance, and those who cannot afford coverage simply go without or apply for government benefits. The health insurance section should spell out the health insurance coverage for both spouses and the minor children. It should also cover payment of unreimbursed expenses and how the parties plan to pay such costs.

EXAMPLE

ARTICLE IX

Health Insurance

9.1 *The Husband has available and agrees to maintain health insurance coverage for himself and the minor children through his employer. Should the Husband leave his employment, the husband agrees to continue to provide health insurance coverage for the minor children unless the Wife is employed and has health insurance coverage available to her for the minor children at a lower cost.*

9.2 *The parties agree that health insurance coverage through the Husband's employer is available to the Wife under COBRA and that the Husband shall pay the premium for the Wife's health insurance coverage for the statutory time period available, unless the Wife obtains employment before the statutory period ends and comparable coverage is available to her through her employment at no cost or at a cost to her that much lower that the cost of COBRA.*

9.3 *The parties agree that after the statutory period for health insurance coverage for the Wife under COBRA expires, the Wife shall be responsible for obtaining and paying for her own health insurance coverage.*

9.4 *The parties shall equally share any unreimbursed medical expenses of the minor children, except that should any or all of the minor children require orthodontic care, the parties shall contribute to the cost of such care in accordance with the percentages established for their respective child support obligations under the Child Support Guidelines*

LIABILITIES

The debts and liabilities of the parties and who will be responsible for their payment must be covered in the separation agreement. The liabilities section should also include a **hold harmless provision** whereby the spouses indemnify each other from any debt incurred by the other.

EXAMPLE

ARTICLE X

Liabilities

10.1 *The parties agree that they will each be responsible for the liabilities on their respective financial affidavits submitted in connection with this pending matter.*

10.2 *The Husband shall indemnify, defend, and hold Wife harmless from any and all other indebtedness, loans, obligations, claims, and causes of action that have, may now, or hereafter be made against Wife on her property as a result of any acts or omissions of Husband, judgments that may be obtained against Husband, debts, guarantees, or obligations incurred by Husband.*

10.3 *The Wife shall indemnify, defend, and hold Husband harmless from any and all other indebtedness, loans, obligations, claims, and causes of action that have, may now, or hereafter be made against Husband on his property as a result of any acts or omissions of Wife, judgments that may be obtained against Wife, debts, guarantees, or obligations incurred by Wife.*

TAXES

The filing of federal and state tax returns is an important issue to be addressed in the agreement. In addition, the question of how the parties will share a refund or pay for an assessment should be determined to avoid surprises later.

EXAMPLE

> ## ARTICLE XI
>
> ### Taxes
>
> 11.1 *With respect to the calendar year of 2005, the parties filed joint tax returns, both federal and state. Pursuant to these returns, the parties owed $0 in federal income tax and owed $750 in state income tax. The payment of $750 was tendered to the Connecticut Commissioner of Revenue Services, by the Husband and Wife.*
>
> 11.2 *The parties agree to equally pay any additional taxes which may hereafter be assessed in connection with either 2004 return and equally divide any refunds or rebates in connection with such returns.*
>
> 11.3 *For the calendar year of 2006, and thereafter, the parties shall file separate tax returns, both federal and state. Each party shall pay and be responsible for all taxes assessed against their respective separate incomes.*

DISCLOSURE

In the disclosure clause, the parties acknowledge that they have had the opportunity to fully discover any data regarding their spouse's income, assets, liabilities, and expenses and that they have accurately disclosed the same.

EXAMPLE

> ## ARTICLE XII
>
> ### Disclosure
>
> 12.1 *The parties acknowledge that they have had the opportunity for full discovery of any and all pertinent data with regard to income, assets, liabilities, and expenses of the other and that each waives his or her right to further discovery based upon the other's representation that they have fully and accurately disclosed to each other all their respective assets, income, and liabilities as set forth in their financial affidavits.*

REPRESENTATION OF THE PARTIES

In the representation section, the parties acknowledge that they have been represented by independent counsel and indicate the name of each attorney. This section may also deal with the issue of attorney's fees and who will be responsible for their payment.

ARTICLE XIII

Representation of the Parties

13.1 *Each party to this AGREEMENT represents and acknowledges that he or she has been represented in negotiations for and in preparation of this AGREEMENT by counsel of his or her own choosing.*

13.2 *Each party has been fully advised by his or her respective attorney, Justine F. Miller, Esq. of New Haven, Connecticut, for the Husband, and Grace A. Luppino, Esq. of New Haven, Connecticut, for the Wife, as to their respective rights and liabilities, each against the other, and to and upon the property and estate of the other in regard to the dissolution of their marriage.*

13.3 *Each party has read this AGREEMENT and has had it fully explained to him or her.*

13.4 *The Husband has agreed to pay his own attorney's fees in the present dissolution action, and he agrees to pay the outstanding balance of $4,120,000 which the Wife owes for her attorney's fees in the present dissolution action.*

MISCELLANEOUS CLAUSES

The miscellaneous section addresses matters of a general nature that might be anticipated to arise, such as questions of governing jurisdictional law, the parties' cooperation in executing documents necessary to facilitate the operation of the separation agreement, a waiver of rights in the other party's estate in the event of death, and provisions to address unexpected occurrences or events.

ARTICLE XIV

Miscellaneous

14.1 *Except as provided herein, the Husband and Wife each hereby waives any right at law or in equity to elect to take against any last will made by the other, including all rights of dower or of curtesy, and hereby waives, renounces, and relinquishes unto the other, their respective heirs, executors, administrators, and assigns forever, all and every interest of any kind or character which either may now have or may hereafter acquire in any real or personal property of the other, whether now owned or hereinafter acquired by either.*

14.2 *Except for any cause of action for divorce, legal separation, or dissolution of marriage or any action or proceeding to enforce the provisions of their Agreement, each party hereby releases and forever discharges the other, and by this Agreement does for himself or herself and his or her heirs, legal representatives, executors, administrators and assigns, release and discharge, and releases the other, with respect to matters arising out of the marital relationship from any and all causes of action, claims, rights, or demands whatsoever in law or in equity, which either of the parties ever had or now has against the other.*

14.3 *The Husband and Wife agree that they will, from time to time, at the request of the other, execute, acknowledge, and deliver any and all further instruments that may be reasonably required to give full force and effect to the provisions of this Agreement.*

14.4 *A waiver of any provision of this Agreement shall be effective only if made in writing and executed with the same formality as this Agreement. The failure of either party to insist upon strict enforcement of any provisions of this Agreement shall not be construed as a waiver of such terms, and such terms shall nevertheless continue in full force and effect.*

14.5 *If any provision of this Agreement is held to be invalid and unenforceable, all other provisions shall nevertheless continue in full force and effect.*

14.6 *This Agreement shall be construed and governed in accordance with the laws of the State of Connecticut.*

14.7 *The parties hereto agree and intend that the Agreement shall be incorporated in full by reference or otherwise in the dissolution proceedings. This Agreement shall merge with any decree of any Court affecting the parties.*

14.8 *This Agreement shall not be modified or altered except by an instrument signed and acknowledged by the Husband and Wife.*

14.9 *This Agreement is simultaneously executed in five (5) counterparts and each of said counterparts shall be original and each of said counterparts shall constitute but one and the same instrument.*

SIGNATURE PROVISIONS

In the signatory section of the separation agreement, each party signs their legal signature, which should conform to the name used in the legal action before the court. Each party's signature is witnessed by two people.

EXAMPLE

IN WITNESS WHEREOF, the parties hereto have hereunto set their respective hands and seals on the day and year first above written.

_____	_____
Witness	*RENEE ANDREWS*
_____	
Witness	
_____	_____
Witness	*JOHN ANDREWS*
_____	
Witness	

ACKNOWLEDGMENT

The acknowledgment section follows the signing and witnessing of the separation agreement. In this section, a notary public or an officer of the court, if allowed to do so in the jurisdiction, will take the acknowledgment of each party. This means that the notary public or court officer will acknowledge that the party signed the document in the presence of witnesses and acknowledge that he or she signed the document and did so freely and without coercion.

STATE OF CONNECTICUT   )
)   *ss.*_____

COUNTY OF NEW HAVEN   )

   On this the 6th day of October, 2006, personally appeared JOHN ANDREWS known to me to be the person whose name is subscribed to the within instrument and acknowledged that he executed the same, for the purposes therein contained, as his own free act and deed, before me.

   IN WITNESS WHEREOF, I hereunto set my hand and official seal.

                                       _____

                                      JUSTINE F. MILLER
                                      Commissioner of the Superior Court

STATE OF CONNECTICUT   )
)   *ss.* _____

COUNTY OF NEW HAVEN   )

   On this the 6th day of October, 2006, personally appeared RENEE ANDREWS known to me to be the person whose name is subscribed to the within instrument and acknowledged that she executed the same, for the purposes therein contained, as her own free act and deed before me.

   IN WITNESS WHEREOF, I hereunto set my hand and official seal.

                                       _____

                                        GRACE A. LUPPINO
                                        Commissioner of the Superior Court

Appendix F includes the entire marital settlement agreement signed by entertainer Madonna and her former husband, Sean Penn.

END OF CHAPTER EXERCISES

Crossword Puzzle

Across

3. part of a separation agreement that indicates that a particular spouse will be responsible for debt incurred during the marriage, that he or she will be solely responsible for its payment, and that the other spouse shall be free and clear of any obligation regarding that debt

5. a contract between spouses who are in the process of obtaining a divorce or a legal separation resolving the various legal issues that arise when a marriage is dissolving; also known as a marital settlement agreement, property settlement, or settlement agreement

6. meeting someone halfway or giving up a position in exchange for something else

7. a formal written indication, from one party to the opposing party, that communicates what the first party is seeking in terms of a divorce settlement

8. an agreement that is no longer a contract between two parties, but a court order that can be modified or enforced through contempt of court proceedings

Down

1. details the client's position on the various legal issues to be resolved, such as property division, alimony, child custody, child visitation and support, maintenance of health and life insurance, distribution of debts and other liabilities, and counsel fees

2. standardized agreement forms or clauses

4. where neither party objects to the court granting a divorce and entering an order of marital dissolution

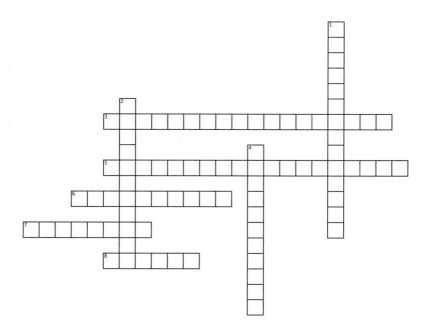

Review Questions

1. What is a proposal?

2. Explain the purpose of a proposal letter.

3. What is a separation agreement?

4. How do family courts view separation agreements?

5. Explain the concept of merging a separation agreement into a dissolution decree.

6. What is meant by the term *compromise*?

7. Describe the resources a paralegal might utilize when drafting a separation agreement.

8. What are boilerplate agreements, and why should the paralegal proceed with caution when using them?

9. How should a paralegal structure a separation agreement?

10. List the basic clauses of a separation agreement.

Cases for Briefing

FARRELL v. FARRELL, 661 So.2d 1257 (Fla. App. 3 Dist. 1995)

IN RE BLACK v. NY STATE AND LOCAL EMPL 30 A. D. 3d 920 [3d Dept 2006]

IN THE MATTER OF ASCH v. ASCH, 30 A. D. 3rd 513 [2d Dept 2006] (NY)

Exploring the Workplace: Activities

SEPARATION AGREEMENT

You are a paralegal working in a family law practice. Your supervising attorney has asked you to prepare a separation agreement that deals with the issue of access for her client Jane Doe. Jane has physical custody of her two minor children, Bobby Doe age six and Melissa Doe age eight. The father, Richard Doe, will share joint legal custody of the children with weekly visits every Friday from 6 PM to Sunday 6 PM and Wednesday from 5:30 PM to 8:30 PM. The father will be entitled to two weeks of nonconsecutive access each year until the youngest child (Bobby) reaches the age of ten. Thereafter, the father will be entitled to two weeks of consecutive access until both children reach the age of majority. Jane has two issues of concern with this agreement:

a. The father wants to take the children. California to visit with their grandparents. Jane wants to have certain conditions placed upon the visit (plane fare, phone calls , etc.).

b. Jane also wants to place reasonable limits on a vacation to Disney World in Florida.

Prepare the section of the separation agreement that deals with "Custody and Access," including all pertinent aspects and specifically addressing the previously mentioned areas of concern.

Websites

http://www.americanvalues.org
http://www.imapp.org
http://www.marriageinstitute

Alternative Dispute Resolution and the Divorce Trial

KEY TERMS

alternative dispute resolution
ADR
appeal
arbitration award
bench trial
Bureau of Vital Statistics form
claim for relief
collaborative divorce
contested hearing
custody affidavit
default trial
dissolve
divorce arbitration
divorce trial
document
final argument
financial disclosure affidavit
habeas corpus

judgment
judicial pretrial conference
mediation
memorandum of understanding
merger
military affidavit
pretrial conference
settlement conference
shuttle mediation
stipulation
testimony
theory of the case
transcript
trial notebook
unconscionable
uncontested hearing
uniform arbitration act
wage execution

The prevailing trend in resolving divorce cases is to encourage the parties to work out their differences privately and amicably. The adversarial process, complete with battling lawyers and harmful words hurled from a witness box, is not the preferred environment for the parties to settle their differences. The reality is that most divorces do not allow the parties the luxury of going their separate ways. Former spouses who may despise each other must still function as parents. A divorce trial that leaves "scorched earth" behind may create wounds that will last long after the lawyers and judges have walked away from the case.

Most jurisdictions now require the parties in a divorce action to participate in some type of **alternative dispute resolution,** or **ADR.** ADR is a method of resolving disputes between parties without resorting to a trial. While every marriage must be dissolved by a judge, the actual divorce trial will be either contested or uncontested. When the parties work out an agreement through alternative dispute resolution, the divorce trial is an uncontested proceeding and it takes a judge a matter of minutes to review the agreement and go through the legal motions of dissolving the marriage.

There are many benefits to alternative dispute resolution. The first is that an amicable divorce is less expensive. The cost of any form of ADR pales in comparison to the legal fees charged for a contested divorce case. Matters resolved through ADR take less time than countless court hearings. Staying out of court also helps reduce the emotional costs. This saves the parties from having to take the witness stand, facing harsh cross-examination and possibly saying something they will later regret or that will have long lasting effects. A professional trained in ADR can sometimes help the parties get to the root of their dispute and encourage a "win-win" compromise. The ADR process also is better for the children. They are not stuck between two parents who are in the midst of litigation and may be spared an additional layer of stress in an already difficult situation. Trained professionals help the parties focus on their goals as parents and encourage them to make decisions that are in the best interest of the children. Another benefit to ADR is privacy, as these meetings are conducted in private. Courtrooms are open to the public and divorce trial proceedings, as well as appeals, are published and easily accessible on the Internet. Some forms of ADR also give the parties some control over the outcome of their case, whereas the results of an adjudicated proceeding are in the hands of a judge.

TYPES OF ALTERNATIVE DISPUTE RESOLUTION IN FAMILY CASES

There are several types of alternative dispute resolution options available for divorce cases. Not all of these options work for every case, so the legal professionals have to determine which one is more suitable, given the client's needs and willingness to participate.

SETTLEMENT CONFERENCE

The first type of ADR is called a **settlement conference.** A settlement conference is a meeting with both lawyers and their respective clients with the specific goal to settle the case without court intervention. During a settlement conference, the parties, with the assistance of their attorneys, attempt to reach an agreement by discussing the issues in their case and finding some type of resolution. This method is useful when the parties are able to at least be in the same room together, share equal bargaining power, and do not require the assistance of a mental health professional. The end goal is an amicable agreement in their case that will be presented to a judge on the day of the final hearing.

Divorce Mediation

Mediation is a confidential, structured process in which a neutral third party assists the parties in resolving their differences and reaching an agreement. Mediation is appropriate where the parties need help in resolving alimony, child custody, visitation, and complicated issues of property and debt distribution. Mediation is also appropriate for resolving postjudgment matters, such as changes in parenting plans and child support. Mediation is not marriage counseling or psychotherapy, but rather a short-term conflict resolution alternative to court litigation.

Mediation is either voluntary or mandatory. Parties who choose voluntary mediation seek out such services on their own for the purpose of avoiding litigation, and its inherent financial and emotional costs. Voluntary mediation requires the parties to seek private mediation services from a qualified professional. The respective parties pay for private mediation services. Courts in many states require mandatory mediation before the court will even hear a contested divorce case. (See Exhibit 13–1 for an example of Connecticut's Court-Annexed Mediation Referral and Order form.) A court-ordered private mediator or court personnel trained in such matters might conduct the mediation. Costs vary from state to state. Whether voluntary or mandatory, the divorce mediation process takes several sessions to complete. More sessions may be necessary depending on the complexity of the case.

A divorce mediator, the neutral third party in the mediation process, may be a mental health professional or lawyer trained in helping parties identify issues of mutual concern, discuss possible solutions, and work out an agreement that is mutually acceptable. There are attorneys and mental health counselors who work together as co-mediators, combining their respective areas of expertise. A mediator guides the parties toward arriving at their own solutions. The parties, not the mediator, determine the outcome. The purpose behind this practice is that parties who participate in decision making are happier with the outcome and more likely to honor such agreements. Paralegals may also become divorce mediators by participating in training courses focusing on mediation techniques and the relevant law. There are currently no states that certify or license divorce mediators. In addition to participating in training courses, persons interested in offering divorce mediation services should join a reputable professional organization. The Academy of Family Mediators, the Association of Family and Conciliation Courts, and the Society of Professionals in Dispute Resolution are national organizations. Individual states may also have comparable organizations that set professional standards, require a minimum level of training for membership, follow a code of ethics, and continue members' education through group-sponsored programs.

Lawyers who offer mediation services cannot act as counsel for one or both parties. Such representation would be considered a conflict of interest. The lawyer-mediator must make it clear to the parties that he or she will not represent either party, but rather serve as a neutral facilitator in helping them resolve their issues. The distinction of the attorney's role as mediator and not advocate should be memorialized in writing in a contract between parties and the mediator.

Once the lawyer-mediator has facilitated the process, he or she will prepare a **memorandum of understanding,** a plain-language, nonbinding document containing the agreement of the parties on the various issues relevant to their case. The parties must then take this document to their respective attorneys, who will prepare a formal separation agreement to be filed with the court and incorporated into the divorce decree. The separation agreement is binding on the parties once the court incorporates it into its decree. It is important for the parties to have their own attorney who will explain the legal implications of the mediated agreement, advocate for any modifications, and process the case through the court system. It is not uncommon for one of the parties to file a *pro se* appearance where money is an issue. Sometimes, both parties will use a mediator, draft their own separation agreement, and appear before the judge *pro se.*

As long as they are willing to submit to the process and their primary concern is the welfare of the children, many divorcing couples benefit from the voluntary mediation process. Some cases, however, are inappropriate for mediation services. Mediation will not work where:

- There is a history of physical, emotional, financial or sexual abuse. In these cases, the abused spouse may be intimidated or fear the consequences of speaking his or her mind.

- There is a history of alcohol or substance abuse that would impair the afflicted party from participating in the process.

- One or both parties want things their way and are unwilling to compromise or work toward mutually agreeable solutions.

- Parties are hiding assets and are not truthful in their disclosures.

- One or both parties are extremely angry and want revenge. There is no way to mediate with such persons unless they can put their anger aside and work toward more noble goals.

Where the state's family courts mandate mediation services, an attorney representing a client with a history of domestic violence may request for some type of **shuttle mediation.** In this process, the parties will meet separately with the mediator, who then shuttles between the parties in attempt to broker an agreement. If the client is not comfortable with this process, the attorney may make a motion to the court, arguing that the case is not appropriate for any type of alternative dispute resolution option and should proceed directly to trial.

COLLABORATIVE LAW DIVORCE

Collaborative divorce is a fairly new concept in comparison to other forms of ADR in family matters. In cases where the parties need the strong advocacy of an attorney but wish to protect themselves and their children from the emotional trauma inherent in divorce litigation, and avoid lengthy proceedings and their high costs, the collaborative process is an option. It is a team approach to divorce dispute resolution where both parties employ the services of a collaborative divorce attorney, financial planner, and mental health professional. Other professionals may be hired, such as vocational experts, when the case warrants creative input from other disciplines. While the prospect of paying fees to each of these professionals may worry some, the reality is that a long, protracted divorce will drain much more of the marital assets.

In a collaborative law divorce, the couple and their respective attorneys agree in advance of the collaborative process to collaborate on resolving the matter and that they will not litigate. The agreement signed by the couple and their attorneys will include a provision stating that in the event the couple fails to resolve their dispute, the attorneys will not represent them in a contested hearing and they must now find new counsel. This clause strongly encourages the parties to work on resolving their case. The agreement will also include a provision stating that all of the experts who worked on the case are disqualified as witnesses and that their work product is inadmissible in court unless an agreement to the contrary is signed. The attorneys, however, will provide new counsel with the client file and any other relevant documents. The disclosures made by the parties during the collaborative process are confidential in nature, except for threats to harm another or claims of child abuse, which must be reported to the appropriate state child protection agency. The parties also agree in advance to make full and honest disclosures regarding their financial matters.

Attorneys who practice collaborative law should be trained in resolving matters in a nonadversarial manner and are an essential component to the process. The attorney's role in the process is to provide advice to his or her client on legal matters as well as work with the other attorney toward crafting an amicable separation or settlement agreement. The mental health professional is essential in helping the client through what can be a very emotional time. Financial planners are essential in helping the client determine how the divorce will affect their financial future and how to minimize problems before they materialize. The parties are free to bring whoever can assist the parties in creative problem solving. The emphasis of the teams is not adversarial, but rather a search for "win-win" solutions.

DIVORCE ARBITRATION

There are some divorce cases where resolution by settlement conference, mediation, or collaborative divorce is not an option. Though some parties are unable to work out a resolution and need a third party to decide their case, they do not want prolonged court proceedings. The parties may also want to save on legal fees as well as have their case heard in a more informal setting. This type of case may be suitable for arbitration.

In **divorce arbitration,** the parties present their evidence before a neutral third party who will render a decision in the case. The arbitrator is either a retired judge or an attorney experienced in divorce cases. The arbitrator renders an opinion called an **arbitration award.** Depending on the agreement of the parties or state law, the award will either be binding or nonbinding on the parties. If binding, the arbitration award will be filed with the court and treated as if the parties had tried their case before a judge. It is important to check state statutes regarding divorce arbitration. Most jurisdictions, with some variation, follow the **Uniform Arbitration Act,** which strictly limits appeals of arbitrated matters. The parties, however, may enter an agreement to the contrary prior to the arbitration proceeding to include certain appeal rights.

SHUTTLE DIPLOMACY

In *Miller v. Miller,* the arbitrator conducted the hearing by positioning the parties in separate rooms and shuttling back and forth. Both spouses agreed to the use of this procedure. The wife later objected, filing a motion to set aside the award based on the argument that she did not have the opportunity to present evidence or take testimony. Applying Michigan's Domestic Relations Arbitration Act, the Supreme Court of that state held that arbitration and trial proceedings do not require the same formalities and that parties are free to agree to "shuttle" arbitration.

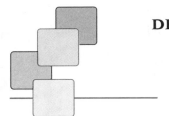

DEBRA LEA MILLER V. JOHN THOMAS MILLER

707 N.W.2D 341, 474 MICH. 27(2005)

SUPREME COURT OF MICHIGAN

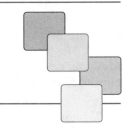

This case presents the question whether the Domestic Relations Arbitration Act (DRAA) requires a formal hearing during arbitration comparable to that which occurs in traditional trial proceedings. We conclude that it does not.

Also at issue is whether a court order to which the parties have stipulated in writing can satisfy the act's requirement of a written agreement to arbitrate. We conclude that it can. Therefore, we reverse the judgment of the Court of Appeals, which ruled to the contrary on both issues, and we reinstate the arbitration award and the judgment of divorce.

THE FACTUAL AND PROCEDURAL HISTORY

Plaintiff filed for divorce in January 2001. After failed settlement conferences in the circuit court, on December 4, 2001, both parties stipulated in writing to entry of an order sending all issues in the case to binding arbitration.

The arbitrator put the parties in separate rooms during the arbitration proceedings. He shuttled between them, gathering the necessary information and hearing the respective arguments. Both parties agreed to this procedure.

At the end of the day, plaintiff asked the arbitrator for additional sessions. He denied the request, expressly noting in his written award that plaintiff had failed to raise anything new to justify further proceedings. When plaintiff made a second request, the arbitrator gave her three days to provide an outline of what she would present at the additional proceedings. She supplied, instead, voluminous material. Rather than schedule more hearings, the arbitrator reviewed

plaintiff's material, modified the award, and issued the final binding arbitration award.

Plaintiff filed a motion in court to set aside the arbitration award on the basis that the arbitrator had failed to conduct a "hearing" as required by the DRAA. She also claimed that no arbitration agreement existed. The court rejected plaintiff's claims and entered a judgment of divorce. In a split published decision, the Court of Appeals reversed the judgment of the circuit court and vacated the arbitration award. It held that the DRAA required a formal hearing and that none occurred during the arbitration. *Miller v. Miller*, 264 Mich App 497; 691 NW2d 788 (2004).

THE APPROPRIATE STANDARD OF REVIEW

The two issues on appeal are matters of statutory interpretation that we review de novo. *People v. Kimble*, 470 Mich 305, 308–309; 684 NW2d 669 (2004). When interpreting a statute, our goal is to give effect to the Legislature's intent as determined from a review of the language of the statute. *People v. Koonce*, 466 Mich 515, 518; 684 NW2d 153 (2002).

Defendant asks us to review the Court of Appeals decision not to enforce the arbitration award. We review such decisions de novo to determine whether the arbitrators exceeded their powers. See *Gordon Sel-Way, Inc v. Spence Bros, Inc*, 438 Mich 488, 496–497; 475 NW2d 704 (1991). Arbitrators exceed their powers whenever they act beyond the material terms of the contract from which they draw their authority or in contravention of controlling law. *DAIIE v. Gavin*, 416 Mich 407, 433–434; 331 NW2d 418 (1982).

WHAT CONSTITUTES A HEARING UNDER THE DRAA

MCL 600.5081 is the statutory provision that governs vacation and modification of arbitration awards under the DRAA. MCL 600.5081(2) provides:

> If a party applies under this section, the court shall vacate an award under any of the following circumstances:
> a. The award was procured by corruption, fraud, or other undue means.
> b. There was evident partiality by an arbitrator appointed as a neutral, corruption of an arbitrator, or misconduct prejudicing a party's rights.
> c. The arbitrator exceeded his or her powers.
> d. The arbitrator refused to postpone the hearing on a showing of sufficient cause, refused to hear evidence material to the controversy, or otherwise conducted the hearing to prejudice substantially a party's rights.

The Court of Appeals concluded that the arbitrator violated MCL 600.5081(2)(d). It reasoned that the informality of the hearing prejudiced plaintiff's rights. The question is whether, in proceedings under the DRAA, the statute precludes hearings being conducted as the hearing was conducted in this case.

In reaching its decision, the Court of Appeals majority relied primarily on MCL 600.5074(1), which provides:

> An arbitrator appointed under this chapter *shall hear* and make an award on each issue submitted for arbitration under the arbitration agreement subject to the provisions of the agreement. [Emphasis added.]

The DRAA does not define the term "hear" or "hearing." Moreover, it sets no procedural requirements for arbitration. Rather, it specifically eschews them. For example, MCL 600.5077 requires, with certain exceptions, that the arbitrator not make an official record of most arbitration proceedings. This purposeful requirement of little or no record shows that the Legislature intended not to require specific procedures in arbitration proceedings. Without a record, reviewing courts cannot assess what procedures have been followed.

The Legislature's failure to provide specific arbitration procedures is consistent also with tradition. Historically, judicial review of arbitration awards is highly limited. *Gavin*, 416 Mich 433–434. This Court has characterized arbitration procedures as "informal and sometimes unorthodox. . . ." *Id.* at 429. Consequently, courts should not speculate why an arbitrator ruled in one particular manner. *Id.*

Rather than employ the formality required in courts, parties in arbitration are able to shape the parameters and procedures of the proceeding. The DRAA requires that they first sign an agreement for binding arbitration delineating the powers and duties of the arbitrator. MCL 600.5072(1)(e).

The act also contemplates that the parties will discuss with the arbitrator the scope of the issues and how information necessary for their resolution will be produced. MCL 600.5076. The act contemplates that the parties will decide what is best for their case. Nowhere in the DRAA are procedural formalities imposed that restrict this freedom.

This Court has consistently held that arbitration is a matter of contract. "It is the agreement that dictates the authority of the arbitrators." *Rowry v. Univ of Michigan*, 441 Mich 10; 490 NW2d 305 (1992). In this case, the Court of Appeals decision infringes on the parties' recognized freedom to contract for binding arbitration.

It restricts the parties' freedom to decide how the arbitration hearing should be conducted. Plaintiff presents no convincing argument that the Legislature intended all DRAA hearings to approximate traditional court hearings. We know of none. It is inappropriate for a court to read into a statute something that was not intended. *AFSCME v. Detroit*, 468 Mich 388, 412; 662 NW2d 695 (2003).

Significantly, in this case, the parties specifically agreed to allow the arbitrator to conduct the hearing in two separate rooms. If the parties and the arbitrator thought that this was the best way to hold their hearing, they were at liberty to make that agreement. Because it is the agreement of the parties that dictates arbitration, the Court of Appeals should not have altered the agreement. *Rowry*, 441 Mich 10.

THE SUFFICIENCY OF THE PARTIES' WRITTEN ARBITRATION AGREEMENT

Plaintiff argued below that no written arbitration agreement existed in this case. Defendant disagreed. Although the Court of Appeals majority did not reach this issue directly, it listed as alternative grounds for possible relief that the stipulated order did not constitute a written arbitration agreement. *Miller*, 264 Mich App 507 n. 12. We disagree.

As we noted earlier, the DRAA requires a written arbitration agreement setting out the subject of the arbitration and the arbitrator's powers. MCL 600.5071 and MCL 600.5072(1)(e). Here, the parties entered into a written agreement satisfying these requirements when they stipulated to entry of the particularized order for binding arbitration that the court in due course entered.

The order lists the issues for arbitration. It clearly delineates the arbitrator's powers and duties. Accordingly, it is sufficient to satisfy the requirements of MCL 600.5071 and MCL 600.5072 (1)(e).

Nothing in the DRAA mandates that there be an agreement separate from the stipulated order. This is consistent with the informal and sometimes unorthodox nature of arbitration. *Gavin,* 416 Mich 429. As long as the parties agree to some document that meets the minimal requirements of MCL. 600.5071 and MCL 600.5072 (1)(e), the agreement is sufficient. Therefore, we reverse the decision of the Court of Appeals that reached the contrary conclusion.

CONCLUSION

We hold that the Domestic Relations Arbitration Act does not require that the formality of a hearing in arbitration proceedings approximate that of a hearing in court. Arbitration is by its nature informal. The appropriate structure for an arbitration hearing is best decided by the parties and the arbitrator. A procedure by which the arbitrator shuttles between the parties in separate rooms questioning and listening to them satisfies the act's requirement of a hearing.

We also hold that no written agreement beyond the order for binding arbitration is required (1) if the parties stipulate to entry of the order and the order meets the criteria of MCL 600.5071 and MCL 600.5072 (1)(e), and (2) if the parties satisfy MCL 600.5072 (1)(a) to (d) on the record.

Therefore, we reverse the judgment of the Court of Appeals and reinstate the arbitration award and the judgment of divorce.

THE PARALEGAL'S ROLE IN ALTERNATIVE DISPUTE RESOLUTION

In all forms of alternative dispute resolution, the most important role for the paralegal is that of information gathering and analysis. Family law is a fact-driven field of practice. Divorce cases are decided on a case-by-case basis because every family and its particular financial and social structure is different. Paralegals may assist the attorney in the ADR process by:

- having knowledge of all forms of ADR available in their jurisdiction.
- compiling files on various reputable and reliable ADR professionals.
- preparing state-specific forms required for mandatory ADR procedures.
- monitoring clients who are required by state law to attend mandatory mediation and parenting classes and following up on their compliance.
- scheduling ADR conferences with the relevant parties.
- preparing and processing discovery requests.
- helping the client respond to discovery requests.
- reviewing the client's discovery as well as that of the opposing party.
- assisting the attorney at settlement conferences and collaborative law sessions.
- drafting mediation agreements between the lawyer-mediator and clients.
- drafting memorandums of understanding in mediation cases.
- drafting collaborative law agreements between the attorney and client.
- drafting separation agreements in accordance with agreements reached through settlement conferences, mediation, or collaborative law sessions.

THE DIVORCE TRIAL

At this stage, the parties have either reached an agreement or plan to litigate some or all of their issue in a **divorce trial,** the process in which both parties present their case to the court for its final hearing. Divorce trials are for the most part

bench trials, which means that the trial is conducted before a judge, not a jury. In some jurisdictions, such as New York and Texas, the parties can demand a jury trial in divorce cases. In a bench trial the judge is both the trier of fact and law. The family court judge is knowledgeable in the area of domestic relations and his role is to apply the law, which includes statutory and case law, to the particular facts in the case before him and render a decision that is fair to both parties.

Divorce trials are open to the public so anyone can sit in and observe the case. Courtrooms may be sealed upon motion of the parties to protect children of the marriage when the trial issues are of a particularly sensitive nature. Divorce files are also open to the public and may be viewed in local courthouses at the clerk's office.

Divorce trials are either uncontested or contested. Whether the case is contested or uncontested, the paralegal must send a formal notice to the court indicating that the case is ready for the trial list. (See Exhibit 13–2.)

UNCONTESTED HEARING

In an **uncontested hearing,** the parties have either reached an agreement regarding the issues surrounding the dissolution of their marriage (i.e., alimony, property division, child custody and support, attorney's fees) or one party is defaulted for failure to appear. A **default trial** takes place when one of the parties to an action has failed to appear at the scheduled trial date even though she has received proper notice of the proceedings. In this case, the court will proceed with a default hearing and sever the marriage. It is important that the respondent/defendant file a cross-complaint so in the event the petitioner/plaintiff does not appear, the court can proceed on the respondent/defendant's cross-complaint.

Most divorce cases proceed as uncontested matters. Many couples resolve their major issues through negotiations between themselves, through their respective attorneys, or with a professional mediator. The parties then preserve their agreement in writing. The case must then be put on the court calendar as an uncontested hearing.

Every jurisdiction has specific procedures for requesting a trial date in either an uncontested or contested dissolution matter. The paralegal should become familiar with his particular state's requirements for getting a case on the court calendar. In addition, some jurisdictions may also provide preprinted forms to facilitate this process.

Uncontested divorce trials are very brief in duration. The court will first confirm service of process on the defendant spouse. This means that the judge determines whether service of the divorce complaint/petition was adequately made on the defendant/respondent. In the case where there is a nonappearing defendant, the moving party must provide the court with a **military affidavit** in accordance with the Soldiers and Sailors Relief Act 50 USC §520 (1982) to prove that the defendant is currently not serving in one of the armed forces. (SeeExhibit 13–3.) This requires contacting each branch of the military to determine whether or not the defendant is in the armed forces. When requesting a military affidavit, the paralegal should provide the defendant's name, address, Social Security number, and date of birth. In addition, a small fee must accompany each request.

Some jurisdictions do not require the parties to appear in court if the divorce is uncontested or if there is a default. In these jurisdictions the parties are merely required to file the appropriate paperwork with the court.

In matters where the parties have worked out a settlement or separation agreement, the plaintiff/petitioner will be called to the witness stand and put under oath. The plaintiff's attorney will question her briefly on the allegations made in the complaint/petition, which is necessary to establish the statutory grounds for a dissolution of marriage. The judge may also direct some questions to the parties.

If the parties have executed the separation agreement, the original is presented to the court and reviewed by the judge. Separation agreements are usually approved by the court unless the terms of the agreement are deemed by the court to be **unconscionable,** unfair, or one sided. The court must determine if the parties are aware of the contents of the agreement, that they understand it, that it is their free and voluntary act, that it was not made under fraud or duress, and that the assets have been fully disclosed. Provisions regarding alimony and property division will not be scrutinized as carefully as those provisions dealing with child custody, support, or visitation. The court also has an interest in determining what economic position the parties will be left in after the divorce. If the court finds the agreement unconscionable, it will order the parties to go back to the drawing board and reconsider certain provisions.

If the court accepts the parties' agreement by finding it to be fair and equitable, the court will first dissolve the marriage, then the court, upon request of the parties, will incorporate the parties' agreement into the divorce decree. This is known as a **merger.** Once the settlement agreement has been merged with the divorce decree, the terms of the agreement are now considered court orders.

A merger affords the parties with the postjudgment remedies of contempt of court proceedings and modification. Without a merger, the settlement agreement is a contract between the parties, who will be left with contract remedies in order to enforce or change their agreement. If a spouse fails to comply with the terms of a separation agreement that has been merged into the divorce decree, the aggrieved spouse may seek contempt of court proceedings to enforce its provisions. A merger also allows parties to seek modification of certain provisions as long as they can prove that there has been a substantial change in circumstances since the entry of the original decree.

CONTESTED HEARING

Parties that have been unable to reach an agreement regarding issues of alimony, property division, visitation, and child custody and support will have to let the judge make those decisions. A disputed divorce trial is known as a **contested hearing.** Although contested trials give the client their "day in court," they can also be very stressful and their outcome uncertain.

Parties who have negotiated a settlement agreement are more likely to be content with the final results because they actually had some degree of participation in its formation and are more likely to cooperate with its terms because it was agreed to voluntarily. Once a case has been turned over to a judge, there is no telling what the result will be.

Contested hearings may also increase the parties' hostility toward each other. This has a particularly devastating result when children are caught in the middle. Contested hearings can also be very expensive. Clients incur additional legal fees and expenses such as sheriff's fees, expert witness fees, court costs, transcript fees, appraisal reports, investigations, or evaluations prepared by third parties.

Why, then, despite these consequences, do some divorces end up in a contested trial? The trial process provides a forum where opposing parties can vigorously litigate issues of law and fact before an impartial third party. Unfortunately, the hostility surrounding a broken marriage can often spill into the courts. Some parties find that a proposed settlement is unfair and refuse to accept it. The other spouse refuses to change or modify his position, hence the parties reach a stalemate. Sometimes clients have unrealistic expectations of what the legal system can do for them and insist on going to trial. Others wish to use the threat of trial to intimidate a spouse who may not wish to have every sordid detail of the marriage exposed in public. Others still play out their anger toward their spouse in the legal system by refusing to cooperate or compromise on anything and instead contest every single issue possible.

If the case cannot be settled and it looks like it will proceed as a contested matter, the appropriate forms must be filed to request a trial date.

Some jurisdictions require that parties in contested matters attend a **judicial pretrial conference.** The pretrial conference takes place before a judge. It is not a trial. The purpose of the judicial pretrial conference is to help parties come to an agreement. The judge's role is to tell the parties how she would rule if this matter were to be tried before her. If parties agree to the judge's proposal, an agreement will be drafted and the parties will bring the agreement before the court. Another function of the judicial pretrial conference is to marrow the issues to be litigated in cases where there is no agreement in sight.

If the case cannot be resolved and instead heads for trial, a **pretrial conference** or mandatory settlement conference may be scheduled. (Exhibit 13–4 illustrates a notice to Melissa Carrey scheduling a settlement conference and ordering her and her attorney to have certain documents ready for trial.) The purpose of the pretrial conference is to streamline the trial process. At the pretrial conference, the parties will:

1. **Exchange witness lists.** This will assist the parties in preparation of cross-examination and impeachment of the opposing party's witnesses. It will also help anticipate witnesses' testimony.

2. **Disclose exhibits to be filed.** Parties can review in advance exhibits that will be entered as evidence and determine which exhibits may be entered into evidence by agreement and which ones will be opposed.

3. **Narrow the issues to be tried.** Even though the divorce is contested, there may be issues that the parties can agree on or can stipulate to.

4. **Establish if an interpreter is needed for the proceedings.** A party may not be able to speak or understand the English language or may require sign language to be used. The pretrial conference serves to give court personnel advance notice of such needs so they can make arrangements to have an interpreter present.

5. **Establish if a habeas corpus is needed.** A writ of *habeas corpus* may be necessary so that an incarcerated party may be transported by the state's correction department for trial.

6. **Determine the role of the child's attorney.**

7. **Determine whether children will testify and under what circumstances.**

If disagreements still exist after a pretrial conference, a trial date will be scheduled. The goal of the trial process is to arrive at the truth. The way we arrive at the truth in our American system of jurisprudence is through the adversarial system. Both parties, represented by competent counsel, battle it out before an impartial third party known as a judge. The rules of evidence dictate which information can be admitted and which excluded so that evidence offered at trial is reliable and untainted. The problem with the adversarial system is that it assumes that both lawyers are equally competent, that the judge has no biases or prejudices, and that both sides have enough funds in their war chest to afford expert witnesses, evaluations, appraisals, investigators, and every legal maneuver available to present their case.

Unfortunately this is not always the case. Some attorneys are better than others and just because a judge puts on a black robe does not mean that he is saturated with the wisdom of Solomon. Clients do not always possess the funds to pay for the presentation of a perfect case and may have to settle for what is realistic.

As mentioned earlier, parties who go to trial take a risk when turning their decision-making power over to the judge. They have now lost the ability to control their destiny in terms of the dissolution of their marriage.

THE PARALEGAL'S ROLE IN TRIAL PREPARATION

The process of trial preparation begins on the day of the initial client interview. Only a clairvoyant will know whether or not a case will go to trial. Clients will, at times, inform the attorney that the parties have worked out an agreement and there are no problems. This, however, is never a sure thing. The amicable agreement of today can turn into the contested bloodbath of tomorrow.

The attorney will need to develop the theory of the case. The **theory of the case** is the legal justification for the client's position and for the relief she is seeking. A thorough review of the discovery materials will help formulate some type of case strategy.

Family court dockets can be extremely crowded and judges appreciate a well-prepared, well-researched, and well-organized case that does not take up time with matters that have already been resolved.

Once a theory of the case has been developed, the lawyer and paralegal must assemble the necessary evidence to present the client's case to the court. A client's case is proven by presenting evidence that will support the client's claim. The client's case is developed through the evidentiary vehicles of testimony and documents.

Testimony is often given during a divorce trial. A list of witnesses is prepared to determine who will testify at trial. In a divorce case, the client spouse will be the primary witness and he will tell his story to the court. Other witnesses may also be called to testify: expert witnesses such as physicians and mental health professionals, social workers, teachers, appraisers, accountants, and investigators. Lay witnesses such as family members, friends, neighbors, coworkers, employers, and/or supervisors may also testify.

When calling a witness other than a client, it is necessary for the party calling that witness to subpoena the witness to trial. A subpoena is a document ordering a witness to appear under penalty of law to provide testimony at a legal proceeding. (See Exhibit 13–5.) A paralegal may be in charge of preparing the subpoenas and arranging for service of these orders by a sheriff. The paralegal must also keep track of subpoenas to make sure they have been properly served. Failure to subpoena a party may result in her not appearing for trial. Records also need to be subpoenaed. Witnesses also need to be prepared by the attorney to testify.

Documents that may be used at trial include the following:

- financial records of parties already produced through discovery,
- any court-ordered evaluations that are part of the court file,
- additional psychological or psychiatric reports that either party seeks to have admitted in support of their position, and
- appraisals of assets, an independent financial evaluation of business interests, licenses, goodwill, and pensions.

Once the attorney has determined which types of evidence will be used at trial, the next step is to prepare the **trial notebook.** The trial notebook provides a way to organize materials important to the case in a manner that makes them readily available for use at trial. There is nothing more embarrassing for an attorney than having to fumble and leaf through stacks of unorganized documents during a trial. It gives the client and the court the impression that the attorney did not prepare adequately.

The trial notebook is not necessarily a physical notebook, although a notebook can be used if preferred. Some attorneys organize their trial notebooks by designating a series of file folders to contain certain information. These file folders will then be placed in a large folder or box to facilitate easy access during trial. Other attorneys may prefer to use commercially or self-prepared trial notebooks. The trial notebook may contain a variety of subfiles organized such that they facilitate easy access to the information.

The parties may also be required to submit certain documents to the court at the time of trial that may be prepared by the paralegal. Please note that filing requirements vary from state to state. These documents include:

1. An updated sworn **financial disclosure affidavit,** indicating the income, expenses, assets, and liabilities of the client. (See Exhibit 13–6.)
2. A **custody affidavit** indicating that there is no other proceeding pending in another court that affects the custody of the minor children. If a proceeding is pending, the paralegal must indicate where and the nature of the proceedings. (See Exhibit 13–7.)
3. A **claim for relief,** which is a statement filed by a party indicating what he wants in terms of a disposition in the case. (See Exhibit 13–8.)
4. **Wage execution** forms for the purpose of facilitating alimony and child support payments through automatic deductions from the obligor's paycheck. (See Exhibit 13–9.)
5. State-specific **Bureau of Vital Statistics forms** designed for the purpose of collecting statistical information on divorcing couples. (See Exhibit 13–10.)
6. **Stipulations,** which are written agreements where parties agree that certain facts are true or that certain procedures are to be followed.

The client should be notified by phone and then in writing regarding the trial date. The attorney should set up an appointment with the client prior to trial for the purpose of reviewing testimony and explaining the trial process to the client.

The attorney should also review the exhibits she intends to introduce through the client so the client becomes familiar with them and prepared to testify. The client should be given directions either to the courthouse or to meet the attorney at the office. The client should also be informed to dress conservatively as if he or she were attending a religious service. A conservative appearance conveys reverence and respect for the court.

DAY OF THE TRIAL

Some attorneys allow their paralegals to assist at trial. Although a paralegal may not question witnesses, argue motions, make opening and closing arguments, or raise objections, paralegals can perform many important tasks at trial. At trial, the paralegal will sit at the counsel table with the attorney and client. Remember that the paralegal's status must be communicated to the court so that neither the judge nor opposing party is under the impression that the paralegal is an attorney.

The divorce trial will be heard by a judge, who will preside over the hearing. Parties may be referred to a hearing officer, referee, or a special master in courts that utilize these alternative decision makers to resolve the overflow of cases. As mentioned earlier, a divorce trial is open to the public unless the court has ordered the courtroom sealed to protect particularly sensitive cases, and in some jurisdictions, the parties can demand a jury trial.

The plaintiff or petitioner will be the first to put on his case and call his witnesses to the stand. The opposing party will then have the opportunity to cross-examine the plaintiff's witnesses. Once the plaintiff has rested his case, the defendant/respondent will be able to proceed with his case and present his witnesses. During the course of the trial, the paralegal may make notes during each witness's testimony. This is one of the most important functions of a paralegal during the trial. It is important that the lawyer focus his attention on the testimony in order to make the appropriate objections or argue with opposing counsel regarding the admission or exclusion of evidence. If the note-taking process is delegated to the paralegal, then the attorney can concentrate on the trial. Taking notes during testimony is essential for the purpose of preparing closing arguments and cross-examination. A paralegal may also assist at trial by dealing with the client. A client should be given a legal pad and pen and instructed to write down any questions or comments that arise during trial. This lets the client express himself without distracting the attorney.

The paralegal may also help keep track of exhibits, pass materials to the attorney, and deal with impatient witnesses waiting to testify. Paralegals may also run errands such as photocopying, making quick legal research trips to the court library, and making phone calls to witnesses or the office.

After testimony, each attorney argues why the court should rule in his or her client's favor. This is known as **final argument.** The court may decide the case immediately or render its decision at a later date. Sometimes the court will require the parties to prepare briefs or a memorandum of law on particular issues to assist the court in making its decision.

If the court renders its decision immediately after trial, the court must first **dissolve** the marriage—that is, declare that the spouses are no longer married. The court will then rule on the issue of child support, property division, alimony, attorney's fees, and debts. One of the parties will be ordered to prepare the judgment, which will be signed by the opposing party and the court. The **judgment** delineates the orders made by the court pursuant to the court's decision after trial and becomes a permanent part of the court file. (See Exhibit 13–11.)

A **transcript** of the trial may be necessary if the decision was rendered at the close of trial to facilitate the preparation of the judgment or the preparation of an **appeal** of the case to a higher court. The paralegal may have the responsibility of ordering the transcript and dealing with the court reporter's office that will be responsible for its preparation. The paralegal may also be required to draft the judgment in accordance with local rules.

EXHIBIT 13–1

COURT-ANNEXED
MEDIATION REQUEST

JD-CL-61 Rev. 3-06

INSTRUCTIONS

1. *For a list of mediators, check the website under "MEDIATION."*
2. *Complete the Case Information section.*
3. *Mail/Fax the referral to the Mediation Coordinator at the address shown below.*
4. *The Mediation Assignment section is to be completed by the Mediation Coordinator and a notice of assignment is sent to all counsel and pro se parties of record.*

STATE OF CONNECTICUT
SUPERIOR COURT
www.jud.ct.gov

TO: Mediation Coordinator, 225 Spring St., Wethersfield, CT 06109 or fax to (860) 563-8134

CASE INFORMATION

NAME OF CASE	DOCKET NO. ☐ CV ☐ FA
	JUDICIAL DISTRICT OF

CASE TYPE *(e.g., Contract, Dissolution of Marriage, etc.)*	TRIAL DATE	EST. LENGTH OF TIME FOR SESSION

PLAINTIFF'S TRIAL COUNSEL/PRO SE *(Print Name, Firm Name and Address)*	TELEPHONE NUMBER
	FAX NUMBER

DEFENDANT'S TRIAL COUNSEL/PRO SE *(Print Name, Firm Name and Address)*	TELEPHONE NUMBER
	FAX NUMBER

CHILD'S COUNSEL, IF ANY *(Print Name, Firm Name and Address)*	TELEPHONE NUMBER
	FAX NUMBER

INSURANCE CARRIER, IF ANY *(Print Name and Address)*	TELEPHONE NUMBER
	FAX NUMBER

PREFERRED MEDIATOR(S)

1) _____ 2) _____ 3) _____

AVAILABLE SCHEDULING

1) _____ 2) _____ 3) _____

4) _____ 5) _____ 6) _____

MEDIATION ASSIGNMENT

NAME OF MEDIATOR	JURIS NO. OF MEDIATOR	LOCATION OF SESSION

DATE/TIME OF SESSION

NOTICE TO COUNSEL AND PRO SE PARTIES OF RECORD

1. Counsel and parties are advised that mediation will not delay the progress of the case or interfere with scheduled events, i.e., trials, jury selection, etc.
2. Mediation is a voluntary nonbinding process. Counsel and parties are expected to participate in good faith and make an effort to resolve outstanding issues.
3. The requirements of the mediation session are printed on the back/page 2 of this form.

(continued on back/page 2)

EXHIBIT 13–1 Continued

Mediation Requirements

- Once the mediation session is confirmed, a notice will be sent to all parties stating the Mediator's requirements in regard to the position summation. The summation <u>MUST</u> be submitted to the Mediator no later than the date stated in the notice. Late submittal may result in cancellation of the mediation at the Mediator's discretion.

  The Mediator may request copies of pleadings and motions.

- Trial counsel and pro se parties of record are required to attend. Plaintiffs and defendants are required to attend. However, in civil matters, defendants who are represented by insurance companies need not attend unless the claim is in excess of the coverage, but the claims representatives with authority to settle must attend. In insurance carrier cases, the order for the defendant's appearance should be determined on a case-to-case basis. Failure to attend may result in the imposition of sanctions unless excused in advance by the Mediator. The Mediator may waive any requirement.

- The mediation session is confidential. Information related to the mediation may not be placed in the court file without the agreement of the parties. Only the referral form and stipulations for judgment may become part of the court file.

- As a general proposition, there should not be ex parte conversation with the mediator outside the mediation process and only in the process as agreed by the parties.

- At the conclusion of the session, the Mediator will communicate the outcome to the Mediation Coordinator.

Continuance Policy

- Continuances are allowed only for extreme hardship and must be ordered by the Mediation Coordinator after consultation with the Mediator.

- Any continuance request must be in writing and submitted to the Mediation Coordinator with copies to all counsel and pro se parties of record.

- The request must note whether the request is by agreement of the parties.

- Counsel will be notified of the decision and will be responsible for notifying all other parties.

- Questions may be directed by telephone to the Mediation Coordinator at (860) 563-9435.

EXHIBIT 13–2 Sample request for trial form.

ATTORNEY OR PARTY WITHOUT ATTORNEY (NAME AND ADDRESS)	TELEPHONE NUMBER:	FOR COURT USE ONLY
ATTORNEY FOR *(Name):*		

SUPERIOR COURT OF CALIFORNIA, COUNTY OF SANTA CLARA

STREET ADDRESS:
MAILING ADDRESS: 191 North First Street
CITY AND ZIP CODE: San Jose, CA 95113
BRANCH NAME:

PETITIONER:

RESPONDENT:

OTHER PARENT/CLAIMANT:

REQUEST FOR TRIAL **(Family Law)**	CASE NUMBER:
☐ Dissolution ☐ Domestic Partnership ☐ Legal Separation ☐ Nullity ☐ Parentage ☐ Other Family Law : _____	DEPARTMENT NUMBER:

1. How long do you think your trial will last? _____ check one: ☐ hour(s) ☐ day(s)

2. What has not been agreed upon between you and the other party?:
   ☐ Custody/Visitation   ☐ Child Support   ☐ Spousal Support
   ☐ Contempt   ☐ Property Characterization   ☐ Arrearages
   ☐ Property Valuation   ☐ Property Valuation Date   ☐ Reimbursement
   ☐ Date Of Separation   ☐ Property Division   ☐ Set-Aside
   ☐ Attorney's Fees & Costs   ☐ Other: _____

3 Discovery (getting information about/from the other party):
   a. Has discovery been completed? ☐ Yes ☐ No
   b. What discovery still needs to be done? ☐ Interrogatories ☐ Depositions ☐ Document Production
   c. How long do you think it will take to finish discovery by both sides: _____

4 Petitioner has served Respondent with ☐ Preliminary Declaration of Disclosure ☐ Yes ☐ No
   Petitioner has served Respondent with ☐ Final Declaration of Disclosure ☐ Yes ☐ No
   Respondent has served Petitioner with ☐ Preliminary Declaration of Disclosure ☐ Yes ☐ No
   Respondent has served Petitioner with ☐ Final Declaration of Disclosure ☐ Yes ☐ No

5 Do you want a:
   a. Settlement Officer Conference? ☐ Yes ☐ No
   b. Trial on separate issues? ☐ Yes ☐ No   If yes, what issues: _____
   _____

6 Have parties and/or counsel met to discuss settlement? ☐ Yes ☐ No

7 Is the Department of Child Support Services involved on the issue of child support? ☐ Yes ☐ No

   If yes, which county?_____ What is the court case number (if different from this case):_____

Date: _____

☐ Attorney for ☐ Petitioner ☐ Respondent ☐ Other

REQUEST FOR TRIAL
(Family Law)

EXHIBIT 13–2 Continued

PROOF OF SERVICE BY MAIL (C.C.P. 1013a)

I mailed a copy of the Request for Trial in a sealed envelope as follows:

a. Mailed from:_____(city)_____(state)

b. On (date):_____

c. To:_____(Name of party or attorney served)

d. Address:_____

City:_____State:_____Zip:_____

Server's Information:

Name:_____

Address:_____

City:_____State:_____Zip:_____

(*If you are a registered process server*):

County of Registration_____ Registration Number:_____

I am over the age of 18 and not a party to this case.

I declare under penalty of perjury under the laws of the State of California that the information above is true and correct.

Dated:_____   _____

                                         (Signature of Person Doing the Mailing)

EXHIBIT 13–3 Sample military affidavit.

State of Minnesota

District Court

County	

Judicial District:
Court File Number:
Case Type: Dissolution

In Re the Marriage of:

_____

Name of Petitioner

And

_____

Name of Respondent

**Affidavit of
Non-Military Status**

STATE OF MINNESOTA   )
COUNTY OF _____)SS
       (County where Affidavit signed)

_____ being duly sworn, says:

I am the Petitioner in this action.

To the best of my knowledge, Respondent is not now, nor was Respondent at the date of service of the _Summons and Petition for Dissolution of Marriage_, in the military or naval service of the United States.

Dated: _____

_____

Signature

Name: _____

Street Address: _____

City/State/Zip: _____

EXHIBIT 13–4 Sample notice of trial date and pretrial conference.

```
 1   NORMAN M. DOLIN, ESQ., SBN 30475
     LAW OFFICES OF NORMAN M. DOLIN
 2   1925 Century Park East, Suite 2200
     Los Angeles, CA 90067-2723
 3   Tel: (310) 552-9338
                                              LO     CO       RT
 4   Attorney for Petitioner, JAMES EUGENE CARREY    FEB 18  1994

 5                                            EDWARD          CLERK
                                                   A  R
 6                                            BY M  DEN  A  DEPUTY

 7

 8               SUPERIOR COURT OF CALIFORNIA

 9             FOR THE COUNTY OF LOS ANGELES

10

11   In Re Marriage of:           )   CASE NO.  BD 135499
                                   )
12   PETITIONER:   JAMES   EUGENE  )   NOTICE   OF   TRIAL   DATE,
                   CARREY          )   MANDATORY    SETTLEMENT
13   and                          )   CONFERENCE DATE, AND ORDER
                                   )
14                                 )   Trial:
     RESPONDENT:   MELISSA  JANE   )   Date:  May 11, 1994
15                 CARREY          )   Time:  8:30 a.m.
                                   )   Dept:  2B
16   _____)
                                       Mandatory  Settlement
17                                     Conference:
                                       Date:  April 21, 1994
18                                     Time:  8:30 a.m.
                                       Dept:  2
19

20   TO RESPONDENT, MELISSA JANE CARREY AND TO HER ATTORNEYS OF RECORD:

21        PLEASE TAKE NOTICE that trial in the above-captioned matter is

22   set for May 11, 1994, at 8:30 a.m., in Department 2B of the

23   Superior Court located at 111 North Hill Street, Los Angeles,

24   California.

25        PLEASE TAKE FURTHER NOTICE that the Mandatory Settlement

26   Conference in the above-captioned matter is set for April 21, 1994,

27   at 8:30 a.m. in Department 2 of the Superior Court located at 111

28   North Hill Street, Los Angeles, California.


     Carrey\NotTRI.MSC            1
```

EXHIBIT 13–4 Continued

1   PLEASE NOTE THE COURT HAS MADE THE FOLLOWING FURTHER ORDERS:

2   1.   All discovery, including depositions of all experts,

3 shall be pursuant to the provisions of §2024 <u>Code of Civil</u>

4 <u>Procedure</u>.

5   2.   At least seven (7) calendar days before the first trial

6 date, all counsel and parties in pro per shall exchange with each

7 other the following in writing:

8   a.   A new trial brief discussing in detail the

9 disputed issues, approximate tax consequences.

10   b.   Lists of names of all witnesses to be called at

11 trial.   Except for good cause shown, failure to so disclose shall

12 preclude undisclosed witnesses from testifying.

13   c.   Lists of exhibits as described in Los Angeles

14 Superior Court Civil Trials Manual Section 75.   Except for good

15 cause shown, failure to so disclose shall preclude admission of

16 undisclosed exhibits.

17   3.   Counsel and parties in propria persona are ordered to

18 premark their proposed exhibits in accordance with Section VIII

19 (Trial Preparation) of the Family Law Manual of Procedures.

20   4.   Counsel or parties in propria persona are to comply with

21 CCP §2025(Q)(i) in identifying deposition transcripts to be used at

22 trial.

23 Dated: February 17, 1994   Respectfully submitted,

24   LAW OFFICES OF NORMAN M. DOLIN

25

26   BY: _____

27   Norman M. Dolin
                      Attorney for Petitioner,

28   JAMES EUGENE CARREY

EXHIBIT 13–5 Sample subpoena.

SUBPOENA/CIVIL
JD-CL-43 Rev. 3-06
C.G.S. § 52-143, 52-144
Pr. Bk. Secs. 7-19, 24-22

STATE OF CONNECTICUT
SUPERIOR COURT
www.jud.ct.gov

INSTRUCTIONS: Do NOT use this subpoena if the witness is being summoned by the state or by the attorney general or an assistant attorney general or by any public defender or assistant public defender acting in his/her official capacity.

COURT USE ONLY
SUBISSU

NAME OF CASE	DOCKET NO.

☐ Judicial District	☐ Housing Session	☐ G.A. No. ____	☐ Small Claims Area	ADDRESS OF COURT *(No., street and town)*

TO: *(Name and address)*

DATE AND TIME YOU ARE TO APPEAR	TIME ___ . m.	REPORT TO	☐ CLERK'S OFFICE ☐ COURTROOM NO. ☐ PERSON REQUESTING SUBPOENA

BY AUTHORITY OF THE STATE OF CONNECTICUT, you are hereby commanded to appear before the Superior Court in session at the above address on the date indicated above or to such day thereafter and within sixty days hereof on which the action named above is legally to be tried, to testify what you know in said action pending in the court.

YOU ARE FURTHER COMMANDED TO BRING WITH YOU AND PRODUCE:

HEREOF FAIL NOT, UNDER PENALTY OF THE LAW.
To any proper officer or indifferent person to serve and return.

NAME OF PERSON REQUESTING SUBPOENA	TELEPHONE NO.

SIGNED *(Clerk, Commissioner of Superior Court)*	ON *(Date)*	AT

NOTICE TO THE PERSON SUMMONED

You must report to the court at the time and address shown above and remain until this case is disposed of and you are discharged by the court. Present this subpoena when you report.

If you do not appear in court on the day and at the time stated, or on the day and at the time to which your appearance may have been postponed or continued by order of an officer of the court, and one day's attendance and traveling fees have been tendered to you, the court may order that you be arrested. In addition, if the aforementioned fees have been paid to you and you fail to appear and testify, without reasonable excuse, you shall be fined not more than twenty-five dollars and pay all damages to the aggrieved party. **The party requesting the subpoena is responsible for paying the witness fees.**

Any questions regarding this subpoena should be directed to the person who requested it.

RETURN OF SERVICE

JUDICIAL DISTRICT OF _____ ss. _____ , Connecticut	DATE

Then and there I made service of the within subpoena not less than eighteen hours prior to the time designated for the person summoned to appear, by reading the same in the presence and hearing/leaving a true and attested copy hereof in the hands/at the last usual place of abode of each of the within-named persons, viz:	**FEES**
	COPY
	ENDORSEMENT
	SERVICE
	TRAVEL *(Show miles & amount)*

ATTEST *(Signature of proper officer or indifferent person)*	TITLE *(If applicable)*	**TOTAL**

DISTRIBUTION: ORIGINAL - Court   COPY1 - Witness   COPY2 - File

447

EXHIBIT 13-6 Sample financial disclosure affidavit.

FL-155

Your name and address or attorney's name and address:	TELEPHONE NO.:	*FOR COURT USE ONLY*

ATTORNEY FOR *(Name):*

SUPERIOR COURT OF CALIFORNIA, COUNTY OF

STREET ADDRESS:

MAILING ADDRESS:

CITY AND ZIP CODE:

BRANCH NAME:

PETITIONER/PLAINTIFF:

RESPONDENT/DEFENDANT:

OTHER PARENT:

FINANCIAL STATEMENT (SIMPLIFIED)	CASE NUMBER:

NOTICE: Read page 2 to find out if you qualify to use this form and how to use it.

1. a. ☐ My only source of income is TANF, SSI, or GA/GR.
   b. ☐ I have applied for TANF, SSI, or GA/GR.
2. I am the parent of the following number of natural or adopted children from this relationship . . . . _____
3. a. The children from this relationship are with me this amount of time . . . . _____ %
   b. The children from this relationship are with the other parent this amount of time . . . . _____ %
   c. Our arrangement for custody and visitation is *(specify, using extra sheet if necessary):*
4. My tax filing status is: ☐ single ☐ married filing jointly ☐ head of household ☐ married filing separately.
5. My current gross income *(before taxes)* per month is . . . . $ _____

   Attach 1 copy of pay stubs for last 2 months here (cross out social security numbers)

   This income comes from the following:
   ☐ Salary/wages: Amount before taxes per month . . . . $ _____
   ☐ Retirement: Amount before taxes per month . . . . $ _____
   ☐ Unemployment compensation: Amount per month . . . . $ _____
   ☐ Workers' compensation: Amount per month . . . . $ _____
   ☐ Social security: ☐ SSI ☐ Other Amount per month . . . . $ _____
   ☐ Disability: Amount per month . . . . $ _____
   ☐ Interest income (from bank accounts or other): Amount per month . . . . $ _____
   I have no income other than as stated in this paragraph.
6. I pay the following monthly expenses for the children in this case:
   a. ☐ Day care or preschool to allow me to work or go to school . . . . $ _____
   b. ☐ Health care not paid for by insurance . . . . $ _____
   c. ☐ School, education, tuition, or other special needs of the child . . . . $ _____
   d. ☐ Travel expenses for visitation . . . . $ _____
7. ☐ There are *(specify number)* _____ other minor children of mine living with me. Their monthly expenses
   that I pay are . . . . $ _____
8. I spend the following average monthly amounts *(please attach proof):*
   a. ☐ Job-related expenses that are not paid by my employer *(specify reasons for expenses on separate sheet)* $ _____
   b. ☐ Required union dues . . . . $ _____
   c. ☐ Required retirement payments (not social security, FICA, 401k or IRA) . . . . $ _____
   d. ☐ Health insurance costs . . . . $ _____
   e. ☐ Child support I am paying for other minor children of mine who are not living with me . . . . $ _____
   f. ☐ Spousal support I am paying because of a court order for another relationship. . . . . $ _____
   g. ☐ Monthly housing costs: ☐ rent or ☐ mortgage . . . . $ _____
      If mortgage: interest payments $_____ real property taxes $_____
9. Information concerning ☐ my current employment ☐ my most recent employment:
   Employer:
   Address:
   Telephone number:
   My occupation:
   Date work started:
   Date work stopped *(if applicable):*   What was your gross income *(before taxes)* before work stopped?:

Page 1 of 2

Form Approved for Optional Use
Judicial Council of California
FL-155 [Rev. January 1, 2004]

FINANCIAL STATEMENT (SIMPLIFIED)

Family Code, § 4068(b)
www.courtinfo.ca.gov

American LegalNet, Inc.
www.USCourtForms.com

EXHIBIT 13–6 Continued

PETITIONER/PLAINTIFF: RESPONDENT/DEFENDANT: OTHER PARENT:	CASE NUMBER:

10. My estimate of the other party's gross monthly income *(before taxes)* is . . . . $ _____

11. My current spouse's monthly income *(before taxes)* is . . . . $ _____

12. Other information I want the court to know concerning child support in my case *(attach extra sheet with the information)*.

13. ☐ I am attaching a copy of page 3 of form FL-150, *Income and Expense Declaration* showing my expenses.

I declare under penalty of perjury under the laws of the State of California that the information contained on all pages of this form and any attachments is true and correct.

Date:

_____
(TYPE OR PRINT NAME)

▶

_____
(SIGNATURE OF DECLARANT)

☐ PETITIONER/PLAINTIFF   ☐ RESPONDENT/DEFENDANT

INSTRUCTIONS

Step 1: Are you eligible to use this form? *If your answer is YES to any of the following questions, you may NOT use this form:*

- Are you asking for spousal support (alimony) or a change in spousal support?
- Is your spouse or former spouse asking for spousal support (alimony) or a change in spousal support?
- Are you asking the other party to pay your attorney fees?
- Is the other party asking you to pay his or her attorney fees?
- Do you receive money (income) from any source other than the following?

  - Welfare (such as TANF, GR, or GA)
  - Salary or wages
  - Disability
  - Unemployment

  - Interest
  - Workers' compensation
  - Social security
  - Retirement

- Are you self-employed?

If you are eligible to use this form and choose to do so, you do not need to complete the *Income and Expense Declaration* (form FL-150). Even if you are eligible to use this form, you may choose instead to use the *Income and Expense Declaration* (form FL-150).

Step 2: Make 2 copies of each of your pay stubs for the last two months. If you received money from other than wages or salary, include copies of the pay stub received with that money.
Privacy notice: If you wish, you may cross out your social security number if it appears on the pay stub, other payment notice or your tax return

Step 3: Make 2 copies of your most recent federal income tax form.

Step 4: Complete this form with the required information. Type the form if possible or complete it neatly and clearly in black ink. If you need additional room, please use plain or lined paper, 8½-by-11", and staple to this form.

Step 5: Make 2 copies of each side of this completed form and any attached pages.

Step 6: Serve a copy on the other party. Have someone other than yourself mail to the attorney for the other party, the other party, and the local child support agency, if they are handling the case, 1 copy of this form, 1 copy of each of your stubs for the last two months, and 1 copy of your most recent federal income tax return.

Step 7: File the original with the court. Staple this form with 1 copy of each of your pay stubs for the last two months. Take this document and give it to the clerk of the court. Check with your local court about how to submit your return.

Step 8: Keep the remaining copies of the documents for your file.

Step 9: Take the copy of your latest federal income tax return to the court hearing.

It is very important that you attend the hearings scheduled for this case. If you do not attend a hearing, the court may make an order without considering the information you want the court to consider.

FL-155 [Rev. January 1, 2004]   **FINANCIAL STATEMENT (SIMPLIFIED)**   Page 2 of 2

EXHIBIT 13–7 Sample custody affidavit.

FL-105/GC-120

ATTORNEY OR PARTY WITHOUT ATTORNEY *(Name, State Bar number, and address):*	FOR COURT USE ONLY

TELEPHONE NO.:   FAX NO. *(Optional):*

E-MAIL ADDRESS *(Optional):*

ATTORNEY FOR *(Name):*

SUPERIOR COURT OF CALIFORNIA, COUNTY OF

STREET ADDRESS:

MAILING ADDRESS:

CITY AND ZIP CODE:

BRANCH NAME:

PETITIONER:

RESPONDENT:

DECLARATION UNDER UNIFORM CHILD CUSTODY JURISDICTION AND ENFORCEMENT ACT (UCCJEA)	CASE NUMBER:

1. **I am a party** to this proceeding to determine custody of a child.
2. ☐ My present address is not disclosed. It is confidential under Family Code section 3429. I have listed the address of the children presently residing with me as confidential.
3. *(Number):* _____ minor children are subject to this proceeding as follows:
   (Insert the information requested below. The residence information must be given for the last FIVE years.)

a. Child's name		Place of birth	Date of birth	Sex
Period of residence	Address	Person child lived with *(name and present address)*		Relationship
to present	☐ Confidential			
to				
to				
to				
to				

b. Child's name		Place of birth	Date of birth	Sex
☐ Residence information is the same as given above for child a. *(If NOT the same, provide the information below.)*				
Period of residence	Address	Person child lived with *(name and present address)*		Relationship
to present	☐ Confidential			
to				
to				
to				

c. ☐ Additional children are listed on Attachment 3c. *(Provide all requested information for additional children.)*

Page 1 of 2

Form Approved for Optional Use
Judicial Council of California
FL-105/GC-120 [Rev. July 1, 2006]

DECLARATION UNDER UNIFORM CHILD CUSTODY JURISDICTION AND ENFORCEMENT ACT (UCCJEA)

Family Code, § 3400 et seq.
Probate Code, §§ 1510(f), 1512
www.courtinfo.ca.gov

American LegalNet, Inc.
www.USCourtForms.com

EXHIBIT 13–7 Continued

SHORT TITLE:	CASE NUMBER:

4. Have you participated as a party or a witness or in some other capacity in another litigation or custody proceeding, in California or elsewhere, concerning custody of a child subject to this proceeding?

　　☐ No ☐ Yes　*(If yes, provide the following information):*

　　a. Name of each child:

　　b. I was a: ☐ party ☐ witness ☐ other *(specify):*

　　c. Court *(specify name, state, location):*

　　d. Court order or judgment *(date):*

5. Do you have information about a custody proceeding pending in a California court or any other court concerning a child in this case, other than that stated in item 4?

　　☐ No ☐ Yes *(If yes, provide the following information):*

　　a. Name of each child:

　　b. Nature of proceeding: ☐ dissolution or divorce ☐ guardianship ☐ adoption ☐ other *(specify):*

　　c. Court *(specify name, state, location):*

　　d. Status of proceeding:

6. ☐ One or more domestic violence restraining /protective orders are now in effect. (Attach a copy of the orders if you have one.)
　　The orders are from the following court or courts *(specify county and state):*

　　a. ☐ Criminal: County/state: _____　c. ☐ Juvenile: County/state: _____
　　　Case No. *(if known):* _____　　　　　Case No. *(if known):* _____

　　b. ☐ Family: County/state: _____　d. ☐ Other: County/state: _____
　　　Case No. *(if known):* _____　　　　　Case No. *(if known):* _____

7. Do you know of any person who is not a party to this proceeding who has physical custody or claims to have custody of or visitation rights with any child in this case?

　　☐ No ☐ Yes *(If yes, provide the following information):*

a. Name and address of person	b. Name and address of person	c. Name and address of person
☐ Has physical custody ☐ Claims custody rights ☐ Claims visitation rights	☐ Has physical custody ☐ Claims custody rights ☐ Claims visitation rights	☐ Has physical custody ☐ Claims custody rights ☐ Claims visitation rights
Name of each child	Name of each child	Name of each child

I declare under penalty of perjury under the laws of the State of California that the foregoing is true and correct.

Date:

_____　　▶　_____
　　　　(TYPE OR PRINT NAME)　　　　　　　　　　　　(SIGNATURE OF DECLARANT)

8. ☐ Number of pages attached after this page:

NOTICE TO DECLARANT: You have a continuing duty to inform this court if you obtain any information about a custody proceeding in a California court or any other court concerning a child subject to this proceeding.

**DECLARATION UNDER UNIFORM CHILD CUSTODY
JURISDICTION AND ENFORCEMENT ACT (UCCJEA)**

EXHIBIT 13–8 Sample claim for relief.

DOCKET NO. FA 96-123456   : SUPERIOR COURT

BRONSON, RODNEY   : JUDICIAL DISTRICT OF NEW HAVEN

V.   : AT NEW HAVEN

BRONSON, EVELYN   : DECEMBER 8, 2005

DEFENDANT'S PROPOSED CLAIMS FOR RELIEF

1. **ALIMONY**—The parties each waive any right to alimony.

2. **REAL PROPERTY**—The marital home will be listed for sale and the parties shall divide the net proceeds equally.

3. **CUSTODY**—The parties shall share joint legal and physical custody of the minor children.

4. **PENSION**— The parties shall each retain their respective pensions.

THE DEFENDANT,
EVELYN BRONSON

BY: _____
GRACE A LUPPINO, ESQ.
HER ATTORNEY
555 MAIN AVENUE
NEW HAVEN, CT 06511
(203) 333-3333
JURIS NO. 160000

ORDER

The foregoing motion having been heard, it is hereby ORDERED:

GRANTED/DENIED
THE COURT

BY: _____
JUDGE

CERTIFICATION

This is to certify that a true copy of the foregoing motion was mailed, postage prepaid, on this date to all counsel and pro se parties of record on this _____ day of _____ , 2000, as follows:

Justine F. Miller
22 Park Place
New Haven, CT 06522

_____
Grace A. Luppino, Esq.
Commissioner of the Superior Court

EXHIBIT 13–9 Sample wage execution form for facilitating alimony and child support payments by means of automatic deductions.

☐ **ORDER/NOTICE TO WITHHOLD INCOME FOR CHILD SUPPORT**
☐ **NOTICE OF AN ORDER TO WITHHOLD INCOME FOR CHILD SUPPORT**

☐ Original   ☐ Amended   ☐ Termination   Date: _____

State/Tribe/Territory __Connecticut_____
City/Co./Dist./Reservation _____
☐ Non-governmental entity or individual _____
Case Number _____

_____	RE: _____
Employer's/Withholder's Name	Employee's/Obligor's Name (Last, First, MI)
_____	_____
Employer's/Withholder's Address	Employee's/Obligor's Social Security Number
_____	_____
_____	Employee's/Obligor's Case Identifier
_____	_____
Employer's/Withholder's Federal EIN Number (if known)	Obligee's Name (Last, First, MI)

ORDER INFORMATION - This Order is based on the support or withholding order from _____
You are required by law to deduct these amounts from the employee's/obligor's income until further notice.

$ _____ Per _____ current child support
$ _____ Per _____ past-due child support - Arrears greater than 12 weeks? ☐ yes   ☐ no
$ _____ Per _____ current cash medical support
$ _____ Per _____ past-due cash medical support
$ _____ Per _____ spousal support
$ _____ Per _____ past-due spousal support
$ _____ Per _____ other (specify) _____
for a total of $ _____ per _____ to be forwarded to the payee below.

You do not have to vary your pay cycle to be in compliance with the support order. If your pay cycle does not match the ordered payment cycle, withhold one of the following amounts:

$ _____ per weekly pay period. $ _____ per semimonthly pay period (twice a month).
$ _____ per biweekly pay period (every two weeks). $ _____ per monthly pay period.

REMITTANCE INFORMATION - When remitting payment, provide the pay date/date of withholding and the case identifier. If the employee's/obligor's principal place of employment is Connecticut, begin withholding no later than the first pay period occurring 14 days after the date of service or, in the case of a payer of income other than an employer, begin withholding no later than the date of periodic payment occurring 14 days after the date of service. Send payment within 7 working days of the pay date/date of withholding. The total withheld amount, including your fee, may not exceed _____ % of the employee's/obligor's aggregate disposable weekly earnings.

If the employee's/obligor's principal place of employment is not Connecticut, for limitations on withholding, applicable time requirements, and any allowable employer fees, follow the laws and procedures of the employee's/obligor's principal place of employment (see #3 and #9, ADDITIONAL INFORMATION TO EMPLOYERS AND OTHER WITHHOLDERS).

Make check payable to: **Connecticut - CCSPC** (Note: CCSPC is an abbreviation for Centralized Child Support Processing Center)
Send check to: **Connecticut - CCSPC, P.O. Box 990032, Hartford, CT 06199-0032**
If remitting payment by EFT/EDI, call **1-888-233-7223 (option 3)** before first submission. Use this FIPS code: **0900003**
Bank routing number code (EFT Payment): **ABA 053101626** Bank account number (EFT Payment): **2000013946793**

If this is an Order/Notice to Withhold:	**If this is a Notice of an Order to Withhold:**
Print Name _____	Print Name _____
Title of Issuing Official _____	Title (if appropriate) _____
Signature and Date _____	Signature and Date _____
☐ IV-D Agency ☐ Court	☐ Attorney ☐ Individual ☐ Private Entity
☐ Attorney with authority under state law to issue order/notice.	

NOTE: Non-IV-D Attorneys, individuals, and non-governmental entities must submit a Notice of an Order to Withhold and include a copy of the income withholding order unless, under a state's law, an attorney in that state may issue an income withholding order. In that case, the attorney may submit an Order/Notice to Withhold and include a copy of the state law authorizing the attorney to issue an income withholding order/notice.

IMPORTANT: The person completing this form is advised that the information on this form may be shared with the obligor.

JD-FM-1 Rev. 1/05 (OMB 0970-0154)   **Page 1 of 3**

EXHIBIT 13–9 Continued

CASE NO. *(To be completed by preparer)*

ADDITIONAL INFORMATION TO EMPLOYERS AND OTHER WITHHOLDERS

☐ If checked, you are required to provide a copy of this form to your employee/obligor. If your employee works in a state that is different from the state that issued this order, a copy must be provided to your employee/obligor even if the box is not checked.

1. **Priority:** Withholding under this Order or Notice has priority over any other legal process under state law (or tribal law, if applicable) against the same income. If there are federal tax levies in effect, please notify the contact person below. (See #10 below.)

2. **Combining Payments:** You may combine withheld amounts from more than one employee's/obligor's income in a single payment to each agency/party requesting withholding. You must, however, separately identify the portion of the single payment that is attributable to each employee/obligor.

3. **Reporting the Paydate/Date of Withholding:** You must report the paydate/date of withholding when sending the payment. The paydate/date of withholding is the date on which the amount was withheld from the employee's wages. You must comply with the law of the state of employee's/obligor's principal place of employment with respect to the time periods within which you must implement the withholding and forward the support payments.

4. **Employee/Obligor with Multiple Support Withholdings:** If there is more than one Order or Notice against this employee/obligor and you are unable to honor all support Orders or Notices due to federal, state or tribal withholding limits, you must follow the state or tribal law/procedure of the employee's/obligor's principal place of employment. You must honor all Orders or Notices to the greatest extent possible. (See #9 below.)

5. **Termination Notification:** You must promptly notify the Child Support Enforcement (IV-D) Agency and/or the contact person listed below when the employee/obligor no longer works for you. Please provide the information requested and return a complete copy of this Order or Notice to the Child Support Enforcement (IV-D) Agency and/or the contact person listed below. (See #10 below.)

THE EMPLOYEE/OBLIGOR NO LONGER WORKS FOR: _____

EMPLOYEE'S/OBLIGOR'S NAME: _____ CASE IDENTIFIER: _____

DATE OF SEPARATION FROM EMPLOYMENT: _____

LAST KNOWN HOME ADDRESS: _____

NEW EMPLOYER/ADDRESS: _____

6. **Lump Sum Payments:** You may be required to report and withhold from lump sum payments such as bonuses, commissions, or severance pay. If you have any questions about lump sum payments, contact the Child Support Enforcement (IV-D) Agency.

7. **Liability:** If you have any doubts about the validity of the Order or Notice, contact the agency or person listed below. (See #10 below.) If you fail to withhold income as the Order or Notice directs, you are liable for both the accumulated amount you should have withheld from the employee's/obligor's income and any other penalties set by state or tribal law/procedure. Pursuant to C.G.S. § 52-362(f), you have a legal duty to make deductions from the obligor's income and pay any amounts deducted as required by this withholding order. If you do not, legal action may be taken against you. If such an action is taken, you may be liable for the full amount not withheld since receipt of proper notice. You may also be subject to a finding of contempt by the court or family support magistrate for failure to honor any terms of this withholding order.

8. **Anti-discrimination:** You are subject to a fine determined under state or tribal law for discharging an employee/obligor from employment, refusing to employ, or taking disciplinary action against any employee/obligor because of a child support withholding. Pursuant to C.G.S. § 52-362(j), if the obligor is your employee, you must not discipline, suspend, or discharge him/her because this withholding order has been served upon you. If you do unlawfully take action against your employee, you may be liable to pay such employee all of his/her lost earnings and employment benefits from the time of your action to the time that the employee is reinstated. In addition, a fine up to one thousand dollars may be imposed on any employer who discharges from employment, refuses to employ, takes disciplinary action against or discriminates against an employee subject to a support order for withholding because of the existence of such withholding order and the obligations or additional obligations which it imposes upon the employer.

9. **Withholding Limits:** For state orders, you may not withhold more than the lesser of: 1) the amounts allowed by the Federal Consumer Credit Protection Act (CCPA) (15 U.S.C. § 1673(b)); or 2) the amounts allowed by the state of the employee's/obligor's principal place of employment. The federal limit applies to the aggregate disposable weekly earnings (ADWE). ADWE is the net income left after making mandatory deductions such as: state, federal, local taxes, Social Security taxes, statutory pension contributions, and Medicare taxes. The Federal CCPA limit is 50% of the ADWE for child support and alimony, which is increased by 1) 10% if the employee does not support a second family; and/or 2) 5% if arrears greater than 12 weeks. Pursuant to C.G.S. § 52-362, certain income of the obligor cannot be withheld to satisfy this withholding order. First, only "disposable income" may be subjected to this withholding. Disposable income for the purpose of this withholding order means that part of the earnings of an individual remaining after deduction from that income of amounts required to be withheld for the payment of federal, state, and local income taxes, employment taxes, normal retirement contributions, union dues and initiation fees, and group life and health insurance premiums. Second, 85% of the first $145.00 per week of disposable income are legally exempt from this withholding order. Use the table on page 3, SECTION II, to compute the obligor's disposable income each week and the amount available for withholding. See page 3, SECTION II, for additional information on computing withholding.

For tribal orders, you may not withhold more than the amounts allowed under the law of the issuing tribe. For tribal employers who receive a state order, you may not withhold more than the amounts allowed under the law of the state that issued the order.

Child(ren)'s Name(s) and Additional Information: _____

_____

10. If you or your employee/obligor have any questions, contact: _____

by telephone at _____ by FAX at _____

or by Internet at _____

EXHIBIT 13–9 Continued

CASE NO. *(To be completed by preparer)*

SECTION I *(To be completed by preparer)*

Support Category *("X" one)*

- [ ] **A.** Obligor is supporting a spouse or dependent child other than the spouse or child with respect to whose support the order is issued.
- [ ] **B.** Obligor is not supporting a spouse or dependent child other than the spouse or child with respect to whose support the order is issued.
- [ ] **C.** Obligor is supporting a spouse or dependent child other than the spouse or child with respect to whose support the order is issued AND there is an arrearage of greater than 12 weeks in length.
- [ ] **D.** Obligor is not supporting a spouse or dependent child other than the spouse or child with respect to whose support the order is issued AND there is an arrearage of greater than 12 weeks in length.

SECTION II *(To be completed by payer of income)*

ADDITIONAL INFORMATION FOR CONNECTICUT PAYERS OF INCOME

Pursuant to C.G.S. § 52-362, certain income of the obligor cannot be withheld to satisfy this withholding order. First, only "disposable income" may be subjected to this withholding. Disposable income for the purpose of this withholding order means that part of the earnings of an individual remaining after deduction from that income of amounts required to be withheld for the payment of federal, state and local income taxes, employment taxes, normal retirement contributions, union dues and initiation fees, and group life and health insurance premiums. Second, 85% of the first $145.00 per week of disposable income are legally exempt from this withholding order. Use the following table to compute the obligor's disposable income each week and the amount available for withholding.

1. Obligor's gross income per week.. $_____
2. Federal income tax withheld... $_____
3. Federal employment tax.. $_____
4. State income tax withheld .... $_____
5. Local income tax withheld... $_____
6. Normal retirement contribution .... $_____
7. Union dues and initiation fees.. $_____
8. Group life insurance premium.. $_____
9. Health insurance premium .... $_____
10. Total allowable deductions *(add lines 2-9)* .... $_____
11. WEEKLY DISPOSABLE INCOME *(subtract line 10 from line 1)*..................... $_____
12. Weekly Disposable Income minus 85% of the first $145.................. $_____
13. Refer to Support Category checked in SECTION I above and enter:

    50% of Weekly Disposable Income if box A is checked
    60% of Weekly Disposable Income if box B is checked } $_____
    55% of Weekly Disposable Income if box C is checked
    65% of Weekly Disposable Income if box D is checked

14. Amount available for withholding *(lesser of lines 12 and 13)* $_____

The instructions below must be followed to determine the amount of weekly withholding. Refer to "Order Information" on the first page of this "Order to Withhold Income for Child Support" and line 14 above.

15. **Amount of withholding - to be computed weekly:**
    Deduct weekly the total withholding order specified in the "Order Information" on the first page or the amount specified in line 14 above, whichever is less.

SECTION III *(To be completed by Clerk)*

TO ANY PROPER OFFICER: You are hereby ordered to make due service of this Order (3 pages) on the payer of income to the obligor named on the first page of the Order.

TO PAYER OF INCOME: You are hereby ordered to deduct from the income due the obligor named on the first page of the Order and to make payable as prescribed on the Order, the amount you calculated above. You are further ordered to comply with all other requirements of the Order.

DATE OF COURT ORDER	NAME OF JUDGE, FAMILY SUPPORT MAGISTRATE	
SIGNED *(Judge, Family Support Magistrate, Asst. Clerk, SEO, Authorized DSS Personnel)*		DATE SIGNED

EXHIBIT 13–9 Continued

ADVISEMENT OF RIGHTS

Re: Income Withholding

I. You have the right to present any evidence to the court as to why an order for withholding effective immediately should not be ordered.

II. EXEMPTIONS: If your income is subject to a withholding order, a portion of your income will not be withheld. Only disposable income is subject to a withholding order. Disposable income means that part of the income of an individual remaining after deduction from that income of amounts required to be withheld for the payment of federal, state and local income taxes, employment taxes, normal retirement contributions, union dues and initiation fees and group life and health insurance premiums. The amount withheld may not exceed the maximum amount permitted under section 1673 of title 15 of the United States Code: If you are supporting a spouse or dependent child other than the spouse or child with respect to whose support the order is issued, the maximum amount of your disposable income that may be withheld is 50% of such income, unless you are twelve weeks or more in arrears in which case the maximum is 55% of such income. If you are not supporting a spouse or dependent child other than the spouse or child with respect to whose support the order is issued, the maximum amount of your disposable income that may be withheld is 60% of such income unless you are twelve weeks or more in arrears in which case the maximum is 65%. In no event, however, under state law may you be left with less than 85% of the first $145 of disposable income per week.

III. You have the right to claim the exemptions listed above or any other applicable state or federal exemptions with respect to income withholding orders.

IV. The computation of the amount withheld will be done by the payer of the income based on information supplied by the court. If you believe that an incorrect amount of your income is being withheld due to incorrect information being supplied to the payer of the income and you would like the amount withheld modified, you must request a court hearing.

V. You have a right to seek a modification of, or raise a defense to, the support order by filing a proper motion with the court.

This is to certify that this document was read to me or read by me in a language that I understand. A copy of this statement has been given to me.

_____   _____
Signature   Date

This is to attest that the above document was signed in my presence.

_____   _____
Signature/Title   Date

Check the box below if the parties have completed the "Waiver" on the back/page 2 of this form.

☐ "Waiver of Right to Immediate Income Withholding Order" completed on back/page 2.

JD-FM-71 Rev. 6-03
C.G.S. § 52-362

EXHIBIT 13–9 Continued

WAIVER OF RIGHT TO IMMEDIATE INCOME WITHHOLDING ORDER

NAME OF CASE			DOCKET NO.	

The undersigned parties agree that a contingent and not an immediate income withholding order shall issue in this case.

OBLIGOR	DATE SIGNED	OBLIGEE		DATE SIGNED
OTHER	DATE SIGNED	OTHER		DATE SIGNED
WITNESS	DATE SIGNED	WITNESS		DATE SIGNED

EXHIBIT 13–10 Sample form for collecting statistical information about divorcing couples.

DISSOLUTION OF MARRIAGE REPORT

JD-FM-181 Rev. 10-06
P.B. § 25-58

STATE OF CONNECTICUT
SUPERIOR COURT
www.jud.ct.gov

INSTRUCTIONS
1. To be completed by the Attorney for the Plaintiff or, if Pro Se, by the Plaintiff.
2. Clerk to complete section 2.

PART 1 *(To be completed by Attorney for the Plaintiff)*

HUSBAND

NAME OF HUSBAND *(First, middle, last)*

USUAL RESIDENCE *(Number and street)* | CITY OR TOWN

COUNTY | STATE | BIRTHPLACE *(State or Foreign Country)* | DATE OF BIRTH *(Mo., Day, Year)*

WIFE

NAME OF WIFE *(First, middle, last)* | MAIDEN NAME *(Last name only)*

USUAL RESIDENCE *(Number and street)* | CITY OR TOWN

COUNTY | STATE | BIRTHPLACE *(State or Foreign Country)* | DATE OF BIRTH *(Mo., Day, Year)*

MARITAL HISTORY

PLACE OF THIS MARRIAGE *(City)* | COUNTY | STATE

DATE OF MARRIAGE *(Mo., Day, Year)* | APPROXIMATE DATE COUPLE SEPARATED *(Month, Year)*

NUMBER OF CHILDREN BORN ALIVE OF THIS MARRIAGE | NUMBER OF CHILDREN STILL LIVING | NUMBER OF CHILDREN UNDER 18 YEARS OF AGE

PLAINTIFF ☐ HUSBAND ☐ WIFE | CSSD FAMILY SERVICES EVALUATION ☐ YES ☐ NO | CSSD FAMILY SERVICES MEDIATION ☐ YES ☐ NO

PUBLIC ASSISTANCE RECIPIENT ☐ YES ☐ NO | AMOUNT OF ASSISTANCE MONTHLY

ATTORNEY FOR MINOR CHILD(REN) ☐ YES ☐ NO | GUARDIAN AD LITEM FOR MINOR CHILD(REN) ☐ YES ☐ NO

ATTORNEY FOR PLAINTIFF (IF APPLICABLE) *(Name)* | ATTORNEY'S ADDRESS (IF APPLICABLE) *(No., street, city, state, zip code)*

INFORMATION FOR STATISTICAL PURPOSES ONLY: (To be completed by Attorney for the Plaintiff or, if Pro Se, by the Plaintiff)

RACE *(White, Black, Native American, etc., specify)*	NO. OF THIS MARRIAGE *(First, Second, etc. specify)*	IF PREVIOUSLY MARRIED, HOW MANY ENDED BY		EDUCATION - SPECIFY HIGHEST GRADE COMPLETED		
		DEATH	DIVORCE OR ANNULMENT	ELEMENTARY *(0,1,2,3, thru 8)*	HIGH SCHOOL *(1,2,3, or 4)*	COLLEGE *(1,2,3, 4 or 5+)*
HUSBAND	FOR HUSBAND	FOR HUSBAND	FOR HUSBAND	HUSBAND	HUSBAND	HUSBAND
WIFE	FOR WIFE	FOR WIFE	FOR WIFE	WIFE	WIFE	WIFE

PART 2 *(To be completed by the Clerk of Superior Court)*

DECREE

DATE OF DECREE *(Mo., Day, Year)* | TYPE OF DECREE ☐ ABSOLUTE DIVORCE ☐ ANNULMENT | DATE WRIT RETURNABLE *(Month, Year)*

COUNTY OF DECREE | DOCKET NO. FA | LEGAL GROUNDS FOR DISSOLUTION *(Specify)*

CASE CONTESTED ☐ YES ☐ NO | CUSTODY OF MINOR CHILDREN TO ☐ HUSBAND ☐ WIFE ☐ JOINT ☐ NOT APPLICABLE

DECREE GRANTED TO ☐ HUSBAND ☐ WIFE | TITLE OF OFFICIAL | SIGNED *(Clerk or Assistant Clerk)*

EXHIBIT 13–11 Sample judgment in a divorce trial.

1   At the *Matrimonial/IAS* Part _____
                                                          of New York State Supreme Court at
2   the Courthouse, _____
3   County, on _____.

Present:

4   Hon. _____ *Justice/Referee*
     --X

5

6   Plaintiff,   Index No.: _____
                                                      Calendar No.: _____
     -against-
                                                      JUDGMENT OF DIVORCE

7   Defendant.
     --X

8   This action was submitted to *the referee / this court* for consideration this date (on inquest

of _____).

9   The Defendant was served   *personally/by publication/pursuant to court order dated*

_____ *within/outside*   the State of New York.

10   Plaintiff presented a verified complaint.

11   The Defendant has   *not appeared and is in default   /   appeared and waived his or her*

right to answer.

12   The Court accepted   *written/oral*   proof of non-military service.

13   The Plaintiff's address is _____, and social security

number is _____. The Defendant's address is _____,

and social security number is _____.

14   Now on motion of _____, the   *attorney for*   Plaintiff, it is:

15   ORDERED AND ADJUDGED that the Referee's Report, if any, is confirmed, and it is

further

(Form UD-11)

EXHIBIT 13–11 Continued

16   ORDERED AND ADJUDGED that   *Plaintiff/Defendant*   shall have a judgment

dissolving the marriage on the evidence found in the Findings of Fact and Conclusions of Law based

upon DRL §170 subd. _____, and it is further

17   ORDERED AND ADJUDGED that   *Plaintiff/Defendant*   shall have custody of the

children of the marriage, i.e.:

18   <u>Name</u>   <u>Date <u>of</u> Birth</u>

            _____   _____

            _____   _____

            _____   _____

            and it is further

19   ORDERED AND ADJUDGED that the existing Family Court Order(s) under Index No(s).

_____ shall be continued.

20   ORDERED AND ADJUDGED that   *Plaintiff/Defendant*   shall pay to *Plaintiff/Defendant*

the sum of _____ per *week/month* for maintenance commencing on _____ and

on _____ *day of each week/the first day of each month*   thereafter, and it is further

21   ORDERED AND ADJUDGED that   *Plaintiff/Defendant*   shall pay to *Plaintiff/Defendant*

the sum of _____ per *week/month* for child support commencing on _____ and

on _____ *day of each week/the first day of each month*   thereafter, and it is further

22   ORDERED AND ADJUDGED that   *Plaintiff/Defendant*   shall pay to *Plaintiff/Defendant*

the sum of _____ per *week/month* for child care expenses as follows:_____

_____, and it is further

23   ORDERED AND ADJUDGED that   *Plaintiff/Defendant*   shall pay to *Plaintiff/Defendant*

the sum of _____ per *week/month*   for future   reasonable   health   care   as   follows:

_____, and it is further

(Form UD-11)

EXHIBIT 13–11 Continued

24   ORDERED AND ADJUDGED that *Plaintiff/Defendant* shall pay to *Plaintiff/Defendant*

the sum of _____ per *week/month* for *present/future post-secondary / private / special /*

enriched education for the children as follows: _____,

and it is further

25   ORDERED AND ADJUDGED that this Judgment of Divorce shall serve as a Qualified

Medical Support Order where a child support determination is being made, and it is further

26   ORDERED AND ADJUDGED that the minor children shall be enrolled and entitled to

receive health insurance benefits as described below:

_____

_____

_____

27   ORDERED AND ADJUDGED that the relative legally responsible to supply health

insurance benefits is:

_____

_____

_____

28   ORDERED AND ADJUDGED that the relative legally responsible to supply health insurance

benefits is eligible under the following available group health plan or plans:

_____

_____

_____

_____

and shall provide health insurance benefits to the minor children *until the minor children reach the*

age of _____ / *until* _____.

29   ORDERED AND ADJUDGED that the *agreement/stipulation* dated _____,

a copy which is attached, and incorporated by reference into this judgment shall *survive and not*

(Form UD-11)

EXHIBIT 13–11 Continued

merge/not survive and merge in this judgment, and the parties hereby are directed to comply with

every legally enforceable term and provision of such *agreement/stipulation;* and it is further

30   ORDERED AND ADJUDGED that the Family Court shall be granted concurrent jurisdiction

with the Supreme Court with respect to the issues of maintenance, child support, custody and

visitation, and it is further

31   ORDERED AND ADJUDGED that *(insert any transfers of monies, property or mandates*

*of the court that may need enforcement):*_____

_____

_____

32   ORDERED AND ADJUDGED that either party may resume the use of a pre-marriage name

as follows _____.

33   Dated:
                              ENTER:

                                        _____
                                             J.S.C./Referee

                                        _____
                                             CLERK

(Form UD-11)

EXHIBIT 13–11 Continued

1 SUPREME COURT OF THE STATE OF NEW YORK
COUNTY OF _____
---X

2,3   Index No.:_____
                       Plaintiff.

        -against-
                                   NOTICE OF ENTRY

4
                       Defendant.
---X
STATE OF NEW YORK   }
                           ss:
5   COUNTY OF_____   }

         PLEASE TAKE NOTICE that the attached is a true copy of a judgment of divorce in

6 this matter that was entered in the Office of the Clerk of the Supreme Court, _____

7 County, on the _____ day of _____, 20____.

8 Date:_____
9   _____
                                   Plaintiff

10   _____
                               _____
                               _____
                               _____
                               Address

11 TO:

_____
Defendant/Attorney for Defendant

_____
_____
_____
_____
      Address

(Form UD-12)

END OF CHAPTER EXERCISES

Crossword Puzzle

Across

2. a sworn statement of the income, expense, assets, and liabilities of the parties in a divorce case

4. required to be filed under the Soldiers and Sailors Relief Act

7. disputed divorce trial

8. a confidential, structured process in which a neutral third party assists the parties in resolving their differences and reaching an agreement

9. a team approach to divorce dispute resolution in which both parties agrue to collaborate on resolving the matter and that they will not litigate.

10. a method of resolving disputes between parties without resorting to a trial

11. a trial conducted before a judge with no jury

12. a plainlanguage, nonbinding document containing the agreement of the parties on the various issues relevant to their case, prepared by a lawyer-mediator

13. a meeting with the judge scheduled to preside over a contested matter, as well as the attorneys and their clients; the purpose of this meeting is to assist the parties in reaching an agreement on some or all of the issues in the case to either avoid a trial or narrow down the matters that need to be litigated

14. the parties will meet separately with the mediator, who shuttles between the parties trying to broker an agreement

15. a meeting with both lawyers and their respective clients with the specific goal being to settle the case without court intervention

Down

1. a term describing an unfair or one-sided agreement

3. a divorce trial in which one of parties has failed to appear despite having received notice of the proceedings

5. an opinion rendered by an arbitrator

6. a model arbitration act passed by most jurisdictions that which strictly limits appeals of arbitrated matters

Review Questions

1. Name and describe the forms of alternative dispute resolution discussed in this chapter.

2. If you and your spouse were getting divorced, what form of dispute resolution would you use? Explain your reasons for choosing this option.

3. What is the paralegal's role in alternative dispute resolution?

4. What is the paralegal's role at the trial?

5. How does the trial notebook assist the attorney at trial?

Case for Briefing

PATEL v. PATEL , 359 S.C. 515, 599 S.E.2d 114 (2004) (An interesting case that took eight years and thousands of dollars to resolve!)

Exploring the Workplace: Activities

1. Search the Internet and determine the various documents that must be filed in your state at a divorce trial.

2. Read *"Deconstructing the Divorce Mediation Process: One Practitioner's Approach,"* by Anju

D. Jessani, at **http://www. divorcesource. com/NJ/ARTICLES/ jessani17.html** and explain what actually happens during the divorce mediation process.

3. Go to **http://www.adrlawinfo.com/familydivorce.html** and find your jurisdiction's statutes on divorce mediation. Explain the mediation options available in your state.

4. Read and summarize the *Model Standards for Family Divorce Mediation* at **http://www. adrlawinfo.com/familydivorce.html**

5. You work as a paralegal for the Law Office of Peter Panzarella, an attorney and divorce mediator in your state. Delores and Arthur Fleming have retained the services of Attorney Panzarella to mediate their custody issues. Both parties wish to avoid the costs of a contested divorce trial and resolve their dispute amicably for their children's sake. Using the sample mediation agreements found at the following websites, draft a mediation agreement in this case.

http://www.divorcemediation.norwalk.ct. us/mediation agreement.htm
http://www.smartmediator.com/pg1030.cfm

CHAPTER

14

Postjudgment Divorce Matters

KEY TERMS

arrearage

modification

contempt citation

forum shopping

motion for contempt

motion to modify

motion to modify alimony

motion to modify child support

motion to modify custody

motion to modify visitation

motion to open the judgment

nonmodifiable

order to show cause

Parental Kidnapping
Prevention Act (PKPA)

postjudgment matters

substantial change in
circumstances

Uniform Child Custody
Jurisdiction Act (UCCJA)

Uniform Child Custody
Jurisdiction and Enforcement
Act (UCCJEA)

Uniform Interstate Family
Support Act (UIFSA)

The entry of a final dissolution decree does not always end the litigation in a particular case. A spouse ordered to pay alimony or child support may cease making payments, either voluntarily or involuntarily. The circumstances of the parties may have also changed substantially since the date of the original divorce decree, thus requiring a change in the original order.

A large part of a family lawyer's practice involves **postjudgment matters.** Hence, this chapter focuses on postjudgment matters, which consist of **modifications** to an original order, enforcement of court orders, and motions to open the judgment. Appeals are also postjudgment matters, but because appeals are covered in basic civil litigation courses they are not addressed here.

The dissolution decree contains some provisions that constitute the final resolution of an issue, and hence cannot be modified. Other provisions are modifiable and are subject to the court's continuing jurisdiction until certain events occur.

NONMODIFIABLE TERMS OF THE DISSOLUTION DECREE

A final decree of dissolution usually contains a section that deals with the distribution of marital assets or property. The separation agreement sets forth a final unappealable disposition of assets. Therefore, property distribution awards are **nonmodifiable.** If parties agree that one spouse will transfer all of his or her right and title to the family residence, once this agreement is made a part of the divorce judgment, the transferring party usually may not come back at a later date to modify or reverse this arrangement. Only if a spouse alleges and can prove fraud in the making of the divorce agreement will the court consider reopening and modifying the disposition of issues deemed final and nonmodifiable. This will require the aggrieved spouse to file a **motion to open the judgment,** requesting that a new trial be granted.

If alimony is awarded as a one-time lump sum and is labeled nonmodifiable in the divorce decree, then the spouse paying the lump sum is released from any future obligation to provide maintenance or support for the ex-spouse regardless of her future need for assistance, no matter how urgent. Lump-sum alimony is nonmodifiable even if it is to be paid in installments. If lump sum alimony is to be paid in installments, and the separation agreement or judgment of the court specifies the number of installments to be paid and the amount of each such installment, the court may determine that a modification of the payment arrangement is necessary to avoid substantial financial hardship for the payer. In making that determination the courts will look for a substantial change in the circumstances of the payer, such as loss of employment, loss of income-generating assets that are not the result of the payer's intentional alienation or dissipation of these assets, and changes in a child support obligation based upon a change in the circumstances of the party or the "deviation" criteria that result in an upward deviation of the child support obligation.

EXCEPTIONAL CIRCUMSTANCES UNDER WHICH NONMODIFIABLE TERMS OF THE DISSOLUTION DECREE HAVE BEEN MODIFIED

There have been infrequent but significant instances where a court has granted a party's motion to modify a clause or term of the separation agreement or dissolution decree that was originally deemed nonmodifiable.

This is especially true where a separation agreement has provided that the alimony obligation is nonmodifiable as to the amount. Either a substantial change in the circumstances of one of the parties or a significant increase in the cost of living since the entry of the judgment would be a compelling reason for the court to override the nonmodifiability provision of an alimony order. There have also been instances where the court has overridden the clause regarding nonmodifiability of the term of alimony when the payee spouse has developed a severe medical problem, can no longer work, and still has minor children.

CONTROLLING PROVISIONS OF STATE OR FEDERAL LAW AND THE EFFECT ON NONMODIFIABILITY OF CHANGES IN THESE LAWS

The operation of provisions in federal or state law or changes in federal or state law may result in the modifiability of provisions of a dissolution judgment that previously was nonmodifiable.

In the early 1980s the U.S. Supreme Court held that federal law precluded state courts from dividing military retirement benefits under state community property laws. (See *McCarty v. McCarty*, 453 U.S. 210, 101 S.Ct. 2728, 69 L.Ed.2d 589 (1981). Subsequently, the Uniformed Services Former Spouses Protection Act (USFSPA), 10 U.S.C. §1408 was enacted by Congress. Contained within the USFSPA was a specific provision that allowed for the retroactive application of the law, changing the status of military retirement benefits to divisible. As a result, those individuals whose judgments of dissolution had entered between the time *McCarty* was decided and the enactment of the USFSPA were granted the right to seek a portion of the military retirement benefits. However, it is noted that it is within the sound discretion of the court to determine whether such a modification should be granted. Though this is an extremely rare circumstance, it may in the future occur again.

STATUTORY PROVISIONS THAT CONTROL IN THE ABSENCE OF A SPECIFIC WAIVER

In any situation regarding the obligations of one spouse to another for alimony that fails to include a triggering event that would terminate said alimony, statutory provisions relating to the modification or termination of alimony shall control. In *In Re: Marriage of Thornton*, 95 Cal.App. 4th 251 (2002), the court held that the omission of express language regarding the termination of alimony upon remarriage did not prevent the payer husband from obtaining an order terminating the alimony obligation as of the date of the wife's remarriage because California law specifically requires that any waiver of the statutory provisions must be in writing.

MODIFIABLE TERMS OF THE DISSOLUTION DECREE

Let's now take a look at the terms of a dissolution decree that can be modified.

MODIFICATION OF ALIMONY

In determining the modifiability of alimony, the parties must look to the original alimony award. The original award was either agreed on by the parties in a separation agreement or ordered by the court in a contested hearing where the parties could not agree on the issue of alimony. The court can modify alimony unless it is barred from doing so under the separation agreement or decree of dissolution.

If an order for alimony requires a spouse to pay the other spouse a fixed amount of money periodically, such as every week or every month, either the paying spouse or the receiving spouse may bring the matter back to the court to request either an increase or a decrease in the periodic amount ordered. In either case, the moving party will usually allege, as grounds, a change in their circumstances or a change in the other party's circumstances. The moving party must prove that since the date of the original order, there has been a **substantial change in circumstances** requiring a modification of the original order.

If either party waived alimony at the time of the dissolution, they are forever barred from returning to court and asking for alimony in the future. If a party was awarded nominal alimony of one dollar per year, this will allow the recipient spouse to return to court at a later date and request a modification of the original one-dollar alimony award. If a party was awarded rehabilitative alimony, either the separation agreement or court order after trial will indicate its modifiability. Reimbursement alimony is typically nonmodifiable since modifiability would defeat the purpose of "reimbursing" a spouse.

Arrearages, or amounts of unpaid alimony due to the recipient spouse, are nonmodifiable. A recipient spouse has a vested property right in the arrearage that cannot be changed by the court.

Motion to Modify Alimony

A party brings his or her request to the court's attention by filing a **motion to modify** the court's previous alimony order. (See Exhibits 14–1 and 14–2.) In this motion, the moving party alleges that a substantial change in circumstances has occurred since the date of the original decree, requiring the court to reopen the case and modify its original order.

In many jurisdictions, if a party files this motion within six months after the entry of the dissolution decree, the party need only file the motion with the court and serve, by mail, a copy of the motion to the attorney who represented the other spouse in the dissolution action. This avoids the need for service of the motion by a sheriff. The attorney must also serve by mail a copy on the attorney for the children if the children were represented by counsel in the action.

If more than six months has elapsed, the moving party must serve additional documents on the ex-spouse, along with the motion to modify. In many jurisdictions, the moving spouse must serve an **order to show cause** on the ex-spouse (See Exhibit 14–1). This document must usually be personally served by a sheriff or other individual authorized to serve process. The **motion to modify alimony** will accompany the rule to show cause, which will already have identified a hearing date set by the court clerk. Some courts have preprinted forms and simplified procedures, allowing parties to appear *pro se.* (See Exhibit 14–2.)

After service is complete, the papers must be filed with the court and an entry fee must be paid, the amount of which depends on the jurisdiction. Sheriff's fees and attorney's fees must also be paid by the client. Therefore, bringing an action to modify parts of the divorce judgment can be costly.

Grounds for Modification of Alimony

Grounds for all modifications are broadly known as a substantial change in circumstance. What constitutes a substantial change? In matters relating to alimony, changed circumstances refers to an actual or assumed change in the financial status or capability of either party. For instance, if a spouse-husband was earning a high salary when the alimony order was entered and he subsequently loses his job and now works for a much lower rate, he can move to have the court lower the amount previously ordered based on his loss of ability to pay. Similarly, if a spouse-wife was receiving alimony and had a high-paying job that she had to leave because of illness, she may petition the court to increase the amount her ex-husband must pay to her.

When the court addresses a request to modify alimony, the court looks at the financial status of each of the parties and tries to make a decision that is reasonable under the circumstances. Both spouses are expected to provide for themselves according to ability to do so. If a spouse, male or female, has been making alimony payments consistent with the court order to an able-bodied nonworking spouse and the paying spouse suddenly—say, through a significant job promotion—experiences a large increase in earned income, the nonworking spouse may bring a motion to modify alimony upward. The court, however, may find that since the nonworking spouse never sought employment, the previous award sufficiently satisfied the spouse's financial need and that the other spouse should not be penalized because his or her ability and hard work has resulted in greater financial remuneration.

The change in circumstances must also be involuntary. If, for example, a husband ordered to pay alimony voluntarily quits his job and then shows up in court with a motion to modify alimony, the court will not be very sympathetic. If a recipient spouse runs up charges on a credit card, she cannot later come in to court and ask for a modification, since she created the financial problem.

The following circumstances may constitute sufficient grounds for modification of alimony:

- deteriorating health of the payer or recipient spouse,
- increased cost of living,
- loss of employment,
- remarriage or cohabitation of recipient spouse,
- pay raises,
- winning the lottery,
- retirement,
- employment changes (i.e., downsizing),
- rehabilitation of recipient spouse, and
- unforeseen economic circumstances.

MODIFICATION OF CHILD SUPPORT

The court has continuing jurisdiction in child support matters and may entertain modifications until its jurisdiction ends. The family court has the right to order child support for each child until the child reaches the age of majority. As with alimony, a custodial parent may file a **motion to modify child support** if that spouse can prove a substantial change in circumstances since the date of the original order. A noncustodial parent paying child support may also move to modify an existing court order if he can prove a change in circumstances. The moving party must file motions similar to those discussed in the earlier section regarding modification of alimony. If a modification is warranted, the court will make the change in the child support award pursuant to that jurisdiction's child support guidelines. Child support arrearages, however, are unmodifiable.

When addressing a motion to decrease the amount obligated to pay, the court usually does not extinguish the arrearage and will order that continuing payments, whether the same or lower, include an additional amount to pay off any unpaid back alimony or child support. Alternately, the court may order that the total of the back amounts owed be paid to the recipient spouse within a reasonable time, such as thirty or sixty days.

The following circumstances may constitute sufficient grounds for modification of child support:

- cost of living increases—as children grow, their expenses increase (i.e., clothing, food, extracurricular activities),
- custody change—if the noncustodial parent moves for custody and prevails,
- an increase or decrease in either parent's income,
- change in the child's health requiring unusual or extraordinary expenses, and
- increased or onset of costs for special education, tutoring, or day care.

Substantial Change in Circumstances and Child Support Orders

The State of Connecticut has established a "rule of thumb" to determine whether a party seeking a modification of child support orders has met the "substantial change of circumstances" criteria for a modification. The rule of thumb is that there must be a 15 percent change in the support obligation itself, not the income of either or both of the parties. It would be advisable for a paralegal to know whether the state in which he is practicing has such a rule of thumb and, if so, what the rule says.

Modification of Custody and Visitation

Custody and visitation orders are always modifiable. The courts, however, will not disturb a custody or visitation order unless the moving party can prove that there has been a substantial change in circumstances *and* that a modification to the existing custody or visitation situation is in the best interest of the child or that the court did not have certain facts available at the time of entering the original order of custody. The substantial change of circumstances must have occurred after the date of the original order. The court will not entertain any evidence that has already been introduced at the divorce trial. New evidence must be such that justifies a **motion to modify custody** or a **motion to modify visitation;** the court will not tolerate a disgruntled parent retrying the custody matter through the mask of a modification.

The following circumstances may constitute sufficient grounds for modification of custody or visitation:

- the child becomes old enough to choose a custodian,
- either parent's remarriage or cohabitation,
- a change in the child's needs,
- the parent's lifestyle adversely affecting the child,

- a parent's or child's health issues,
- abuse or neglect, and
- the custodial parent's relocation.

In some states, a guardian ad litem or attorney for the minor child, appointed or retained during the *pendent lite* period, may be ordered to continue in that capacity for so long as the court shall have jurisdiction over issues of custody and visitation.

In January 2006, the State of Connecticut added to its Rules of Court a requirement that a party seeking postjudgement modification of orders relating to custody, visitation, or parental responsibility shall append a Request for Leave (see Exhibit 14–1) to the motion. In addition, the Rules require that a sworn statement of the moving party or other individual having personal knowledge reciting the factual and legal basis for the requested modification also be filed. (See Conn. Rules of Court §25-26[g]). This was enacted in order to allow the court to make a preliminary determination of whether the motion for modification had merit, thereby stemming the tide of frivolous motions.

RELOCATION OF CUSTODIAL PARENT

Because mobility is a characteristic of our society today, many dissolution decrees anticipate the possible relocation of a custodial parent and the consequences. Many dissolution decrees provide that a custodial parent may not move out of the jurisdiction without giving the noncustodial parent sufficient advance notice so that the noncustodial parent will have sufficient time if he or she desires to bring this proposed move to the attention of the court and object to this move as being contrary to the child's best interest. If the noncustodial parent brings such a motion before the court, the matter may be referred to the family relations division for a study and recommendation to the court. The noncustodial parent's chances of prevailing will be greater if that parent demonstrates the strength and value of the child's relationship with the noncustodial parent and with other significant individuals within the jurisdiction such as grandparents or uncles and aunts. On the other hand, if the noncustodial parent has played only an inconsistent and erratic role in the child's life, the court may not find that the child's best interests will be compromised by an out-of-state move.

In the past, in a decree for divorce or dissolution, a judge would sometimes order the custodial parent not to move out of the state with the children. While the parent was free to travel as he or she pleased, the children could not be moved out of the jurisdiction. Unfortunately, life isn't that simple and circumstances arise requiring a return to court to address the original order barring relocation. Let's say the mother is the custodial parent and her original decree states that she shall not remove the children from the state. Mother remarries and her new spouse is offered a job in another state. Mother must return to court to get permission to take the children out of the state or she will be in contempt of court. The court now must address the issue of relocation pursuant to a two-prong test:

1. Is the original decree modifiable?
2. If modifiable, is the relocation in the best interest of the children?

The court must look at the original decree and determine if the court-ordered limitation on the custodial parent's freedom to relocate with the children is modifiable or whether the original order was a final, nonmodifiable, nonappealable part of the judgment, as is the case with the distribution of marital assets. While child custody is always modifiable, the issue of one parent relocating with the children may be limited by the court in that it deprives the other parent of contact and access to the children. The burden is on the moving party to prove to the court whether the original decree is modifiable. A review of the original decree and/or transcript may reveal that the issue is explicitly addressed and there is no dispute as to its modifiability. If the issue is unclear, then the court must make a decision based on the evidence offered and arguments of the parties. In the case illustrated earlier, if the decree is deemed nonmodifiable, the relocation of the children is barred. If modifiable, then the court moves to the second prong of the test, which is determining if the relocation is in the best interest of the children.

If the custodial parent prevails on the argument that the limitation on the custodial parent's freedom to have the child take up residence out of state is modifiable, then the burden falls on the noncustodial parent to demonstrate that such a move would not be in the child's best interest. At this point, the custodial parent may offer evidence to refute the noncustodial parent's evidence that such a move would compromise the child's best interest and the custodial parent may introduce evidence that such a move will enhance the child's best interest.

STATUTES

Regulations regarding the relocation of a custodial parent have recently been legislated and will soon be codified as a part of the Connecticut General Statutes.

CONNECTICUT PUBLIC ACT (P.A. 06-168)

An Act Concerning the Relocation of Parents Having Custody of Minor Children (Effective October 1, 2006).

(a) In any proceeding before the Superior Court arising after the entry of a judgment awarding custody of a minor child and involving the relocation of either parent with the child, where such relocation would have a significant impact on an existing parenting plan, the relocating parent shall bear the burden of proving, by a preponderance of the evidence, that (1) the relocation is for a legitimate purpose, (2) the proposed location is reasonable in light of such purpose, and (3) the relocation is in the best interests of the child.

(b) In determining whether to approve the relocation of the child under subsection

(a) of this section, the court shall consider but such consideration shall not be limited to: (1) Each parent's reasons for seeking or opposing the relocation; (2) the quality of the relationships between the child and each parent; (3) the impact of the relocation on the quantity and quality of the child's future contact with the nonrelocating parent; (4) the degree to which the relocating parent's and the child's life may be enhanced economically, emotionally, and educationally by the relocation; and (5) the feasibility of preserving the relationship between the nonrelocating parent and the child through suitable visitation arrangements.

This act, once codified, represents a deviation from the prior case law which governed the burden of proof in relocation cases. In *Ireland v. Ireland*, 246 Conn. 413 (1998) the Connecticut Supreme Court determined the appropriate burdens of proof for each of the parties. In *Ireland*, once the relocating parent made a *prima facie* showing of the first two criteria set forth in subsection (a) above, the burden shifted to the nonrelocating parent to show, by a preponderance of the evidence, that the relocation was not in the best interests of the minor child.

ENFORCEMENT OF COURT ORDERS

If the court has ordered a spouse to make periodic payments of alimony or child support and the spouse ceases to make these payments, the other spouse may file a motion for contempt to bring this matter to the court's attention. Enforcement of child support orders was addressed in Chapter 8.

If a party fails to make court-ordered payments, the receiving spouse should first write a letter to the paying spouse stating the arrearage owed and demanding payment of that arrearage. If that does not get a response and the party continues to fail to comply with a court order, the receiving spouse may bring this to the court's attention by filing a **motion for contempt** or **contempt citation.** (See Exhibits 14–3 and 14–4.) In family law disputes, common motions for contempt include motions for contempt for failure to pay alimony or child support or motions for contempt against the custodial parent for withholding visitation from the noncustodial parent, or motion for contempt against the noncustodial parent for not complying with visitation orders by bringing the child back late, picking the child up late, or engaging in inappropriate activities while the child is visiting.

Sometimes, one or the other party may not be happy with the visitation arrangements under a court order that provided only for the "right of reasonable visitation." What is "reasonable" is a subjective judgment—what one party thinks is reasonable, the other party may not. Therefore, the unhappy party may not be successful in proving that the other party is in contempt of the court order. Therefore, a motion for contempt is not the appropriate legal vehicle to use in resolving this matter. Instead, one party or the other may file a motion to modify visitation and ask the court to modify its ruling from "reasonable visitation" to a definite schedule for weekly visitation and a specific visitation schedule for holidays, school year vacations, and summer vacations. This is usually needed when the parties are unable to resolve these types of issues on their own.

CHILD SUPPORT ENFORCEMENT REMEDIES

Many states, including West Virginia, Colorado, and Oregon, have enacted legislation whereby nonpayment of support can result in a criminal contempt proceeding against the delinquent obligor.

In 1997 the federal government enacted the **Uniform Interstate Family Support Act (UIFSA)** (see Appendix D), which has been adopted by all fifty states, Washington D.C., and most territories. As a result of this act, questions regarding jurisdiction, "choice of law," and "authority to modify in support matters have been virtually eliminated. One of the most important provisions of UIFSA is the adoption of a uniform Wage Assignment Form (see Exhibit 14–5). The failure of an employer to respond to a wage assignment will mean that it will be subject to federal jurisdiction and severe penalties for the failure to comply.

SUSPENSION OF PASSPORT

UIFSA provides for the suspension of an obligor's passport when the arrearage owed exceeds $5,000. The information is provided by the individual states to the State Department. In the event that an obligor owes more that $5,000, he will not be permitted to leave the country until such time as the obligation has been paid to an amount such that it is less than $5,000. A well-paid business professional who must travel abroad on a regular basis as part of his job may find that failure to remain current with child support may result in suddenly not being able to leave the country due to suspension. This is an embarrassing but effective way to see that affluent obligors who neglect to support their children will experience curtailment of significant activities unless they pay their child support.

OTHER SANCTIONS

Among the sanctions that may be imposed upon a delinquent child support obligor are the following: driver's license suspension, professional and occupational license suspension, seizure of bank accounts, seizure of workers' compensation or personal injury awards, conversion of child support arrearages to judgments and levying of liens upon personal and real property, reporting of child support arrearages to credit bureaus, federal and/or state income tax refund offsets, seizure of lottery winnings, and incarceration. In addition to utilizing these sanctions, some states, including the state of California, charge interest on the child support arrearage.

WAGE WITHHOLDING ORDERS (EXECUTIONS)

Pursuant to federal law, a wage withholding order for support enters in all cases that involve state assistance. Whether to obtain such an order when state assistance is not involved is a matter of decision for the court and/or the parties.

A wage withholding order is executed by the court and served upon the obligor's employer, who must then begin to withhold from the obligor's pay the court-ordered support amount. The employer must send it directly to the state's enforcement agency or the payee. This method works reasonably well, provided an obligor remains with the same employer. Problems with this system include delays in the receipt of payments by the payee as a result of delays in forwarding payment by the employer and the processing of payments by the state enforcement agency. Additionally, because a wage execution does not automatically follow an obligor, in many states the duty to notify a new employer of a support obligation falls upon the obligor. This can present great difficulties if the obligor does not disclose to his new employer the existence of a wage withholding order.

Fortunately, some states have developed a system that allows the wage withholding order to follow the obligor. California, for instance, has instituted a tracking system whereby each employer must report the Social Security number of each new hire to a central child support agency. If the new hire is included in the database, the agency will automatically forward notice of the wage withholding order to the employer, and the order will become effective upon the new employer.

Though this method is highly controversial, it is also very effective because (1) it is successful in tracking the employment movements of obligors, and (2) it provides a cost-effective way for the state to be reimbursed for assistance payments made for the benefit of the children of obligors.

SUSPENSION OF DRIVER'S LICENSES AND PROFESSIONAL LICENSES

Many states—California, New York, Arizona, and New Jersey included—now permit suspension of the driver's licenses and professional licenses of delinquent obligors. The trigger for reinstatement of the various licenses varies from state to state; however, the result is the same. The license is suspended and the obligor may not engage in those activities for which the license is required until such time as a specified percentage or dollar amount of the child support or alimony arrearage is paid. In some instances, a history of current payments is maintained for a specified period.

FEDERAL AND/OR STATE INCOME TAX OFFSETS

In accordance with the Welfare Reform Act of 1998, all states are required to report to the Internal Revenue Service all those who are delinquent in their child support and/or alimony payments. In accordance with federal law, the Internal Revenue Service will, upon the meeting of certain criteria, divert payment of any refund due the delinquent obligor to the state agency charged with collection of child support. This is known as a federal income tax offset. Many states have also developed a similar system for the diversion of state income tax refunds to the state agency charged with the collection of child support paymens.

INCARCERATION

In some states, delinquent obligors face incarceration when they are found in contempt of court for ignoring a support order. However, the delinquent obligor is frequently given the opportunity to "purge" himself of the contempt by paying a certain amount of the past-due child support. This amount is within the sound discretion of the court. In order to purge oneself of the contempt the delinquent obligor is given a certain date by which he must make the ordered payment or face incarceration. Alternatively, upon a finding of contempt, the delinquent obligor may be incarcerated immediately and remain so until the ordered payment is made. In extreme circumstances, where a delinquent obligor has a significant history of willful noncompliance and cannot show that he was unable to pay the child support as it became due, a court may simply order the delinquent obligor incarcerated until such time as the arrearage is paid in full.

KIDNAPPING AND CROSSING STATE LINES

Occasionally, a parent flees with a child from the jurisdiction to parts unknown. A custodial parent may abruptly move out of state and fail to give the noncustodial parent information as to where the custodial parent and children are now living. Sometimes, a noncustodial parent may have the child legally in his or her possession during an agreed-on visitation period but then refuse to return the child at the end of the visiting period.

For instance, in one case a noncustodial father had the right to take his children to his residence in a neighboring state for a school vacation visitation. When the visitation period ended, the father refused to return the children. The mother sought legal counsel only to find that the father was not guilty of kidnapping because when he took the children, he had the legal right to do so. Instead, under the laws of the custodial parent's state, the noncustodial parent was merely guilty of a misdemeanor known as interference with custodial rights, and the state would not seek extradition on such a minor criminal violation.

The custodial parent was forced to obtain the services of a lawyer in the neighboring state, who had to bring an action there to enforce an out-of-state decree. The noncustodial parent countered by bringing a custodial action in that jurisdiction, and a custody trial was held several months later in the neighboring state. During the entire period, the children remained with the parent who kept them away from the custodial parent, and by the time of the trial had become so attached to that parent and the extended family members that they did not wish to leave that parent. Thus, the court deemed that it was in the children's best interest to remain where they were.

The advent of the **Uniform Child Custody Jurisdiction Act (UCCJA)** of 1968 changed this situation. Under this act, if a noncustodial parent took a child while under the custodial parent's control, and then failed to return the child after a visitation period ended, the custodial parent had the right to have law enforcement officials in the other jurisdiction arrest the noncustodial parent and arrange for the children's return to the custodial parent. This new law has resulted in fewer kidnapping and custodial interference cases—when the whereabouts of the noncustodial parent and children are known. However, where a noncustodial parent simply disappears, the custodial parent will receive no relief until the noncustodial parent and the children are located.

Many children who are kidnapped have been kidnapped by noncustodial parents. Alternately, sometimes a custodial parent and children will simply disappear or vanish to avoid having to deal with an abusive or difficult noncustodial parent. In several cases, mothers or fathers have disappeared with children when they believed that the noncustodial parent was sexually abusing the children. In at least one instance, a mother who came out of hiding with her child was willing to go to jail because her infraction had allowed her to successfully protect her child from the child's sexually abusive father.

All fifty states have adopted the UCCJA. As an additional response to the parental kidnapping dilemma, the federal government passed the **Parental Kidnapping Prevention Act (PKPA),** U.S.C. §1738A, in 1980. The PKPA was enacted by Congress because states had very different laws regarding the enforcement of another jurisdiction's custody decrees. Lack of a uniform system throughout the country encouraged parents dissatisfied with an original custody order to flee the jurisdiction and seek modification of the original order in another state. This is known as **forum shopping.** Under the PKPA, a new state court must give full faith and credit to a custody order entered in another state and cannot modify that order as long as one of the child's parents resides in that jurisdiction.

The PKPA and UCCJA had conflicting provisions that caused much confusion and litigation in the legal community. In 1997, the **Uniform Child Custody Jurisdiction and Enforcement Act (UCCJEA)** was drafted by the National Conference of Commissioners on Uniform State Laws in hopes of rectifying the inconsistencies between the PKPA and UCCJA. Some of the highlights of the UCCJEA include the following:

- simplification of the procedures necessary for registering an original state's order in a new state,
- prohibiting a new state (enforcing state) from modifying an original state's custody decision; the new state can only enforce the original order,
- a *habeas corpus* remedy requiring a return of the child by the parent violating a custody or visitation order,
- granting the enforcing court the authority to issue a warrant to physically take the child into custody if there are fears that the parent will harm the child or flee the state, and
- assistance of state prosecutors or attorneys general in the enforcement of the orders in civil proceedings and in locating the child. Prosecutors can pursue criminal actions if the parent violated a criminal law in the process.

Appendix G of this book includes the full text of the UCCJEA.

EXHIBIT 14–1 Sample Postjudgment application and order to show cause to reopen and modify alimony.

<table>
<tr>
<td>

REQUEST FOR LEAVE
JD-FM-202 Rev. 8-06
P.B. Sec. 25-26

</td>
<td>

STATE OF CONNECTICUT
SUPERIOR COURT
www.jud.ct.gov

</td>
</tr>
</table>

INSTRUCTIONS

<table>
<tr>
<th>TO PREPARER</th>
<th>TO RESPONDING PARTY</th>
<th>TO CLERK</th>
</tr>
<tr>
<td>

1. If you would like to file a motion for modification, complete Sections I and II and attach your motion for modification to this form.
2. Have this form served with the attached motion for modification on the opposing party and return it to the court.
3. If you are representing yourself and the other party does not have an appearance in this case, bring this form to court clerk's office for completion of Section II.B.

</td>
<td>

1. If you choose to object to this Request for Leave, complete Sections III and IV on page 2.
2. Provide a copy to the other party and return this form to the court.

</td>
<td>

1. Send notice to all appearing parties of the court's order regarding this request.
2. If Request for Leave is granted, upon receipt of filing fee for the motion for modification, assign hearing date if necessary and retain a copy for court file.

</td>
</tr>
</table>

JUDICIAL DISTRICT OF	AT *(Address of court)*		DOCKET NO.
PLAINTIFF'S NAME *(Last, first, middle initial)*		DEFENDANT'S NAME *(Last, first, middle initial)*	

SECTION I—REQUEST FOR LEAVE (PERMISSION) TO FILE

1. I am the ☐ PLAINTIFF   ☐ DEFENDANT   in this case and I am requesting leave (permission) to file the attached motion for modification, in which the factual and legal basis has been sworn.

2. In the attached motion, I am requesting modification of the *(Check all that apply)*:

   ☐ Final order for custody that is dated: _____

   ☐ Final order for visitation that is dated: _____

   ☐ Parental responsibility plan that is dated: _____

FOR COURT USE ONLY
* R E Q M O D *

SIGNED *(Attorney or Pro Se Party)*	TYPE OR PRINT NAME OF PERSON SIGNING	DATE SIGNED
ADDRESS *(No., street, town or city, state and zip code)*		TELEPHONE NO. *(Area code first)*

SECTION II—NOTICE *(Check either A or B below)*

☐ **A - CERTIFICATION** *(Check and complete if responding party has an appearance on file.)*

I certify that I mailed or delivered a copy of this request to:	NAME	DATE MAILED/DELIVERED
ADDRESS *(No., street, town or city, state and zip code)**		
SIGNED *(Attorney or Pro Se Party)*	TYPE OR PRINT NAME OF PERSON SIGNING	DATE SIGNED

*If necessary, attach additional sheet with name of each party served and the address at which service was made.

☐ **B - INSTRUCTION TO PROPER OFFICER** *(Check and complete if responding party does not have an appearance on file.)*
TO ANY PROPER OFFICER:
By the Authority of the State of Connecticut, you must serve a true and attested copy of the above Request on the below named person in one of the ways required by law and file proof of service with this court.

NAME OF PERSON TO BE SERVED	ADDRESS	
SIGNED *(Assistant Clerk, Comm. Sup. Ct.)*		DATE SIGNED

NOTICE OF RIGHT TO OBJECT AND APPEAR

If you do not file an objection to this Request for Leave within ten days of the date of service of this request, the request may be determined by the court with or without hearing. To object, fill out Sections III and IV on page 2 of this form, provide a copy to any pro se party and/or attorney who has filed an appearance in this case, and return this form to the court clerk's office prior to expiration of the ten day period. If you do not file an objection or an Appearance in this case, you may not receive notice of the scheduling of a hearing, if any, and the Request for Leave may be granted.

Page 1 of 2

EXHIBIT 14-1 Continued

PLAINTIFF'S NAME *(Last, first, middle initial)*	DEFENDANT'S NAME *(Last, first, middle initial)*	DOCKET NO.

SECTION III—OBJECTION AND APPEARANCE BY RESPONDING PARTY

FOR COURT USE ONLY

* O B J E C T *

☐ I hereby object to the filing of the attached motion for modification for the following reason(s):

_____

_____

_____

_____

_____

_____

☐ Enter the appearance of:

NAME OF ATTORNEY, LAW FIRM OR PRO SE PARTY	JURIS NO. *(If attorney or law firm)*
ADDRESS OF ATTORNEY, LAW FIRM OR PRO SE PARTY	TELEPHONE NO. *(Area code first)*
SIGNED *(Attorney or Pro Se Party)*	DATE SIGNED

SECTION IV—CERTIFICATION BY RESPONDING PARTY

I certify that I mailed or delivered a copy of this objection to:	NAME	DATE MAILED/DELIVERED

ADDRESS *(No., street, town or city, state and zip code)**

SIGNED *(Attorney or Pro Se Party)*	TYPE OR PRINT NAME OF PERSON SIGNING	DATE SIGNED

*If necessary, use the space below to list the name of each party served and the address at which service was made.

SECTION V—COURT ORDER

☐ The request for leave is **GRANTED.**

☐ The request for leave is **DENIED.**

☐ It is hereby **ORDERED THAT:**

_____

_____

_____

_____

_____

BY THE COURT	DATE OF ORDER

JD-FM-202 (back/page 2) Rev. 8-06   **Page 2 of 2**

EXHIBIT 14–2 Sample preprinted form requesting a modification to a divorce decree.

MOTION FOR MODIFICATION JD-FM-174 Rev. 1-06 C.G.S. § 46b-86, P.B. §§ 25-26, 25-30, 25-57, 25-65	**STATE OF CONNECTICUT** **SUPERIOR COURT** www.jud.ct.gov	**COURT USE ONLY** **MFMOD**

(Check one)

☐ **Before judgment**   ☐ **After judgment** *(If you are asking the court to modify a final [after judgment] custody or visitation order and/or a parental responsibility plan, you must attach a Request for Leave form (JD-FM-202) to this motion and complete the SWORN STATEMENT section on page 2.)*

JUDICIAL DISTRICT OF	AT *(Town)*	DOCKET NO.

PLAINTIFF'S NAME *(Last, first, middle initial)*	DEFENDANT'S NAME *(Last, first, middle initial)*

PLAINTIFF'S ADDRESS *(No., street, city, state, zip code)*	DEFENDANT'S ADDRESS *(No., street, city, state, zip code)*

TYPE OF MOTION TO MODIFY
☐ CHILD SUPPORT   ☐ ALIMONY   ☐ CUSTODY   ☐ VISITATION   ☐ PARENTAL RESPONSIBILITY PLAN   ☐ OTHER *(Specify):* _____

I am the ☐ PLAINTIFF ☐ DEFENDANT. I respectfully represent that:

1. This Court issued an order dated _____ directing the ☐ plaintiff ☐ defendant to:
   (Complete all that apply)

PAY CHILD SUPPORT IN THE AMOUNT OF:	PAY ALIMONY IN THE AMOUNT OF:	HAVE CUSTODY OF THE CHILD/CHILDREN: *(Check one)* ☐ JOINT ☐ SOLE
PER	PER	
HAVE VISITATION OR PARENTING TIME AS FOLLOWS: *(Attach a copy of the visitation schedule if available)*		PRIMARY RESIDENCE WITH
OTHER:		

2. *(Check appropriate box(es) and explain briefly why you are seeking a modification)*

   ☐ Since the date of the order, the circumstances concerning this case have changed substantially as follows:

   ☐ The final order for child support is substantially different from the Child Support Guidelines as follows:

I ask the Court to modify the current order as follows: *(Check all that apply)*

CHILD SUPPORT *(You must file a Financial Affidavit (JD-FM-6) at least 5 days before the hearing. You must file an Affidavit Concerning Children (JD-FM-164) before the Court will act, and a completed child support and arrearage guidelines worksheet and an Advisement of Rights Re: Income Withholding (JD-FM-71) at the hearing.)*

☐ Increase   ☐ Decrease the amount of child support to be paid.   ☐ Order immediate income withholding.

ALIMONY *(You must file a Financial Affidavit (JD-FM-6) at least 5 days before the hearing. You must file an Advisement of Rights Re: Income Withholding (JD-FM-71) at the hearing.)*

☐ Increase   ☐ Decrease the amount of alimony to be paid.

CUSTODY *(If after judgment, you must attach a completed Request for Leave (JD-FM-202) to this motion. You must file a Financial Affidavit (JD-FM-6) and a completed child support and arrearage guidelines worksheet at the hearing. You must file an Affidavit Concerning Children (JD-FM-164) before the Court will act.)*

☐ Modify custody as follows:

VISITATION *(If after judgment, you must attach a completed Request for Leave (JD-FM-202) to this motion. You must file a Financial Affidavit (JD-FM-6) at the hearing. You must file an Affidavit Concerning Children (JD-FM-164) before the Court will act. You must file a completed child support and arrearage guidelines worksheet at the hearing.)*

☐ Modify visitation (parenting time) as follows:

PARENTAL RESPONSIBILITY PLAN *(If after judgment, you must attach a completed Request for Leave (JD-FM-202) to this motion.)*

☐ Modify parental responsibility plan as follows:

OTHER *(Please be specific):*

☐ _____

SIGNATURE	PRINT NAME	DATE SIGNED
ADDRESS *(No., street, city, state, zip code)*		TELEPHONE *(Area code first)*

(Continued on back/page 2)   Check appropriate court: ☐ Superior Court   ☐ Family Support Magistrate Division

EXHIBIT 14–2 Continued

PLAINTIFF'S NAME (Last, first, middle initial)	DEFENDANT'S NAME (Last, first, middle initial)	DOCKET NO.

NOTE: If you are now or have ever been a recipient of state assistance, you must send a copy of this motion to: The Office of the Attorney General, 55 Elm Street, Hartford, CT 06106

SWORN STATEMENT

(Complete only if you are asking the court to modify a final order [after judgment] of custody or visitation and/or parental responsibility plan.)

I certify that the factual and legal basis for the modification is true and accurate to the best of my knowledge and belief.

SIGNED (Moving party or other person having personal knowledge of the facts recited herein)

Subscribed and sworn to before me on:	DATE	SIGNED (Notary, Comm. of Superior Court, Assistant Clerk)

CERTIFICATION

I certify that I mailed or delivered a copy of this motion to:	NAME*	DATE MAILED/DELIVERED

ADDRESS (No., street, city, state, zip code)*

SIGNATURE	PRINT NAME	DATE SIGNED

*If necessary, attach additional sheet with name of each party served and the address at which service was made.

ORDER FOR HEARING AND SUMMONS (To be completed by clerk, if applicable)

The Court orders that a hearing be held at the time and place shown below. The Court also orders the

☐ plaintiff   ☐ defendant   to give notice to the opposing party of the Motion and of the time and place where the court will hear it, by having a true and attested copy of the Motion and this Order served on the opposing party by any proper officer at least **12 days** before the date of the hearing. Proof of service shall be made to this Court at least **six days** before the date of hearing.

HEARING TO BE HELD AT →	SUPERIOR COURT, JUDICIAL DISTRICT OF	**EXHIBIT 14–3**	DATE
	COURT ADDRESS	ROOM NO.	TIME

TO ANY PROPER OFFICER:

By the Authority of the State of Connecticut, you must serve a true and attested copy of the above Motion and Order For Hearing on the below named person in one of the ways required by law at least **12 days** before the date of the hearing, and file proof of service with this Court at least **six days** before the hearing.

PERSON TO BE SERVED	ADDRESS	
BY THE COURT	ASSISTANT CLERK	DATE SIGNED

ORDER

The court has heard this motion and orders it   ☐ **GRANTED**   ☐ **DENIED.**

BY THE COURT (Judge/F.S.M./ Assistant Clerk)	DATE ORDERED

FOR COURT USE ONLY

FEE FOR MOTION TO MODIFY: ☐ PAID   ☐ WAIVED

JD-FM-174 (Back/Page 2) Rev. 1-06

EXHIBIT 14–3

APPLICATION FOR CONTEMPT ORDER, INCOME WITHHOLDING, AND/OR OTHER RELIEF

JD-FM-15 Rev. 4-05
C.G.S. §§ 46b-215, 46b-220, 46b-231, 52-362

**STATE OF CONNECTICUT
SUPERIOR COURT**
www.jud.state.ct.us

COURT USE ONLY
CITWFRD

INSTRUCTIONS

TO ATTORNEY OR PRO SE PARTY
1. *Prepare original and two copies.*
2. *Obtain day of week for appearance from clerk.*
3. *Keep a copy for your files.*
4. *Forward original to the clerk.*
5. *After the clerk returns the signed original, forward to proper officer for service.*

TO SUPPORT ENFORCEMENT OFFICER
1. *Complete "Application" and "Order and Summons."*
2. *Forward to proper officer for service.*
3. *Keep a copy for your files.*
4. *Return original to clerk after service.*

TO CLERK
1. *Check all information for accuracy.*
2. *Sign the "Order" and "Summons"*
3. *Return original to preparer.*

TO PROPER OFFICER
See instructions on reverse/page 2.

APPLICATION

Application is made to issue to the below-named Respondent a(n):	"X" ALL THAT APPLY ☐ CONTEMPT ORDER	☐ INCOME WITHHOLDING	☐ PLAN TO PAY PAST-DUE SUPPORT	☐ ORDER TO PARTICIPATE IN WORK ACTIVITIES

NAME OF CASE *(Plaintiff vs. Defendant)*   DOCKET NO.

JUDICIAL DISTRICT   ADDRESS OF COURT *(Number, street, and town)*

NAME OF PETITIONER *(Applicant)*   ADDRESS OF PETITIONER *(Number, street, and town)*

NAME OF RESPONDENT   ADDRESS OF RESPONDENT *(Number, street, and town)*

DATE JUDGMENT/AGREEMENT	AMOUNT OF ORDER $	TOTAL BALANCE OWED $	DELINQUENCY $	AS OF *(Date)*

HEALTH INSURANCE ORDERED
☐ NOT MADE AVAILABLE   ☐ NOT MAINTAINED

CONTRIBUTIONS NOT MADE
☐ CHILD CARE   ☐ UNREIMBURSED MEDICAL EXPENSES

I certify that the above information is true to the best of my knowledge and belief: SIGNED *(Petitioner or Support Enforcement Officer)*   DATE SIGNED

ORDER AND SUMMONS

It is hereby ordered that the above-named respondent appear before the Superior Court/Family Support Magistrate Division at:

ADDRESS OF SUPERIOR COURT/FAMILY SUPPORT MAGISTRATE DIVISION	ON *(Day of week)*	DATE *(Mo., day, yr.)*	TIME *(A.M./P.M.)*

to show cause why said respondent should not be held in contempt of court for failure to pay support and/or the child care or unreimbursed medical expense contributions and/or provide/maintain health insurance as ordered by the court or Family Support Magistrate, and/or to show cause why an income withholding, license suspension, and/or an order for a plan to pay any past-due support or an order to participate in work activities should not issue against said respondent.

To: Any Proper Officer
BY AUTHORITY OF THE STATE OF CONNECTICUT, you are hereby commanded to make service of this application and order on the above-named respondent according to law at least twelve (12) days, inclusive, before the court appearance "Date" indicated below.

Hereof fail not but due service and return make.

BY THE COURT/FAMILY SUPPORT MAGISTRATE DIVISION	☐ J. ☐ F.S.M	SIGNED *(Assistant Clerk, Support Enforcement Officer)*	DATE SIGNED

NOTICE TO RESPONDENT *(To be completed by proper officer)*

1. **You have been summoned to appear in court at:**

ADDRESS OF SUPERIOR COURT/FAMILY SUPPORT MAGISTRATE DIVISION	ON *(Day of week)*	DATE *(Mo., day, yr.)*	TIME *(A.M./P.M.)*

2. **If you fail to appear in court on the court appearance date and time shown above, a capias may be issued for your arrest and/or an income withholding may issue against your income.**

3. The Superior Court and any Family Support Magistrate may issue an order to suspend the professional, occupational, recreational, commercial driver's and/or motor vehicle operator's license of a delinquent child support obligor and may order a plan for payment of any past-due support and/or participation in work activities. A "delinquent child support obligor" is (A) an obligor who owes overdue support, accruing after the entry of a court order, in an amount which exceeds ninety (90) days of periodic payments on a current support or arrearage payment order; (B) an obligor who has failed to make court ordered medical or dental insurance coverage available within ninety (90) days of the issuance of a court order or who fails to maintain such coverage pursuant to court order for a period of ninety (90) days; or (C) an obligor who has failed, after receiving appropriate notice, to comply with subpoenas or warrants relating to paternity or child support proceedings.

ORDER *(For use by Court/Family Support Magistrate Division only)*

The foregoing motion having been heard and it being found that the Respondent is in arrears as of *(date)* _____ in the

amount of $ _____ it is hereby ORDERED:

(order continues on reverse/page 2)

BY THE COURT/FAMILY SUPPORT MAGISTRATE DIVISION	☐ J. ☐ F.S.M.	SIGNED *(Assistant Clerk)*	DATE OF ORDER

(continued...)   **CONTEMPT ORDER/INCOME WITHHOLDING**

EXHIBIT 14–3 Continued

(Continuation of Order)

INSTRUCTIONS TO PROPER OFFICER

1. If applicable, fill in information required in the "Order and Summons" section and the "Notice to Respondent" section on front before making service.
2. Serve the copy on the respondent.
3. Complete the "Return of Service" section below and return.

RETURN OF SERVICE

Then and there by virtue of the original application, and by order of the Court/Family Support Magistrate Division,
I served the Respondent with a true and attested copy of the original application, order and summons by
(specify method of service)
_____

The within and foregoing is the original application, order and summons with my doings thereon endorsed.

SIGNED (State Marshal, Support Enforcement Off., Proper Officer)	PRINT NAME AND TITLE OF SIGNER	DATE SERVED

COPY _____
ENDORSEMENT _____
SERVICE _____
TRAVEL _____
TOTAL _____

A TRUE AND ATTESTED COPY, ATTEST: _____
(State Marshal or proper officer)

JD-FM-15 *(Back)* Rev. 4-05

EXHIBIT 14–4

MOTION FOR CONTEMPT
JD-FM-173 Rev. 2-2001
C.G.S. § 46b-87 § 46b-220 P.B. § 25-27

STATE OF CONNECTICUT
SUPERIOR COURT

COURT USE ONLY
MFCONTP

(Check one) ☐ Before Judgment (pendente lite) ☐ After Judgment

JUDICIAL DISTRICT OF	AT *(Town)*	DOCKET NO.
PLAINTIFF'S NAME *(Last, First, Middle Initial)*	DEFENDANT'S NAME *(Last, First, Middle Initial)*	
PLAINTIFF'S ADDRESS *(No., street, city, state, zip code)*	DEFENDANT'S ADDRESS *(No., street, city, state, zip code)*	

I, the ☐ PLAINTIFF ☐ DEFENDANT, respectfully represent that this Court issued an order on _____
(month, day, year)

directing the ☐ plaintiff ☐ defendant to *(complete only the information below that applies to the order(s) you claim was/were disobeyed):*

PAY CHILD SUPPORT IN THE AMOUNT OF	PAY ALIMONY IN THE AMOUNT OF	TOTAL BALANCE OWED	AS OF *(Date)*
per	per		

HAVE VISITATION OR PARENTING TIME AS FOLLOWS: *(Attach a copy of the visitation schedule if available)*

PAY MEDICAL BILLS OR PROVIDE HEALTH INSURANCE AS FOLLOWS

OTHER:
_____
_____
_____

The ☐ plaintiff or ☐ defendant has disobeyed the court order in the following ways: *(Please be specific. Include the amount of any arrears claimed due as of the date of this motion or a date specifically identified.)*

_____
_____
_____

I ask the Court to find the ☐ plaintiff ☐ defendant in contempt. I certify that the above information is true to the best of my knowledge.

SIGNATURE*	DATE	TELEPHONE *(Area Code first)*

CERTIFICATION *(Complete if motion is filed before judgment (pendente lite))*

I certify that I mailed/delivered a copy of this motion to:	NAME**	DATE MAILED/DELIVERED
ADDRESS *(No., street, city, state, zip code)*		
SIGNATURE	PRINT NAME	DATE SIGNED

**If necessary, attach additional sheet with name of each party served and the address at which service was made.

ORDER TO ATTEND HEARING AND NOTICE *(TO BE COMPLETED BY THE COURT)*

The court orders ☐ the plaintiff ☐ the defendant to attend a hearing at the time and place shown below to show why you are not in contempt. The Court also orders the ☐ plaintiff ☐ the defendant to give notice to the opposing party of the Motion and of the time and place where the Court will hear it, by having a true and attested copy of the Motion and this Order served on the opposing party by any proper officer at least **12 days** before the date of the hearing. Proof of service shall be made to this Court at least **six days** before the hearing.

BY THE COURT *(Judge/Assistant Clerk)*	DATE SIGNED

HEARING TO BE HELD AT →	SUPERIOR COURT, JUDICIAL DISTRICT OF	DATE	TIME
	COURT ADDRESS	ROOM NO. *(If known)*	TELEPHONE *(Area code first)*

If you do not attend the court hearing, a civil arrest order (capias) may be issued against you.

(Continued on back/page 2)   *Check appropriate court: ☐ Superior Court   ☐ Family Support Magistrate Division

485

EXHIBIT 14–4 Continued

SUMMONS

TO ANY PROPER OFFICER:

By the Authority of the State of Connecticut, you must serve a true and attested copy of the above Motion and Order to Attend Hearing on the below named person in one of the ways required by law at least **12 days** before the date of the hearing, and file proof of service with this Court at least **six days** before the hearing.

PERSON TO BE SERVED	ADDRESS	
ASSISTANT CLERK		DATE SIGNED

ORDER

The Court has heard the above Motion and finds that the ☐ plaintiff ☐ defendant:

☐ **is not in contempt.** ☐ **is in contempt in the following way(s):**

☐ owes arrears as of _____ in the amount of _____ .

☐ other *(specify):* _____

_____

IT IS ORDERED:

☐ payment in the amount of _____ for current support and _____ on arrears by *(date)* _____ .

☐ income withholding in the amount of _____ .

☐ suspension of professional, occupational, recreational, or driver's license with a 30-day stay (attach "License Suspension Order," Form JD-FM-153)

☐ posting of a surety bond

☐ incarceration

☐ attorney's fees

☐ marshal's fees

☐ this matter is continued to _____ at _____ .
  (date)   *(time)*

☐ other *(specify):* _____

BY THE COURT (*Judge/FSM*)	SIGNED (*Assistant Clerk*)	DATE OF ORDER

RETURN OF SERVICE

I left a true and attested copy of the Motion for Contempt ☐ personally with the defendant ☐ personally with the plaintiff

☐ at the current home of the ☐ defendant or ☐ plaintiff at _____
  (Number, street, town or city)

The original Motion is attached.

NAME AND TITLE	COUNTY	DATE OF SERVICE

MARSHAL'S USE ONLY

FEE INFORMATION:

COPY _____

ENDORSEMENT _____

SERVICE _____

TRAVEL _____

TOTAL _____

JD-FM-173 *(Back)* Rev. 2-2001

EXHIBIT 14–5

□ **ORDER/NOTICE TO WITHHOLD INCOME FOR CHILD SUPPORT**
□ **NOTICE OF AN ORDER TO WITHHOLD INCOME FOR CHILD SUPPORT**

□Original   □Amended   □Termination   Date:_____
□State/Tribe/Territory_____
   City/Co./Dist./Reservation_____
□Non-governmental entity or Individual _____
   Case Number_____

_____   RE:_____
   Employer's/Withholder's Name   Employee's/Obligor's Name (Last, First, MI)

_____   _____
   Employer's/Withholder's Address   Employee's/Obligor's Social Security Number

_____
_____   Employee's/Obligor's Case Identifier

_____   _____
Employer's/Withholder's Federal EIN Number (if known)   Obligee's Name (Last, First, MI)

ORDER INFORMATION: This document is based on the support or withholding order from _____.
You are required by law to deduct these amounts from the employee's/obligor's income until further notice.
$_____ Per _____ current child support
$_____ Per _____ past-due child support - Arrears greater than12 weeks? □yes □no
$_____ Per _____ current cash medical support
$_____ Per _____ past-due cash medical support
$_____ Per _____ spousal support
$_____ Per _____ past-due spousal support
$_____ Per _____ other (specify) _____
for a total of $_____ per _____ to be forwarded to the payee below.
You do not have to vary your pay cycle to be in compliance with the support order. If your pay cycle does not match the ordered payment cycle, withhold one of the following amounts:
$_____per weekly pay period. $_____per semimonthly pay period (twice a month).
$_____per biweekly pay period (every two weeks).$_____per monthly pay period.

REMITTANCE INFORMATION: When remitting payment, provide the pay date/date of withholding and the case identifier. If the employee's/obligor's principal place of employment is _____, begin withholding no later than the first pay period occurring_____ days after the date of _____. Send payment within_working days of the pay date/date of withholding The total withheld amount, including your fee, may not exceed_____% of the employee's/obligor's aggregate disposable weekly earnings.

If the employee's/obligor's principal place of employment is not _____, for limitations on withholding, applicable time requirements, and any allowable employer fees, follow the laws and procedures of the employee's/obligor's principal place of employment (see #3 and #9, ADDITIONAL INFORMATION TO EMPLOYERS AND OTHER WITHHOLDERS).

Make check payable to:_(Payee and Case identifier)_____Send check to: _____. If remitting payment by EFT/EDI, call _____before first submission. Use this FIPS code:_____:
Bank routing number: _____Bank account number:_____.

If this is an Order/Notice to Withhold:	**If this is a Notice of an Order to Withhold:**
Print Name _____	Print Name_____
Title of Issuing Official_____ Mandatory_____	Title (if appropriate)_____
Signature and Date _____	Signature and Date_____
□ IV-D Agency □Court	□ Attorney □Individual □Private Entity

□ Attorney with authority under state law to issue order/notice.
NOTE: Non-IV-D Attorneys, individuals, and non-governmental entities must submit a Notice of an Order to Withhold and include a copy of the income withholding order unless, under a state's law, an attorney in that state may issue an income withholding order. In that case, the attorney may submit an Order/Notice to Withhold and include a copy of the state law authorizing the attorney to issue an income withholding order/notice.

EXHIBIT 14–5 Continued

ADDITIONAL INFORMATION TO EMPLOYERS AND OTHER WITHHOLDERS

☐ If checked, you are required to provide a copy of this form to your employee/obligor. If your employee works in a state that is different from the state that issued this order, a copy must be provided to your employee/obligor even if the box is not checked.

1. **Priority:** Withholding under this Order or Notice has priority over any other legal process under state law (or tribal law, if applicable) against the same income. If there are federal tax levies in effect, please notify the contact person listed below. (See 10 below.)

2. **Combining Payments:** You may combine withheld amounts from more than one employee's/obligor's income in a single payment to each agency/party requesting withholding. You must, however, separately identify the portion of the single payment that is attributable to each employee/obligor.

3. **Reporting the Paydate/Date of Withholding:** You must report the paydate/date of withholding when sending the payment. The paydate/date of withholding is the date on which the amount was withheld from the employee's wages. You must comply with the law of the state of employee's/obligor's principal place of employment with respect to the time periods within which you must implement the withholding and forward the support payments.

4. **Employee/Obligor with Multiple Support Withholdings:** If there is more than one Order or Notice against this employee/obligor and you are unable to honor all support Orders or Notices due to federal, state, or tribal withholding limits, you must follow the state or tribal law/procedure of the employee's/obligor's principal place of employment. You must honor all Orders or Notices to the greatest extent possible. (See 9 below.)

5. **Termination Notification:** You must promptly notify the Child Support Enforcement (IV-D) Agency and/or the contact person listed below when the employee/obligor no longer works for you. Please provide the information requested and return a complete copy of this Order or Notice to the Child Support Enforcement (IV-D) Agency and/or the contact person listed below. (See 10 below.)
    THE EMPLOYEE/OBLIGOR NO LONGER WORKS FOR:_____
    EMPLOYEE'S/OBLIGOR'S NAME: _____CASE IDENTIFIER: _____
    DATE OF SEPARATION FROM EMPLOYMENT: _____
    LAST KNOWN HOME ADDRESS: _____
    NEW EMPLOYER/ADDRESS: _____

6. **Lump Sum Payments:** You may be required to report and withhold from lump sum payments such as bonuses, commissions, or severance pay. If you have any questions about lump sum payments, contact the Child Support Enforcement (IV-D) Agency.

7. **Liability:** If you have any doubts about the validity of the Order or Notice, contact the agency or person listed below under 10. If you fail to withhold income as the Order or Notice directs, you are liable for both the accumulated amount you should have withheld from the employee's/obligor's income and any other penalties set by state or tribal law/procedure.
    _____
    _____

8. **Anti-discrimination:** You are subject to a fine determined under state or tribal law for discharging an employee/obligor from employment, refusing to employ, or taking disciplinary action against any employee/obligor because of a child support withholding.
    _____
    _____

9. **Withholding Limits:** For state orders, you may not withhold more than the lesser of: 1) the amounts allowed by the Federal Consumer Credit Protection Act (15 U.S.C. § 1673(b)); or 2) the amounts allowed by the state of the employee's/obligor's principal place of employment. The federal limit applies to the aggregate disposable weekly earnings (ADWE). ADWE is the net income left after making mandatory deductions such as: state, federal, local taxes, Social Security taxes, statutory pension contributions, and Medicare taxes. The Federal CCPA limit is 50% of the ADWE for child support and alimony, which is increased by 1) 10% if the employee does not support a second family; and/or 2) 5% if arrears greater than 12 weeks.
    For tribal orders, you may not withhold more than the amounts allowed under the law of the issuing tribe. For tribal employers who receive a state order, you may not withhold more than the amounts allowed under the law of the state that issued the order.

    Child(ren)'s Names and Additional Information:_____
    _____
    _____

10. If you or your employee/obligor have any questions, contact_____by telephone at
    _____by Fax at _____or by internet at_____.

EXHIBIT 14–6

NOTICE TO NONAPPEARING OBLIGOR
OF INCOME WITHHOLDING ORDER

JD-FM-70 Rev. 9-99
Gen. Stat. § 52-362, 15 U.S.C. 1673
P.A. 99-193 § 6

INSTRUCTIONS

1. *Upon issuance of a withholding order effective immediately, complete original and one copy.*
2. *Serve original on obligor in accordance with General Statute § 52-57 or by certified mail, return receipt requested.*
3. *Retain copy for file.*

(Name and mailing address of obligor)

TO:

CONNECTICUT SUPERIOR COURT

NAME OF CASE

NAME AND ADDRESS OF COURT	DOCKET NO.

AMOUNT OF SUPPORT ORDER

DATE OF SUPPORT ORDER	AMOUNT OF INCOME UPON WHICH THE SUPPORT ORDER IS BASED

A SUPPORT ORDER in the above amount has been issued against you.

The support order is to be enforced by an **INCOME WITHHOLDING ORDER.**

An Income Withholding Order against your earnings, **EFFECTIVE IMMEDIATELY**, has been issued as part of the support order.

SOME OF YOUR INCOME IS EXEMPT from withholding. Only disposable income is subject to an Income Withholding Order. "Disposable income" means that part of the income of an individual remaining after deduction from that income of amounts required to be withheld for the payment of federal, state and local income taxes, employment taxes, normal retirement contributions, union dues and initiation fees and group life and health insurance premiums. The amount withheld may not exceed the maximum amount permitted under section 1673 of title 15 of the United States Code: If you are supporting a spouse or dependent child other than the spouse or child with respect to whose support the order issued, the maximum amount of your disposable income that may be withheld

is 50% of such income, unless you are twelve weeks or more in arrears in which case the maximum is 55% of such income. If you are not supporting a spouse or dependent child other than the spouse or child with respect to whose support the order issued, the maximum amount of your disposable income that may be withheld is 60% of such income, unless you are twelve weeks or more in arrears in which case the maximum is 65%. In no event, however, under state law, may you be left with less than 85% of the first $145 of disposable income.

YOU HAVE THE RIGHT TO A HEARING, upon motion to the court, to claim any other applicable state or federal exemption, or to offer any evidence as to why the Income Withholding Order effective immediately should not continue in effect.

THE AMOUNT OF INCOME received by you which formed the basis for the support order against you is shown above. **YOU HAVE A RIGHT TO MOVE TO MODIFY THE SUPPORT ORDER** if your income has changed substantially or if the support order substantially deviates from the child support guidelines established pursuant to General Statute § 46b-215a.

SIGNED *(Dependent or attorney)*	PRINT NAME OF PERSON SIGNING AT LEFT	DATE SIGNED

489

END OF CHAPTER EXERCISES

Crossword Puzzle

Across

4. a document alerting the court to the other party's failure to comply with the court's earlier order and request that the court provide relief

6. a change or adjustment to a previous court order

7. modifications to an original order, enforcement of court orders, and motions to open judgments

8. amounts due by court order but unpaid; also know as back alimony

Down

1. statute requiring a state to honor the original support order of another state rather than entering a new order or modifying the existing order to conform to its guidelines for determining the amount of support

2. statue enabling a custodial parent to ultimately obtain child support from the noncustodial parent residing in another state by instituting certain procedures

3. the type of order issued by a court that cannot be changed, regardless of the circumstances

5. where one party in an action does not comply with the court's order

Review Questions

1. What parts of a dissolution decree are modifiable and what parts are not modifiable? Why are some parts modifiable and others not?

2. Discuss the facts that could constitute "changed circumstances" in terms of a modification of alimony or child support.

3. What are some changes in circumstances that could merit a modification of a custody order or a modification of a visitation order?

4. List the events included in your state's statutory provision or in its controlling case law that will precipitate an end to the payment of alimony.

5. What is a rule to show cause, and when is it used in a postjudgment family matter?

6. What is an arrearage?

7. What are some of the measures various states provide to "encourage" a delinquent obligor to pay the outstanding arrearage and remain current on alimony and child support payments?

8. Discuss the remedies available to a custodial parent when the noncustodial parent leaves the jurisdiction and ceases to pay child support.

9. Discuss the remedies available to a custodial parent when the noncustodial parent has fled the jurisdiction with a minor child.

10. Discuss the Uniform Child Custody Jurisdiction Enforcement Act (UCCSEA) and the remedies it provides.

11. What factors does a court consider when allowing a custodial parent to move out of the jurisdiction with a minor child?

12. What is the difference between parental kidnapping and the misdemeanor known as custodial interference?

Cases for Briefing

Compare the following cases that deal with different aspects of the same issue:

In re: Marriage of Thorlin, 155 Ariz. 357 (App. 1987)

Flynn v. Rogers, 172 Ariz. 62 (1992)

For an example of the factors courts consider in making postjudgment custody and visitation determinations, consider the following:

Gil v. Gil, 94 Conn. App. 306 (2006)

Palmer v. Palmer, 284 A.D.2d 612 [3d Dept. 2001] (New York)

In the Matter of Hamm-Jones v. Jones, 14 A.D.3d [3d Dept. 200?] (New York)

In the Matter of Lopez v. Robinson, 23 A.D. 3d 1034 (New York)

In re: Marriage of Bates, Ill.2D 489 (2004)

For examples of how different state courts decide relocation issues, consider the decisions of the following jurisdictions:

In re: Marriage of Sobol, 342 Ill. App.3d 363 (2003)

In re: Marriage of Brown & Yana, 37 Cal. 4th 1116 (2006)

Exploring the Workplace: Activities

1. Research your state's case law and statutes to see what criteria the family courts use to decide whether a parent with physical custody of the minor children may move out of the state. Present a fact pattern under which the court is likely to grant the parent's request.

2. You work as a paralegal for a firm in Louisiana. Your supervising attorney asks you to research the state's position regarding the enforcement of the Uniformed Services Former Spouse's Protection Act, in which a separation agreement provides that the nonmilitary spouse will take no share of the other spouse's pension.

3. Your firm represented Mr. Collier in a dissolution proceeding three years ago. This morning he called the office very upset because he just received a notice from the Department of Motor Vehicles stating that the registration for his recreational motor home has been revoked because he has not paid his child support in a year and owes more than $8,000. He tells you that his former spouse had not let the children visit him since Thanksgiving, which was over eight months ago, and that because of this he has not been motivated to pay child support. He also tells you that recently, his former spouse told him that he may take his three children for two weeks' vacation as soon as school ends, which will be in less than a month. He planned to take the children to Disneyworld in his recreational vehicle and they would camp in a nearby state park. He has already told the children and they are elated. He cannot afford airfare and hotel accommodations for himself and the children, so if he does not get his registration reinstated, they will not be able to go and the children will be heartbroken. He doesn't understand how the state can do this to him, and he wants to know what he can do about it.

You relay this information to your supervising attorney. She asks you to research the background on this state initiative and also to research what steps Mr. Collier must take to get his registration back. Prepare an interoffice memorandum for your supervisor that includes this information.

CHAPTER 15

Child Protection and Adoption

KEY TERMS

abandonment

abuse

adoption

Armstrong v. Manzo

child protection agency

clear and convincing evidence

hotline

investigative child protection worker

mandatory reporter

neglect

open adoption agreement

open adoption

parens patriae

petition to adopt

second parent adoptions

service (performance) agreement

specific steps (expectations)

stepparent adoption

temporary custody

termination of parental rights

treatment worker

INTEGRITY OF THE FAMILY

The U.S. government has recognized the integrity of the family unit. In the Supreme Court case *Stanley v. Illinois,* 405 U.S. 645, 92 S. Ct. 1208, 31 L. Ed. 2d 551 (1972), the Court maintained that family preservation is a priority and that the U.S. Constitution protects family integrity. However, this protection is not absolute. It must be balanced against states' obligations to protect children.

STATES' OBLIGATIONS TO PROTECT CHILDREN

In some instances, a child's health, safety, and physical and emotional well-being are in peril by virtue of being in an intact family. Sometimes one parent or both parents may behave in a neglectful or abusive manner toward a child or may simply allow or not attempt to prevent neglectful or abusive conditions. For instance, a parent may physically abuse a child by hitting and spanking the child in a way that inflicts physical injury on the child. Similarly, a parent may inflict mental abuse on a child by words or conduct that threaten and intimidate or ridicule and humiliate the child. Parents are neglectful of their children when they fail to adequately provide for the child's nutritional, medical, or educational needs or allow the child to live in conditions that are unsanitary or in a home that is uninhabitable due to the absence of heat, hot water, or electricity. A child left to sleep continuously on a urine-soaked, stained mattress in dirty bedclothes is a neglected child.

A parent is expected to take a child for regular physical examinations and make sure that the child's immunizations are up to date. A parent is expected to take a child to the doctor when the child has a serious illness, suffers a serious injury, or has a chronic health problem that requires periodic monitoring.

Parents must provide their children with adequate housing that is warm, clean, and large enough to accommodate all family members without excessive crowding in either living quarters or sleeping space.

DETECTING CHILD NEGLECT AND CHILD ABUSE

When parents fail to provide a safe and nurturing environment for their children, the state intervenes to protect the children. The state possesses the authority for such action under the legal doctrine of ***parens patriae.*** This Latin term is literally translated as "the parent of the country." In reality, this doctrine gives the state the right to protect children and persons with disabilities when their parent or legal guardian has failed to do so. However, before the state acts, the state must have reason to believe that intervention is needed. The fact that a child needs protection must come to the state's attention, usually through a complaint or referral by a third party.

Every state has a **child protection agency** that is charged with intervening in a family unit when neglect or abuse is known or suspected. In many states, this agency is known as the Department of Children and Families (DCF), the Department of Children and Youth Services (DCYS), the Department of Health and Rehabilitative Services (HRS), or by a similar type of name.

The child protection agency receives complaints from a variety of sources. Certain professionals and paraprofessionals are **mandatory reporters,** meaning that by law, under penalty of law, they are required to report any signs of suspected child **abuse** or **neglect.** These persons include school personnel such as classroom teachers, school nurses, counselors, and social workers; and medical personnel, specifically pediatricians, general practitioners, emergency room personnel, medical social workers, and other hospital department staff. If a teacher sees a child with suspicious bruises, for example, the teacher must report this to the local child protection agency. Similarly, if a child is brought to the emergency room with a suspicious injury or illness, the local child protection agency must be called.

Sometimes a neighbor or a family member will report suspected child neglect or abuse by calling the child protection agency's emergency **hotline.** States have established central hotlines that provide a twenty-four-hour toll-free number for reporting suspected child abuse. Occasionally, the caller to a hotline will identify himself or herself, especially if the caller is a blood relative and wants to serve as a placement resource for the child if removal from the home becomes an option. More frequently, the caller may wish to remain anonymous and refuse to give his or her name. If the anonymous caller sounds credible, the child protection agency will investigate the complaint.

INVESTIGATION OF A COMPLAINT OF CHILD NEGLECT OR CHILD ABUSE

When a child protection staffperson decides that an incoming complaint warrants follow-up, an **investigative child protection worker** will visit the family, unannounced, and assess the physical living conditions and the emotional environment of the family. Through asking questions and observing the premises and condition of the children, the worker will decide whether or not the allegations can be substantiated.

If the allegations are not substantiated, no action is taken. However, the complaint is documented so that if another complaint is made in the future, knowledge of the previous complaint may alert the worker to move quickly and to conduct a more intensive investigation. If allegations are substantiated, the state will intervene. The type and degree of intervention will be determined by the seriousness of the situation.

SERVICE AGREEMENT APPROACH

If a worker goes to a home and finds that the children are at risk for not being properly cared for, the investigative worker may recommend that the children remain in the home but that a case be opened with the agency and that a **treatment worker** be assigned to the case and family. The treatment worker will meet with the parents and the children and communicate to the parents what they must do so that their children will not be removed from their home.

The worker may make a list of things that must be corrected. These items will be incorporated into a **service agreement** or **performance agreement** that the worker will ask the parent or parents to sign. For instance, the worker will indicate that the parents must take their children to the doctor and keep current with immunizations. If the parents indicate that they have a substance abuse problem, the worker will indicate that the parents must go to a treatment program; if food or clothing for the children is not sufficient, the worker may try to help the clients budget and also put them in touch with social service providers and government agencies for financial assistance, food stamps, medical insurance, and other benefits.

After the agreement is in place, the worker will visit the family regularly and if the problems are corrected and all is well, the case will be closed. As long as the worker has concerns, the case will remain open and if, at any time, the situation worsens and the risk to the children's health and safety increases, the worker may initiate a more intense intervention.

ORDER OF TEMPORARY CUSTODY

If at any time a worker suspects that children may be in a situation of imminent harm or danger, the worker will seek authorization from his or her supervisor to apply to the child protection court for an order that gives the child protection agency **temporary custody** of the children. This order enables the worker to remove the children from the home and place them in temporary foster care. The parents are then notified that within five to seven days, a court hearing will be held to determine whether the children are to remain in the state's custody.

Frequently, at the same time the parents are notified of the impending court hearing, the parents are also served with a legal petition in which the child protection agency as the petitioner alleges that the children are being neglected and requesting that the children be committed to the appropriate state agency for a statutorily mandated period of time. This petition usually contains a notice of a hearing on the neglect petition and the date of the hearing. This hearing date will be scheduled for a date after the date of the hearing on the order of temporary custody.

Prior to the temporary custody hearing, the child protection court appoints an attorney or guardian *ad litem* to represent the interests of the children. The parents are notified that they should obtain their own legal representation. If the parents cannot afford an attorney and if their income falls within certain guidelines, the court provides them with an attorney paid for by the judicial system.

At the temporary custody hearing, the attorney for the child protection agency, usually an attorney from the state's attorney general's office, has to prove that the children would be placed in immediate, imminent harm if they were to be returned to their parents at that time. The parents' attorney introduces evidence and testimony to rebut the state's arguments. The children's attorney has a chance to cross-examine the witnesses of both the state and the parents, and also may wish to present witnesses and evidence in support of either confirmation of the custody order or revocation, depending on what the children's attorney believes will best promote the children's interest.

After all evidence is presented and closing arguments are heard, the judge rules either to confirm the order of temporary custody or to revoke that order and allow the children to be returned to the parents. If the custody order is confirmed, the children will remain in the state's custody until the underlying neglect matter is adjudicated. If the order is revoked, the underlying neglect matter will remain. Although the children will be allowed to return home, the parents must return for further court proceedings, which may include a trial on the neglect petition. If the state prevails at the neglect trial or if the parents choose to forego their right to a trial and either admit or plead no contest to the allegations of neglect, the children will be adjudicated as neglected children. The court then makes a disposition that could result in the children being committed for a statutory period or in the children remaining in the home under state supervision for a period of several months.

EFFORTS FOR REUNIFICATION OF THE CHILD WITH THE PARENTS

When a court commits a child to the care and custody of the state's child protection agency, the court is frequently called on to order that specific requirements be met before the child may be returned to the parents. These requirements, which are often known as **specific steps** or **expectations,** are drawn up by the representative of the child protection agency. The parents sign the document containing these steps to acknowledge that they know what the court expects them to do and to acknowledge that they will participate in the activities the state requires in order to be reunified with their child.

SPECIFIC STEPS

The expectations or specific steps may include requirements such as the parent completing a substance abuse treatment program, attending parenting classes, or undergoing domestic violence counseling. The steps usually include general requirements such as the requirement that the parents visit their child as frequently as the child protection agency permits; that the parents keep their whereabouts known to the child protection agency and to their attorney; that the parents obtain a means of legal income and adequate housing; and that the parents have no involvement or no further involvement with the criminal justice system.

If a parent has completed all of the specific steps to the satisfaction of the child protection agency, the parent's attorney may bring a motion to revoke the commitment before the court before the statutory commitment period ends. If the state agrees that all expectations have been met or if the child's attorney demonstrates by a preponderance of the evidence that the parent has fulfilled all of the expectations, the court may revoke the commitment and order that arrangements be made to reunify the child and parent as soon as possible.

EXTENSION OF COMMITMENT

If a parent is unable to meet the requirements set for reunification within the statutory twelve-month commitment period, the child protection agency will file a motion or a petition to extend the period of custodial commitment for an additional statutory period. The parent may oppose this extension of commitment. Unless an agreement or compromise is reached between the state and the parent, the parent's attorney may request an evidentiary hearing on the motion for extension. At that hearing, the state presents evidence that the parent has not completed the specific steps needed to be fulfilled for reunification. The parent's attorney presents evidence to the contrary, which demonstrates that the parent has complied with the child protection agency's requirements and that the child's best interest will be served by reunifying parent and child.

If the court is persuaded that the parent has completed all requirements for reunification and if the court is persuaded that it will be in the child's best interest to return the child home, the extension will be denied and the child protection agency will have to reunify the child with the parents before the state's custodial commitment expires. Conversely, if the child protection agency proves that the parent has not complied with the court-ordered specific steps and has failed to fulfill the expectations required for reunification, the court will extend the commitment.

If following this period or perhaps even during this commitment period, the child protection agency has reason to believe that there is little chance that within a reasonable period of time the parent will be able to meet the conditions needed for reunification, the child protection agency will make a determination that reunification is no longer the agency's goal. At this point, the agency will look for other options. Such options include transferring of guardianship of the child to one of either of the parents' relatives; placing the child in a long-term foster care arrangement, especially if the child is older or has special needs and requires considerable therapeutic treatment; or terminating the natural parents' rights and the placement of the child in the agency's preadoption program. The most drastic option the child protection agency may elect is the bringing of an action to terminate the parent's parental rights to the child.

TERMINATION OF PARENTAL RIGHTS

A **termination of parental rights** is a court proceeding that severs the legal bond between a parent and his or her biological or legally adopted child. A court of appropriate jurisdiction may terminate or permanently remove all legal rights a parent possesses in connection with his or her child. Rights may be terminated as to both parents or only as to one parent. Specially, upon the effective date of termination, the parent will no longer have the following legal rights and responsibilities that are part of the parent/child relationship: The parent will no longer have a duty to support the child; nor will the parent have the right to inherit from the child or the legal right to participate in any decisions whatsoever regarding the health, education, or welfare of the child.

VOLUNTARY TERMINATION OF PARENTAL RIGHTS

A voluntary termination of parental rights occurs when a natural parent or an adoptive parent consents to having a court of appropriate jurisdiction terminate all legal rights a parent possesses regarding her relationship to a minor child. An individual's parental rights may be terminated only through a court proceeding. If the parent consents to the termination, the court proceeding is fairly short and uncomplicated. The judge asks the parent whether she wishes to have her parental rights severed. The judge canvasses the parent to make sure that the parent's consent is being freely given, without being pressured in any way to do so. The judge also informs the parent of each of the rights the parent will be relinquishing.

If the parent is represented by counsel in this matter, the judge may also ask the parent whether her attorney discussed the matter thoroughly with her and whether the parent is satisfied with the legal representation the attorney provided. Following this canvassing, the judge announces that the parent's rights have been terminated and the proceeding ends shortly thereafter.

INVOLUNTARY TERMINATION OF PARENTAL RIGHTS

An involuntary termination of parental rights proceeding involves a trial. The state or the child protection agency must bring a petition before the court seeking termination of parental rights. In this petition, the state will allege that one or more statutory grounds exist to provide the legal justification for the court to terminate the parent's rights.

GROUNDS FOR TERMINATION OF PARENTAL RIGHTS

Each state has its own set of statutory grounds for termination. Many states include grounds such as parental abandonment, absence of a parent/child relationship, and failure of the parent to rehabilitate to a degree where the parent can achieve a meaningful role in the child's care and upbringing. Parental consent is also usually a statutory ground. In order for the court to grant the state's petition for termination of parental rights, the state must prove at least one statutory ground by **clear and convincing evidence.** This term connotes a very high evidentiary standard of proof that requires a higher degree of certainty than the preponderance of the evidence standard required for a judicial finding of neglect.

CONSIDERATION OF THE CHILD'S BEST INTERESTS

If the court finds that the state has met its evidentiary burden and that one or more of the necessary grounds have been proven, the court must then go one step further and determine through the evidence whether it is in the child's best interest to terminate the parent's rights or whether additional time should be allowed to give the parent time to rectify whatever situations gave rise to the existence of the grounds for termination.

If the court decides to allow a parent a specific additional amount of time in which to do what is necessary for reunification with the child, the child protection agency will retain custody during this time period and the court will outline what requirements the parent will have to meet by the end of the additional time period. On the other hand, if the court decides that additional time is not warranted, the court will issue an order terminating the parent's rights. If the parental rights of both parents have been terminated, the child will be free to be adopted.

ADOPTION

Adoption is the legal procedure that makes a person or persons the legal parent or parents of a minor child who is not their natural child. In some states, the adoption procedure takes place in family court. In other states, the adoption is done in a court known as probate court or surrogates court.

AGENCY ADOPTIONS

There are two types of adoption agencies, public adoption agencies and private adoption agencies. Public agencies are usually a component of the state government's child protection agency. For instance, when parental rights to a minor child have been severed in response to a petition brought by a state's child protection agency, frequently, the child protection agency itself facilitates the child's adoption through the branch of the agency specializing in adoptions. When the parents voluntarily consent to termination of their parental rights and the state child protection agency is not directly involved, the adoption is often handled by a private agency, sometimes one that the parents themselves have selected.

PUBLIC ADOPTION AGENCIES

A public agency adoption usually addresses the adoption of children already committed to the state's custody. These children have been placed in foster care following court proceedings. Upon the termination of parental rights, the state becomes the statutory parent of the child and remains the child's statutory parent until the child is adopted. Sometimes, the child's foster parents may seek to adopt the child. If the foster parents meet the criteria for adopting the child, they are frequently given preference, especially if the child has been in their care for a period of time and has bonded with the foster family. If the foster family is unwilling or unable to adopt the child, the agency will transfer the child's file to the agency's preadoption unit, where an assigned worker will attempt to find suitable adoptive parents from the list of individuals and couples who have registered to be considered as adoptive parents.

Public agencies have many older children who have been in foster care for months or even years. Some of these children are available for adoption. A prospective adoptive parent who is willing to adopt an older child may face a shorter wait than the prospective parent who is seeking an infant or a very young child.

The children who are involuntarily committed to the care of a child protection agency are not available for adoption while the agency's goal for the child is reunification with the natural parents and, as discussed, the natural parents are usually given a reasonable period of time in which to complete the court-ordered steps required for reunification. Individuals seeking to adopt infants are more likely to have success by going to a private adoption agency or seeking out private adoption opportunities.

PRIVATE ADOPTION AGENCIES

A private adoption agency must be licensed and follow certain statutory and administrative regulations that govern the adoption process. Individuals and couples who register with either public or private adoption agencies must undergo rigorous examinations. Agency workers conduct home visits to assess the physical and emotional environment the prospective adoptive parents can provide for a child. Many agencies conduct intensive home studies to determine the appropriateness of placing a particular child with a particular family.

Once the decision is made to place a child with a family, the agency monitors the placement for several months to ensure that the placement meets the child's needs. When this provisional period ends and the agency approves the placement as permanent, the prospective adoptive parents file a **petition to adopt** or a similar document in probate or surrogates court. The court will request that the agency file a report. If the agency report is favorable and supports the adoption, the court will grant the adoption petition.

PRIVATE ADOPTIONS

A private adoption is an adoption that takes place without the intervention of an agency. In a private adoption, the child's natural parents agree voluntarily to sever their parental rights so that a particular person or couple may adopt their child. The adoption is frequently facilitated by an attorney or by the natural parents' doctor.

The private adoption must be approved by the court, and many states require that a state agency child protection worker investigate the proposed adoption and file a report with the court as to the advisability of permitting the adoption. The court reviews the report prior to making a decision and will usually not approve the adoption unless the report is favorable.

STEPPARENT ADOPTION

One of the most common types of adoption is a **stepparent adoption.** This is where an individual who marries a divorced or widowed person adopts his or her spouse's children. In these cases, the noncustodial parent relinquishes his or her parental rights. This includes the right to inherit from a child's estate; the right to visitation; the right to make decisions regarding health, education, and religious upbringing; and the obligation to pay child support. The procedures for a stepparent adoption are similar to those of independent adoptions in general, except that some courts have streamlined the process by eliminating waiting periods and the necessity for a home study conducted by state officials. The home study screening in a stepparent adoption is not as extensive as that conducted in an independent adoption.

In order to adopt a stepchild, a stepparent must obtain consent from both biological parents. Consent is needed so the court can terminate the noncustodial parent's rights and legalize the adoption with the stepparent. The custodial parent's rights remain intact in a stepparent adoption. While obtaining consent from the custodial parent may be easy, as he or she is generally in favor of the adoption, the same may not be said of the noncustodial parent. A stepparent's attempt to adopt a stepchild may be unsuccessful if the biological, noncustodial parent raises an objection. There may be legal grounds in some jurisdictions for a stepparent to prevail—such as the noncustodial parent's willful failure to pay child support, abandonment, or parental abuse or neglect of the child. Legal **abandonment** is defined in many states as failure to have contact with a child or provide that child with support for one continuous year. If the noncustodial parent calls the child sporadically and sends cards or visits occasionally, this does not satisfy the definition of abandonment. The procedure is relatively easy when the noncustodial parent is deceased, since the parental rights are terminated by death.

Not all stepparent adoptions are heard in a state's family court. In the State of Connecticut, for example, the state's probate courts have jurisdiction over these matters. In other states, adoptions may be heard by the surrogacy courts. It is important to determine which court in the state may hear a stepparent adoption.

The next step in processing a stepparent adoption through the state courts is to file a petition in the appropriate court. Laws and forms to process stepparent adoptions vary from state to state. It is also important to give notice to all the parties involved. This includes conducting a diligent search for the noncustodial parent, who may have been absent from the child's life. It is best to exhaust all avenues to find the noncustodial parent and provide him or her with notice. This will spare any emotional trauma and legal challenges later on should the noncustodial parent raise any objections.

In the landmark U.S. Supreme Court case of *Armstrong v. Manzo,* 380 U.S. 545 (1965), the Court held that lack of notice to the noncustodial father violated his rights to due process. In *Armstrong,* the mother, who had custody of the minor child, remarried. Two years later, her new husband filed stepparent adoption papers. The mother informed the juvenile court that the biological father had not financially supported the child during this two-year period. The mother also told the court that she was not aware of his whereabouts. Based on her representations, the juvenile court granted the stepparent's petition for adoption. When the biological father heard of the news, he filed a petition to annul the adoption and, at a hearing before the juvenile court, also presented evidence that he had in fact met his child support obligations. The juvenile court denied his petition, the Texas

Appellate Court affirmed the lower court decision, and the Texas Supreme Court refused to hear the case. The father's appeal to the U.S. Supreme Court proved successful. The Court agreed with the father's argument that his right to due process was violated. The Court held that father's due process rights would be protected by vacating the order and granting him a new hearing.

The Court must also determine that a stepparent adoption is in the child's best interest. If the child is old enough to be involved in the decision process, he or she should be involved. The child's opinion is very important. If the child has a relationship with the noncustodial parent, that child may be conflicted about the adoption. The child may feel less conflicted if there is little or no relationship with the noncustodial parent. In some jurisdictions, a child who is of sufficient statutory age must also consent to the adoption in writing.

Gay stepparents and heterosexual domestic partners may in some jurisdictions use procedures for stepparent adoption. In the State of Massachusetts, where same-sex couples can legally marry, same-sex spouses may also be able to adopt their partner's children. California statutes allow registered domestic partners to use the same streamlined adoption procedures available to stepparents. Following is California's stepparent adoption statute.

California Family Code Section 9000-9007

9000. (a) A stepparent desiring to adopt a child of the stepparent's spouse may for that purpose file a petition in the county in which the petitioner resides.

(b) A domestic partner, as defined in Section 297, desiring to adopt a child of his or her domestic partner may for that purpose file a petition in the county in which the petitioner resides.

(c) The caption of the adoption petition shall contain the names of the petitioners, but not the child's name. The petition shall state the child's sex and date of birth and the name the child had before adoption.

(d) If the child is the subject of a guardianship petition, the adoption petition shall so state and shall include the caption and docket number or have attached a copy of the letters of the guardianship or temporary guardianship. The petitioners shall notify the court of any petition for guardianship or temporary guardianship filed after the adoption petition. The guardianship proceeding shall be consolidated with the adoption proceeding.

(e) The order of adoption shall contain the child's adopted name, but not the name the child had before adoption.

(f) If the petitioner has entered into a postadoption contact agreement with the birth parent as set forth in Section 8616.5, the agreement, signed by the participating parties, shall be attached to and filed with the petition for adoption.

(g) For the purposes of this chapter, stepparent adoption includes adoption by a domestic partner, as defined in Section 297.

9001. (a) The probation officer, qualified court investigator, licensed clinical social worker, licensed marriage family therapist, or, at the option of the board of supervisors, the county welfare department in the county in which the adoption proceeding is pending shall make an investigation of each case of stepparent adoption. The court may not make an order of adoption until after the probation officer, qualified court investigator, licensed clinical social worker, licensed marriage family therapist, or county welfare department has filed its report and recommendation and they have been considered by the court.

(b) Unless ordered by the court, no home study may be required of the petitioner's home in a stepparent adoption. The agency conducting the investigation or any interested person may request the court to order a home study or the court may order a home study on its own motion.

(c) "Home study" as used in this section means a physical investigation of the premises where the child is residing.

9002. In a stepparent adoption, the prospective adoptive parent is liable for all reasonable costs incurred in connection with the stepparent adoption, including, but not limited to, costs incurred for the investigation required by Section 9001, up to a maximum of seven hundred dollars ($700). The court, probation officer, qualified court investigator, or county welfare department may defer, waive, or reduce the fee if its payment would cause economic hardship to the prospective adoptive parent detrimental to the welfare of the adopted child.

9003.(a) In a stepparent adoption, the consent of either or both birth parents shall be signed in the presence of a notary public, court clerk, probation officer, qualified court investigator, or county welfare department staff member of any county of this state. The notary public, court clerk, probation officer, qualified court investigator, or county welfare department staff member before whom the consent is signed shall immediately file the consent with the clerk of the court where the adoption petition is filed. The clerk shall immediately notify the probation officer or, at the option of the board of supervisors, the county welfare department of that county.

(b) If the birth parent of a child to be adopted is outside this state at the time of signing the consent, the consent may be signed before a notary or other person authorized to perform notarial acts.

(c) The consent, when reciting that the person giving it is entitled to sole custody of the child and when acknowledged before the notary public, court clerk, probation officer, qualified court investigator, or county welfare department staff member, is prima facie evidence of the right of the person signing the consent to the sole custody of the child and that person's sole right to consent.

(d) A birth parent who is a minor has the right to sign a consent for the adoption of the birth parent's child and the consent is not subject to revocation by reason of the minority.

9004. In a stepparent adoption, the form prescribed by the department for the consent of the birth parent shall contain substantially the following notice:

"Notice to the parent who gives the child for adoption: If you and your child lived together at any time as parent and child, the adoption of your child through a stepparent adoption does not affect the child's right to inherit your property or the property of other blood relatives."

9005. (a) Consent of the birth parent to the adoption of the child through a stepparent adoption may not be withdrawn except with court approval. Request for that approval may be made by motion, or a birth parent seeking to withdraw consent may file with the clerk of the court where the adoption petition is pending, a petition for approval of withdrawal of consent, without the necessity of paying a fee for filing the petition. The petition or motion shall be in writing, and shall set forth the reasons for withdrawal of consent, but otherwise may be in any form.

(b) The court clerk shall set the matter for hearing and shall give notice thereof to the probation officer, qualified court investigator, or county welfare department, to the prospective adoptive parent, and to the birth parent or parents by certified mail, return receipt requested, to the address of each as shown in the proceeding, at least 10 days before the time set for hearing.

(c) The probation officer, qualified court investigator, or county welfare department shall, before the hearing of the motion or petition for withdrawal, file a full report with the court and shall appear at the hearing to represent the interests of the child.

(d) At the hearing, the parties may appear in person or with counsel. The hearing shall be held in chambers, but the court reporter shall report the proceedings and, on court order, the fee therefor shall be paid from the county treasury. If the court finds that withdrawal of the consent to adoption is reasonable in view of all the circumstances and that withdrawal of the consent is in the child's best interest, the court shall approve the withdrawal of the consent. Otherwise the court shall withhold its approval.

Consideration of the child's best interest shall include, but is not limited to, an assessment of the child's age, the extent of bonding with the prospective adoptive parent, the extent of bonding or the potential to bond with the birth parent, and the ability of the birth parent to provide adequate and proper care and guidance to the child. If the court approves the withdrawal of consent, the adoption proceeding shall be dismissed.

(e) A court order granting or withholding approval of a withdrawal of consent to an adoption may be appealed in the same manner as an order of the juvenile court declaring a person to be a ward of the juvenile court.

9006. (a) If the petitioner moves to withdraw the adoption petition or to dismiss the proceeding, the court clerk shall immediately notify the probation officer, qualified court investigator, or county welfare department of the action.

(b) If a birth parent has refused to give the required consent, the adoption petition shall be dismissed.

9007. The prospective adoptive parent and the child proposed to be adopted shall appear before the court pursuant to Sections 8612 and 8613.

GAY ADOPTION

Same-sex couples today are not only seeking legal recognition of their unions, but also legal recognition as parents of the children they raise. Legal custody of a child protects both the rights of the parent and the rights of the child in the event of the dissolution of the relationship between the parents, intrusion by other relatives or the state, or death of one of the same-sex parents.

Same-sex couples, in one way or another, have always created families that have included children. Some gay men or lesbians leave heterosexual marriages with custody of their children and form family units with their partners without legal protections. Lesbians may use artificial insemination and gay men may hire surrogates to carry and deliver a child on their behalf. In the past, when homosexuality was deep in the closet, gay and lesbian parents adopted as "single persons" and explained away the same-sex partner as a roommate or member of the family. Perjury or lying under oath is a crime, so this type of subterfuge should never be recommended to a client. More and more same-sex couples are adopting children through the same channels used by heterosexual couples. Some couples have gone the traditional route of adopting through a state agency, while others have become parents through international adoptions. Their ability to adopt depends largely on state or international laws, as well as the attitudes of social workers, lawyers, judges, and adoption agency personnel.

Utah, Mississippi, and Florida have enacted statutes that expressly ban adoptions by same-sex couples. The State of Arkansas bans same-sex adoption by state agency rules. Florida Statute 63.042(3), for example, states "[n]o person eligible to adopt under this statute may adopt if that person is a homosexual." California, Connecticut, the District of Columbia, Illinois, Indiana, Massachusetts, New Jersey,

New York, Pennsylvania, and Vermont allow same-sex couples to enter into joint adoptions. Other states allow what is known as **second parent adoptions.** In these jurisdictions, one partner of a same-sex couple adopts the child and the other partner files for co-parent status. Once a legal bond has been created through a second parent or joint adoption, a same-sex partner now has the right to make decisions regarding the child's health, education, and welfare, as well as the responsibility of providing the child with financial support, similar to heterosexual parents.

In most states, the issue of whether a same-sex parent may adopt is left up to the presiding judge. Because of the subjective nature of applying the best interest of the child standard in adoption cases, a same-sex couple may be at a disadvantage if the court is in any way opposed to the gay lifestyle.

OPEN ADOPTION

An **open adoption** is an adoption where the biological parents, the adoptive parents, and sometimes the children are known to each other. This is contrary to an independent adoption where the parties have no knowledge of the others' identity. The advantages of an open adoption are to maintain a child's relationship with the birth family, as long as doing so is in the child's best interest. Most adopted children, at some point in their lives, want the truth about their family of origin, which may include the desire to reconnect with their parents and other relatives. Open adoptions provide the adoptive parents and the child with an extensive medical history of the child's birth family. This information is necessary for the child to receive adequate health care treatment throughout his or her life.

Informal open adoptions have existed since the beginning of time, where relatives have stepped in to care for the children of family members when they are unable to do so. The biological and adoptive parents may be aware of the other's identity under the following circumstances:

1. The biological parents may have specifically chosen the adoptive parents to adopt their children and therefore may know them personally. For example, biological parents who cannot care for their children or have had their parental rights terminated due to the abuse, neglect, or abandonment of a child may identify relatives who are willing and able to assume legal responsibility of the child.

2. The biological parents may have chosen an adoptive couple after having been provided with information about the prospective parents and their ability to provide the child with a loving home. This is usually done through a private or state agency. While the parties do not know each other by identity, the biological parents receive some personal assurances that they have chosen a good home for their child.

3. Another situation is where there is contact between the biological and adoptive parents and possibly the child. The degree of contact between the parties depends on the level of comfort of the parties. The degree of contact, arranged by agreement, may take the form of:
   (a) a picture of the child sent by the adoptive parents to the biological parents once or twice a year;
   (b) letters, phone calls, or emails sent by the adoptive parents regarding the child;
   (c) in-person visits with the children; and
   (d) contact with the child.

THE OPEN ADOPTION AGREEMENT

Biological parents who enter into an open adoption are not the child's legal parent because their parental rights have been severed by a court of law. The adoptive parents now have legal custody and guardianship of the child. The **open adoption agreement** is a contract entered into between one or both biological parents and the adoptive parents, prior to the adoption proceeding, that grants the biological parent(s) the right to continue some type of relationship with the child or to have information regarding the child's development and well-being. The first step in drafting an open adoption agreement is to determine the state law regarding these contracts.

Some states allow the parties to enter into an enforceable agreement regarding postadoption contact with the child or adoptive parents. The State of Washington, for example, has legislated that the parties may enter into a legally binding open adoption contract.

Revised Code of Washington 26.33.295

1. Nothing in this chapter shall be construed to prohibit the parties to a proceeding under this chapter from entering into agreements regarding communication with or contact between child adoptees, adoptive parents, and a birth parent or parents.

2. Agreements regarding communication with or contact between child adoptees, adoptive parents, and a birth parent or parents shall not be legally enforceable unless the terms of the agreement are set forth in a written court order entered in accordance with the provisions of this section. The court shall not enter a proposed order unless the terms of such order have been approved in writing by the prospective adoptive parents, any birth parent whose parental rights have not previously been terminated, and, if the child is in the custody of the department or a licensed child-placing agency, a representative of the department or child-placing agency. If the child is represented by an attorney or guardian ad litem in a proceeding under this chapter or in any other child-custody proceeding, the terms of the proposed order also must be approved in writing by the child's representative. An agreement under this section need not disclose the identity of the parties to be legally enforceable. The court shall not enter a proposed order unless the court finds that the communication or contact between the child adoptee, the adoptive parents, and a birth parent or parents as agreed upon and as set forth in the proposed order, would be in the child adoptee's best interests.

3. Failure to comply with the terms of an agreed order regarding communication or contact that has been entered by the court pursuant to this section shall not be grounds for setting aside an adoption decree or revocation of a written consent to an adoption after that consent has been approved by the court as provided in this chapter.

4. An agreed order entered pursuant to this section may be enforced by a civil action and the prevailing party in that action may be awarded, as part of the costs of the action, a reasonable amount to be fixed by the court as attorneys' fees. The court shall not modify an agreed order under this section unless it finds that the modification is necessary to serve the best interests of the child adoptee, and that: (a) The modification is agreed to by the adoptive parent and the birth parent or parents; or (b) exceptional circumstances have arisen since the agreed order was entered that justify modification of the order.

Other jurisdictions, such as the State of Oregon, for example, may allow the parties to enter into nonbinding agreements.

Oregon Statutes 109.305

1. The rule that statutes in derogation of common law are to be strictly construed does not apply to the adoption laws of this state.
2. Nothing in the adoption laws of this state shall be construed to prevent the adoptive parents, the birth parents and the child from entering into a written agreement, approved by the court, to permit continuing contact between the birth relatives and the child or the adoptive parents. As used in this subsection, "birth relatives" includes birth parents, grandparents, siblings and other members of the child's birth family.
3. Failure to comply with the terms of an agreement made under subsection (2) of this section is not grounds for setting aside an adoption judgment or revocation of a written consent to an adoption.

4.(a) An agreement made under subsection (2) of this section may be enforced by a civil action. However, before a court may enter an order requiring compliance with the agreement, the court must find that the party seeking enforcement participated, or attempted to participate, in good faith in mediating the dispute giving rise to the action prior to filing the civil action.

(b) The court may modify an agreement made under subsection (2) of this section if the court finds that the modification is necessary to serve the best interests of the adopted child, that the party seeking modification participated, or attempted to participate, in good faith in mediation prior to seeking modification of the agreement and that:

(A) The modification is agreed to by all parties to the original agreement; or

(B) Exceptional circumstances have arisen since the parties entered into the agreement that justify modification of the agreement.

The paralegal may be given the task of drafting the open adoption agreement. In addition to becoming familiar with any state law on the subject, the paralegal must also review the relevant case law interpreting the statute to get further insight on how to draft a valid open adoption agreement. A paralegal may also review an open adoption agreement on behalf of a client at the attorney's request. Knowledge of the law is equally important regardless of whether the office represents the biological parents, adoptive parents, or the child. When reviewing the document on behalf of the minor child, the guiding principle is always the best interest of the child.

Once the relevant law of the jurisdiction is reviewed, the biological parents and their respective attorneys should establish the terms of the contract by determining the type of open adoption, the frequency of the contact, and the duration of the visits or phone calls. A paralegal must be clear regarding the terms agreed upon by the parties before drafting the open adoption agreement.

END OF CHAPTER EXERCISES

Crossword Puzzle

Across

2. a court proceeding that severs the legal bond between a parent and his or her biological or legally adopted child

3. professionals and paraprofessionals required, under penalty of law, to report suspected child abuse

5. a form of adoption in which one partner of a same-sex couple adopts the child and the other partner files for co-parent status

7. where an individual who marries a divorced or widowed person adopts his or her spouse's children

8. a legal procedure that makes a person or persons the legal parent or parents of a minor child who is not their natural child

9. failure to have contact with a child or have provided that child with support for one continuous year

10. a form of adoption in which the biological parents, the adoptive parents, and sometimes the children are known to each other

Down

1. a state agency charged with intervening in the family unit when child neglect or abuse is known or suspected

4. a contract entered into between one or both biological parents and the adoptive parents, prior to the adoption proceeding, that grants the biological parent(s) the right to continue some type of relationship with the child or to have information regarding the child's development and well-being

6. U.S. Supreme Court case decided in 1965 in which the Court held that lack of notice to the noncustodial father violated his rights to due process

Review Questions

1. Does the U.S. Constitution guarantee absolute protection of the integrity of the family?

2. What is the function of a state child protection agency?

3. What is the state social worker's role in investigating allegations of child abuse and neglect?

4. What are the legal grounds for terminating a parent's parental rights?

5. Define adoption, open adoption, and stepparent adoption.

Case for Briefing

Remkiewicz v. Remkiewicz, 180 Conn.114, 120, 429 A.2d 1035 (1980)

Exploring the Workplace: Activities

1. You work as a paralegal in the Law Firm of Capone, Ulto, & Torello in your state. Monique Fallon and Thomas Gallagher are clients of the firm. She was divorced three years ago and has two boys, ages eight and nine. Her ex-husband, William Fallon, moved out of state after the divorce and has not had any contact with either the ex-wife or the children. He does, however, pay child support, which is deducted from his paycheck under a wage withholding order. Ms. Fallon married Mr. Gallagher two years ago. He is wonderful with the children and treats them as if they were his own. The children call him "Dad." Mr. Gallagher wants to adopt the children; Ms. Fallon is in full agreement with this idea and so are the children.

After researching your state law through Internet or state-specific sources, determine the procedure for processing a stepparent adoption and determine which court has jurisdiction over these matters. If Mr. Fallon does not consent to the stepparent adoption, what are the chances that his parental rights will be terminated under your jurisdiction's statute? Prepare an interoffice memorandum for your supervising attorney, Lori Ulto. Visit the National Adoption Information Clearinghouse website at **http://naic.acf.hhs.gov/**.

You will find links to state laws under "General Resources, Law and Legal Issues."

2. Using the above-referenced website, research your state's statute on mandatory reporters. What persons in your jurisdiction are required to report suspected child abuse and neglect? What is the penalty in your state for failure of a mandatory reporter to file a report of suspected child abuse and neglect? Must the report be in writing? What is the time frame for filing a report?

3. You work as a paralegal for the Law Office of Jonathan Mack in your state. Clients Evelyn Wynn and Rona Gomez are seeking the advice of Attorney Mack in a gay adoption issue. Evelyn Wynn has a child from a previous heterosexual marriage. The child's biological father is deceased.

Ms. Wynn has been diagnosed with early stage breast cancer. Her prognosis looks good and she is responding quite well to her treatments. This scare has prompted both women to discuss the possibility of Ms. Gomez adopting the child as either a joint or co-parent. They would like some advice on their rights and options in your state. Using the Internet or state-specific sources, prepare an interoffice memorandum for Attorney Mack outlining Ms. Gomez's rights and whether adoption is possible.

APPENDIX A

Arizona and California Premarital Agreement Acts

Arizona Uniform Premarital Agreement Act

Ariz. Rev. Stat. § 25-201 *et seq.*

25-201. Definitions

In this article, unless the context otherwise requires:

1. "Premarital agreement" means an agreement between prospective spouses that is made in contemplation of marriage and that is effective on marriage.
2. "Property" means an interest, present or future, legal or equitable, vested or contingent, in real or personal property, including income and earnings.

25-202. Enforcement of premarital agreements; exception

A. A premarital agreement must be in writing and signed by both parties. The agreement is enforceable without consideration.

B. The agreement becomes effective on marriage of the parties.

C. The agreement is not enforceable if the person against whom enforcement is sought proves either of the following:

   1. The person did not execute the agreement voluntarily.
   2. The agreement was unconscionable when it was executed and before execution of the agreement that person:
      (a) Was not provided a fair and reasonable disclosure of the property or financial obligations of the other party.
      (b) Did not voluntarily and expressly waive, in writing, any right to disclosure of the property or financial obligations of the other party beyond the disclosure provided.

      (c) Did not have, or reasonably could not have had, an adequate knowledge of the property or financial obligations of the other party.

D. If a provision of a premarital agreement modifies or eliminates spousal support and that modification or elimination causes one party to the agreement to be eligible for support under a program of public assistance at the time of separation or marital dissolution, a court, notwithstanding the terms of the agreement, may require the other party to provide support to the extent necessary to avoid that eligibility.

E. An issue of unconscionability of a premarital agreement shall be decided by the court as a matter of law.

F. If a marriage is determined to be void, an agreement that would otherwise have been a premarital agreement is enforceable only to the extent necessary to avoid an inequitable result.

25-203. Scope of agreement

A. Parties to a premarital agreement may contract with respect to:
1. The rights and obligations of each of the parties in any of the property of either or both of them whenever and wherever acquired or located.
2. The right to buy, sell, use, transfer, exchange, abandon, lease, consume, expend, assign or create a security interest in, mortgage, encumber, dispose of or otherwise manage and control property.
3. The disposition of property on separation, marital dissolution, death or the occurrence or nonoccurrence of any other event.
4. The modification or elimination of spousal support.
5. The making of a will, trust or other arrangement to carry out the provisions of the agreement.
6. The ownership rights in and disposition of the death benefit from a life insurance policy.
7. The choice of law governing the construction of the agreement.
8. Any other matter, including their personal rights and obligations, not in violation of public policy or a statute imposing a criminal penalty.

B. The right of a child to support may not be adversely affected by a premarital agreement.

25-204. Amendment or revocation of agreement

After marriage, a premarital agreement may be amended or revoked only by a written agreement signed by the parties. The amended agreement or the revocation is enforceable without consideration.

25-205. Limitation of actions

A statute of limitations applicable to an action asserting a claim for relief under a premarital agreement is tolled during the marriage of the parties to the agreement. However, equitable defenses limiting the time for enforcement, including laches and estoppel, are available to either party.

California Premarital Agreement Act

California Family Law Code Section 1615(c)

A. A premarital agreement is not enforceable if the party against whom enforcement is sought proves either of the following:
1. That party did not execute the agreement voluntarily.
2. The agreement was unconscionable when it was executed and, before execution of the agreement, all of the following applied to that party:
    (a) That party was not provided a fair, reasonable, and full disclosure of the property or financial obligations of the other party.
    (b) That party did not voluntarily and expressly waive, in writing, any right to disclosure of the property or financial obligations of the other party beyond the disclosure provided.
    (c) That party did not have, or reasonably could not have had, an adequate knowledge of the property or financial obligations of the other party.
B. An issue of unconscionability of a premarital agreement shall be decided by the court as a matter of law.
C. For the purposes of subdivision (a), it shall be deemed that a premarital agreement was not executed voluntarily unless the court finds in writing or on the record all of the following:
1. The party against whom enforcement is sought was represented by independent legal counsel at the time of signing the agreement or, after being advised to seek independent legal counsel, expressly waived, in a separate writing, representation by independent legal counsel.
2. The party against whom enforcement is sought had not less than seven calendar days between the time that party was first presented with the agreement and advised to seek independent legal counsel and the time the agreement was signed.
3. The party against whom enforcement is sought, if unrepresented by legal counsel, was fully informed of the terms and basic effect of the agreement as well as the rights and obligations he or she was giving up by signing the agreement, and was proficient in the language in which the explanation of the party's rights was conducted and in which the agreement was written. The explanation of the rights and obligations relinquished shall be memorialized in writing and delivered to the party prior to signing the agreement. The unrepresented party shall, on or before the signing of the premarital agreement, execute a document declaring that he or she received the information required by this paragraph and indicating who provided that information.
4. The agreement and the writings executed pursuant to paragraphs (1) and (3) were not executed under duress, fraud, or undue influence, and the parties did not lack capacity to enter into the agreement.
5. Any other factors the court deems relevant.

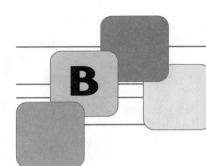

APPENDIX

Qualified Domestic Relations Order
(Jim Carrey)

1 Paul L. Basile, Jr.
   (State Bar No. 050078)
2 Attorney at Law
   11400 West Olympic Boulevard, Ninth Floor
3 Los Angeles, California 90064-1507
   Telephone: (310) 478-2114
4
   Special Tax Counsel
5

FILED
LOS ANGELES SUPERIOR COURT

JUN 1 4 1994

EDWARD M. KRITZMAN, CLERK

L. A. Belmonte

BY R. A. BELMONTE, DEPUTY

8   SUPERIOR COURT OF THE STATE OF CALIFORNIA

9   FOR THE COUNTY OF LOS ANGELES

10

11 In Re the Marriage of:

12 JAMES EUGENE CARREY,

13   Petitioner,

14   and

15 MELISSA JANE CARREY,

16   Respondent.

17

Case No: BD 135 499

STIPULATED QUALIFIED DOMESTIC RELATIONS ORDER RE AFTRA RETIREMENT PLAN

18   WHEREAS, Petitioner, JAMES EUGENE CARREY, and Respondent, MELISSA

19 JANE CARREY, were married to each other on March 28, 1987, and separated on June 15,

20 1993;

21   WHEREAS, this Court has personal jurisdiction over both Petitioner and

22 Respondent and jurisdiction over the subject matter of this Order and this dissolution of

23 marriage action;

24   WHEREAS, Petitioner, Respondent, and the Court intend that this Order

25 shall be a Qualified Domestic Relations Order (a "QDRO") as that term is used in the

26 Retirement Equity Act of 1984, P.L. No. 98-397 (the "Act"); and

27   WHEREAS, Petitioner and Respondent have stipulated that the Court shall

28 enter the following Order:

1   NOW, THEREFORE, IT IS HEREBY ORDERED BY THE COURT as

2 follows:

3   1.   As used in this Order, the following terms shall apply:

4   a.   "Participant" refers to the Petitioner, JAMES EUGENE

5 CARREY, whose last known address is c/o JOHN RIGNEY,

6 RIGNEY/FRIEDMAN BUSINESS MANAGEMENT, 12400 Wilshire Boulevard,

7 Suite 850, Los Angeles, California 90025, whose social security number is ▮▮▮

8 ▮▮▮▮, and whose date of birth is January 17, 1962.

9   b.   "Alternate Payee" refers to the Respondent, MELISSA

10 JANE CARREY, whose last known address is c/o JOHN RIGNEY,

11 RIGNEY/FRIEDMAN BUSINESS MANAGEMENT, 12400 Wilshire Boulevard,

12 Suite 850, Los Angeles, California 90025, whose social security number is

13 ▮▮▮▮▮, and whose date of birth is July 8, 1960.

14   c.   "Plan" refers to the AFTRA RETIREMENT PLAN, as

15 amended, the Trustee of which is the Board of Trustees of the AFTRA

16 RETIREMENT PLAN, and the assets of which are currently held by said

17 Trustee.

18   d.   "Plan Administrator" refers to the Board of Trustees of

19 the AFTRA RETIREMENT PLAN.

20   2.   The Alternate Payee is the spouse of Participant until the herein

21 marriage has been dissolved.

22   3.   This order is entered pursuant to the California Family Law Act,

23 Section 2500 *et seq.* of the California Family Law Code.

24   4.   The Alternate Payee shall be entitled to share in the benefits of the

25 Plan as follows:

26   a.   The Alternate Payee shall receive a monthly pension,

27 commencing on the date when the Participant attains Normal Retirement Age

28 (as defined in the Plan) in an amount equal to one-half (1/2) of the

Participant's accrued benefit as of the date of separation (June 15, 1993) to which the Participant would be entitled on normal retirement age computed on a single life annuity basis and multiplied by a fraction, the numerator of which is the number of months of the Participant's participation in the Plan between the date of marriage (March 28, 1987) and the date of separation (June 15, 1993), and the denominator of which is the total number of months of the Participant's participation in the Plan as of the Participant's Normal Retirement Age. If the Participant retires earlier than at Normal Retirement Age, the date of the Participant's actual retirement shall be used in the foregoing calculation in place of Normal Retirement Age.

  b.   If the Participant dies before payments have commenced to the Alternate Payee, then, whether or not the Participant is survived by a spouse (other than the Alternate Payee) and whether or not the Participant has met the eligibility requirements for a pension, the Alternate Payee shall receive monthly payments in an amount equal to the monthly amount payable to a surviving spouse under the Plan, if any, multiplied by a fraction, the numerator of which is the number of months of the Participant's participation in the Plan between the dates of marriage and separation, and the denominator of which is the total number of months of the Participant's participation in the Plan as of the time of the Participant's death. The remainder of the monthly amount payable under the Plan, and no more, shall be paid to the Participant's spouse or designated beneficiary, as the case may be.

  c.   With respect to the Alternate Payee's entitlements under Paragraph 4(a) above, the amount thereof shall be calculated on the basis of a single life annuity with the Participant's life as the measuring life, but the Alternate Payee may elect to have the Alternate Payee's share paid to the Alternate Payee in actuarially adjusted monthly amounts over the Alternate

Payee's lifetime. If the Alternate Payee does not so elect, payments to the Alternate Payee shall cease on the Participant's death. If the Alternate Payee does not so elect and the Alternate Payee predeceases the Participant, the remaining payments of the Alternate Payee's entitlement, if any, shall be made to the beneficiary designated by the Alternate Payee in writing and filed with the Plan Administrator, provided that any such beneficiary qualifies as an alternate payee of the Participant pursuant to ERISA §206(d)(3)(K). Similarly, if the Alternate Payee predeceases the Participant and dies before payments have commenced, the Alternate Payee's entitlement, if any, shall be paid to the Alternate Payee's designated beneficiary or beneficiaries and·in the form designated by the Alternate Payee in writing and filed with the Plan Administrator, such payment to be made at the time it would have been made to the Alternate Payee if the Alternate Payee were still living, provided that any such beneficiary qualifies as an alternate payee of the Participant pursuant to ERISA §206(d)(3)(K).

d.   Notwithstanding any provision of the Plan, payment of benefits to the Alternate Payee shall not be suspended by reason of the Participant's returning to covered employment after retiring.

5.   At the Alternate Payee's election, the Alternate Payee may receive the Alternate Payee's benefits at the earliest time permissible under the Plan consistent with the methods set forth in this Order. If such election is made prior to the Participant's date of retirement, the date when the Alternate Payee makes the election shall be used in place of the Participant's date of retirement in calculating the denominator of the fraction expressed in Section 4(a) of this Order. If the Alternate Payee dies before making such election and before payments have commenced to the Alternate Payee, such election may be made by the Alternate Payee's designated beneficiary, provided that any such beneficiary qualifies as an alternate payee of the Participant pursuant to ERISA §206(d)(3)(K).

6.   The Participant and the Alternate Payee shall be separately responsible

1 for income taxes attributable to the payments received by each of them under the Plan.

2   7.   This Order is intended to be a QDRO made pursuant to the Act, has

3 been determined to be a QDRO by the signature of the Plan Administrator below, and its

4 provisions shall be administered and interpreted in conformity with the Act. If the Act is

5 amended or the law regarding QDROs is otherwise changed or modified, then the parties

6 hereto shall immediately take such steps as are necessary to amend this QDRO to comply

7 with any such changes, amendments, or modification to the Act or laws regarding QDROs.

8   8.   The Court shall retain jurisdiction over this matter to amend this Order

9 in order to establish and/or maintain its qualification as a QDRO under the Act and to

10 carry out the terms and conditions of this Order.

11

12 Dated: 4/20/94

           JAMES EUGENE CARREY, Petitioner

13

14 Dated: 1/20/94

           MELISSA JANE CARREY, Respondent

15

16 APPROVED AS TO FORM AND CONTENT:

17 Dated: 5/26/97

           LAW OFFICES OF NORMAN M. DOLIN

18

19   By:
           NORMAN M. DOLIN
           Attorney for Petitioner,

20   JAMES EUGENE CARREY

21

22 Dated: 4/20/94

           SIMKE, CHODOS, SILBERFELD & ANTEAU, INC.

23

24   By:
            RONALD W. ANTEAU,
           Attorney for Respondent,

25   MELISSA JANE CARREY

26

27

28

1 Dated: 6-1-94

Board of Trustees of the
AFTRA RETIREMENT PLAN

By: _____
Plan Administrator

5 THE CLERK IS ORDERED TO ENTER THIS ORDER.

7 JUN 1 4 1994

Dated: _____

_____
JUDGE OF THE SUPERIOR COURT

JAMES D. ENDMAN
Judge Pro Tem

1 | Paul L. Basile, Jr.
(State Bar No. 050078)
2 | Attorney at Law
11400 West Olympic Boulevard, Ninth Floor
3 | Los Angeles, California 90064-1507
Telephone: (310) 478-2114
4 |
5 | Special Tax Counsel

FILED
LOS ANGELES SUPERIOR COURT
MAY 2 6 1994
EDWARD M. KRITZMAN, CLERK
BY R. A. BELMONTE, DEPUTY

8 | SUPERIOR COURT OF THE STATE OF CALIFORNIA

9 | FOR THE COUNTY OF LOS ANGELES

10 |

11 | In Re the Marriage of:

Case No: BD 135 499

12 | JAMES EUGENE CARREY,

STIPULATED QUALIFIED
DOMESTIC RELATIONS ORDER
RE SCREEN ACTORS GUILD-
PRODUCERS PENSION PLAN

13 | Petitioner,

14 | and

15 | MELISSA JANE CARREY,

16 | Respondent.

17 |

18 | WHEREAS, Petitioner, JAMES EUGENE CARREY, and Respondent, MELISSA

19 | JANE CARREY, were married to each other on March 28, 1987, and separated on June 15,

20 | 1993;

21 | WHEREAS, this Court has personal jurisdiction over both Petitioner and

22 | Respondent and jurisdiction over the subject matter of this Order and this dissolution of

23 | marriage action;

24 | WHEREAS, Petitioner, Respondent, and the Court intend that this Order

25 | shall be a Qualified Domestic Relations Order (a "QDRO") as that term is used in the

26 | Retirement Equity Act of 1984, P.L. No. 98-397 (the "Act"); and

27 | WHEREAS, Petitioner and Respondent have stipulated that the Court shall

28 | enter the following Order:

- 1 -

1 NOW, THEREFORE, IT IS HEREBY ORDERED BY THE COURT as

2 follows:

3   1.   As used in this Order, the following terms shall apply:

4   a.   "Participant" refers to the Petitioner, JAMES EUGENE

5 CARREY, whose last known address is c/o JOHN RIGNEY,

6 RIGNEY/FRIEDMAN BUSINESS MANAGEMENT, 12400 Wilshire Boulevard,

7 Suite 850, Los Angeles, California 90025, whose social security number is ▮▮

8 ▮▮▮▮, and whose date of birth is January 17, 1962.

9   b.   "Alternate Payee" refers to the Respondent, MELISSA

10 JANE CARREY, whose last known address is c/o JOHN RIGNEY,

11 RIGNEY/FRIEDMAN BUSINESS MANAGEMENT, 12400 Wilshire Boulevard,

12 Suite 850, Los Angeles, California 90025, whose social security number is

13 ▮▮▮▮▮, and whose date of birth is July 8, 1960.

14   c.   "Plan" refers to the SCREEN ACTORS GUILD-PRODUCERS

15 PENSION PLAN, as amended (a non-contributory defined benefit plan), the

16 Trustee of which is the Board of Trustees of the SCREEN ACTORS GUILD-

17 PRODUCERS PENSION PLAN, and the assets of which are currently held by

18 said Trustee.

19   d.   "Plan Administrator" refers to BRUCE L. DOW, or his

20 successor duly appointed by the Trustee.

21   2.   The Alternate Payee is the spouse of Participant until the herein

22 marriage has been dissolved.

23   3.   This order is entered pursuant to the California Family Law Act,

24 Section 2500 *et seq.* of the California Family Law Code.

25   4.   The Alternate Payee shall be entitled to share in the benefits of the

26 Plan as follows:

27   a.   The Alternate Payee shall receive a monthly pension,

28 commencing on the date when the Participant retires under the Plan in an

amount equal to one-half (1/2) of the monthly pension to which the Participant would be entitled on that date computed on a single life annuity basis and multiplied by a fraction, the numerator of which is the number of years of Pension Credit (as defined in the Plan) earned by the Participant between the date of marriage (March 28, 1987) and the date of separation (June 15, 1993), and the denominator of which is the total number of years of the Participant's Pension Credit at the Participant's date of retirement. In computing the numerator, the Pension Credit for the year of marriage and the year of separation shall be prorated on a daily basis.

b.   With respect to the Alternate Payee's entitlement under Section 4(a) of this Order, the amount thereof shall be calculated on the basis of a single life annuity with the Participant's life as the measuring life and shall be paid to the Alternate Payee in actuarially adjusted monthly amounts over the Alternate Payee's lifetime. If the Alternate Payee dies before the Alternate Payee has received sixty (60) monthly payments, monthly payments shall be made to the beneficiary or beneficiaries designated by the Alternate Payee in writing and filed with the Plan Administrator until a total of sixty (60) monthly payments have been made. If no beneficiary declaration is on file at the Alternate Payee's death or if no designated beneficiary survives until the Alternate Payee's entitlement is paid in full, the unpaid balance of the Alternate Payee's entitlement shall be paid to the Alternate Payee's estate.

c.   If the Participant dies before payments have commenced to the Alternate Payee, then, whether or not the Participant is survived by a Qualified Spouse (as defined in the Plan), the Alternate Payee (or the Alternate Payee's designated beneficiary if the Alternate Payee shall have predeceased the Participant) shall receive an amount equal to one-half (1/2) of the Death Benefit (as defined below) multiplied by a fraction the

1   numerator of which is the same as the numerator expressed in Section 4(a)

2   of this Order and the denominator of which is the total number of Pension

3   Credit at the Participant's death. The Death Benefit shall be the amount

4   described in Section 1(a) of Article V of the Plan if the Participant dies

5   before attaining age sixty-five (65) or the amount described in Section 1(b) of

6   Article V of the Plan if the Participant dies after attaining age sixty-five (65).

7   In either case, the amount payable to the Alternate Payee (or the Alternate

8   Payee's beneficiary) shall be paid in a lump sum or in monthly installments

9   as the Alternate Payee (or the Alternate Payee's beneficiary) shall elect in

10   accordance with said Sections of the Plan; provided, however, that if the

11   amount of the Alternate Payee's entitlement is $3,500 or less, it shall be

12   payable only in a lump sum.

13   5.   Notwithstanding the provisions of Section 9 of Article VIII of the Plan,

14   payment of benefits to the Alternate Payee shall not be suspended by reason of the

15   Participant's returning to covered employment after retiring.

16   6.   At the Alternate Payee's election, the Alternate Payee may receive the

17   Alternate Payee's benefits at the earliest time permissible under the Plan consistent with the

18   methods set forth in this Order. If such election is made prior to the Participant's date of

19   retirement, the date when the Alternate Payee makes the election shall be used in place of

20   the Participant's date of retirement in calculating the denominator of the fraction expressed

21   in Section 4(a) of this Order. If the Alternate Payee dies before making such election and

22   before payments have commenced to the Alternate Payee, such election may be made by

23   the Alternate Payee's designated beneficiary.

24   7.   The Participant and the Alternate Payee shall be separately responsible

25   for income taxes attributable to the payments received by each of them under the Plan.

26   8.   This Order is intended to be a QDRO made pursuant to the Act, has

27   been determined to be a QDRO by the signature of the Plan Administrator below, and its

28   provisions shall be administered and interpreted in conformity with the Act. If the Act is

1 amended or the law regarding QDROs is otherwise changed or modified, then the parties

2 hereto shall immediately take such steps as are necessary to amend this QDRO to comply

3 with any such changes, amendments, or modification to the Act or laws regarding QDROs.

4   9.   The Court shall retain jurisdiction over this matter to amend this Order

5 in order to establish and/or maintain its qualification as a QDRO under the Act and to

6 carry out the terms and conditions of this Order.

7

8 Dated: _4/20/94_

         JAMES EUGENE CARREY, Petitioner

9

10 Dated: _4/20/94_

         MELISSA JANE CARREY, Respondent

11

12 APPROVED AS TO FORM AND CONTENT:

13 Dated: _4/26/94_

         LAW OFFICES OF NORMAN M. DOLIN

14

15   By: _____

         NORMAN M. DOLIN

16   Attorney for Petitioner,

         JAMES EUGENE CARREY

17

18 Dated: _4/20/94_

         SIMKE, CHODOS, SILBERFELD & ANTEAU, INC.

19

20   By: _____

         RONALD W. ANTEAU,

21   Attorney for Respondent,

         MELISSA JANE CARREY

22

23 Dated: _5/19/94_

24   BRUCE L. DOW,

         Plan Administrator

25

26

27

28

1 | THE CLERK IS ORDERED TO ENTER THIS ORDER.

2

3 | Dated: _____ MAY 2 6 1994 _____

JUDGE OF THE SUPERIOR COURT

4

5 | JAMES D. ENDMAN
                             Judge Pro Tem

6

7

8

9

10

11

12

13

14

15

16

17

18

19

20

21

22

23

24

25

26

27

28

APPENDIX C

Massachusetts Child Support Guidelines

COMMONWEALTH OF MASSACHUSETTS
ADMINISTRATIVE OFFICE
OF THE
TRIAL COURT
BOSTON 02108

CHILD SUPPORT GUIDELINES

The attached CHILD SUPPORT GUIDELINES supersede any previous Guidelines and are effective February 15, 2006.

Robert A. Mulligan
Chief Justice for Administration and Management

COMMONWEALTH OF MASSACHUSETTS

ADMINISTRATIVE OFFICE
OF THE TRIAL COURT

CHILD SUPPORT GUIDELINES

THERE SHALL BE A PRESUMPTION THAT THESE GUIDELINES APPLY IN ALL CASES SEEKING THE ESTABLISHMENT OR MODIFICATION OF A CHILD SUPPORT ORDER. A SPECIFIC, WRITTEN FINDING THAT THE GUIDELINES WOULD BE UNJUST OR INAPPROPRIATE AND THAT THE BEST INTERESTS OF THE CHILD HAVE BEEN CONSIDERED IN A PARTICULAR CASE SHALL BE SUFFICIENT TO REBUT THE PRESUMPTION IN THAT CASE. THESE GUIDELINES APPLY TO CURRENT CHILD SUPPORT ONLY. THEY DO NOT APPLY TO ALIMONY, THE DIVISION OF MARITAL PROPERTY, THE PAYMENT OF ARREARS, RESTITUTION, OR REIMBURSEMENT.

THESE REVISED GUIDELINES, IN AND OF THEMSELVES, DO NOT CONSTITUTE A SUFFICIENT CHANGE OF CIRCUMSTANCES TO WARRANT A MODIFICATION OF THE CHILD SUPPORT ORDER.

The child support guidelines are formulated to be used by the justices of the Trial Court, whether the parents of the children are married or unmarried, in setting temporary, permanent or final orders for current child support, in deciding whether to approve agreements for child support, and in deciding cases that are before the court to modify existing orders. A modification may be allowed upon showing a discrepancy of 20% or more between an established order and a proposed new order calculated under these guidelines. The presumption establishing a proposed new order may be rebutted in cases where the amount of support required under the guidelines is due to the fact that the amount of the current support order resulted from a rebuttal of the guideline amount and there has not been a change in the circumstances which resulted in a rebuttal of the guideline amount. The guidelines are intended to be of assistance to members of the bar and to litigants in determining what level of payment would be expected of them given the relative income levels of the parties. In all orders where an order for child support is requested, a guideline worksheet must be filled out, regardless of the income of the parties.

In establishing these guidelines, due consideration has been given to the following principles:

1) To minimize the economic impact on the child of family breakup;
2) To encourage joint parental responsibility for child support in proportion to, or as a percentage of income;
3) To provide the standard of living the child would have enjoyed had the family been intact;
4) To meet the child's survival needs in the first instance, but to the extent either parent enjoys a higher standard of living to entitle the child to enjoy that higher standard;
5) To protect a subsistence level of income of parents at the low end of the income range whether or not they are on public assistance;
6) To take into account the non-monetary contributions of both the custodial and non-custodial parents;
7) To minimize problems of proof for the parties and of administration for the courts; and
8) To allow for orders and wage assignments that can be adjusted as income increases or decreases.

I. INCOME DEFINITION

A.   For purposes of these guidelines income is defined as gross income from whatever source. Those sources include, but are not limited to, the following:

1) salaries and wages, including overtime and tips, and income from self-employment, except in certain instances, see B below;
2) commissions;
3) severance pay;
4) royalties;
5) bonuses;
6) interest and dividends;
7) income derived from business/partnerships;
8) social security;
9) veterans' benefits;
10) insurance benefits, including those received for disability and personal injury;
11) workers' compensation;
12) unemployment compensation;
13) pensions;
14) annuities;
15) income from trusts;
16) capital gains in real and personal property transactions to the extent that they represent a regular source of income;
17) spousal support received from a person not a party to the order;
18) contractual agreements;
19) perquisites or in kind compensation to the extent that they represent a regular source of income;
20) unearned income of children, in the court's discretion;
21) income from life insurance or endowment contracts;
22) income from interest in an estate, either directly or through a trust;
23) lottery or gambling winnings received either in a lump sum or in the form of an annuity;
24) prizes or awards;
25) net rental income; and
26) funds received from earned income credit.

B.   In individual cases, the court may choose to disregard overtime income or income derived from a second job. However, consideration of such income may be appropriate in certain instances such as those where such income constituted a regular source of income when the family was intact.

II. FACTORS TO BE CONSIDERED IN SETTING THE CHILD SUPPORT ORDER

A.   RELATIONSHIP TO ALIMONY OR SEPARATE MAINTENANCE PAYMENTS

So long as the standard of living of the children is not diminished, these guidelines do not preclude the court from deciding that any order be denominated in whole or in part as alimony or as a separate maintenance payment. It is the responsibility of counsel representing the parties to present the tax consequences of proposed orders to the court.

B.   CLAIMS OF PERSONAL EXEMPTIONS FOR CHILD DEPENDENTS

In setting a support order, the court may make an order regarding the claims of personal exemptions for child dependents between the parties to the extent permitted by law.

C.   MINIMUM AND MAXIMUM LEVELS

The guidelines recognize the principle that, in many instances, to maintain a domicile and a reasonable standard of living for the minor children, the custodial parent will choose to work. In those cases, a disregard of gross income of the custodial parent is to be applied up to a maximum of $20,000. The formula in these guidelines is intended to be adjusted where the income of the custodial parent exceeds the $20,000 disregard after consideration of day care expenses.

These guidelines are also intended to ensure a minimum subsistence level for those non-custodial parents whose income is less than $100 per week. However, it is the obligation of all parents to contribute to the support of their children. To that end, in all cases, a minimum order of $80.00 per month ($18.46 per week) should enter. This minimum should not be construed as limiting the court's ability to set a higher order, should circumstances permit.

Where the court makes a determination that either or both of the parties is either purposely unemployed or underemployed, the section of these guidelines entitled ATTRIBUTION OF INCOME should be consulted.

These guidelines are not meant to apply where the combined gross income of the parties exceeds $135,000 or where the gross income of the non-custodial parent exceeds $100,000. In cases where income exceeds these limits, the court should consider the award of support at the $100,000/$135,000 level as a minimum presumptive level of support to be awarded. Additional amounts of child support may be awarded at the judge's discretion.

D.   CUSTODY AND VISITATION

1)   Custody

These guidelines are based upon traditional custody and visitation arrangements. Where the parties agree to shared physical custody or the court determines that shared physical custody is in the best interests of the children, these guidelines are not applicable. The guidelines also are not meant to apply to cases in which there is split physical custody, i.e., each parent has physical custody of one or more children.

2)   Visitation

These guidelines recognize that children must be allowed to enjoy the society and companionship of both parents to the greatest extent possible. The court may adjust the amount of child support beyond the 2 percent range (see SECTION III (A), BASIC ORDER) after taking into consideration the parties' actual time sharing with the children and the relative resources, expenses, and living standards of the two households.

In some instances the non-custodial parent may incur extraordinary travel related expenses in order to exercise court ordered visitation rights. To foster parental involvement with the children, the court may wish to consider such extraordinary expenses in determining the support order.

E.   CHILD CARE CREDIT

The basic child support obligation set out in the guidelines includes the non-custodial parent's share of child care expenses. Child care expenses are not seen as a separate support item and responsibility for them resides with the custodial parent.

February 15, 2006

The reasonable cost of child care (costs as defined by 26 U.S.C. § 21, I.R.C. § 21) actually paid is to be subtracted from the custodial parent's gross income before the disregard formula is applied.

F.   AGE OF THE CHILDREN

To reflect the costs of raising children, age has been broken down into three groups: 0-12, 13-18, and over 18. A single adjustment to the basic order should be made based on the age of the oldest child for whom support is to be ordered. The support order where the oldest child is 12 or under should be the basic support order according to the schedule. Where the oldest child is between the ages of 13 and 18, the order should be increased by 10 percent of the basic order amount. For cases involving children over the age of 18, to the extent permitted by the General Laws, the amount of the order, if any, will be left to the court's discretion.

Where the parties file an agreement with the court that allows for private payment between the parties, it is suggested that the incremental age issue be addressed in the agreement.

G.   HEALTH INSURANCE, UNINSURED, AND EXTRAORDINARY MEDICAL EXPENSES

1)   Health Insurance

When the court makes an order for child support, the court shall determine whether the obligor under the order has health insurance on a group plan available to him/her through an employer or organization or has health insurance or other health coverage available to him/her at a reasonable cost that may be extended to cover the child for whom support is ordered. When the court makes a determination that the obligor has such coverage, the court shall include in the support order a requirement that the obligor exercise the option of additional coverage in favor of such child, unless the obligee already has provided such coverage for the child at a lesser cost (except for health insurance funded under public assistance programs), or has and prefers to continue such coverage irrespective of cost.

If family health coverage is to be provided by the obligor, the support order should be reduced by one half the cost of family coverage. It is the responsibility of the obligor under the support order who is seeking such a reduction in the order to produce proof satisfactory to the court of the existence of such family coverage under the plan, or no such reduction shall be allowed. However, there shall be no reduction if the obligor has a preexisting family health insurance policy which could be amended to name the additional dependents to the policy at no cost to the obligor. Should health insurance not be provided for any period for which it is ordered, the credit for the premium payment shall be revoked and the order shall be increased by the amount of the credit during the period of noncompliance.

If family health coverage is provided by the obligee, the support order should be increased by one half the cost of the coverage. It is the responsibility of the obligee who is seeking an increase in the order to produce proof satisfactory to the court of the existence of such family coverage under the plan, or no such increase shall be allowed. However, there shall be no increase if the obligee has a preexisting family health insurance policy which could be amended to name the additional dependents at no cost to the obligee. Should health insurance not be provided for any period for which it is ordered, the increase allowed for the premium payment shall be revoked and the order shall be decreased during the period when health insurance is not provided.

2)   Routine Uninsured Medical and Dental Expenses

The custodial parent shall be responsible for the payment of the first $100 per child per year for routine uninsured medical and dental expenses. For amounts above that limit, the court shall allocate costs on a case by case basis. No reduction in the child support order should be allowed.

3)   **Uninsured Extraordinary Medical and Dental Expenses**

The payment of uninsured extraordinary medical and dental expenses incurred by the minor children, absent agreement of the parties, shall be treated on a case by case basis. (Example: orthodontia, psychological/psychiatric counseling, etc.) In such cases, where the court makes a determination that such medical and dental services are necessary and are in the best interests of the child, consideration toward a reduction in the child support order should be given.

H.   ATTRIBUTION OF INCOME

If the court makes a determination that a party is earning substantially less than he or she could through reasonable effort, the court may consider potential earning capacity rather than actual earnings. In making this determination, the court shall take into consideration the education, training, and past employment history of the party. These standards are intended to be applied where a finding has been made that the party is capable of working and is unemployed, working part-time or is working a job, trade, or profession other than that for which he/she has been trained.

This determination is not intended to apply to a custodial parent with children who are under the age of six living in the home.

I.   PRIOR ORDERS FOR SUPPORT

To the extent that prior orders for spousal and child support are **actually** being paid, the court should deduct those payments from the gross income before applying the formula to determine the child support order. This section applies only to orders for child support for children **other than** those who are the subject of the pending action.

J.   EXPENSES OF SUBSEQUENT FAMILIES

In instances where the non-custodial parent has remarried and has children by a subsequent marriage, the court should examine such circumstances closely to determine in the allocation of available resources whether consideration beyond Part II, Section I (Prior Orders for Support) should be given when the custodial parent of children borne of the first marriage, or subsequent marriages appears before the court seeking a modification of the existing child support order. Expenses of a subsequent family may be used as a defense to a request to modify an order seeking an increase in the existing order, but such expenses should not be considered a reason to decrease existing prior orders. In actions pursuant to G.L. c. 209C, this paragraph shall be construed to apply equally to children born out of wedlock.

III. CHILD SUPPORT OBLIGATION SCHEDULE

A.   BASIC ORDER

The basic child support obligation, based upon the income of the non-custodial parent is as follows:

GROSS WEEKLY INCOME	NUMBER OF CHILDREN		
	1	2	3
$ 0-$100	Discretion of the court, but not less than $80 per month		
$101-$280	21%	24%	27%
$281-$750	$59 + 23%	$67 + 28%	$76 + 31%
	(% refers to all dollars over $280)		
$751-max	$167 + 25%	$199 + 30%	$222 + 33%
	(% refers to all dollars over $750)		

For children in excess of 3 covered by the order, the support shall be no less than that for 3 children; should a judge order support at the 3 child level, written findings shall describe the circumstances of the particular case which warrant the minimum order.

Within the discretion of the court, and in consideration of the totality of the circumstances of the parties, the Basic Order may be either increased or decreased by 2%. An adjustment of 2% shall not be considered a deviation.

B.   AGE DIFFERENTIAL

The above orders are to be increased to reflect the cost of raising older children. The following is intended to be applied to the age of the oldest child in the household for whom support is sought under the pending action.

AGE OF OLDEST CHILD	PERCENTAGE INCREASE
0-12	Basic Order Applies
13-18	Basic Order + 10% of Basic Order
Over 18	Discretion of the court (and if statute permits)

C.   CUSTODIAL PARENT INCOME ADJUSTMENT

Where the custodial parent works and earns income in excess of $20,000 after consideration of child care expenses, the support order is to be reduced by the percentage that the excess represents in relation to the combined incomes of both parents minus the custodial parent's disregard.

CHILD SUPPORT GUIDELINES WORKSHEET

Court Docket #:_____   Date Worksheet Completed: _____

All provisions of the Guidelines should be reviewed prior to the completion of the worksheet. These Guidelines will apply in cases where combined gross income of both parties does not exceed $135,000 and where the gross income of the non-custodial parent does not exceed $100,000. **Worksheets shall be completed for all cases.**

1. BASIC ORDER
   a. Non custodial gross weekly income (less prior support orders actually paid for child/family other than the family seeking this order)
   b. Basic Child Support Order from chart (Attachment A)   _____   (A) _____

2. ADJUSTMENT FOR AGE OF CHILDREN
   a. If age of oldest child is 13 - 18, calculate 10% times (A)
   b. Adjusted order (A) + (2 a)   _____   (B)_____

3. CUSTODIAL PARENT INCOME ADJUSTMENT
   a. Custodial parent gross income (annual)   _____

   b. Less $20,000   - $20,000

   c. Less annual child care cost   - _____

   d. Custodial adjusted gross   _____

   e. Non custodial gross (annual)   _____

   f. Total available gross (d) +(e)   _____

   g. Line 3(d) _____ Line 3 (f)_____

   h. 3 (d) divided by 3 (f)   _____ %

   I. Adjustment for custodial income
      (Line 3 h %) X (B)   (C) _____

4. CALCULATION OF FINAL ORDER
   a. Adjusted order, (B) above   (B)_____

   b. Less adjustment for (C) above   (C) - _____

   c. Less 50% weekly cost to obligor of family group health insurance [Section G. 1]   - _____
              Or
      Plus 50% weekly cost of obligee's family group health insurance [Section G. 1]   + _____

5. **WEEKLY SUPPORT ORDER (B) - (C) $\pm$ 4 (c)** $ _____

February 15, 2006

SAMPLE WORKSHEET

Court Docket #:___02D0109_____   Date Worksheet Completed:__May 3, 2002___

Non custodial parent gross annual income	$40,000 ($769/week)
Weekly support paid - child of prior marriage	$40
Custodial parent gross annual income	$28,000
2 Children covered by order, ages 6 and 8	
Annualized day care cost	$4,160
Non custodial weekly cost family group health insur.	$24

1. BASIC ORDER
   a. Non custodial gross weekly income (less prior
      support orders actually paid for child/family
      other than the family seeking this order)   ___729___
   b. Basic Child Support Order from chart
      (Attachment A)   (A) ___193___

2. ADJUSTMENT FOR AGE OF CHILDREN
   a. If age of oldest child is 13 - 18,
      calculate 10% times (A)   ___0___
   b. Adjusted order (A) + (2 a)   (B) ___193___

3. CUSTODIAL PARENT INCOME ADJUSTMENT
   a. Custodial parent gross income (annual)   ___28,000___

   b. Less $20,000   - $20,000

   c. Less annual child care cost   ___- 4,160___

   d. Custodial adjusted gross   ___3,840___

   e. Non custodial gross (annual)   ___40,000___

   f. Total available gross (d) +(e)   ___43,840___

   g. Line 3(d) _3840___ Line 3 (f) _43840___

   h. 3 (d) divided by 3 (f)   ___.09_%

   I. Adjustment for custodial income
      (Line 3 h %) X (B)   (C) ___17___

4. CALCULATION OF FINAL ORDER
   a. Adjusted order, (B) above   (B) ___193___

   b. Less adjustment for (C) above   (C) - ___17___

   c. Less 50% weekly cost to obligor of family
      group health insurance [Section G. 1]   ___- 12___
                  Or
      Plus 50% weekly cost of obligee's family
      group health insurance [Section G. 1]   +_____

5. **WEEKLY SUPPORT ORDER (B) - (c) ± 4 (c)** $_____164___

Attachment A

BASIC CHILD SUPPORT ORDER			

Non-Custodial Gross Weekly Income	Number of Children			Non-Custodial Gross Weekly Income	Number of Children		
	1	2	3		1	2	3
0-100	Not less than 18.46						
101	21	24	27	325	69	80	90
105	22	25	28	330	70	81	92
110	23	26	30	335	72	82	93
115	24	28	31	340	73	84	95
120	25	29	32	345	74	85	96
125	26	30	34	350	75	87	98
130	27	31	35	355	76	88	99
135	28	32	36	360	77	89	101
140	29	34	38	365	79	91	102
145	30	35	39	370	80	92	104
150	32	36	40	375	81	94	105
155	33	37	42	380	82	95	107
160	34	38	43	385	83	96	109
165	35	40	45	390	84	98	110
170	36	41	46	395	85	99	112
175	37	42	47	400	87	101	113
180	38	43	49	405	88	102	115
185	39	44	50	410	89	103	116
190	40	46	51	415	90	105	118
195	41	47	53	420	91	106	119
200	42	48	54	425	92	108	121
205	43	49	55	430	94	109	122
210	44	50	57	435	95	110	124
215	45	52	58	440	96	112	126
220	46	53	59	445	97	113	127
225	47	54	61	450	98	115	129
230	48	55	62	455	99	116	130
235	49	56	63	460	100	117	132
240	50	58	65	465	102	119	133
245	51	59	66	470	103	120	135
250	52	60	68	475	104	122	136
255	54	61	69	480	105	123	138
260	55	62	70	485	106	124	140
265	56	64	72	490	107	126	141
270	57	65	73	495	108	127	143
275	58	66	74	500	110	129	144
280	59	67	76	505	111	130	146
281	59	67	76	510	112	131	147
285	60	68	78	515	113	133	149
290	61	70	79	520	114	134	150
295	62	71	81	525	115	136	152
300	64	73	82	530	116	137	154
305	65	74	84	535	118	138	155
310	66	75	85	540	119	140	157
315	67	77	87	545	120	141	158
320	68	78	88	550	121	143	160

Attachment A

BASIC CHILD SUPPORT ORDER							

Non-Custodial Gross Weekly Income	Number of Children			Non-Custodial Gross Weekly Income	Number of Children		
	1	2	3		1	2	3
555	122	144	161	785	176	210	234
560	123	145	163	790	177	211	235
565	125	147	164	795	178	212	237
570	126	148	166	800	180	214	238
575	127	150	167	805	181	216	240
580	128	151	169	810	182	217	242
585	129	152	171	815	183	218	243
590	130	154	172	820	184	220	245
595	131	155	174	825	186	222	247
600	133	157	175	830	187	223	248
605	134	158	177	835	188	224	250
610	135	159	178	840	190	226	252
615	136	161	180	845	191	228	253
620	137	162	181	850	192	229	255
625	138	164	183	855	193	230	257
630	140	165	184	860	194	232	258
635	141	166	186	865	196	234	260
640	142	168	188	870	197	235	262
645	143	169	189	875	198	236	263
650	144	171	191	880	200	238	265
655	145	172	192	885	201	240	267
660	146	173	194	890	202	241	268
665	148	175	195	895	203	242	270
670	149	176	197	900	204	244	272
675	150	178	198	905	206	246	273
680	151	179	200	910	207	247	275
685	152	180	202	915	208	248	276
690	153	182	203	920	210	250	278
695	154	183	205	925	211	252	280
700	156	185	206	930	212	253	281
705	157	186	208	935	213	254	283
710	158	187	209	940	214	256	285
715	159	189	211	945	216	258	286
720	160	190	212	950	217	259	288
725	161	192	214	955	218	260	290
730	162	193	216	960	220	262	291
735	164	194	217	965	221	264	293
740	165	196	219	970	222	265	295
745	166	197	220	975	223	266	296
750	167	199	222	980	224	268	298
751	167	199	222	985	226	270	300
755	168	200	224	990	227	271	301
760	170	202	225	995	228	272	303
765	171	204	227	1000	230	274	304
770	172	205	229	1005	231	276	306
775	173	206	230	1010	232	277	308
780	174	208	232	1015	233	278	309

Attachment A

BASIC CHILD SUPPORT ORDER

Non-Custodial Gross Weekly Income	Number of Children			Non-Custodial Gross Weekly Income	Number of Children		
	1	2	3		1	2	3
1020	234	280	311	1255	293	350	389
1025	236	282	313	1260	294	352	390
1030	237	283	314	1265	296	354	392
1035	238	284	316	1270	297	355	394
1040	240	286	318	1275	298	356	395
1045	241	288	319	1280	300	358	397
1050	242	289	321	1285	301	360	399
1055	243	290	323	1290	302	361	400
1060	244	292	324	1295	303	362	402
1065	246	294	326	1300	304	364	404
1070	247	295	328	1305	306	366	405
1075	248	296	329	1310	307	367	407
1080	250	298	331	1315	308	368	408
1085	251	300	333	1320	310	370	410
1090	252	301	334	1325	311	372	412
1095	253	302	336	1330	312	373	413
1100	254	304	338	1335	313	374	415
1105	256	306	339	1340	314	376	417
1110	257	307	341	1345	316	378	418
1115	258	308	342	1350	317	379	420
1120	260	310	344	1355	318	380	422
1125	261	312	346	1360	320	382	423
1130	262	313	347	1365	321	384	425
1135	263	314	349	1370	322	385	427
1140	264	316	351	1375	323	386	428
1145	266	318	352	1380	324	388	430
1150	267	319	354	1385	326	390	432
1155	268	320	356	1390	327	391	433
1160	270	322	357	1395	328	392	435
1165	271	324	359	1400	330	394	436
1170	272	325	361	1405	331	396	438
1175	273	326	362	1410	332	397	440
1180	274	328	364	1415	333	398	441
1185	276	330	366	1420	334	400	443
1190	277	331	367	1425	336	402	445
1195	278	332	369	1430	337	403	446
1200	280	334	370	1435	338	404	448
1205	281	336	372	1440	340	406	450
1210	282	337	374	1445	341	408	451
1215	283	338	375	1450	342	409	453
1220	284	340	377	1455	343	410	455
1225	286	342	379	1460	344	412	456
1230	287	343	380	1465	346	414	458
1235	288	344	382	1470	347	415	460
1240	290	346	384	1475	348	416	461
1245	291	348	385	1480	350	418	463
1250	292	349	387	1485	351	420	465

Attachment A

BASIC CHILD SUPPORT ORDER							
Non-Custodial Gross Weekly Income	Number of Children			Non-Custodial Gross Weekly Income	Number of Children		
	1	2	3		1	2	3
1490	352	421	466	1710	407	487	539
1495	353	422	468	1715	408	488	540
1500	354	424	470	1720	410	490	542
1505	356	426	471	1725	411	492	544
1510	357	427	473	1730	412	493	545
1515	358	428	474	1735	413	494	547
1520	360	430	476	1740	414	496	549
1525	361	432	478	1745	416	498	550
1530	362	433	479	1750	417	499	552
1535	363	434	481	1755	418	500	554
1540	364	436	483	1760	420	502	555
1545	366	438	484	1765	421	504	557
1550	367	439	486	1770	422	505	559
1555	368	440	488	1775	423	506	560
1560	370	442	489	1780	424	508	562
1565	371	444	491	1785	426	510	564
1570	372	445	493	1790	427	511	565
1575	373	446	494	1795	428	512	567
1580	374	448	496	1800	430	514	568
1585	376	450	498	1805	431	516	570
1590	377	451	499	1810	432	517	572
1595	378	452	501	1815	433	518	573
1600	380	454	502	1820	434	520	575
1605	381	456	504	1825	436	522	577
1610	382	457	506	1830	437	523	578
1615	383	458	507	1835	438	524	580
1620	384	460	509	1840	440	526	582
1625	386	462	511	1845	441	528	583
1630	387	463	512	1850	442	529	585
1635	388	464	514	1855	443	530	587
1640	390	466	516	1860	444	532	588
1645	391	468	517	1865	446	534	590
1650	392	469	519	1870	447	535	592
1655	393	470	521	1875	448	536	593
1660	394	472	522	1880	450	538	595
1665	396	474	524	1885	451	540	597
1670	397	475	526	1890	452	541	598
1675	398	476	527	1895	453	542	600
1680	400	478	529	1900	454	544	602
1685	401	480	531	1905	456	546	603
1690	402	481	532	1910	457	547	605
1695	403	482	534	1915	458	548	606
1700	404	484	536	1920	460	550	608
1705	406	486	537	1923	460	551	609

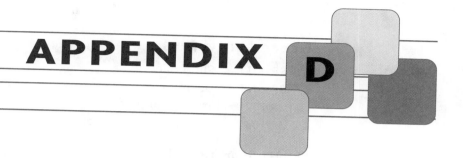

APPENDIX D

Florida Uniform Interstate Family Support Act

Florida Uniform Interstate Family Support Act Chapter 88

Part I

General Provisions

88.0011 Short title. This act shall be known and may be cited as the "Uniform Interstate Family Support Act."

History. s. 1, ch. 96–189.

88.1011 Definitions. As used in this act:

(1) "Child" means an individual, whether over or under the age of majority, who is or is alleged to be owed a duty of support by the individual's parent or who is or is alleged to be the beneficiary of a support order directed to the parent.

(2) "Child support order" means a support order for a child, including a child who has attained the age of majority under the law of the issuing state.

(3) "Duty of support" means an obligation imposed or imposable by law to provide support for a child, spouse, or former spouse, including an unsatisfied obligation to provide support.

(4) "Home state" means the state in which a child lived with a parent or a person acting as parent for at least 6 consecutive months immediately preceding the time of filing of a petition or comparable pleading for support and, if a child is less than 6 months old, the state in which the child lived from birth with any of them. A period of temporary absence of any of them is counted as part of the 6-month or other period.

(5) "Income" includes earnings or other periodic entitlements to money from any source and any other property subject to withholding for support under the law of this state.

(6) "Income-withholding order" means an order or other legal process directed to an obligor's employer or other debtor, as defined by the income deduction law of this state, or payor as defined by s. 61.046, to withhold support from the income of the obligor.

(7) "Initiating state" means a state from which a proceeding is forwarded or in which a proceeding is filed for forwarding to a responding state under this act or a law or procedure substantially similar to this act, the Uniform Reciprocal Enforcement of Support Act, or the Revised Uniform Reciprocal Enforcement of Support Act.

(8) "Initiating tribunal" means the authorized tribunal in an initiating state.

(9) "Issuing state" means the state in which a tribunal issues a support order or renders a judgment determining parentage.

(10) "Issuing tribunal" means the tribunal that issues a support order or renders a judgment determining parentage.

(11) "Law" includes decisional and statutory law and rules and regulations having the force of law.

(12) "Obligee" means:

(a) An individual to whom a duty of support is or is alleged to be owed or in whose favor a support order has been issued or a judgment determining parentage has been rendered;

(b) A state or political subdivision to which the rights under a duty of support or support order have been assigned or which has independent claims based on financial assistance provided to an individual obligee; or

(c) An individual seeking a judgment determining parentage of the individual's child.

(13) "Obligor" means an individual, or the estate of a decedent:

(a) Who owes or is alleged to owe a duty of support;

(b) Who is alleged but has not been adjudicated to be a parent of a child; or

(c) Who is liable under a support order.

(14) "Register" means to record or file a support order or judgment determining parentage in the Registry of Foreign Support Orders of the circuit court, or other appropriate location for the recording or filing of foreign judgments generally or foreign support orders specifically.

(15) "Registering tribunal" means a tribunal in which a support order is registered.

(16) "Responding state" means a state in which a proceeding is filed or to which a proceeding is forwarded for filing from an initiating state under this act or a law or procedure substantially similar to this act, the Uniform Reciprocal Enforcement of Support Act, or the Revised Uniform Reciprocal Enforcement of Support Act.

(17) "Responding tribunal" means the authorized tribunal in a responding state.

(18) "Spousal-support order" means a support order for a spouse or former spouse of the obligor.

(19) "State" means a state of the United States, the District of Columbia, Puerto Rico, the United States Virgin Islands, or any territory or insular possession subject to the jurisdiction of the United States. The term includes:

(a) An Indian tribe; and

(b) A foreign jurisdiction that has enacted a law or established procedures for issuance and enforcement of support orders which are substantially similar to the procedures under this act, the Uniform Reciprocal Enforcement of Support Act, or the Revised Uniform Reciprocal Enforcement of Support Act, as determined by the Attorney General.

(20) "Support enforcement agency" means a public official or agency authorized to seek:

(a) Enforcement of support orders or laws relating to the duty of support;

(b) Establishment or modification of child support;

(c) Determination of parentage; or

(d) To locate obligors or their assets.

(21) "Support order" means a judgment, decree, or order, whether temporary, final, or subject to modification, for the benefit of a child, a spouse, or a former spouse, which provides for monetary support, health care, arrearages, or reimbursement, and may include related costs and fees, interest, income withholding, attorney's fees, and other relief.

(22) "Tribunal" means a court, administrative agency, or quasi-judicial entity authorized to establish, enforce, or modify support orders or to determine parentage.

History. s. 1, ch. 96–189; s. 13, ch. 97–170.

88.1021 Tribunal of state. The circuit court or other appropriate court, administrative agency, quasi-judicial entity, or combination is the tribunal of this state.

History. s. 1, ch. 96–189; s. 14, ch. 97–170.

88.1031 Remedies cumulative. Remedies provided by this act are cumulative and do not affect the availability of remedies under other law.

History. s. 1, ch. 96–189.

Part II

Jurisdiction

88.2011 Bases for jurisdiction over nonresident. In a proceeding to establish, enforce, or modify a support order or to determine parentage, a tribunal of this state may exercise personal jurisdiction over a nonresident individual or the individual's guardian or conservator if:

(1) The individual is personally served with citation, summons, or notice within this state;

(2) The individual submits to the jurisdiction of this state by consent, by entering a general appearance, or by filing a responsive document having the effect of waiving any contest to personal jurisdiction;

(3) The individual resided with the child in this state;

(4) The individual resided in this state and provided prenatal expenses or support for the child;

(5) The child resides in this state as a result of the acts or directives of the individual;

(6) The individual engaged in sexual intercourse in this state and the child may have been conceived by that act of intercourse;

(7) The individual asserted parentage in a tribunal or in a putative father registry maintained in this state by the appropriate agency; or

(8) There is any other basis consistent with the constitutions of this state and the United States for the exercise of personal jurisdiction.

History. s. 2, ch. 96–189.

88.2021 Procedure when exercising jurisdiction over nonresident. A tribunal of this state exercising personal jurisdiction over a nonresident under s. 88.2011 may apply s. 88.3161 (special rules of evidence and procedure) to receive evidence from another state, and s. 88.3181 (assistance with discovery) to obtain discovery through a tribunal of another state. In all other respects, parts III through VII of this chapter do not apply and the tribunal shall apply the procedural and substantive law of this state, including the rules on choice of law other than those established by this act.

History. s. 2, ch. 96–189.

88.2031 Initiating and responding tribunal of state. Under this act, a tribunal of this state may serve as an initiating tribunal to forward proceedings to another state and as a responding tribunal for proceedings initiated in another state.

History. s. 2, ch. 96–189; s. 15, ch. 97–170.

88.2041 Simultaneous proceedings in another state.

(1) A tribunal of this state may exercise jurisdiction to establish a support order if the petition or comparable pleading is filed after a petition or comparable pleading is filed in another state only if:
    (a) The petition or comparable pleading in this state is filed before the expiration of the time allowed in the other state for filing a responsive pleading challenging the exercise of jurisdiction by the other state;
    (b) The contesting party timely challenges the exercise of jurisdiction in the other state; and
    (c) If relevant, this state is the home state of the child.
(2) A tribunal of this state may not exercise jurisdiction to establish a support order if the petition or comparable pleading is filed before a petition or comparable pleading is filed in another state if:
    (a) The petition or comparable pleading in the other state is filed before the expiration of the time allowed in this state for filing a responsive pleading challenging the exercise of jurisdiction by this state;
    (b) The contesting party timely challenges the exercise of jurisdiction in this state; and
    (c) If relevant, the other state is the home state of the child.

History. s. 2, ch. 96–189.

88.2051 Continuing exclusive jurisdiction.

(1) A tribunal of this state issuing a support order consistent with the law of this state has continuing exclusive jurisdiction over a child support order:
    (a) As long as this state remains the residence of the obligor, the individual obligee, or the child for whose benefit the support order is issued; or
    (b) Until all of the parties who are individuals have filed written consents with the tribunal of this state for a tribunal of another state to modify the order and assume continuing exclusive jurisdiction.
(2) A tribunal of this state issuing a child support order consistent with the law of this state may not exercise its continuing jurisdiction to modify the order if the

order has been modified by a tribunal of another state pursuant to this act or a law substantially similar to this act.

(3) If a child support order of this state is modified by a tribunal of another state pursuant to this act or a law substantially similar to this act, a tribunal of this state loses its continuing exclusive jurisdiction with regard to prospective enforcement of the order issued in this state, and may only:

(a) Enforce the order that was modified as to amounts accruing before the modification;

(b) Enforce nonmodifiable aspects of that order; and

(c) Provide other appropriate relief for violations of that order which occurred before the effective date of the modification.

(4) A tribunal of this state shall recognize the continuing exclusive jurisdiction of a tribunal of another state which has issued a child support order pursuant to this act or a law substantially similar to this act.

(5) A temporary support order issued ex parte or pending resolution of a jurisdictional conflict does not create continuing exclusive jurisdiction in the issuing tribunal.

(6) A tribunal of this state issuing a support order consistent with the law of this state has continuing exclusive jurisdiction over a spousal support order throughout the existence of the support obligation. A tribunal of this state may not modify a spousal support order issued by a tribunal of another state having continuing exclusive jurisdiction over that order under the law of that state.

History. s. 2, ch. 96–189; s. 16, ch. 97–170.

88.2061 Enforcement and modification of support order by tribunal having continuing jurisdiction.

(1) A tribunal of this state may serve as an initiating tribunal to request a tribunal of another state to enforce or modify a support order issued in that state.

(2) A tribunal of this state having continuing exclusive jurisdiction over a support order may act as a responding tribunal to enforce or modify the order. If a party subject to the continuing exclusive jurisdiction of the tribunal no longer resides in the issuing state, in subsequent proceedings the tribunal may apply s. 88.3161 (special rules of evidence and procedure) to receive evidence from another state and s. 88.3181 (assistance with discovery) to obtain discovery through a tribunal of another state.

(3) A tribunal of this state which lacks continuing exclusive jurisdiction over a spousal support order may not serve as a responding tribunal to modify a spousal support order of another state.

History. s. 2, ch. 96–189.

88.2071 Recognition of controlling child support order.

(1) If a proceeding is brought under this act and only one tribunal has issued a child support order, the order of that tribunal controls and must be so recognized.

(2) If a proceeding is brought under this act, and two or more child support orders have been issued by tribunals of this state or another state with regard to the same obligor and child, a tribunal of this state shall apply the following rules in determining which order to recognize for purposes of continuing, exclusive jurisdiction:

(a) If only one of the tribunals would have continuing, exclusive jurisdiction under this act, the order of that tribunal controls and must be so recognized.

(b) If more than one of the tribunals would have continuing, exclusive jurisdiction under this act, an order issued by a tribunal in the current home state of the child controls and must be so recognized, but if an order has not been issued in the current home state of the child, the order most recently issued controls and must be so recognized.

(c) If none of the tribunals would have continuing, exclusive jurisdiction under this act, the tribunal of this state having jurisdiction over the parties shall issue a child support order, which controls and must be so recognized.

(3) If two or more child support orders have been issued for the same obligor and child and if the obligor or the individual obligee resides in this state, a party may request a tribunal of this state to determine which order controls and must be so recognized under subsection (2). The request must be accompanied by a certified copy of every support order in effect. The requesting party shall give notice of the request to each party whose rights may be affected by the determination.

(4) The tribunal that issued the controlling order under subsection (1), subsection (2), or subsection (3) is the tribunal that has continuing, exclusive jurisdiction under s. 88.2051.

(5) A tribunal of this state which determines by order the identity of the controlling order under paragraph (2)(a) or paragraph (2)(b) or which issues a new controlling order under paragraph (2)(c) shall state in that order the basis upon which the tribunal made its determination.

(6) Within 30 days after issuance of an order determining the identity of the controlling order, the party obtaining the order shall file a certified copy of it with each tribunal that issued or registered an earlier order of child support. A party who obtains the order and fails to file a certified copy is subject to appropriate sanctions by a tribunal in which the issue of failure to file arises. The failure to file does not affect the validity or enforceability of the controlling order.

History. s. 2, ch. 96–189; s. 17, ch. 97–170.

88.2081 Multiple child support orders for two or more obligees. In responding to multiple registrations, petitions, or comparable pleadings for enforcement of two or more child support orders in effect at the same time with regard to the same obligor and different individual obligees, at least one of which was issued by a tribunal of another state, a tribunal of this state shall enforce those orders in the same manner as if the multiple orders had been issued by a tribunal of this state.

History. s. 2, ch. 96–189.

88.2091 Credit for payments. Amounts collected and credited for a particular period pursuant to a support order issued by a tribunal of another state must be credited against the amounts accruing or accrued for the same period under a support order issued by the tribunal of this state.

History. s. 2, ch. 96–189.

Part III

Civil Provisions of General Application

88.3011 Proceedings under this act.

(1) Except as otherwise provided in this act, this article applies to all proceedings under this act.

(2) This act provides for the following proceedings:
(a) Establishment of an order for spousal support or child support pursuant to part IV;
(b) Enforcement of a support order and income-withholding order of another state without registration pursuant to part V;
(c) Registration of an order for spousal support or child support of another state for enforcement pursuant to part VI;
(d) Modification of an order for child support or spousal support issued by a tribunal of this state pursuant to ss. 88.2031–88.2061;
(e) Registration of an order for child support of another state for modification pursuant to part VI;
(f) Determination of parentage pursuant to part VII; and
(g) Assertion of jurisdiction over nonresidents pursuant to ss. 88.2011–88.2021.

(3) An individual petitioner or a support enforcement agency may commence a proceeding authorized under this act by filing a petition or a comparable pleading in an initiating tribunal for forwarding to a responding tribunal or by filing a petition or a comparable pleading directly in a tribunal of another state which has or can obtain personal jurisdiction over the respondent.

History. s. 3, ch. 96–189; s. 18, ch. 97–170.

88.3021 Action by minor parent. A minor parent, or a guardian or other legal representative of a minor parent, may maintain a proceeding on behalf of or for the benefit of the minor's child.

History. s. 3, ch. 96–189.

88.3031 Application of law of state. Except as otherwise provided by this act, a responding tribunal of this state:

(1) Shall apply the procedural and substantive law, including the rules on choice of law, generally applicable to similar proceedings originating in this state and

may exercise all powers and provide all remedies available in those proceedings; and

(2) Shall determine the duty of support and the amount payable in accordance with the law and support guidelines of this state.

History. s. 3, ch. 96–189; s. 19, ch. 97–170.

88.3041 Duties of initiating tribunal.

(1) Upon the filing of a petition or comparable pleading authorized by this act, an initiating tribunal of this state shall forward three copies of the petition and its accompanying documents or a comparable pleading and its accompanying documents:

(a) To the responding tribunal or appropriate support enforcement agency in the responding state; or

(b) If the identity of the responding tribunal is unknown, to the state information agency of the responding state with a request that they be forwarded to the appropriate tribunal and that receipt be acknowledged.

(2) If a responding state has not enacted this act or a law or procedure substantially similar to this act, a tribunal of this state may issue a certificate or other document and make findings required by the law of the responding state. If the responding state is a foreign jurisdiction, the tribunal may specify the amount of support sought and provide other documents necessary to satisfy the requirements of the responding state.

History. s. 3, ch. 96–189; s. 20, ch. 97–170.

88.3051 Duties and powers of responding tribunal.

(1) When a responding tribunal of this state receives a petition or comparable pleading from an initiating tribunal or directly pursuant to s. 88.3011(3), it shall cause the petition or comparable pleading to be filed and notify the petitioner where and when it was filed.

(2) A responding tribunal of this state, to the extent otherwise authorized by law, may do one or more of the following:

(a) Issue or enforce a support order, modify a child support order, or render a judgment to determine parentage.

(b) Order an obligor to comply with a support order, specifying the amount and the manner of compliance.

(c) Order income withholding.

(d) Determine the amount of any arrearages, and specify a method of payment.

(e) Enforce orders by civil or criminal contempt, or both.

(f) Set aside property for satisfaction of the support order.

(g) Place liens and order execution on the obligor's property.

(h) Order an obligor to keep the tribunal informed of the obligor's current residential address, telephone number, employer, address of employment, and telephone number at the place of employment.

(i) Issue a bench warrant, capias, or writ of bodily attachment for an obligor who has failed after proper notice to appear at a hearing ordered by the tribunal and enter the bench warrant, capias, or writ of bodily attachment in any local and state computer systems for criminal warrants.

(j) Order the obligor to seek appropriate employment by specified methods.

(k) Award reasonable attorney's fees and other fees and costs.

(l) Grant any other available remedy.

(3) A responding tribunal of this state shall include in a support order issued under this act, or in the documents accompanying the order, the calculations on which the support order is based.

(4) A responding tribunal of this state may not condition the payment of a support order issued under this act upon compliance by a party with provisions for visitation.

(5) If a responding tribunal of this state issues an order under this act, the tribunal shall send a copy of the order to the petitioner and the respondent and to the initiating tribunal, if any.

History. s. 3, ch. 96–189; s. 21, ch. 97–170.

88.3061 Inappropriate tribunal. If a petition or comparable pleading is received by an inappropriate tribunal of this state, it shall forward the pleading and accompanying documents to an appropriate tribunal in this state or another state and notify the petitioner where and when the pleading was sent.

History. s. 3, ch. 96–189; s. 22, ch. 97–170.

88.3071 Duties of support enforcement agency.

(1) A support enforcement agency of this state, upon request, shall provide services to a petitioner in a proceeding under this act.

(2) A support enforcement agency that is providing services to the petitioner as appropriate shall:

    (a) Take all steps necessary to enable an appropriate tribunal in this state or another state to obtain jurisdiction over the respondent.

    (b) Request an appropriate tribunal to set a date, time, and place for a hearing.

    (c) Make a reasonable effort to obtain all relevant information, including information as to income and property of the parties.

    (d) Within 10 days, exclusive of Saturdays, Sundays, and legal holidays, after receipt of a written notice from an initiating, responding, or registering tribunal, send a copy of the notice to the petitioner.

    (e) Within 10 days, exclusive of Saturdays, Sundays, and legal holidays, after receipt of a written communication from the respondent or the respondent's attorney, send a copy of the communication to the petitioner.

    (f) Notify the petitioner if jurisdiction over the respondent cannot be obtained.

(3) This act does not create or negate a relationship of attorney and client or other fiduciary relationship between a support enforcement agency or the attorney for the agency and the individual being assisted by the agency.

History. s. 3, ch. 96–189; s. 23, ch. 97–170.

88.3081 Duty of Governor and Cabinet. If the Governor and Cabinet determine that the support enforcement agency is neglecting or refusing to provide services to an individual, the Governor and Cabinet may order the agency to perform its duties under this act or may provide those services directly to the individual.

History. s. 3, ch. 96–189.

88.3091 Private counsel. An individual may employ private counsel to represent the individual in proceedings authorized by this act.

History. s. 3, ch. 96–189.

88.3101 Duties of state information agency.

(1) The Department of Revenue is the state information agency under this act.

(2) The state information agency shall:

(a) Compile and maintain a current list, including addresses, of the tribunals in this state which have jurisdiction under this act and any support enforcement agencies in this state and transmit a copy to the state information agency of every other state.

(b) Maintain a register of tribunals and support enforcement agencies received from other states.

(c) Forward to the appropriate tribunal in the place in this state in which the individual obligee or the obligor resides, or in which the obligor's property is believed to be located, all documents concerning a proceeding under this act received from an initiating tribunal or the state information agency of the initiating state.

(3) Obtain information concerning the location of the obligor and the obligor's property within this state not exempt from execution, by such means as postal verification and federal or state locator services, examination of telephone directories, requests for the obligor's address from employers, and examination of governmental records, including, to the extent not prohibited by other law, those relating to real property, vital statistics, law enforcement, taxation, motor vehicles, driver's licenses, and social security.

History. s. 3, ch. 96–189.

88.3111 Pleadings and accompanying documents.

(1) A petitioner seeking to establish or modify a support order or to determine parentage in a proceeding under this act must verify the petition or comparable pleading. Unless otherwise ordered under s. 88.3121 (nondisclosure of information in exceptional circumstances), the petition or comparable pleading or the documents accompanying either the petition or comparable pleading must provide, so far as known, the name, residential address, and social security numbers of the obligor and the obligee, and the name, sex, residential address, social security number, and date of birth of each child for whom support is sought. The petition must be accompanied by a certified copy of any support order in effect. The petition may include any other information that may assist in locating or identifying the respondent.

(2) The petition must specify the relief sought. The petition and accompanying documents must conform substantially with the requirements imposed by the forms mandated by federal law for use in cases filed by a support enforcement agency.

History. s. 3, ch. 96–189.

88.3121 Nondisclosure of information in exceptional circumstances. Upon a finding, which may be made ex parte, that the health, safety, or liberty of a party or child would be unreasonably put at risk by the disclosure of identifying information, or if an existing order so provides, a tribunal shall order that the address of the child or party or other identifying information not be disclosed in a pleading or other document filed in a proceeding under this act.

History. s. 3, ch. 96–189.

88.3131 Costs and fees.

(1) The petitioner may not be required to pay a filing fee or other costs.

(2) If an obligee prevails, a responding tribunal may assess against an obligor filing fees, reasonable attorney's fees, other costs, and necessary travel and other reasonable expenses incurred by the obligee and the obligee's witnesses. The tribunal may not assess fees, costs, or expenses against the obligee or the support enforcement agency of either the initiating or the responding state, except as provided by other law. Attorney's fees may be taxed as costs, and may be ordered paid directly to the attorney, who may enforce the order in the attorney's own name. Payment of support owed to the obligee has priority over fees, costs, and expenses.

(3) The tribunal shall order the payment of costs and reasonable attorney's fees if it determines that a hearing was requested primarily for delay. In a proceeding under part VI, a hearing is presumed to have been requested primarily for delay if a registered support order is confirmed or enforced without change.

History. s. 3, ch. 96–189.

88.3141 Limited immunity of petitioner.

(1) Participation by a petitioner in a proceeding before a responding tribunal, whether in person, by private attorney, or through services provided by the support enforcement agency, does not confer personal jurisdiction over the petitioner in another proceeding.

(2) A petitioner is not amenable to service of civil process while physically present in this state to participate in a proceeding under this act.

(3) The immunity granted by this section does not extend to civil litigation based on acts unrelated to a proceeding under this act committed by a party while present in this state to participate in the proceeding.

History. s. 3, ch. 96–189.

88.3151 Nonparentage as defense.
A party whose parentage of a child has been previously determined by or pursuant to law may not plead nonparentage as a defense to a proceeding under this act.

History. s. 3, ch. 96–189.

88.3161 Special rules of evidence and procedure.

(1) The physical presence of the petitioner in a responding tribunal of this state is not required for the establishment, enforcement, or modification of a support order or the rendition of a judgment determining parentage.

(2) A verified petition or other comparable pleading, affidavit, document substantially complying with federally mandated forms, and a document incorporated by reference in any of them, not excluded under the hearsay rule if given in person, is admissible in evidence if given under oath by a party or witness residing in another state.

(3) A copy of the record of child support payments certified as a true copy of the original by the custodian of the record may be forwarded to a responding tribunal.

The copy is evidence of facts asserted in it, and is admissible to show whether payments were made.

(4) Copies of bills for testing for parentage, and for prenatal and postnatal health care of the mother and child, furnished to the adverse party at least 10 days before trial, are admissible in evidence to prove the amount of the charges billed and that the charges were reasonable, necessary, and customary.

(5) Documentary evidence transmitted from another state to a tribunal of this state by telephone, telecopier, or other means that do not provide an original writing may not be excluded from evidence on an objection based on the means of transmission.

(6) In a proceeding under this act, a tribunal of this state may permit a party or witness residing in another state to be deposed or to testify by telephone, audiovisual means, or other electronic means at a designated tribunal or other location in that state. A tribunal of this state shall cooperate with tribunals of other states in designating an appropriate location for the deposition or testimony.

(7) If a party called to testify at a civil hearing refuses to answer on the ground that the testimony may be self-incriminating, the trier of fact may draw an adverse inference from the refusal.

(8) A privilege against disclosure of communications between spouses does not apply in a proceeding under this act.

(9) The defense of immunity based on the relationship of husband and wife or parent and child does not apply in a proceeding under this act.

History. s. 3, ch. 96–189.

88.3171 Communications between tribunals. A tribunal of this state may communicate with a tribunal of another state in writing, or by telephone or other means, to obtain information concerning the laws of that state, the legal effect of a judgment, decree, or order of that tribunal, and the status of a proceeding in the other state. A tribunal of this state may furnish similar information by similar means to a tribunal of another state.

History. s. 3, ch. 96–189.

88.3181 Assistance with discovery. A tribunal of this state may:

(1) Request a tribunal of another state to assist in obtaining discovery.

(2) Upon request, compel a person over whom it has jurisdiction to respond to a discovery order issued by a tribunal of another state.

History. s. 3, ch. 96–189.

88.3191 Receipt and disbursement of payments. A support enforcement agency or tribunal of this state shall disburse promptly any amounts received pursuant to a support order, as directed by the order. The agency or tribunal shall furnish to a requesting party or tribunal of another state a certified statement by the custodian of the record of the amounts and dates of all payments received.

History. s. 3, ch. 96–189.

Part IV

Establishment of Support Order

88.4011 Petition to establish support order.

(1) If a support order entitled to recognition under this act has not been issued, a responding tribunal of this state may issue a support order if:
    (a) The individual seeking the order resides in another state; or
    (b) The support enforcement agency seeking the order is located in another state.

(2) The tribunal may issue a temporary child support order if:
    (a) The respondent has signed a verified statement acknowledging parentage;
    (b) The respondent has been determined by or pursuant to law to be the parent; or
    (c) There is other clear and convincing evidence that the respondent is the child's parent.

(3) Upon finding, after notice and opportunity to be heard, that an obligor owes a duty of support, the tribunal shall issue a support order directed to the obligor and may issue other orders pursuant to s. 88.3051.

History. s. 4, ch. 96–189.

Part V

Direct Enforcement of Order of Another State Without Registration

88.5011 Employer's receipt of income-withholding order of another state. An income-withholding order issued in another state may be sent to the person or entity defined as the obligor's employer under the income deduction law of this state or payor as defined by s. 61.046, without first filing a petition or comparable pleading or registering the order with a tribunal of this state.

History. s. 5, ch. 96–189; s. 24, ch. 97–170.

88.50211 Employer's compliance with income-withholding order of another state

(1) Upon receipt of an income-withholding order, the obligor's employer shall immediately provide a copy of the order to the obligor.

(2) The employer shall treat an income-withholding order issued in another state which appears regular on its face as if it had been issued by a tribunal of this state.

(3) Except as otherwise provided by subsection (4) and s. 88.5031, the employer shall withhold and distribute the funds as directed in the withholding order by complying with the terms of the order which specify:

(a) The duration and amount of periodic payments of current child support, stated as a sum certain;

(b) The person or agency designated to receive payments and the address to which the payments are to be forwarded;

(c) Medical support, whether in the form of periodic cash payment, stated as a sum certain, or ordering the obligor to provide health insurance coverage for the child under a policy available through the obligor's employment;

(d) The amount of periodic payments of fees and costs for a support enforcement agency, the issuing tribunal, and the obligee's attorney, stated as sums certain; and

(e) The amount of periodic payments of arrearages and interest on arrearages, stated as sums certain.

(4) An employer shall comply with the law of the state of the obligor's principal place of employment for withholding from income with respect to:

(a) The employer's fee for processing an income-withholding order;

(b) The maximum amount permitted to be withheld from the obligor's income; and

(c) The times within which the employer must implement the withholding order and forward the child support payment.

History. s. 25, ch. 97–170.

88.5031 Compliance with multiple income-withholding orders. If the obligor's employer receives multiple income-withholding orders with respect to the earnings of the same obligor, the employer satisfies the terms of the multiple orders if the employer complies with the law of the state of the obligor's principal place of employment to establish the priorities for withholding and allocating income withheld for multiple child support obligees.

History. s. 26, ch. 97–170.

88.5041 Immunity from civil liability. An employer who complies with an income-withholding order issued in another state in accordance with this article is not subject to civil liability to an individual or agency with regard to the employer's withholding of child support from the obligor's income.

History. s. 27, ch. 97–170.

88.5051 Penalties for noncompliance. An employer who willfully fails to comply with an income-withholding order issued by another state and received for enforcement is subject to the same penalties that may be imposed for noncompliance with an order issued by a tribunal of this state.

History. s. 28, ch. 97–170.

88.5061 Contest by obligor.

(1) An obligor may contest the validity or enforcement of an income-withholding order issued in another state and received directly by an employer in this state in the same manner as if the order had been issued by a tribunal of this state. Section 88.6041, choice of law, applies to the contest.

(2) The obligor shall give notice of the contest to:

(a) A support enforcement agency providing services to the obligee;

(b) Each employer that has directly received an income-withholding order; and

(c) The person or agency designated to receive payments in the income-withholding order, or if no person or agency is designated, to the obligee.

History. s. 29, ch. 97–170.

88.5071 Administrative enforcement of orders.

(1) A party seeking to enforce a support order or an income-withholding order, or both, issued by a tribunal of another state may send the documents required for registering the order to a support enforcement agency of this state.

(2) Upon receipt of the documents, the support enforcement agency, without initially seeking to register the order, shall consider and, if appropriate, use any administrative procedure authorized by the law of this state to enforce a support order or an income-withholding order, or both. If the obligor does not contest administrative enforcement, the order need not be registered. If the obligor contests the validity or administrative enforcement of the order, the support enforcement agency shall register the order pursuant to this act.

History. s. 5, ch. 96–189; s. 30, ch. 97–170.

Note. Former s. 88.5021.

Part VI

Enforcement and Modification of Support Order After Registration

88.6011 Registration of order for enforcement. A support order or an income-withholding order issued by a tribunal of another state may be registered in this state for enforcement.

History. s. 6, ch. 96–189.

88.6021 Procedure to register order for enforcement.

(1) A support order or income-withholding order of another state may be registered in this state by sending the following documents and information to the appropriate tribunal in this state:

(a) A letter of transmittal to the tribunal requesting registration and enforcement.

(b) Two copies, including one certified copy, of all orders to be registered, including any modification of an order.

(c) A sworn statement by the party seeking registration or a certified statement by the custodian of the records showing the amount of any arrearage.

(d) The name of the obligor and, if known:

(1) The obligor's address and social security number.

(2) The name and address of the obligor's employer and any other source of income of the obligor.

(3) A description and the location of property of the obligor in this state not exempt from execution.

(e) The name and address of the obligee and, if applicable, the agency or person to whom support payments are to be remitted.

(2) On receipt of a request for registration, the registering tribunal shall cause the order to be filed as a foreign judgment, together with one copy of the documents and information, regardless of their form.

(3) A petition or comparable pleading seeking a remedy that must be affirmatively sought under other law of this state may be filed at the same time as the request for registration or later. The pleading must specify the grounds for the remedy sought.

History. s. 6, ch. 96–189.

88.6031 Effect of registration for enforcement.

(1) A support order or income-withholding order issued in another state is registered when the order is filed in the registering tribunal of this state.

(2) A registered order issued in another state is enforceable in the same manner and is subject to the same procedures as an order issued by a tribunal of this state.

(3) Except as otherwise provided in this article, a tribunal of this state shall recognize and enforce, but may not modify, a registered order if the issuing tribunal had jurisdiction.

History. s. 6, ch. 96–189.

88.6041 Choice of law.

(1) The law of the issuing state governs the nature, extent, amount, and duration of current payments and other obligations of support and the payment of arrearages under the order.

(2) In a proceeding for arrearages, the statute of limitation under the laws of this state or of the issuing state, whichever is longer, applies.

History. s. 6, ch. 96–189.

88.6051 Notice of registration of order.

(1) When a support order or income-withholding order issued in another state is registered, the registering tribunal shall notify the nonregistering party. The notice

must be accompanied by a copy of the registered order and the documents and relevant information accompanying the order.

(2) The notice must inform the nonregistering party:

(a) That a registered order is enforceable as of the date of registration in the same manner as an order issued by a tribunal of this state.

(b) That a hearing to contest the validity or enforcement of the registered order must be requested within 20 days after the date of mailing or personal service of the notice.

(c) That failure to contest the validity or enforcement of the registered order in a timely manner will result in confirmation of the order and enforcement of the order and the alleged arrearages and precludes further contest of that order with respect to any matter that could have been asserted.

(d) Of the amount of any alleged arrearages.

(3) Upon registration of an income-withholding order for enforcement, the registering tribunal shall notify the obligor's employer pursuant to chapter 61 or other income deduction law of this state.

History. s. 6, ch. 96–189; s. 31, ch. 97–170.

88.6061 Procedure to contest validity or enforcement of registered order.

(1) A nonregistering party seeking to contest the validity or enforcement of a registered order in this state shall request a hearing within 20 days after notice of the registration. The nonregistering party may seek to vacate the registration, to assert any defense to an allegation of noncompliance with the registered order, or to contest the remedies being sought or the amount of any alleged arrearages pursuant to s. 88.6071.

(2) If the nonregistering party fails to contest the validity or enforcement of the registered order in a timely manner, the order is confirmed by operation of law.

(3) If a nonregistering party requests a hearing to contest the validity or enforcement of the registered order, the registering tribunal shall schedule the matter for hearing and give notice to the parties of the date, time, and place of the hearing.

History. s. 6, ch. 96–189; s. 32, ch. 97–170.

88.6071 Contest of registration or enforcement.

(1) A party contesting the validity or enforcement of a registered order or seeking to vacate the registration has the burden of proving one or more of the following defenses:

(a) The issuing tribunal lacked personal jurisdiction over the contesting party;

(b) The order was obtained by fraud;

(c) The order has been vacated, suspended, or modified by a later order;

(d) The issuing tribunal has stayed the order pending appeal;

(e) There is a defense under the law of this state to the remedy sought;

(f) Full or partial payment has been made; or

(g) The statute of limitation under s. 88.6041 precludes enforcement of some or all of the arrearages.

(2) If a party presents evidence establishing a full or partial defense under subsection (1), a tribunal may stay enforcement of the registered order, continue the proceeding to permit production of additional relevant evidence, and issue other appropriate orders. An uncontested portion of the registered order may be enforced by all remedies available under the law of this state.

(3) If the contesting party does not establish a defense under subsection (1) to the validity or enforcement of the order, the registering tribunal shall issue an order confirming the order.

History. s. 6, ch. 96–189.

88.6081 Confirmed order. Confirmation of a registered order, whether by operation of law or after notice and hearing, precludes further contest of the order with respect to any matter that could have been asserted at the time of registration.

History. s. 6, ch. 96–189.

88.6091 Procedure to register child support order of another state for modification. A party or support enforcement agency seeking to modify, or to modify and enforce, a child support order issued in another state shall register that order in this state in the same manner provided in ss. 88.6011–88.6041 if the order has not been registered. A petition for modification may be filed at the same time as a request for registration, or later. The pleading must specify the grounds for modification.

History. s. 6, ch. 96–189.

88.6101 Effect of registration for modification. A tribunal of this state may enforce a child support order of another state registered for purposes of modification, in the same manner as if the order had been issued by a tribunal of this state, but the registered order may be modified only if the requirements of s. 88.6111 have been met.

History. s. 6, ch. 96–189.

88.6111 Modification of child support order of another state.

(1) After a child support order issued in another state has been registered in this state, the responding tribunal of this state may modify that order only if s. 88.6131 does not apply and after notice and hearing it finds that:
    (a) The following requirements are met:
        (1) The child, the individual obligee, and the obligor do not reside in the issuing state;
        (2) A petitioner who is a nonresident of this state seeks modification; and
        (3) The respondent is subject to the personal jurisdiction of the tribunal of this state; or
    (b) The child, or a party who is an individual, is subject to the personal jurisdiction of the tribunal of this state and all of the parties who are individuals have filed written consents in the issuing tribunal for a tribunal of this state to modify the support order and assume continuing exclusive jurisdiction over the order. However, if the issuing state is a foreign jurisdiction that has not enacted a law or established procedures substantially similar to the procedures under this act, the consent otherwise required of an individual residing in this state is not required for the tribunal to assume jurisdiction to modify the child support order.

(2) Modification of a registered child support order is subject to the same requirements, procedures, and defenses that apply to the modification of an order issued by a tribunal of this state and the order may be enforced and satisfied in the same manner.

(3) A tribunal of this state may not modify any aspect of a child support order that may not be modified under the law of the issuing state. If two or more tribunals

have issued child support orders for the same obligor and child, the order that controls and must be so recognized under s. 88.2071 establishes the aspects of the support order which are nonmodifiable.

(4) On issuance of an order modifying a child support order issued in another state, a tribunal of this state becomes the tribunal of continuing exclusive jurisdiction.

History. s. 6, ch. 96–189; s. 33, ch. 97–170.

88.6121 Recognition of order modified in another state. A tribunal of this state shall recognize a modification of its earlier child support order by a tribunal of another state which assumed jurisdiction pursuant to this act or a law substantially similar to this act and, upon request, except as otherwise provided in this act, shall:

(1) Enforce the order that was modified only as to amounts accruing before the modification.

(2) Enforce only nonmodifiable aspects of that order.

(3) Provide other appropriate relief only for violations of that order which occurred before the effective date of the modification.

(4) Recognize the modifying order of the other state, upon registration, for the purpose of enforcement.

History. s. 6, ch. 96–189; s. 34, ch. 97–170.

88.6131 Jurisdiction to modify child support order of another state when individual parties reside in this state.

(1) If all of the parties who are individuals reside in this state and the child does not reside in the issuing state, a tribunal of this state has jurisdiction to enforce and to modify the issuing state's child support order in a proceeding to register that order.

(2) A tribunal of this state exercising jurisdiction under this section shall apply the provisions of parts I and II, this part and the procedural and substantive law of this state to the proceeding for enforcement or modification. Parts III–V, VII, and VIII do not apply.

History. s. 35, ch. 97–170.

88.6141 Notice to issuing tribunal of modifications. Within 30 days after issuance of a modified child support order, the party obtaining the modification shall file a certified copy of the order with the issuing tribunal that had continuing exclusive jurisdiction over the earlier order, and in each tribunal·in which the party knows the earlier order has been registered. A party who obtains the order and fails to file a certified copy is subject to appropriate sanctions by a tribunal in which the issue of failure to file arises. The failure to file does not affect the validity or enforceability of the modified order of the new tribunal having continuing exclusive jurisdiction.

History. s. 36, ch. 97–170.

Part VII

Determination of Parentage

88.7011 Proceeding to determine parentage.

(1) A tribunal of this state may serve as an initiating or responding tribunal in a proceeding brought under this act or a law or procedure substantially similar to this act, the Uniform Reciprocal Enforcement of Support Act, or the Revised Uniform Reciprocal Enforcement of Support Act to determine that the petitioner is a parent of a particular child or to determine that a respondent is a parent of that child.

(2) In a proceeding to determine parentage, a responding tribunal of this state shall apply the procedural and substantive law and rules of this state on choice of law.

History. s. 7, ch. 96–189; s. 37, ch. 97–170.

Part VIII

Interstate Rendition

88.8011 Grounds for rendition.

(1) For purposes of this article, "Governor" includes an individual performing the functions of Governor or the executive authority of a state covered by this act.

(2) The Governor of this state may:

(a) Demand that the Governor of another state surrender an individual found in the other state who is charged criminally in this state with having failed to provide for the support of an obligee; or

(b) On the demand by the Governor of another state, surrender an individual found in this state who is charged criminally in the other state with having failed to provide for the support of an obligee.

(3) A provision for extradition of individuals not inconsistent with this act applies to the demand even if the individual whose surrender is demanded was not in the demanding state when the crime was allegedly committed and has not fled therefrom.

History. s. 8, ch. 96–189.

88.8021 Conditions of rendition.

(1) Before making demand that the Governor of another state surrender an individual charged criminally in this state with having failed to provide for the support of an obligee, the Governor of this state may require a prosecutor of this state to demonstrate that at least 60 days previously the obligee had initiated proceedings for support pursuant to this act or that the proceeding would be of no avail.

(2) If, under this act or a law substantially similar to this act, the Uniform Reciprocal Enforcement of Support Act, or the Revised Uniform Reciprocal Enforcement of Support Act, the Governor of another state makes a demand that the Governor of this state surrender an individual charged criminally in that state with having failed to provide for the support of a child or other individual to whom a duty of support is owed, the Governor may require a prosecutor to investigate the demand and report whether a proceeding for support has been initiated or would be effective. If it appears that a proceeding would be effective but has not been

initiated, the Governor may delay honoring the demand for a reasonable time to permit the initiation of a proceeding.

(3) If a proceeding for support has been initiated and the individual whose rendition is demanded prevails, the Governor may decline to honor the demand. If the petitioner prevails and the individual whose rendition is demanded is subject to a support order, the Governor may decline to honor the demand if the individual is complying with the support order.

History. s. 8, ch. 96–189.

Part IX

Miscellaneous Provisions

88.9011 Uniformity of application and construction. This act shall be applied and construed to effectuate its general purpose to make uniform the law with respect to the subject of this act among states enacting it.

History. s. 9, ch. 96–189.

88.9031 Severability clause. If any provision of this act or its application to any person or circumstance is held invalid, the invalidity does not affect other provisions or applications of this act which can be given effect without the invalid provision or application, and to this end the provisions of this act are severable.

History. s. 9, ch. 96–189.

88.9051 Authority to adopt rules. The department shall have the authority to adopt rules to implement this chapter.

History. s. 38, ch. 97–170.

APPENDIX

E

Restraining Order Roseanne Barr (Formerly Roseanne Arnold)

TROPE AND TROPE
12121 Wilshire Blvd.
Suite 801
Los Angeles, CA 90025-1171
ATTORNEY FOR (name) Petitioner

TELEPHONE NO (310) 207-82_

FOR COURT USE ONLY

ORIGINAL FILED

APR 1 8 1994

**LOS ANGELES
SUPERIOR COURT**

SUPERIOR COURT OF CALIFORNIA, COUNTY OF LOS ANGELES
STREET ADDRESS 111 NORTH HILL ST
MAILING ADDRESS
CITY AND ZIP CODE LOS ANGELES CA 90012
BRANCH NAME CENTRAL

PETITIONER/PLAINTIFF ROSEANNE CHERRIE ARNOLD

RESPONDENT/DEFENDANT: TOM DWAYNE ARNOLD

EX PARTE APPLICATION AND
ORDER TO SHOW CAUSE FOR ☐ MODIFICATION
☐ Child Custody ☐ Visitation ☒ Injunctive Orders
☐ Child Support ☐ Spousal Support ☐ Other (specify):
☐ Attorney Fees and Costs

CASE NUMBER:

BD155482

1. TO (name): TOM DWAYNE ARNOLD
2. YOU ARE ORDERED TO APPEAR IN THIS COURT AS FOLLOWS TO GIVE ANY LEGAL REASON WHY THE RELIEF SOUGHT IN THE ATTACHED APPLICATION SHOULD NOT BE GRANTED. *If child custody or visitation is an issue in this proceeding, Family Code section 3170 requires mediation before or concurrently with the hearing listed below.*

a. Date: 5-27-94 Time: 8:30 ☒ Dept.: 20 ☒ Rm.: 243

b. Address of court ☒ same as noted above ☐ other (specify):

3. IT IS FURTHER ORDERED that a completed Application for Order and Supporting Declaration, a blank Responsive Declaration, and the following documents shall be served with this order:
(1) ☐ Completed Income and Expense Declaration and a blank Income and Expense Declaration
(2) ☐ Completed Property Declaration and a blank Property Declaration
(3) ☐ Points and authorities
(4) ☐ Other (specify):
a. ☐ Time for ☐ service ☐ hearing is shortened. Service shall be on or before (date):
Any responsive declaration shall be served on or before (date):

b. ☒ You are ordered to comply with the temporary orders attached.
c. ☒ Other (specify): *Attorney for Respondent, Nanty Fird, has accepted service of the Petition and OSC on behalf of Respondent.*

ROBERT SCHNIDE
JUDGE PRO TEM

Date: APR 1 8 1994

JUDGE OF THE SUPERIOR COURT

Notice: If you have children from this relationship, the court is required to order payment of child support based on the income of both parents. The amount of child support can be large. It normally continues until the child is 18. You should supply the court with information about your finances. Otherwise the child support order will be based on the information supplied by the other parent.
You do not have to pay any fee to file responsive declarations in response to this order to show cause (including a completed Income and Expense Declaration that will show your finances). The original of the responsive declarations must be filed with the court and a copy served on the other party at least five court days before the hearing date.

Form Adopted by Rule 1285
Judicial Council of California
1285 (Rev. January 1, 1994)

ORDER TO SHOW CAUSE
(Family Law)

Gov. Code § 26826
Family Code §§ 215, 271-272, 2030-2034, 2045, 2254, 4330-4339, 4350, 4370, 4455, 4801, 4809

EXHIBIT D

TEMPORARY RESTRAINING ORDERS
(Attachment to Order to Show Cause)

The person restrained in the first three orders is (name): TOM DWAYNE ARNOLD
Race: White............... Date of birth: 3/6/59......... Sex: Male.......

THE RESTRAINED PERSON

1. [X] shall NOT contact, molest, attack, strike, threaten, sexually assault, batter, telephone, or otherwise disturb the peace of the other party, *and Petitioner shall not contact, molest, threaten, batter, telephone or*

2. [ ] shall move out immediately and shall not return to the family dwelling at (address): *disturb the peace of Respondent*

   [ ] taking only clothing and personal effects needed until the hearing

3. [X] a. must stay at least 100......................... yards away from the other party and the following places.

   (1) [X] Residence of (name): Roseanne Cherrie Arnold
   (address optional): 12916 Evanston Street, Los Angeles, CA 90049

   This order is without prejudice to the time of the OSC hearing. Each party is ordered to stay away from that portion of the

   (2) [X] Place of work of (name): CBS/MTM Studios
   (address optional): Studio City, CA *used exclusively by the other party.*

   (3) [X] The children's school (address optional): *Petitioner is ordered to stay 100 yards from Respondent and 10 yards from Wilshire House, 10001 Wilshire Bl., Los Angeles.*

   (4) [X] Other (specify): Residence of Bill Pentland
   This order without prejudice

   [ ] b. may make contact relating to pickup and delivery of children pursuant to a court order for visitation or a stipulation of the parties arrived at during mediation.

- Any person subject to any of these three restraining orders is prohibited by Penal Code section 12021 from purchasing or receiving or attempting to purchase or receive a firearm. Such conduct may be punishable by a $1,000 fine, imprisonment up to one year, or both.
- Taking or concealing a child in violation of this order may be a felony and punishable by confinement in state prison, a fine, or both.
- Other violations of these orders may also be punishable by fines, imprisonment, or both.

4. [X] **PROPERTY RESTRAINT**

   a. [X] Petitioner [X] Respondent is restrained from transferring, encumbering, hypothecating, concealing, or in any way disposing of any property, real or personal, whether community, quasi-community, or separate, except in the usual course of business or for the necessities of life.
      [ ] The other party is to be notified of any proposed extraordinary expenditures and an accounting of such is to be made to the court.

   b. [X] Both parties are restrained and enjoined from cashing, borrowing against, canceling, transferring, disposing of, or changing the beneficiaries of any insurance or other coverage including life, health, automobile, and disability held for the benefit of the parties or their minor child or children.

   c. [X] Neither party shall incur any debts or liabilities for which the other may be held responsible, other than in the ordinary course of business or for the necessities of life

(Continued on reverse)

TEMPORARY RESTRAINING ORDERS
(Family Law)

Civil Code § 4359

EXHIBIT B

MARRIAGE OF *(last name, first name of parties)*:	CASE NUMBER
ARNOLD, Roseanne and Tom	

TEMPORARY RESTRAINING ORDERS
(Family Law)

5. [X] **PROPERTY CONTROL**

    a. [X] Petitioner [ ] Respondent   is given the exclusive temporary use, possession, and control of the following property the parties own or are buying *(specify)*: 12916 Evanston Street, Los Angeles, CA 90049

    b. [ ] Petitioner [ ] Respondent   is ordered to make the following payments on liens and encumbrances coming due while the order is in effect:

Debt	Amount of payment	Pay to

6. [ ] **MINOR CHILDREN**

    a. Neither party shall remove the minor child or children of the parties

        (1) [ ] from the State of California.

        (2) [ ] other *(specify)*:

    b. [ ] Petitioner [ ] Respondent   shall have the temporary physical custody, care, and control of the minor children of the parties, [ ] subject to the other party's rights of visitation as follows:

7. By the close of business on the date of this order, a copy of this order shall be delivered by the protected person to the law enforcement agency having jurisdiction over the residence of the protected person, who shall provide information to assist in identifying the restrained person. Proof of service of this order on the restrained person shall also be provided to the law enforcement agency. The law enforcement agency having jurisdiction over the plaintiff's residence is *(name and address of agency)*:
Los Angeles Police Department, West Los Angeles Division,

8. [X] A copy of this order shall be given to the additional law enforcement agencies listed below as follows:

    a. [ ] Plaintiff shall deliver.   b. [X] Plaintiff's attorney shall deliver.   c. [ ] The clerk of the court shall mail.

Law enforcement agency	Address
Los Angeles Police Department West Los Angeles Division	1663 Butler Avenue Los Angeles, CA 90025

9. This order is effective when made. The law enforcement agency shall enforce it immediately upon receipt. It is enforceable anywhere in California by any law enforcement agency that has received the order, is shown a copy of it, or has verified its existence on the California Law Enforcement Telecommunications System (CLETS). If proof of service on the restrained person has not been received, the law enforcement agency shall advise the restrained person of the terms of the order and then shall enforce it.

10. [ ] **OTHER ORDERS** *(specify)*:

11. These orders expire on the date of the court hearing unless extended by the court.

Date APR 18 1994

► _____
JUDGE OF THE SUPERIOR COURT

12. The date of the court hearing is *(insert date when known)*:   **EXHIBIT B**   ROBERT SCHNIDE
JUDGE PRO TEM

CLERK'S CERTIFICATE

MARRIAGE OF (last name, first name ~rbes):

ARNOLD, Roseanne and Tc

CASE CLOSED

(THIS IS NOT AN ORDER)

☒ Petitioner ☐ Respondent ☐ Claimant requests the following orders be made:

☐ CHILD CUSTODY   ☐ To be ordered pending the hearing
   a. Child (name and age)   b. Request custody to (name)   c. ☐ Modify existing order
                                                      (1) filed on (date):
                                                      (2) ordering (specify)

2. ☐ CHILD VISITATION   ☐ To be ordered pending the hearing
   a. ☐ Reasonable   d. ☐ Modify existing order
   b. ☐ Other (specify):   (1) filed on (date):
   c. ☐ Neither party shall remove the minor child or children of the parties   (2) ordering (specify):

      (1) ☐ from the State of California. (2) ☐ other (specify):

3. ☐ CHILD SUPPORT (A Wage and Earnings Assignment Order will be issued.)
   a. Child (name and age)   b. Monthly amount   c. ☐ Modify existing order
                                    (if not by guideline)   (1) filed on (date):
                                    $ (2) ordering (specify):

4. ☐ SPOUSAL SUPPORT (A Wage and Earnings Assignment Order will be issued.)
   a. ☐ Amount requested (monthly): $ b. ☐ Modify existing order
   c. ☐ Terminate existing order   (1) filed on (date):
      (1) filed on (date):   (2) ordering (specify):
      (2) ordering (specify):

5. ☐ ATTORNEY FEES AND COSTS a. ☐ Fees. $ b. ☐ Costs: $
6. ☐ RESIDENCE EXCLUSION AND RELATED ORDERS   ☐ To be ordered pending the hearing
   ☐ Petitioner ☐ Respondent must move out immediately and must not return to the family dwelling at
   (address):
   ☐ taking only clothing and personal effects needed until the hearing.
7. ☒ STAY-AWAY ORDERS   ☐ To be ordered pending the hearing
   a. ☐ Petitioner ☒ Respondent must stay at least 100... yards away from applicant and the following places
      (1) ☒ applicant's residence (address optional): 12916 Evanston Street, Los Angeles, CA 90049
      (2) ☒ applicant's place of work (address optional): CBS/MTM Studios, Studio City, CA
      (3) ☐ the children's school (address optional):
      (4) ☐ other (specify):

   b. ☐ Contacts relating to pickup and delivery of children pursuant to a court order or a stipulation of the parties
      arrived at during mediation shall be permitted.
8. ☒ RESTRAINT ON PERSONAL CONDUCT   ☐ To be ordered pending the hearing
   ☐ Petitioner ☒ Respondent
   a. shall not molest, attack, strike, threaten, sexually assault, or otherwise disturb the peace of the other party
      ☒ and any person under the care, custody, and control of the other party

   b. ☒ shall not contact or telephone the other party.
   c. ☐ except that peaceful contacts relating to minor children of the parties shall be permitted.

(Continued on reverse)

Form Adopted by Rule 1285.20
Judicial Council of California
1285.20 (Rev. January 1, 1993)

**APPLICATION FOR ORDER
AND SUPPORTING DECLARATION**
(Family Law)

Case Code 6-1288

EXHIBIT B

MARRIAGE OF (last name, first name of . .es):		NUMBER
_ARNOLD, Roseanne and Tom		

9 ☐ **PROPERTY RESTRAINT** ☐ To be ordered pending the hearing

   a The ☐ petitioner ☐ respondent ☐ claimant be restrained from transferring, encumbering, hypothecating, concealing, or in any way disposing of any property, real or personal, whether community, quasi-community, or separate, except in the usual course of business or for the necessities of life

      ☐ and applicant be notified at least five business days before any proposed extraordinary expenditures and an accounting of such be made to the court.

   b ☐ Both parties are restrained and enjoined from cashing, borrowing against, canceling, transferring, disposing of, or changing the beneficiaries of any insurance or other coverage including life, health, automobile, and disability held for the benefit of the parties or their minor children.

   c ☐ Neither party shall incur any debts or liabilities for which the other may be held responsible, other than in the ordinary course of business or for the necessities of life.

10 ☒ **PROPERTY CONTROL** ☐ To be ordered pending the hearing

   a ☒ Petitioner ☐ Respondent be given the exclusive temporary use, possession, and control of the following property we own or are buying (specify): 12916 Evanston Street, Los Angeles, CA 90049

   b ☐ Petitioner ☐ Respondent be ordered to make the following payments on liens and encumbrances coming due while the order is in effect:

Debt	Amount of payment	Pay to

11 ☒ **LAW ENFORCEMENT AGENCIES** I request that copies of orders be given to the following law enforcement agencies having jurisdiction over the locations where violence is likely to occur.

Law enforcement agency	Address
Los Angeles Police Department	1663 Butler Avenue
West Los Angeles Division	Los Angeles, CA 90025

12 ☐ I request that time for service of the Order to Show Cause and accompanying papers be shortened so that they may be served no less than (specify number): .... days before the time set for the hearing. I need to have the order shortening time because of the facts specified in the attached declaration.

13 ☐ **OTHER RELIEF** (specify):

14 ☒ **FACTS IN SUPPORT** of relief requested and change of circumstances for any modification are (specify):
   ☒ contained in the attached declaration.

I declare under penalty of perjury under the laws of the State of California that the foregoing is true and correct

Date April 16, 1994

ROSEANNE CHERRIE ARNOLD
(TYPE OR PRINT NAME)

_____
(SIGNATURE OF APPLICANT)

1 <u>In re Marriage of ARNOLD</u>   <u>L.A.S.C. Case No. BD</u>

2   <u>DECLARATION OF ROSEANNE ARNOLD</u>

3

4   I, ROSEANNE ARNOLD, declare as follows:

5   1.   I am the Petitioner in the instant action. The

6 facts stated herein are known by me to be true, and if called upon

7 to testify, I could and would testify competently thereto.

8   2.   The Respondent and I married on January 20, 1990.

9 Throughout our marriage, the Respondent has been physically and

10 emotionally abusive toward me. I now realize that I have been a

11 classic battered and abused wife who has tolerated the conduct of

12 the Respondent only because the Respondent has successfully lowered

13 my self-esteem and reduced me into the realm of battered wife

14 syndrome.

15   3.   Throughout our marriage, the Respondent hit me,

16 struck me, has thrown objects at me, pinched me, and verbally

17 abused me. He also has pushed me against walls, while he screams

18 and shouts at me, drowning out any possible plea that I might make

19 for him to stop.

20   4.   I should note that the Respondent has a proclivity

21 and character for violence. He was arrested seven times for

22 drunken and disorderly behavior, assaulting police, and other

23 disorderly and violent conduct as a younger person.

24   5.   In recent months, the Respondent's pattern of

25 violence has grown worse. I am now extremely afraid of him and am

26 extremely afraid for my physical safety. I am gravely concerned

27 that if the Respondent found out that I was filing for dissolution

28 of marriage, and seeking these restraining orders, that he would

TROPE and TROPE
ATTORNEYS AT LAW
12121 WILSHIRE BLVD
LOS ANGELES CA
90025-1171

DECLARATION OF ROSEANNE ARNOLD   **EXHIBIT B**   Page 1

In re Marriage of ARNOLD   L.A.S.C. Case No. BD _____

immediately seek revenge in the form of violent retribution against either me or some person who is important in my life. I am therefore requesting that personal conduct restraining orders be issued ex parte and without notice so as to minimize the possibility of such violent retribution.

6. Most recently, on April 15, 1994, I attempted to have the Respondent barred from access to the studio where I film my television program. I arranged for several security personnel to be present so as to prevent the Respondent from having access to this area. Notwithstanding these efforts, the Respondent gained access to the studio area and assaulted four people in a violent episode. He scratched and hit these individuals.

7. Also on April 15, 1994, the Respondent gained access to my personal residence located at 12916 Evanston Street, Los Angeles, California 90049. Although I have a security system at my residence, and attempted to prevent the Respondent from gaining access thereto, he nonetheless did gain access to the residence and threatened my children, none of whom are of my marriage to the Respondent. My children's names and ages are Brandi Brown (age 23), Jessica Pentland (age 19), Jennifer Pentland (age 17½), and James Pentland (age 15½), who reside with Bill Pentland. I called the police at approximately 3:00 p.m. on April 15, 1994 to seek their assistance in removing the Respondent from my property.

8. Respondent moved out of this residence approximately six months ago pursuant to an agreement we made at that time. He now resides in a condominium located at the Wilshire Towers on Wilshire Boulevard. Since he no longer resides at the residence,

TROPE and TROPE
ATTORNEYS AT LAW
1131 WILSHIRE BLVD
LOS ANGELES CA
90025-1171

DECLARATION OF ROSEANNE ARNOLD

EXHIBIT B   Page 2

1   <u>In re Marriage of ARNOLD   L.A.S.C. Case No. BD</u>

2   I am requesting that I be granted exclusive use, possession and

3   control of the residence located at 12916 Evanston Street. Since

4   the Respondent has moved out and has a residence of his own, this

5   will not pose any burden upon the Respondent.

6   9.   On Saturday, April 9, 1994, my children, the

7   Respondent, and I were driving in my limousine en route to a movie

8   premiere.   Without provocation, the Respondent grew angry and

9   violent, and grabbed my calf and twisted it. This caused me severe

10   pain and left a bruise. He did this in front of my children, which

11   was the first time that he had displayed his violent behavior in

12   front of my children.

13   10.   A few days before that incident, we were in my

14   residence and had an argument. As a result of this argument, he

15   pushed me down on the bathroom floor, put his foot against my back,

16   and pulled at my hair. I was screaming in desperation for him to

17   relent, but he was screaming and shouting and ignoring my pleas.

18   This episode lasted several minutes, and I was extremely frightened

19   for my physical safety, if not my life.

20   11.   Just a few days before this episode, he was in the

21   residence and pushed me up against the wall. He pinned me against

22   the wall and again was screaming loudly at me.

23   12.   This type of pattern of violent and abusive behavior

24   has been recurrent throughout our marriage. However, such episodes

25   of violent and abusive behavior have become more frequent and more

26   violent in recent months. I have finally come to the realization

27   that I must not subject myself to his conduct. My life would be

28   ruined if I continue in this abusive relationship.

DECLARATION OF ROSEANNE ARNOLD   **EXHIBIT R**   Page 3

In re Marriage of ARNOLD   L.A.S.C. Case No. BD _____

13. The Respondent also has engaged in verbal abuse against me. He has constantly referred to me as a "fuckin' bitch" as well as other derogatory comments. He has a proclivity for attempting to humiliate me in public by inappropriately and unnecessarily revealing personal aspects of our life.

14. As a result of the foregoing, I am requesting that restraining orders be issued against the Respondent so that he cannot threaten, harass, annoy, or contact me. I am also requesting that restraining orders be issued to prevent him from coming near my residence or place of work. There is absolutely no reason why the Respondent need go to either of these locations. Again, I am also requesting that these restraining orders be issued on an ex parte basis with no notice, because of the very real possibility that the Respondent will seek violent revenge upon learning of my filing for dissolution and my seeking of these restraining orders.

15. I cannot overemphasize my grave fear of the Respondent and the fear that I have for my physical safety and well-being. This fear extends to individuals that are close to me. For example, Respondent has threatened a security person who works for me, Ben Thomas. He has literally threatened to kill Mr. Thomas.

16. I certainly realize that the revelations that I am making in this declaration will become a matter of public record and will no doubt be exploited by certain parts of the news media, in particular the tabloids. I have often been the subject of humiliating stories in tabloid newspapers. However, I must make

TROPE and TROPE
ATTORNEYS AT LAW
···· ·········
··· ·········· ··
····· ····

DECLARATION OF ROSEANNE ARNOLD   EXHIBIT B   Page 4

1 In re Marriage of ARNOLD   L.A.S.C. Case No. BD

2 these revelations at this time because of the conclusion that I

3 have reached that I cannot continue to live in a classic battered

4 wife syndrome mentality. I am earnestly seeking the assistance of

5 this court to separate myself from the Respondent and to remove his

6 threatening and violent character from my life.

7

8   I declare, under penalty of perjury, under the laws of the

9 State of California, that the foregoing is true and correct.

10   Executed April 16, 1994, at Los Angeles, California.

11

12   _Roseanne Cherrie Arnold_
                                ROSEANNE CHERRIE ARNOLD
13

14

15

16

17

18

19

20

21

22

23

24

25

26

27

28

TROPE and TROPE
ATTORNEYS AT LAW
12121 WILSHIRE BLVD
LOS ANGELES CA
90025 1171

DECLARATION OF ROSEANNE ARNOLD   EXHIBIT B   Page 5

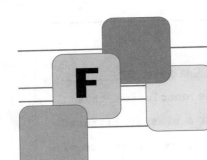

APPENDIX F

Marital Settlement Agreement (Madonna and Sean Penn)

MARITAL SETTLEMENT AGREEMENT

THIS AGREEMENT, made and entered into JANUARY 19 , MCP 1989, by and between SEAN PENN, hereinafter referred to as "Husband", and MADONNA CICCONE PENN, hereinafter referred to as "Wife":

WHEREAS, the parties hereto were lawfully married on August 16, 1985, and ever since then have been, and still are, Husband and Wife; and

WHEREAS, in consequence of unhappy differences and irreconcilable disputes which have arisen between Husband and Wife, as a result of which the parties have separated on December 31, 1988, and have not cohabited together since then, and are no longer living or cohabiting together as husband and wife; and

WHEREAS, there are no minor children who are the issue of the marriage of Husband and Wife; and

WHEREAS, it is the mutual wish and desire of both Husband and Wife to immediately effect, by way of a contract, a full, complete, and final settlement of all of their community property and quasi-community property interests, future and present, and, except as otherwise set forth herein, to irrevocably adjust and determine forever all legal obligations of any nature which may exist in respect to each other and by reason of their said marriage, and to fully and completely resolve any and all issues relating to spousal support. This Agreement shall be effective irrespective of when or if a proceeding for dissolution of marriage is filed, a final decree of dissolution is entered, or this Marital Settlement Agreement is integrated into the decree of dissolution.

NOW, THEREFORE, by reason of the foregoing facts and in consideration of the mutual covenants and provisions hereinafter set forth, it is hereby agreed, by and between the parties, as follows:

PROPERTY AWARDED TO WIFE

MCP

FIRST: Husband hereby releases, sets over and assigns to Wife all right, title and interest and any claim to that certain real property located at *1 WEST 64th STREET*, in the City of New York, State of New York, the legal description of which is attached as Exhibit "A" hereto (herein the "New York Apartment"). Husband shall quitclaim to Wife all of his right, title and interest to the New York Apartment.

PROPERTY AWARDED TO HUSBAND

SECOND: Wife hereby releases, sets over and assigns to Husband all right, title and interest and any claim to that certain real property located at 22271 Carbon Mesa Drive, Malibu,

2

California the legal description of which is attached as Exhibit "B" hereto (herein the "Malibu Residence"). Wife shall quitclaim to Husband all of her right, title and interest to the Malibu Residence. ~~Husband shall pay to Wife, within 180 days from the date of execution of this Agreement, the sum of $_____ in order to equalize the difference in value between the Malibu property and the New York property.~~ Husband shall hold Wife harmless from, and pay all liens and encumbrances of record on the Malibu property and shall indemnify Wife from all claims connected with any such liens or encumbrances.

EXTENT OF COMMUNITY PROPERTY

THIRD: 1.   The parties acknowledge that the only community property, quasi-community property or marital property owned by them is the Malibu Residence and New York Apartment. The parties have by other verbal agreement confirmed to each other their respective separate property interests in all other property owned by either of them. The parties further agree that the only community debt is the indebtedness on the Malibu residence secured by deeds of trust, which indebtedness (as between Husband and Wife) is expressly assumed by Husband.

3

<u>PROPERTY WAIVER</u>

<u>FOURTH</u>: 1. Both parties voluntarily waive the right to require each other to account to the other for any use of funds and property each has received or managed during their marriage or to set out in this Agreement a description of their respective assets and liabilities. Both parties voluntarily and expressly waive any requirement that the other provide a financial statement, or further information, in connection with this Agreement.

2. To the extent that there exists any property of any kind or description, or any interest in any property in the name of either of the parties or under either of their control or held for the benefit of either of them that is not otherwise described and/or disposed of herein, that property, real or personal, wherever situated, is awarded to the party in whose name said property is held or for whose benefit said property is held.

3. Each party hereby waives the right to investigate or value any property, or rights in and to property, either party has acquired during marriage or since the parties' separation.

4. The parties acknowledge and agree that, to the extent that any opportunities to examine, audit and appraise books, records and accounts and business interests of either party

4

has not been exercised, the parties hereby, now and forever, expressly waive the right to do so.

SECTION 1041 OF INTERNAL REVENUE CODE

Fifth: The parties intend and agree that all transfers of property as provided for herein are subject to the provisions of Section 1041, Internal Revenue Code of 195486, as amended, entitled "Treatment of Transfers of Property Between Spouses or Incident to Divorce", that they shall be accounted for and reported on his or her respective individual income tax returns in such a manner so that no gain or loss shall be recognized as a result of the division and transfer of property as provided herein. Each party shall file his or her Federal or State tax returns, and report his or her income and losses thereon, consistent with the foregoing intent of reporting the division and transfers of property as a non-taxable event. In the event either party causes an adjustment to basis to be made to their property that gives rise to any actual or alleged claim or liability for taxes, state or federal, the party making such adjustment shall defend, hold harmless and indemnify the other with respect to any such claim or liability.

5

RELEASE FROM THIRD-PARTY CLAIMS

SIXTH: 1. Husband shall indemnify, defend and hold Wife harmless from any and all other indebtedness, loans, obligations, claims and causes of action that have, may now or hereafter be made against Wife on her property as a result of any acts or omissions of Husband, judgments that may be obtained against Husband, debts, guarantees or obligations incurred by Husband on his own behalf or on behalf of any company, owned or controlled by him.

2. Wife shall indemnify, defend and hold Husband harmless from any and all other indebtedness, loans, obligations, claims and causes of action that have, may now or hereafter be made against Husband or his property as a result of any acts or omissions of Wife, judgments that may be obtained against Wife, debts, guarantees or obligations incurred by Wife on her own behalf or on behalf of any company, owned or controlled by her.

SPOUSAL SUPPORT WAIVER

SEVENTH: Both parties warrant and agree that they have each, individually, consulted with their respective legal counsel concerning their rights to spousal support. Each party is self-supporting and waives the right to claim spousal support, temporary spousal support, family support, maintenance or alimony from the other, now or at any time.

6

ATTORNEY'S FEES, ACCOUNTANT'S FEES AND COSTS

EIGHTH: Each party shall bear his or her own attorney's fees, accountant's fees, appraiser's fees, and all other fees and costs incurred with respect to this Agreement or any action to dissolve the marriage of the parties.

INDEPENDENTLY BINDING

NINTH: This Agreement, and all of its terms and conditions, shall be absolutely binding upon the parties hereto, regardless of whether any action to dissolve the marriage of the parties is filed. The parties agree that this Agreement may be submitted in evidence in any action that may be brought to dissolve their marriage, but its effectiveness is not subject to Court approval. The executory terms hereof may be incorporated into a Judgment of Dissolution of Marriage. The parties declare it to be their intention that this Agreement shall be absolutely binding upon them, regardless of whether this Agreement is ever presented to any court or approved or disapproved by an court.

RELEASE OF CLAIMS

TENTH: Except as otherwise provided in this Agreement, Husband and Wife hereby release the other from any and all liabilities, debts, or obligations of every kind whatsoever

7

including any claims arising out of any tortious conduct, heretofore incurred or hereafter incurred, and from any and all claims and demands of any kind, nature and description.

Further, Husband and Wife agree that this Release extends to all claims of every nature or kind, known or unknown, suspected or unsuspected each may have against the other and each further waives all rights under Section 1542 of the California Civil Code, which provides:

> "A general release does not extend to claims which the creditor does not know or suspect to exist in his favor at the time of executing the release, which if known by him must have materially affected his settlement with the debtor."

RELEASE OF LIABILITY

ELEVENTH: A. Husband hereby warrants to Wife that he has not incurred, and hereby covenants that he will not incur, any liability or obligation on which Wife is liable or may be liable and Husband hereby covenants and agrees that if any claim, action or proceeding shall hereafter be brought seeking to hold Wife liable on account of any debt, liability, act or omission of Husband, he will, at his sole expense, defend Wife against any such claim or demand, whether or not well-founded, and he will hold her free and harmless therefrom. HUSBAND IS NOT RESPONSIBLE MCP FOR PAYING FOR WIFES INDEPENDENT COUNSEL.

8

B.   Wife hereby represents to Husband that she has not incurred, and hereby covenants that she will not incur, any liability or obligation on which Husband is liable or may be liable and Wife hereby covenants and agrees that if any claim, action or proceeding shall hereafter be brought seeking to hold Husband liable on account of any debt, liability, act or omission or Wife, she will, at her sole expense, defend Husband against any such claim or demand, whether or not well-founded, and she will hold him free and harmless therefrom.

RELEASE OF ESTATES AND SURVIVOR BENEFITS

TWELFTH: A.   Husband and Wife hereby waive any and all right to inherit the estate of the other at his or her death, or to take property from the other by devise or bequest, unless under a Will executed subsequent to the effective date hereof, or to claim any family allowance or probate homestead, or to act as administrator or administratrix of the estate of the other, except as the nominee of another person legally entitled to said right, or to act as the executor or executrix under the Will
of the other, unless under a Will executed subsequent to the effective date hereof.

B.   Husband and Wife hereby waive any and all right to receive surviving spouse benefits under any private, non-governmental, pension or retirement plan in which either spouse is a participant.

9

REPRESENTATION OF LEGAL COUNSEL

THIRTEENTH: Each party to this Agreement represents and acknowledges that he or she has been represented in negotiations for and in the preparation of this Agreement by counsel or his or her own choosing.   Each party has read this Agreement and has had it fully explained to him or her.

PROPERTY ACQUIRED AFTER SEPARATION

FOURTEENTH: The parties have separated and have lived apart since December 31, 1988.   It is hereby agreed that any and all property (except the Malibu Residence and the New York Apartment) acquired by Husband and Wife from and after August 16, 1986, the effective date of the Post-Marital Property Agreement, is and shall be the sole and separate property of the one so acquiring the same, and does hereby waive any and all right in or to such acquisitions, as well as future acquisitions made from and after the date of this Agreement and does hereby grant the other all such acquisitions and future acquisitions of property as the sole and separate property of the one so acquiring same.

MCP

ENTIRE UNDERSTANDING

FIFTEENTH: This Agreement constitutes the full and entire understanding of the parties with respect to the parties' community property, ~~quasi-community~~ property and marital property and any prior agreement, understanding or representation concerning the same is hereby terminated and cancelled in its entirety and is of no further force or effect. This provision is to not be understood to limit, or deny the effectiveness of, that certain Separate Property Agreement of even date herewith ~~or the Post-Marital Property Agreement between the parties hereto~~. The parties hereto cannot alter and/or modify this Agreement, except by an instrument in writing executed by them and dated after the effective date hereof. This Agreement includes all of the representations of every kind and nature by the parties.

MODIFICATION

SIXTEENTH: No modification or waiver of any terms of this Agreement shall be valid as between the parties unless in writing and executed with the same formality of this Agreement; no waiver of any breach or default hereunder shall be deemed a waiver of any subsequent breach or default of the same or similar nature, no matter how made or how often occurring.

11

FREE OF COERCION

SEVENTEENTH: Each party hereto acknowledges that they are making this Agreement of their own free will and volition, and acknowledges that no coercion, force, pressure, or undue influence whatsoever has been employed against them in negotiations leading to or the execution of this Agreement, either by any other party hereto or by any other person or persons whomsoever, and declares that no reliance whatsoever is placed upon any representation other than those expressly set forth herein.

COUNTERPARTS

EIGHTEENTH: This Agreement may be executed in counterparts and each such counterpart shall be deemed to be an original.

EXECUTION OF DOCUMENTS AND RESERVATION OF JURISDICTION

NINETEENTH: The parties agree to perform all acts and to execute any documents necessary to effectuate and carry out the terms of this Agreement.

AGREEMENT SURVIVES INVALIDATION OF ANY PART

TWENTIETH: If any portion of this Agreement is held

12

to be illegal, unenforceable, void or voidable by any court, each of the remaining terms shall continue in full force as a separate contract.

RESOLUTION OF ALL ISSUES

TWENTY-FIRST: The parties acknowledge and understand that this Marital Settlement Agreement, and the Separate Property Agreement of even date ~~and the Post-Marital Property Agreement,~~ have resolved all issues between them.

MCP

CHANGES IN THE LAW

TWENTY-SECOND: Subsequent changes in California law, New York law or federal, through legislation or judicial interpretation, that creates or finds additional or different rights and obligations of the parties, shall not affect this Agreement.

PUBLIC RECORDS; INCORPORATION IN MARITAL PROCEEDING

TWENTY-THIRD: In the event that any court action is instituted concerning the subject matter of this Marital Settlement Agreement or in connection with a separation and/or dissolution of marriage, the parties agree that they will sign appropriate stipulations to cause this Marital Settlement Agreement and any and

13

all financial information of the parties to be placed under seal
and not to be made public or part of any record. If the court
directs that this Marital Settlement Agreement and said financial
information to be made a part of the records, then the parties
agree to request the court to place this Agreement and said
financial information under seal and not allow this Agreement or
said financial information to be seen read, reviewed or copied by
anyone without the agreement of the parties, except as may be
necessary to enforce the rights of either of the parties. The
parties further agree that the court ~~shall be requested to approve~~
~~this Marital Settlement Agreement as fair and equitable and to~~ may
make specific orders requiring each party to do all of the things
provided for in this Agreement and further agree that any executory
provisions hereof shall be made a part of any decree entered by the
court in a separation or dissolution proceeding. Notwithstanding
incorporation or approval in any judgment or decree of this Marital
Settlement Agreement or any of its terms, this Marital Settlement
Agreement shall not be affected or altered in any way but shall
continue to be fully independent and viable and enforceable to the
same extent and by the same means and remedies as though such
judgment had not been entered.

MISCELLANEOUS

TWENTY-FOURTH: This Agreement shall be binding upon,
and shall enure to the benefit of the respective legatees,

devisees, heirs, executors, administrators, and assigns and successors in interest of the parties.

Each party agrees to not molest, harass, annoy, injure, threaten or interfere with the other party in any manner whatsoever or interfere with the use, ownership, enjoyment or disposition of any property now or hereafter owned or occupied by the other party.

"Property" as used herein is intended in its broadest and most comprehensive sense and includes real, personal and mixed real and personal property, tangible and intangible, and all earnings, interest, profits, appreciation and proceeds thereof and thereon, and insurance (and proceeds of insurance) thereon.

In the event any party hereto shall commence an action to enforce or receive damages or obtain any relief based on this Agreement, the prevailing party shall be entitled to recover, in addition to all other relief, reasonable attorneys fees fixed by the court in such action or in a separate action brought for that purpose.

IN WITNESS WHEREOF, the parties hereto have executed this Agreement as of the 19th day of January, 1989.

I, MADONNA CICCONE PENN, by my signature hereto, attest to my agreement to the terms and provisions of this Agreement. I have been advised as to the legal effect of the provisions of this Agreement by Michael K. Inglis, independent legal counsel chosen by me, and understand that I am, as a result of this Agreement, relinquishing certain rights as to properties which might and/or would, but for this Agreement, have been determined to be community

15

property, quasi-community property or marital property, or which
I might have been entitled to receive had SEAN PENN died intestate
or as dowry or its statutory equivalent or any other statutory
share of a surviving spouse in the state or country in which he had
died, owned property or was a resident or citizen. I understand
all of the provisions of the Agreement and the rights which I am
relinquishing as a result of the execution of the Agreement and the
benefits I am receiving under the Agreement. I believe the
benefits accruing to me under this Agreement are fair and
reasonable. I have executed the Agreement without any influence
on the part of SEAN PENN or any other party whomsoever and as a
result of my own free volition. No oral statements or inducements,
other than those contained herein, have been made as an inducement
for me to sign this Agreement.

MADONNA CICCONE PENN - "WIFE"

CAT. NO. NN00627
TO 1944 CA (1—83)

(Individual)

TICOR TITLE INSURANCE

STATE OF CALIFORNIA
COUNTY OF __LOS ANGELES__ } SS.

On __January 24, 1989__ before me, the undersigned, a Notary Public in and for
said State, personally appeared __MADONNA CICCONE PENN__
_____ , personally known to me or
proved to me on the basis of satisfactory evidence to be
the person__ whose name __is__ subscribed to the
within instrument and acknowledged that __she__ executed the same.
WITNESS my hand and official seal.

Signature _____

OFFICIAL SEAL
JILL M. NAPOLITANO
NOTARY PUBLIC - CALIFORNIA
LOS ANGELES COUNTY
My Comm. Expires Jan. 25, 1991

(This area for official notarial seal)

STAPLE HERE

I, SEAN PENN, by my signature hereto, attest to my agreement to the terms and provisions of this Agreement. I have been advised as to the legal effect of the provisions of this Agreement by Robert Kaufman, independent legal counsel chosen by me, and understand that I am, as a result of this Agreement, relinquishing certain rights as to properties which might and/or would, but for this Agreement, have been determined to be community property, quasi-community property or marital property, or which I might have been entitled to receive had MADONNA CICCONE PENN dies intestate or as dowry or its statutory equivalent or any other statutory share of a surviving spouse in the state or country in which she died, owned property or was a resident or citizen. I understand all of the provisions of the Agreement and the rights which I am relinquishing as a result of the execution of the Agreement and the benefits I am receiving under the Agreement. I believe the benefits accruing to me under this Agreement are fair and reasonable. I have executed such Agreement without any influence on the part of MADONNA CICCONE PENN or any other party whomsoever and as a result of my own free volition. No oral statements or inducements, other than those contained herein, have been made as an inducement for me to sign the Agreement.

SEAN PENN - "HUSBAND"

17

GENERAL ACKNOWLEDGMENT   NO. 201

State of ___California___

County of ___Los Angeles___ } SS.

On this the __19th__ day of __January__ 19_89_, before me,

___Tracie L. Marcelin___,

the undersigned Notary Public, personally appeared

___Sean Penn___,

☑ personally known to me

☐ proved to me on the basis of satisfactory evidence

to be the person(s) whose name(s) ___is___ subscribed to the within instrument, and acknowledged that ___he___ executed it. WITNESS my hand and official seal.

___Tracie L. Marcelin___

Notary's Signature

OFFICIAL SEAL
TRACIE L MARCELIN
NOTARY PUBLIC - CALIFORNIA
LOS ANGELES COUNTY
My comm. expires NOV 7, 1989

7110 122

NATIONAL NOTARY ASSOCIATION • 23012 Ventura Blvd. • P.O. Box 4625 • Woodland Hills, CA 91364

APPENDIX G

Connecticut Uniform Child Custody Jurisdiction and Enforcement Act

Conn. Gen. Stat. 46b-115 to 46b-115jj

Section 1. This act may be cited as the Uniform Child Custody Jurisdiction and Enforcement Act.

Sec. 2. As used in this act:

(1) "Abandoned" means left without provision for reasonable and necessary care or supervision;

(2) "Child" means an individual who has not attained eighteen years of age;

(3) "Child custody determination" means a judgment, decree, or other order of a court providing for the legal custody, physical custody or visitation with respect to a child. The term includes a permanent, temporary, initial and modification order. The term does not include an order relating to child support or other monetary obligation of an individual;

(4) "Child custody proceeding" means a proceeding in which legal custody, physical custody or visitation with respect to a child is an issue. The term includes a proceeding for dissolution of marriage, divorce, separation, neglect, abuse, dependency, guardianship, paternity, termination of parental rights and protection from domestic violence, in which the issue may appear. The term does not include a proceeding involving juvenile delinquency, contractual emancipation or enforcement under sections 22 to 34, inclusive, of this act;

(5) "Commencement" means the filing of the first pleading in a proceeding;

(6) "Court" means any entity, including the Superior Court or Probate Court in this state, if such entity has jurisdiction to establish, enforce or modify a child custody determination;

(7) "Home state" means the state in which a child lived with a parent or person acting as a parent for at least six consecutive months immediately before the commencement of a child custody proceeding. In the case of a child less than six months old, the term means the state in which the child lived from birth with any such parent or person acting as a parent. A period of temporary absence of any such person is counted as part of the period;

(8) "Initial determination" means the first child custody determination concerning a particular child;

(9) "Issuing court" means the court that has made a child custody determination for which enforcement is sought under this act;

(10) "Issuing state" means the state in which a child custody determination has been made;

(11) "Modification" means a child custody determination that changes, replaces, supersedes or is otherwise made after a previous determination concerning the same child, whether or not it is made by the court that made the prior custody determination;

(12) "Person" shall have the same meaning as contained in subsection (k) of section 1-1 of the general statutes;

(13) "Person acting as a parent" means a person, other than a parent, who: (A) Has physical custody of the child or has had physical custody for a period of six consecutive months, including any temporary absence, any part of which period occurred within one year immediately before the commencement of a child custody proceeding, and (B) has been awarded legal custody by a court or claims a right to legal custody under the laws of this state;

(14) "Physical custody" means the physical care and supervision of a child;

(15) "State" means a state of the United States, the District of Columbia, Puerto Rico, the United States Virgin Islands, or any territory or possession subject to the jurisdiction of the United States.

Sec. 3. This act does not govern an adoption proceeding or a proceeding pertaining to the authorization of emergency medical care for a child.

Sec. 4. A child custody proceeding that pertains to an Indian child as defined in the Indian Child Welfare Act, 25 USC Section 1901 et seq., is not subject to this act to the extent that it is governed by the Indian Child Welfare Act.

Sec. 5. For purposes of this act, any child custody order of a foreign country shall be treated in the manner provided in section 36 of this act.

Sec. 6. A child custody determination made by a court of this state that had jurisdiction under this act binds all persons who have been served in accordance with the laws of this state or notified in accordance with section 8 of this act or who have submitted to the jurisdiction of the court, and who have been given an opportunity to be heard. As to those persons, the determination is conclusive as to all decided issues of law and fact except to the extent the determination is modified.

Sec. 7. If a question of the existence or exercise of jurisdiction under this act is raised in a child custody proceeding, the question, upon request of a party, must be given calendar priority and handled expeditiously.

Sec. 8.

   (a) Notice required for the exercise of jurisdiction over a person outside this state shall be given in a manner reasonably calculated to give actual notice, and may be: (1) By personal delivery outside this state in the manner prescribed for service of process within this state; (2) in the manner prescribed by the law of the place in which the service is made for service of process in that place in an action in any of its courts of general jurisdiction; (3) any form of mail addressed to the person to be served and requesting a receipt; or (4) as directed by the court including publication, if other means of notification are ineffective.

   (b) Except as otherwise provided by any provision of the general statutes, notice under this section shall be served, mailed or delivered or last published at least twelve days before any hearing in this state.

   (c) Proof of service outside this state may be made by affidavit of the individual who made the service, or in the manner prescribed by the law of this state, the order pursuant to which the service is made, or the law of the place in which the service is made. If service is made by mail, proof may be a receipt signed by the addressee or other evidence of delivery to the addressee.

   (d) Except as otherwise provided by any provision of the general statutes, notice is not required if a person submits to the jurisdiction of the court.

Sec. 9.

   (a) A court of this state may communicate with a court in another state concerning a proceeding arising under this act.

   (b) The court may allow the parties to participate in the communication. If the parties are not able to participate in the communication, they must be given the opportunity to present facts and legal arguments before a decision on jurisdiction is made.

   (c) Communication between courts on schedules, calendars, court records and similar matters may occur without informing the parties. A record need not be made of the communication.

   (d) Except as otherwise provided in subsection (c) of this section, a record must be made of a communication under this section. The parties must be informed promptly of the communication and granted access to the record.

   (e) For the purposes of this section, "record" means information that is inscribed on a tangible medium or that is stored in an electronic or other medium and is retrievable in perceivable form.

Sec. 10.

   (a) In addition to other procedures available to a party, a party to a child custody proceeding, guardian ad litem or legal representative of the child may offer testimony of witnesses who are located in another state, including testimony of the parties and the child, by deposition or other means allowable in this state for testimony taken in another state. The court on its own motion may order that the testimony of a person be taken in another state and may prescribe the manner in which and the terms upon which the testimony is taken.

(b) A court of this state may permit an individual residing in another state to be deposed or to testify by telephone, audiovisual means, or other electronic means before a designated court or at another location in that state. A court of this state shall cooperate with courts of other states in designating an appropriate location for the deposition or testimony.

(c) Documentary evidence transmitted from another state to a court of this state by technological means that do not produce an original writing may not be excluded from evidence on an objection based on the means of transmission.

Sec. 11.

(a) A court of this state may request the appropriate court of another state to: (1) Hold an evidentiary hearing; (2) order a person to produce or give evidence pursuant to procedures of that state; (3) order that an evaluation be made with respect to the custody of a child involved in a pending proceeding; (4) forward to the court of this state a certified copy of the transcript of the record of the hearing, the evidence otherwise presented, and any evaluation prepared in compliance with the request; and (5) order a party to a child custody proceeding or any person having physical custody of the child to appear in the proceeding with or without the child.

(b) Upon request of a court of another state, a court of this state may hold a hearing or enter an order described in subsection (a) of this section.

(c) Travel and other necessary and reasonable expenses incurred under subsections (a) and (b) of this section may be assessed against the parties.

(d) A court of this state shall preserve the pleadings, orders, decrees, records of hearings, evaluations and other pertinent records with respect to a child custody proceeding until the child attains eighteen years of age. Upon appropriate request by a court or law enforcement official of another state, the court shall forward a certified copy of those records.

Sec. 12.

(a) Except as otherwise provided in section 15 of this act, a court of this state has jurisdiction to make an initial child custody determination if:

(1) This state is the home state of the child on the date of the commencement of the child custody proceeding;

(2) This state was the home state of the child within six months of the commencement of the child custody proceeding, the child is absent from the state, and a parent or a person acting as a parent continues to reside in this state;

(3) A court of another state does not have jurisdiction under subdivisions (1) or (2) of this subsection, the child and at least one parent or person acting as a parent have a significant connection with this state other than mere physical presence,

and there is substantial evidence available in this state concerning the child's care, protection, training and personal relationships;

(4) A court of another state which is the home state of the child has declined to exercise jurisdiction on the ground that this state is the more appropriate forum under a provision substantially similar to section 18 or section 19 of this act, the child and at least one parent or person acting as a parent have a significant connection with this state other than mere physical presence, and there is substantial evidence available in this state concerning the child's care, protection, training and personal relationships;

(5) All courts having jurisdiction under subdivisions (1) to (4), inclusive, of this subsection have declined jurisdiction on the ground that a court of this state is the more appropriate forum to determine custody under a provision substantially similar to section 18 or section 19 of this act; or

(6) No court of any other state would have jurisdiction under subdivisions (1) to (5), inclusive, of this subsection.

(b) Subsection (a) of this section is the exclusive jurisdictional basis for making a child custody determination by a court of this state.

(c) Physical presence of, or personal jurisdiction over, a party or a child is not necessary or sufficient to make a child custody determination.

Sec. 13.

(a) Except as otherwise provided in section 15 of this act, a court of this state which has made a child custody determination pursuant to sections 12 to 14, inclusive, of this act, has exclusive, continuing jurisdiction over the determination until: (1) A court of this state or a court of another state determines that the child, the child's parents and any person acting as a parent do not presently reside in this state; or (2) a court of this state determines that (A) this state is not the home state of the child, (B) a parent or a person acting as a parent continues to reside in this state but the child no longer has a significant relationship with such parent or person, and (C) substantial evidence is no longer available in this state concerning the child's care, protection, training and personal relationships.

(b) A court of this state which has made a child custody determination but does not have exclusive, continuing jurisdiction under this section may modify that determination only if it has jurisdiction to make an initial determination under section 12 of this act.

Sec. 14.

(a) Except as otherwise provided in section 15 of this act, a court of this state may not modify a child custody determination made by a court of another state unless a court of this state has jurisdiction to make an initial determination under subdivisions (1) to (4), inclusive, of subsection (a) of section 12 of this act and one of the following occurs: (1) The court of the other state determines that it no longer has exclusive, continuing jurisdiction under a provision substantially similar to section 13 of this act; (2) a court of another state determines that a court of this state would be a more convenient forum under a provision substantially similar to section 18 of this act; or (3) a court of this state or another state determines that the child, the child's parents and any person acting as a parent do not presently reside in the other state.

(b) Notwithstanding the provisions of this act, a court of this state may modify a child custody determination made by a court of another state if: (1) The child resides in this state with a parent; (2) the child has been, or is under a threat of being, abused or mistreated by a person who resides in the state which would have jurisdiction under the provisions of this act; and (3) the court of this state determines that it is in the child's best interest to modify the child custody determination.

Sec. 15.

(a) A court of this state has temporary emergency jurisdiction if the child is present in this state and (1) the child has been abandoned, or (2) it is necessary in an emergency to protect the child because the child, a sibling or a parent has been, or is under a threat of being, abused or mistreated. As used in this subsection with respect to a child, "abused" shall have the same meaning as in section 46b-120 of the general statutes.

(b) If there is no previous child custody determination that is enforceable under this act and a child custody proceeding has not been commenced in a court of a state having jurisdiction under a provision substantially similar to section 12, 13 or 14 of this act, a child custody determination made under this section remains in effect until an order is obtained from a court of a state having jurisdiction under a provision substantially similar to section 12, 13 or 14 of this act. A child custody determination made under this section shall be a final determination if: (1) A child custody proceeding has not been or is not commenced in a court of a state having jurisdiction under a provision substantially similar to section 12, 13 or 14 of this act; (2) this state has become the home state of the child; and (3) the child custody determination provides that it is a final determination.

(c) If there is a previous child custody determination that is enforceable under this act or if a child custody proceeding has been commenced in a court of a state having jurisdiction under a provision substantially similar to section 12, 13 or 14 of this act, the court of this state which issues an order pursuant to this section shall specify that such order is effective for a period of time which the court deems adequate to allow the person seeking an order to obtain such order from the other state which has jurisdiction. Such order shall be effective for that period of time specified in the order or until an order is obtained from the other state whichever occurs first.

(d) If the court, in any proceeding commenced pursuant to this section, is informed that a child custody proceeding has been commenced, or that a child custody determination has been made, by a court of another state having jurisdiction pursuant to a provision substantially similar to section 12, 13 or 14 of this act, such court shall immediately communicate with the court of the other state and take appropriate action, including the making of temporary orders for a specified period of time, to resolve the emergency and to protect the safety of the child and the parties.

Sec. 16.

(a) Before a child custody determination is made under this act, notice and an opportunity to be heard in accordance with the standard established in section 8 of this act shall be given to the parties, any parent whose parental rights have not been previously terminated and any person who has physical custody of the child.

(b) This act does not govern the enforceability of a child custody determination made without notice or an opportunity to be heard.

(c) The obligation to join a party and the right to intervene as a party in a child custody proceeding under this act are governed by section 46b-57 of the general statutes.

Sec. 17.

(a) Except as otherwise provided in section 15 of this act, if at the time of the commencement of the proceeding in this state a proceeding concerning the custody of the child has been commenced in a court of another state having jurisdiction pursuant to a provision substantially similar to section 12, 13 or 14 of this act, a court of this state shall not exercise jurisdiction. A court of this state may exercise jurisdiction if the proceeding in the other state has been terminated or is stayed by the court of the other state because such court has determined pursuant to a provision substantially similar to section 18 of this act, that a court in this state is a more convenient forum.

(b) Except as otherwise provided in section 15 of this act, the court shall, after review of relevant information provided to it, determine whether a child custody proceeding has been commenced in another state. If such proceeding has been commenced, the court in this state shall take appropriate action to communicate with the other court and to resolve which court shall have jurisdiction. If the court of this state determines that the court of the other state has jurisdiction pursuant to a provision substantially similar to section 12, 13 or 14 of this act, the court of this state shall stay its proceeding while the court of the other state determines whether the court of this state is the more appropriate forum. If the court of the other state determines that the court of this state is not a more appropriate forum, the court of this state shall dismiss the proceeding.

(c) Except as otherwise provided in section 15 of this act, the court, in a proceeding to modify a child custody determination, shall after review of relevant information provided to it, determine whether a proceeding to enforce the determination has been commenced in another state. If the court determines that such enforcement proceeding has commenced, the court may (1) stay the proceeding for modification pending the entry of an order of the court of the other state enforcing, staying, denying or dismissing the proceeding for enforcement; (2) enjoin the parties from continuing with the proceeding for enforcement; or (3) proceed with the modification under conditions it considers appropriate.

(d) Except as otherwise provided in section 15 of this act, the court, in a proceeding to enforce a child custody determination, shall proceed, with regard to simultaneous proceedings, in accordance with the provisions of section 27 of this act.

Sec. 18.

(a) A court of this state which has jurisdiction under this act to make a child custody determination may decline to exercise its jurisdiction at any time if it determines that it is an inconvenient forum under the circumstances and that a court of another state is a more appropriate forum. The issue of inconvenient forum may be raised upon a motion of a party, the guardian ad litem for the child or the attorney for the child, the court's own motion or a request of another court.

(b) In determining whether a court of this state is an inconvenient forum and that it is more appropriate for a court of another state to exercise jurisdiction, the court shall allow the parties to submit information and shall consider all relevant factors including: (1) Whether family violence has occurred and is likely to continue in the future and which state could best protect the parties and the child; (2) the length of time the child has resided outside this state; (3) the distance between the court in this state and the court in the state that would assume jurisdiction; (4) the relative financial circumstances of the parties; (5) any agreement of the parties as to which state should assume jurisdiction; (6) the nature and location of the evidence required to resolve the pending litigation, including testimony of the child; (7) the ability of the court of each state to decide the issue expeditiously and the procedures necessary to present the evidence; and (8) the familiarity of the court of each state with the facts and issues in the pending litigation.

(c) If a court of this state determines that it is an inconvenient forum and that a court of another state is a more appropriate forum, it shall stay the proceedings upon condition that a child custody proceeding be promptly commenced in another designated state and may impose any other condition the court considers just and proper.

(d) A court of this state may decline to exercise its jurisdiction under this act if a child custody determination is incidental to an action for dissolution of marriage, divorce or another proceeding while still retaining jurisdiction over the dissolution of marriage, divorce or other proceeding.

Sec. 19.

(a) Except as otherwise provided in section 15 of this act, if a court of this state has jurisdiction under this act because a person seeking to invoke its jurisdiction has engaged in unjustifiable conduct, the court shall decline to exercise its jurisdiction unless:

(1) The parents and all persons acting as parents have acquiesced in the exercise of jurisdiction;

(2) A court of the state otherwise having jurisdiction under a provision substantially similar to section 12, 13 or 14 of this act determines that this state is a more appropriate forum under a statute similar to section 18 of this act; or

(3) No court of any other state would have jurisdiction under the criteria specified in sections 12 to 14, inclusive, of this act.

(b) If a court of this state declines to exercise its jurisdiction pursuant to subsection (a) of this section, it may fashion an appropriate remedy to ensure the safety of the child and prevent a repetition of the unjustifiable conduct, including staying the proceeding until a child custody proceeding is commenced in a court having jurisdiction under a provision substantially similar to section 12, 13 or 14 of this act.

(c) If a court dismisses a petition or stays a proceeding because it declines to exercise its jurisdiction pursuant to subsection (a) of this section, it shall assess against the party seeking to invoke its jurisdiction reasonable expenses including costs, communication expenses, attorneys' fees, investigative fees, expenses for witnesses, travel expenses and child care during the course of the proceedings, unless the party from whom fees are sought establishes that the assessment would be clearly inappropriate. The court may not assess fees, costs or expenses against the state unless authorized by law.

Sec. 20.

(a) In a child custody proceeding, each party, in its first pleading or in an attached affidavit, shall give information, if reasonably ascertainable and not confidential under state law, under oath as to the child's present address or location, the places where the child has lived during the past five years, and the names and present addresses of the persons with whom the child has lived during the past five years. The pleading or affidavit must state whether the party:

(1) Has participated, as a party or witness or in any other capacity, in any other proceeding concerning the custody of or visitation with the child and, if so, identify the court, the case number, and the date of the child custody determination;

(2) Knows of any civil or criminal proceeding that could affect the current proceeding, including proceedings for enforcement and proceedings relating to family violence, protective orders, termination of parental rights and adoptions, and if so, identify the court, the case number and the nature of the proceeding; and

(3) Knows the names and addresses of any person not a party to the proceeding who has physical custody of the child or claims rights of legal custody or physical custody of, or visitation with, the child and if so, the names and addresses of those persons.

(b) If the information required by subsection (a) of this section is not provided, the court upon motion of a party or on its own motion may stay the proceeding until such information is provided.

(c) If the party provides any of the information required in subdivisions (1) to (3) of subsection (a) of this section, such party shall also provide any additional information under oath as required by the court. The court may examine the parties under oath as to details of the information provided and other matters pertinent to the court's jurisdiction and the disposition of the case.

(d) Each party has a continuing duty to inform the court of any proceeding in this state or another state that could affect the current proceeding.

(e) If a party alleges in an affidavit or a pleading under oath that the health, safety or liberty of a party or child would be jeopardized by disclosure of identifying information, the information must be sealed and may not be disclosed to the other party or the public unless the court, after a hearing, determines that it is in the interest of justice that such disclosure be made.

Sec. 21.

(a) In a child custody proceeding in this state, the court may order a party to the proceeding who is in this state to appear before the court in person with or without the child. The court may order any person who is in this state and who has physical custody or control of the child to appear in person with the child.

(b) If the court orders the appearance of a party who is outside this state, the court may order that a notice is given in accordance with section 8 of this act and that such notice include a statement directing the party to appear in person with or without the child and informing the party that failure to appear may result in a decision adverse to such party.

(c) The court may enter any orders necessary to ensure the safety of the child or of any person ordered to appear pursuant to this section.

(d) The court may order a party to pay for reasonable and necessary travel and expenses of a party to the child custody proceeding or the child who is outside the state.

Sec. 22. As used in sections 22 to 34, inclusive, of this act, "petitioner" means a person who seeks enforcement of a child custody determination, and "respondent" means a person against whom a proceeding has been commenced for enforcement of a child custody determination.

Sec. 23. A court of this state may enforce an order by a federal court or another state court for the return of a child made pursuant to the Hague Convention on the Civil Aspects of International Child Abduction in accordance with section 38 of this act.

Sec. 24.

(a) A child custody determination issued by a court of another state may be registered in this state, with or without a simultaneous request for enforcement, by sending to the Superior Court in this state: (1) A letter or other document requesting registration; (2) two copies, including one certified copy, of the determination sought to be registered, and a statement under penalty of perjury that to the best of the knowledge and belief of the petitioner the order has not been modified; and (3) except as otherwise provided in section 20, the name and address of the petitioner and any parent or person acting as parent who has been awarded custody or visitation in the child custody determination sought to be registered.

(b) On receipt of the documents required by subsection (a) of this section, the registering court shall cause the determination to be filed as a foreign judgment, together with one copy of any accompanying documents and information, regardless of their form.

(c)　Within five days after the registering court's receipt of the documents required by subsection (a) of this section, the petitioner shall notify the persons named pursuant to subdivision (3) of subsection (a) of this section of the registration of the documents by certified mail, return receipt requested at their respective last-known addresses or by personal service, and provide them with an opportunity to contest the registration in accordance with this section. The notice required in this subsection shall state that: (1) A registered determination is enforceable as of the date of the registration in the same manner as a determination issued by a court of this state; (2) a hearing to contest the validity of the registered determination must be requested within twenty days after service of notice; and (3) failure to contest the registration will, upon proof of notice, result in confirmation of the child custody determination and preclude further contest of that determination with respect to any matter that could have been asserted.

(d)　The respondent must request a hearing within twenty days after service of the notice. At that hearing, the court shall confirm the registered order unless the respondent establishes that: (1) The issuing court did not have jurisdiction under a provision substantially similar to section 12, 13 or 14 of this act; (2) the child custody determination sought to be registered has been vacated, stayed or modified by a court having jurisdiction to do so pursuant to a statute substantially similar to sections 12 to 14, inclusive, of this act; or (3) the respondent was entitled to notice of the proceedings before the court that issued the order for which registration is sought, but such notice was not given in a manner reasonably calculated to give actual notice.

(e)　If a timely request for a hearing to contest the validity of the registration is not made, the registration is confirmed as a matter of law with respect to those who have received proper notice and all persons served must be notified of the confirmation by the petitioner.

(f)　Confirmation of a registered order, whether by operation of law or after notice and hearing, precludes further contest of the order with respect to any matter that could have been asserted at the time of registration.

Sec. 25. A court of this state shall recognize and enforce, but not modify except in accordance with section 14 of this act, a child custody determination of a court of another state if (1) the court of the other state exercised jurisdiction under a provision substantially similar to section 12, 13 or 14 of this act, the determination was made under factual circumstances meeting the jurisdictional standards of the act and the determination has not been modified in accordance with this act, or (2) the child custody determination was registered in this state pursuant to section 24 of this act. A child custody determination which satisfies the criteria in subdivision (1) or (2) of this section shall have the same effect and shall be enforced in the same manner as a child custody determination rendered by the Superior Court.

Sec. 26.

    (a) A court of this state which does not have jurisdiction to modify a child custody determination may issue a temporary order enforcing (1) the visitation schedule made by the court of another state, or (2) the visitation provisions of a child custody determination of another state which does not provide for a specific visitation schedule.

    (b) If a court of this state makes an order pursuant to subdivision (2) of subsection (a) of this section, it shall specify in the order a period that it considers adequate to allow the petitioner to obtain an order from a court having jurisdiction under a provision substantially similar to section 12, 13 or 14 of this act. The order remains in effect until an order is obtained from the other court or the period expires, whichever comes first.

Sec. 27. If a proceeding for enforcement under this act is commenced in a court of this state and the court determines that a proceeding to modify the determination is pending in a court of another state having jurisdiction to modify the determination under a provision substantially similar to section 12, 13 or 14 of this act, the enforcing court shall immediately communicate with the modifying court. The court of this state shall proceed with the action for enforcement of the child custody determination unless the court, after consultation with the modifying court, stays or dismisses the proceeding.

Sec. 28.

    (a) A petitioner seeking to enforce a child custody determination must verify the petition and attach copies of certified copies of all orders or notice sought to be enforced and of any order confirming registration if such child custody determination has been registered.

    (b) A petition for enforcement of a child custody determination shall state: (1) Whether the court that issued the determination identified the jurisdictional basis it relied upon in exercising jurisdiction and, if so, what the basis was; (2) whether the determination for which enforcement is sought has been vacated, stayed or modified by a court whose decision must be enforced under this act and, if so, identify the court, the case number and the nature of the proceeding; (3) whether any proceeding has been commenced that could affect the current proceeding, including proceedings relating to family violence, protective orders, termination of parental rights and adoptions and, if so, identify the court, the case number, and the nature of the proceeding; (4) the present physical address of the child and the respondent, if known; (5) whether relief in addition to the immediate physical custody of the child and attorneys' fees are sought, including a request for assistance from law enforcement officials, and, if so, the relief sought; and (6) if the child custody determination has been registered and confirmed under section 24 of this act, the date and place of registration.

    (c) Upon the filing of a petition, the court shall issue an order directing the respondent to appear in person with or without the child at a hearing, the time and place of which shall be specified, and may enter any order necessary to ensure the safety of the parties and the child. The order shall advise the respondent that at the hearing, the court will order that the petitioner take immediate physical custody of the child and the payment of fees, costs and expenses under section 32, and any other relief that the court may deem appropriate, unless the respondent appears and establishes that: (1) The child custody determination has not been registered and confirmed pursuant to section 24 of this act and (A) the court issuing the order for which enforcement is sought did not have jurisdiction under section 12, 13 or 14 of this act or a provision substantially similar to said sections; (B) the child custody determination for which enforcement is sought has been vacated, stayed or modified by a court having jurisdiction to do so under sections 12 to 21, inclusive, of this act; or (C) the respondent was entitled to notice, but notice of the proceedings before the court that issued the order for which enforcement is sought was not given in accordance with section 8 of this act or in a manner reasonably calculated to provide actual notice; or (2) the child custody determination for which enforcement is sought was registered and confirmed pursuant to section 24 of this act, but has been vacated, stayed or modified by a court of a state having jurisdiction to do so under section 12, 13 or 14 of this act or a provision substantially similar to said sections. The hearing must be held on the next business day after service of the order unless otherwise ordered for good cause shown. The court may extend the date of the hearing at the request of the petitioner.

Sec. 29. Except as otherwise provided in section 31 of this act, the petition and order shall be served upon the respondent and any person who has physical custody of the child by personal service.

Sec. 30.

(a) Unless the court issues a temporary emergency order pursuant to section 15 of this act, the court shall enforce the child custody determination and if appropriate, order the petitioner to take immediate physical custody of the child unless the respondent establishes that: (1) The child custody determination has not been registered and confirmed pursuant to section 24 of this act and (A) the court issuing the order for which enforcement is sought did not have jurisdiction under section 12, 13 or 14 of this act or a provision substantially similar to said sections; (B) the child custody determination for which enforcement is sought has been vacated, stayed or modified by a court having jurisdiction to do so under section 12, 13 or 14 of this act or a provision substantially similar to said sections; or (C) the respondent was entitled to notice, but notice of the proceedings before the court that issued the order for which enforcement is sought was not given in accordance with section 8 of this act or in a manner reasonably calculated to give actual notice; or (2) the child custody determination for which enforcement is sought was registered and confirmed pursuant to section 24 of this act, but has been vacated, stayed or modified by a court of a state having jurisdiction to do so under section 12, 13 or 14 of this act.

(b) The court shall award the fees, costs and expenses as provided in section 32 of this act and may grant additional relief, including a request for the assistance of law enforcement officials.

(c) If a party called to testify refuses to answer on the ground that the testimony may be self-incriminating, the court may draw an adverse inference from the refusal.

(d) A privilege against disclosure of communications between spouses and a defense of immunity based on the relationship of husband and wife or parent and child may not be invoked in a proceeding under sections 22 to 34, inclusive, of this act.

Sec. 31.

(a) Upon the filing of a petition seeking enforcement of a child custody determination, the petitioner may file a verified application for the issuance of an order to take physical custody of the child if the child will suffer imminent, serious physical harm or will be removed from the state. The application for the order shall include the statements required by subsection (b) of section 28 of this act. If the court, after reviewing the petition, testimony of the petitioner or other witnesses and other facts before it, finds there is a substantial likelihood that the child will suffer imminent serious physical harm or be removed from this state, it may issue an order to an appropriate law enforcement official to take physical custody of the child and place the child in the care of an appropriate person pending a hearing pursuant to subsection (b) of this section. In making the decision on placement of the child, the court may impose conditions to ensure the appearance of the child and the person with whom the child is placed at the hearing. Such order shall include the court's findings and the facts upon which the court made its findings. The petition and the order shall be served upon the respondent at the time the child is taken into physical custody or immediately thereafter.

(b) The court shall hold a hearing on the petition on the next business day after the order and the petition is served unless there are compelling circumstances.

Sec. 32. The court shall award the prevailing party, necessary and reasonable expenses incurred by or on behalf of the party, including costs, communication expenses, attorneys' fees, investigative fees, expenses for witnesses, travel expenses, and child care during the course of the proceedings, unless the party from whom fees or expenses are sought establishes that the award would be clearly inappropriate.

Sec. 33. A court of this state shall accord full faith and credit to an enforcement order issued by another state in accordance with statutes substantially similar to this act which enforces a child custody determination by a court of another state unless the order has been vacated, stayed or modified by a court having jurisdiction to do so under sections 12 to 21, inclusive, of this act.

Sec. 34. An order enforcing a child custody determination may not be stayed pending appeal unless the court enters a temporary emergency order under section 15 of this act.

Sec. 35. Subsection (a) of section 46b-124 of the general statutes is repealed and the following is substituted in lieu thereof:

(a) All records of cases of juvenile matters, as defined in section 46b-121, except delinquency proceedings, or any part thereof, and all records of appeals from probate brought to the superior court for juvenile matters pursuant to subsection (b) of section 45a-186, including studies and reports by probation officers, social agencies and clinics, shall be confidential and for the use of the court in juvenile matters, and open to inspection or disclosure to any third party, including bona fide researchers commissioned by a state agency, only upon order of the Superior Court, except that (1) the records concerning any matter transferred from a court of probate pursuant to section 45a-623 or subsection (g) of section 45a-715 or any appeal from probate to the superior court for juvenile matters pursuant to subsection (b) of section 45a-186 shall be available to the court of probate from which such matter was transferred or from which such appeal was taken, (2) such records shall be available to (A) the attorney representing the child or youth including the Division of Public Defender Services in any proceeding in which such records are relevant, (B) the parents or guardian of the child or youth until such time as the child or youth reaches the age of majority or becomes emancipated, (C) an adult adopted person in accordance with the provisions of sections 45a-736, 45a-737 and 45a-743 to 45a-757, inclusive, (D) employees of the Division of Criminal Justice who in the performance of their duties require access to such records, (E) employees of the judicial branch who in the performance of their duties require access to such records, (F) another court under the provisions of [section 46b-111] subsection (d) of section 11 of this act, (G) the subject of the record, upon submission of satisfactory proof of the subject's identity, pursuant to guidelines prescribed by the Office of the Chief Court Administrator and provided the subject has reached the age of majority or has been emancipated, and (H) the Department of Children and Families. Any record or any part thereof forwarded by said court or any of its employees to any persons, governmental and private agencies, and institutions, shall not be disclosed, directly or indirectly, to any third party not specified in subsection (c) of this section save upon order of said court or except in the report required under section 54-76d or 54-91a.

Sec. 36. As used in sections 37 and 38 of this act: "Foreign child custody determination" means any judgment, decree or other order of a court or tribunal of competent jurisdiction of a foreign state providing for legal custody, physical custody or visitation with respect to a child. The term includes a permanent, temporary, initial and modification order. The term does not include an order relating to child support or other monetary obligation of an individual.

Sec. 37. A court of this state shall treat a foreign child custody determination made under factual circumstances in substantial conformity with the jurisdictional standards of this act, including reasonable notice and opportunity to be heard to all affected persons, as a child custody determination of another state under sections 1 to 21, inclusive, of this act, unless such determination was rendered under child custody law which violates fundamental principles of human rights or unless such determination is repugnant to the public policy of this state.

Sec. 38. A court of this state shall enforce a foreign child custody determination or an order of a federal court or another state court for return of a child under The Hague Convention on the Civil Aspects of International Child Abduction made under factual circumstances in substantial conformity with the jurisdictional standards of this act, including reasonable notice and opportunity to be heard to all affected persons, as a child custody determination of another state under sections 22 to 34, inclusive, of this act, unless such determination was rendered under child custody law which violates fundamental principles of human rights or unless such determination is repugnant to the public policy of this state.

Sec. 39. Sections 46b-90 to 46b-114, inclusive, of the general statutes are repealed.

Sec. 40. This act shall take effect July 1, 2000.

APPENDIX H

Guides for Distance Learning and Legal Research

Distance Learning

Distance learning presents you with wonderful opportunities for learning, growing, and expanding your personal and professional horizons. At the same time, it provides you with a number of unique challenges. The whole world is your classroom, yet you don't have the physical presence of classmates. The flexibility and excitement of this kind of learning can build your confidence while it develops your mind. However, it may sometimes seem overwhelming or lonely. We have included this appendix to help make your distance learning experience rewarding, invigorating, and successful.

Do's and Don'ts

- **DO** stay motivated. Write down your goals. Join Internet legal networks. Access online universities and associations. Keep a journal of your obstacles and successes. Reward yourself for work well done.

- **DO** become proficient in using the Internet. Really learn to navigate the World Wide Web. This technology provides abundant useful and free resources for your research. Learn how to use the search engines (particularly Google, Yahoo, Infos-eek, Snap, and Lycos). Utilize newsgroups; participate in forums.

- **DO** learn "netiquette"; for example, writing in all capital letters is considered yelling. A number of websites will teach these skills (look up "netiquette" in Google for a list of places). Remember that when you write your reader does not have the luxury of seeing your body language or hearing the tone of your voice.

- **DON'T** isolate yourself. Consider joining a local paralegal association, attending trials, and contacting your local courthouse for copies of forms.

- **DON'T** be afraid of new ideas—even radical new ideas.
- **DO** expect to feel overwhelmed or discouraged *sometimes.*
- **DON'T** give in to negative self-talk or challenging material. You can do it!
- **DO** make suggestions to your school. **DO** ask them for help when you need to.
- **DO** ask for support from your family and friends.
- **DO** be flexible, open-minded, and willing to learn new ideas and "roll with the punches."
- **DO** have fun, be creative, and study well.

Distance Learning Support, Mentoring, and Study Aid Sites

Distance Learning Support and Mentoring

http://maxpages.com/edsupport
Provides help in the areas of studying, note-taking, reading, and comprehending challenging material: as well as test-taking, outlining, grammar, and writing skills. Includes advice on time management and balancing priorities. Offers virtual one-on-one tutoring and mentoring support for distance learners and nontraditional students. Check this one out!

Brain Dancing for Students

http://braindance.com/
Provides tips on how to enhance memory, improve reading, manage information, enhance mental clarity, and optimize web browsing. Great site!

Eggleston's Distance Education Resources

http://www.the-eggman.com
Provides extensive information about and links to distance learning support services, consultants, newsgroups, government resources, and more.

Study Guide for Distance Education

http://www.gwu.edu/~etl/deguide
Provides general information about distance education. Topics include "Fundamentals of Distance Education" and "The Distance Education Student."

Distance Learning on the Net

http://www.hoyle.com/distance
Provides descriptions of and links to distance education sites. Very user-friendly. Excellent guide.

Distance Education Clearinghouse

http://www.uwex.edu/disted/
Provides articles, bibliography, resources, and general information about distance education.

Legal Research

HOT LEGAL WEBSITES

Take advantage of any links these sites provide. Cross-reference. Use keywords in general search engines (Google, Yahoo, etc.) to find more! If you don't know where to find a particular search engine, use the default engine in your computer and type in the name of the search engine you're looking for. If your search does not reveal the site you are looking for, try typing the address without the *www* prefix or try adding the suffix *html* or *htm*.

LEGAL RESEARCH SITES

Nolo Press Self-Help Law Center

http://www.nolo.com
Discusses *how* to do legal research. A must see!

LawCrawler

http://www.lawcrawler.com
Use keywords to find documents for your subject. Provides links directly to sites.

Findlaw

http://www.findlaw.com
Allows user to search specific areas and continually narrow down and focus research.

Lawsource, Inc.

http://www.lawsource.com
Lets you research by jurisdiction. Includes Canada and Mexico.

Law Journal Extra!

http://www.ljx.com
Contains electronic versions of print periodicals, employment information, and law firm listings.

Law Guru

http://www.lawguru.com
Provides links to specific areas of legal research.

FastSearch

http://www.fastsearch.com
Includes four search engines—be sure to click on "the law engine."

UNIVERSITIES AND LAW SCHOOLS

Chicago—Kent College of Law: **http://www.kentlaw.edu**
Cornell Law School: **http://www.law.cornell.edu/**
Emory Law Library: **http://www.law.emory.edu/library/**

COURTS, COURT INFORMATION, AND GOVERNMENT AGENCIES

Court Decisions on the Web

http://www.stanford.edu/library/
Allows user to choose jurisdiction and find decisions. Provides state, national, and international data.

The Courthouse

http://www.ljextra.com
Provides access to circuit court database (Supreme, federal, and state).

Internal Revenue Service Home Page

http://www.irs.gov
Home of the IRS. Can access general tax information and specific treasury regulations.

Legal and Government Forms

Findlaw's forms collections and indexes: **http://www.findlaw.com**
The 'Lectric Library's forms room: **http://www.lectlaw.com**

PROFESSIONAL ASSOCIATIONS

American Bar Association: **http://www.abanet.org**
Association of Legal Administrators: **http://www.alanet.org**
National Association of Legal Assistants: **http://www.nala.org**
National Federation of Paralegal Associations: **http://www.paralegals.org**

LEGAL EMPLOYMENT

Law Journal Extra! Law Employment Center

http://www.lawjobs.com
Draws from ads in various law journals. Regional focus (New York, New Jersey, Connecticut, Massachusetts).

The Legal Employment Search Site

http://www.legalemploy.com
Connected to employment section of Yahoo.

RESEARCHING FAMILY LAW ONLINE

ABA Center on Children and the Law: **http://www.abanet.org/child/home.html**
ABA Commission on Domestic Violence: **http://www.abanet.org/domviol/home.html**

ABA Family Law Section: **http://www.abanet.org/family/home.html**

ABA Tables Summarizing the Law in the Fifty States (Family Law): **http://www.abanet.org/family/familylaw/tables.html**

Megalaw.com Adoption: **http://www.megalaw.com/top/adoption.php**

Association for Children for Enforcement of Support: **http://www.childsupport-aces.org/**

Child Custody and Divorce Resources State by State: **http://custodysource.com/state.htm**

Children's Rights: **http://www.megalaw.com/top/children.php**

Internet Law Library—Domestic Relations: General: **http://www.lectlaw.com/inll/97.htm**
Links to family law, state by state, as well as federal laws impacting children.

Coalition for the Restoration of Parents Rights: **http://www.parentsrights.com/**

Legal Database: **http://www.legal-database.com/**

Legal Information Institute (Cornell University Law School): **http://www.seniorlaw.com/** Senior Law Homepage

Divorcenet.com: **http://www.divorcenet.com/index_html**

National Congress for Fathers & Children: **http://www.ncfc.net/index.html**

Court-Appointed Special Advocates for Children: **http://www.casanet.org/**

National Senior Citizens Law Center: **http://www.nsclc.org/**

Alliance for Non-Custodial Parents Rights: **http://www.ancpr.org/**

Findlaw: Family Law: **http://www.findlaw.com/01topics/15family/stateagencies.html**

Project for the Improvement of Child Support Litigation Technology: **http://www.findlaw.com/01topics/15family/ stateagencies.html**

State-by-State Family Law Forms and Guidelines: **http://www.findlaw.com/01topics/15family/statefam.html**

Legal Information Institute (Cornell University Law School): **http://www.law.cornell.edu/topics/Table_Marriage.htm**
Includes state marriage laws.

Child Support Guidelines: **http://www.supportguidelines.com/main.html**

Unmarried Couples and the Law: **http://www.palimony.com/**

MegaLaw Family Law Center: **http://www.megalaw.com/top/family.php**

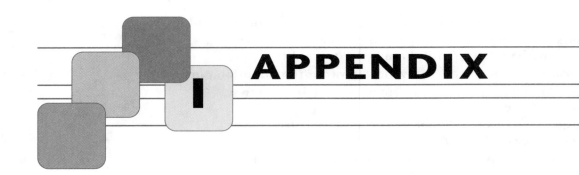

APPENDIX

I

Answers to Crossword Puzzles

Chapter 1

Chapter 2

Chapter 3

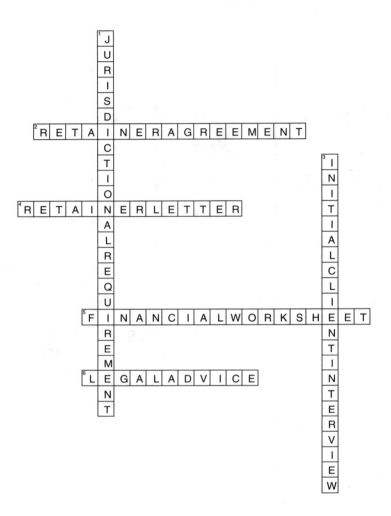

1. JURISDICTIONALREQUIREMENT

2. RETAINERAGREEMENT

3. INITIALCLIENTINTERVIEW

4. RETAINERLETTER

5. FINANCIALWORKSHEET

6. LEGALADVICE

Chapter 4

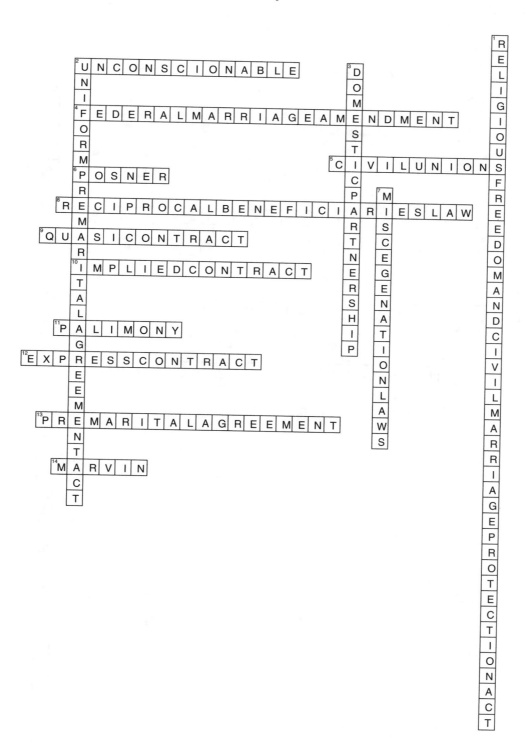

Chapter 5

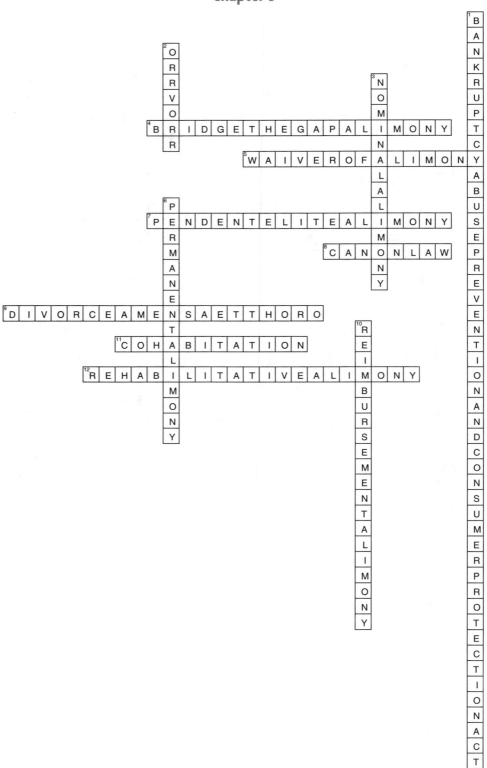

Chapter 6

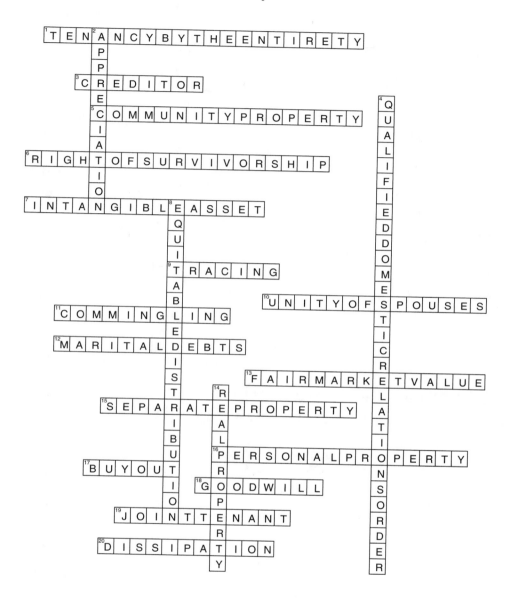

Chapter 7

Across

3. INVITROFERTILIZATION
6. ARTIFICIALINSEMINATION
8. SURROGATEMOTHER
9. LEGALCUSTODY
10. PARENTALALIENATIONSYNDROME
12. PARENTALALIENATION
13. UCCJEA
14. SAID
15. TROXELVGRANVILLE
16. VIRTUALVISITATION

Down

1. HOMESTATE
2. CAPA
4. MANDATORYPARENTINGEDUCATIONPROGRAMS
5. PARENSPARRIAE
7. CUSTODYEVALUATIONS
10. PHYSICALCUSTODY
11. PARENTINGPLAN

Chapter 8

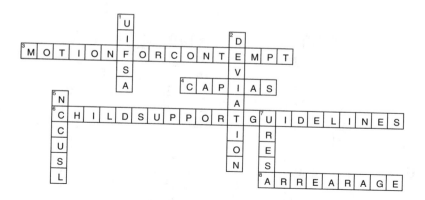

Chapter 9

Chapter 10

Chapter 11

Chapter 12

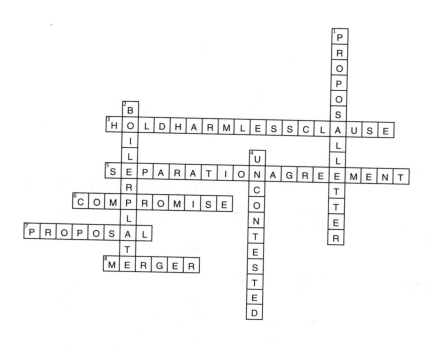

Chapter 13

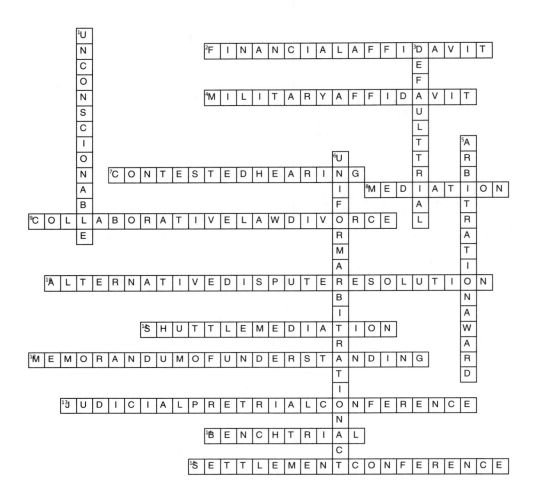

Chapter 14

Chapter 15

Across

2. TERMINATION OF PARENTAL RIGHTS
3. MANDATORY REPORTERS
5. SECOND PARENT ADOPTION
7. STEPPARENT ADOPTION
8. ADOPTION
9. ABANDONMENT
10. OPEN ADOPTION

Down

1. CHILD PROTECTION AGENCY
4. OPEN ADOPTION AGREEMENT
6. ARMSTRONG V MANZ

GLOSSARY

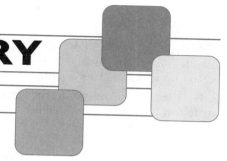

abandonment   failure to have contact with a child or have provided the child with support for one continuous year

abode   residence

abode service   service on a defendant by leaving a copy of the pleadings at his or her home

abuse   physically harmful treatment

administrative enforcement   action by a state or federal agency, rather than a court

Administrative Procedure Act   a federal statute that allows a person appearing before a federal administrative agency to be represented by an attorney or, if the agency permits, "by other qualified individual"

adoption   a legal procedure that makes a person or persons the legal parent or parents of a minor child who is not their natural child

adultery   voluntary sexual intercourse of a married person with a person other than the offender's spouse; one of the legal grounds to establish fault in a divorce proceeding

affidavit   a signed, sworn statement

affidavit of publication   a signed, sworn statement that a legal notice was printed

affinity   related by marriage

alienation of affection   where a husband or wife contends that a third party has become romantically or sexually involved with his or her spouse and interfered with or broken up the marriage

alimony   a sum of money, or other property, paid by a former spouse to the other former spouse for financial support, pursuant to a court order, temporary or final, in a divorce proceeding; also known as spousal maintenance or spousal support

alimony in gross   a support payment made in one single payment; also known as lump sum alimony

allowable deductions   taxes, debts, and allowable expenses that must be deducted from a spouse's gross income to determine net income

annulment   a judicial decision that a valid marriage does not exist or never existed between a person and another party

answer   a document in which each of the allegations contained in the numbered paragraphs of a complaint is responded to

antenuptial agreement   a contract entered into by the prospective spouses regarding their rights during the marriage and in the event of a divorce; also known as a premarital or prenuptial agreement

appearance   a document stating that a person has come into a court action as a party or an attorney representing a party

application for a prejudgment remedy   where a party asks the court to take some action before a judgment in the case is rendered

Armstrong v. Manzo   U.S. Supreme Court case decided in 1965 where the Court held that lack of notice to the noncustodial father violated his rights to due process

arrearage   amounts due by court order but unpaid; also known as back alimony

attorney-client privilege   the ethical rule stating that attorneys cannot disclose information related to the representation of a client, with certain exceptions

attorney's fees   the amount charged by a lawyer to a client for undertaking his or her case

authorized practice of law   general criteria for obtaining a license to practice law required by state statute

Bankruptcy Abuse Prevention and Consumer Protection Act   new federal bankruptcy law passed on April 20, 2005 (with most provisions effective October 17, 2005) legislating significant changes impacting divorce litigation

bench trial   a trial conducted before a judge, not a jury

beneficiary   the person for whom a trustee holds legal title to property

best interest of the child   standard that opened the contest for custody not only to fathers but also to other potential caregivers when the child's well-being or interests could be best served by such a custody determination

bigamy   being married to two people at the same time

billable hours   the amount of time expended on a particular case, which can later be billed to that client

body   the part of a complaint that contains the necessary factual information that establishes the jurisdiction of the court and identifies the grounds on which the divorce is being sought

boilerplate   standardized agreement forms or clauses

breach of promise to marry   where a man promises to marry a woman to gain favor and then fails to do so

bridge-the-gap alimony   short-term, lump sum alimony awarded to a spouse for the purpose of transitioning from married to single status

Bureau of Vital Statistics form   a form that is filled out and sent to the state in order to keep track of certain information regarding divorcing couples

buyout   where the pension of one spouse is valuated and the employee spouse gives cash to the nonemployee spouse in exchange for any interest the nonemployee spouse may have in the employee spouse's pension

canon law   the church's body of law or rules that determine man's moral obligations to man, to woman, and to God

capias   a document empowering a sheriff to arrest a nonappearing, noncustodial parent and bring him or her to jail and to court

caption   the initial section of a complaint that contains the names of the parties, the name and division of the court, the docket number or the return date of the action, and the date the complaint was drawn up

certification   page accompanying a court document stating that a copy of the document was sent on a specific date to all counsel of record and *pro se* appearing parties (if any)

child protection agency   a state agency charged with intervening when abuse or neglect is known or suspected

Child Support Enforcement Amendments   federal laws passed to enable mothers to collect child support and ease the social welfare burden on the taxpayers

child support guidelines   statutorily enacted formulas for determining the amount the noncustodial parent must pay for the support of each child

church courts   courts that had the jurisdiction to hear some matters that could also be heard in the general state courts; however, they had exclusive jurisdiction over all family-related legal matters; also known as ecclesiastical courts

civil code   the system of Spanish and French concepts of marital property law existing on the European mainland; also known as the *code civile*

civil unions   a separate category of legal recognition that grants same sex-couples marriage rights available to heterosexual couples, in the states of Vermont and Connecticut; civil unions are a way for same-sex couples to formalize their relationship and take advantage of the same state rights afforded to heterosexual couples

claim for relief   a statement filed by a party indicating what he or she wants in terms of a disposition in the case

clear and convincing evidence   a high evidentiary standard of proof that requires a higher degree of certainty than the preponderance of evidence standard required for a judicial finding of neglect and lower than the beyond a reasonable doubt standard required in criminal matters

COBRA   see *Consolidated Omnibus Budget Reconciliation Act*

code   a set of written rules that establishes the guid lines for attorneys in their interactions with clients, courts, staff, and their obligations to the general public

cohabitation   unmarried parties living together as if married

cohabitation agreement   contracts entered into by unmarried persons who live together or plan to live together

combined net income   the figure arrived at when each parent's net income is added together to determine child support; also known as total net income

common law marriage   a marriage created without a license or ceremony

community property   a system of property division that assumes that both husband and wife contributed to the accumulation of marital assets

competency   the duty to exercise a reasonable degree of care and skill commonly used by other attorneys engaged in a similar area of practice

complaint   a grievance filed with a disciplinary body against an attorney; also, a document that commences an action when the opposing party is served; also known as a petition

compromise   meeting someone halfway or giving up a position in exchange for something else

concurrent ownership   when property is held by two or more persons together; also known as joint ownership

confidential   information that is privileged; that is, not everyone is allowed access to it

confidentiality the ethical rule that protects communications between attorneys and their clients

confidentiality agreement an arrangement between an attorney and a client that certain information the client may divulge will be kept secret

conflict of interest any activity that may divide the attorney's loyalty and compromise his or her independent judgment

consanguinity related by blood

Consolidated Omnibus Budget Reconciliation Act 26 USC sec. 4980B(f) (COBRA) a federal law that enables a nonemployee spouse to continue his or her health insurance coverage provided by his or her spouse's employer for a period of three years after a divorce, as long as the nonemployee spouse pays the premium

constructive trust trust imposed by the court to avoid unjust enrichment when there is no intent between the parties

contempt where one party in an action does not comply with the court's order

contempt proceeding a civil proceeding that a party may commence to force the payor spouse to comply with the court's order when the party entitled to alimony is not paid

contested a disputed divorce trial

contingent fees an arrangement that entitles attorneys to a percentage of the financial outcome of the case, be it a judgment or settlement

cooling-off period the statutorily mandated time period following the initiation of divorce proceedings during which no final decree may be entered

cost of living clause provides for increases in the alimony payments due to the increase of payor's income and an increase in the cost of living, which obviates the need for the parties to go back to court for modifications; also known as an escalation clause

costs of litigation include filing fees, sheriff's fees, deposition costs, expert witness fees, and excessive photocopying and mailing costs

counterclaim an allegation presented by the defendant against the plaintiff

court calendar a small printed booklet or a set of pages that contains a number of cases listed according to parties and docket number and indicates the order in which cases will be heard

court-entry fee an amount of money required to file a complaint in court; also known as a filing fee

covenant marriage an alternative type of marriage that can be summarized as requiring premarital counseling, a return to fault-based grounds in order to dissolve the marriage, counseling before going through divorce, the signing of a covenant contract, and longer mandatory waiting periods

creditor a party to whom a sum of money is owed; also known as an obligee

cross-claim where the defendant-spouse assumes the role of a plaintiff by bringing a cross-action or countersuit for dissolution in which the party makes allegations and asks the court to grant him or her the relief of a dissolution or divorce and orders regarding custody, child support, alimony, and property division; also known as a cross-complaint

cross-complaint see *cross-claim*

cross-examination when the opposing party's lawyer has the opportunity to question the opposing party

custodial parent the parent with whom the child primarily resides

custody affidavit an affidavit indicating that there is no other proceeding pending in another court that affects the custody of the minor children

debt a sum of money owed to another party

debtor the party responsible for the money that is owed; also known as an obligor

deep pocket the term applied to characterize the defendant in a lawsuit who has the financial resources to absorb a civil suit for monetary damages

default judgment where one party "wins" the dissolution or divorce suit by failure of the other party to act

default trial where one of the parties to an action has failed to appear at the scheduled trial date even though he or she has received proper notice of the proceedings; the court proceeds with a hearing and severs the marriage

defendant the party against whom an action is brought

Defense of Marriage Act (DOMA) a federal law passed in response to attempts on the part of gay-rights activists to require states to recognize same-sex marriages; DOMA defines marriage for federal purposes

deny in a court proceeding, where the judge refuses to grant the motion of one of the parties

deponent the person who is being questioned at a deposition

deposition a procedure in which one party's attorney orally questions an opposing party or a nonparty witness who has sworn under oath to answer all questions truthfully and accurately to the best of his or her knowledge and ability

desertion where one spouse abandons his or her duties toward the other; one of the legal grounds to establish fault in a divorce proceeding

deviation from the guideline when the parties agree between themselves that one or the other will pay more or less of the statutorily determined amount

direct examination the initial questioning by the party's own attorney

disciplinary board bodies that may sanction or punish attorneys for engaging in conduct that violates the state's code of professional conduct

disclosure the process of the parties revealing the full extent and current values of all their assets

discovery the process or stage in a civil litigation matter during which information is gathered by each party for use in their case against the other party

discovery tools ways in which attorneys may gather information for use in their case against another party

discrete tasks representation or **unbundled legal services** clients purchase legal services on a task-by-task basis. The client and attorney agree by contract as to what services the lawyer will provide in exchange for a fee

discretion of the court where the court has the power to make the alimony decision and an appellate court will not reverse that decision unless the judge somehow abused his or her discretion

dissipation depletion of the marital assets by waste

dissolution of marriage is the phrase many jurisdictions use to formally define the word "divorce"

divorce the complete severance of the marital relationship, allowing the parties to go their separate ways, including the right to remarry; also known as divorce *a vinculo matrimonii*

divorce *a mensa et thoro* divorce from bed and board, which did not sever the marriage, but just enabled the spouses to live separate and apart; also known as divorce

divorce *a vinculo matrimonii* the complete severance of the marital relationship, allowing the parties to go their separate ways, including the right to remarry

divorce trial a trial in which both parties present their case to the court for its final hearing

docket control system a system of one or more calendars that helps an attorney keep track of the various court dates and deadlines

documents the papers associated with a case

domestic partnership is a committed relationship between two persons of the same gender, who reside together and support each other, in a mutually exclusive partnership

domestic partnership laws grant same-sex couples a way to formalize their relationship and gain certain rights and privileges under state law

domestic support obligations the phrase created by Congress under the Bankruptcy Abuse Prevention and Consumer Act that replaced the terms *alimony*, *child support*, and *property settlements* in the Bankruptcy Code

domicile residing in a state with the intent to permanently remain

duplicative referring to discovery, something that has already been asked for

earned retainer amount from the retainer which the attorney may keep in proportion to the amount of work expended on the client's file

ecclesiastical courts courts that had the jurisdiction to hear some matters that could also be heard in the general state courts; however, they had exclusive jurisdiction over all family-related legal matters; also known as church courts

emancipation acquiring adult status; a youth may be emancipated by operation of law, that is, on his or her birthday by reaching the age of majority or by court order at a younger age

Employee Retirement Income Security Act (ERISA) a federal statute passed in 1974 to protect employees and their pensions in case the employer declared bankruptcy or went out of business

equitable distribution a system allowing family courts to distribute property acquired during marriage on the basis of fairness, as opposed to ownership

equity the fair market value of the property minus any encumbrances

ERISA see *Employee Retirement Income Security Act*

escalation clause provides for increases in alimony payments due to the increase of payor's income and an increase in the cost of living, obviating the need for the parties to go back to court for modifications; also known as a cost of living clause

ethical wall when a paralegal cannot discuss a case with anyone in the office or have access to the file because of the possibility of conflict of interest

ex parte a Latin term meaning "by one party" or "for one party"

ex parte **proceeding** a court hearing conducted in response to one party's *ex parte* motion or petition. The opposing party is not present during an *ex parte* proceeding because such proceedings are generally filed in an emergency situation

expert witness a person with specialized knowledge who is called to testify in court

express contract an agreement between the parties regarding the specific terms

expressed trusts a trust in which the terms have been negotiated by the parties

fair market value the price a buyer is willing to pay a seller in exchange for a property

family relations unit trained social workers who work for the court and conduct studies and apply child development and child psychology concepts to make custody and visitation recommendations; also known as the family services division

family services division see *family relations unit*

family support payments the term given to regular, periodic payments a payor spouse makes to the other spouse for the financial maintenance of both the ex-spouse and children

Federal Marriage Amendment a proposed amendment to the U.S. Constitution that would ban same-sex marriage; attempts to pass the amendment in 2005 were unsuccessful

fees the amount the attorney will charge the client, based on the skill and experience of the attorney, the simplicity or complexity of the client's matter, cost of similar service in the community, the result obtained, the reputation of the attorney, and whether the matter is contested or uncontested

filing fee an amount of money required to file a complaint in court; also known as a court entry fee

final argument where each attorney argues why the court should rule in his or her client's favor

financial affidavits a sworn statement that enumerates the party's sources of income, earned and unearned, the party's expenses, necessary and optional, and all of the party's assets and liabilities

financial disclosure affidavit a sworn statement indicating the income, expenses, assets, and liabilities of a client

financial worksheet focuses on the client's income, expenses, assets, and liabilities, be they joint or separate; enables the attorney to begin assessing the extent of the marital estate

fixed schedule definite dates and time frames set aside for the purpose of allowing a noncustodial parent to visit with a child

flat fee an arrangement whereby a fixed dollar amount is agreed on and charged for the entire case

former client–current opponent upon an attorney or paralegal switching jobs, discovering that his or her new employer is representing the opponent in a former client's case

freelance paralegal independent contractor who works for a number of attorneys on an as-needed basis

front loading where the majority of property settlements in a divorce case are made in the first three years after the divorce

full faith and credit clause part of the U.S. Constitution that states that all states must honor the public acts, records, and judicial proceedings of every other state

fundamental right a right either expressed in the Constitution or one that the Supreme Court has stated may be inferred (implied) from the existing rights

grant in a court proceeding, when the judge decides to allow a party's request or motion

grievance a complaint filed with a disciplinary body against an attorney

grievance committees state bar associations that regulate the legal profession through disciplinary bodies

gross income the sum of all available sources of income

habeus corpus a document that allows an incarcerated party to be transported by a state's correctional department for trial

habitual intemperance where one party frequently and repeatedly becomes intoxicated; one of the legal grounds to establish fault in a divorce proceeding

hold harmless clause part of a separation agreement that indicates that a particular spouse will be responsible for a debt incurred during the marriage, that he or she will be solely responsible for its payment, and the other spouse shall be free and clear of any obligation regarding that debt

hotline twenty-four-hour telephone number established for the reporting of suspected child abuse and neglect

hourly basis billing the client for each hour of time spent working on a client's file, including, but not limited to, research, drafting documents, phone calls, travel, office visits, trial preparation, and interviewing witnesses

implied-in-fact contract an agreement in which the intention of the parties is inferred by their conduct

implied partnership in the case of a cohabitating couple that works on a business enterprise owned by one of the parties, the court recognizes an implied partnership

implied trust a legal relationship in which the trustee holds legal title to property for the benefit of the beneficiary

in personam jurisdiction personal service over the defendant; it means that once the defendant is served with the initial pleadings, the court may enter orders and enforce judgments against that individual

in rem jurisdiction   the power of the courts to actually dissolve the marriage

incarceration in a penal institution   confinement in a jail or prison; one of the legal grounds to establish fault in a divorce proceeding

incompatibility   the no-fault ground for divorce; may be also be referred to as irreconcilable differences, irretrievable breakdown, or irremediable breakdown

initial client interview   the first meeting between a client and an attorney or paralegal at which basic information to start work on a case is gathered

institutionalization for mental illness   confinement to a sanitarium or asylum; one of the legal grounds to establish fault in a divorce proceeding

integrated bar associations   affiliations of state bar associations where membership is mandatory

interrogatories   requests for disclosure of all real and personal property owned by a spouse either in his or her own name or owned jointly with the spouse or with another person or entity

investigative child protection worker   social worker representing the state child protection agency who makes the initial investigation of suspected child abuse or neglect and determines whether the state should take further action to protect the child

irreconcilable differences   the no-fault ground for divorce; may be also be referred to as incompatibility, irretrievable breakdown, or irremediable breakdown

irrelevant   not having anything to do with the matter at hand

irremediable breakdown   the no-fault ground for divorce; may be also be referred to as incompatibility, irreconcilable differences, or irretrievable breakdown

irretrievable breakdown   the no-fault ground for divorce; may be also be referred to as incompatibility, irreconcilable differences, or irremediable breakdown

IRS recapture rule   applies when the parties do not wish to have alimony taxed as income or deducted; should be indicated in the settlement agreement

joint custody   arrangement in which parents are equally responsible for the financial, emotional, educational, and health-related needs of their children

joint ownership   when two or more persons hold property together; also known as concurrent ownership

joint tenancy with rights of survivorship   where each party owns equal interests in property and at the death of one of the joint tenants, his or her interest automatically passes to the remaining parties

judgment   the orders made by a court pursuant to the court's decision after trial; orders become a permanent part of the court file

judicial pretrial   a conference that takes place before a judge, not a trial, to help the parties try to come to an agreement before the trial starts; also known as a pretrial conference

juris number   the attorney's license number

jurisdiction   describes the court's control or power over a specific geographic territory; it also refers to the power of the courts to hear and resolve a dispute

legal advice   advising a client of his or her specific legal rights and responsibilities, and either predicting an outcome or recommending that the client pursue a particular course of action

legal custody   where both parents are the children's legal guardians and, as such, have the right to make decisions regarding their children's health, education, and welfare

legal grounds   prior to the passage of no-fault divorce laws, where a spouse seeking a divorce was required to have facts proving that the other spouse was at fault

legal separation   an action brought by a spouse who wishes to avoid the legal, social, or religious ramifications of a divorce but nevertheless wishes to live apart from his or her spouse

limited scope retainer agreement   a contract for legal services between the attorney and client where the attorney limits the scope of representation with the client's consent

living expenses   any monies for client's personal use that may not be advanced to a client by the attorney

lump sum alimony   a support payment made in one single payment; also known as alimony in gross

malpractice   negligent legal representation; representation that is below the standard of the professional community and could result in damage to the client

mandatory reporter   a professional who is required by state statute to report suspected child abuse or neglect

marital assets   the property acquired during a marriage

marital debts   the liabilities incurred by either spouse during a marriage

marital settlement agreement   a contract between spouses who are in the process of obtaining a divorce or a legal separation resolving the various legal issues that arise when a marriage is dissolving; also known as a property settlement, separation agreement, or settlement agreement

marriage a marriage is defined as the joining together of one man and one woman in a civil contract

marriage certificate a document prepared by the official performing the marriage; most jurisdictions require the bride and groom, the person officiating the marriage, and one or two witnesses to sign the marriage certificate after the completion of the ceremony; in some jurisdictions, the marriage certificate is filed with the clerk upon completion of the marriage and in others it is incorporated into the marriage license

marriage license a document issued by the county clerk that authorizes a couple to get married

marriage statute a law passed by a state legislature that indicates who may marry

Married Women's Property Acts statutes that eliminated the disadvantages of married women and gave them the right to control their own earnings, bring lawsuits, be sued, own their own property, enter into contracts, and function in a legal capacity

mediation where the parties meet and attempt to resolve the pending issues surrounding their dissolution of marriage action with the assistance of a trained third party, either court-provided and free, or privately engaged and paid

memorandum of law a written document presented to the court that states a party's argument in a case and supports that argument with specific case law and statutes

mental cruelty where one spouse tries to cause psychological harm to the other; one of the legal grounds to establish fault in a divorce proceeding

merger an agreement that is no longer a contract between the two parties, but rather a court order, which can be modified or enforced through contempt of court proceedings

migratory divorces people flocking to a particular jurisdiction to get divorced because of the short divorce residency requirements

military affidavit a sworn statement that serves as proof that the defendant is currently not serving in one of the armed forces

miscegenation laws statute that prohibited interracial marriages

Model Rules of Professional Conduct a prototype for attorney's ethics written by the American Bar Association as a model for states that wish to adopt them

modification a change or adjustment to a previous court order

modification of alimony the issue of whether spousal support may be either increased or decreased after the original order has been entered due to a substantial change in one spouse's circumstances

motion a written document that asks the court to take some type of action

motion day one or two days of the week that courts set aside to hear motions brought before the court; also known as the short calendar

motion for alimony, *pendente lite* where a party to a dissolution proceeding asks the court to grant support payments to him or her for the duration of the case

motion for child support, *pendente lite* where a party to a dissolution proceeding asks the court to have the other party pay child maintenance for the duration of the case

motion for contempt a document that alerts the court to the other party's failure to comply with the court's earlier order and requests that the court provide relief

motion for custody, *pendente lite* where a party to a dissolution proceeding asks the court to have possession of the children for the duration of the case

motion for disclosure of assets requests disclosure of all real and personal property owned by a spouse either in his or her own name or owned jointly with the spouse or with another person or entity

motion for exclusive possession of the marital home, *pendente lite* where a party to a dissolution proceeding asks the court to allow him or her to stay in the home, without the other party, for the duration of the case

motion for modification where a party asks that orders entered by the court be changed when there has been a substantial change in the one of the party's circumstances from the time the original order was entered; also known as a motion to modify

motion for modification of child support a document requesting the court to order the noncustodial parent to pay higher periodic child support payments, so that less of the custodial parent's income will be needed for the child

motion for payment of mortgage payments and insurance premiums, *pendente lite* where a party to a dissolution proceeding asks the court to have the other party pay for certain bills for the duration of the case

motion for protective order where a party asks the court to prevent the other party from coming in contact with him or her

motion for use of the automobile, *pendente lite* where a party to a dissolution proceeding asks the court to have sole use of the couple's automobile for the duration of the case

motion to compel examination a document that asks the court to force the opposing party to submit to an examination

motion to freeze marital assets where a party asks the court to stop any transactions of the marital property from taking place

motion to modify where a party asks that orders entered by the court be changed when there has been a substantial change in one of the party's circumstances from the time the original order was entered; also known as a motion for modification

motion to modify alimony where a party asks that orders for spousal support entered by the court be changed when there has been a substantial change in one of the party's circumstances from the time the original order was entered; also known as a motion to modify support

motion to modify custody where a party asks that orders regarding child custody entered by the court be changed when there has been a substantial change in one of the party's circumstances from the time the original order was entered

motion to modify support where a party asks that orders for spousal support entered by the court be changed when there has been a substantial change in one of the party's circumstances from the time the original order was entered; also known as a motion to modify alimony

motion to modify visitation where a party asks that orders for child visitation entered by the court be changed when there has been a substantial change in one of the party's circumstances from the time the original order was entered

motion to restrain party from entering marital residence where a party asks the court to order that the other party be forbidden to enter the home where that party is living

moving party the person bringing the motion to court

multiple representation where one lawyer is hired to represent both parties to a case

National Association of Legal Assistants (NALA) voluntary national, state, and local paralegal association that has established its own ethical codes

National Federation of Paralegal Professionals (NFPA) voluntary national, state, and local paralegal association that has established its own ethical codes

neglect the failure of a parent to adequately provide for the child's nutritional, educational, or medical needs, or allowing a child to live in conditions that are unsanitary or dangerous

net income the dollar amount remaining after allowable deductions are subtracted from the gross income

no-fault divorce in order to obtain a divorce, a litigant traditionally had to prove one of the statutory fault grounds or no divorce was granted; in 1969, the California legislature enacted the first no-fault divorce, which required parties only to prove that they had irreconcilable differences and there was no hope of reconciliation; currently, all fifty states have some form of no-fault divorce provisions where one of the parties only has to allege that the marriage has broken down and that there is no hope of reconciliation in order for the court to dissolve a marriage

no-fault divorce laws a modification of existing divorce laws to include the ground that the marital union or marital relationship had broken down irretrievably

nominal alimony alimony in the amount of $1.00 per year; the purpose of nominal alimony is to allow the spouse to preserve his or her right to return to court in the event there is a change in circumstances

noncustodial parent the parent who does not have the child living with him or her on a full-time basis

nonmodifiable orders issued by a court that cannot be changed, regardless of the circumstances

nonvested in an employee pension plan, when the right to the employer portion of the funds has not yet attached

notice of deposition a document that alerts a party that he or she will be required to submit to examination by the opposing attorney

notice of filing of interrogatories a document that alerts the court that a party has asked the opposing party to answer a set of written questions

notice of responding to and/or objecting to interrogatories a document that alerts the court that the answering party has either answered the written questions or objects to one or more of the questions

notice to appear for a deposition to disclose assets a document that requires a party to appear in order to be questioned, under oath, on the previous disclosure to determine whether it completely revealed all of the party's assets

objection a document used when a party is in opposition to an action the court or the opposition has taken

obligee a party to whom a sum of money is owed; also known as a creditor

obligor the party responsible for money that is owed; also known as a debtor

offset when an employee-spouse agrees to transfer his or her interest in other marital assets in exchange for the full ownership of his or her pension benefits

open adoption an adoption where the biological parents, the adoptive parents, and sometimes the children are known to each other

open adoption agreement a contract entered into between one or both biological parents and the adoptive parents, prior to the adoption proceeding, that grants the biological parent(s) the right to continue some type of relationship with the child or have access to information regarding the child's development and well-being

order a statement that sets forth the judge's decision on a particular motion before the court

order of temporary custody a court order enabling the state to remove children from their home and place them in relative or foster care, when they are in imminent danger

overbroad too general; not specific enough

padding unjustifiably increasing the number of hours actually spent on a client's case

palimony a lawsuit for support filed against a cohabitating partner

partnership during a marriage, when the efforts and personal and financial resources of the parties are pooled for the benefit of the marriage

paternity action where the petitioning party, usually the child's mother but occasionally the father, requests that the court hold a hearing to establish whether a particular man is the child's biological father

patria potestas in ancient civilizations, where fathers possessed absolute right to the possession of their children and could even sell the children or put them to death if desired

pendancy period the time during court proceedings before judgment is rendered

pendente lite **alimony** payments made during the pendency of the divorce with the purpose of providing temporary financial support for the spouse; also known as temporary alimony

pendente lite **motion** a motion granting relief only for the duration of the court action, before judgment is rendered

pension a retirement benefit acquired by an employee

periodic alimony term applied to court-ordered payments that are to be made to a spouse on a regular basis

permanent alimony the term applied to court-ordered payments that are to be made to a spouse on a regular and periodic basis and that terminate only on the death, remarriage, or cohabitation of the other spouse or on court order

personal property anything other than real property that can be touched and is movable

petition a document that commences the action when the opposing party is served; also known as a complaint

petitioner the party who brings a court action against another; also known as the plaintiff

physical cruelty actual personal violence of one spouse toward another; one of the legal grounds to establish fault in a divorce proceeding

physical custody when a parent has actual bodily possession of the children

plaintiff the party who brings a court action against another; also known as the petitioner

pleading documents that state the plaintiff's claims giving rise to the dissolution action and the defendant's responses or defenses to such claims

polygamy having multiple spouses

postmajority support agreements that frequently address payment for college tuition or other postsecondary education; payment for the maintenance of post-majority adult children with special needs; and payment of medical and dental insurance coverage for dependent adult children while they are students or when they are newly employed but not yet eligible for coverage at work

postnuptial agreement agreements made *after* the marriage has been performed in which the elements are similar to those of prenuptial agreements

prayer for relief the plaintiff's request for a dissolution and for court orders, when appropriate, regarding property distribution, alimony, child custody, and support of the minor children

premarital agreement a contract entered into by the prospective spouses regarding their rights during the marriage and in the event of a divorce; also known as an antenuptial agreement or prenuptial agreement

premium a monetary sum paid on an annual or installment basis for malpractice insurance coverage

prenuptial agreement a contract entered into by the prospective spouses regarding their rights during the marriage and in the event of a divorce; also known as an antenuptial agreement or premarital agreement

prereturn date relief where a plaintiff spouse needs and may seek immediate relief or court intervention as soon as the complaint is served

pretrial conference a meeting that takes place before a judge, not a trial, to help the parties try to come to an agreement before the trial starts; also known as a judicial pretrial

primary caregiver the individual who has done most of the significant parenting of the child since birth or for the several preceding years

privilege a court-conferred right permitting parties in a lawsuit to keep confidential any information exchanged between themselves and another person in instances where there was a special type of relationship between themselves and the other person that promoted an expectation of trust, confidentiality, and privacy

pro hac vice where a state may grant an attorney special permission to handle one particular case

pro per individuals who represent themselves in court; also known as *pro se*

pro se see *pro per*

property settlement a contract between spouses who are in the process of obtaining a divorce or a legal separation resolving the various legal issues that arise when a marriage is dissolving; also known as a marital settlement agreement, separation agreement, or settlement agreement

proposal a formal written indication, from one party to the opposing party, that communicates what the first party is seeking in terms of a divorce settlement

proposal letter details the client's position on the various legal issues to be resolved, such as property division, alimony, child custody, visitation and support, maintenance of health and life insurance, distribution of debts and other liabilities, and counsel fees

psychological parent the parent who has had the child since the child's birth and/or who has spent the most meaningful time with the child, has bonded most fully with the child, and who has provided the most psychological nurturing of the child

public policy a belief generally held by a majority of the public as to the desirability or rightness or wrongness or certain behavior

Qualified Domestic Relations Order (QDRO) a court order served on the pension administrator ordering the plan to distribute a specified portion of the pension funds to the nonemployee spouse

quasi-contract contractual obligations that are imposed on the parties by the court, but no actual contract has been entered into by the parties

REA see *Retirement Equity Act*

real property land and anything affixed to it

reasonable rights of visitation a very flexible arrangement that requires the parties to work out their own schedule for visitation with children

Reciprocal Beneficiaries Law a Hawaii law that grants residents who are eighteen or older and not allowed to marry under state law the right to register and benefit from hospital visitation rights, legal standing to sue in wrongful death cases, as well as property and inheritance rights.

reciprocity where one state may extend to attorneys in a different state the right to practice law in its jurisdiction in exchange for the other state's granting the same privilege to attorneys in their state

redirect after cross-examination, where the party's attorney may question the witness on any subject covered in the cross-examination testimony

rehabilitative alimony spousal support that is awarded for a limited period of time to give the spouse the opportunity to become self-sufficient

reimbursement alimony where a nondegreed spouse may be compensated for his or her contribution to the student spouse's attainment of an advanced degree that results in an enhanced earning capacity

release a document that indicates the client has given his or her attorneys the permission to disclose information to another party

Religious Freedom and Civil Marriage Protection Act a proposed California bill allowing same-sex couples to marry; vetoed by Governor Arnold Schwarzenegger in September of 2005

request a document that asks the court to take some type of action; it is automatically granted by the court thirty days after filing, absent the opposing party's objection

request for admission where a party formally asks that an opposing party admit the truth of some fact or event that will inevitably be proved at trial

request for an order attacking known assets a document asking the court to freeze the opposing party's property in order to prevent dissipation of those assets

request for production of documents where a party formally asks that the other party present certain papers for use in a case

requesting party the party asking the court to take some action

requests for physical and mental examination where a party formally asks that the other party have a physical and/or psychiatric examination

residency the domicile of the parties

respondeat superior the doctrine that states an employer is responsible for negligence and other torts committed by his or her employees when the acts are committed during the scope of their employment

respondent the party against whom an action is brought

responding party the party who must produce discovery documents

resulting trust where only one party provides the funds for property, while title is in the other party's name

retainer payment made in advance to an attorney

retainer agreement a contract between the law firm and the client whereby the law firm agrees to provide specified legal services in exchange for monetary compensation; also known as a retainer letter

retainer letter see *retainer agreement*

Retirement Equity Act of 1984 (REA) a federal statute determining the manner in which states may divide a pension at the time of divorce

return date a date in the near future by which the complaint must be returned to the court clerk's office and filed with the court

Revised Uniform Reciprocal Enforcement Act of 1968 (RURESA) where a custodial parent may ultimately obtain child support from the noncustodial parent residing in another state by instituting certain procedures

rule to show cause a document commanding a party to appear and argue as to why his or her motion should be granted

rules of court a jurisdiction's official publication containing the procedural codes of the jurisdiction

rules of ethics standards of conduct that a profession demands from its members

RURESA see *Revised Uniform Reciprocal Enforcement Act*

same-sex marriage marriage between two people of the same gender

sanctions punishment issued to attorneys for engaging in conduct that violates the state's code of professional conduct

second glance doctrine consideration of what circumstances exist at the time of enforcement of a prenuptial agreement in order to protect spouses from changes in circumstances that occurred since the date of the formation of the prenuptial agreement

second parent adoptions a form of adoption where one partner of a same-sex couple adopts the child and the other partner files for co-parent status

secular courts courts administered by the state, as opposed to church, or ecclesiastical, courts

separate maintenance an action that affirms the continuation of a marriage and enforces the legal obligations of each spouse in the marriage

separate property property acquired by a spouse *prior* to the marriage, or after the marriage by a gift, inheritance, or will, designated to that particular spouse alone

separation agreement a contract between spouses who are in the process of obtaining a divorce or a legal separation resolving the various legal issues that arise when a marriage is dissolving; also known as a marital settlement agreement, property settlement, or settlement agreement

service by publication when a sheriff puts a legal notice in the newspaper in the city, town, or general area where the defendant was last known to reside, or where the defendant is now thought to be residing

service of process formal delivery of the initial pleadings

service or performance agreement a document signed by a parent or parents in a child protection case in which the parent agrees to accomplish certain tasks

settlement the practice of negotiating areas of disagreement and, through compromise, reaching an agreement to present to the court

settlement agreement a contract between spouses who are in the process of obtaining a divorce or a legal separation resolving the various legal issues that arise when a marriage is dissolving; also known as a marital settlement agreement, property settlement, or separation agreement

sham or **green card marriage** a U.S. citizen agrees to a marriage for monetary compensation

shared custody arrangement where a child resides with one parent for a certain number of days a week and a certain number of days with the other parent

sheriff's return a signed statement from a sheriff stating that he or she made proper service of a court document

short calendar one or two days of the week that courts set aside to hear motions brought before the court; also known as motion day

simplified divorce procedure a form of low-cost divorce enacted by a number of states that is sometimes referred to as summary process or divorce by mutual consent; the parties in these states must appear before the court to dissolve their marriage

sole custody where one parent has exclusive custody of a child

sole ownership property owned by an individual alone

solicitation actively seeking persons in need of legal services, either by mail or in person, unless there already exists an attorney–client relationship or a family relationship

special defenses part of a defendant's answer in which he or she cites unusual or extraordinary circumstances as part of his or her defense

split custody arrangement where one parent has sole custody of the child for a part of each calendar year, and the other parent has sole custody for the remaining portion of the year

spousal maintenance   a sum of money, or other property, paid by a former spouse to the other former spouse for financial support, pursuant to a court order, temporary or final, in a divorce proceeding; also known as alimony or spousal support

spousal support   see *spousal maintenance*

standing   a term that describes whether a party has a legal right to request an adjudication of the issues in a legal dispute

stepparent adoption   where an individual who marries a divorced or widowed person adopts his or her spouse's children

stipulations   written agreements where parties agree that certain facts are true or that certain procedures will be followed

subject matter jurisdiction   the court's power to actually hear a divorce case

subpoena   a legal document signed by an officer of the court that requires the person receiving it to appear under penalty of law at the time, date, and place indicated on the document

subscription   part of a court document that confirms the truth and accuracy of allegations and confirms the veracity of the party making these allegations; also known as the verification

substantial change in circumstances   an actual or assumed alteration in the financial status or capability of either party

summary dissolution of marriage   simplified procedures for obtaining a divorce in cases where the parties have little or no assets, no children, were married for a relatively short period of time, and both want the divorce; all that is required in these jurisdictions, if you meet the requirements, is the filing of official documents with the appropriate court without the assistance of attorneys

summons   a one-page preprinted form on which the names and addresses of parties and the name and address of the court are inserted and that directs the defendant to appear in court and answer allegations in a complaint

tax-deferred   when taxes on the income produced by the pension will not be paid until the monies are withdrawn

temporary alimony   payments made during the pendency of the divorce with the purpose of providing temporary financial support for a spouse; also known as *pendente lite* alimony

tenancy by the entirety   a form of co-ownership that can only exist between a husband and wife and cannot be severed by either co-owner

tenancy in common   where each party owns an undivided interest in certain property, has equal rights to its use and enjoyment, and may dispose of their share by gift, will, or sale

tender years doctrine   the theoretical justification for the placing of children with their mother

termination of parental rights   a court proceeding that severs the legal bonds between a parent and his or her biological child

testimony   evidence given by a witness under oath or affirmation

theory of the case   the legal justification for a client's position and for the relief he or she is seeking

third-party intervenor   a party who is not one of the main parties in a dispute

time sheet   a record of work performed on behalf of a client that will be billed to the client on a periodic basis; also known as a time slip

time slip   see *time sheet*

title   a party's ownership interest in property

total net income   the figure arrived at when each parent's net income is added to determine child support; also known as combined net income

transcripts   an official copy of the record of proceedings in a trial or hearing

transmutation   the transformation of separate property to marital property

treatment worker   social worker representing the state child protection agency who works with the family on a long-term basis by putting essential services in place and visiting the family on a regular basis

trial notebook   a method of organizing the materials prepared for trial in a manner that makes them readily available for use at trial

trustee   a person who holds legal title to property for the benefit of another

UIFSA   see *Uniform Interstate Family Support Act*

unauthorized practice of law (UPL)   when a nonattorney engages in any activity that the state UPL statute prohibits. Anyone engaging in the unauthorized practice of law can be prosecuted in criminal court

unbundled legal services or **discrete tasks representation**   clients purchase legal services on a task-by-task basis; the client and attorney agree by contract as to what services the lawyer will provide in exchange for a fee

unconscionable   an agreement that is so unfair to one party that the court will refuse to enforce it

uncontested   where neither party objects to the court granting a divorce and entering an order of marital dissolution

unearned retainer   any part of a retainer left over after the attorney has completed his or her work that must be returned to the client

Uniform Interstate Family Support Act (UIFSA) where the noncustodial parent's state must honor the original support and may not enter a new order or modify the existing order to conform to its guidelines for determining the amount of support

Uniform Premarital Agreement Act   a model act drafted by the National Conference of Commissioners on Uniform State Laws that provides states with model legislation addressing the issues necessary to create a valid premarital agreement

Uniform Reciprocal Enforcement Act (URESA) where a custodial parent may ultimately obtain child support from the noncustodial parent residing in another state by instituting certain procedures

unity of spouses   the English common law system used to determine the division of marital property on dissolution of a marriage, which stated that, on marriage, a husband and wife merged into a single legal entity—the husband

UPL   see *unauthorized practice of law*

value   what the marital property is worth

venue   the proper divorce court within the state in which to file the initial divorce complaint on petition

verification   part of a court document that confirms the truth and accuracy of allegations and confirms the veracity of the party making these allegations; also known as the subscription

vested   in an employee pension plan, entitles the employee to the employer's contribution portion provided that the employee has worked for the employer for an enumerated number of years

vicarious liability   where an employer is responsible for negligence and other torts committed by his or her employees when the acts are committed during the scope of their employment

visitation   the time allotted for the noncustodial parent to spend with the child

void ab initio   invalid from its inception

void marriage   a marriage that is invalid at the time of its creation

voidable marriage   a marriage that is invalid at its inception but remains in effect unless the court terminates it

wage execution   serves the purpose of facilitating alimony and child support payments through automatic deductions from the obligor's paycheck

waiver   where the parties agree not to seek an alimony award in a divorce case

waiver of alimony   one or both of the spouses may wish to waive or relinquish their right to ask for alimony

willful contempt   when the recipient spouse proves that the payor spouse has the means to make weekly payments but purposefully and deliberately fails to do so

work product   the notes, materials, memoranda, and written records generated by an attorney, as well as the written records of the attorney's mental impressions and legal theories concerning a case

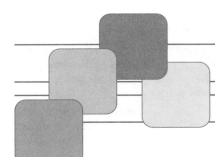

INDEX